Turbo Pascal®:

The Complete Reference

Turbo Pascal®:
The Complete Reference

Stephen K. O'Brien

BORLAND·OSBORNE/McGRAW·HILL
PROGRAMMING SERIES

Osborne **McGraw-Hill**
2600 Tenth Street
Berkeley, California 94710
U.S.A.

For information on translations and book distributors outside of the
U.S.A., write to Osborne **McGraw-Hill** at the above address.

A complete list of trademarks appears on page 797.

Turbo Pascal®: The Complete Reference

 234567890 DODO 898

ISBN 0-07-881290-9

To Rita, Abbie, Fina, and Wing

**C
O
N
T
E
N
T
S**

Turbo Pascal: The Complete Reference is an indispensable tool for anyone who develops programs in Turbo Pascal Version 4.0 and earlier. Experienced and novice programmers alike will want this desktop reference at their fingertips while they work. Author Stephen K. O'Brien provides answers to the most frequently-asked questions about programming in Turbo Pascal. As a bonus, he presents routines that will be a welcome addition to any programmer's library.

You can rely on this book both for the thoroughness with which it covers the subject and for the lucidity of the explanations. All aspects of Turbo Pascal programming—from accessing DOS services to writing terminate-and-stay-resident programs—are included. Special attention is paid to telecommunications, a common use of Turbo Pascal, and to interfacing Turbo Pascal with assembly language. The procedures and functions are well written and extremely useful, and even the most complex processes are accompanied by easy-to-understand examples that users can follow to write their own programs.

Stephen K. O'Brien has been programming in Turbo Pascal since its launch by Borland in 1983. Now he provides you with everything you need to know to develop programs in Turbo Pascal efficiently and productively in one concise, easy-to-use volume.

Philippe Kahn
Chief Executive Officer
Borland International, Inc.

FOREWORD

Thanks are due to all the people at Osborne/McGraw-Hill and Borland International who contributed their efforts to this book. Special thanks go to Nancy Carlston, Lindy Clinton, and Fran Haselsteiner for keeping the project on track from beginning to end, and to Wing-Kit Cheung, programmer emeritus, who, I am conviced, dines on silicon.

ACKNOWLEDGMENTS

Before Turbo Pascal first appeared, microcomputer programmers had some difficult choices to make. They could use BASIC, which came with their computers, or they could buy compilers. But BASIC is slow and unstructured, good compilers were expensive, and many like me, had spent their entire budget on the computer itself.

Then came Turbo Pascal, the first microcomputer compiler to provide programmers with an integrated programming environment at a reasonable price. While most other compilers required separate programs for editing, compiling, and linking, Turbo Pascal combined these functions in one seamless package. The result has been world-wide acceptance of Turbo Pascal as both a great programming system and the standard against which other compilers are measured.

Now, with Version 4.0, Turbo Pascal takes a giant leap forward. Gone are the 64K limit on code, the need to recompile every bit of code every time you made a small change, and a host of other limitations. Turbo Pascal 4.0 is the compiler Pascal programmers have been waiting for.

About the Book

This book is intended for all Turbo Pascal programmers. It covers all aspects of the compiler, including both Version 3.0 and 4.0 throughout the text. Both beginners and advanced programmers will find useful information ranging from dynamic allocation to memory-resident programming. But the book is primarily designed as a reference to provide information quickly and concisely on a broad range of topics.

Chapters 1 through 11 cover fundamental aspects of programming in Turbo Pascal. Topics include program structure, using files, and commonly used algorithms such as sorting, merging, and searching. Chapters 12 through 18 delve into such advanced concepts as assembly language, DOS and BIOS services, and interrupt programming. Chapters 19 through 22 provide a reference guide to the Turbo Pascal toolboxes: Database, Graphix, Editor, and Numerical Methods. Chapter 23 focuses just on Turbo Pascal 4.0.

Diskette Package

All the programs listed in this book, as well as additional programs and routines, are available on either 5 1/4-inch or 3 1/2-inch diskettes. The source code is written for both Version 3.0 and Version 4.0. To order your diskette, send $35.00 in check or money order with the order form on this page.

Please send me the diskette that accompanies *Turbo Pascal: The Complete Reference*. My payment of $35.00 in check or money order is enclosed.

Name _____

Address _____

City _____ State _____ ZIP _____

Disk size   ☐ 5 1/4-inch   ☐ 3 1/2-inch

Solo Flight Software, Inc., 217 East 84th Street, Suite 194, New York, New York 10028

This is solely the offering of Stephen K. O'Brien, Solo Flight Software, Inc. Osborne/McGraw-Hill takes no responsibility for the fulfillment of this offer.

Programming: A Fast Start

**O
N
E**

If you are using Turbo Pascal for the first time, this chapter is for you. In it you will discover the fundamentals of the Turbo Pascal system and, at the same time, write and run your first programs. Do not be too concerned about understanding everything presented in this chapter; even simple programming concepts take time to sink in. Just take your time, get comfortable with the system, try the sample programs, and experiment on your own.

A Simple Turbo Pascal Program

The best way to start is by writing your first program. To start Turbo Pascal, make sure you are logged in to the drive and directory in which the TURBO.COM and TURBO.MSG files reside. At the DOS prompt, type **TURBO** and press RETURN. When the prompt **Include error messages (Y/N)?** appears, type **Y**.

On your screen, you see the Turbo Pascal Main menu. To enter a program, type **E** (for edit). Turbo Pascal needs the name of the file you want to work on, so type in the work-file name **Prog1** and press RETURN.

Other than the editor's status line, which appears at the very top, the screen is empty. Now type in the following Turbo Pascal program, which will display one line of text on your computer's screen:

```
Program Prog1;
Begin
WriteLn('This is my first program.');
End.
```

If you make a typing mistake as you enter the program, use the arrow keys on the numeric keypad to position the cursor at the error, press DEL to delete the error, and then retype the correct letters.

Now that you have entered the program, hold down the CTRL key and type **K** and then **D** to get back to the Main menu prompt (>). Hereafter, this book refers to key combinations like this as CTRL-KD. Now it is time to run your program. Type **R** and your monitor will show these two lines:

Running
This is my first program.

Turbo Pascal displays the first message, **Running**, whenever a program is run from within the Turbo Pascal system. The second line, **This is my first program.**, is the message the program displays on the monitor.

While it is small, this program contains elements common to all Turbo Pascal programs. It has a program heading, **Program Prog1**, which identifies it. It also has a program block that begins with **Begin** and ends with **End**, as shown in Figure 1-1.

A Turbo Pascal program always starts at the first **Begin** statement of the program block and executes all the statements, one by one, until it reaches the final **End** statement.

```
                      ┌─►Begin
Program Block ─┤        WriteLn('This is my first program.');
                      └─►End.
```

Figure 1-1.   A simple program block

The program block in the example just given contains only one statement:

WriteLn ('This is my first program.');

WriteLn is a Turbo Pascal standard procedure that prints numbers and strings of characters to the screen, the printer, or a disk file, and then returns to the beginning of the next line. Inside the parentheses of the **WriteLn** statement are the items to be printed. While in this case the **WriteLn** procedure prints only one line, it is capable of printing more than one item at a time. Figure 1-2 shows an example of a **WriteLn** statement that prints three separate "strings."

A *string* is any combination of characters that is enclosed in single quotation marks. Commas separate the strings, or *parameters*, that are passed to the **WriteLn** procedure. Note that the second string, which consists of two blank characters, creates a space between the first and third strings. When this statement is executed, the result looks like this:

This is one string. This is another string.

Like **WriteLn**, the procedure **Write** also displays strings and numbers. When you use **Write**, the cursor remains on the same line as the information written, while **WriteLn** moves the cursor to the beginning of the next line.

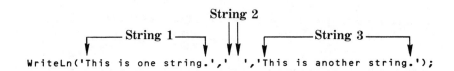

Figure 1-2.   Writing more than one string with WriteLn

Adding Variables to a Program

To write a more useful program, you need to know about *variables*. Variables are places in your computer's memory that hold values, such as numbers or strings. You can give a variable almost any name you want, but it is best to choose a name that describes the information the variable holds. For example, you might call a variable that holds the name of a customer **CustomerName** and define it as follows:

    CustomerName : String[50];

Here, **CustomerName** is the variable identifier, because it identifies by name the place in RAM where a value is stored. **String [50]** identifies it as a string and indicates that the **CustomerName** variable cannot exceed 50 characters.

Var is a Turbo Pascal *reserved word* that indicates the beginning of variable declarations. There are many other reserved words in Turbo Pascal, such as **Integer**, **Begin**, **End**, and so on. (Appendix G contains a complete list of Turbo Pascal reserved words.) These words are central to the Turbo Pascal language, and therefore you cannot redefine them. These examples illustrate illegal attempts to use reserved words as variable identifiers:

    Var
        Begin : Integer;
        Real : String[50];

Variables can hold numbers (*integers* and *reals*), single characters (*char*), groups of characters (*strings*) or true/false indicators (*Boolean*). While designed for different purposes, these variable types share one common characteristic—their value can be changed (or varied) using an *assignment statement*.

Assignment statements set variables to particular values. For example, the statement

CustomerName := 'John Doe'

takes the string 'John Doe' and stores it in the **string** variable **CustomerName**. Note that the assignment statement uses the := operator, which is known as the *assignment operator*.

Variables and Input

The assignment statement is just one way to set the value of a variable; the **ReadLn** procedure is another. But unlike assignment statements, **ReadLn** gets its value from the person who uses the program. The **ReadLn** statement causes a program to stop and wait until the user types in the data and presses RETURN. **ReadLn** then takes the input and assigns it to a variable named in the **ReadLn** statement. For example, the statement **ReadLn(CustomerName)** waits for the user to type in a string, accepts a string, and stores it in the variable **CustomerName**.

The sample program shown below demonstrates how **ReadLn** obtains input and stores it in variables.

```
Program PROG2;
Var
  i : Integer;
  s : String[20];

Begin
ClrScr;
Write('Enter a number: ');
ReadLn(i);
```

```
WriteLn('Your number is ',i);

WriteLn;

Write('Enter a string: ');
ReadLn(s);
WriteLn('Your string is ',s);
End.
```

To enter **Prog2**, open a new work file by pressing **W** at the Turbo Pascal prompt. Enter the work-file name **Prog2** and press RETURN. Now press **E** to call up the Turbo Pascal editor, and begin typing the program as shown. When done, press CTRL-KD to return to the Main menu; then type **R** to run the program.

As soon as the program starts, the **ClrScr** command clears the screen, and the program displays **Enter a number:** on your monitor. Type the number **9** and press RETURN. The program now displays **Your number is 9**, skips one line on the screen, and displays **Enter a string:**. When you type **ABC** and press RETURN, the program displays **Your string is ABC**.

Prog2 uses two variables: **i** (an integer) and **s** (a string). Integers are numerical values with no decimal place. In this case, **s** is defined as **String[20]**, which means that it cannot hold more than 20 characters.

The three lines listed in the following illustration demonstrate how your program can receive input.

```
Write('Enter a number: ');◄────────Displays the prompt


ReadLn(i);◄──────────────────────Accepts input


WriteLn('Your number is ',i);◄──Confirms input
```

The first line prompts the user for input by asking for a number. The prompt **Enter a number:** is displayed by using the **Write** procedure, as opposed to **WriteLn**. Keeping the cursor on the same line as the prompt tells the user that the program is waiting for input.

You respond to the prompt by typing in a number, which is captured by the **ReadLn** statement and stored in **i**. When Turbo Pascal executes the statement **ReadLn(i)**, the program waits for the user to type characters and press RETURN. The program assigns whatever the user types to the integer variable **i**. The last statement confirms the input by displaying both a message and the contents of **i**.

If the **ReadLn** statement detects an error in the input, it notifies you and halts the program. For example, run **Prog2** again, but when it asks for a number, type **ABC** and press RETURN. Turbo Pascal detects an *input/output (I/O) error* and displays this message:

```
Enter a number: ABC

I/O error 10, PC=2D8D
Program aborted

Searching
  9 Lines

Run-time error position found. Press <ESC>
```

In this case, the I/O error number is 10, which is an error in the numeric format. In other words, **ABC** is not a valid integer. (I/O and other Turbo Pascal errors are described in Appendix A.)

When Turbo Pascal encounters an I/O or run-time error, it searches through your program to locate the point at which the error occurred. Once it finds the error, Turbo Pascal tells you to press ESC: after you do so, it calls up the editor with your program already loaded and the cursor pointing to the error.

The next statement in **Prog2** demonstrates the use of the **WriteLn** statement with no parameters. When executed, this statement simply writes a CR/LF (carriage-return linefeed) combination to the computer monitor, which places the cursor on the first position of the next line.

The next three lines again prompt you for input. This time, the program assigns input to a string variable, which is subsequently displayed along with a text literal.

```
Write('Enter a string: ');
ReadLn(s);
WriteLn('Your string is ',s);
End.
```

Simple Turbo Pascal Arithmetic

Prog3 demonstrates how arithmetic is used in Turbo Pascal programs and introduces another data type called **real**. Like integers, **real** variables are numbers; unlike integers, they can have decimal places. They can also be much larger than integers: the maximum value for an integer is 32,767, while for reals it is 1.0E38, or a 1 with 38 zeros after it.

```
Program PROG3;
Var
   Number1,
   Number2,
   AddResult,
   SubResult,
   MultResult,
   DivResult    : Real;

Begin
Write('Enter a number: ');
ReadLn(number1);
Write('Enter another number: ');
ReadLn(number2);

AddResult  := Number1 + Number2;
SubResult  := Number1 ┌ Number2;
MultResult := Number1 * Number2;
DivResult  := Number1 / Number2;


WriteLn('Number1 + Number2 = ',AddResult);
WriteLn('Number1 ┌ Number2 = ',SubResult);
WriteLn('Number1 * Number2 = ',MultResult);
WriteLn('Number1 / Number2 = ',DivResult);

WriteLn;
```

```
WriteLn('Number1 + Number2 = ',AddResult:10:3);
WriteLn('Number1 - Number2 = ',SubResult:10:3);
WriteLn('Number1 * Number2 = ',MultResult:10:3);
WriteLn('Number1 / Number2 = ',DivResult:10:3);
End.
```

Prog3 prompts the user for two real values, which are assigned to **Number1** and **Number2** and then used in four arithmetic operations:

AddResult	:= Number1 + Number2;
SubResult	:= Number1 − Number2;
MultResult	:= Number1 * Number2;
DivResult	:= Number1 / Number2;

After completing the computations, **Prog3** writes out the results in two different formats. For example, if you enter the numbers 2 and 3, then the first format statement

WriteLn('Number1 + Number2 = ',AddResult);

results in the following output:

Number1 + Number2 = 5.0000000000E+00

This is the default format for real numbers and is also known as *scientific notation*. The first part of the number (5.0000000000) is the value of the **real**, and the second part (+00) is the power of 10, to which the first part is raised. In other words, the number 5.0000000000E+00 can be expressed as 5.0 times 10 to the 0 power. Since 10 to the 0 power equals 1, the result is equal to 5.0.

The second set of **WriteLn** statements in **Prog3** writes real numbers with a format that you specify. For example, in the statement

WriteLn('Number1 + Number2 = ',AddResult:10:3);

the variable **AddResult** is followed by the format **:10:3**. This format tells Turbo Pascal to print the **real** variable right-justified in a field that is 10 spaces wide and has 3 decimal places, as illustrated here.

Print position	1	2	3	4	5	6	7	8	9	10
Output						5	.	0	0	0

If the number printed requires more than the 10 spaces allocated, the program prints the entire number, taking as many spaces as needed.

Repeating Statements with Loops

A loop is a mechanism that allows you to repeat a statement or series of statements. Turbo Pascal provides several ways of creating loops. The program in Figure 1-3 demonstrates two of them, the For-Do loop and the Repeat-Until loop.

You need three things to write a loop: a starting point, an ending point, and an integer variable, which is used as a counter. In the For-Do loop definition

For i := 1 To 5 Do

i is the counter, 1 is the starting point, and 5 is the ending point.

When the loop starts, the program sets **i** to 1 and increases it by 1 every time the loop repeats; after the fifth time through the loop, **i** is incremented to 6. Since 6 is greater than the ending point specified in the For-Do loop, the loop ends and the program proceeds with the first statement that follows the For-Do loop block.

```
          Program PROG4;
          Var
             NumberArray : ARRAY [1..5] Of Integer;
             Average : Real;
             i : Integer;

          Begin
          For i := 1 To 5 Do ◄──────────┐        After the
For-Do ┌──► Begin                       │        For-Do loop
Loop ──┤    Write('Enter a number: ');  │        executes five
Block └─►  ReadLn(NumberArray[i]);       ├──── times, the
          End;                          │        program skips
                                        │        to this
          Average := 0; ◄───────────────┘        statement

          i := 1;


Repeat- ┌──► Repeat
Until ──┤   Average := Average + NumberArray[i];
Loop  └─►  i := i + 1;
           Until i > 5;

          Average := Average / 5;
          WriteLn('The average is: ',Average:0:2);
          End.
```

Figure 1-3.   Using loops

Prog4 also demonstrates a second type of loop, known as the Repeat-Until loop. Compared with For-Do loops, Repeat-Until loops require a little more work. First, initialize the counter to the starting point; in this case, the starting point is 1. Second, increment the counter after each pass through the loop. Finally, explicitly test the value of the counter at the end of the loop.

For all this work, Repeat-Until loops do have advantages. For one thing, you do not need to know before you write the loop how many times it will execute. Repeat-Until loops repeat until the condition specified in the Until line is satisfied. Another advantage is that you can test for more than one condition at the same time, as is shown in this example:

```
Repeat
i := i + 1;
j := j + 1;
Until (i > 100) Or (j = 50);
```

If either of the tests in the **Until** statement is found to be true, the program exits the Repeat-Until loop.

Using Disk Files

Since you want your program to be able to store data, you need to learn to use disk files. Turbo Pascal makes using disk files easy. **Prog5** presents an example of how to use disk files.

```
Program PROG5;
Var
   i,j : Integer;
   f : Text;
   r : Real;

Begin
Assign(f,'squares.dat');
Rewrite(f);

For i := 1 To 20 Do
  WriteLn(f,sqr(i):10);

Reset(f);
For i := 1 To 20 Do
  Begin
  ReadLn(f,j);
  WriteLn(i:4,' squared is ',j:4);
  End;

Close(f);
End.
```

The program creates a text file that contains the squares of the first 20 positive integers and then rereads this file and writes a report to the screen.

Prog5 introduces the Turbo Pascal reserved word **Text**. A disk file that holds mainly words and sentences, a text file can also hold numbers. **Prog5** declares the file identifier **f** to be of type **Text**, which means that you can write data to **f** or read data in from **f**, depending on what your program needs to do.

Before you use a physical disk file, first assign it to a file variable. Do this with the **Assign** command as follows:

```
Assign (f, 'SQUARES.DAT');
Rewrite(f);
```

Assign links the physical file SQUARES.DAT with the **Text** file **f**. The **Rewrite** statement prepares the file to accept data. If the physical file SQUARES.DAT does not exist, the **Rewrite** command creates it. If it does exist, **Rewrite** destroys the contents of the file. Once a file has been rewritten, it is ready for output. **Prog5** writes data to **f** with this statement:

```
WriteLn(f,sqr(i):10);
```

This is the same **WriteLn** procedure used in earlier program examples, but this time the first parameter is the **Text** file **f**, which tells Turbo Pascal that everything written by this statement goes to this file.

Before you can read information from a file, it must be reset with the **Reset** statement, which opens the file and prepares it for reading. Once the file is reset, the **ReadLn** statement can be used to read from it.

As you read through this book, you will find in-depth discussions of the concepts you just learned, as well as information on many advanced topics. Turbo Pascal offers a number of powerful features that may take some time to fully grasp. Read, experiment, have fun, and you will become an accomplished programmer before you know it.

Getting Started with Turbo Pascal Version 4.0

Turbo Pascal Version 4.0 users must follow a slightly different procedure than that for Version 3.0 users. To start Version 4.0, type **TURBO** at the DOS prompt and press RETURN. You will soon see a screen that looks like Figure 1-4.

Turbo Pascal 4.0 divides the screen into two windows. The top window, the Edit window, is where you type in your programs. The bottom window, the Output window, contains the words and messages that your program creates.

The Turbo Pascal 4.0 menu, located at the top of the screen, offers five choices—File, Edit, Run, Compile, and Options. For now, you need to use only the Edit and Run

```
     File      Edit      Run      Compile      Options
  ┌─────────────────────────────── Edit ──────────────────────────────┐
  │  Line 1      Col 1    Insert Indent      C:NONAME.PAS              │
  │                                                                    │
  │                                                                    │
  │                                                                    │
  │                                                                    │
  │                                                                    │
  │                                                                    │
  │                                                                    │
  │                                                                    │
  │──────────────────────────── Output ───────────────────────────────│
  │ C:\tp>turbo                                                        │
  │                                                                    │
  │                                                                    │
  └────────────────────────────────────────────────────────────────────┘
  F1-Help  F2-Save  F3-Load  F5-Zoom  F6-Output  F9-Make  F10-Main menu
```

Figure 1-4.   Turbo Pascal 4.0 main screen

options. The others are described fully in Chapter 2.

When you first start it, Turbo Pascal 4.0 puts you in Edit mode. In the Edit mode you can enter or change source-code files just as in Turbo Pascal Version 3.0. A partial sample program would look like that shown in Figure 1-5.

The editor in Turbo Pascal 4.0 uses the same commands as Version 3.0. Turbo Pascal 4.0 also assigns uses to the computer's function keys for quick access to features like help screens, saving and loading files, changing windows, and the like.

Turbo Pascal 4.0 is highly compatible with Version 3.0: using Turbo Pascal 4.0, you can run any of the programs in this chapter and most throughout the book. In most cases you will have to add the following new line of code to the beginning of existing Version 3.0 programs to make them work with Version 4.0.

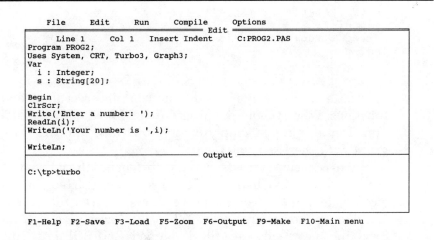

Figure 1-5.   Turbo Pascal 4.0 Edit window with program loaded

```
Uses CRT, Turbo3, Graph3;
```

This line tells Turbo Pascal 4.0 to include units named Crt, Turbo3, and Graph3 into your program. These units provide the functions needed to make your programs run correctly. The following program listing illustrates how to insert the line in a program:

```
Program PROG2;
Uses CRT, Turbo3, Graph3;
Var
   i : Integer;
   s : String[20];

Begin
ClrScr;
Write('Enter a number: ');
ReadLn(i);
WriteLn('Your number is ',i);

WriteLn;

Write('Enter a string: ');
ReadLn(s);
WriteLn('Your string is ',s);
End.
```

Units are segments of code that contain procedures and functions. When you need a procedure or function that is contained in a unit, you simply include that unit into your program with the **Uses** statement.

The concept of units is new to Turbo Pascal and is explained fully in Chapter 3. But, just to get started, here is a complete unit that contains procedures that control the size of the cursor on your screen. When you save this unit in a disk file, make sure the file is named CURSOR.PAS (the filename should match the name of the unit).

```
Unit Cursor;

(*************************************************)
Interface
(*************************************************)
```

```
Uses DOS;

Procedure CursorOff(Stype : Char);
Procedure CursorOn(Stype : Char);
Procedure CursorBig(Stype : Char);
Procedure ScreenType(Var Stype : Char);

(*************************************************)
Implementation
(*************************************************)

Procedure CursorOff;
Var
  Regs : Registers;

Begin
FillChar(Regs,SizeOf(Regs),0);
With Regs Do
  Begin
  AH := $01;
  CH := $20;
  CL := $20;
  End;
Intr($10, Regs);
End;

(*******************************************)

Procedure CursorOn;
Var
  Regs : registers;

Begin
FillChar(Regs,sizeof(Regs),0);
With Regs Do
  Begin
  CH := 6;
  CL := 7;

  if Stype = 'M' then
    Begin
    CH := CH+6;
    CL := CL+6;
    end;

  AH := $01;
  End;
Intr($10, Regs);
End;

(*******************************************)
```

```
Procedure CursorBig;
Var
  Regs : registers;
Begin
FillChar(Regs,sizeof(Regs),0);
With Regs Do
  Begin
  CH := 0;
  If Stype = 'M' then
    CL := 13
  Else
    CL := 7;
  AH := $01;
  end;
Intr($10, Regs);
End;

(************************************************)

Procedure ScreenType;
Var
  Regs : registers;
Begin
FillChar(Regs,sizeof(Regs),0);
Regs.AH := $0F;
Intr($10,Regs);
If Regs.AL = 7 Then
  Stype := 'M'
Else
  Stype := 'C';
End;

(************************************************)

end. (* of Unit Cursor *)
```

Note how the unit is much like a Pascal program. It starts with a name line, ends with the **End.** statement, and has a body. The body is broken into two parts—the interface section and the implementation section. You must have both parts in any unit you write.

To control the cursor, the program calls a BIOS routine with the statement:

```
Intr($10,Regs);
```

Intr is the Turbo Pascal function that calls BIOS services; **$10** is the hexadecimal value of the service we want (the video service); and **Regs** is a variable that passes information to the BIOS service. In this case, **Regs** tells BIOS that we want to change the size of the cursor and also says what size the cursor should be.

Now that you have defined your unit, type in the following program, which demonstrates the use of the cursor control procedures.

```
Program TestCursor;
Uses Dos,
     Cursor,
     CRT,
     Turbo3;
Var
  Stype : Char;

Begin
ScreenType(Stype);
WriteLn('Screen Type is: ',Stype);
ReadLn;

CursorBig(Stype);
WriteLn('Big Cursor');
ReadLn;

CursorOff(Stype);
WriteLn('No Cursor');
ReadLn;

CursorOn(Stype);
WriteLn('Small Cursor');
ReadLn;
End.
```

When you compile and run the program **TestCursor**, the procedures from the unit Cursor will be included in your program. Run this program to see how the cursor changes.

The Turbo Pascal
Programming
System

One of the reasons Turbo Pascal is so enjoyable to use is its integrated programming system. Once you are in the Turbo Pascal system, you can edit, compile, run, and debug your programs without having to go back to the DOS prompt. This chapter covers the most important topics for beginners — starting Turbo Pascal, using the editor, and compiling a program.

Getting Started

To start Turbo Pascal, type **TURBO** at the DOS prompt and press RETURN. Turbo Pascal immediately displays the screen shown in Figure 2-1. This screen tells you the version of Turbo Pascal you are using and the current display mode. In this case, the version is 3.02A and the default display mode is selected.

```
- - - - - - - - - - - - - - - - - - - - - - - - - - - - - - - - - -
  TURBO Pascal system            Version 3.02A
                                        PC-DOS

  Copyright (C) 1983,84,85,86 BORLAND Inc.
- - - - - - - - - - - - - - - - - - - - - - - - - - - - - - - - - -

  Default display mode


  Include error messages (Y/N)?
```

Figure 2-1.   Turbo Pascal's opening screen

At the bottom of the screen is the question **Include error messages (Y/N)?** If you decide not to load the error messages and type **N**, Turbo Pascal will flag mistakes with indecipherable codes. Since it is obviously much better for Turbo Pascal to describe the errors in English, you should always answer **Y** to this question. Why then does Turbo Pascal ask you this question at all?

This question was a legitimate one when most computers had no more than 64K of RAM. When memory was expensive, it sometimes made sense to exclude error messages in order to save space for programs. Today, few computers have less than 128K of RAM, making this small savings unimportant.

The Turbo Pascal Main Menu

After loading the error messages, Turbo Pascal brings you to the Main menu. This is the heart of the Turbo Pascal system, providing access to all the program's features. The Main menu looks like that shown in Figure 2-2. The first two lines tell you which drive and directory you are currently logged to: drive C in the \TURBO directory.

```
Logged drive: C
Active directory: \TURBO

Work file:
Main file:

Edit      Compile  Run   Save

Dir       Quit   compiler Options

Text:      0 bytes
Free: 62024 bytes

>
```

Figure 2-2.   The Turbo Pascal Main menu

Next are the *work file* and the *main file*. The work file is the file that is currently loaded into the Turbo Pascal editor. The main file, if specified, is the file that will be compiled. Use the main file when your programs are large and require separate source-code files. If you do not specify a main file, the compiler uses the work file.

The two lines at the bottom, **Text** and **Free**, are *memory-usage indicators*. These indicators tell you how much memory you have used and how much is left. Since you have not loaded a work file yet, all memory is free, that is, unused. Turbo Pascal can work on source files as large as 62,024 bytes (60K). If you do not load the error messages, the work space increases by 1462 bytes. As you can see, loading the error messages does not use much memory.

The Main menu itself lists the functions Edit, Compile, Run, Save, Dir, Quit, and compiler Options. You can select any of the seven functions by typing the appropriate character for each function. You can tell which character to type by looking for the uppercase character in the menu selections. Thus, you type **E** for Edit, **O** for compiler Options, and so on.

Edit (E)

The Edit option brings you into the Turbo Pascal editor, a simplified word processor you can use to create and change Turbo Pascal *program files*, also known as *source-code files*. Program files can be saved on your disk with the filename you selected. If you do not supply an extension to the filename yourself, Turbo Pascal automatically adds the default filename extension .PAS (for example, a file named **TEST** becomes **TEST.PAS**).

Compile (C)

Though programs are written in programming languages, computers only understand special codes called *machine language*. The Turbo Pascal compiler translates your source-code file into machine language. Once your program has compiled, you can run it to see how it works.

Run (R)

The Run function allows you to do two jobs at the same time. First, it compiles the program (unless it was just compiled). Second, it runs the program. Run is the function that makes Turbo Pascal special. Most compilers require that you edit your code with one program, compile it with another, and then run it from the DOS prompt. With Turbo Pascal, you can run and compile your programs as soon as you edit them without leaving the Turbo Pascal system.

Save (S)

The Save function stores the current work file to disk and automatically backs up the previous file. If you do not specify a file extension when you save a file, Turbo Pascal adds the default extension .PAS. The backup file always has the filename extension .BAK.

Dir (D)

The Dir function in Turbo Pascal works like the DOS Dir command: it lists filenames in any directory, allowing wild-card characters to select the filenames.

Quit (Q)

Selecting Quit ends your Turbo Pascal session and returns you to the DOS prompt. If, prior to quitting, you did not save the current work file, Turbo Pascal will ask you if you want to do so before it ends the session.

Compiler Options (O)

When you select the compiler Options function, Turbo Pascal presents the *compiler Options menu*. This menu, shown in Figure 2-3, comprises three features that can help you as you program—Compile Type, Command-line Parameters, and Find Run-time Error. The Quit selection simply returns you to the main menu, saving any changes you made at this menu.

```
compile -> Memory
           Com-file
           cHn-file


command line Parameters:


Find run-time error   Quit

>
```

Figure 2-3.   The compiler Options menu

Compile Type

As the menu indicates, Turbo Pascal can compile your program in one of three ways—into memory, a *command file*, or a *chain file*. Selecting the Memory option sets Turbo Pascal in *direct mode*, in which you can run programs without leaving the Turbo Pascal system. In this mode, however, Turbo Pascal does not store the compiled version of the program in a disk file.

The second compile option is Com-file, which tells Turbo Pascal to compile your program into a command file with the .COM filename extension (for example, TEST.COM). A command file is special because it can be run from the DOS prompt without the aid of the Turbo Pascal system.

The third compile option is cHn-file, which is short for chain file. Like a command file, a chain file is compiled by Turbo Pascal, and the results are stored on your disk with the .CHN filename extension (for example, TEST.CHN). Unlike a command file, however, a chain file cannot be run on its own but must be called from another Turbo Pascal program. You can use chain files when your program exceeds Turbo Pascal's limit of 64K for code space.

The compiler Options menu next displays the Command-line Parameters option. If you have used your computer for more than a few minutes, you have used command-line parameters. A simple example is the following DOS command:

    COPY A: C:

COPY is the name of the DOS program that copies files. The command line has two parameters, A: and C:. The Copy program reads these parameters from the command line to know where to copy from and to.

You can write a Turbo Pascal program that uses command-line parameters. When you start your program from the DOS prompt, it is easy to include your command-line parameters—simply type them in after the name of the program:

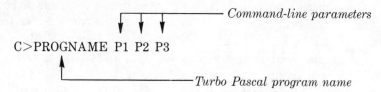

Command-line parameters

C>PROGNAME P1 P2 P3

Turbo Pascal program name

But what if you are running your program in direct mode? To run a program with command-line parameters in the direct mode, select the command-line parameters function by typing **P** at the compiler Options menu. Turbo Pascal displays the following prompt:

Parameters:

Enter your command-line parameters as shown below and press RETURN:

Parameters: P1 P2 P3

Once entered, the command-line parameters remain stored in memory. When you run a program in direct mode, Turbo Pascal feeds the parameters to the program as if they had been entered on the command line.

The last option on the compiler Options menu is Find Run-time Error. All but the most trivial programs have bugs at first. Some bugs are worse than others, and a few are so bad that the program will abort immediately when it finds them. These bugs are called *run-time errors*, and when Turbo Pascal finds one, you will see a message like this:

Run-time error 02, PC=2DAF
Program aborted

This message tells you what type of error occurred—code 02h in this case. The lowercase "h" after the code number indicates that it is in hexadecimal format. The message also tells you the approximate location of the error in the program. In this example, the error occurred at position 2DAFh. In addition, the message thoughtfully informs you that your program has aborted, a fact that should be readily apparent.

Translations of the run-time error codes can be found in Appendix A. You will find there that error condition 02h means that the program attempted to divide a number by zero. Division by zero is a subtle, yet serious, error, and one you should check for in your programs.

If you get a run-time error while running a program in direct mode, you will receive messages like these:

```
Run-time error 02, PC=2D79
Program aborted

Searching
  7 Lines

Run-time error position found. Press <ESC>
```

When run-time errors are found while a program is running in direct mode, Turbo Pascal searches for the point in the program where the error occurred. As it searches, the line numbers are displayed on the screen. When Turbo Pascal finds the error position, press ESC. Turbo Pascal calls the editor with the appropriate file loaded and points to the approximate location in the source code where the error occurred.

In direct mode, Turbo Pascal does the work for you. If you are running the program from the DOS prompt, however, the process is different. When your program aborts with a run-time error, record the PC value displayed on your screen. This value indicates the position in your program

where Turbo Pascal encountered the run-time error.
To locate the error,

1. Start Turbo Pascal.

2. Select Compiler Options from the Main menu.

3. Select the Find Run-time Error option from the compiler Options menu.

4. Enter the PC value.

Turbo Pascal will now find the location of the error just as it would in direct mode.

While Turbo Pascal accurately locates run-time errors under normal circumstances, problems can occur when you use *overlays*. Overlays stretch the memory of your computer by allowing several segments of your program to share the same memory. Because of this overlapping of memory, several procedures can share the same PC value. When tracking a run-time error in an overlaid procedure, Turbo Pascal might erroneously point to the wrong section of code. Keep this in mind when debugging programs with overlaid procedures.

The Turbo Pascal Editor

At the heart of Turbo Pascal is the editor, a simplified word processor for writing and editing Turbo Pascal programs. The editor's commands are patterned after WordStar. Touch typists enjoy the fact that they can execute all the editor's functions without moving their hands from the home position. Others prefer to use function keys to initiate special features.

To accommodate this preference, the TINST.COM program on the Turbo Pascal diskette provides the ability to redefine a function to any key. Unfortunately, it is difficult to do this. A better method for redefining the editor's function keys is SuperKey, a program from the maker of Turbo Pascal. With SuperKey, you can create not only your own command format but also powerful macrocommands that help to speed your programming. In fact, even if you like the editor's default command format, SuperKey can increase your productivity substantially.

The Status Line

To enter the editor, type **E** at the Main menu. If you have not yet identified a work file, Turbo Pascal asks you to do so before it allows you to enter the editor.

Once in the editor, the top line of the screen looks something like this:

Line 1   Col 1   Insert   Indent C:TEST.PAS

This is the *status line*, and it contains some important information. First, it tells you at which line and column of your source code the cursor is positioned. This is important for judging the size of your program and correctly aligning indentations.

Next is the *insert/overwrite indicator*. In insert mode, any text to the right of the cursor is pushed over to make room for the characters you type. In overwrite mode, the characters you type replace the text to the right.

The word **Indent** tells you that the *auto-indent* feature is on. When you enter a line and press RETURN, the auto-indent feature moves the cursor to the next line, directly beneath the first character of the line you just entered. This feature helps keep blocks of code properly indented as you write a program. The auto-indent feature can be turned off, in which case the word **Indent** disappears from the status line.

The last item on the status line is the name of the work file you are editing. If you do not specify a filename extension, Turbo Pascal adds the default extension .PAS.

Turbo Pascal Editor Commands

Like WordStar, most of the editor's commands are executed by holding down CTRL and pressing one or two other keys. Some Turbo Pascal editor commands differ from WordStar, however, so you should be completely familiar with how the Turbo Pascal editor works.

Cursor-Movement Commands

You can move the cursor by using either the keys on the numeric keypad or CTRL with character keys. Using the numeric keypad is fairly straightforward. The up-arrow key moves the cursor up one line, the right-arrow key moves the cursor right one character, and so on.

While the numeric keypad is adequate, you may prefer the alternate method of cursor control, the *cursor-control diamond.* The keys E, D, X, and S form a diamond on the left side of the keyboard, as shown here:

```
Q W E R T Y U I O P
 A S D F G H J K L
  Z X C V B N M
```

By holding down CTRL and pressing these keys, you get the same functions as the arrow keys on the numeric keypad but within easier reach of the home position. Pressing CTRL-E moves the cursor up one line, and CTRL-D moves the cursor one character to the right. (The convention CTRL-E means

holding down the control key and pressing the E key.)
Here are the cursor movements and the keys that you should
press:

Cursor Movement	Keypad Key	CTRL Key
Move up one line	up arrow	CTRL-E
Move down one line	down arrow	CTRL-X
Move right one character	right arrow	CTRL-D
Move left one character	left arrow	CTRL-S

Extended Cursor-Movement Commands

Other commands allow you to move the cursor by more than
one character or line at a time. For example, to move up or
down by one screen, use PGUP and PGDN on the numeric keypad or press CTRL-R or CTRL-C. Likewise, CTRL-F (or CTRL-
right arrow) moves the cursor to the next word, and CTRL-A
(or CTRL-left arrow) moves the cursor to the previous word.

Some cursor-control commands can be invoked only
from the keyboard; they have no equivalent key on the
numeric keypad. For example, you can scroll the text up or
down by pressing CTRL-Z or CTRL-W.

The TAB key (or CTRL-I) is unusual because it uses the
line above the cursor to determine how far to move. If there
is text on the line above and to the right of the cursor, pressing the tab key will move the cursor to the space corresponding to the beginning of the next word in the previous line.

Here is a summary of the extended cursor-movement
keys:

Cursor Movement	Keypad Key	CTRL Key
Move up by one screen	PGUP	CTRL-R
Move down by one screen	PGDN	CTRL-C
Move to beginning of next word	CTRL-right arrow	CTRL-F
Move to beginning of previous word	CTRL-left arrow	CTRL-A

Cursor Movement	**Keypad Key**	CTRL **Key**
Scroll page up	None	CTRL-Z
Scroll page down	None	CTRL-W
Move to beginning of next word on the line above	TAB	CTRL-I

Once you know these commands, you can move the cursor quickly and with little effort.

Block Operations

Block operations are so called because they work on an entire block of text. A block can be as small as a single character or as large as an entire file. With these commands you can copy, move, or delete a block of code, write a block to a disk file, or read a disk file into the editor.

All block operations work in essentially the same way. First, place the cursor at the beginning of the block of text you want to work with and press CTRL-KB. Then move the cursor to the end of the block and press CTRL-KK. To set it apart from the rest of the text, Turbo Pascal changes the display of the defined block to low video.

If you are moving or copying a block, move the cursor to the new position and press CTRL-KC to copy or CTRL-KV to move the block. To delete the block of text, press CTRL-KY. Once you copy or move a block, it remains displayed in low video until you press CTRL-KH.

Here is a summary of the block operations:

Action	CTRL **Key**
Mark the beginning of a block	CTRL-KB
Mark the end of a block	CTRL-KK
Mark a single word	CTRL-KT
Copy a block to the current cursor position	CTRL-KC
Move a block to the current cursor position	CTRL-KV

Action	CTRL Key
Write a block to a disk file	CTRL-KW
Read a disk file	CTRL-KR
Delete a block	CTRL-KY
Turn off block markers	CTRL-KH

Moving a block of text from one file into another file requires several steps.

1. In the source file, mark the block of text you want to move and press CTRL-KW.

2. Turbo Pascal displays **Write block to file:** at the top of the screen and waits for you to enter a filename. Type in a filename and press RETURN.

3. Exit from the editor by pressing CTRL-KD and change the work file to the file you want to move the text into.

4. Return to the editor by typing **E**.

5. Move to the place in the program where you want the new text to appear.

6. Press CTRL-KR.

7. Turbo Pascal displays **Read block from file:**. Enter the name of your temporary file and press RETURN. The block of text is inserted into your code.

Quick Commands

Some of the editor's commands already discussed can be "quickened" by preceding them with Q. For example, CTRL-R moves the cursor up by one page, while CTRL-QR moves the cursor to the beginning of the file. Other examples of how to quicken commands are shown below:

Cursor Movement	CTRL Key
To top of file	CTRL-QR
To bottom of file	CTRL-QC
To left of line	CTRL-QS

Cursor Movement	CTRL Key
To right of line	CTRL-QD
To beginning of a block	CTRL-QB
To the end of a block	CTRL-QK
To the last cursor position	CTRL-QP

Inserting and Deleting

As mentioned previously, the Turbo Pascal editor has two typing modes, insert and overwrite. In insert mode, the characters you type are inserted in the current line, and text to the right of the cursor is shifted over to make room for the new text. In overwrite mode, the characters you type replace the existing text. You can tell what mode you are in by looking at the status line at the top of the screen, where the word **Insert** or **Overwrite** appears. To change from one mode to the other, press CTRL-V. Whenever this command is called, the status line is changed to display the current mode.

You can delete text in a number of ways. One way is to use the **Block-delete** command (CTRL-KY) discussed earlier. But for small deletions, it is better to use the special commands listed here:

Action	Key
Delete character left	DEL
Delete character under cursor	CTRL-G
Delete to the end of the word	CTRL-T
Delete to the end of the line	CTRL-QY

Find/Search and Replace

Keeping track of variables and procedures is tough, and the bigger the program, the tougher it gets. The editor's **Find** command can help. You tell it what to look for, and it finds it for you.

For example, to find every place the variable **counter** appears, press CTRL-QF. Immediately, the editor prompts you for the text to search for. After typing in **counter** and pressing RETURN, the editor asks for options. Type **U** to indicate that you want to search regardless of case. When you hit RETURN again, the search begins.

In a few seconds, the editor stops at the first match it finds. To search for the next occurrence, press CTRL-L. That's all there is to it.

The three options available for the **Find** command, each represented by a single letter, are listed below:

Letter	Option
B	Start the search at the present location, but work backward toward the beginning of the file.
U	Ignore differences in case. When the U option is selected, Turbo Pascal considers "APPLE," "apple," and "ApPlE" to be identical.
W	Search only for whole words. When this is specified, the editor distinguishes between "car" and "cartoon."

The **Search-and-Replace** command is very similar to the **Find** command. But the **Search-and-Replace** command not only finds something, it also replaces it.

To start the **Search-and-Replace** command, press CTRL-QA. The editor prompts you for the text you want to search for. You are then asked to enter the replacement text. Finally, enter the options. The **Search-and-Replace** command uses the same three options as the **Find** command, plus these two additional options:

Letter	Option
G	Start search from the beginning of the file, regardless of the present cursor position.
n	Indicates the number of times to repeat the operation. For example, to perform a search and replace on the next three cases (but not on the subsequent cases), you would enter **n3**.

If you specify the **G** option alone, the editor asks you to confirm each change before it is made. If you specify **n** with a number, the editor will not ask for confirmation but will search for and replace the text as many times as the number you specified.

Note that if you select both the **G** and **n** options at the same time, the command runs through the entire file without stopping. This is useful if you are sure you want to make the changes throughout the file. To speed up the search-and-replace operation as it is running, press ESC followed by RETURN.

Aborting a Command

Some editor commands, such as the **Search-and-Replace** command, require you to enter some information (for example, a filename, a string to search for, and so on). If you want to abort or cancel a command instead of completing it, press CTRL-U and then ESC.

Other Editor Commands

There are two other commands in the Turbo Pascal editor that you may never have occasion to use. The first command, CTRL-QI, turns off the auto-indent feature. When you press the RETURN key in the editor, the auto-indent feature positions the cursor beneath the first character in the preceding line.

Turning off this feature brings the cursor back to the left side of the screen after each line. The status line changes to reflect changes in auto-indent mode.

The other command, CTRL-QL, restores a line to its previous form after you make changes to it. This resembles an undo command (sorely lacking in the editor) but it is extremely limited. The command only works while you are still on the line you made changes to. Once the cursor leaves the line, CTRL-QL does nothing. In addition, the command cannot restore a line that was deleted with the CTRL-Y command.

Returning to the Menu

When you are finished editing, you can return to the Main menu by pressing CTRL-KD. This does not save your program, however. To ensure that you do not lose your work, type **S** (for Save) at the Main menu as soon as you exit the editor.

Using SideKick with the Turbo Pascal Editor

Because the editor does not provide windows, it is a good idea to use a program called SideKick with the Turbo Pascal editor. The SideKick notepad creates a window in the Turbo Pascal editor. This allows you to view another part of the source code or another file without moving from your position in the program. In addition to the notepad feature, SideKick provides a table of ASCII codes and a calculator that can translate between decimal, hexadecimal, and binary numbers.

One word of caution about using the SideKick notepad as a window. The file that you load into the SideKick notepad is separate from the file you are editing in Turbo Pascal. As a result, changes made in one file are not reflected in the other file. Therefore, always make changes in the Turbo Pascal editor and use the notepad only as a viewing window into a file.

The Turbo Pascal Compiler

The *compiler* is the key component in the Turbo Pascal programming system. It translates your source code into a program the computer can run. Turbo Pascal's compiler is characterized by several strong points.

First and foremost, Turbo Pascal is one of the fastest compilers around. Part of Turbo Pascal's compilation speed can be attributed to the small size of the compiler. Many other compilers are huge, requiring multiple files to operate. The Turbo Pascal compiler, in contrast, takes up fewer than 40,000 bytes, including both the editor and the compiler, and it operates completely out of RAM.

Besides speed, another hallmark of a good compiler is compact code. Compared with other Pascal compilers, Turbo Pascal generates compact code. The more compact the code, the more program you can squeeze into the limited RAM space.

Finally, Turbo Pascal's execution speed is excellent. Keep in mind, however, that while execution time is important, the program's user will be far more concerned about presentation and ease of use than about a few microseconds here or there. Besides, a program's efficiency depends as much on the programmer's skills as it does on the efficiency of the compiler.

The Turbo Pascal compiler does have weak points. For example, the compiler has to start over from the beginning of the program whenever it encounters a compile error. If a program contains ten compile errors, it must be compiled ten times to find them all. The impact of this flaw increases as a program grows in size.

This problem could be avoided if Turbo Pascal supported

separate compilation units, which are compiled apart from the main program. The units are later linked to create an executable program. As a result, when you make a change in the code, you only have to compile the segment with the change.

Another weak point is the limitation on code space. Even with the use of overlays, 64K is used up surprisingly fast. Very simply, a compiler as good as Turbo Pascal should be able to address a larger code space.

Compiling a Program

Once you have written a Pascal program, exited from the editor with the CTRL-KD command, and saved the program at the Main menu, you can compile your program. You have two choices: compile and run the program in direct mode or compile the program to a command file and run it from the DOS prompt.

Direct Mode

Running in direct mode is easy. Simply type **C** at the Main menu and the program compiles. Assuming that no compile errors are encountered, you need only type **R** to run the program. You can even skip half the process by typing **R** from the start. This compiles and runs your program in one step.

Once a program starts in direct mode, it runs just as it would from the DOS prompt, with one exception. If the program uses the **Chain** or **Execute** commands, which pass control from one Turbo Pascal program to another, it will run into problems. But when you run a program while still in the Turbo Pascal system, you are not allowed to give up control of the program by using the **Chain** and **Execute** commands.

Compiling a Command File

Command files are program files that end with the .COM filename extension and can be run from the DOS prompt, without the aid of the Turbo Pascal system.

To compile your program to a command file, follow these steps:

1. At the Main menu, type **O** for Compiler Options.

2. To select the Com-file option, type **C**.

3. To return to the Main menu, type **Q**.

4. To begin compiling the program, type **C**.

When the program has finished compiling, the screen displays the following messages:

```
Compiling --> C:TEST.COM
   120 lines

Code:        0003 paragraphs (    48 bytes), 0D25 paragraphs free
Data:        0002 paragraphs (    32 bytes), 0FDA paragraphs free
Stack/Heap:  0400 paragraphs ( 16384 bytes) (minimum)
             A000 paragraphs (655360 bytes) (maximum)
```

The first two lines tell you that the file is TEST.COM and that the source code consists of 120 lines. The messages that follow tell you about the program's memory requirements, which are expressed in terms of hexadecimal (h) paragraphs, each paragraph containing 16 bytes of memory. The number of bytes is also expressed in decimal format.

In the example above, the program requires 3h paragraphs (48 bytes) of code space and 2h paragraphs (32 bytes) of data space. This leaves 0D25h paragraphs (53,840 bytes) free in the code segment and 0FDAh paragraphs (64,928 bytes) free in the data segment.

Turbo Pascal limits a program's code and data segments to 64K (65,536 bytes). Keeping this in mind, a little arithmetic with these numbers yields surprising results, as shown here:

	Code Segment	Data Segment
Used	48	32
Free	53840	64928
Total	53888	64960

When the used and free space are added, the result is actually 54K — not the 64K that was promised. What happened?

In the code segment, the Turbo Pascal run-time library adds about 10K to every program. The Turbo Pascal run-time library contains all the standard procedures and functions for input, output, arithmetic, and so on. The data segment is much less restrictive. You only lose about 500 bytes of memory here, which is used for Turbo Pascal "overhead."

The last two lines of the compiler messages have to do with the *stack* and the *heap*. The stack and the heap are *dynamic data* spaces, which means that they grow and shrink according to the demands of the program. Like the code and data segments, the stack segment is limited to 64K. The heap, on the other hand, has no defined limit and can use all the memory the computer has available (up to 640K).

Because the stack and heap spaces are dynamic, they do not have a fixed number of bytes allocated to them. Instead, Turbo Pascal gives these two segments a range, that is, a minimum and a maximum amount of memory they can operate in. In the example given earlier, the stack and heap spaces have a minimum requirement of 400h paragraphs (16,384 bytes) and a maximum of A000h paragraphs (655,360 bytes).

Computing Program Memory Requirements

With the numbers provided by the compiler messages, you can estimate the minimum amount of RAM needed to run the program. Simply add the code-segment size, the data-segment size, the minimum stack and heap values, and the size of the Turbo Pascal run-time library. In the example given earlier, the total is as follows:

Code segment	48
Data segment	32
Stack/Heap	16,648
Run-time library	11,648
Data segment overhead	576
Total	28,952

As you can see, you need at least 28,952 bytes free to run this program but you may need more. Remember that programs ask for space on the stack and the heap as it is needed. If a program requires more than the minimum of 16,648, it looks for more memory. If the extra memory is not available, the program aborts.

Changing Program Memory Requirements

When you first start Turbo Pascal, the memory control values are set to the following default values:

Minimum code segment size:	0000h (max 0D28h paragraphs)
Minimum data segment size:	0000h (max OFDCh paragraphs)
Minimum free dynamic memory:	0400h paragraphs
Maximum free dynamic memory:	A000h paragraphs

The code and data segments are both set to a minimum of zero bytes, while dynamic memory is given a minimum of 400h paragraphs and a maximum of A000h paragraphs.

You can control how much memory your program uses by setting your own minimums for the code and data segments. The minimum and maximum for dynamic memory (the stack and heap) can also be changed.

You can change memory defaults in either the Com-file or cHn-file mode. There is no reason, however, to ever set the options on a chain file, since a chain file conforms to the segments of the .COM file that calls it. Always use the default options when compiling to a chain file.

To change memory defaults for a .COM file, select the memory value you want to change by typing the appropriate key: **O** for code-segment size, **D** for data-segment size, **I** for minimum dynamic memory, and **A** for maximum dynamic memory.

O	Change code-segment size
D	Change data-segment size
I	Change minimum dynamic memory
A	Change maximum dynamic memory

The value you enter must equal the number of hexadecimal paragraphs. For example, to set the minimum code segment to 1000 bytes, you need to convert 1000 bytes to hex paragraphs: Divide 1000 by 16 and convert to hexadecimal (SideKick's calculator comes in handy here). The result is 3Eh. Now type **O** for cOde segment and enter **3E**.

You may be surprised to find that the number displayed is 316h. Why did Turbo Pascal change 3Eh to 316h? Because it added the run-time library (2D8h paragraphs) to your value. Similarly, when you enter an amount for the minimum data segment, the overhead value of 24h paragraphs is added to your hexadecimal value; 10h becomes 34h.

The run-time library overhead is not added to the minimum and maximum settings for dynamic memory. For these, the number you enter is the number you get.

When to Change Memory Defaults

Normally, you do not need to alter the default memory values. The exceptions are when you use chain files, when you run a program on top of your program, or when you want to specify a minimum amount of memory for your program to run.

Memory Requirements for Chain Files

When a program is compiled to a .COM file, the data and code segments must be large enough to accommodate the largest data and code segments found in any of the chain files. The figures below illustrate code and segment sizes for three chain files:

Program Name	Code Size	Data Size
TEST1.CHN	0006h	0007h
TEST2.CHN	0006h	017Eh
TEST3.CHN	00BAh	0007h

The largest code-segment size is 00BAh paragraphs, while the largest data-segment size is 017Eh paragraphs. Accordingly, when you compile the .COM file that calls these chain files, the minimum code-segment and data-segment sizes must be set to no less than these values.

Setting a Maximum Memory Requirement

You can temporarily suspend the execution of a Turbo Pascal program, run another program on top of it, and then return to the Turbo Pascal program. To do this, you must set dynamic memory to a maximum value; otherwise, the Turbo Pascal program grabs all the available memory when it starts up, and none is left over to run the other program.

Setting a Minimum Memory Requirement

If a program uses a lot of space on the heap, make sure the computer that will run the program has enough RAM to support your dynamic allocations. By specifying a minimum amount of dynamic space when you compile a program, you effectively prevent anyone from running your program on a computer that does not have enough memory.

Compiling a Chain File

As you know, Turbo Pascal limits its code space to 64K, of which you can use only 54K. If you are writing a large program, you can easily exhaust your code space, even if you use overlays. But if you break up the program into segments and create chain files, each segment is allocated its own code and data space. Then, instead of calling the procedure as you normally would, execute the chain file.

Passing Variables to a Chain File

Once called from another Turbo Pascal program, a chain file executes like an entirely new program. Because Turbo Pascal does not initialize a program's data space, you can pass global variables from the command file to the chain file with all the values intact. To do this successfully, you must make the declaration sections of the command file and the chain file the same, as shown in Figure 2-4.

In this example, the values in variables **a**, **x**, and **b** will be preserved after calling the chain file. Variables **s** and **g** will not preserve their values, however, because eliminating the integer variable **c** throws off the match between the two declarations. If you insert an integer variable in the chain-file declarations before the **s**, then **s** and **g** will retain their values.

This process of passing values through matching global declarations works in the other direction as well. If a chain file executes a command file with matching global values, the values are passed to the command file.

While they have their place, chain files do have some drawbacks. First, they take time to start up. Even for small chain files, this time can be considerable. Second, calling a chain file is a one-way trip: you cannot jump back into the

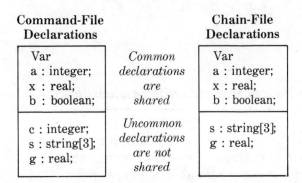

Figure 2-4.   Command- and chain-file declarations

calling program. At best, you can execute the calling program at the end of the chain file and pass information to the calling program via a temporary disk file. It works like this:

1. The command file calls the chain file.

2. The chain file executes.

3. Before ending, the chain file creates a temporary file and writes information in it that is passed to the command file.

4. The chain file executes the command file and finishes.

5. The command file starts up and checks whether the temporary file exists. If it does, the command file knows that it has been executed from a chain file.

6. The command file opens the temporary file, reads its contents, and then erases the file.

7. The command file uses the contents of the temporary file to return to the point where it called the chain file.

Compared with overlays, chain files are clumsy, complicated, and inefficient. Nonetheless, there are times when a chain file can be useful.

The Turbo Pascal Version 4.0 Environment

With Turbo Pascal 4.0, Borland introduces a new programming environment. Pull-down menus are one of the features of this new environment; they are menus that appear from the top of the screen when you highlight a choice on the Main menu. In addition, you will find the screen divided into two parts—the Edit window and the Output window. Finally, Turbo Pascal 4.0 makes use of your computer's function keys. Figure 2-5 shows a list of the function keys and their uses at the bottom of the screen.

These changes mark a departure from earlier versions of Turbo Pascal and aim to make the system easier to use. Experienced Turbo Pascal programmers may find the changes cumbersome at first but after a few hours will find an overall improvement in their programming.

The Main Menu

Turbo Pascal 4.0 displays a Main menu at the top of the screen. Because the Main menu is always visible, you always have access to all of Turbo Pascal's features. The choices on the Main menu are File, Edit, Run, Compile, and Options. You make your choice in one of two ways. You can highlight the choice you want by using the right- and left-arrow keys and pressing RETURN, or you can simply press the key corresponding to the first letter of the name of the choice. For example, to select the File option, you could simply press **F**.

```
    File      Edit     Run     Compile    Options
                                 Edit
        Line 1      Col 1    Insert Indent      C:NONAME.PAS







                              Output
C:\tp>turbo




 F1-Help  F2-Save  F3-Load  F5-Zoom  F6-Output  F9-Make  F10-Main menu
```

Figure 2-5.   Function keys used in Turbo Pascal 4.0

The File Selection

The File option from the Main menu is used to select new files to edit, save files you have already edited, or change directories, for example. Descriptions of each of the File options follows.

Load   The load option reads a disk file into the Turbo Pascal Edit window. If the filename you enter does not exist, a new file will be created.

Pick   Turbo Pascal 4.0 keeps a list of the eight files you edited most recently. When you select the Pick option, Turbo Pascal displays this list and lets you pick the file you want. The Pick option is especially helpful when you are editing multiple source files.

New   The New option clears the Edit window and sets the filename to NONAME.PAS. When you save the file, Turbo Pascal will ask you for a name.

Save   The Save option writes the file currently in the editor to disk.

Write to   The Write to option writes the contents of the editor to a file that you specify.

Directory   The Directory option lets you specify the directory entries you wish to see and then displays them on the screen.

Change dir   The Change dir option allows you to change the default directory.

OS shell   If you type O, Turbo Pascal 4.0 will temporarily halt and display the DOS prompt. At the DOS prompt, you can perform DOS functions or run other programs. You return to Turbo Pascal by typing **EXIT**.

Quit   The Quit option terminates your session with Turbo
Pascal 4.0.

The Edit Selection

When you select Edit from the Main menu, Turbo Pascal
moves you from the Main menu into the Edit window. In the
Edit window, you can enter and change source code just as
you would in any version of Turbo Pascal. To return to the
Main menu from the Edit window, press either ^KD or F10.

The Run Selection

When you select Run from the Main menu, Turbo Pascal will
compile, link, and run your program without leaving the
Turbo system. This is very similar to the Run feature in Version 3.0.

The Compile Selection

This selection allows you to compile a program to memory or
to disk much like the Compile option in Version 3.0. Version
4.0, however, offers the following additional features.

Compile   This feature compiles and links your source
program.

Make   Make creates an executable file with the .EXE
extension. As Turbo Pascal compiles your program, it checks
to see if any units were altered since they were last compiled.
If a unit has been altered, Turbo Pascal will recompile it.

Build   Build works like the Make option except that all
units are forced to be recompiled, even if they haven't been

altered since they were last compiled.

Destination   Your compiled code can be stored in a disk file or in memory. Compiling a program to memory is faster than compiling it to disk, but the program compiled to memory will not be saved when you end your session. You can select the destination by highlighting **Destination** and pressing RETURN.

Find error   When a Turbo Pascal program encounters a run-time error, the program will display a memory location in the form **xxxx:xxxx** and then terminate. You can use the Find error option to locate the the error by entering the memory location as it is displayed.

Primary file   Selecting a primary file is the same as selecting a main file in Version 3.0—Turbo Pascal will always start compiling from the primary file.

Get info   This option displays information about the program you are currently working on. Information includes the primary file, the current file, the size of the file, the number of lines compiled, the code size, the data size, the stack size, the minimum and maximum heap limits, and a few other bits of useful information.

The Options Selection

Turbo Pascal 4.0 offers extended control over the programming environment via the Options selection. With this selection you can control compiler directives, directories to search for files, and command-line parameters. You can also save your options in a file and retrieve them whenever you change programs.

Compiler   Compiler directives are special codes you insert in programs to control the type of code Turbo Pascal creates. Some directives can enable error checking while others select certain options. Using the Compiler option, you can set these compiler directives without putting the codes in the program itself.

The Compiler option is also used to set the memory requirements for your program. You can set the stack size for up to 64K and the lower and upper heap limits.

Environment   This selection allows you to select the Auto Save Edit option and the Backup Source Files option. You should normally leave these on so you don't accidentally lose valuable source code. The Environment option allows you to set Tab size, Screen size (25 lines, 43-line EGA, and 50-line VGA), and Zoom windows, and includes a toggle to retain or not retain the saved screen.

Directories   With the Directories option, you can tell Turbo Pascal where to look for certain files. You can have separate directories for the Turbo Pascal program files, your executable code, include files, unit files, and object files.

Parameters   The Parameters option allows you to specify command-line parameters that are passed to your program when it is run from memory.

Load options   With this option, you load a configuration file into Turbo Pascal. A configuration file contains information on which directories to use, settings for compiler directives, and other options you have selected.

Save options   This feature stores the current Turbo Pascal configuration in a configuration file. You can load this file back into memory whenever you want. This saves time since you don't have to reset all the configuration options every time you start to program.

The Turbo Pascal 4.0 Screen

Turbo Pascal 4.0 divides the screen into two portions—the Edit window and the Output window. The Edit window displays the source file currently loaded into the editor. The Output window displays a portion of the screen as it looked before the Turbo Pascal system started. As you run programs, you can see the results in the Output window.

To move from the Main menu line to the Edit window, simply press **E** or highlight the word **Edit** and press RETURN. You can switch between the Edit window and the Output window by pressing F6. When you are in the Output window, you cannot enter any information, but you can scroll the screen up and down to view its entire contents.

When you are in the Edit window, you can press F5 to remove the Output window and use the entire screen for editing. Likewise, if you press F5 when in the Output window, the entire screen will display output.

Function Keys

Turbo Pascal 4.0 makes good use of the PC's function keys. The functions of these keys are displayed at the bottom of the screen and control such features as help, saving and loading files, switching windows, and the Make compiler option. The F10 key is especially important because it activates the Main menu.

Fundamental Concepts
of Turbo Pascal
Programming

Goto-less Programming
Turbo Pascal and Standard Pascal
Strong Typing of Variables in Pascal
Procedures and Functions
Functions Versus Procedures

Two of the most important programming languages today, Pascal and BASIC, started out as teaching tools. It is there that the similarity between the two languages ends. Comparing the two will help you understand what Pascal is all about.

In the early 1970s, a major movement in programming began. Known as *structured programming*, this approach stressed breaking a program down into manageable pieces, and then assembling those pieces into a program with a coherent, logical flow.

Pascal, developed by Niklaus Wirth, was designed to teach structured programming skills to future programmers. By enforcing a strict set of rules regarding the declaration of variables, program structure, and flow of control, Pascal steered aspiring programmers toward good programming habits. In addition, Pascal provided a wide range of programming tools that made writing good, clear code much easier than was possible with COBOL or Fortran.

BASIC, on the other hand, was developed as an easy-to-learn language for nonprogrammers. It was not intended to produce good programming habits but to get nontechnical people to write simple programs. The result is a language that one can learn quickly and be able to write simple programs. Unfortunately, BASIC encourages poor programming habits and unreadable code. It is significant that the improved versions of BASIC resemble Pascal.

Goto-less Programming

One of the main goals of Niklaus Wirth was to eliminate the need for the Goto statement. Students of programming, who are generally taught structured programming from the outset, might be surprised at just how pervasive and destructive the **Goto** command is. It allows programmers to jump anywhere within a program regardless of consistency in the program flow. Debugging and maintaining programs full of Goto's is very difficult. Pascal eliminated the need for the Goto statement entirely by providing powerful control structures, which both increased program readability and eliminated a lot of unforeseen errors.

Turbo Pascal and Standard Pascal

While standard Pascal had many strong points, it was never fully developed for use in commercial applications. It lacked useful input and output functions and sorely needed string types. Nonetheless, this version of Pascal was considered the standard for the world.

Borland recognized both the strengths and the weaknesses of standard Pascal and updated the language substantially. The result is a rich language that provides the programmer with the logical structure of standard Pascal plus an extensive set of tools.

In making these additions, Borland broke away from the

Pascal standard, a move that prompted criticism from some quarters. Despite this, Turbo Pascal and its extensions have become the standard international microcomputer Pascal.

Strong Typing of Variables in Pascal

Pascal is often called a *strong-typed language*. This means that you cannot mix different types of variables arbitrarily. In assignment statements, the values on the right must be compatible in type with the corresponding variable on the left. For example, if the variable **i** is defined as an integer, the following statement would be illegal:

   i := 1.0 + 2;

The value **1.0** is a real value and cannot be used in an assignment statement for an integer because using a real value to evaluate an integer variable goes against the properties of a strong-typed language. Observing the strong-typing rules helps avoid errors in programming. Turbo Pascal is less picky about strong typing than standard Pascal, but you still have to follow these rules:

1. A **real** cannot be used directly in an assignment statement for an **integer** or **byte**. The **real** must first be converted to an **integer** by using the Trunc or Round standard functions.

2. An **array** can be assigned to another **array** only when the two have the same range and type.

3. A variable that is passed to a procedure or function must be defined as the same type as the variable defined in the procedure or function. This rule can be relaxed for **string** variables by using the **V** compiler directive.

Strong typing as implemented in Turbo Pascal is relatively unrestrictive, yet it still helps programmers avoid unnecessary errors.

Procedures and Functions

The logic of modular programming states that it is easier to write a good program if you break it down into small chunks. In Pascal, these chunks are called *procedures* or *functions*. One reason this approach is easier than writing one long program is that each procedure and function can be written and tested independently from the main program. Once you are sure the procedure is functioning correctly, it can be integrated into the main program without concern. In addition, Pascal allows you to pass variables into the function or procedure, further increasing the modularity of the program.

```
Program ProcDemo;
Var
   x, y : Integer;

   Procedure Subtract;  ◄────   Procedure name

   Begin ◄────
   x := x - 1;
   y := y - 1;          ├──   Code block
   End; ◄────

Begin
x := 5;
y := 10;
Subtract;  ◄────────────   Call to procedure
end.
```

Figure 3-1.   A Turbo Pascal procedure declaration

Defining Procedures in Pascal

To define a procedure in Pascal, you need at least two things: a name for the procedure and a block of code. The example in Figure 3-1 is a simple procedure definition that provides both ingredients.

The Pascal reserved word **Procedure** tells the compiler that a procedure is about to be defined. The next identifier is the name of the procedure, **Subtract**. Later, the program will call this procedure by using its name.

Subtract decrements the value of variables **x** and **y** by 1. In the example, **x** and **y** are initialized to 5 and 10, respectively. Upon returning from **Subtract**, **x** is equal to 4 and **y** is equal to 9. **Subtract** can use **x** and **y** because they are *global variables*. Global variables are those variables declared in the program block and, as a result, can be used by any procedure in the program.

Passing Parameters to a Procedure

The example in Figure 3-1 works for global variables **x** and **y** only. If you want to decrement any other pair of variables, you're out of luck. You can expand the usefulness of this procedure by defining parameters. Then, you can use the same procedure for any two integer variables. The following example shows the revised procedure with the **Subtract** parameters.

```
Program ProcDemo2;
Var
  q, w, x, y : Integer;

  Procedure Subtract(a : Integer; Var b : Integer);
  Begin
  a := a - 1;
  b := b - 1;
  End;

Begin
x := 5;
y := 10;
```

```
q := 1;
w := 4;
Subtract(x,y);
Subtract(q,w);
End.
```

Note that the procedure name is now followed by a list of two parameters—**a** and **b**—both of which are integers. When **Subtract** is called, the program passes two integer values to the procedure. In the statement **Subtract(x,y)**, **x** supplies the value for parameter **a**, and **y** supplies the value for parameter **b**. Thus, **x** and **y** are the parameters being passed to the procedure. Once inside the procedure, **a** takes the value of **x** and **b** takes the value of **y**. The same logic applies to the second call to **Subtract**, where **q** and **w** are passed as parameters.

While the procedure **Subtract** decrements each parameter by one, the effect on **x** will be different than on **y**. In the procedure definition, parameter **b** is preceded by the Pascal reserved word **Var**, while **a** is not. Parameters preceded by **Var** are called *reference parameters;* those without it are called *value parameters*.

Reference Parameters

When a variable is passed to a procedure as a reference parameter, changes made to that variable remain even after the procedure has ended. In the preceding example, the global variable **y**, with a value of 10, is passed to the procedure as parameter **b**. The procedure subtracts 1 from **b**, giving a value of 9. When the procedure ends, **b** is passed back to the main program, where it retains the value of 9.

Changes made to reference parameters within a procedure remain in effect even after the procedure has ended because Turbo Pascal passes not the variable's value, but the variable's address in memory. In other words, a change made to **b** is really made to the location in memory where the original variable (in this case, the variable **y**) is stored.

In short, the reference parameter and the actual variable passed to the procedure are one and the same; that is, they share the same position in memory. Therefore, any change made to the reference parameter is stored as a permanent change in the actual variable.

Value Parameters

Value parameters are different from reference parameters. When a value parameter is passed to a procedure, a temporary copy of the variable is placed in memory. Within the procedure, only the copy is used. When the value of the parameter is changed, it only affects the temporary storage; the actual variable outside the procedure is never touched.

In the preceding illustration, **a** is a value parameter because it is not preceded by the reserved word **Var**. When the program starts, **x** is initialized to 5. When **Subtract** is called, a copy of **x** is made in temporary storage, and the copy is then passed to the procedure. Parameter **a**, then, points to the temporary storage location, not to the actual location of **x**. Therefore, when **a** is decremented, only the value in temporary storage is affected. At the end of the procedure, the value in temporary storage is discarded and the global variable **x** retains the original value of 5.

Functions Versus Procedures

Both procedures and functions provide modularity to your programs. Both are self-contained units and both can use parameters. The difference between functions and procedures, illustrated by the following examples, is in how they return values.

```
Procedure Square(x : Real;Var x2 : Real);
Begin
x2 := x * x;
End;

Function Square(x : Real) : Real;
Begin
Square := x * x;
End;
```

The procedure **Square** passes two parameters. The first parameter, **x**, is the number to be squared and the second, **x2**, is the result. The procedure multiplies parameter **x** by itself and assigns the result to the parameter **x2**. Because **x2** is a reference parameter, its new value is retained when the procedure ends.

The function Square produces basically the same result as the procedure. However, the function does not store the result in a parameter, but passes it back through the function itself. To clarify the difference, examine how the two would be used in a program:

Using the Procedure Square
$$Square(x, x2);$$
or
$$Square(x, x2);$$
$$if\ x2 > 100\ then\ ...$$

Using the Function Square
$$x2 := Square(x);$$
or
$$if\ Square(x) > 100\ then\ ...$$

A function can (and must) be used in an assignment, comparison, or arithmetic expression. Another way of looking at it is that functions are like variables whose value depends on the parameters that are passed to them.

Procedures, on the other hand, cannot be used in assignment, comparison, or arithmetic expressions. At most, a procedure can return a variable that can be used in expressions.

Both functions and procedures have their strong points. Functions are generally preferred when one clearly identifiable result is desired. In the preceding example, a function makes more sense than a procedure since obtaining the squared value is the objective. A procedure, rather than implying a specific result, performs an operation that may return many or no results. In the end, experience is the best guide in deciding between functions and procedures.

Passing Parameters of Different Types

Variables that are passed to a procedure or function must match the type declaration of their respective parameters. If, for example, a parameter is declared to be an **integer**, you cannot pass a **real** type through it. A procedure declaration that includes the standard Turbo Pascal scalars follows.

```
Procedure Example (i : Integer;
                   r : Real;
                   b : Boolean;
                   x : Byte);
```

User-defined types, such as **strings**, can also be used to define parameters, as shown below.

```
Program ProcDemo3;
Type
  Str255 = String[255];
  Str80 = String[80];

Var
  St1 : Str255;
  St2 : Str80;

  Procedure Blank(Var s : Str255);
  Begin
  s := '';
  End;
```

```
Begin
Blank(St1); (* legal *)
Blank(St2); (* not legal *)
End.
```

Note that the parameter s is defined by using the type definition supplied by the user. Note also that you can pass strings to the procedure only if they have been defined as the same type. Thus, **St2** cannot be passed because it is defined as **Str80**, not **Str255**. This is a result of Pascal's strong typing.

Clearly, it would be preferable to pass any type of string into this procedure. This can be done by using the {**$V-**} compiler directive, which turns off string-type checking. With the {**$$-**} compiler directive disabled, Turbo Pascal allows you to pass any type of string variable through any type of string parameter. Compiler directives are discussed in detail in Chapter 4.

Passing Set Parameters

Sets, another type of user-defined type, follow the same rules that apply to strings. An example of a set used as a parameter is shown in the following illustration:

```
Program ProcDemo4;
Type
  CharSet = Set Of Char;

Var
  Ch : Char;
  UpCaseChar : CharSet;

  Function TestChar(Ch : Char; TestSet : CharSet) : Boolean;
  Begin
  TestChar := Ch in TestSet;
  End;

Begin
Ch := 'A';
UpCaseChar := ['A'..'Z'];
If TestChar(Ch,UpCaseChar) Then WriteLn(ch);
End.
```

The user-defined type **CharSet** is used to define a parameter in TestChar. When the function is called, the variable **UpCaseChar** is passed to the function as parameter **TestSet**.

Passing Untyped Parameters

Parameters defined using a data type (such as **real**, **integer**, and so on) are appropriately called *typed parameters*. Turbo Pascal also allows you to use *untyped parameters*. The advantage of untyped parameters is that you can pass variables of any type of data into them —**strings**, **reals**, **integers**, **booleans**, and any other data type are all legal.

How is it that an untyped parameter can accept any data type? To understand this, think about typed parameters. When you define a typed parameter, you tell Turbo Pascal what type of data to expect. Thus, Turbo Pascal can easily determine if a mismatch exists between the variable type and the parameter type. When you use untyped parameters, however, the procedure or function has no idea what it is you are passing to it. The procedure accepts whatever is passed to it and expects the programmer to know how to handle it. Because of this, untyped parameters must be used carefully. Consider the example in Figure 3-2.

Parameter **x** (a reference parameter) has no type associated with it. Therefore, **x** is an untyped parameter. The reserved word **Var** is necessary because all untyped parameters must be reference parameters.

While **x** is clearly a parameter, it cannot be used directly by the procedure. Why not? The procedure does not know what **x** is, so it cannot use the parameter.

Instead of using **x**, you must declare a variable in the procedure that is **Absolute** at **x**. This means that the variable you declare will reside at exactly the same address as **x**. In Figure 3-2, **y** is defined as an **integer** that is located at the same place in memory as **x**. Now, you can use variable **y** in place of **x**.

When this procedure is called, any type of variable can be passed to this procedure and the procedure will treat the

---

```
Procedure Example(Var x);
Var
  y : Integer Absolute x;
Begin

WriteLn(y);
```
*Legal: **y** is of type **Integer***

```
WriteLn(x);
```
Illegal: x has no type

```
End;
```

Figure 3-2.   Legal and illegal untyped parameters

variable as an integer. What does that mean? Suppose you pass a string into the procedure. Since y is an integer, and an integer is two bytes long, the procedure will take the first two bytes of the string and treat them as an integer value. Of course, the integer value will have absolutely no relation to the value of the string. If you pass a string with the value "TEXT" into the procedure, the integer value will be 21,500 — a totally arbitrary value.

So why use untyped parameters? In certain and very few instances, untyped parameters are useful. One example, a procedure that compares two variables to see if they are equal, is shown in the following illustration:

```
(*$V-*)
Program CompareData;
Var
  i1,i2 : Integer;
  r1,r2 : Real;
  s1,s2 : String[255];

Function Compare(Var x,y; kind : Char) : Integer;
Var
  aString : String[255] Absolute x;
  bString : String[255] Absolute y;
```

```
    aReal : Real Absolute x;
    bReal : Real Absolute y;

    aInteger : Integer Absolute x;
    bInteger : Integer Absolute y;

Begin
  Case kind Of

    'R' : (* Real *)
      Begin
      If aReal > bReal Then
        Compare := 1
      Else If aReal < bReal Then
        Compare := -1
      Else
        Compare := 0;
      End;

    'I' : (* Integer *)
      Begin
      If aInteger > bInteger Then
        Compare := 1
      Else If aInteger < bInteger Then
        Compare := -1
      Else
        Compare := 0;
      End;

    'S' : (* String *)
      Begin
      If aString > bString Then
        Compare := 1
      Else If aString < bString Then
        Compare := -1
      Else
        Compare := 0;
      End;

  End; (* of case *)
End;

Begin
r1 := 10000.0;
r2 := -33.0;
WriteLn(Compare(r1,r2,'R'));

i1 := 100;
i2 := 200;
WriteLn(Compare(i1,i2,'I'));
```

```
s1 := 'Xavier';
s2 := 'Smith';
WriteLn(Compare(s1,s2,'S'));

End.
```

This example passes two variables at a time into the function Compare. The variables are passed as untyped parameters and are subsequently redefined as **real**, **integer**, and **string** variables. The third parameter, **kind**, is a character denoting the type of the first two parameters. An **S** indicates **string**, **R** indicates **real**, and **I** indicates **integer**.

By checking the value of **kind**, the procedure knows whether to compare strings, reals, or integers. The final result, then, is a generalized procedure that can compare any two variables of type **integer**, **real**, or **string**. The only restriction is that you must tell the procedure what type of variable you are comparing.

Passing Literal Values

In the examples so far, only variables have been passed as parameters to functions. It is also possible to pass a literal value, such as an actual number or a string enclosed in quotation marks, to a procedure. Figure 3-3 shows how the numeric literal 3.0 is passed to the function Square. The

```
Function Square(x : Real) : Real;
Begin
Square := x * x;
End;                                    The literal value 3.0 is passed
                          ◄─────────     to the function
Begin
WriteLn(Square(3.0));
End.
```

Figure 3-3.   Passing a literal value to a procedure

function performs just as it would if a variable were passed to it.

The following example illustrates how a string literal is passed to a procedure:

```
Procedure WriteUpCase(st : Str255);
Var
  i : Integer;
Begin
For i := 1 To Length(st) Do
  st[i] := UpCase(st[i]);
WriteLn(st);
End;

Begin
WriteUpCase('This is a string literal');
End.
```

This procedure takes the string passed to it, converts it to all uppercase characters, and writes it out. In the preceding example, the string passed is a literal, but the procedure would accept a string variable as well. Note, however, that you can pass literal values and string literals to value parameters only, not to reference parameters.

Procedures and the Scope of Variables

In BASIC and some other programming languages, all variables are *global*, that is, all variables can be referred to at any point throughout the program. Pascal supports global variables but also provides local variables. These are variables that exist within a limited portion of the program, also known as the *scope of a variable*. By limiting the scope of variables, unwanted side effects are eliminated.

The scope of a variable is determined by the block in which it is declared, as illustrated in the program shown in Figure 3-4.

Variable **x** is global in scope because it is defined within the program block, not within a function or procedure block. The variable **y**, defined within **Procedure A**, is limited in

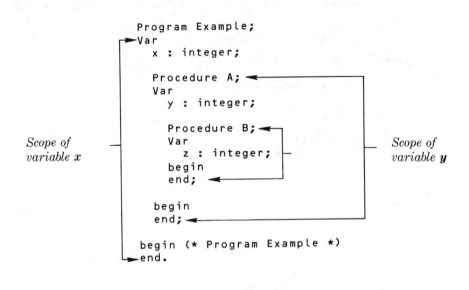

```
            Program Example;
          ►Var
               x : integer;

               Procedure A;  ◄──────────────────┐
            Var                                  │
               y : integer;                      │
                                                 │
               Procedure B; ◄─┐                  │
            Var               │                  │
               z : integer; ──┤                  │
            begin             │                  │
            end; ◄────────────┘                  │
                                                 │
            begin                                │
            end; ◄───────────────────────────────┘

            begin (* Program Example *)
          ►end.
```

Scope of   *Scope of*
variable x   *variable y*

Figure 3-4.   Determining the scope of a variable

scope and can only be referred to within the scope of **Procedure A**.

Finally, variable **z**, defined within **Procedure B**, is even more limited in scope: it can only be referred to within the scope of **Procedure B**. Therefore, **Procedure B** can use variables **x**, **y**, and **z**; and **Procedure A** can use both variable **x** and variable **y**, but not variable **z**. The main program, the most limited of all, can refer only to variable **x**.

Variables at different levels can share the same name. However, giving variables the same name limits the scope of one of the two. This is demonstrated in Figure 3-5.

This program contains three variables named **x**. In the program block, **x** is an integer variable, while in **Proc1** it is a string variable. **Proc1** cannot access the global variable **x** because it has already defined its own variable with the same name. When **Proc2** refers to **x**, it uses the variable defined in **Proc1** because **Proc2** is declared within **Proc1**.

```
Program DoubleName;
Var
  x : Integer; ◄─────────────────────────┐
                                          │
  Procedure Proc1;                        │
  Var                                     │
    x : String[20]; ◄──────────┐          │
                               │          │
    Procedure Proc2;           │          │
    Begin                      │          │
    x := 'Bill';               │          │
    End;                       │          │
                               │          │
  Begin                        │          │
  x := 'Jones'; ◄──────────────┘          │
  End;                                     │
                                           │
Begin                                      │
x := 1; ◄──────────────────────────────────┘
End.
```

Figure 3-5.   Declaring variables with the same name

Turbo Pascal
Program Structure

The Program Heading
The Data Section
The Code Section
More on Program Blocks
Include Files
Overlays
Chain Files
Turbo Pascal Version 4.0
  Program Structure

A place for everything and everything in its place. This saying accurately describes Pascal, an orderly language consisting of well-defined sections, each of which serves a specific purpose. The major sections of a Pascal program are the *program heading*, *data section*, and the *code section*, whose components are shown in Figure 4-1.

The Program Heading

The first two lines in a Turbo Pascal program generally consist of the *program name* and the *compiler directives*. Both are optional, but for the sake of program documentation, it is preferable to include them.

As the first line in the program, the *program heading* does no more than identify the name of the program and

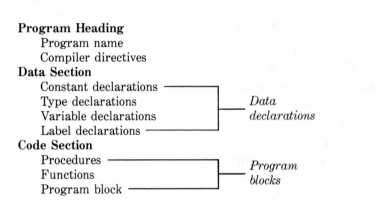

Program Heading
    Program name
    Compiler directives
Data Section
    Constant declarations
    Type declarations
    Variable declarations
    Label declarations
Code Section
    Procedures
    Functions
    Program block

Data declarations

Program blocks

Figure 4-1.   The structure of a Turbo Pascal program

whether it will be using input, output, or both. A typical program heading follows:

    Program ProgName(Input,Output);

The second line of the program contains the *compiler directives*, which can play an active and vital role in Turbo Pascal programs, controlling various types of error checking and input/output control. Although beginners can often ignore compiler directives entirely, more advanced programmers must understand how to use these options to get the most out of Turbo Pascal.

How to Enable or Disable Compiler Directives

Specific compiler directives are identified by single letters (uppercase or lowercase). For example, **K** specifies the stack-checking directive, **R** sets up index range checking, **I** controls input/output error checking, and so on. The format for enabling or disabling a compiler directive is a dollar sign followed by the directive and either a plus sign (to enable) or a minus sign (to disable); these characters are enclosed in comment delimiters (parentheses with asterisks or braces). The following are examples of valid compiler directive statements:

```
(*$I-*)
                    These are the same
{$i-}

(*$i-,k+,u-,c+*)
```

The first two statements both disable input/output error checking. As you can see from the examples, either type of comment delimiter (braces or parentheses with asterisks) can be used; the case of the directive (upper or lower) is unimportant. The third example specifies four compiler directives at once. It disables input/output error checking, enables stack checking, disables user-interrupts, and enables console I/O control. Note that in this statement, the dollar sign appears before the first directive only.

Although they are usually placed directly after the program heading, compiler directives can be included at any point in a program. Turbo Pascal assigns default values to any compiler directives not explicitly specified by the programmer.

Compiler Directive B: I/O Mode Selection

In Turbo Pascal input and output are directed to physical devices through the use of logical devices and files. *Physical devices* are printers, disk drives, and so on. *Logical devices* are programming inventions that correspond to physical devices; for example, the logical device KBD: corresponds to the physical keyboard, and the logical device LST: corresponds to the printer. A *file* is any organized collection of information identified by a filename. The relationship between physical devices, logical devices, and files is depicted in Figure 4-2.

Turbo Pascal provides six logical devices and eight *standard files*, or files that are always set aside for use with the logical devices. When a Turbo Pascal program starts, the standard files Input and Output are assigned to the CON: device, which in turn is associated with the computer keyboard for input and the computer screen for output. When compiler directive **B** is enabled—by using {$B+}—Turbo Pascal standard files Input and Output are assigned to the logical device CON:. The default is **B**+. When the compiler directive **B** is disabled—by using {$B−}—standard files Input and Output are assigned to the logical device TRM:.

Compiler Directive C: Console I/O Control

The console, a logical device that in Turbo Pascal is used for standard I/O, consists of two physical devices—the computer monitor and keyboard. When compiler directive **C** is enabled

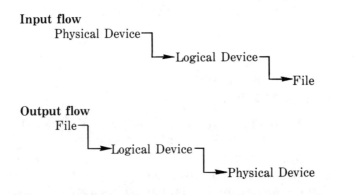

Figure 4-2.   Physical and logical devices in Turbo Pascal

with the statement {$C+}, the console interprets two control codes from the keyboard, CTRL-C and CTRL-S. Pressing CTRL-C when the program is waiting for input from the console aborts the program, at which point Turbo Pascal displays the following messages:

> User Break, PC=2D9F
> Program aborted

This message simply confirms that the program has been aborted at the user's request. The PC value indicates the point in the program at which the CTRL-C command was detected.

Pressing CTRL-S during output to the console (that is, the computer monitor) stops the program temporarily so you can read what is on the screen before it scrolls off the top. Pressing CTRL-S again allows the program to continue.

Note that the **C** directive is global to an entire program and cannot be changed once it is set. In addition, it must be declared before the main program block begins; otherwise, the default value (**C** directive enabled) will apply.

Finally, the CTRL-C and CTRL-S commands are crude program-control tools and, as such, their use should be restricted to program development and testing. More elegant control mechanisms (discussed later) offer a more user-friendly approach with less risk of terminating a program accidentally.

Compiler Directive I: I/O Error Checking

The **I** compiler directive, which is used to check for I/O errors in your program, is enabled with the statement {$I+}. The default is **I+**. Perhaps the most common type of Turbo Pascal error, I/O errors are also among the most dangerous. Undetected, they can produce unpredictable results in a program that appears to be operating normally.

If the **I** directive is enabled and your program detects an

I/O error, Turbo Pascal displays the following message:

I/O error 01, PC=2DB9
Program aborted

This message tells you that an I/O error occurred and specifies the type of error. In this case, the error is type 01h, which means that the file you tried to use does not exist. (The numerous types of I/O errors are described in detail in Appendix A.) The PC value indicates the point in the program at which the error was detected.

Enabling the **I** compiler directive is not the best way to handle I/O errors. A more effective method is to disable the **I** directive with the statement {$I−} and trap I/O errors yourself. Techniques for trapping I/O errors are covered in Chapter 9, "Turbo Pascal Files."

Compiler Directive R:
Index Range Checking

When you define an array or a string, you also set a legal range, or limit, for it. For example, a string defined as **String[20]** can only go up to 20 characters. Likewise, an array defined as **Array [1..100] of Char** can only have 100 characters.

What happens if you try to call up characters that exceed the limit? If the **R** compiler option is enabled, Turbo Pascal generates a run-time error and displays the following message:

Run-time error 90, PC=2DBB
Program aborted

Index range errors never occur in a properly functioning program, but they can be common during early stages of program development. To protect yourself against them, always enable the **R** compiler directive while developing a program. The default for the compiler directive is **R**−. To enable this directive, use the statement {**$R**+}.

One final point about compiler directive **R**: when enabled, it significantly increases the size of your compiled program and slows its execution. To maximize efficiency, disable the **R** compiler directive before compiling the final version of the program. To disable this compiler directive, use the statement {**$R**−}.

Compiler Directive V: Var-Parameter Type Checking

As discussed in Chapter 2, when you pass a string to a procedure as a reference parameter, Turbo Pascal expects the string type to match the parameter type exactly. For example, you cannot pass a variable of **String[30]** into a reference parameter of **String[20]**.

This limitation is inconvenient since it requires that all strings that are passed to a procedure be of the same type as the parameter. The {**$V**−} compiler directive relaxes the parameter type checking on strings passed as reference parameters, allowing any type of string to be passed to any type of string reference parameter. The default is **V**+.

Compiler Directive U: User Interrupt

One of the most frustrating experiences in programming is watching a computer freeze up while a program is running. This situation allows you only one choice: reboot and lose all changes made to your source code that were not saved to disk. The **U** compiler directive is a lifesaver at times like these. When enabled—with {**$U**+}—it allows you to interrupt the program at any point by pressing CTRL-C. The default is **U**−. To enable it, use the statement {**$U**+}.

The **U** directive is much more powerful than the **C** directive, which only allows program interrupts during console input. The price for this power is a marked decrease in the execution speed of your program. Nevertheless, you should use this compiler directive any time there is a chance that a malfunction will force you to reboot.

Compiler Directive K: Stack Checking

When a Turbo Pascal program begins, it allocates a certain amount of memory to be used by the code segment and the data segment. The memory left over, as is shown in Figure 4-3, is shared by the stack and the heap, two work spaces that store temporary variables.

As more variables are allocated to them, the heap grows upward in memory and the stack grows downward. Under extreme conditions (for example, if your program allocates too many pointer variables), the stack and the heap, which compete for the limited space in memory, can collide. If you enable the **K** compiler directive, Turbo Pascal generates a run-time error after the collision. This type of error (FFh) is called a *stack/heap collision,* and its error message looks something like this:

Run-time error FF, PC=2DA9
Program aborted

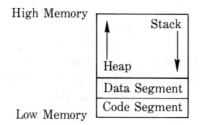

Figure 4-3.   Memory organization in Turbo Pascal

Because this is a serious error, the **K** compiler directive should always be enabled during program development. The default is **K+**. To enable this directive, use the statement {**$K+**}. Unfortunately, like the **R** compiler directive, the **K** compiler directive increases the size of your compiled program and slightly decreases your program's execution speed.

For more information on the use of the stack and the heap, see Chapter 7, "Program Control Structures."

The Data Section

After you insert the program heading and the compiler directives into your program, you are ready to begin the data section. In this section, you declare all the data elements (such as labels, constants, types, and variables) that your program uses.

Constant Declarations

As discussed in Chapter 2, many values remain constant throughout an entire program. Using constant identifiers (such as DaysPerWeek and HoursPerDay) simplifies your programs. Constants also simplify program modification. For a change to be reflected throughout a program, you need to change the value of the constant only once.

The Turbo Pascal *reserved word* **Const** signals the beginning of a constant-declaration block. (Reserved words are those used solely by Turbo Pascal; they cannot be defined by users as identifiers.)

You have two choices of constants in Turbo Pascal: untyped and typed. An untyped constant is declared with the following syntax: an identifier followed by an equal sign, a literal value (numeric or text), and a semicolon, as shown in the following example:

```
CONST
  DaysPerWeek = 7;
  HoursPerDay = 24;
  Message = 'Good Morning';
```

Typed constants are declared similarly, except that the type definition is inserted between the identifier and the equal sign, as shown in the following example:

```
CONST
  DaysPerWeek : Integer = 7;
  Message : String[20] = 'Good Morning';
  Interest : Real = 0.14;
```

If you are concerned about code space, you should use a typed constant rather than an untyped constant. Untyped constants take up more space because the constant identifier is replaced by the literal value when the program is compiled. In the example of untyped constants above, Turbo Pascal would replace every identifier **Message** with the string literal "**Good Morning**".

Typed constants, on the other hand, take up only as much space as the data type requires. Any time your program uses a typed constant, it refers to only one memory location.

Type Declarations

In the type-declaration block, denoted by the Turbo Pascal reserved word **Type**, you can invent your own customized data types to declare variables and parameters to procedures.

The general form for type declarations is an identifier followed by an equal sign, the data type, and a semicolon, as shown here:

```
Type

  PayType   = (Salary,HourlyRate);

  Customer = Record
    Name : String[30];
    Age : Integer;
    Income : Real;
```

```
    End;

MaxString = String[255];

NameList = Array [1..100] Of String[30];
```

The ability to create customized data types is one of Pascal's most powerful features and is discussed throughout this book.

Variable Declarations

Variables are values that can change. To begin a variable-declaration block, type the reserved word **Var**.

You can define variables by using standard Turbo Pascal data types (for example, boolean, real, integer) or customized ones created in the **Type** section. The format for variable declarations is nearly the same as that used for **Type** declarations, but the identifier is followed by a colon rather than an equal sign.

```
Var
    i, j, k : Integer;
    x, y, z : Real;
    BeyondLimit : Boolean;
    Ad : AdType;

    Book : Record
        Title : String[20];
        TotPages : Integer;
        Text : Array [1..10000] Of String[20];
        End;
```

The definition of the variable **Book** uses the Record type, which allows you to group more than one data element into a single variable.

Label Declarations

Labels are used to mark points in a program. Using the **Goto** statement together with a label, you can force the program flow to jump from place to place. Many programmers consider the use of the **Goto** statement bad programming technique because it leads to messy, unstructured programs.

Begin the label-declaration block by typing the reserved word **Label**. The declarations themselves consist simply of identifiers that are separated by commas and terminate with a semicolon, as shown here.

```
Label
    EndOfProgram, NextStep;
```

When used in your program, the label is followed by a colon (for example, EndOfProgram:). Statements following the label are executed whenever a **Goto** statement branches to that label.

The Code Section

The third major part of a Turbo Pascal program is the code section. It is the largest portion of the program and contains the step-by-step instructions that make the program work.

The code section always contains a program block and often contains procedures and functions. Blocks, delimited by the Turbo Pascal reserved words **Begin** and **End**, contain the instructions that assign values to variables, create logical branching, call other procedures and functions, and so on. In Turbo Pascal, the part of the program that executes first, the program block, is defined at the end of the program, as shown in Figure 4-4.

The program in Figure 4-5, which computes the weekly pay for a group of employees, demonstrates all the fundamental characteristics of a Turbo Pascal program. The program heading and the compiler directives are at the top. The data section declares constants, variables, user-defined data types, and a label. Procedures and functions are declared in the code section.

At the heart of this program is the user-defined record type **EmployeeType**. This record, containing basic informa-

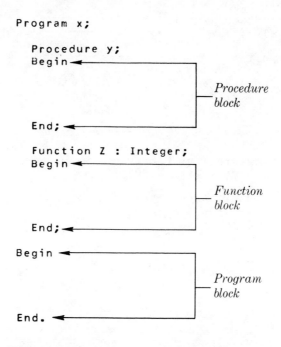

```
Program x;

    Procedure y;
    Begin

    End;

    Function Z : Integer;
    Begin

    End;

Begin

End.
```

*Procedure
block*

*Function
block*

*Program
block*

Figure 4-4.   Organization of the code section

tion about an employee, defines the array **Employee**. This array contains 100 employee records, each of which is a record of type **EmployeeType**. A customized data type (the constant **Employees**) defines the array. If the number of employees changes, all you need to do is change the definition of this constant.

The main program block in Figure 4-5 consists of a loop that executes once for every employee. Each iteration, or execution, of the loop calls the procedure **CalcPay**, which calculates the pay for the employee. When the procedure ends, the main program block tests to make sure that the result, **TotalPay**, is less than zero, since clearly no one should (or could) be paid a negative amount. If the result is less than

```
        Program Payroll;               ──────────── Program heading
        (*$v-,k-,r-*)         ──────────────────── Compiler directives

        Const  ────────────────────────────── Declaration of constants

          BonusRate = 0.07;
          Employees = 60;


        Type  ────────────────────────── Declaration of user-defined types

          EmployeeType = Record
            Name : String[30];
            Id : Integer;
            HourlyRate : Real;
            HoursWorked : Integer;
            GetsBonus : Boolean;
            TotalPay : Real;
            end;

          MaxStr = String[255];


        Var  ──────────────────────────────── Declaration of variables

          Employee : Array [1..Employees] of EmployeeType;
          i : Integer;
          s : MaxStr;

        Label  ──────────────────────────────── Declaration of label

          EndOfProgram;


        (*******************************************)

        Procedure CalcPay(Var Employee : EmployeeType);

          Function CalcBonus(Pay : Real) : Real;
          Begin
          CalcBonus :=  Pay + (Pay * BonusRate);
          End;
```

Data Section

Code Section

Figure 4-5.   A typical Turbo Pascal program

```
    Begin
    Employee.TotalPay := Employee.HoursWorked *

Employee.HourlyRate;
    if Employee.GetsBonus then
      Employee.TotalPay := CalcBonus(Employee.TotalPay);
    End;

(*******************************************)

    Procedure WriteReport(Employee : EmployeeType);
    Begin
    writeln('Name:        ',Employee.name);
    writeln('Total Pay: ',Employee.TotalPay:0:2);
    writeln;
    End;

(*******************************************)

Begin
for i := 1 to Employees do
  Begin
  CalcPay(Employee[i]);
  If Employee[i].TotalPay < 0 then
    Begin
    Writeln('Error: Total pay less than zero');
    Goto EndOfProgram;
    End;
  WriteReport(Employee[i]);
  End;

EndOfProgram:
End.
```

Main program block

Figure 4-5.   A typical Turbo Pascal program (*continued*)

zero, the program jumps to the **EndOfProgram** label and terminates. If, however, the amount of **TotalPay** is in the correct range, the program calls the procedure **WriteRe-**

port, which writes the employee's name and the total amount paid.

More on Program Blocks

Pascal is known as a block-structured language, that is, a language in which every statement in a program belongs to a specific block of code. A simple program can consist of only one block, as shown here:

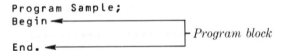

```
Program Sample;
Begin
                                    Program block
End.
```

The program block is the lowest level in the program: it is the foundation upon which you can build more layers. In the preceding example, the entire program exists at the program-block level. When you add procedures and functions to a program, you add more levels, as shown in Figure 4-6. This program consists of three blocks—one program block and two procedure blocks—but has only two levels. Because both procedures are nested within the program block, they are both level-2 procedures, as the indentation suggests.

By nesting procedures within other procedures, you can add even more levels to the program. In Figure 4-7, for example, procedure **Proc1A** is nested inside procedure **Proc1** to form a third level in the program.

Nesting procedures creates "privacy" among procedures. A procedure that is nested inside another is private to that procedure. Keeping procedures private can decrease programming errors by limiting the use of a procedure to a specific section of your program.

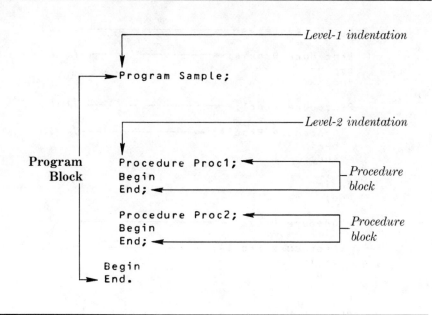

Figure 4-6.   Adding levels to a Turbo Pascal program

Procedural Scope

Note that Figure 4-7 contains three procedures named **Proc1A**: the first is at level 2; the other two are at level 3 nested within the procedures **Proc1** and **Proc2**.

Although these three procedures have the same name, each is treated as a distinct entity. A call to **Proc1A** in the program block executes the level-2 procedure, while calls made within **Proc1** and **Proc2** refer to their respective nested procedures.

Two rules govern the scope of procedures:

1. A program may call a procedure within the block

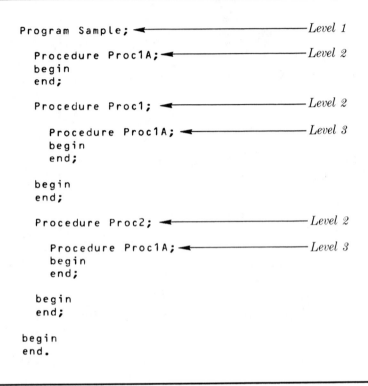

```
Program Sample;  ◄────────────────── Level 1

    Procedure Proc1A; ◄────────────── Level 2
    begin
    end;

    Procedure Proc1; ◄─────────────── Level 2

        Procedure Proc1A; ◄────────── Level 3
        begin
        end;

    begin
    end;

    Procedure Proc2; ◄─────────────── Level 2

        Procedure Proc1A; ◄────────── Level 3
        begin
        end;

    begin
    end;

begin
end.
```

Figure 4-7.   Nesting procedures within procedures

where it is declared and within any subblock nested in that block.

2. The exception to Rule 1 occurs when the program declares another procedure of the same name in a higher-level subblock.

In Figure 4-7, the level-2 procedure **Proc1A** would normally extend its scope into **Proc1** and **Proc2**. But because the program declares the same procedure name in **Proc1** and **Proc2**, the scope of the level-1 procedure is limited to the first level.

Procedural Precedence

In some languages (notably C), the order in which you declare procedures makes no difference. In Turbo Pascal, a language far more orderly than C, you cannot call procedures until you have declared them. (The only exception to this is when you use forward declarations, which are discussed in the next section.) For example, in Figure 4-7, **Proc2** can call **Proc1**, but **Proc1** cannot call **Proc2**.

The rule of procedural precedence is based on the logic that a complex idea is best built from simple ideas. In other words, a program should be built from small, simple procedures that are combined to form increasingly complex procedures. A programmer should see a continual evolution from the beginning to the end of a Turbo Pascal program, culminating in the program block, which may well consist of only a few procedure calls.

Forward Declarations

While procedural precedence enforces a desirable order in a program, there are times when you simply need to refer to a procedure before you declare it. For these cases, Turbo Pascal provides the **FORWARD** declaration, which informs the compiler that a procedure exists before it specifies what the procedure does. A forward declaration consists of the normal procedure heading followed by the word **FORWARD** and a semicolon. The body of the procedure is declared later, at which point only the name of the procedure, and not the entire program heading, is declared.

Figure 4-8 shows an example of a forward-declared procedure. In this case, **Step2** and **Step1** both call each other—something not allowed by procedure precedence but overcome by the forward declaration of **Step2**.

If you try to run this program, make sure you use the (*$U+*) compiler directive so you can break out of the endless loop.

```
Program Endless_Loop;
(*$u+*)
Var
  i : Integer;

  Procedure Step2(i : integer); FORWARD;     ← The entire
                                               heading
                                               goes here
  Procedure Step1(i : integer);
  Begin
  i := i + 1;
  WRITELN(i);
  Step2(i);
  End;
                                             Only the
  Procedure Step2;  ←───────────────────── procedure name
  Begin                                      is declared here
  i := i + 1;
  WRITELN(i);
  Step1(i);
  End;

Begin
i := 1;
step1(i);
End.
```

Figure 4-8.   Using a forward declaration

Include Files

The Turbo Pascal editor cannot hold more than 62K of text at any one time. If your program exceeds this limit, you have to break it into pieces by storing it in multiple files. When you compile the program, the include-file directive pulls all the pieces together from these multiple files. The include-file directive is also useful when you have standard libraries of frequently used routines.

To include a file in a Pascal program, type a left parenthesis or brace followed by an asterisk, $I, the name of the

Include file is PROCS.INC

```
Procedure ListFiles;
Var
   i : Integer;
Begin
End;
```

Main program file is MAIN.PAS

```
Program Main;
(*$I Procs.Inc*)
Begin
ListFiles;
End.
```

Figure 4-9.   Using an include file

file to be used, and a right parenthesis or brace. For example, the sample directive **(*$I Procs.Inc*)** tells Turbo Pascal to read the include file PROCS.INC as if the text were written in the program. Another example of how to include a file is shown in Figure 4-9.

Here, the main program file (MAIN.PAS) makes a call to the procedure ListFiles, yet ListFiles is defined not in the file MAIN.PAS but in the file PROCS.INC. The include statement in MAIN.PAS tells the compiler to read in PROCS. INC at that point and use its code as part of the program.

Overlays

There is no limit to the size of a Turbo Pascal source code when you use include files. The limitation is in the size of a program you can compile: Turbo Pascal restricts a program's total code space to 64K. If you try to compile a program that exceeds this limit, the compiler will stop and display this message:

Error 98: Memory overflow. Press <ESC>

Reducing the size of your code can be easily accomplished with overlays.

How Overlays Work

Overlays let you "shoehorn" large programs into Turbo Pascal's 64K code limit by allowing more than one procedure to share the same memory space. Consider the following:

```
Program OverTest;

    Overlay Procedure ProcA;
    Begin
    End;

    Overlay Procedure ProcB;
    Begin
    End;

Begin
End.
```

Here, procedures **ProcA** and **ProcB** are overlaid. They both execute by using the same area of memory but not at the same time. When **ProcA** is needed, it is loaded into memory from the overlay file and executed. If **ProcB** is called subsequently, it is loaded into memory, replacing **ProcA**.

Remember that both procedures cannot be active in memory at the same time; in other words, **ProcB** cannot include a call to **ProcA**. If it does, Turbo Pascal will load **ProcA**, wiping out **ProcB** in the process and probably causing your computer to hang. Be very careful to ensure that your program contains no conflicting overlay calls.

When it is executing overlaid procedures, Turbo Pascal allocates only as much space in the code segment as needed by the largest of the overlaid procedures. For example, if **ProcA** requires 15K of RAM and **ProcB** requires just 3K, Turbo Pascal sets aside 15K in the code segment for **ProcA** and **ProcB** to share. By using overlays, you would save 3K in the code segment. Memory savings increase as you use overlaid procedures that are similar in size and as more procedures are overlaid.

When your program calls an overlaid procedure, the procedure has to be loaded into memory from disk. This takes time and is the trade-off you make to reduce code size. Using overlays wisely, however, can minimize the cost in speed. First, overlaying seldom-used procedures minimizes the impact on the overall execution speed of the program; you will barely notice the time required to load such procedures. If, however, the overlay needs to be loaded every few minutes (or seconds), the impact will be much greater.

Second, you should avoid *thrashing* as much as possible. Thrashing occurs when repeated calls to overlaid procedures cause excessive loading from the disk, leading it to "thrash" back and forth. To eliminate thrashing, the overlays should be restructured so that both procedures can be present in memory at the same time, that is, they should be put in separate overlay files, as discussed in the following section.

Implications for Program Structure

Turbo Pascal considers all contiguous overlaid procedures to be part of the same overlay. If, however, two overlaid procedures are separated by a procedure that is not overlaid, as in Figure 4-10, the two are considered to be separate overlays.

In Figure 4-10, if procedure C had been overlaid, then all five of the procedures would have been included in one overlay. As it stands, however, procedure C separates the overlaid files, forcing two different overlays. One advantage of separate overlays is that the procedures in one overlay can

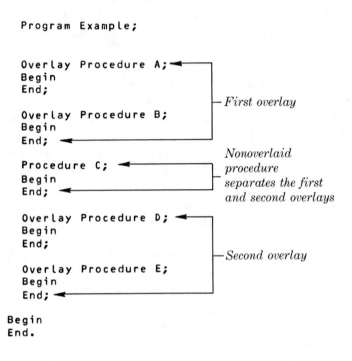

```
Program Example;

Overlay Procedure A;
Begin
End;

Overlay Procedure B;
Begin
End;

Procedure C;
Begin
End;

Overlay Procedure D;
Begin
End;

Overlay Procedure E;
Begin
End;

Begin
End.
```

First overlay

Nonoverlaid procedure separates the first and second overlays

Second overlay

Figure 4-10. Separating overlays

safely call the procedures in another overlay because they do not share the same memory. For example, in Figure 4-10, there is no danger in procedure **E** calling procedure **A**. The shared-memory conflict only applies to procedures in the same overlay.

When the program in Figure 4-10 is compiled, three files are produced. If the source file is named TEST.PAS, the compiled files will be as follows:

TEST.COM Code that is not overlaid
TEST.000 Code for procedures A and B
TEST.001 Code for procedures D and E

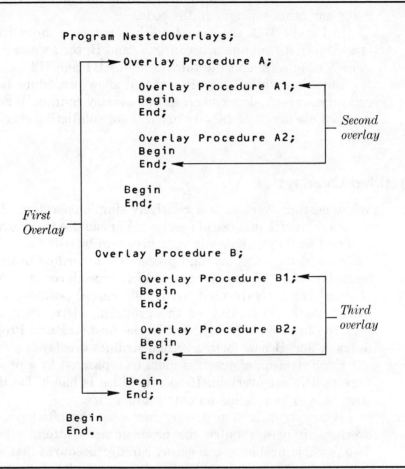

Figure 4-11.   Nested overlays

Nested Overlays

There are two different approaches to implementing overlays in a program—nested and stratified. You create *nested overlays* when you overlay procedures within the scope of their procedures. They are easy to use; simply put the word **Over-**

lay in front of the procedure declaration. You do not need to make any other changes in the code.

In Figure 4-11, the nested overlays result in three overlays. The first contains procedures **A** and **B**, the second contains **A1** and **A2**, and the third contains **B1** and **B2**.

Note that while Turbo Pascal will allow procedure **B** to call procedure **A**, doing so creates an overlay conflict. Whenever you use overlays, be sure to check for conflicting overlay calls.

Stratified Overlays

While nesting overlays is a relatively simple operation, it is not the most efficient use of overlays. You can use fewer overlays and save more space in your program by using *stratification*, which groups overlaid procedures according to their level. Consider Figure 4-12, in which procedures **A1**, **A2**, **B1**, and **B2** are extracted from their nested positions and moved to the beginning of the program. Here, they are declared to be one overlay, that is, the first stratum. Procedures **A** and **B** now form a second-stratum overlay.

Each stratum of overlays must be separated by a procedure that is not overlaid. If no procedure is handy for this purpose, you can define an empty procedure.

While stratification greatly increases the efficiency of overlays, it does require the programmer's attentiveness. Two possible problems can occur. First, procedures that are extracted from their nested positions become global in scope. You must ensure that this does not cause any conflicts in the program. Second, it is much easier to create illegal overlay calls with stratified overlays. Here again, proper attention is needed to avoid a problem.

Chain Files

In addition to overlays, Turbo Pascal offers another method of overcoming its 64K code limit: chain files. A chain file is a

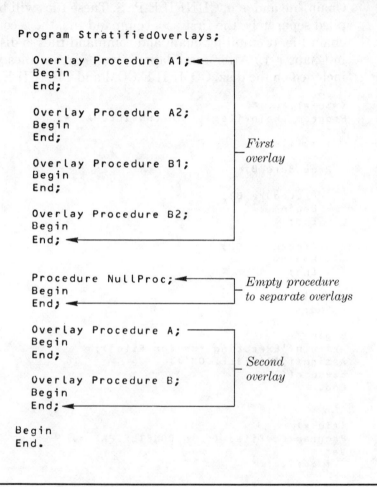

```
Program StratifiedOverlays;
    Overlay Procedure A1;
    Begin
    End;

    Overlay Procedure A2;
    Begin
    End;

    Overlay Procedure B1;
    Begin
    End;

    Overlay Procedure B2;
    Begin
    End;


    Procedure NullProc;
    Begin
    End;

    Overlay Procedure A;
    Begin
    End;

    Overlay Procedure B;
    Begin
    End;

Begin
End.
```

First
overlay

Empty procedure
to separate overlays

Second
overlay

Figure 4-12.   Stratified overlays

separate program that is called from another Turbo Pascal program. It divides a program into separately compiled units, each of which gets its own 64K code segment.

To understand how a chain file is created, examine the following program, in which two separate Turbo Pascal programs have been created. One is called ComFile and is contained in a file called COMFILE.PAS. The other is called

ChainFile and is in CHNFILE.PAS. These files will be compiled separately, the first as a command file, the second as a chain file. (Compiling chain and command files is discussed in Chapter 1.) After compilation, two program files will be included on the disk, COMFILE.COM and CHNFILE.CHN.

```
(*$u+*)
Program ChainFile; (* in CHNFILE.PAS *)
Var
  f : File;

  Procedure B;

    Procedure B1;
    Begin
    End;

    Procedure B2;
    Begin
    End;

  Begin
  End;

Begin
Writeln('Executing the Com File');
Assign(f,'COMFILE.COM');
Execute(f)
End.


(*$u+*)
Program ComFile; (* in COMFILE.PAS *)
Var
  f : File;

  Procedure A;

    Procedure A1;
    Begin
    End;

    Procedure A2;
    Begin
    End;

  Begin
  End;
```

```
Begin
Writeln('Executing the chain file');
Assign(f,'CHNFILE.CHN');
Chain(f)
End.
```

Invoking a chain file from a command file is a two-step process. First, the chain file must be assigned to an untyped file variable. In the example program, this is done with the statement **Assign(f,'CHNFILE.CHN')**, which assigns the physical file CHNFILE.CHN to file **f**. Next, the command **Chain(f)** transfers control to the chain file.

To invoke the command file from the chain file requires a similar process. The **Assign** command attaches the command file to an untyped file variable, and the execute statement passes control to the command file.

These programs create an endless loop because each one calls the other. If you try to run these programs, be sure to include the **(*$U+*)** compiler directive so you can break out of the loop.

Turbo Pascal Version 4.0 Program Structure

Turbo Pascal 4.0 introduces some major changes in program structure from Version 3.0. For one thing, overlays and chain files are not allowed. Fortunately, the need for overlays is eliminated because Version 4.0 can use all your PC's memory—up to 640K.

Another major change is the introduction of units. Units are portions of code that are compiled separately from the main program. The major advantage of having units is that you no longer need to recompile an entire program when you make a small change, only the units affected by the change are recompiled. This saves much time and increases your productivity.

Turbo Pascal Units

Programmers who have used Modula 2 will find Turbo Pascal units familiar. A unit contains one or more procedures and functions. You can compile, test, and debug a unit separately from a main program. Once the unit is completely debugged and compiled for the last time, it need never be recompiled. Instead, Turbo Pascal links the unit to programs that use it. Linking a unit takes far less time than compiling a unit.

Units are like programs unto themselves and follow a strict format—a unit name line, an interface section, and an implementation section.

The Unit Name

The first line in any unit must declare the unit and define its name, as shown here:

```
Unit Prnt;
```

The name of the unit is arbitrary but must match the name of the file that contains it. For example, if the unit is named Prnt, the file that contains source code of the unit must be named PRNT.PAS. The .PAS extension identifies the file as a source-code file. Turbo Pascal will compile the unit to the filename with a .TPU (Turbo Pascal unit) extension. If the unit name is different from the filename, the main program will have a problem finding the .TPU file. By using the **U** compiler directive, you can tell Turbo Pascal where to find the unit. For example, if a unit named Ptr is contained in a file named XUNIT.PAS, Turbo Pascal will create a file named XUNIT.TPU. The following demonstrates how to call this unit from a program:

```
Program TESTPRTR;
uses
 {*U XUNIT*}
   PRTR;
Being...End.
```

The Interface Section

After the unit name declaration comes the interface section. As its name implies, the interface section is the part of the unit that connects it with other units and programs. Sometimes the interface section is called the visible portion of the unit because other units and programs have access to the information contained there.

The interface section consists primarily of the header information for the procedures contained in the unit. A typical unit interface section is shown here:

```
Unit Math;
Interface
  Function Add(a,b : integer) : Integer;
  Procedure Multiply(x,y : integer;
                     Var z : integer);
```

Notice that the bodies of the procedure and function are not present—only the header is. This is similar to the way a **FORWARD** declaration is written. The point is that other programs do not need to know how the procedure works; they only need to know how to call the procedure. That information is contained in the header.

The interface section can also be used to declare global variables and to declare the use of other units, as shown here:

```
Unit Math;
Interface
  Uses Dos, Crt;
  Var
    a,b,c : integer;
  Function Add(a,b : integer) : Integer;
  Procedure Multiply(x,y : integer;
                     Var z : integer);
```

In the preceding example, the interface unit declares the use of two units, Dos and Crt. This means that the Math unit will have the full use of any procedure or function present in the Dos and Crt units. This unit also declares three integer variables—a, b, and c. These variables are global to the extent that they are available to other units and programs that use the Math unit.

You can, however, run into problems here. If the main program and a unit both have global variables of the same name, the main program variables will override the unit variables, and the variables in the unit will be global to that unit only. You must, therefore, be careful about how you declare global variables in a unit's interface section.

The Implementation Section

The third section of a unit, the implementation section, contains the body of the procedures and functions declared in the interface section, as shown here:

```
Unit Math;

Interface

   Function Add(a,b : integer) : Integer;

   Procedure Multiply(x,y : integer;
                      Var z : integer);

Implementation

   Function Add;
   begin
   Add := a + b;
   end;


   Procedure Multiply;
   begin
   z := x * y;
   end;

End.
```

Notice that the procedure and function declarations in the implementation section contain only the name and not the entire heading. Again, this follows the rules used in **FORWARD** declarations. Note that the unit file is terminated with an **End.** statement.

Global variables can be declared within an implementation section, but these variables will be global to the unit only and not accessible to any other unit or program.

Compiling Units

Once you have written the source code for a unit, you compile it just as you would a program. The compiled unit will be stored in a file with the same name but with the .TPU extension. Now you can use the unit in a program as demonstrated here:

```
Program TestMath;
Uses Math;
Var
  a,b,c : Integer;

Begin
a := 1;
b := 2;
WriteLn(Add(a,b));

Multiply(a,b,c);
WriteLn(c);
End.
```

The program **TestMath** contains the statement **Uses Math;**, which tells the compiler to allow the program to use any of the procedures and functions in this unit. Though the program is compiled from beginning to end, the unit is not — it is simply linked to the program by Turbo Pascal. As a result, using units decreases compilation time dramatically.

Turbo Pascal 4.0 Compiler Directives

With Turbo Pascal 4.0, Borland introduces some new compiler directives, described here.

Compiler Directive B:
Short-circuit Boolean evaluation (Default is B—)

Short-circuit Boolean evaluation reduces the time it takes your computer to determine whether an expression is true or false. Normally you will want this directive enabled since it produces much more efficient code.

Compiler Directive D:
Debug Information (Default is D+)

When the **D** compiler directive is enabled, Turbo Pascal generates a file of information that relates object code to source code. When a run-time error occurs, Turbo Pascal uses this information to locate the error in the source code.

Compiler Directive F:
Force Far Calls (Default is F—)

When the **F** directive is enabled, all function and procedure calls are generated as far calls. A far call is not necessary when the location of the call and the procedure being called are in the same segment. You should normally leave this directive disabled since Turbo Pascal is programmed to select far calls only when necessary.

Compiler Directive L:
Link Buffer (Default is L+)

The link buffer is a portion of memory that is used to speed up the linking process at the end of compilation. Enabling this directive will speed up your compilation time but use some memory in the process.

Compiler Directive L:
Link Object File (Usage: {$L CURSOR.OBJ})

In Turbo Pascal 4.0, external procedures must be defined in .OBJ files, not in .BIN files as implemented in Version 3.0 and before. The L compiler directive tells Turbo Pascal that the named file is to be linked into the program. Note that the object module must be an Intel Relocatable Object file. External declarations are made as in Version 3.0.

Compiler Directive M:
Memory Allocation Sizes (Usage: {$M stacksize, heapmin, heapmax})

In Turbo Pascal 4.0, you can, and in many cases you must, set the size of the stack and heap in order for your programs to run properly. You can specify the sizes of these segments with the **M** compiler directive. The default state is {$M 16384, 0, 655360}, which means the stack is 16K, the minimum amount of memory on the heap is 0K, and the maximum amount of memory on the heap is 640K.

Compiler Directive N:
Numeric Co-processor (Default is N−)

Turbo Pascal 4.0 has two models for floating-point math. When **N** is disabled (N−), real-type calculations are performed by the 8088; when **N** is enabled (N+), real-type calculations using variables declared as type **single**, **double**, **extended**, and **comp** are performed by using the 8087 math coprocessor chip.

Compiler Directive S:
Stack Overflow Checking (Default is S+)

When enabled, the S directive checks for stack overflow conditions. In Turbo Pascal 3.0, this was controlled by the **K** compiler directive.

Compiler Directive T:
TPM File Generation (Default is T—)

Enabling the **T** directive tells Turbo Pascal 4.0 to generate a
.TPM file when a program is compiled to disk. The **T** directive is effective only when compiling a program (not a unit)
to disk (not to memory).

Compiler Directive U:
Unit File Name (Usage: {$U filename})

The **U** directive will allow you to tell Turbo Pascal the
name of the file the unit is in. The {$U *filename*} must be in
the **Uses** statement, just before the unit name.

The unit concept and the extended compiler directives
are part of Turbo Pascal's growth as a language. Once you
learn to use these new tools, you will find that your program
development time will decrease and the efficiency of your
programs will increase.

FIVE

Turbo Pascal
Data Types

Standard Data Types
Constants
Sets
User-Defined Data Types
New Data Types for Turbo Pascal Version 4.0

Pascal provides programmers with a rich set of data types, each serving a specific purpose. Some Turbo Pascal variables come as standard equipment, while others are defined by the user. This chapter covers Turbo Pascal variables and how to use them.

Standard Data Types

Turbo Pascal offers six standard data types. **Bytes** are used for small, unsigned numbers; **integers** for numbers without decimal places; **reals** for numbers with decimal places; **booleans** to express true and false conditions; and **char** types to hold characters. In addition to the standard data types found in Pascal, Turbo Pascal provides a **string** data type. This chapter discusses the standard data types offered by Turbo Pascal and how they can be used.

Byte

A variable of type **byte** occupies one byte. A **byte** is an unsigned numeric value that can range from 0 to 255. In arithmetic expressions, a **byte** variable can be substituted for an integer as long as the value does not exceed the byte's numeric range.

When the value assigned to a **byte** exceeds 255, the variable's value loops around to a lower value. For example, adding 1 to a **byte** variable with a value of 255 results in 0.

Integer

Like **bytes**, **integers** hold numerical values that have no decimal places. Because they are two bytes (16 bits) in length, integers can range in value from $-32,768$ to $32,767$. Also like **bytes**, **integers** loop around when they exceed the limit; thus, when you add 1 to an **integer** that has the value $32,767$, its new value will be $-32,768$.

Real

Any numerical variable that holds values greater than $32,767$, less than $-32,768$, or contains a fractional amount must be **real**. The **real** data type, also known as the **floating-point** type, requires six bytes of storage and can range in value from 10E-38 to 10E38. The *Turbo Pascal Reference Manual* explains that **reals** have a "40-bit mantissa and an 8-bit 2's exponent." Luckily, you do not need to know what that means unless you are writing floating-point operations in assembler.

Because of their complex structure, arithmetic operations involving reals take far longer to execute than do operations on integers or bytes, which are stored in their binary numerical equivalents.

While Turbo Pascal implements **reals** quite well, some unexpected results can occur under extreme situations, such as when unusually large numbers are used. The most common problem with **reals**, a rounding error, is exacerbated in Turbo Pascal because it has no support for long **reals** (long **reals** are twice as precise as standard reals). Because Turbo Pascal **reals** hold only 11 significant digits, any number greater than 1.0 E10 is truncated. For example, if you set a **real** to the value 9999999999999999.0, the value stored is 9.9999999999E15, or 9999999999900000.0; the least significant digits are lost. Similarly, if you try to add 1 to large numbers, the value of the **real** variable remains unchanged because the 1 will be truncated. Incrementing very large **reals**, then, must be done with care or you may get incorrect results.

Another common problem encountered with **reals** is the overflow condition, which occurs when you try to assign too large a number to a **real** variable. The *Turbo Pascal Reference Manual* states that an overflow condition resulting from an arithmetic operation causes a run-time error in the program. This is not entirely true. For example, if 1 is added to a **real** variable with the maximum value of 1.0E38, the value remains 1.0E38 and no execution error is detected. Even though an overflow condition clearly exists, the program does not halt execution. This is because a **real** can store only 10 decimal places. That means that the smallest number you can add to change the number 1.0E38 is 1.0E28; numbers smaller than that have no effect.

The limit of 1.0E38 on **reals** is not valid under all conditions. For example, a **real** with a value of 1.0E38 can be incremented by adding the value 1.0E37. When the total reaches the value 1.7E38, an overflow condition occurs.

On the other hand, an overflow condition can occur when you might not expect it. If a **real** variable with the maximum value of 1.0E38 is multiplied by 1.0, the value should not change and there should be no overflow error. Even so, Turbo Pascal detects an overflow condition and halts execution.

Admittedly, you are not likely to encounter such extreme conditions regularly; in most cases you will never come close to the limit of **reals** in Turbo Pascal. Still, it is worth being aware of these exceptional cases, and perhaps future versions of Turbo Pascal will provide a **long real** type to help overcome these anomalies.

For greater numerical accuracy, Turbo Pascal offers Turbo-87 and TurboBCD, both of which extend the range and the number of significant digits stored in a **real**. Turbo-87 **reals** are 8 bits long, resulting in 16 significant digits and a range of 4.19E−307 to 1.67E+308. TurboBCD stores real numbers in Binary Coded Digit format, which gives 18 sig-

nificant digits and a range of 1E−63 to 1E+63. Both of
these, however, pose their own problems. Programs compiled
with Turbo-87, for example, can be run only on computers
that have the 8087 math coprocessor, a chip specially designed
for mathematical computations. Turbo BCD **reals**, on the
other hand, do not require the 8087 math coprocessor, but
they cannot use most Turbo Pascal standard arithmetic functions (for example, SIN, COS, and so forth). Both Turbo-87
and TurboBCD are discussed in Appendix C.

Char

Like the **byte** type, the **char** (character) data type occupies
one byte of storage in memory. Unlike the **byte** variable,
however, a **char** variable cannot be used directly in arithmetic expressions. It is used instead for manipulating and
comparing text, as well as in string-assignment statements.

String

The **string** data type stores text information. A **string** variable can be from 1 to 255 characters long, but it occupies one
byte in memory more than its defined length. For example, if
a **string** variable is declared to be 10 characters in length (**S
: String[10]**;), the variable occupies 11 bytes in memory. This
is because the first byte in a **string** keeps track of the length
of the string currently stored in the variable (and so is called
the *length byte*). If a 10-character **string** variable contains the
word "HELLO", the first byte in memory holds the binary
value 5, indicating that the variable contains five characters.
The last five bytes are ignored by Turbo Pascal's string-
manipulation procedures. The memory allocated to the **string**
variable would look like this:

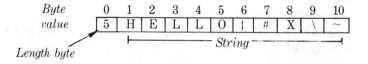

Note that the first byte is not the character "5" but the number 5 in binary (00000101), and that the last five bytes in the string contain random data.

Maintaining a length byte requires quite a bit of overhead. As a result, string-manipulation statements tend to be among the slowest in Turbo Pascal. Yet the alternative implementation of strings, such as in C, is even less efficient. In C, the character array (the equivalent of the Pascal **string** type) has no length byte. Consequently, any time a program needs to know the length of a string, it has to calculate it by counting every character until a delimiter is reached.

The only problem with Borland's implementation of the **string** type is the limitation to 255 characters. The addition of a **long string** type would be welcome.

Constants

Turbo Pascal does not initialize variables when a program starts up. As a result, there is no way of telling what value a variable has until you assign one.

Constants, on the other hand, are assigned values when the program starts. To illustrate the importance of constants, consider the example of a program that computes interest on loans. The program uses a fixed interest rate of 7%, which appears about 100 times within the program. At the same time, a variable interest rate of 7% also appears frequently in the program. To change all the fixed-rate values from 7% to 8% would require checking each occurrence of the number 7, deciding if the number is a fixed or a variable rate, and changing the value manually.

If, on the other hand, a constant named **FixedRate** (or some other appropriate name) is declared, changing the value throughout the program would be accomplished by simply changing the declaration.

Untyped and Typed Constants

Turbo Pascal provides two types of constants, untyped and typed. Untyped constants are true constants in that Turbo Pascal does not allow their value to be altered. Typed constants, on the other hand, can change in value (just as variables can).

To understand how typed constants got their name, consider the sample declarations shown here.

```
CONST

   I = 100;
   R = 15.23;
   S = 'TEXT';

   II : integer = 100;
   RR : real = 15.23;
   SS : string[4] = 'TEXT';
```

— *Untyped constants*

— *Typed constants*

A definition of a typed constant contains the type declaration (for example, **integer, real, string**) and can be used in assignment statements. Untyped constants cannot be used in assignment statements, as is shown here.

Correct
```
CONST
   S : STRING[4] = 'TEXT';
BEGIN
S := 'AAAA';
END.
```

Incorrect
```
CONST
   S = 'TEXT';
BEGIN
S := 'AAAA';
END.
```

Since Turbo Pascal provides both constants and variables, what is the intrinsic value of a typed constant? Some programmers prefer to initialize all variables to specific values when a program starts. This avoids the unpredictable results that can occur when a variable is not properly assigned.

This approach does have a major drawback. Constants reside in the code segment, while variables reside in the data segment. Code space is much more valuable than data space for two reasons. First, code space tends to be used up much faster than data space unless extremely large arrays are being used. Second, if a program runs out of space in the data segment, it can push variables onto the stack and heap. It is therefore better programming practice to use constants sparingly and use explicitly initialized variables whenever possible.

One other difference between typed and untyped constants concerns their use as parameters to a procedure. Either constant can be passed as a value parameter without any difficulty; however, only a typed constant can be passed by reference.

Sets

In Turbo Pascal, a *set* is a group of related numbers or characters. Sets are primarily used to see if a character or number belongs to the set. For example, you might define a set that consists of the capital letters from A to Z and then use the set to check if other characters in the program are included in it. If a character is included in the set, you know it is uppercase. A discussion of numeric and character sets follows.

Numeric Sets

Numeric sets can consist only of integers (actually byte values). The sets include any integers from 0 to 255; such numbers as -1 and 256 exceed the range established by Turbo Pascal. Here are two examples of numeric set definitions:

Zero Through Nine : Set of 0..9;

FullRange : Set of Byte;

In the first line, Zero Through Nine can include any combination of integers from 0 to 9, but the number 10 cannot be included because it is outside the range of the set.

In the second line, no range is specified for the set FullRange; the definition specifies only that the set consists of bytes. Later in the program, the programmer can define FullRange to be any numeric subset with a statement such as this:

    FullRange := [0..9];

Now, the set FullRange has the same elements as Zero Through Nine.

Character Sets

Character sets can consist only of characters. Like numeric sets, the maximum range of character sets is from 0 (00h) to 255 (FFh). The major difference between numeric sets and character sets is that character sets can be directly compared with character variables. Here are two examples of character-set definitions:

    UpperCase : Set Of 'A'..'Z';
    AllChars : Set Of Char;

The set UpperCase can legally include any combination of uppercase characters from "A" (ASCII code 65) to "Z" (ASCII code 90). Thus, the character "a" (ASCII code 97) could not be included in this set.

The second set, AllChars, is defined as a "Set Of Char." This means that this set can include any combination of characters from 0 to 255.

Sets of User-Defined Elements

Lastly, a set can consist of elements defined by the user. These elements are neither numeric nor character and must be listed individually. The maximum number of elements allowed, as before, is 255. Here is an example of a user-defined set:

Ingredients : Set Of (eggs, milk, butter, flour);

All operations on sets of user-defined elements follow the same rules as all other sets.

Sets and Memory Allocation

Sets can use a maximum of 32 bytes of storage, the equivalent of 256 individual bits. This is what limits the scope of a set to the range 0 to 255. If your set has only a few elements, it uses only a few bytes, and allocating the full 32 bytes would be wasteful.

Sets are automatically reduced in size. For example, a set defined as follows

X : 1..5 ;

needs only one byte, so Turbo Pascal allocates just one byte for the set. The values in the byte are allocated as follows:

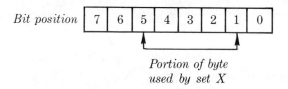

*Portion of byte
used by set X*

The arrows indicate the part of the byte used to store the set. When an element is present in a set, the appropriate bit is turned on (that is, set to 1). To illustrate how the memory would represent the presence of elements in a set, consider the following set assignment:

X := [1..3,5];

This statement assigns the elements 1, 2, 3, and 5 to set X. In memory, this assignment creates the following bit pattern:

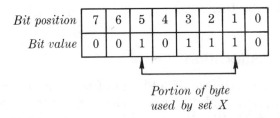

Portion of byte
used by set X

The ones in the bit value portion of this illustration indicate the presence of an element in the set. They are found in the 1, 2, 3, and 5 positions of the byte, which correspond precisely to the assignment statement.

Since Turbo Pascal needs only one byte to store set X, the remaining 31 bytes are used for other purposes. Only three bits of memory (the 0, 6, and 7 positions) are wasted. To further illustrate the storage of sets, consider the following set definition:

X : Set Of 7..8;

This set comprises only two elements but requires two bytes of storage. Why? Because the set straddles a byte boundary, as shown in the following illustration.

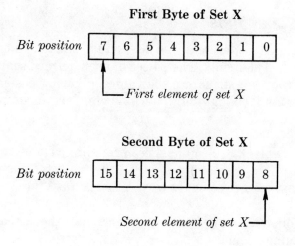

First Byte of Set X

Bit position | 7 | 6 | 5 | 4 | 3 | 2 | 1 | 0 |

First element of set X

Second Byte of Set X

Bit position | 15 | 14 | 13 | 12 | 11 | 10 | 9 | 8 |

Second element of set X

The first element (7) is in the first byte, while the second element (8) is in the second byte. Two bytes are used, 30 bytes are eliminated, and 14 bits are wasted.

It is possible to create a compiler that eliminates this kind of wasted memory, but such a compiler would increase the size of the compiled programs and slow down execution. Wisely, Borland decided to accept a minimal amount of waste in return for faster execution and smaller code.

User-Defined Data Types

One of the most powerful aspects of Turbo Pascal is its ability to define customized data types. By tailoring data structures to a program's specific algorithms, you can increase your program's readability and simplify its maintenance. User-defined data types fall into one of three categories: user-defined scalars, records, and arrays.

User-Defined Scalar Type

A user-defined scalar requires one byte of memory and can have up to 256 elements. The power of user-defined scalars is that the programmer names the values, allowing easier programming and debugging. The following are examples of enumerated sets:

```
Color : (black,brown,blue,green,red,pink,yellow,white);
Sex : (Male, Female);
Occupation : (Doctor, Lawyer, other);
```

The following code excerpt demonstrates the readability of user-defined scalars:

```
IF occupation = doctor THEN
   color := black
ELSE IF occupation = lawyer THEN
   color := blue
ELSE
   color := red
```

Without user-defined scalars, the programmer must develop coding schemes to represent the values (for example, 1 = doctor, 2 = lawyer, 3 = other). When the number of coded variables is large, it is difficult to keep track of the different value meanings.

Each element of a user-defined scalar equates to a byte value according to its position in the enumerated set, with the first element having a value of 0. In the preceding examples of enumerated sets, the color black has the value 0, while the color white has the value 7. To determine the current value of color, use the Turbo Pascal standard function Ord. If the color is currently black, then the statement **Ord (Color)** returns the value 0; if it is white, it returns 7. If you wish, you can assign this value to a numeric variable, as is done next, where the variable **i** will be equal to 1 after the assignment statement:

```
VAR
  i : INTEGER;
  Color : (black,brown,blue,green,red,yellow,white);
BEGIN
color := brown;
i := ORD(color);
END.
```

While transforming a user-defined scalar to a numeric value is easy, the opposite is not true. In the following example, the statement **Color := i** is illegal:

```
VAR
  i : INTEGER;
  Color : (black,brown,blue,green,red,yellow,white);
BEGIN
i := 1;
Color := i;  (* Illegal statement *)
END.
```

To resolve this illegal statement simply, you can use the Turbo Pascal standard function Fillchar, which is discussed in greater detail later in Appendix H. The following example shows the proper way to assign a numeric value (integer or byte, not real) to an enumerated set.

```
VAR
  i : INTEGER (* or BYTE *);
  Color : (black,brown,blue,green,red,yellow,white);

BEGIN
i := 1;
FILLCHAR(color,1,i);
END.
```

Records

A record is a combination of other data types into a new data type. The next example exhibits a typical record definition:

```
VAR
  Customer : RECORD
              Name : STRING[30].
              Address : STRING[60];
              Age : INTEGER;
              Income : REAL;
              Married : BOOLEAN;
              END;
```

Using records has two advantages. First, all data elements for a single record are logically connected to each other. This makes it easier to keep track of things. Second, some operations, such as assignments and file operations, can be performed on an entire record, eliminating the need to refer to each element in the record.

Using records in assignment statements is straightforward. You can access elements in a record in one of two ways: by explicit reference or implicit reference using the reserved word **With**, as shown in Figure 5-1. The statement

Rec1.b := 1;

is an example of explicit reference because both the record name and the element name, separated by a period, appear in the assignment. In an implicit reference, using the reserved word **With**, you do not need to repeat the record name in each assignment statement. The assignment statement

Rec2 := Rec1;

assigns every element in Rec1 to the corresponding element in Rec2.

Implicit references can be nested so that one **With** statement refers to more than one record, as shown in Figure 5-2. The statement

With Rec2, Rec1 Do

allows the programmer to reference elements in both records

```
PROGRAM x;
VAR
  Rec1,Rec2 : RECORD
     a : STRING[20];
     b : INTEGER;
     x : REAL;
     END;


BEGIN

Rec1.a := 'sss';
Rec1.b := 1;
Rec1.x := 123.23;

WITH Rec1 DO
  BEGIN
  a := 'sss';
  b := 1;
  x := 123.23;
  END;



Rec2 := Rec1;


WITH Rec2 DO
  BEGIN
  WRITELN(a);
  WRITELN(b);
  WRITELN(x);
  END;

END;
```

These segments do exactly the same thing

Record-to-record block assignment

*Output using the **With** option*

Figure 5-1.   Using the With statement with records

implicitly. Problems can arise, however. In Figure 5-2, Rec1 and Rec2 both have an element "a". This ambiguous reference does not tell Turbo Pascal which record element is being referred to. Thus, the compiler assumes that the

```
PROGRAM x;
VAR
  Rec1 : RECORD
    a : STRING[20];
    b : INTEGER;
    x : REAL;
    END;

  Rec2 : RECORD
    a : STRING[20];
    r1, r2 : REAL;
    END;

BEGIN
WITH Rec1 DO
  BEGIN
  a := 'sss';
  b := 1;
  x := 123.23;
  END;

WITH Rec2 DO
  BEGIN
  a := 'xxx';
  r1 := 20.0;
  r2 := 10.0;
  END;

WITH Rec2, Rec1 DO
  BEGIN
  a := a;
  x := r1 * r2;
  END;

WITH Rec2 DO
WITH Rec1 DO
  BEGIN
  a := a;
  x := r1 * r2;
  END;

WITH Rec1 DO
  BEGIN
  WRITELN(a);
  WRITELN(b);
  WRITELN(x);
  END;
END.
```

These segments do exactly the same thing

Figure 5-2. Nested With statements

ambiguous element belongs to the last record that contains that element. In Figure 5-2, the assignment statement

a := a;

assumes that both elements are from Rec1. In short, it assumes that the statement means

Rec1.a := Rec1.a.

Variant Records

Turbo Pascal allows programmers to produce what are known as *variant records*. Variant records are records that can change; they are a combination of a record type and the Turbo Pascal logical operator **Case**. Variant records are explored more fully in Chapter 6 under the general discussion of the **Case** operator.

Arrays

Any data type, whether standard or user defined, can be extended into an *array*. An array is a variable that repeats a data type a specified number of times. To define an array, follow this general format:

Variable Name : Array [lower limit..upper limit] of Data Type;

The lower limit and the upper limit are any legal integer values in which the upper limit is greater than the lower limit.

Arrays are usually used when a program includes a list of recurring elements. For example, to hold a year's worth of stock prices, define the array as follows:

Price : Array [1..365] of Real;

To refer to a specific price, indicate which element in the

array you want. For example, to set the price on the tenth day in the year, you would use

Price[10] := 34.50;

The lower limit of an array does not have to be 1. It makes more sense to start the array at a value that corresponds to the context of your data. If you were measuring the conductivity of a metal with a temperature range of −100° to +100° C, you would define the array as

Conductivity : Array [− 100 . . 100] of real;

The range of the array now matches the functional range of temperatures (assuming that the measurements will be taken at whole-number intervals).

Another example of an array that matches its data is one that stores the average incomes of people age 35 to 65. An array defined as

Average Income : Array [35 . . 65] of real;

would do the trick.

Multidimensional Arrays

Any arrays defined to have more than one dimension are considered to be *multidimensional arrays*, although they rarely exceed three dimensions. Two-dimensional arrays, sometimes called *matrices*, are quite common, especially in multivariate statistics. For example, when measuring the conductivity of a metal, the following two-dimensional arrays could be used, assuming that the temperature intervals are not whole numbers:

TempConductivity : Array [1 . . 200, 1 . . 2] of real;

The best way to think about this array is to visualize a table of columns and rows: the first dimension in the array

	1 **Temperature**	**2** **Conductivity**
1	−99.34	12.3
2	−97.76	12.2
3	−96.01	11.9
.		
.		
.		
200	99.01	2.9

Table 5-1.   Sample Temperature and Conductivity Readings

(1..200) provides the rows, and the second dimension (1..2) provides the columns. Going row by row, all you need to do is put the temperatures in one column and the matching conductivity ratings in another, as shown in Table 5-1.

To assign a value in a multidimensional array, specify both dimensions, as shown in the following two statements:

```
TempConductivity[1,1] := −99.34;
TempConductivity[1,2] := 12.3;
```

To refer to the first pair of observations, specify both the row and the column. In this example, the first temperature reading is "TempConductivity[1,1]," while the corresponding conductivity rating is "TempConductivity[1,2]."

Substitute for Multidimensional Arrays

These examples of multidimensional arrays should make one thing clear—it is hard to keep track of what values are in which column. There is simply no clue given in the array itself. Because it is preferable to deal with variables that have meaningful names, Turbo Pascal vides an alternative to multidimensional arrays: arrays of records. The following example shows why these arrays are better than the multidimensional ones:

```
Observation : ARRAY [1..200] OF RECORD
   Temperature : REAL;
   Conductivity : REAL;
   END;
```

Arrays of records create clear definitions; it is immediately apparent that the RECORD definition in the preceding illustration defines a series of observations consisting of temperatures and conductivities. These can be referred to by name in the following manner:

Observation[1].Temperature
Observation[1].Conductivity

Whenever you use multidimensional arrays, consider the possibility that you may be able to substitute an array of a record type that does the job, yet improves program clarity.

New Data Types for Turbo Pascal Version 4.0

Turbo Pascal Version 4.0 introduces new and important data types for both scalars and reals. The new scalar types are **word**, **ShortInt**, and **LongInt**.

word

The **word** data type is sometimes referred to as an unsigned integer. Like the integer data type, a **word** comprises two bytes. Integers, however, use the highest order bit to indicate the sign of the number, whereas **word** data types use no sign bit. This gives **word** variables a range from 0 to 65535.

ShortInt

The **ShortInt** (short integer) data type can be thought of as a signed byte. It uses one byte of storage but treats the high-order bit as a sign bit. This gives the **ShortInt** variable a range of −128 to 127.

LongInt

Perhaps the most significant addition to Turbo Pascal's data types is the **LongInt** (long integer). **LongInt** variables utilize four bytes of storage and have a range of −2,147,483,648 to 2,147,483,647. Consequently, you can use long integers in many places where you would have otherwise used a real variable. This is especially important because calculations that use integers take less time than those that use real variables.

In addition to offering new scalar types, Turbo Pascal 4.0 offers five types of reals: **real** (same as Version 3.0), **single**, **double**, **extended**, and **comp**. Unfortunately, the **single**, **double**, **extended**, and **comp** types can only be used if your computer has an 8087 math coprocessor chip.

single

The **single** data type, the least precise of the new real data types, utilizes four bytes and has a range of 1.5E−45 to 3.4E38.

double

The **double** data type occupies eight bytes and ranges from 5.0E−324 to 1.7E308.

extended

The **extended** data type is ten bytes long and can range from −2E+63 +1 to 2E+63 −1.

comp

While the **comp** data type is technically a real variable, it acts like an integer in that it contains only whole numbers. The **comp** data type uses eight bytes and can range from $-2E+63 +1$ to $2E+63 -1$.

Constants

Turbo Pascal 4.0 makes one small but significant change in the implementation of typed constants. Previously, typed constants were stored in the code segment. With Version 4.0, typed constants are stored in the data segment.

Arithmetic and Logic in Turbo Pascal

Arithmetic in Turbo Pascal
Logical Operators

Intelligence and number-crunching power are characteristics long associated with computers, an association reinforced by the names of such computer languages as FORTRAN (from Formula Translator) and ALGOL (from Algorithmic Logic). Pascal continues in this vein: it is named after Blaise Pascal, a seventeenth-century mathematician, and provides powerful arithmetic functions and extensive logic commands.

Arithmetic in Turbo Pascal

Turbo Pascal arithmetic is based on the concept of an expression or equation. An expression consists of a combination of identifiers, numerical values, numeric functions, and operators, all of which result in a specific numeric value. If that sounds too complicated, consider this well-known expression:

$$2 + 2$$

This has all the elements of a mathematical expression — numeric values and an operator (the plus sign) — but it is not a Pascal statement. In Pascal, an expression must be part of either an assignment statement or a logical statement.

A numerical assignment statement computes a value from an expression and stores the value in a numeric variable. An example of an arithmetic assignment statement is

Result := 2 + 2;

When this statement is executed, Turbo Pascal calculates the right-hand side of the statement and assigns the result in the variable **Result**.

An arithmetic expression in a logical statement is similar, except that the expression does not result in a numerical value but in a true or false condition. For example, the logical statement

If Result =(2 + 2) then...

does not change the value in the variable result. Rather, Turbo Pascal adds the two numbers and compares them to the value that is already in **Result**. In this case, if **Result** is equal to 4, then the expression is true; if not, it is false. Logical structures are discussed more fully later in this chapter.

Note that the assignment operator in Pascal is :=, while in logical statements it is =. This might seem to be a trivial distinction, but there is a rationale behind it: an assignment statement does not imply equality. In arithmetic, a statement such as $X = X + 1$ is simply incorrect. In Pascal, however, the statement **X := X + 1** is perfectly legal. Remember, this assignment statement does not say "X is equal to X + 1"; it says, "Take the value of X + 1 and assign it to the variable X."

Integer and Real Expressions

In Turbo Pascal, arithmetic expressions result in either an integer value or a real value. For an expression to yield an integer result, two conditions must be met. First, all the operands in the expression must be integers. Second, if division is performed, the **Div** operator must be used instead of the / character.

Any expression that is not an integer expression is, by default, a real expression. Even if an expression has 50 integer operands and only 1 real operand, the expression results in a real value. The following illustration shows examples of both integer and real expressions:

```
Program Math1;
Var
   i,j,k : integer;
   x,y,z : real;

begin

i := 1 + j;
j := 3 div i;
k := (i + k) div (3 * j);

x := 1.0 + j;
y := 3 / i;
z := (i + k) div (3 * j);

end.
```

Integer expressions

Real expressions

Hierarchy of Arithmetic Operators

The order of precedence dictates that multiplication and division are performed before addition and subtraction and that any operation in parentheses is done first. Turbo Pascal follows these rules: it has four hierarchical levels of arithmetic operators, as shown here:

Level 1: Unary Minus, Unary Plus *←Highest priority*

Level 2: Parentheses

Level 3: Multiplication, Division

Level 4: Addition, Subtraction *←Lowest Priority*

A *unary minus* is the sign that directly precedes a number and indicates that the number is negative. For example, the minus sign in the number -3 is a unary minus. When used in arithmetic expressions, the unary minus can lead to statements such as

Result := 1 − −3,

in which case, **Result** is equal to 4.

Turbo Pascal also supports the unary plus. While the unary plus has absolutely no impact on the value of the number, the fact that it is supported means that a statement such as

Result := 1 − +2

is perfectly legal. Please note, however, that the unary plus operator is not an indicator of absolute value (the absolute value of a negative number is its positive equivalent). If a unary plus precedes a variable with a negative value, the variable remains negative.

The second level in the hierarchy of Turbo Pascal arithmetic operators is parentheses. Following the order of precedence, operations within parentheses are executed before operations outside parentheses. To clarify this rule, consider the following two expressions:

A := 3 * 4 + 5;
A := 3 * (4 + 5);

In the first case, the multiplication operator takes precedence, so that 3 * 4 is evaluated first, yielding 12, and 5 is added to 12 for a final result of 17. In the second case, the operation within the parentheses takes precedence over the multiplication operator, so that 4 + 5 is evaluated first, yielding 9, and 9 is multiplied by 3 for a final result of 27.

You should use parentheses to increase clarity, even when they are not strictly necessary. For example, the following two expressions yield the same result, yet the parentheses in the latter make it more readable:

$$r := a + b * c * d + x + y / r;$$
$$r := a + (b * c * d) + x + (y / r);$$

Integer Versus Real Arithmetic

The last two levels in the hierarchy of arithmetic operators are multiplication and division (level 3) and addition and subtraction (level 4). It is at this point that Turbo Pascal's strong typing forces a separation between integer arithmetic and real arithmetic.

Integer Arithmetic

The rules of integer arithmetic apply when an expression is assigned to an integer variable. All operators in an integer expression must be either integers or reals converted to integers using the Turbo Pascal standard function Trunc. The program shown next provides examples of both legal and illegal integer arithmetic statements.

```
Program IntegerMath;
Var
   i,j,k : integer;
   x,y,z : real;

Begin

(* Legal Statements*)

i := 10 + j;
j := i DIV k;
k := j + round(x) + trunc(y/z);

(* Illegal Statements*)

i := 10.0 + j;
j := i / k;
k := j + x + y / z;
End.
```

Note that numeric literals are not allowed to have decimal places in integer expressions.

Round and Trunc are Turbo Pascal standard functions that convert real values into integer values, but they work in slightly different ways. The Round function rounds a real value to the nearest integer. If the decimal portion is below 0.5, the real value is rounded down; otherwise, it is rounded up. For example, the result of Round(10.49) is the integer value 10, while Round(10.5) returns the value 11.

The Trunc standard function truncates a real value, chopping off any decimal places. Therefore, the result of Trunc(10.99) is 10. With the Round and Trunc standard functions, you can freely mix reals within integer expressions.

Special Integer Operators

The integer-division operator **Div** is replaced by the slash character for floating-point arithmetic. The following integer operators, however, have no counterpart for floating-point operations: **Mod, And, Or, Xor, Shl, Shr.**

The **Mod** operator returns the remainder of integer division. For example, 7 **Div** 2 yields 3; the remainder of 1 is lost. The **Mod** operator, however, discards the dividend and returns the remainder. Therefore, 7 **Mod** 2 returns 1.

The remaining integer operators—**And, Or, Xor, Shl,** and **Shr**—are familiar to anyone who has used Assembler. These are also known as *bit-manipulation operators* since they are usually used not for arithmetic but to alter the values of specific bits in a byte or integer variable. To understand how these operators work, it is necessary to know what a byte and integer look like in memory.

A byte consists of eight bits, each bit capable of storing only two values: 0 and 1. Because bits can store only two numbers, they are base-two numbers. Consider the equivalent binary and decimal numerical values in Table 6-1. (Binary numbers are typically indicated by a lowercase b appended to the digits.) Note that the highest value a byte can hold is 255.

Decimal	Binary
0	00000000b
1	00000001b
2	00000010b
3	00000011b
10	00001010b
100	01100100b
255	11111111b

Table 6-1.   Binary and Decimal Equivalents

Integers consist of two bytes. As a result, their numerical range extends far beyond the limit of 255 that a single byte can hold. The largest possible two-byte integer value is 65,535, or 11111111 11111111b. In Turbo Pascal, however, the leftmost bit in an integer determines the sign of the number; 0 indicates a positive number, 1 a negative number. As a result, the largest integer value in Turbo Pascal is 32,767, or 01111111 11111111b, and the smallest integer value is −32,768, or 11111111 11111111b. For the sake of simplicity, the bit-manipulation operators are illustrated with byte values rather than integers; the general concepts apply equally to both.

The And, Or, and Xor Operators

The **And, Or,** and **Xor** operators compare each bit in two different byte variables and return a third byte variable as the result. The value of the resulting byte depends on the type of the comparison.

The **And** operator compares each bit in two bytes one-by-one and stores the result in a third byte. If the comparison finds both bits are on, the corresponding bit in the third byte is also turned on (that is, set to a value of 1). If the bits compared are not both on, the corresponding bit in the third byte is turned off.

```
PROGRAM AndOperator;
VAR
  Byte1, Byte2, Byte3 : BYTE;
BEGIN
Byte1 := 77;
Byte2 := 62;
Byte3 := Byte1 AND Byte2;
WriteLn (Byte3);
END.
```

Bit position	7	6	5	4	3	2	1	0
Byte1	0	1	0	0	1	1	0	1
And	↓	↓	↓	↓	↓	↓	↓	↓
Byte2	0	0	1	1	1	1	1	0
Gives	↓	↓	↓	↓	↓	↓	↓	↓
Byte3	0	0	0	0	1	1	0	0

Figure 6-1.   Bit manipulation using the And operator

Figure 6-1 gives an example of the **And** command. Byte1 is **And**ed with Byte2, yielding Byte3. Bit 0 in Byte1 is on, but it is off in Byte2. Because only one, and not both, of these bits is on, bit 0 in Byte3 is turned off. Bit position 2 is different in that it is on in both Byte1 and Byte2. Therefore, bit 2 in Byte3 is turned on.

Like the **And** operator, the **Or** operator compares each bit in two bytes and stores the result in a third byte. However, the bit in the third byte is turned on if the comparison finds either bit or both bits in Byte1 and Byte2 are on. The corresponding bit in the third byte is turned off only if both of the bits compared are off.

In Figure 6-2, Byte1 is **Or**ed with Byte2, yielding Byte3. Bit 0 in Byte1 is on, but in Byte2 it is off. Because the **Or** operator requires only one of the bits to be on, bit 0 in Byte3 is turned on. In this example, the only bit position that fails the **Or** test is bit position 7. Because bit 7 is off in both Byte1 and Byte2, bit 7 in Byte3 is also turned off.

```
PROGRAM OrOperator;
VAR
   Byte1, Byte2, Byte3 : BYTE;
BEGIN
Byte1 := 77;
Byte2 := 62;
Byte3 := Byte1 OR Byte2;
WriteLn (Byte3);
END.
```

Bit position	7	6	5	4	3	2	1	0
Byte1	0	1	0	0	1	1	0	1
Or	↓	↓	↓	↓	↓	↓	↓	↓
Byte2	0	0	1	1	1	1	1	0
Gives	↓	↓	↓	↓	↓	↓	↓	↓
Byte3	0	1	1	1	1	1	1	1

Figure 6-2.   Bit manipulation using the Or operator

The **Xor** comparison is true if one bit, and only one bit, is on between two bytes. If both bits are on or both bits are off, the comparison fails and the corresponding bit in the third byte is turned off.

In Figure 6-3, Byte1 is **XOR**ed with Byte2. Bit 0 is on in Byte1 and off in Byte2. Because only one of the bits is on, the comparison is true, and bit 0 in Byte3 is turned on. On the other hand, bits 2 and 7 are turned off in Byte3 because bit 2 is on in both Byte1 and Byte2 and bit 7 is off in both bytes.

The Shl and Shr Operators

As their names suggest, the operators **Shift-left (Shl)** and **Shift-right (Shr)** shift the bits in a byte left or right. A byte can be shifted left or right a maximum of eight times, at which point all the bits are set to zero. When a byte is shifted left by 1, each bit in the byte moves one position to the left.

```
PROGRAM XorOperator;
VAR
   Byte1, Byte2, Byte3 : BYTE;
BEGIN
Byte1 := 77;
Byte2 := 62;
Byte3 := Byte1 XOR Byte2;
WriteLn (Byte3);
END.
```

Bit position	7	6	5	4	3	2	1	0
Byte1	0	1	0	0	1	1	0	1
Xor	↓	↓	↓	↓	↓	↓	↓	↓
Byte2	0	0	1	1	1	1	1	0
Gives	↓	↓	↓	↓	↓	↓	↓	↓
Byte3	0	1	1	1	0	0	0	1

Figure 6-3. Bit manipulation using the Xor operator

The leftmost bit is lost, and a zero appears in the rightmost position, as displayed below:

```
Program ShiftLeft;
Var
   i : Byte;

Begin
i := 255;        (* i equals 11111111b *)
i := i SHL 1;    (* i equals 11111110b *)
i := i SHL 1;    (* i equals 11111100b *)
i := i SHL 1;    (* i equals 11111000b *)
i := i SHL 1;    (* i equals 11110000b *)

i := i SHL 4;    (* i equals 00000000b *)
End.
```

Shift-right (Shr) operates in the same way as **Shift-left**, but it works in the opposite direction. When a byte is shifted to the right, the rightmost bit is lost and the leftmost bit is set to zero.

While they are considered arithmetic in nature, bit-manipulation operators are not often used for computations. More often, they test or set specific bit values. The following listing contains several procedures that use bit-manipulation operators.

```pascal
Program BinaryDemo;
Type
  Binstr = String[8];
Var
  i : Integer;
  b : Byte;

(*****************************************)

Function Binary(b : Byte) : Binstr;
{
This function accepts a byte parameter and returns
a string of eight ones and zeros indicating the binary
form of the byte.
}
Var
  i : Integer;
  bt : Byte;
  s : Binstr;
Begin
bt := $01;
s := '';
For i := 1 TO 8 DO
  Begin
  If (b AND bt) > 0 Then
    s := '1' + s
  Else
    s := '0' + s;
  bt := bt SHL 1;
  End;
Binary := s;
End;

(*****************************************)

Procedure SetBit(Position, Value : Byte; Var ChangeByte : Byte);
{
This procedure sets a particular bit in the byte ChangeByte to
either 1 or 0. The bit is specified by Position, which can range
from 0 to 7.
}
Var
  bt,
  i : Byte;
Begin
bt := $01;
bt := bt SHL Position;
If Value = 1 Then
  ChangeByte := ChangeByte OR bt
Else
  Begin
  bt := bt XOR 255;
```

```
   ChangeByte := ChangeByte AND bt;
   End;
End;

(****************************************)

Function BitOn(Position, TestByte : Byte) : Boolean;
{
This function tests to see if a bit in TestByte is turned on
(equal to one). The bit to test is indicated by the parameter
Position, which can range from 0 (right-most bit) to 7
(left-most bit). If the bit indicated by Position is turned on,
the BitOn is returns TRUE.
}
Var
   bt,
   i : Byte;
Begin
bt := $01;
bt := bt SHL Position;
BitOn := (bt AND TestByte) > 0;
End;

(****************************************)

Begin
Clrscr;
WriteLn;
WriteLn('Demonstrate binary conversion.');
Write('Enter a number (0 - 255): ');
ReadLn(b);
WriteLn('Binary equivalent is: ',binary(b));
WriteLn;
Write('Press Return to Continue...');
ReadLn;


Clrscr;
WriteLn;
WriteLn('Demonstrate SetBit procedure.');
WriteLn;
b := 0;
For i := 0 TO 7 DO
   Begin
   SetBit(i,1,b);
   WriteLn(binary(b));
   End;
For i := 0 TO 7 DO
   Begin
   SetBit(i,0,b);
```

```
   WriteLn(binary(b));
   End;
WriteLn;
Write('Press Return to Continue...');
ReadLn;

   Clrscr;
   b := 1;
   WriteLn;
   WriteLn('Byte value is: ',binary(b));
   WriteLn('Test if the bit 0 is turned on.');
   If BitOn(0,b) Then
     WriteLn('Bit is on.')
   Else
     WriteLn('Bit is off.');
   End.
```

Procedure **Binary** converts a byte value into a string of ones and zeros that represent the bits. Procedure **SetBit** turns on or off any individual bit in a byte. The last procedure, the Boolean function **BitOn**, tests whether a particular bit in a byte is turned on.

Real Arithmetic

An arithmetic expression yields a floating-point result under two conditions: when the expression contains any floating-point operands and when division is executed with the slash (/) operator. Floating-point operands are any identifiers defined as Real or any numeric literal with decimal places (for example, 10.2). The following program listing, which comprises examples of both integer and floating-point expressions, highlights the small differences between the two expression types.

```
Program Math1;
Var
  i,j,k : Integer;
  x,u,z : Real;

Begin
j := i div k; (* integer expression *)
x := i / k;   (* floating-point expression *)

j := i + 3;   (* integer expression *)
x := i + 3.0; (* floating-point expression *)

j := i + k;   (* integer expression *)
x := i + z;   (* floating-point expression *)


x := 10 * 10          (* Integer expression. Will be
                         converted to floating point. *)

x := 10000 * 10000;   (* Integer expression. Will be
                         converted to floating point, but
                         value will be incorrect. *)

x := 10000 * 10000 * 1.0; (* Floating-point expression.
                             Value will be correct. *)
End.
```

The last two statements in the preceding listing point out a potential source of error in programs. Consider the assignment statement

x := 10 * 10;

The right side of the statement, which is an integer expression, is evaluated as an integer before being converted into a floating-point value.

A problem arises when the result of the integer expression exceeds the maximum integer value of 32,767. In the statement

x := 10000 * 10000;

the integer expression overflows the maximum integer value before being converted to a real. As a result, x is incorrectly assigned the value −7936. To eliminate this error, include a floating-point operand in the expression. The expression is then evaluated as a floating-point expression.

In the preceding program listing, the solution is to multiply the expression by 1.0. This forces the expression to be evaluated as a floating-point value, thereby producing the correct result.

Arithmetic Functions

Turbo Pascal provides a rich set of standard arithmetic functions that give easy access to complex computations. These are as follows:

ABS(num)   Returns the absolute value of the number passed as a parameter. The value passed can be either **integer** or **real**, and the value returned will match the type of the parameter: If the **num** is an integer, then **ABS** returns an integer.

ARCTAN(num)   Returns the arc tangent of **num**. **Num** can be either a real or an integer, but the result is a real.

COS(num)   Returns the cosine of **num**, where **num** is either a real or an integer, and the result is a real.

EXP(num)   Computes the exponential of **num**. **Num** is a real or an integer; the result is a real. **Exp** produces an overflow error when **num** is greater than 88 or less than −88.

FRAC(num)   This is the fractional part of **num**. **Num** can be a real or an integer, although integers always return a value of zero. The result is a real. **Frac** also returns zero for any number raised to 1.0E10 power.

HI(NUM)   Returns an integer whose high-order byte is zero and whose low-order byte contains the high-order byte of **num**. **Num** must be an integer.

INT(num)   Returns the nonfractional portion of **num**. **Num** may be either a real or an integer. If **num** is an integer, the function does not change the value, but it does produce a real.

LO(NUM)   Returns an integer whose high-order byte is zero and whose low-order byte contains the low-order byte of **num**. **Num** must be an integer.

LN(num)   Calculates the natural logarithm of **num**. **Num** can be either a real or an integer but it must be greater than zero.

ORD(var)   Returns the relative value of any scalar, including type **Char**. The result is an integer.

PRED(num)   Decrements the integer **num** by one. The result is an integer.

RANDOM   Returns a random value with a lower limit of zero and less than one. The result is a real.

RANDOM(num)   Computes a random number from an integer-type **num**. The random number will be an integer, and its value will be greater than or equal to zero but less than **num**.

ROUND(num)   Returns the value of **num**, rounded to the nearest whole number. **Num** is a real, while the result is an integer.

SIN(num)   Computes the sine of **num**. **Num** can be a real or an integer; the result is a real.

SQR(num)   Returns the square of **num**. **Num** can be a real or an integer; the result is a real. An overflow error occurs when **num** exceeds 1.0E18.

SQRT(num)   Computes the square root of **num**. **Num** can be a real or an integer; the result is a real.

SUCC(num)   Increments the integer **num** by one. The result an integer.

TRUNC(num)   Returns the value of **num** with the decimal portion removed. **Num** is a real, and the result is an integer.

You can also write your own numeric functions. The following listing contains two valuable numerical functions; the first computes the cumulative normal probability density function of a number and the second raises a number to a power.

```
Program NumberFunctions;

(****************************************************)

Function n(X : Real) : Real;
(*Computes the Cumulative Normal Probability Density Function*)
Var
  x2, t, y1, y2, y3, y4, y5, z, R : Real;

Begin
If x > 13.0 Then
  Begin
  n := 1.0;
  Exit;
  End;

If x < -13.0 Then
  Begin
  n := 0.0;
  Exit;
  End;

y1 := 1.0/(1.0+(0.2316419*ABS(X)));
y2 := y1*y1; y3 := y2*y1; y4 := y3*y1; y5 := y4*y1; x2 := X*X;
z := 0.3989423*EXP(-x2/2.0);
R := 1.330274*y5-1.821256*y4+1.781478*y3-0.356538*y2+0.3193815*y1;
t := 1.0-z*R;
If X > 0 Then
  n := t
Else
  n := 1-t;
End;

(*******************************************************)

Function x_to_y(X, y : Real) : Real;
Var
  r : Real;

Begin
r := y*LN(X);
If r > 88.0296 Then
  r := 88.0296;

If r < -88.0296 Then
  r := -88.0296;

X_to_y := EXP(r);
End;

(*******************************************************)
```

```
Begin
WriteLn('3 to power of 2 is: ',x_to_y(3, 2):0:4);
WriteLn;
WriteLn('Cumulative Normal Probability Density Function of
        2 = ',n(2):0:4);
End.
```

The function **n** produces a run-time error when the value of **x** is larger than 13 or smaller than −13. As protection, the procedure tests **x** to make sure its value is between −13 and 13. If **x** is not in this range, the function is assigned a default value (1 if over 13; 0 if under −13). The **Exit** statement forces the procedure to skip remaining statements in the procedure block.

Logical Operators

Turbo Pascal supports the following logical operators:

=	Equal to
<>	Not equal to
<	Less than
>	Greater than
<=	Less than or equal to
>=	Greater than or equal to
Not	Negation of condition
Case	Multiple comparison

Strictly speaking, **Case** is a statement and not an operator. Yet it is so closely allied with the logical operators discussed in this section that it makes sense to include it here.

Logical operators are generally used in **If-Then** statements, which test to determine whether adjacent statements should be executed. This is an example of an **If-Then** statement:

> If a > b Then
> WriteLn('A is greater than B');

In this example, **a** and **b** are **integer** variables. If **a** equals 5 and **b** equals 2, then the test **a** > **b** will be true and the line following the statement will execute.

The **Not** operator negates the result of a logical test. For example, if **a** > **b** is evaluated as true, then **Not a** > **b** will be false. For any test using the **Not** operator, there is an equivalent test without it. For example, **Not a** > **b** is the same as **a** <= **b**.

An **If-Then** statement can control the execution of more than one statement by using **Begin** and **End** to create a block of code. In the example below, if **a** is greater than **b**, all the statements between the **Begin** and **End** statements will execute:

```
If a > b Then
  Begin
  WriteLn('A is greater than B');
  b := a;
  End;
```

The **If-Then** statement can be extended with the Turbo Pascal reserved word **Else**. If the condition tested fails, the program executes the code following the **Else** clause, as shown in this example:

```
If a > b Then
  Begin
  WriteLn('A is greater than B');
  b := a;
  End
Else
  Begin
  WriteLn('A is not greater than B');
  a := b;
  End;
```

Note that the statement preceding the **Else** clause is not terminated with a semicolon. Turbo Pascal considers the **Else** clause to be a continuation of one long statement, so a semicolon indicating the end of a statement is inappropriate.

To create *multiple-condition branching*, you can give an **If-Then** statement more than one **Else** clause. This is useful when you test a variable against many possible values.

```
If a = 1 Then
   Begin
   WriteLn('A equals 1');
   End
Else If a = 2 Then
   Begin
   WriteLn('A equals 2');
   End
Else If a = 3 Then
   Begin
   WriteLn('A equals 3');
   End
Else If a = 4 Then
   Begin
   WriteLn('A equals 4');
   End;
```

Case Operator

An alternative to multiple **Else-If** statements is the **Case** statement, which is specifically designed to handle tests that require multiple conditions. A typical **Case** statement looks like this:

```
Case a Of

   1 : WriteLn('a equals 1');

2..4 : Begin
       WriteLn('a is between 2 and 4');
       WriteLn('Case statements can specify ranges.');
       End;

   5 : WriteLn('a equals 5');
```

```
Else Begin
    WriteLn('a is not between 1 and 5');
    WriteLn('The Case statement supports the Else clause');
    End;

End; (* of case *)_
```

Case statements are easier to read than extended **If-Then-Else** statements and are more flexible because they allow you to specify a range of values, such as 2...4.

Note, however, that because it uses only simple data types, the **Case** statement is more restrictive than the **If-Then** statement. Therefore, you cannot use **real** or **string** data types with the **Case** statement.

Using the Case Operator in Variant Records

Declaring **record** data types is discussed in Chapter 5. This section discusses how the **Case** operator can be used within the **record** data type to create what is called a *variant record.*

Variant records are intended to conserve space as well as create data structures that more precisely reflect the entities they represent. For example, consider the use of the variant record in the following listing:

```
Program VariantRecord;
Type
  VehicleType = (Car, Boat, Plane);
  VehicleRec = Record
    IDnumber : Integer;
    Price    : Real;
    Weight   : Real;

    Case Kind : VehicleType Of

    Car : (MilesPerGallon : Integer;
           Odometer : Real);

    Boat : (Displacement : Real;
            Length : Integer);
```

```
      Plane : (Engines : Integer;
               Seats : Integer);

   End;

Var
   Vehicle : VehicleRec;

Begin
Vehicle.IDnumber := 123;
Vehicle.Price := 12000;
Vehicle.Weight := 1200;
Vehicle.Kind := Car;
Vehicle.MilesPerGallon := 21;
Vehicle.Odometer := 75000.0;

With vehicle DO
   Begin
     Case kind Of

     Car:
       Begin
       WriteLn(MilesPerGallon);
       WriteLn(Odometer);
       End;

     Boat:
       Begin
       WriteLn(Displacement);
       WriteLn(Length);
       End;

     Plane:
       Begin
       WriteLn(Engines);
       WriteLn(Seats);
       End;
     End;
   End;
End.
```

Notice how the record contains separate sections pertaining to different types of transportation. Because of this flexibility, variant records can cover broad classes of things, yet still retain specific detailed information.

The fields under Car, Boat, and Plane comprise a total of four integers and two reals—20 bytes in total. But the variant portions of the records share the same memory. Since the largest single block of memory used by a variant portion of the record is eight bytes (a real and an integer), only eight bytes are allocated to the variant part of the record.

The field named Kind is known as the *tag field*. The tag field helps keep track of which part of the variant record is in use. When a tag field is used, the variant record is known as a *discriminated union* because the tag field can discriminate which portion of the variant record should be used.

Another type of variant record is the *free union*, or a variant record that does not have a tag field. COBOL programmers will feel at home with free unions because they resemble COBOL's redefined fields.

The program example below presents an example of a free-union variant record.

```
Program FreeUnion;
Type
   CharByte = Record
     Case Integer Of
     1 : (Characters : Array [1..10] Of Char);
     2 : (Numbers : Array [1..10] Of Byte);
     End;
Var
   CB : CharByte;
Begin
With CB DO Characters[1] := 'A';
With CB DO WriteLn(Numbers[1]);
End.
```

Notice that the variant record definition has no tag field; only a data type, **integer**, is specified. The lack of a tag field means no tag value is stored and that you can refer to any of the variant elements without restriction.

This example program is special because the variant record defines one array in two different ways. The 10-byte array in one line is defined as an array of characters, while in the next line it is defined as an array of bytes. Since these arrays share the same memory (because they are the variant part of the record), you can refer to the elements in the arrays as either characters or numbers. This is demonstrated in the program block. Notice where a character is assigned to the first element in the array using the identifier **Characters**, and then the element is written out as a number using the identifier **Numbers**.

Turbo Pascal's variant records, numerous logical operators, and powerful arithmetic functions make it one of the best languages for writing scientific, statistical, and financial programs. But even less demanding applications benefit from the clarity, structure, and variety of operators that Turbo Pascal provides.

SEVEN

Program Control Structures

Condition Statements
Decision Making and Conditional Branching
Conditional Branching with the Case Statement
Repetitive Control Structures
Unstructured Branching

This chapter discusses the various control structures Pascal provides, the ways they are used, and their good and bad points.

The least complicated Turbo Pascal program starts at the first **Begin** statement of the program block, executes each statement in order, and stops when it hits the final **End** statement. This straightforward program structure is illustrated in the following program:

```
Program PayRoll;
Var
   TotalPay,
   HourlyRate,
   HoursWorked : Real;

Begin
Write('Enter your hourly rate: ');
Readln(HourlyRate);
Write('Enter the number of hours you worked: ');
Readln(HoursWorked);
TotalPay := HourlyRate * HoursWorked;
Writeln('Your total pay is: $',TotalPay:0:2);
End.
```

Programming tasks can rarely be expressed in such simple terms, however. The preceding program, for example, does not take into account that people often work more than 40 hours per week, entitling them to overtime pay.

You can express additional complexity by using *control structures*. Control structures give programs the ability to act differently under different situations. Adding a control structure (in this case, the **If-Then** statement) to the program above gives it the ability to compute overtime pay:

```
Program PayRoll2;
Var
   TotalPay,
   HourlyRate,
   HoursWorked,
   OvertimeHours : Real;

Begin
Write('Enter your hourly rate: ');
Readln(HourlyRate);
Write('Enter the number of hours you worked: ');
Readln(HoursWorked);

OvertimeHours := 0.0;
If (HoursWorked > 40.0) Then
   Begin
   OvertimeHours := HoursWorked - 40.0;
   HoursWorked := 40.0;
   End;

TotalPay := (HourlyRate * HoursWorked) +
            (1.5 * HourlyRate * OvertimeHours);

Writeln('Your total pay is: $',TotalPay:0:2);
End.
```

Here, the **If-Then** statement tests whether an individual put in any overtime by comparing the number of hours worked to 40. If the number of hours is greater than 40, overtime pay is clearly due. The expanded equation includes the calculation of overtime pay at 1.5 times the standard rate.

Condition Statements

All Turbo Pascal control structures, with the major exception of the **GoTo** statement, have one thing in common: they do something based on the evaluation of a *condition state-*

ment. A condition statement, also known as a *Boolean state-ment,* is any expression that results in either a true or false condition. In **For-Do** statements, explained later in this chapter, the condition is implied, but for all other control structures (**If-Then, While-Do, Repeat-Until**), the condition statement is explicitly defined.

Condition statements can consist of direct comparisons:

```
age > 12
name = 'Jones'
x < y
```

or they can include calculations:

```
x > (y * 12)
(x−15) < > (y * 12) + Sqr(z)
```

or they might have multiple conditions:

```
(age > 12) and (name = 'Jones');
```

All Boolean expressions have a common element: they have a left side that is compared with a right side using a logical operator. Logical operators were discussed briefly in Chapter 6 but are presented here again:

>	Greater than
<	Less than
>=	Greater than or equal to
<=	Less than or equal to
=	Equal to
<>	Not equal to

These operators can be used to compare any two expressions when the operands are compatible. For example, it is illegal to compare a real with a string, or a string to an integer. You can, however, mix reals, integers, and bytes in Boolean expressions because they are all numeric types.

Simple Boolean expressions, those that use only one operator, are easy to understand. For example, the Boolean expression (i > 0) is clearly understood to mean "i is greater than 0." Complications arise, however, when you combine multiple expressions with the **And** or **Or** operators. The following program illustrates the kind of unexpected results that can occur:

```
Program IntegerOr;
Var
  i,j : Integer;

Begin
i := 9;
j := -47;
WriteLn(i or j > 0);
WriteLn((i > 0) or (j > 0));
End.
```

This program writes out the result of two Boolean expressions. Both expressions are legal and appear to test if either **i** or **j** is greater than zero. Since **i** is assigned a value greater than zero, you might expect both expressions to be true. Appearances can be deceiving, however: the result of the first Boolean expression is false.

To understand why the first expression is false, you must understand Turbo Pascal's hierarchy of operators. Arithmetic operators (+, −, *, /, Div) are always executed before logical operators (**And, Or, Xor**). The **And** and **Or** operators, however, can serve as either arithmetic or logical operators, depending on how they are used. In the preceding example, the **Or** operator is positioned between two integers, which tells Turbo Pascal to treat it as an arithmetic **Or**. When **i** equals 9 and **j** equals −47, the arithmetic result of **i Or j** is −39. Since −39 is less than 0, the result of the Boolean expression is false.

The program's second Boolean expression, on the other hand, separates the tests of **i** and **j** into two distinct Boolean expressions and clarifies the separation with parentheses. (In general, parentheses make Boolean expressions more readable and less prone to error.) In this case, the **Or** operator is treated as a logical operator. First **i** is compared to 0, which results in true. Then **j** is compared to 0, resulting in false.

Finally, the two results are combined with the **Or** operator, giving an overall true result.

The Not Operator

The **Not** operator negates a Boolean expression. If the result is true, the **Not** operator reverses the result to false. For example, $(10 > 0)$ is true, but **Not** $(10 > 0)$ is false.

While the **Not** operator can be useful, it is never required. For every Boolean expression that uses the **Not** operator, there is an equivalent expression that does not. For example, the expression **Not (Age > 65)** can be replaced by the expression **(Age <= 65)**. The **Not** operator sometimes increases the readability of a Boolean expression, but it is better to avoid it because it unnecessarily complicates a Boolean expression and thus increases the possibility of introducing errors in your program.

Boolean Functions in Control Structures

If a control statement requires an especially complex Boolean expression or if the same Boolean expression is used in many control statements throughout your program, you should create a Boolean function that contains the expression. Using the Boolean function in place of the expression decreases your coding and reduces errors. For example, the following program uses the Boolean function Qualifies to determine whether a potential site for a store is a good candidate:

```
Program SiteEvaluation;
Var
   CarsPerHour,
   PopulationDensity,
   TaxRate,
   LandCostPerSquareFoot,
   LaborCostPerHour : real;

Function Qualifies : Boolean;
```

```
Begin
Qualifies := (CarsPerHour > 1000) and
             (PopulationDensity > 5000) and
             (TaxRate < 0.10) and
             (LandCostPerSquareFoot < 150) and
             (LaborCostPerHour < 6.50)
End;

begin
Write('Enter number of cars per hour: ');
Readln(CarsPerHour);
Write('Enter population density per square mile: ');
Readln(PopulationDensity);
Write('Enter Tax Rate: ');
Readln(TaxRate);
Write('Enter land cost per square foot: ');
Readln(LandCostPerSquareFoot);
Write('Enter labor cost per hour: ');
Readln(LaborCostPerHour);

If Qualifies then
  writeln('Good site!')
else
  writeln('Forget it.');
end.
```

The following Boolean expression is complex:

(CarsPerHour $>$ 1000) and
(PopulationDensity $>$ 5000) and
(TaxRate $<$ 0.10) and
(LandCostPerSquareFoot $<$ 150) and
(LaborCostPerHour $<$ 6.50)

By isolating it in a function, you can substitute the identifier **Qualifies** wherever the full Boolean statement would normally go. This reduces the possibility for error (and the amount of typing you have to do) and makes it easier to modify the program since all changes can be done in the function itself; these modifications are automatically reflected throughout the program.

Decision Making and Conditional Branching

Based on information provided to it, a program can choose between different courses of action. However, if you want your program to make decisions, you must specifically tell it what information it will use, how to evaluate the information, and what course of action to follow. This type of programming is often called *conditional branching* because programs that use this method branch in different directions based on a condition (that is, the evaluation of data).

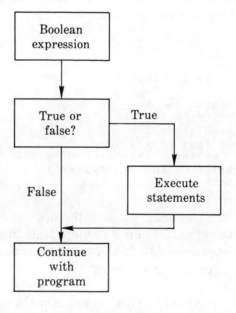

Figure 7-1.   Flowchart of If-Then statement

The If-Then Statement

The simplest form of conditional branching is the **If-Then** statement, which causes a program to execute a block of code if a condition is true. This process is described schematically in Figure 7-1.

The first thing an **If-Then** statement does is to evaluate the information provided to it in the form of a Boolean statement. If, for example, the Boolean statement is (Age > 21), the information is contained in the variable **age**, which is compared with the test value 21.

The evaluation produces one of two possible results — true or false. If the statement is true, the program executes the block of code that immediately follows the **If-Then** statement. If the result is false, the program skips the block. Consider the following example:

```
Program TestAge;
Var
   age : Integer;

Begin
Write('Enter age: ');
Readln(age);
If (age >= 21) then
   Writeln('This person is not a minor');
Writeln('End of Program');
End.
```

The program asks the user to enter a number (an age), then the **If-Then** statement tests to see if **age** is greater than or equal to 21. If the result of the test is true, the program executes the statement

WriteLn('This person is not a minor.');

The program executes the second **WriteLn** statement regardless of the result of the **If-Then** statement. In this example, only one statement follows the **If-Then** test. If you want to conditionally execute more than one statement, use **Begin** and **End** to indicate what statements are included.

For example, the expanded version of **TestAge**, shown here, writes two lines when **age** is greater than or equal to 21:

```
Program TestAge;
Var
  age : Integer;

Begin
Write('Enter age: ');
Readln(age);
If (age >= 21) then
  Begin
  Writeln('This person is not a minor.');
  Writeln('This person is ',age,' years old.');
  End;
Writeln('End of Program.');
End.
```

The **Begin** and **End** statements tell Turbo Pascal to execute both of the enclosed **WriteLn** statements when **age** is greater than or equal to 21. Although the **Begin** and **End** statements are not required when only one statement is to be executed conditionally, you might want to include them for the sake of program clarity and consistency.

The If-Then-Else Statement

The **If-Then** statement provides just one branch, which executes when the Boolean statement is true. Many times, a program requires two branches: one that executes if true, the other if false. This situation is shown in Figure 7-2, where a program executes different blocks of code depending on the outcome of an evaluation.

To express this situation in Turbo Pascal code, you must use the control structure of an **If-Then-Else** statement. This statement works as follows: if an evaluation is true, the block of code that follows the **Then** statement executes; if not true, the block of code that follows the **Else** statement executes. In either case, when the selected block of code terminates, program control skips to the end of the **If-Then-Else** statement, as depicted here:

```
Program TestAge;
Var
  age : Integer;

Begin
Write('Enter age: ');
Readln(age);
If (age >= 21) then
  Begin
  Writeln('This person is not a minor');
  Writeln('This person is ',age,' years old');
  End
Else
  Begin
  Writeln('This person is a minor');
  Writeln('This minor is ',age,' years old');
  End;
Writeln('End of Program');
End.
```

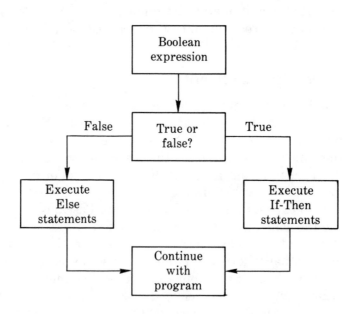

Figure 7-2.   Flowchart of If-Then-Else statement

As in the earlier examples, the following statements are executed when **age** is greater than or equal to 21:

```
WriteLn('This person is not a minor');
WriteLn('This person is ',age,' years old');
```

If **age** is less than 21, the program executes these two statements:

```
WriteLn('This person is a minor');
WriteLn('This minor is ',age,' years old');
```

When writing code that uses **If-Then-Else** statements, do not terminate the **End** that precedes the **Else** with a semicolon (see the preceding program, **TestAge**). Turbo Pascal considers the entire **If-Then-Else** structure to be one continuous statement, and semicolons appear only at the end of a statement.

Extending the If-Then-Else Statement

The **If-Then** structure provides one branch, and the **If-Then-Else** structure provides two. But what happens when you need to express a series of conditions? In such cases, you can extend **If-Then-Else** with the **Else-If** statement. **Else-If** statements allow you to chain Boolean statements, giving your program the ability to multiple branch (see Figure 7-3). The key element of this figure is the path that the program takes when it finds the first Boolean expression to be false. Instead of executing a block of code, the program evaluates a second Boolean expression; it is here that the **Else-If** statement comes into play. If this expression is also false, the program executes the final block of code.

The following sample program demonstrates how **Else-If** can create multiple branches:

```
Program PrintGradeMessage;
Var
   grade : Char;
```

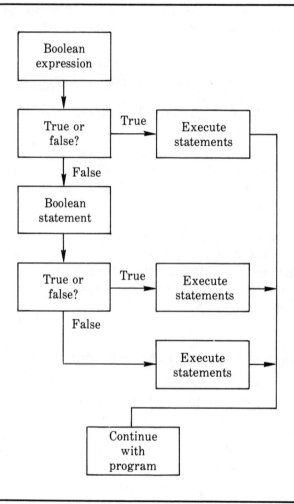

Figure 7-3.   Multiple branching

```
Begin
Write('Enter your grade: ');
Readln(grade);
Grade := Upcase(grade);

If grade = 'A' then
  Writeln('Excellent.')
Else If grade = 'B' then
```

```
  Writeln('Getting there.')
Else If grade = 'C' then
  Writeln('Not too bad.')
Else If grade = 'D' then
  Writeln('Just made it.')
Else If grade = 'F' then
  Writeln('Summer school!')
Else
  Writeln('That''s not a grade.');
End.
```

This program asks the user to enter a grade (A, B, C, D, or F) and prints a message that comments on the grade entered. The program's five Boolean expressions result in a total of six branches. (The sixth branch is the statement that follows the final **Else.**)

As you can see by now, the **If-Then-Else** structure is extremely powerful, allowing you to build a tremendous amount of intelligence into your programs.

Nested If-Then Statements

One way to allow your program to consider two or more separate conditions before embarking on a course of action is to nest the **If-Then** statements. Figure 7-4 depicts the flow of a nested **If-Then** statement.

A nested **If-Then** statement can produce very complex branching schemes. Consider this problem: you are running a game of chance using a box full of black and white marbles. A player takes two marbles from the box at random and, depending on the combination of colors chosen, he or she is paid at the following rate:

First Marble	Second Marble	Payoff
White	White	0:1
White	Black	2:3
Black	White	1:1
Black	Black	2:1

If the first marble is white and the second is white, the

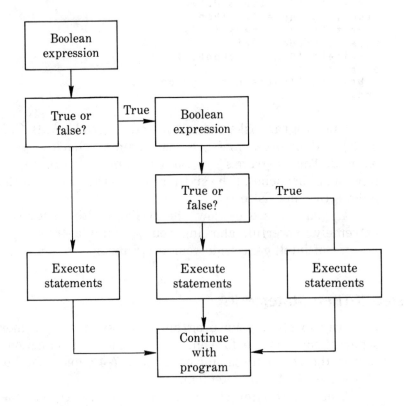

Figure 7-4.   Nested If-Then statements

gambler loses everything. If white is first and black is second, he or she loses two-thirds of the bet. If black is followed by white, the gambler breaks even. Two black marbles doubles the bet.

To code this game in Turbo Pascal, use the **If-Then-Else** statement, as shown here:

```
Program Bet;
Var
  FirstMarble,
  SecondMarble : (black,white);
  i   : Integer;
  Bet : Real;

Begin
repeat

i := random(2);
fillchar(FirstMarble,1,i);

i := random(2);
fillchar(SecondMarble,1,i);

Write('Enter amount of bet: ');
Readln(Bet);

If (FirstMarble = white) and (SecondMarble = white) then
  Begin
  Bet := Bet * 0.0;
  Writeln('First Marble is White; Second Marble is White');
  End
Else If (FirstMarble = white) and (SecondMarble = black) then
  Begin
  Bet := Bet * (2 / 3);
  Writeln('First Marble is White; Second Marble is Black');
  End
Else If (FirstMarble = black) and (SecondMarble = white) then
  Begin
  Bet := Bet * 1.0;
  Writeln('First Marble is Black; Second Marble is White');
  End
Else (* (FirstMarble = black) and (SecondMarble = black) *)
  Begin
  Bet := Bet * 2.0;
  Writeln('First Marble is Black; Second Marble is Black');
  End;
Writeln('You get $',Bet:0:2,' back.');
Writeln;
Writeln;
until i > 100;
End.
```

The program explicitly refers to each of the four possible combinations of black and white marbles. It will work just fine, but it could be coded more efficiently in this format:

```
If (FirstMarble = white) then
  Begin

  (*****************************************)
  (* Beginning of nested If-Then statement. *)
  (*****************************************)
```

```
    if (SecondMarble = white) then
      Begin
      Bet := Bet * 0.0;
      Writeln('First Marble is White; Second Marble is White');
      End
    Else (* SecondMarble = black *)
      Begin
      Bet := Bet * (2 / 3);
      Writeln('First Marble is White; Second Marble is Black');
      End
   End
 Else (* FirstMarble = black *)
    Begin

    (******************************************)
    (* Beginning of nested If-Then statement. *)
    (******************************************)

    If SecondMarble = white) then
      Begin
      Bet := Bet * 1.0;
      Writeln('First Marble is Black; Second Marble is White');
      End
    Else (* SecondMarble = black *)
      Begin
      Bet := Bet * 2.0;
      Writeln('First Marble is Black; Second Marble is Black');
      End;
    End;
 End;
```

The preceding program's first-level **If-Then** statement tests for the color of the first marble, and its second-level, or nested, statement tests the color of the second marble. Rather than testing both marbles in each **If-Then** statement, the nested **If-Then** structure separates the tests.

The first example evaluates up to three Boolean statements before it finds the correct branch. Since each Boolean statement contains two comparisons, the program may execute as many as six comparisons before coming to a result.

The second example never tests more than two Boolean statements in one pass. Thus, your program does less work and gives results more quickly than it would otherwise. While the time saved by the sample program is too small to be noticeable, it can be significant in programs with nested **If-Then** statements that are repeated many times.

Conditional Branching with the Case Statement

If you often use simple data types (that is, no **reals** or **strings**) in your programs, you can use the Turbo Pascal **Case** statement in place of the **If-Then** statement. **Case** provides a logical and clear structure for multiple branching. Here is a typical use of the **Case** statement:

```
Program CaseExample;
Var
   number1,
   number2  : Real;
   operator : Char;
   st,st1,st2 : String[80];
   p,
   code : Integer;

Procedure Compute;
Begin
st1 := '';
st2 := '';
p := 1;

Write('Enter a formula: ');
Readln(st);

(* Pick up the first number *)

While (st[p] = ' ') and (p <= length(st)) do
   p := p + 1;
While (st[p] <> ' ') and (p <= length(st)) do
   Begin
   st1 := st1 + st[p];
   p := p + 1;
   end;


(* Pick up the operator *)

While (st[p] = ' ') and (p <= length(st)) do
   p := p + 1;
Operator := st[p];
   p := p + 1;
```

```
(* Pick up the second number *)

While (st[p] = ' ') and (p <= length(st)) do
  p := p + 1;
While (st[p] <> ' ') and (p <= length(st)) do
  Begin
  st2 := st2 + st[p];
  p := p + 1;
  end;

(* Convert number strings to reals *)

Val(st1,number1,code);
Val(st2,number2,code);

(* Perform computations *)

  Case operator of
  '+' : writeln(number1 + number2:0:3);
  '-' : writeln(number1 - number2:0:3);
  '*' : writeln(number1 * number2:0:3);
  '/' : writeln(number1 / number2:0:3);
  End;

End;

Begin

  Repeat
  Compute;
  Until st = '';

End.
```

This program asks for a string that contains a simple formula (for example, 2 + 2). It extracts the numbers and the operator from the string, converts the extracted strings into real values, and then uses the **Case** statement to perform the correct calculation.

An especially powerful feature of the **Case** statement is its ability to interpret ranges, as shown here:

```
Program CaseWithRanges;
Var
  key : Char;

Begin
Write('Press a key: ');
Read(kbd,key);
Writeln;
```

```
Case key of

'A'..'Z' :
  Writeln('You pressed an uppercase letter');

'a'..'z' :
  Writeln('You pressed a lowercase letter');

'0'..'9' :
  Writeln('You pressed a numeric key');

 Else
    Begin
    Writeln('You pressed an unknown key');
    Writeln('Try again.');
    End;

End;

End.
```

When the user of this program presses a key, the **char** variable **key** stores the character. The **Case** statement then evaluates the character according to the ranges specified; if the character falls between A and Z, the program knows it must be an uppercase letter. The last statement in the **Case** structure is preceded by **Else**, which provides a default branch for variables that do not fit into any of the specified categories. Any time a character is not in one of the ranges A..Z, a..z, or 0..9, the program executes the statement that follows **Else**.

Repetitive Control Structures

Most programs require a method of repeating a block of code. One way is simply to write as many statements as you need, as in the program in Figure 7-5, which reads in five numbers and writes out the sum.

All those **ReadLn** statements are not only inefficient, but

```
Program NoLoop;
Var
  Numbers : Array [1..5] of Real;
  Sum : Real;
Begin
Write('Enter a Number: ');
Readln(Numbers[1]);
Write('Enter a Number: ');
Readln(Numbers[2]);
Write('Enter a Number: ');
Readln(Numbers[3]);
Write('Enter a Number: ');
Readln(Numbers[4]);
Write('Enter a Number: ');
Readln(Numbers[5]);

Sum := Numbers[1] + Numbers[2] + Numbers[3] +
       Numbers[4] + Numbers[5];
Writeln('The sum is: ',sum:0:2);
End.
```

Figure 7-5.   A program without looping structures

they also produce a very limited program, one that must have five numbers entered, no more, no less. To improve this program, you can use one of Turbo Pascal's three looping control structures.

For-Do Loop

The For-Do loop is a particularly powerful looping structure. Nearly every programming language provides some form of this structure, but Turbo Pascal's implementation of it is superior to that of most other languages.

When coding a For-Do loop, you must specify a starting point, an ending point, and an **integer** variable to be used as a counter. A typical For-Do loop statement might look like this:

```
For i := 1 to 100 do
   Begin
   {
   Statements
   }
   End;
```

The first time Turbo Pascal executes this For-Do loop, it sets **i** equal to 1 and executes the block of code following the loop statement. When it has executed the last statement in the block, the loop increases **i** by one. When **i** exceeds the upper limit (in this case, 100), the loop terminates, and control passes to the next line in the program. But as long as **i** is less than or equal to 100, Turbo Pascal continues to execute the block of code.

Figure 7-6 shows an updated version of the program in Figure 7-5. Adding For-Do loops to a program substantially reduces the amount of code needed.

Repeat-Until Loop

While the For-Do loop clearly improves the program, it still must read five numbers, and no more or no less than five numbers, to run properly. You can eliminate this restriction by using the Repeat-Until loop.

This is the general format for the Repeat-Until loop:

```
Repeat
{
Statements
}
Until (Boolean condition);
```

```
Program ForDoLoop;
Var
  i : Integer;
  Numbers : Array [1..5] of Real;
  Sum : Real;
Begin
Sum := 0;
For i := 1 to 5 do
  Begin
  Write('Enter a Number: ');
  Readln(Numbers[i]);
  End;

For i := 1 to 5 do
  Sum := Sum + Numbers[i];
Writeln('The sum is: ',sum:0:2);
End.
```

Figure 7-6. A program with For-Do loops

The word **Repeat** tells Turbo Pascal to execute statements until it reaches the Until instruction. Turbo Pascal then evaluates the Boolean expression or function in the Until instruction, and if the expression is not true, the program goes back to the Repeat instruction and continues executing the block of code.

The main advantage of the Repeat-Until loop is that it does not require you to specify a set number of iterations in advance: it continues to repeat until the Boolean expression is true.

The following sample program is a refined version of the previous example. This program allows you to enter from 0 to 5 numbers, which are then summed:

```
Program RepeatUntilLoop;
Var
  i : Integer;
  Numbers : Array [1..5] of Real;
  Sum : Real;
Begin
Sum := 0;
i := 0;
```

```
Repeat
Write('Enter a Number: ');
i := i + 1;
Readln(Numbers[i]);
Until (i = 5) or (Numbers[i] = 0);

For i := 1 to i do
  Sum := Sum + Numbers[i];
Writeln('The sum is: ',sum:0:2);
End.
```

In this example, the Repeat-Until loop terminates under two conditions: when **i** equals five or the number entered is zero. For example, if you enter the numbers 1, 3, and 0, the program exits from the Repeat-Until loop without asking for the fourth and fifth numbers. The For-Do loop that calculates the sum is the same as the one in the previous program, but in this program the upper limit is set to the integer variable **i**, which counts the number values the user enters. Therefore, the For-Do loop executes once for each number entered.

While-Do Loop

The While-Do loop is similar to the Repeat-Until loop, except the While-Do loop tests a Boolean condition *before* it executes any statements in a block. The following code shows the sample program with a While-Do loop:

```
Program WhileDoLoop;
Var
  i : Integer;
  Numbers : Array [1..5] of Real;
  Sum : Real;
Begin
Sum := 0;
i := 1;
Write('Enter a Number: ');
Readln(Numbers[i]);

While (Numbers[i] <> 0) and (i < 5) do
  Begin
  Write('Enter a Number: ');
  i := i + 1;
  Readln(Numbers[i]);
  End;
```

```
For i := 1 to i do
  Sum := Sum + Numbers[i];
Writeln('The sum is: ',sum:0:2);
End.
```

If the While-Do loop finds that the Boolean expression is not true, Turbo Pascal executes the block of code that follows the While-Do block.

Unstructured Branching

The term *unstructured branching* describes what happens when a program jumps from one point to another, whether or not you specify a Boolean condition to control the jump. (This process is also known as *direct transfer* or *unconditional branching:* The latter term is misleading because a condition can be included.) Turbo Pascal performs unstructured branching when it encounters a **Goto** statement that refers to a declared label. The **Goto** statement transfers control to a particular point in a program, which is marked with a label. The following program shows an example of unstructured branching:

```
Program GoToExample;
Var
  i : Integer;
  ch : Char;

Label
  Retry,
  Stop,
  DoLoop,
  Next,
  Male,
  Female;

Begin
Retry:
Write('What is your sex: ');
Readln(ch);
ch := Upcase(ch);
If Not (ch In ['F','M']) Then
  Goto Retry;
```

```
If ch = 'M' Then
  Goto Male
Else
  Goto Female;


Male:
Writeln('Sex is Male');
Goto DoLoop;


Female:
Writeln('Sex is Female');

DoLoop:
i := 1;

Next:
i := i + 1;
If i > 10 Then
  Goto Stop;
Writeln('i = ',i);
Goto Next;

Stop:
End.
```

Labels are declared with the Turbo Pascal reserved word **Label**, followed by the label identifiers, which are separated by commas and terminated with a semicolon. When a label is placed in a program block, it is followed by a colon.

To execute a **Goto** statement, simply specify the label to which the code is to branch. For example, the instruction

Goto Female;

tells Turbo Pascal to skip directly to the point in the program where the label Female is located. In the preceding program, some of the **Goto** statements are preceded by Boolean condition statements, while others stand alone.

Those who are accustomed to programming in Turbo Pascal will find this program both stilted and inelegant because they know that it can be written more easily and clearly with Turbo Pascal's control structures. As discussed earlier, the Pascal language was developed to do away with the **Goto** statement. The language supports the statement, but the general consensus is that it leads to bad programming habits.

Of course, the **Goto** statement can be used responsibly, and programming style should not be viewed as inviolable. Still, years of badly written, poorly maintained, and incomprehensible programs have convinced most programmers to avoid the **Goto** statement. Compare the previous program with the program below:

```
Program GoToExample;
Var
   i : Integer;
   ch : Char;

Begin
  Repeat
  Write('What is your sex: ');
  Readln(ch);
  ch := Upcase(ch);
  Until (ch In ['F','M']);

If ch = 'M' Then
  Writeln('Sex is Male');
Else
 Writeln('Sex is Female');

For i := 1 to 10 do
  Writeln('i = ',i);
End.
```

As you can see, the program is clearer and more compact without the **Goto** statements. Yet these examples do not fully communicate the extent of the problems caused by **Goto** statements. When a program full of **Goto**s grows in size, its logical flow becomes nearly undecipherable.

Given all of this, does it ever make sense to use the **Goto** statement? In certain cases, yes, but only when you place the label close to the **Goto** that branches to it. Here is an example of a program with a valid use of a **Goto** statement:

```
Program MathError;
Var
   Numbers1,
```

```
    Numbers2,
    Numbers3 : Array [1..100] of Integer;


Procedure Divide;
Var
    i : Integer;
Label
    DivideEnd;

Begin
For i := 1 To 100 Do
    Begin
    If Numbers2[i] = 0 Then
        Begin
        Writeln('Error: Division by zero');
        Goto DivideEnd;
        End;
    Numbers3[i] := Numbers1[i] div Numbers2[i];
    End;
DivideEnd:
End;

Begin
Divide;
End.
```

This program relies on three arrays of integers. The procedure **Divide** divides the elements in one array by the elements in another and assigns the result to an element in a third array. Whenever you divide in Turbo Pascal, you risk a run-time error if the divisor is zero, so the program first tests the divisor to see if it is zero, in which case the **Goto** statement is used to branch to the end of the procedure. This is a valid use of the **Goto** statement because not only is the distance between the **Goto** statement and the label small but also the logic behind the statement is clear. Nonetheless, the following structure is an example of more elegant and precise code:

```
i := 0;
    repeat
    i := i + 1;
    If (Numbers2[i] <> 0) Then
        Numbers3[i] := Numbers1[i] div Numbers2[i]
```

```
else
  Writeln('Error: Division by zero');
Until (i = 100) or (Numbers2[i] = 0);
```

```
for i := 1 To 100 Do
  begin
  If (Numbers2[i] = 0) Then
    Begin
    Writeln('Error: Division by zero');
    Exit;
    End;
  Numbers3[i] := Numbers1[i] div Numbers2[i];
  End;
```

The first routine uses the Repeat-Until loop to provide both a means to increment **i** and to exit if the divisor is found to be zero. The second routine uses **Exit**, a standard Turbo Pascal procedure. Strictly speaking, **Exit** is an unconditional branching statement because it ignores the normal path of execution for the block of code.

Turbo Pascal offers both structured and unstructured methods for creating clear, concise applications. This variety of tools makes programming in Turbo Pascal especially rewarding, allowing you the flexibility to develop a personal programming style while encouraging you to learn good programming habits.

EIGHT

Pointers and Dynamic Memory Allocation

Turbo Pascal Memory Allocation
The Heap and Pointers
Using Pointers with Complex Data Types
The @ Operator in Turbo Pascal Version 4.0
A Word on Segments

Turbo Pascal uses different parts, or segments, of your computer's memory for different purposes. One part holds the instructions your computer executes, while the others store data. Each of these segments performs a specific role, and you must understand these roles and how the segments work before you can master advanced programming concepts.

Turbo Pascal Memory Allocation

Turbo Pascal divides your computer's memory into four parts—the code segment, the data segment, the stack segment, and the heap. Technically, the stack and the heap are not entirely separate since they share the same block of memory, but they operate as separate entities.

While the data segment is clearly dedicated to data storage, data can also be stored in the other three memory locations. The code segment, for example, holds Turbo Pascal typed constants. The stack and heap, on the other hand, hold dynamic data, which is data that is needed temporarily and then discarded. This chapter discusses the role of the stack and the heap and how you can use *dynamic allocation* in your programs.

DOS Memory Mapping Conventions

The first step in understanding how Turbo Pascal manages memory is to learn something about the internal workings of your microcomputer. A computer has a certain amount of RAM (Random Access Memory). Let's say yours has 256 kilobytes. A kilobyte represents 1024 bytes, so your 256K computer really has a total of 262,144 bytes of RAM.

When your program first starts, it sets up a segment that holds the program's instructions (the code segment), a segment to hold the program's data (the data segment), and a segment to hold temporary data (the stack segment). As the instructions in the code segment execute, they manipulate data in both the data segment and the stack segment.

How does the program know at which byte these three segments begin? For that matter, how does a program locate any particular byte in memory? By using addresses. Every byte has an *address*, a 16-bit integer that has a value from 0 to 65,536. When a program needs to "access" a particular byte, it uses the address to find the byte's location in memory.

If a computer's address consisted of a single integer, you could not address more than 64K (65,536 bytes) of RAM. This was the case for the early 8-bit microprocessors.

The advent of 16-bit processors, particularly the Intel 8086/88 family, ushered in a new memory-addressing scheme, known as *segmented addressing*. Segmented addressing uses two integers to specify a particular byte: one that represents the segment and the other the offset. Think of segments as blocks on a street and offsets as the houses on each block.

Each segment holds 64K of RAM. The 8086/88 processors have 16 segments, resulting in 1,048,560 bytes (1 *megabyte*) of addressable memory. However, DOS limits the amount of memory your computer can use to 640K.

Segments and Offsets

Turbo Pascal provides two standard functions, Seg and Ofs, that make it easy to explore memory addressing on your PC.

Seg provides the segment in which a variable resides, and Ofs provides its offset. The program below uses these functions to display the addresses of four variables:

```pascal
Program Addresses;
Type
  StType = String[10];
Var
  i : Integer;
  s : String[5];
  r : Real;
  c : Char;

Type
  St4 = String[4];

(************************************************)

Function IntToHex(i : integer) : St4;
Var
 hexstr : String[8];
 b : Array [1..2] Of Byte Absolute i;
 bt : Byte;

(************************************************)

Function Translate(b : Byte) : Char;
Begin
If b < 10 Then
  Translate := Chr(b + 48)
Else
  Translate := Chr(b + 55);
End;

(************************************************)

Begin
hexstr := '';
hexstr := hexstr + Translate(b[2] shr 4);
hexstr := hexstr + Translate(b[2] and 15);
hexstr := hexstr + Translate(b[1] shr 4);
hexstr := hexstr + Translate(b[1] and 15);
IntToHex := hexstr;
end;

(************************************************)

Begin
ClrScr;
Writeln('Integer: ',IntToHex(Seg(i)),':',IntToHex(Ofs(i)));
Writeln('String:  ',IntToHex(Seg(s)),':',IntToHex(Ofs(s)));
Writeln('Real:    ',IntToHex(Seg(r)),':',IntToHex(Ofs(r)));
Writeln('Char:    ',IntToHex(Seg(c)),':',IntToHex(Ofs(c)));
End.
```

This program defines four variables of different types and then displays the addresses of each of the variables. For example, the statement **Seg(i)** finds the segment of variable **i**, while **Ofs(i)** returns the offset.

The function IntToHex accepts an integer parameter and returns the hexadecimal value as a string of four characters. Segments and offsets are always shown in hexadecimal format, eliminating all problems that Turbo Pascal might encounter in displaying addresses.

Note: Because Turbo Pascal interprets integers as signed values, it allows integers to range in value from −32768 to 32767. Segments and offsets are unsigned integers ranging from 0 to 65535. Therefore, Turbo Pascal expresses a high memory address as a negative integer. The function IntToHex gets around Turbo Pascal's interpretation of the integer by accessing each byte in an integer individually.

When you run the previous program, your screen will show the following messages, though you will see different numbers because your computer may be configured differently.

```
Integer:    3E39:0262
String:     3E39:0264
Real:       3E39:026A
Char:       3E39:0270
```

As you can see, all the variables, which are global, have the same segment. (Global variables all reside in the data segment.) Furthermore, the distance between offsets exactly matches the number of bytes needed to store each variable type. For example, an integer starts at offset 0262h and requires two bytes of storage; the next variable in line (a string) starts at offset 0264h.

Turbo Pascal typed constants are stored in the code segment. Untyped constants also exist in the code segment, but they are considered part of the computer instructions. For this reason, untyped constants do not have addresses.

Variables that are declared in procedures and functions are stored on the stack, a dynamic data storage area. When a program calls a procedure, Turbo Pascal allocates space on the stack for the procedure's local variables. As Turbo Pascal adds variables to the stack, the stack grows downward in memory. When the procedure ends, Turbo Pascal discards these variables and frees the memory to be used again.

The fourth segment in Turbo Pascal memory, the heap, is a dynamic data area that you control. The heap allows efficient use of memory because it eliminates the need to preserve all the data structures throughout a program; instead, you can create a variable on the heap at one point, remove it from the heap at another, and then reuse the space for another variable at still another place.

As you add data structures to the heap, the heap grows upward in memory. Because they grow toward each other, the stack and the heap can "collide." If Turbo Pascal detects a stack/heap collision, it generates a run-time error and stops the program. Techniques for avoiding this situation are discussed later in this chapter.

The following program demonstrates how data can exist in any of the four Turbo Pascal segments:

```
Program Segments;
Const
  y : Integer = 100;
Type
  StType = String[80];
Var
  r1,r2 : Real;
  x : Integer;
  p : ^Integer;

Type
  St4 = String[4];

(***********************************************)

Function IntToHex(i : integer) : St4;
var
 hexstr : string[8];
 b : array [1..2] of byte absolute i;
 bt : byte;

(***********************************************)

Function Translate(b : byte) : Char;
Begin
```

```
if b < 10 then
   Translate := Chr(b + 48)
else
   Translate := Chr(b + 55);
End;

(**********************************************)

begin
hexstr := '';
HexStr := HexStr + Translate(b[2] shr 4);
HexStr := HexStr + Translate(b[2] and 15);
HexStr := HexStr + Translate(b[1] shr 4);
HexStr := HexStr + Translate(b[1] and 15);
IntToHex := HexStr;
end;

(**********************************************)

Procedure ShowCodeVariable;
Begin
Writeln;
Writeln('The location of constant y is ',
        IntToHex(seg(y)),':',
        IntToHex(ofs(y)));

Writeln('This is in the code segment.');
End;



(**********************************************)

Procedure ShowDataVariable;
Begin
Writeln;
Writeln('The location of global variable x is ',
        IntToHex(seg(x)),':',
        IntToHex(ofs(x)));

Writeln('This is in the data segment.');
End;

(**********************************************)

Procedure ShowStackVariable;
Var
   i : Integer;
Begin
Writeln;
Writeln('The location of variable i is ',
        IntToHex(seg(i)),':',
        IntToHex(ofs(i)));
```

```
Writeln('This is in the stack segment.');
End;

(**********************************************)

Procedure ShowHeapVariable;
Begin
Writeln;
Writeln('The location of pointer variable p is ',
        IntToHex(seg(p^)),':',
        IntToHex(ofs(p^)));

Writeln('This is on the heap.');
End;

(**********************************************)

Begin
ClrScr;
Writeln('Addresses are shown in the format Segment:Offset.');
New(p);
ShowCodeVariable;
ShowDataVariable;
ShowHeapVariable;
ShowStackVariable;
End.
```

When you run this program, your terminal will display
output that looks something like this:

> Addresses are shown in the format Segment:Offset.
> The location of constant y is 5972:2D70
> This is in the code segment.
> The location of global variable x is 5C8D.026E
> This is in the data segment.
> The location of pointer variable p is 5CB5:0000
> This is on the heap.
> The location of variable i is 6940:FFF6
> This is in the stack segment.

Each of the four variables in this example resides in a
different segment. The first location, that of constant **y**, is in
the code segment located at 5972h. The variable **x** is located
in the data segment (5C8Dh). Pointer variable **p** was placed
on the heap with the statement **New(p)**. The address of this

dynamic variable shows that its address is 5CB5h, just above the data segment.

The last variable listed is a local variable declared within a procedure. All local variables get stored on the stack, and in this example the stack segment begins at 6940h.

Figure 8-1 provides a schematic diagram of Turbo Pascal's memory. The lines separating the segments are matched with the hexadecimal values from the sample program. The code and data segments are located in low memory. The stack and the heap occupy all the high memory that is left over. The diagram also demonstrates that the stack grows downward and the heap grows upward. While the stack and the heap share the same area of memory, they must never overlap.

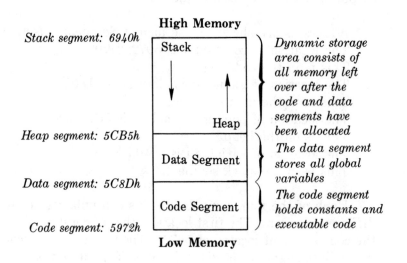

Figure 8-1.   Turbo Pascal memory allocation

The Heap and Pointers

Most variables you declare in Turbo Pascal are static, that is, memory is allocated to them from the time the program starts until it ends. The heap, on the other hand, uses dynamic data types known as **pointers**. Pointer variables are dynamic because you can create them and dispose of them while a program is running. In short, different pointer variables can use and reuse memory on the heap.

Using pointer variables on the heap offers two main advantages. First, it expands the total amount of data space available to a program. The data segment is limited to 64K, but the heap is limited only by the amount of RAM in your computer.

The second advantage of using pointer variables on the heap is that it allows your program to run with less memory. For example, a program might have two very large data structures, but only one of them is used at a time. If these data structures are declared globally, they reside in the data segment and occupy memory at all times. However, if these data structures are defined as pointers, they can be put on the heap and taken off as needed, thus reducing your program's memory requirements.

The Pointer Variable

A pointer variable does not hold data in the same way that other variables do. Instead, it holds the address that points to a variable located on the heap. Suppose you have a pointer variable named **px** that holds the address of an integer. Now, you can use **px** to point to the integer, but **px** itself is not the integer. If you are confused, this example, which demonstrates the simple use of a pointer variable, may help. The following program listing demonstrates the simple use of a pointer variable:

```
Program PointerDemo;
Var
  i : ^Integer;
```

```
   j : integer absolute i;

(***********************************************)
Type
  St4 = String[4];
Function IntToHex(i : integer) : St4;
Var
 hexstr : String[8];
 b : Array [1..2] Of Byte Absolute i;
 bt : Byte;

(***********************************************)

Function Translate(b : Byte) : Char;
Begin
If b < 10 Then
  Translate := Chr(b + 48)
Else
  Translate := Chr(b + 55);
End;

(***********************************************)

Begin
hexstr := '';
hexstr := hexstr + Translate(b[2] shr 4);
hexstr := hexstr + Translate(b[2] and 15);
hexstr := hexstr + Translate(b[1] shr 4);
hexstr := hexstr + Translate(b[1] and 15);
IntToHex := hexstr;
end;

(***********************************************)

Begin
ClrScr;
New(i);
i^ := 100;
Writeln('The value of i is: ',IntToHex(j));
Writeln('The value that i points to is: ',i^);
Dispose(i);
End.
```

The ^ placed before the data type in the definition tells Turbo Pascal to define i as a pointer variable:

    i : ^Integer;

When the program starts, the heap is a blank slate. Before you can use pointer **i**, you must use the statement **New(i)** to tell Turbo Pascal to assign an address on the heap to the pointer **i**. **Dispose(i)**, which appears at the end of the program, is the opposite of **New(i)**. **Dispose** effectively takes a variable off the heap, allowing memory to be used for other variables.

Once you place it on the heap, you can use the variable in **Assignment** and **Arithmetic** statements by adding the ^ symbol to the identifier:

    i^ := 100;

The ^ tells Turbo Pascal that you are referring to the variable on the heap and not to the pointer itself. What would happen if the statement were **i := 100**? This statement changes the value of the pointer, not the value of the variable on the heap. Now, **i** points to memory location 100 rather than to its proper location.

When you run the preceding program, your terminal displays the following messages:

    The value of i is: 0000
    The value that i points to is: 100

The first line displays the address that the pointer is holding. In this case the address is 0000, indicating that this variable is the first to be placed on the heap. The second line is the value of **i^**, the variable at address 0000 on the heap.

New and Dispose

When you allocate and dispose of dynamic variables, what actually happens in the heap? Figure 8-2 describes the process of allocation and deallocation. In the figure, Turbo Pas-

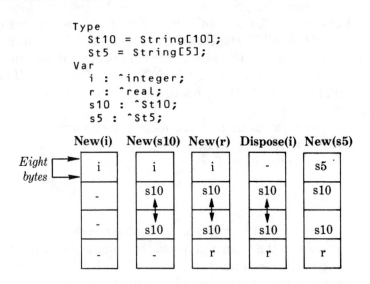

```
Type
  St10 = String[10];
  St5 = String[5];
Var
  i  : ^integer;
  r  : ^real;
  s10 : ^St10;
  s5  : ^St5;
```

Figure 8-2.   Dynamic allocation using New and Dispose

cal declares four pointer variables: one integer, one real, and two strings, one 5 and the other 10 bytes long. The columns, which represent memory on the heap, are divided into 8-byte segments. Turbo Pascal always allocates memory on the heap in 8-byte segments. Thus, when the program executes the statement **New(i)**, the heap provides 8 bytes, even though the integer requires only 2 bytes.

In the second column, Turbo Pascal allocates a string of 10 bytes to the heap. Because this string requires 11 bytes of storage (10 characters plus the length byte), the heap allocates two 8-byte chunks. In short, the heap always provides as many 8-byte chunks of memory as are necessary to contain the data structure put on the heap. When you allocate many small data structures, this is very wasteful, but you can keep waste to a minimum by using the heap only for large data structures.

The third column in Figure 8-2 shows the additional allocation of a real variable, requiring one 8-byte chunk. The next column demonstrates the impact of the **Dispose** statement. When Turbo Pascal disposes **i**, the 8-byte chunk that **i** was using is released for use by other dynamic variables. This creates a "hole" in the heap. In order to use this portion of memory again, the data structure must fit into this hole. If not, Turbo Pascal must allocate memory elsewhere on the heap.

In the fifth column, Turbo Pascal allocates a string of 5 bytes to the heap. Because this variable fits into the hole left by **i**, Turbo Pascal fills the hole with the string.

Using **New** and **Dispose** requires careful planning and rigorous testing. One common error is to reallocate the same variable on the heap. For example, the two following statements

```
New(i);
New(i);
```

both allocate an integer on the heap, but only one of the integers can be accessed as a variable. You not only cannot access the first integer, you cannot even get rid of it. Since the **i** pointer points to the second integer, it cannot be used to dispose the first variable. Always make sure that each **New** is matched by a **Dispose**.

Mark and Release

Turbo Pascal offers an alternative to using **New** and **Dispose** to dynamically allocate memory: **Mark** and **Release**. Instead of leaving holes in the heap the way **New** and **Dispose** do, **Mark** and **Release** lop off an entire end of the heap from a particular point onward. This process is demonstrated in the following program:

```
Program HeapRelease;
Type
  atype = Array [1..100] Of Char;
```

```
Var
  HeapTop : ^Integer;
  a1,a2,a3 : ^atype;

Begin
Clrscr;
Mark(HeapTop);

Writeln('Initial free memory: ',Memavail);
Writeln;
Writeln('----------------');
Writeln;

New(a1);
Writeln('Free memory after allocating a1: ',Memavail);
New(a2);
Writeln('Free memory after allocating a2: ',Memavail);
New(a3);
Writeln('Free memory after allocating a3: ',Memavail);
Writeln;
Writeln('----------------');
Writeln;

Release(HeapTop);
writeln('Free memory after release: ',Memavail);
end.
```

This program allocates three pointer variables—**a1**, **a2**, and **a3**—and uses the Memavail standard function to display the amount of free memory left over. Memavail calculates the total amount of memory available to the heap and the stack and returns the amount in the number of paragraphs (a paragraph is 16 bytes). For example, if Memavail returns a value of 20, that means there are 320 bytes (20 paragraphs $\times$ 16 bytes) left for the stack and the heap to use.

The previous program uses a pointer variable named **HeapTop** to keep track of the point from which you release memory. The statement **Mark(HeapTop)** stores the current address of the top of the heap to the pointer **HeapTop**. The program calls **Mark(HeapTop)** prior to placing any variables on the heap. As a result, when it calls **Release(Heap-Top)**, it deallocates all the variables on the heap, freeing the memory for another use. Running the program results in the following messages:

```
Initial free memory: 5934

. . . . . . . . . . . . . .

Free memory after allocating a1: 5928
Free memory after allocating a2: 5921
Free memory after allocating a3: 5915

. . . . . . . . . . . . . .

Free memory after release: 5934
```

As you can see, each time a variable is placed on the heap, the amount of available memory decreases. When **Release(HeapTop)** is called at the end of the program, the amount of free memory reverts to the initial amount. If you had marked the **HeapTop** pointer after **a1** was allocated, only the memory for **a2** and **a3** would be released.

Note that **Dispose** and **Release** are incompatible methods of recovering memory. You can choose to use one or the other, but never use both in the same program.

GetMem and FreeMem

A third method of dynamic memory allocation is **GetMem** and **FreeMem**. These are much like **New** and **Dispose** in that they allocate and deallocate memory one variable at a time. The special value of **GetMem** and **FreeMem** is that you can specify how much memory you want to allocate regardless of the type of variable you are using. However, you cannot control exactly how much memory Turbo Pascal allocates on the heap for your variable. For example, you can allocate 100 bytes to an integer with the statement

GetMem(i,100);

In response to this, Turbo Pascal allocates 104 bytes, not 100. Why? Recall that Turbo Pascal allocates heap space in 8-byte chunks. Thus, 104 bytes is the smallest amount of memory that accommodates the 100 bytes requested and also is evenly divisible by 8.

Variables allocated with **GetMem** are deallocated with the **FreeMem**, as shown below:

```
GetMem(i,20);
i := x + y;
WriteLn(i);
FreeMem(i,20);
```

The number of bytes specified in the **FreeMem** statement must match that in the **GetMem** statement. Do not use **Dispose** in place of **FreeMem**; if you do, the heap will become hopelessly unsynchronized.

Using Pointers with Complex Data Types

Since the heap is generally used to access large data spaces, pointer variables are generally used with large, complex data structures. Defining a complex data structure as a pointer is a two-step process:

```
Type

   CustPtr = ^CustRec;

   CustRec = Record
     Name : String[25];
     Address : String[30];
     City: String[30];
     State: String[2];
     Zip: String[5];
     End;

Var

   Cust : CustPtr;
```

Here, the statement

CustPtr = ^CustRec;

defines **CustPtr** as a pointer to **CustRec**. Note that **CustRec** has not yet been defined. Declaring pointers is the one case in which Turbo Pascal allows you to refer to a data structure before it is defined. The variable **Cust** is then defined as type **CustPtr**.

Linked Lists

The easy way to manage a list is to define an array. One problem with arrays, however, is that you always have to allocate enough space for the maximum possible number of elements. As a result, you either define very large arrays and waste memory or define small arrays and limit the power of your program. Pointers provide an alternative to arrays— *linked lists*.

Data items in a linked list have pointers that keep track of the order of the list. *Singly linked lists* use one pointer that points to the record that comes next. *Doubly linked lists* have pointers in both directions, so that each data item is linked to the one before it and the one after it.

Figure 8-3 shows the structure of a singly linked list. Each record contains data and a pointer. The pointers indicate which record comes next in the list. The pointer of the last record is set to Nil, indicating there are no more records in the list.

To change the order of the list, only the pointer values need to be changed. In Figure 8-3, the pointer in Data 1 is changed to point to Data 3, and Data 3 is made to point to Data 2. Now, the pointer in Data 2 points to Nil, indicating that this is the last record in the list.

Building a linked list in a Turbo Pascal program requires considerable effort. Even so, it is a skill worth learning since many advanced sorting and searching routines use linked lists to increase their speed and maximize memory usage.

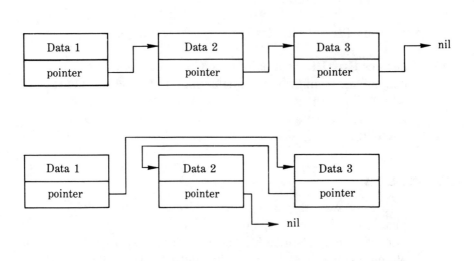

Figure 8-3. A singly linked list

A data item in a singly linked list must have a *forward referencing pointer* that tells Turbo Pascal where it can find the next data item in the list. The following record definition includes a forward-referencing pointer named **Next**:

```
CustPtr = ^CustRec;
CustRec = Record
   Name    : String[20];
   Address : String[40];
   City    : String[20];
   State   : String[2];
   Next    : CustPtr;
   End;
```

CustPtr points to the record **CustRec**. The record **Cust-Rec**, in turn, contains a field named Next, which is defined as **CustPtr**.

You, not Turbo Pascal, are responsible for maintaining pointers correctly, and this takes a bit of doing. First, you must keep track of where your list begins and ends. You must also know where the program currently is in the list and where the next data record is located.

A typical singly linked list requires at least three pointers: one to point to the beginning of the list, one to point to the current record, and one to point to the previous record. The following definition shows how these pointers might be defined:

Var
FirstCust,
PrevCust,
CurrentCust : CustPtr;

If you want to process the list sequentially from beginning to end, you must know the location of the first link in the list. **PrevCust**, which points to the link preceding the current link, makes the pointer called **Next** point to the next record.

A new link in a linked list must be connected to the previous link. The very first link, however, has no previous link and is, therefore, an exception. How does a program know if it is creating the first link or some other link? When the program begins, you must initialize the pointer **FirstCust** to Nil:

FirstCust := Nil;

The procedure that creates new links tests **FirstCust** to see if it is equal to Nil. If it is, the program knows this is the first link in a linked list and processes it appropriately. The following program segment demonstrates how these pointers create a linked list.

```
If FirstCust = Nil Then
  Begin
  New(CurrentCust);
  FirstCust := CurrentCust;
  CurrentCust^.next := Nil;
  End
Else
  Begin
```

```
PrevCust := CurrentCust;
New(CurrentCust);
PrevCust^.next := CurrentCust;
CurrentCust^.next := Nil;
End;
```

The **If-Then-Else** statement checks to see if this is the first link in the list (**FirstCust = Nil**). If so, the program creates a **CurrentCust** record and sets **FirstCust** equal to **CurrentCust**. It sets the Next field in **CurrentCust** equal to Nil because there is no next link in the chain at this time.

The second time through, **FirstCust** is not equal to Nil since it was previously set equal to **CurrentCust**. Therefore, the program skips to the **Else** branch, where it sets the pointer **PrevCust** equal to **CurrentCust** and creates a new **CurrentCust**. At this time, the program is using all three position pointers: **CurrentCust** points to the newly created link, **PrevCust** points to the preceding link, and **FirstCust** points to the first link in the list. After it creates the new **CurrentCust**, the program sets the Next field in **PrevCust** to point to the new link. The elements of these lists are linked by the connection of one record to another with a pointer field.

The following program shows how a singly linked list creates and manipulates a list of customer names and addresses:

```
Program SimpleLink;
Type
  CustPtr = ^CustRec;
  CustRec = Record
    Name : String[20];
    Address : String[40];
    City : String[20];
    State : String[2];
    Next : CustPtr;
    End;
Var
  FirstCust,
  PrevCust,
```

```
   CurrentCust : CustPtr;
   ch : Char;

(*************************************)

Procedure AddRecord;

(*************************************)

Procedure EnterData;
Begin
With CurrentCust^ Do
  Begin
  Write('Enter customer name: ');
  Readln(name);
  Write('Enter address: ');
  Readln(Address);
  Write('Enter city: ');
  Readln(City);
  Write('Enter  state: ');
  Readln(state);
  End;
End;

(*************************************)

Begin
ClrScr;
If FirstCust = Nil Then
  Begin
  New(CurrentCust);
  EnterData;
  FirstCust := CurrentCust;
  PrevCust := CurrentCust;
  CurrentCust^.next := Nil;
  End
Else
  Begin
  PrevCust := CurrentCust;
  New(CurrentCust);
  EnterData;
  PrevCust^.next := CurrentCust;
  CurrentCust^.next := Nil;
  End;
End;

(*************************************)

Procedure ListRecords;
Begin
CurrentCust := FirstCust;
While CurrentCust <> Nil Do
  Begin
  With CurrentCust^ Do
    Writeln(name,', ',address,', ',city,', ',state);
```

```
      CurrentCust := CurrentCust^.Next;
    End;
Writeln;
Write('Press RETURN...');
Readln;
End;

(***************************************)

Begin
FirstCust := Nil;

  Repeat
  ClrScr;
    Repeat
    Write('A)dd a customer, L)ist customers, Q)uit: ');
    Read(kbd,ch);
    Writeln;
    ch := Upcase(ch);
    Until ch In ['A','L','Q'];

  If ch = 'A' Then
    AddRecord
  Else If ch = 'L' Then
    ListRecords;

  Until ch = 'Q';
End.
```

The procedure **ListRecords** demonstrates how to process a linked list sequentially. The essential parts of the code are shown below.

```
CurrentCust := FirstCust;
While CurrentCust <> Nil Do
  Begin
  (* Statements *)s
  CurrentCust := CurrentCust^.Next;
  End;
```

The procedure sets pointer **CurrentCust** equal to **First-Cust**, the first item in the list. Next, a While-Do loop repeats a block of code until the pointer **CurrentCust** is Nil, indicating that the program has reached the end of the list. Within the block of code, the last statement

CurrentCust := CurrentCust^.Next;

causes **CurrentCust** to point to the next item in the list.

Even a cursory review of the previous program illustrates the added complexity of using a linked list instead of a standard array. Every time the program needs a new record, it must create it and set up all the appropriate links. And if you want to move backward through a singly linked list, you simply cannot do it.

Doubly Linked Lists

Doubly linked lists maintain links in both directions, allowing you to process the list backward or forward. This requires another pointer field (**Prev**) in the record definition, as shown below:

```
CustRec = Record
  Name : String[20];
  Address : String[40];
  City : String[20];
  State : String[2];
  Prev,
  Next : CustPtr;
  End;
```

The **Prev** pointer keeps track of the link preceding the current one, while the **Next** pointer keeps track of the next link.

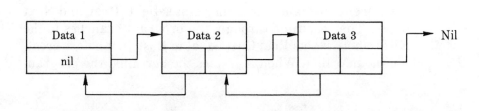

Figure 8-4.   A doubly linked list

While they are more powerful than singly linked lists, doubly linked lists require you to write even more code. Compare the doubly linked list in Figure 8-4 to the singly linked list in Figure 8-3. Adding the *backward referencing pointer* doubles the number of linkages to maintain.

Doubly linked lists require position pointers to keep track of both the beginning and the end of the list. When a new link is created, you must keep track of the location of the first record, the last record, the current record, and the record prior to the current record. The following program segment illustrates this process:

```
If FirstCust = Nil Then
   Begin
   New(CurrentCust);
   FirstCust := CurrentCust;
   LastCust := CurrentCust;
   PrevCust := CurrentCust;
   CurrentCust^.next := Nil;
   CurrentCust^.prev := Nil;
   End
Else
   Begin
   PrevCust := LastCust;
   New(CurrentCust);
   PrevCust^.next := CurrentCust;
   CurrentCust^.next := Nil;
   CurrentCust^.prev := PrevCust;
   LastCust := CurrentCust;
   LastCust^ := CurrentCust^;
   End;
```

When **FirstCust** is equal to zero, the program sets the position pointers **FirstCust**, **LastCust**, and **PrevCust** equal to **CurrentCust**, and it sets the pointer fields **Prev** and **Next** to Nil. The next time through, the program branches to the **Else**, where it sets **PrevCust** equal to **LastCust** before creating the new link. When it creates the new link, the program sets the **Prev** pointer to **PrevCust** and the **Next** pointer in **PrevCust** to **CurrentCust**. This establishes the double link that allows processing in either direction.

The program below uses doubly linked lists to manage a list of names and addresses. Two features to pay attention to are the ability to sort the list and write out the list in reverse order.

```
Program DoubleLink;
Type
  CustPtr = ^CustRec;
  CustRec = Record
    Name : String[20];
    Address : String[40];
    City : String[20];
    State : String[2];
    Prev,
    Next : CustPtr;
    End;
Var
  FirstCust,
  LastCust,
  PrevCust,
  CurrentCust : CustPtr;
  ch : Char;

(***************************************)

Procedure AddRecord;

(***************************************)

Procedure EnterData;
Begin
With CurrentCust^ Do
  Begin
  Write('Enter customer name: ');
  Readln(name);
  Write('Enter address: ');
  Readln(Address);
  Write('Enter city: ');
  Readln(City);
  Write('Enter   state: ');
  Readln(state);
  End;
End;

(***************************************)

Begin
```

```
ClrScr;
If FirstCust = Nil Then
  Begin
  New(CurrentCust);
  EnterData;
  FirstCust := CurrentCust;
  LastCust := CurrentCust;
  PrevCust := CurrentCust;
  CurrentCust^.next := Nil;
  CurrentCust^.prev := Nil;
  End
Else
  Begin
  PrevCust := LastCust;
  New(CurrentCust);
  EnterData;
  PrevCust^.next := CurrentCust;
  CurrentCust^.next := Nil;
  CurrentCust^.prev := PrevCust;
  LastCust := CurrentCust;
  LastCust^ := CurrentCust^;
  End;
End;

(**************************************)

Procedure ListRecords;
Var
  ch : Char;

(**************************************)

Procedure ListForwards;
Begin
CurrentCust := FirstCust;
While CurrentCust <> Nil Do
  Begin
  With CurrentCust^ Do
    Writeln(name,', ',address,', ',city,', ',state);
  CurrentCust := CurrentCust^.Next;
  End;
End;

(**************************************)

Procedure ListBackwards;
Begin
CurrentCust := LastCust;
While CurrentCust <> Nil Do
  Begin
```

```
      With CurrentCust^ Do
        Writeln(name,', ',address,', ',city,', ',state);
      CurrentCust := CurrentCust^.Prev;
      End;
End;

(************************************)

Begin
  repeat
  Write('F)orwards or B)ackwards, Q)uit: ');
  Read(kbd,ch);
  Writeln;
  ch := upcase(ch);
  Until (ch In ['F','B','Q']);

If ch = 'F' Then
  ListForwards
else If ch = 'B' Then
  ListBackwards;
Writeln;
Write('Press RETURN...');
Readln;
End;

(**************************************)

Procedure SortRecords;
Var
  NextRec,FarCust : CustPtr;
  SortDone : Boolean;

Begin

  Repeat
  CurrentCust := FirstCust;
  PrevCust := Nil;
  SortDone := true;

  While CurrentCust^.next <> Nil Do
    Begin
    NextRec := CurrentCust^.next;

    If CurrentCust^.Name > NextRec^.Name Then
      Begin
      SortDone := False;

      If NextRec^.next <> Nil Then
        Begin
        FarCust := NextRec^.next;
```

```
        FarCust^.prev := CurrentCust;
        End
      Else
        FarCust := Nil;

      If CurrentCust^.prev = Nil Then
        Begin
        FirstCust := NextRec;
        PrevCust := Nil;
        End
      Else
        Begin
        PrevCust := CurrentCust^.prev;
        PrevCust^.Next := NextRec;
        End;

      CurrentCust^.next := FarCust;
      CurrentCust^.prev := NextRec;

      NextRec^.next := CurrentCust;
      NextRec^.prev := PrevCust;
        CurrentCust := FirstCust;
        End
      else
        CurrentCust := CurrentCust^.Next;
      End;

  Until SortDone;

LastCust := CurrentCust;
Writeln;
Write('Press RETURN...');
Readln;
End;

(*************************************)

Begin
FirstCust := Nil;

  Repeat
  ClrScr;
    Repeat
    Write('A)dd a customer, L)ist customers, S)ort, Q)uit: ');
    Read(kbd,ch);
    Writeln;
    ch := Upcase(ch);
    Until ch In ['A','L','S','Q'];

  If ch = 'A'Then
    AddRecord
  Else If ch = 'L' Then
```

```
    ListRecords
  Else If ch = 'S' Then
    SortRecords;

  Until ch = 'Q';
End.
```

Dynamic memory allocation is a powerful tool. It allows you to expand your program's data space while opening the door to linked lists and other dynamic data structures. But there is a price to pay. Linked lists maximize the efficient use of memory, but impose considerable overhead and require much more time to develop. In the end, dynamic data structures are best used when the benefits they provide are certain to outweigh the costs of developing and using them. Such programs include database applications that benefit from using as much memory as possible, but must be able to run on computers that have small amounts of memory.

The @ Operator in Turbo Pascal Version 4.0

Turbo Pascal 4.0 makes one addition to dynamic memory allocation: the @ operator. The @ operator returns the address, in pointer format, of a formally declared variable. For example, in the code shown below, **i** is declared an integer, and **b** is a pointer to an array of two bytes.

```
Program Test;
Type
  B_Type : Array [1..2] Of Byte;
Var
  i : Integer;
  b : ^B_Type;
```

```
Begin
i := 0;
b := @i;
Writeln(b^[1],' ',b^[2]);
End.
```

The statement **b := @i** assigns the address of the variable **i** to the pointer **b**. In other words, the @ operator points **b** to the memory location of **i**. The statement

```
Writeln(b^[1],' ',b^[2]);
```

prints out the two bytes of **i** as separate byte variables. The @ operator simplifies the use of pointers when they are used to overlay other variables in memory.

A Word on Segments

Turbo Pascal 4.0 utilizes separately compiled units. Each unit in the program has its own code segment. In Version 3.0, on the other hand, only one code segment existed for an entire program. The presence of multiple code segments might be confusing if you are not aware of this change in Turbo Pascal.

Turbo Pascal Files

File Handling Concepts
Turbo Pascal Text Files
Disk Files and Buffers
Typed Files
Untyped Files
Erasing and Renaming Files
Input and Output in Turbo Pascal Version 4.0

A computer that does not store programs and data on disks is little more than a powerful calculator. People who bought early microcomputers without disk drives soon found this out—when they turned their computers off, their work disappeared. Of course, your computer does have at least a floppy disk drive and possibly a hard disk drive. This allows you to take advantage of Turbo Pascal's powerful disk file operations. Learning to use disk files is vital to producing useful programs, and Turbo Pascal helps by supporting three basic types of disk files: *text, typed,* and *untyped*. This chapter discusses how you create and use these kinds of files.

File Handling Concepts

All Turbo Pascal files, regardless of type, share common characteristics. First, all files are used for either input or output. Input is when a program takes data from a file and uses it in the program; output stores the results of a program in a file or sends the results to a *device* such as a terminal or printer. While it is possible for a file to be used for both input and output, this is an exception to the rule.

Files can be stored on floppy diskettes and hard disk drives. There are, of course, other storage media (tape, optical disks, RAM disks, and so on), but they are less common. DOS requires that every file have a name of one to eight characters. Filenames can also include a three-letter *extension* that usually helps describe the contents of a file. For example, the Turbo Pascal program file is named TURBO .COM. The .COM filename extension tells DOS that this is a program file that can be executed from the DOS prompt. Turbo Pascal source files (the files you create with the Turbo Pascal editor) generally have the .PAS filename extension (for example, PROG1.PAS).

If a file is stored in a DOS directory, the directory path is also part of the filename. If, for example, the file PROG1.PAS is in the Turbo directory on drive C:, the full description or *pathname* of the filename is C:\TURBO\PROG1.PAS. DOS filename conventions are discussed in detail in the DOS user's manual. You should be thoroughly familiar with these conventions before using Turbo Pascal files.

Turbo Pascal Text Files

Text files consist of lines that are terminated by a carriage return and linefeed (CR/LF) and which contain characters, words, and sentences, as shown in Figure 9-1. The CR/LF combination (ASCII codes 10 and 13) is known as a delimiter: A delimiter marks the end of some element, such as a field, record, or in this case, the end of a line.

You can tell if a file consists of text by using the DOS command **Type**. For example, your Turbo Pascal diskette comes with a program text file called LISTR.PAS. If you type **TYPE LISTER.PAS** at the DOS prompt and press RETURN, the file is displayed on the screen in a readable form. If, on the other hand, you try to display a nontext file (such as TURBO.COM) in the same way, you will see only gibberish.

File Name: TEXT.DAT

Line 1 → This is an example of a line of text.[CR/LF]
Line 2 → Every line in a text file ends with a[CR/LF]
Line 3 → carriage return and linefeed.[CR/LF]
Line 4 → [CR/LF]
Line 5 → Even empty lines, like the one above.[CR/LF]
Line 6 → 50 12.23 0.23 40343 332324[CR/LF]

Figure 9-1.   A typical text file

Text-File Identifiers

Before you work with text files, you must declare a *text-file identifier* in your program. Text-file identifiers are declared just like variable identifiers, except that the Turbo Pascal reserved word **Text** is used. An example of a text-file declaration is shown below.

    Program TextFile;
    Var
    TxtFile : Text;

In this illustration, **TxtFile** is a variable identifier of type **Text**. Before using **TxtFile** for input or output, you must assign it to a disk file. A typical **Assignment** statement looks like this:

    Assign(TxtFile,'TEXT.DAT');

Once **TxtFile** is assigned to TEXT.DAT, the disk file is never referred to by name again: all file operations refer to the identifier **TxtFile**.

After you assign a file identifier to a disk file, prepare the disk file with one of three Turbo Pascal commands—

Reset, **Rewrite**, or **Append**. **Reset** opens the disk file and prepares it as an input file. Only input commands can be used on a file that has been reset. Any attempt to write to a **Reset** file generates an I/O (input/output) error.

The **Reset** command also positions the *file pointer*, a counter that keeps track of a program's position in a file, at the beginning of the file. This causes all input to start at the very beginning of the file and move forward from there.

An attempt to **Reset** a file that does not exist generates an I/O error. You can override the I/O error, if desired, by disabling the **i** compiler directive with the statement {$$-}.

Rewrite and **Append** both prepare a text file for output, but they function in different ways. When an existing file is prepared with **Rewrite**, its contents are erased and the file pointer is placed at the beginning of the file. If the file identifier is assigned to a nonexisting file, the **Rewrite** command creates a file with the name given in the **Assignment** statement. The **Append** command, on the other hand, preserves the contents of a file and positions the file pointer at the very end of the file. As a result, any data added to the file is appended to what is already there.

As with the **Reset** statement, should you attempt to use **Append** on a file that does not exist, Turbo Pascal generates an I/O error.

When you are finished using a file for either input or output, you must close the file. The **Close** command performs this task and performs several other tasks in the process. **Close** makes sure that all data in temporary buffers is stored to disk. This is known as *flushing the buffer* and is discussed in detail later in this chapter.

The **Close** command also frees up a DOS *file handle*. A file handle is a mechanism that DOS provides to programs that helps manage file operations. When you **Reset** or **Rewrite** a file, DOS allocates a file handle to Turbo Pascal. Because DOS limits the number of file handles, you cannot have more than 15 Turbo Pascal files open at one time. Closing files keeps the supply of file handles plentiful. Lastly, the **Close** command updates the DOS file directory to reflect the file's size, time, and date.

```
Program FileTime;
Var
  TxtFile : Text;

Begin
Assign(TxtFile,'TEXT.DAT');  ◄──── Links TxtFile to the file TEST.DAT

Reset(TxtFile); ◄──────────────── Prepares TxtFile to be read

Rewrite(TxtFile); ◄────────────── Prepares TxtFile to be written to

Close(TxtFile); ◄──────────────── Closes TxtFile, updates DOS directory


Append(TxtFile); ◄─────────────── Reopens TxtFile for additional output


Close(TxtFile); ◄─────────────── Final closing ensures
                                  that all output is saved
End.
```

Figure 9-2.   Opening text files

Once closed, a file cannot be used for input or output until it is opened again with **Reset**, **Rewrite**, or **Append**. The link between the file identifier and the disk file, however, remains in force even after the file is closed. Therefore, to reopen a file, it is not necessary to repeat the **Assign** command. This process is illustrated in Figure 9-2.

Reading Strings from Text Files

Once a text file is reset, you can extract information from it with the **Read** and **ReadLn** procedures. Examples of text-file input can be seen in the following program, in which the disk file TEXT.DAT is linked to the file identifier **TxtFile**.

```
Program Text1;
Var
  TxtFile : Text;
  s : String[10];

Begin
Assign(TxtFile,'TEXT.DAT');
Reset(TxtFile);

ReadLn(TxtFile,s);
Writeln(s);

Read(TxtFile,s);
Writeln(s);

Close(TextFile);
End.
```

Subsequently, **TxtFile** is prepared for reading with the **Reset** command. The first input operation in this program example is the statement

ReadLn(TxtFile,s)

which tells Turbo Pascal to read characters from the current line in the file and place them into the string variable **s**. After the characters are read, the file pointer skips any remaining characters on the line and moves to the beginning of the next line in the file.

When reading in a string from a text file with the **ReadLn** procedure, three possible situations can occur:

1. There are exactly enough characters left in the line to fill the string to its maximum length.

2. There are not enough characters left in the line to fill the string to its maximum length.

3. There are more characters left in the line than are needed to fill the string to its maximum length.

In the first two cases, Turbo Pascal reads in all the characters left in the line, assigns them to **s**, and then moves the file pointer to the beginning of the next line. The string length is set equal to the number of characters read.

In the third case, Turbo Pascal reads in as many characters as necessary to fill the **string** variable and then moves the file pointer to the next line. Any characters between the end of the string and the end of the line are discarded.

The **Read** procedure operates much like the **ReadLn** procedure, but after it reads in a string, **Read** places the file pointer just after the last character read; it does not move the file pointer to the beginning of the next line. If the **Read** procedure encounters a CR/LF (or just a simple carriage return), indicating the end of the line has been reached, it stops reading characters and also does not advance the file pointer until a **ReadLn** procedure is used.

Reading Multiple Strings per Line

A single **ReadLn** procedure can read in several strings at one time. For example, the statement

ReadLn(TxtFile,s1,s2,s3)

reads characters from the current line and fills the string variables **s1**, **s2**, and **s3** in order. If the line being read is

"This is a line of characters"

and the string variables are all of type **String[5]**, the strings would be assigned values as follows:

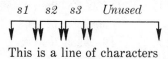

This is a line of characters

Reading Numbers from Text Files

Text files can store not only words and sentences, but also numeric data. Numbers, however, are not stored in their binary form but as characters. For example, in RAM, the integer value 20,545 is stored as two bytes with a binary value of 0101000001000001. But in a text file, the number is stored as the characters "2","0","5","4","5", requiring a total of five bytes. When reading the number 20,545 from a text file, Turbo Pascal translates the number from a string of characters into binary integer format.

As it reads a number from a text file, Turbo Pascal skips the blank characters in a line until it finds a nonblank character. It then reads in characters until it encounters either another nonblank character or a CR/LF. When the characters are read in, Turbo Pascal combines the characters into an alphanumeric string and converts the string into either an integer or a real value, depending on the type of variable being used. If the conversion is successful, the number is assigned to the variable; if it is not successful, Turbo Pascal generates an I/O error.

To learn how numbers are read from text files, examine the numeric text file TEST.DAT in Figure 9-3. This file contains three columns of numbers. The first column is integers, the second real numbers in decimal format, and the third

11	27.53	6.4144900000E+02
21	50.83	1.1843390000E+03
31	74.13	1.7272290000E+03
41	97.43	2.2701190000E+03
51	120.73	2.8130090000E+03
61	144.03	3.3558990000E+03
71	167.33	3.8987890000E+03
81	190.63	4.4416790000E+03
91	213.93	4.9845690000E+03
101	237.23	5.5274590000E+03

Figure 9-3.   TEST.DAT, a numeric text file

real numbers in scientific notation. You can read the three numbers on each line of the file by employing the following statements:

```
Read (TxtFile,i2);
Read(TxtFile,r1);
ReadLn(TxtFile,r2);
```

or by using the equivalent single statement:

```
ReadLn(TxtFile,i,r1,r2);
```

Turbo Pascal assigns the first number found in a line to the integer variable **i** and the next two numbers to real variables **r1** and **r2**.

The following program contains a routine that reads the numerical file TEST.DAT and calculates the average of each column of figures:

```
Program ComputeAverages;
Var
  f : Text;

  i,count : Integer;

  imean,
  r1,r2,
  r1mean,
  r2mean : Real;

Begin
Assign(f,'test.dat');
Reset(f);

count := 0;
imean := 0;
r1mean := 0;
r2mean := 0;

While Not Eof(f) Do
  Begin
  ReadLn(f,i,r1,r2);
  WriteLn(i:10,' ',r1:10:3,' ',r2:10:3);

  count := count + 1;
```

```
   imean := imean + i;
   r1mean := r1mean + r1;
   r2mean := r2mean + r2;
   End;

imean := imean / count;
r1mean := r1mean / count;
r2mean := r2mean / count;

Writeln;
WriteLn(imean:10:3,' ',r1mean:10:3,' ',r2:10:3);
Close(f);
End.
```

This program introduces the Turbo Pascal standard function Eof, which stands for end-of-file. Eof is a Boolean function that is true only when the file pointer is at the end of your file. It can be used to repeat input commands so that an entire file is processed from beginning to end. In the previous example, the statement

While Not Eof(f) Do

tells Turbo Pascal to execute the next block of code until Eof(f) returns true, that is, until the last character in the file is read.

The function Eoln tests for the end of a line. Eoln is true under two conditions: when the file pointer encounters a carriage return and when the file pointer reaches the end of a file. You can use Eoln to read each character in a line one by one, as is shown in Figure 9-4. Eoln reads the characters in a line and writes them out on separate lines.

SeekEof and SeekEoln

To give you even more control over text files, Turbo Pascal offers SeekEof and SeekEoln. Like their counterparts Eof and Eoln, SeekEof returns true at the end of a file and SeekEoln returns true at the end of a line. These functions have a unique capability to skip over ASCII characters in the range 0 to 32 when testing for end-of-file or end-of-line. This range includes the standard ASCII control characters as

```
Program ReadChar;

Var
  f : Text;
  i : Integer;
  c : Array [1..1000] Of Char;


Begin
Assign(f,'TEST.TXT');
Reset(f);

While Not Eof(f) Do          ◄───── Continue for the entire file
  Begin
  While Not Eoln(f) Do       ◄───── Continue until next carriage return
    Begin
    Read(f,Ch);
    Writeln(Ch);
    End;
  ReadLn(f);                 ◄───── Skip past the carriage return,
  End;                               to beginning of the next line


Close(f);
End.
```

Figure 9-4.   Reading characters from a text file

well as the blank character. Consequently, SeekEof returns true even when there are characters left in the file, so long as those characters are blank or control codes.

Errors in Numeric Input

If the format of a number read from a text file is incorrect, the program produces an I/O error. For example, reading the number 50,000 into an integer variable would cause an error because the largest integer allowable is 32,767. Similarly, reading the number 32.1 into an integer variable would cause an error because of the decimal place, which is illegal for integers. Real variables pose fewer restrictions since numbers can be read with or without a decimal place or in scientific notation.

Writing Text Files

A text file can be used for output after being prepared with the **Rewrite** or **Append** procedures, as discussed earlier in this chapter. Once prepared, the **Write** or **WriteLn** procedures output the file. The first parameter in these procedures, the text-file identifier, tells Turbo Pascal where to send the data. It is followed by any number of variable identifiers or literal values to be output. For example, the following statements write the line "**Jones 21**" to the text file identified as **TxtFile**.

```
name := 'Jones';
i := 21;
WriteLn(TxtFile,name,' ',i);
```

Write and **WriteLn** normally output values without any special formatting. Adding a colon and a number after the parameter, however, specifies that the value is to be right-justified in a space defined by the number. For example, these statements

```
Name := 'Johnson';
WriteLn(Name);
WriteLn(Name:20);
WriteLn(Name:4);
```

result in the following output:

```
Johnson
             Johnson
Johnson
```

The first **WriteLn** statement is unformatted, so the

value is written left-justified. The second statement tells Turbo Pascal to create a field 20 characters wide and to right-justify the value within this field. Since the name "Johnson" is seven characters long, Turbo Pascal right-justifies the name by preceding it with 13 blanks. The third statement is also formatted, but the field width of 4 is less than the length of the value itself. When this occurs, the formatting has no effect.

Integers follow the same output formatting as strings: a single colon followed by the correct number of spaces to right-justify the number. Reals, however, can be formatted with either one or two parameters. The first parameter determines the width of the field in which the number will be right justified, and the second determines the number of decimal places. The program listed below demonstrates various formats for real numbers and their results.

```
Program RealFormat;
Var
  r : Real;
Begin
r := 123.23;
Writeln(r);            (* Result:     1.2323000000E+02  *)
Writeln(r:0);          (* Result: 1.2E+02              *)
Writeln(r:10);         (* Result: 1.2323E+02           *)
Writeln(r:10:2);       (* Result:        123.23        *)
Writeln(r:0:0);        (* Result: 123                  *)
End.
```

Disk Files and Buffers

Reading from and writing to a disk file is one of the slowest operations a computer performs. The time it takes for a disk drive to locate data seems like years to a microprocessor. Small chunks of memory called *buffers* are set aside for data to be used in disk operations. Buffers speed up processing by reducing the number of disk reads and writes. For example, suppose a program reads five characters from a text file with the following statements:

```
Read(TxtFile,Ch1);
Read(TxtFile,Ch2);
Read(TxtFile,Ch3);
Read(TxtFile,Ch4);
Read(TxtFile,Ch5);
```

If the input is not buffered, the program must go to the disk for each character read. If, however, the program picks up all five characters with the first **Read** statement and stores them in a buffer, the buffer can distribute the characters to the next four **Read** statements without having to access the disk.

Turbo Pascal provides text files with a standard 128-byte buffer. Every time a program reads data from a text file, the buffer is filled with 128 bytes, even if you only ask for 10. Of course, you will never know the extra bytes are in memory since Turbo Pascal takes care of all that for you.

When you process large text files, the standard 128-byte buffer is inadequate. Turbo Pascal allows you to expand a text file's buffer by specifying the size in the text-file definition. For example, the definition

```
FastFile : TEXT[512];
```

specifies a buffer of 512 bytes. The maximum size of a text-file buffer is 32,767 bytes (the maximum size of an integer), though you rarely need a buffer that exceeds 1024 bytes.

Flushing a File

When writing to a buffered file, Turbo Pascal actually sends the data to an output buffer. When the buffer is filled, the entire contents are written to the disk at one time.

To force Turbo Pascal to empty an output buffer before it is filled, use the **Flush** procedure. The statement **Flush(f)** forces any data in the **f** buffer to be saved to disk immediately, thus eliminating any possibility that the data will be lost. Closing an output file automatically flushes the output buffer.

Typed Files

Typed files are files that contain data of a particular type, such as integers, reals, records, and so on. These valuable files can make your programming easier and more efficient. In fact, typed files provide far faster input and output than do text files.

Unlike text files, which are unstructured, typed files have a rigid structure that is dependent on, and defined by, the type of data they hold. In the example below, the file identifier **f** is declared as a typed file called File of Real.

```
Program TypedFile;
Var
     f : File Of Real;
```

This declaration tells Turbo Pascal that this file will be used to store only real numbers. In fact, this file will store real numbers in the same format in which they are stored in RAM. Herein lies the reason that typed files are fast: because they bypass all the translation and conversion processes that data undergoes within text files, they can transfer the data directly to memory.

For example, a file that is declared to be of type integer knows that it is to store only integers; the data within it does not have to be converted into integers before it can be processed.

Records and Untyped Files

Because they are not made up of lines, as are text files, typed files cannot use the **ReadLn** and **WriteLn** statements. But, if typed files are not organized into lines, how are they organized? Untyped files are organized into records, each data item representing one record. The length of a record corresponds to the number of bytes required to store the data type. In the previous example, the file stores numbers of type real. Since a real number requires six bytes in Turbo Pascal, the record length for the file is six bytes: the first six bytes of the file contain the first record (real number), the next six contain the second record, and so on. For integers, numbers that require just two bytes, an untyped file is organized into two-byte records.

The following program shows how a typed file is declared, used for output, and then used for input:

```
Program RealFile;
Var
   r : Real;
   f : File Of Real;
Begin
Assign(f,'REAL.DAT');
Rewrite(f);

r := 100.234;
Write(f,r);

r := 32.23;
Write(f,r);

r := 9894.40;
Write(f,r);

Reset(f);

While Not Eof(f) do
   Begin
   Read(f,r);
   Writeln(r:0:3);
   End;
End.
```

This program writes out a total of three real numbers. Since each real number requires six bytes, the size of the file is 18 bytes. You can confirm this with the **Dir** command at the DOS prompt.

Strings and Typed Files

Typed files can also be a string type, but this is very different from a text file. Even though both are designed to hold strings, the way they store strings is what separates them. Consider the following example:

```
Program OutputCompare;
Var
   TxtFile : Text;
   StringFile : File Of String[10];
   s : String[10];

Begin
Assign(TxtFile,'OUTPUT.TXT');
Rewrite(TxtFile);
Assign(StringFile,'OUTPUT.STR');
Rewrite(StringFile);

s := 'ABCD';

Write(TxtFile,s);
Write(StringFile,s);

Close(TxtFile);
Close(StringFile);
End.
```

The program declares two files, one Text and the other type File Of String[10]. Both files are prepared for output and the string 'ABCD' is written to both. This is where the similarity ends.

In the case of the Text file, Turbo Pascal writes the letters A, B, C, and D and nothing more, as shown here:

A	B	C	D

In the typed file, however, Turbo Pascal stores the string in its full form: the length byte, the legitimate characters in the string (ABCD), and any garbage characters that fill out the remaining six bytes of storage, as shown here:

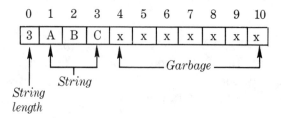

This example demonstrates that string files require more space than text files because the record includes the string length byte as well as any garbage bytes.

Typed Files and Speed

The data stored in a typed file has exactly the same form that it has when it is stored in RAM. This fact leads to a tremendous increase in input/output performance when compared to text-file processing. Why? Because every time Turbo Pascal uses a text file, some time is wasted while numbers are converted into characters and back again and strings are stripped of their length byte and any unused bytes. Data from typed files, on the other hand, can be read directly into RAM without any transformation. That means less work for the computer and, as a result, faster processing.

More Complex Typed Files

Just as you can define your own data types, you can also define a file to hold these data types. For example, a record of data type **customer** with fields Name, Address, and Telephone could be stored in a file as defined in the following program:

```
Program RecordFile;
Type
  CustomerRec = Record
    Name : String[30];
```

```
      Address : String[40];
      Telephone : String[10];
      End;

Var
   Customer : CustomerRec;
   CustFile : File Of CustomerRec;

Begin
Assign(CustFile,'CUST.DAT');
Reset(CustFile);

While Not Eof(CustFile) Do
   Begin
   Read(CustFile,Customer);
   With Customer Do
     Begin
     Writeln(Name,'  ',Address,' ',Telephone);
     End;
   End;
Close(CustFile);
End.
```

Because the file is declared to be of the same type as the record Customer, it is possible to read and write a complete record at a time. This increases speed because you do not have to read or write each item of the record separately.

Untyped Files

Untyped files are an especially powerful tool provided by Turbo Pascal. While text files assume that a file consists of lines terminated with CR/LF, and typed files assume that a file consists of a particular type of data structure, untyped files make no assumptions about the structure of the data in a file. You can read data from an untyped file into any data type you want.

Because Turbo Pascal makes no assumptions about the format of the data, the transfer from disk to your data structure is immediate. This is why untyped files are used for applications requiring high-speed input and output.

The following example, which copies the contents of one file to another, demonstrates a typical use of untyped files. As you can see, two file identifiers, **SourceFile** and **DestFile**, are declared to be of type **File**. Untyped files get their name from the fact that the reserved word **File** is not followed by a type specification, as is the case with typed files.

```
Program CopyFile;
Var
   SourceFile,
   DestFile    : File;
   RecordsRead : Integer;
   Buffer : Array [1..10C00] Of Byte;

Begin
Assign(SourceFile,'FILE.OLD');
Reset(SourceFile,1);

Assign(DestFile,'FILE.NEW');
Rewrite(DestFile,1);

BlockRead(SourceFile,Buffer,SizeOf(Buffer),RecordsRead);

While RecordsRead > 0 Do
   Begin
   BlockWrite(DestFile,Buffer,RecordsRead);
   BlockRead(SourceFile,Buffer,SizeOf(Buffer),RecordsRead);
   End;

Close(SourceFile);
Close(DestFile);
End.
```

Unlike text and typed files, the **Reset** and **Rewrite** statements for untyped files can take a second parameter, the record size. For example, the statement

Reset(SourceFile,1)

prepares the file to be read and specifies that the record length is 1 byte. This makes sense since the data structure is an array of bytes. If the data structure were an array of integers, you could set the record length to 2. While Turbo Pascal does not require you to match the record length to the size of the data type you are using, doing so makes programming easier. Note that if you do not specify a record length in the **Reset** or **Rewrite** statements, Turbo Pascal assigns a default record length of 128 bytes. Reading and writing to untyped files requires two special Turbo Pascal standard procedures, **BlockRead** and **BlockWrite**. In the previous example, the statement

BlockRead(SourceFile, Buffer,SizeOf(Buffer),
RecordsRead);

takes four parameters. The file identifier **SourceFile** is first. The second parameter specifies the data structure into which the data will be placed. In the example, the data structure is the array of bytes **Buffer**.

The third parameter specifies the number of records to read. In the example, the record size was set to 1 byte by the **Reset** statement. The data structure **Buffer**, however, is 10,000 bytes in length. To completely fill **Buffer**, then, you have to read in 10,000 records. You could simply write in the number **10000** as the third parameter, but the Turbo Pascal standard function SizeOf offers a better alternative. SizeOf returns the number of bytes used by a specific data structure. For example, if **i** is an Integer, then SizeOf(i) returns the value 2 because integers require two bytes of storage. In the example, the statement **SizeOf(Buffer)** returns 10,000 because that is the number of bytes **Buffer** uses. By using the SizeOf function, you can change the size of the buffer without having to change **BlockRead** statements.

The fourth and last parameter in the **BlockRead** statement is the integer variable **RecordsRead**. When the **BlockRead** statement executes, it attempts to read in the number of records specified (10,000 in the example). However, if the file pointer is close to the end of the file, you may actually read fewer than 10,000 records. **RecordsRead** tells you exactly how many records were read by the **BlockRead** statement. When **RecordsRead** equals zero, the end of the file has been reached.

BlockWrite operates much the same as **BlockRead**, except that there are only three parameters. The file identifier comes first, followed by the data structure used for the output. The third parameter is the number of records to write to the file. In the example program CopyFile, **RecsRead** specifies the number of records to write because you want to write out exactly what was read in.

Procedures for Typed and Untyped Files

Nontext files (that is, typed and untyped files) are also known as *random access files*, meaning that records in a file can be accessed in nonsequential order. If you want to, you can read the third record first, then the tenth record, and the first record after that. This is done in a two-step process: first position the file pointer at the correct record, then read the record. This is demonstrated in the following program, which creates a typed data file and then reads the records back in nonsequential order.

```
Program DataBaseFile;
(*$$-*)
Type
  MaxStr  = String[255];
  CustRec = Record
    Name : String[30];
    Age  : Integer;
    Income : Real;
    End;

Var
  Cust : CustRec;
  CustFile : File Of CustRec;

(*********)

Procedure AddRec(NameIn : MaxStr;AgeIn : Integer;IncomeIn : Real);
Begin
With Cust Do
  Begin
  Name := NameIn;
  Age := AgeIn;
```

```
Income := IncomeIn;
Write(CustFile,Cust);
End;
End;

(**********)

Procedure DumpRec;
Begin
WriteLn;
With Cust Do
  Begin
  WriteLn('Name:    ',Name);
  WriteLn('Age:     ',Age);
  WriteLn('Income: ',Income:0:0);
  End;
End;

(**********)

Begin
ClrScr;
Assign(CustFile,'CUSTFILE.DAT');
Rewrite(CustFile);

AddRec('Jones',30,23000.0);
AddRec('Adams',65,34000.0);
AddRec('Smith',21,18000.0);


Reset(CustFile);
WriteLn('The number of records in the file is: ',FileSize(CustFile));

(*********************************************************************)
(* Write out the contents of the third record in the file. Because *)
(* the first record in a file is number 0, the third record is     *)
(* number 2.                                                        *)
(*********************************************************************)

Seek(CustFile,2);
Writeln;
Writeln;
Writeln('This is record number: ',FilePos(CustFile));
Read(CustFile,Cust);
DumpRec;

(***********************************************************)
(* Write out the contents of the first record in the file. *)
(***********************************************************)

Seek(CustFile,0);
Writeln;
Writeln;
Writeln('This is record number: ',FilePos(CustFile));
Read(CustFile,Cust);
DumpRec;
```

```
(****************************************************************)
(* Write out the contents of the second record in the file. *)
(****************************************************************)
Seek(CustFile,0);
Writeln;
Writeln;
Writeln('This is record number: ',FilePos(CustFile));
Read(CustFile,Cust);
DumpRec;

(*********************************************)
(* Change the contents of the first record *)
(*********************************************)
Seek(CustFile,0);
AddRec('Arnold',32,43000.0);

Seek(CustFile,0);
Writeln;
Writeln;
Writeln('This is record number: ',FilePos(CustFile));
Read(CustFile,Cust);
DumpRec;

Close(CustFile);
End.
```

The **Seek** statement moves the file pointer to the beginning of the third record. Note that the third record is referred to as number 2 in the **Seek** statement because Turbo Pascal typed files begin with record 0. When the file pointer is in place, you can read the record as you normally would. After the **Read** is executed, the file pointer is automatically moved to the beginning of the next record. In this case, the third record is the last record in the file. Any attempt to read beyond the end of the file results in an I/O error.

An example of a nonsequential **Read** is shown by the following two statements:

```
Seek(CustFile,2);
Read(CustFile,Cust);
```

Two other standard functions, FileSize and FilePos, are also used. FileSize returns the total number of records in the file; FilePos returns the current position of the file pointer.

An especially powerful feature of random access files is the ability to update records at any point in the file. This is demonstrated at the end of the previous example program (titled DataBaseFile), where the information in the first record is changed and then displayed. What is particularly noteworthy is that the **Write** procedure is used without a preceding **Rewrite** statement. This seems to go against the rule that a file must be prepared with **Rewrite** before you can add data to it. For nontext files, the **Rewrite** command is only necessary to create the file. Once the file exists, the **Reset** command allows you to both read and write to the file.

Erasing and Renaming Files

Sophisticated file management requires the ability to rename and erase files without going back to the DOS prompt. Turbo Pascal provides two procedures to do just that. To rename a file, first assign a file to a file variable, then call the **Rename** procedure with the new name specified:

```
Assign(f,'FILE.OLD');
Rename(f,'FILE.NEW');
```

The **Erase** procedure works essentially the same way.

Assign the disk file to a file identifier and then call the **Erase** procedure.

```
Assign(f,'FILE.OLD');
Erase(f);
```

The following program provides a simple method for renaming and erasing files. When you start the program, three choices are presented: rename a file, erase a file, or quit.

```
Program FileControl;
Var
   File1 : File;
   Name1,
   Name2 : String[255];
   Choice : Char;

Begin
   Repeat
   Write('R)ename, E)rase, Q)uit: ')
   Readln(Choice);

     Case Upcase(Choice) Of
     'R':
       Begin
       Write('Name of file to rename: ');
       Readln(Name1);
       Write('New name for the file: ');
       Readln(Name2);
       Assign(File1,Name1);
       Rename(File1,Name2);
       End;
     'E':
       Begin
       Write('Name of file to erase: ');
       Readln(Name1);
       Assign(File1,Name1);
       Erase(File1);
       End;
     End; (* of case *)

   Until Upcase(Choice) = 'Q';
End.
```

Make a selection by typing **R**, **E**, or **Q** and pressing RETURN. When renaming a file, enter the name of the existing file as well as the new name for the file. Erasing a file requires only that you enter the name of the file to be erased.

Input and Output in Turbo Pascal Version 4.0

Some of the rules for input and output have been changed in Turbo Pascal 4.0. One change is the way in which you assign a buffer to a text file. In Version 3.0, you could define 1K buffer for a text file with the declaration

```
Var
  F : Text[1024];
```

This declaration is not supported in Version 4.0. Instead you must declare a buffer and then link it to a text file with the procedure **SetTextBuf** as shown here:

```
Type
  buftype =  Array[1..1024] of Char;


Var
  F : Text;
  Buf: buftype;

Begin
Assign(F, 'TEXTFILE');
SetTextBuf(F, Buf);
rewrite(F);
```

If you want to buffer more than one text file at a time, you must set up separate buffers for each file. You must also call **SetTextBuf** before any input or output is performed, and you should declare your buffer globally. If you link a text file to a buffer that is declared within a procedure, the buffer will disappear when the procedure ends. Any further output to or input from this file will be erroneous.

Other changes have been made regarding DOS devices. Turbo Pascal Version 3.0 supported the CON:, TRM:, and LIST: devices. Version 4.0 replaces these with CON, PRN, LPT1, LPT2, and LPT3. PRN, LPT1, LPT2, and LPT3 refer to the printer, while CON is the console display for output and the keyboard for input.

The LST device still functions for printer output if your program uses the Printer unit. This is demonstrated in the following program segment:

```
Program Prnt;

Uses Printer;

Begin
Writeln(lst,'This is a test');
End.
```

Without the Printer unit, the reference to **lst** will create a compile error.

General Programming Techniques: Strings, Recursion, and Files

Using Strings in Turbo Pascal
Using Recursion in Turbo Pascal
Input/Output Considerations in Turbo Pascal

A carpenter can build many houses of different shapes and sizes using the same tools and techniques. Like carpenters, programmers use the same tools over and over to perform common programming tasks. A well-stocked programming toolbox is a sure sign of an experienced programmer. This chapter introduces several useful tools that can make your programming easier and better.

Using Strings in Turbo Pascal

The Turbo Pascal **string** data type (which is described in Chapter 5) is a powerful and frequently used data structure. While it is most commonly used to hold words and messages, a string can perform far more interesting tasks.

As you may recall, a string consists of a length byte followed by as many bytes as are defined in the string declaration. For example, **STRING[4]** declares a 5-byte data type: one length byte followed by four character bytes.

One of the reasons that the **string** type is so powerful is that it can be processed in two different ways: by directly manipulating its individual elements or by using one of the Turbo Pascal standard functions and procedures for strings. Both methods (each of which is discussed in this chapter) have advantages, depending on the circumstances.

Standard Procedures and Functions for Strings

Because they require a great many character manipulations, string-handling procedures are sometimes difficult to write. Turbo Pascal eliminates the need to write these character-by-character manipulations by providing powerful standard functions, making string manipulation an easy job.

Chr or Char

The standard function **Chr** (or **Char**) accepts an integer parameter and returns its equivalent ASCII value. For example, because ASCII code 65 represents the character "A", the statement **Char(65)** returns **A**.

While it is not a string procedure, the **Chr** function is frequently used with string statements, especially those with unusual characters. For example, the following program writes out a string with a double exclamation point, a character represented by ASCII code 19.

```
Program DoubleExclamation;
var
   s : string[20];
begin
s := 'Wow' + Chr(19);
writeln(s);
end.
```

Upcase

Upcase, another character-level function, accepts a single lowercase alphabetic character from a to z and returns its uppercase equivalent. If the character is not lowercase and alphabetic, **Upcase** returns the character unchanged.

Concat

Concatenation is the combination of several strings into a single string. Turbo Pascal offers two ways to concatenate strings: **Concat** and the **Plus** (+) operator.

The standard function **Concat** accepts any number of strings as parameters and returns them as one string. This program shows how to use this function:

```
Program Concatenate;
Var
   s1,s2,s3 : string[80];
begin
s1 := 'This is the beginning -';
s2 := '- This is the end.';
s3 := Concat(s1,s2);
writeln(s3);
end.
```

In this example, strings **s1** and **s2** are passed into **Concat**, where they are combined and assigned to **s3**. When **s3** is written out, the message displayed is

This is the beginning—This is the end.

Most programmers prefer to use the **Plus** operator to concatenate their strings, primarily because it is simpler to use and produces more readable code, as shown here:

```
Program Concat;
Var
   s1,s2,s3,s4,s5 : string[80];
begin
s1 := 'This is ';
s2 := 'all one ';
s3 := 'sentence.';

s4 := s1 + s2 + s3;
writeln(s4);
end.
```

The statement

s4 := s1 + s2 + s3

produces the same result as

s4 := Concat(s1,s2,s3)

but the **Plus** operator is cleaner looking and easier to type.

With both **Concat** and the **Plus** operator, the concatenated string is truncated when the total length of the concatenated strings exceeds the maximum length of the receiving string.

Copy

The standard function **Copy** extracts a substring from a larger string. To use **Copy**, you must know where in the larger string you want to start copying and how many characters you want to copy. For example, the statement **Copy(s,12,3)** tells Turbo Pascal to return three characters from string s starting with character 12.

The following program uses the **Copy** function to write a long string as a column ten characters wide.

```
Program Concat;
Var
   s : string[80];
   i : integer;

begin
s := 'This is a long line that will be written out in a column.';
i := 1;
while i < length(s) do
   Begin
   Writeln(copy(s,i,10));
   i := i + 10;
   End;
end.
```

When you run this program, the output looks like this:

```
This is a
long line
that will
be written
out in a
column.
```

Each line in the output, except the last line, contains ten characters, including blank characters. The last line contains only seven characters because this is all that remained at the end of the sentence. If you attempt to copy beyond the end of the string, you get either a partial result or no characters at all, but Turbo Pascal does not generate an error.

Delete

The **Delete** procedure removes characters from a string. As with **Copy**, you must specify the starting point in the string and the number of characters to delete. For example, the statement **Delete(s,5,3)** tells Turbo Pascal to delete three characters from string s starting at the fifth character.

Insert

The **Insert** procedure inserts a substring into another string. Three parameters are passed into **Insert**: the substring to insert, the string into which the substring will be inserted, and the position of the insertion. For example, the statement **Insert(s1, s2, 4)** tells Turbo Pascal to insert string **s1** into **s2** starting at the fourth character. This sample program illustrates both **Delete** and **Insert**:

```
Program Insert;
Var
   s1,s2 : string[80];
```

```
begin
s1 := 'A';
s2 := '1234567890';
Insert(s1,s2,3);
Writeln(s2);
Delete(s2,3,1);
Writeln(s2);
end.
```

This program displays the string '12A34567890', showing that **A** has been inserted into the third character in the string. The statement **Delete(s2,3,1)** then removes the **A** from the string and displays it once again.

Length

The standard function **Length** returns the number of characters currently held in a string variable. Thus, if a string **s** is equal to 'This is a string.   ', then **Length(s)** will be equal to 20. The three blanks at the end of the string are counted as part of the string.

Pos

When you want to know if one string is contained in another, Turbo Pascal can tell you this with the standard function **Pos**. Consider the following example:

```
Program Pos;
Var
  s : String[80];
begin
s := 'This is a test string';
clrscr;
writeln('The position of ''test'' in s is: ',pos('test',s));
writeln('The position of ''TEST'' in s is: ',pos('TEST',s));
end.
```

This program displays the following messages:

The position of 'test' in s is: 11
The position of 'TEST' in s is: 0

The first message confirms that the word "test" is located at the eleventh character of the larger string. The second message simply shows that **Pos** returns zero when a match is not found.

Str and Val

Str and **Val**, two closely related standard procedures, are frequently used in programs that process numerical input and output. **Str** converts a number into a string, and **Val** converts a string into a number.

Str takes two parameters: a number (integer or real) and a string variable. The number can be formatted according to Turbo Pascal conventions. Examples of **Str** statements and their results are shown in Figure 10-1.

The first **Str** statement — **Str(10,s)** — converts an integer to a string with no formatting. The statement **Str(10:4,s)**, on the other hand, is formatted as right-justified in a field four spaces wide. The resulting string, therefore, consists of two blank characters before the number 10.

Formatting real numbers is a bit more complicated. When a real number is unformatted, **Str** produces a string in

```
Var
   s : String[20];
```

Statement	Result
Str(10,s);	'10'
Str(10:4,s);	' 10'
Str(3.2,s);	' 3.2000000000E+00'
Str(3.2:0,s);	'3.2E+00'
Str(3.2:15:3,s);	' 3.200'

Figure 10-1.   Results of the Str procedure

scientific notation. For example, **Str(3.2,s)** sets s equal to ' 3.2000000000E+00'. Note that a string begins with two blanks and contains all significant digits. If, however, the real is formatted to a field width of 0—**Str(3.2:0,s)**—the result is '3.2E+00'. In this case, only the essential digits are present, and no blanks are added to the string. The final example, **Str(3.2:15:3,s)**, creates a 15-character string with three decimal places: '   3.200'.

The **Val** procedure accepts three parameters: the string to convert into a number, the numeric variable to receive the value, and an integer variable used to flag errors. The following sample program shows how to use the **Val** procedure:

```
Program StringToNumber;
Type
  MaxStr = String[20];
Var
  r : Real;
  code : Integer;

(*****************************************)

Procedure WriteNumber(s : MaxStr);
Begin
Val(s,r,code);
If code = 0 Then
  Writeln(r:0:3)
Else
  Writeln('Error in numeric conversion');
End;

(*****************************************)

Begin
WriteNumber('123.23');
WriteNumber('s123.23');
End.
```

At the heart of the sample program is the statement **Val(s,r,code)**, which attempts to convert string s into a valid real number. If s contains a valid number in the correct format, the conversion will be successful and **code** will set to zero; if s contains an invalid number, **code** will be set to a nonzero value.

Valid	Invalid	Reason
'12'	'1x2'	String contains nonnumeric character
'-1.32'	' -1.32'	String contains a blank character
'3.2E+00'	'3.2E+00 '	String contains a blank character

Table 10-1.   Valid and Invalid Strings for Numeric Conversion

To be valid for numeric conversions, a string must meet these conditions:

1. It must contain a number in integer, real, or scientific notation.

2. It must not contain any blank, alphabetic, or other characters not used in numeric representation. The "E" used in scientific notation is an exception.

Table 10-1 shows examples of both valid and invalid strings for numeric conversion. As you can see, a string must be in a proper form before it can be converted.

A final point on converting strings to numbers: if you try to convert a string that contains a valid real number (for example, 1.32) into an integer, Turbo Pascal generates an error. The safest approach in such cases is to convert all numeric strings into reals and then convert the real to an integer with the **Round** or **Trunc** functions.

Direct Manipulation of Characters

While the Turbo Pascal string procedures are powerful, they do have limitations. For example, to change a string to all uppercase characters, you must process the string yourself. This is not a difficult task; a string, after all, is nothing more than an array of characters with a length byte in position zero. The following program shows how you can process strings. It contains the function **UpCaseStr**, which accepts a string parameter, changes all lowercase letters to uppercase, and then returns the string:

```
Program UpperCase;
Type
  MaxStr = String[255];
Var
  s : MaxStr;

(*******************)

Function UpCaseStr(s : MaxStr) : MaxStr;
Var
  i,j : Integer;
Begin
j := ord(s[0]);
For i := 1 To j Do
  s[i] := Upcase(s[i]);
UpCaseStr := s;
End;

(*******************)

Begin
s := 'abc';
writeln(UpCaseStr(s));
End.
```

The first statement in the function **UpCaseStr** is

j := ord(s[0])

where s is defined as **String[255]**. But **s[0]** appears to be outside the range **1..255**. How can this be? Whatever their length, all strings have a character at position zero that contains the length of the string. The statement **ord(s[0])** converts that character into its equivalent byte value so that it can be assigned to the integer **j**. The same thing could have been accomplished with the statement **j := Length(s)**.

The next part of the procedure processes the string from the first character to the last. A character that is referred to individually in a string (for example, **s[2]**) can be substituted for a variable of type **Char** in any expression. Thus, the **Upcase** procedure, which takes a parameter of type **Char**, can accept individual characters from a string.

```
For i := 1 To j Do
   s[i] := Upcase(s[i]);
```

When all characters in the string are uppercase, the function passes the altered string back to the program.

Manipulating the Length Byte

You can play some tricks with strings by altering the value of the length byte. This lets you lengthen or shorten a string without assigning a new value. For example, consider this block of code:

```
s := 'ABCDEFG';
s[0] := Chr(3);
Writeln(s);
```

When the string 'ABCDEFG' is assigned to variable s, Turbo Pascal sets the length to ASCII code 7. The next line, however, changes the length byte to ASCII code 3. The **Chr** function is used because Turbo Pascal considers the length byte to be a character. Thus, when the statement **WriteLn(s)** is executed, the output is **ABC**. In Turbo Pascal, changing the length byte changes the string.

On the other hand, changing characters in the string directly does not change the length byte, as illustrated by this code segment:

```
s := 'ABC';
s[4] := 'D';
s[5] := 'E';
Writeln(s);
```

The first statement assigns the string 'ABC' to the variable and sets the length byte to ASCII code 3. The next two statements change the value in positions 4 and 5 of the string, but this does not affect the length byte. Therefore, the statement **WriteLn(s)** displays **ABC**, not **ABCDE**.

Direct manipulation of strings has many practical uses, such as the creation of strings for special text displays. For example, the following program uses an 80-character string that contains the double horizontal line character (ASCII code 205) to split the screen in half:

```
Program SplitScreen;
Type
   MaxStr = String[255];
Var
   Divider : MaxStr;

Begin
Clrscr;
FillChar(Divider,Sizeof(Divider),205);
Divider[0] := Chr(80);

Gotoxy(1,14);
Write(Divider);

Gotoxy(1,7);
Write('This is the upper portion of the screen.');

Gotoxy(1,21);
Write('This is the lower portion of the screen.');
End.
```

The first statement in the procedure,

    FillChar(Divider,Sizeof(Divider),205);

fills the entire string, from position 0 to position 255, with the ASCII value 205. To make the string fill one line of the screen, however, the length byte must be 80. Therefore, the length byte is set to 80 with the statement

    Divider[0] := Chr(80);

Now the string can be written to the screen, providing an attractive divider. In other places in the program, you might want to use the same string, but in shorter lengths, perhaps only 10 or 20 characters. Just change the length byte according to your needs; you do not have to change the characters because they are already set properly.

Resolving Programming Problems with Strings

Now that you understand how to manipulate string variables, you can put them to use. The rest of this section is devoted to some of the more common programming problems that can be resolved by creatively using strings.

A Search and Replace Procedure

From their earliest days, microcomputers have been associated with word processing and text editing. It is not surprising, therefore, that Turbo Pascal provides string procedures that closely resemble the features of a word processor. These procedures allow you to locate a combination of letters in a string, delete that combination, and replace it with another, as shown here:

```
Program SearchAndReplace;
Var
   BigString : String[255];
   FindString,
   ReplaceString : String[20];
   i : Integer;

Begin
FindString := 'Steve';
ReplaceString := 'John';
BigString := 'Tell Steve to pay me the five dollars he owes me.';

Writeln(BigString);
i := Pos(FindString,BigString);
Delete(BigString,i,Length(FindString));
Insert(ReplaceString,BigString,i);
Writeln(BigString);
End.
```

This program uses four string procedures: **Pos, Delete, Insert,** and **Length**. The substring 'Steve' is contained in the larger string starting at the sixth character. Therefore, the statement

i := Pos(FindString,BigString);

assigns the value 6 to **i**.

Now that you know where in the larger string the substring is located, you can remove it with **Delete**. This is accomplished with the following statement:

Delete(BigString,i,length(FindString));

In this case, the substring is the string variable **FindString**, which holds the value 'Steve.' The first parameter, **BigString**, contains **FindString**; the second parameter indicates the position of **FindString** in **BigString**. **Length(FindString)**, the third parameter, uses the standard function **Length** to tell the program how many characters to delete.

Because **FindString** is equal to 'Steve,' **Length(FindString)** is equal to 5. Thus, the **Delete** statement tells Turbo Pascal to delete five characters from **BigString**, starting with the sixth character.

Finally, the following statement inserts the second substring (**ReplaceString**) in **BigString** at exactly the same position as the other string.

Insert(ReplaceString,BigString,i);

This tells Turbo Pascal to insert **ReplaceString** into the **BigString** at position **i**.

Now that you know how the program works, you should be able to guess how it will look when it runs. The program first writes out **BigString** in its original form. It then substitutes 'John' for 'Steve' and writes **BigString** out again, as shown here:

Tell Steve to pay me the five dollars he owes me.
Tell John to pay me the five dollars he owes me.

Thus, by combining four of the string-processing procedures, you are able to perform a rather complex piece of programming with only a few lines of code.

Personalizing Messages

Obviously you cannot write a complete word-processing program with these few functions. You can, however, put the search-and-replace principle to some clever uses. For example, suppose you want to add a personal touch to a program by inserting the user's name into some of the messages your computer displays. To do this, you need to know the user's name, in what strings it is to be inserted, and where it goes in those strings.

First, set a general rule: the @ character in a string indicates where the user's name should be placed. If the name is 'John', the string 'Hello, @' would become 'Hello, John'. You can place the @ character anywhere you want the name to appear. The following sample program demonstrates how to do this:

```
Program InsertName;
Type
   Str255 = String[255];
Var
   Message1,
   Message2,
   Message3 : String[255];
   Name : String[20];


Function WriteMessage(s,name : Str255) : Str255;
Var
   i : Integer;
Begin
i := Pos('@',s);
if i > 0 then
   begin
   Delete(s,i,1);
   Insert(name,s,i);
   end;
WriteMessage := s;
End;

Begin
Message1 := 'Hello, @';
Message2 := 'This message is unchanged.';
Message3 := 'This message, @, has been changed.';
```

```
ClrScr;
Write('Enter your name: ');
Readln(Name);

writeln(WriteMessage(message1,name));
writeln(WriteMessage(message2,name));
writeln(WriteMessage(message3,name));
End.
```

One problem with this program is that every time it encounters the @ character in a message, it replaces it with the user's name. For example, in the message 'This is the @ character, @.', you want the first @ to print as is and the second @ to change the individual's name. Unfortunately, **WriteMessage** will change the first @ and leave the second unchanged. Therefore, you should choose a character that will not be used in its literal form in messages.

Error-free Data Entry

Converting strings to numbers has one very important application: checking for errors in numbers entered by a user. For example, the code for a program that asks a user to enter his or her age may look like this:

```
Var
   Age : Integer;
Begin
Write('Enter age: ');
Readln(Age);
End.
```

The problem with this code is that if a user enters invalid numbers or numbers with spaces, Turbo Pascal generates a run-time error and aborts the program. Avoid this situation by having the user enter the number into a string and then convert the string into a number. If the conversion fails, the user entered an invalid number, and you can ask for input again. The following program illustrates this method:

```
Program EnterNumber;
Var
  Age,Code : integer;
  AgeString : String[10];
Begin
  Repeat
  Write('Enter your age: ');
  Readln(AgeString);
  Val(AgeString,Age,Code);
  If Code <> 0 then
    Write(^g);              (* Make the computer beep *)
  Until Code = 0;
Writeln('Your age is : ',age);
End.
```

In this example, when the user enters his or her age into the string variable **AgeString**, the program attempts to convert **AgeString** into the integer **Age**. If the conversion fails, the integer variable **Code** is set to a value other than zero. When this occurs, the program writes the character ^g, which makes the terminal beep, and continues the loop until the user enters a valid number.

Is this method foolproof? Unfortunately, no. The **Val** procedure has one fault—if the string being converted is blank, *no conversion is performed, yet **Code** is returned equal to zero.* This means that the user can press RETURN, and the program will accept it as a valid number. To eliminate this possibility, still more code must be added to your program, so that the conversion looks like this:

```
Readln(AgeString);
If AgeString = '' then
  begin
  Age := 0
  Code := -1;
  end
else
  Val(AgeString,Age,Code);
```

If the user enters a null string by pressing RETURN, the program will catch this error and continue asking for input. Of course, no user will be zero years old, but your program must be able to properly handle any numeric input it receives.

Removing Blanks

As mentioned previously, blank characters at the beginning or end of a numeric string cause a numeric conversion to fail. The string ' 10 ', for example, cannot be converted to a numeric value unless the blanks at both ends are removed. This can be accomplished with the procedure **StripBlanks**, as shown here:

```
Program NoBlanks;
Type
   MaxStr = String[255];
Var
   s : MaxStr;
   i,code : Integer;

(********************************)

Procedure StripBlanks(Var s: MaxStr);
Begin
While (s[1] = ' ') And (Length(s) > 0) Do
   Delete(s,1,1);
While (s[Length(s)] = ' ') And (Length(s) > 0) Do
   Delete(s,length(s),1);
End;

(********************************)

begin
s := '    20    ';
StripBlanks(s);
Val(s,i,code);
Writeln('Value is: ',i);
end.
```

This program passes a string into **StripBlanks** as a reference parameter, so whatever changes are made to the string are retained after the procedure ends. **StripBlanks** consists of two While-Do loops that control a **Delete** statement. The first loop is shown here:

```
While (s[1] = ' ') And (Length(s) > 0) Do
    Delete(s,1,1);
```

This loop removes blanks from the front of a string by repeatedly deleting the first character from the string. Every time a blank is deleted, the new first character is tested to see if it is blank. The loop ends when it encounters a nonblank first character or when the length of the string has been reduced to zero.

The second loop removes characters from the end of the string with the statement

```
While (s[Length(s)] = ' ') And (Length(s) > 0) Do
    Delete(s,length(s),1);
```

Here, **s[Length(s)]** points to the last character in the string s, while **Delete(s,length(s),1)** removes it.

These are just a few examples of how strings can be used to solve tricky programming problems. As you program, you will discover many more.

Using Recursion in Turbo Pascal

Recursion is a technique wherein a procedure, in the process of performing its tasks, makes calls to itself. How can a procedure make calls to itself? It is a difficult concept to grasp, even for experienced programmers. Recursion can best be described by the classic example, the *factorial function*. The factorial of integer **n** is the cumulative product of all integers from 1 to n. For example, the factorial of 2 is 1×2, while the factorial of 3 is $1 \times 2 \times 3$. The nonrecursive factorial function would be coded as follows:

```
Function Factorial(n : integer) : Real;
Var
 r : Real;
 i : Integer;
Begin
r := 1;
for i := 2 To n Do
  r := r * i;
Factorial := r;
End;
```

The calculation in this nonrecursive example is straight-forward: **r**, originally set equal to 1, is repeatedly multiplied by successive integer values up to and including **n**. Compare this to this recursive version:

```
Function Factorial(n : integer) : Real;
Begin
if n = 0 then
  Factorial := 1
else
  Factorial := n * Factorial(n-1);
End;
```

The recursive version works by repeatedly multiplying **n** by the factorial of the number just preceding it. While the recursive version is more elegant and intellectually appeal-ing, most programmers find the nonrecursive version easier to understand and code. Which is better? That depends on several things.

On the negative side, recursive procedures have a major weak point: each time a procedure calls itself, Turbo Pascal must set up space on the stack for temporary storage. This not only slows a procedure's execution but also increases the danger of a stack/heap collision.

On the other hand, some algorithms are so naturally adapted to a recursive structure that forcing them into a nonrecursive form just does not make sense. A good example of such an algorithm is a function that evaluates a mathe-matical expression stored in a string. The following program shows how the recursive process follows the flow of the underlying algorithm. Study it carefully.

```
Program Calculator;
Type
  MaxCompStr = String[255];
Var
  i : Integer;
  formula : String[80];
  p : Integer;
  result : Real;
  error : Boolean;

(********************)

Function ComputeFormula(Var P : Integer;
                        Strg : MaxCompStr;
                        Var error : Boolean) : Real;

Var
  r : Real;
  i, index,
  BreakPoint : Integer;
  Ch : Char;

(********************)

Procedure Eval(Var Formula : MaxCompStr;
               Var Value : Real;
               Var BreakPoint : Integer);
Const
  Numbers : Set Of Char = ['0'..'9','.'];
Var
  P : Integer;
  Ch : Char;

(********************)

Procedure NextP;
Begin
  Repeat
  P := P+1;
  IF P <= Length(Formula) Then
    Ch := Formula[P]
  Else
    Ch := 13;
  Until (Ch <> ' ');
End;

(******************************************)

Function Expr : Real;
Var
  E : Real;
  Operator : Char;
```

```
(*****************************************)

Function SmplExpr : Real;
Var
  S : Real;
  Operator : Char;

(*****************************************)

Function Term : Real;
Var
  T : Real;

(*****************************************)

Function S_Fact : Real;

(*****************************************)

Function Fct : Real;
Var
  fn : String[20];
  l,start: Integer;
  F : Real;

(*****************************************)

Procedure process_as_number;
var
  code : Integer;
Begin
Start := P;
  Repeat
  NextP
  Until Not(Ch In Numbers);
IF Ch = '.' Then
  Repeat
  NextP
  Until Not(Ch In Numbers);
IF Ch = 'E' Then
  Begin
  NextP;
    Repeat
    NextP
    Until Not(Ch In Numbers);
  End;
Val(Copy(Formula, Start, P-Start), F, code);
End;

(*****************************************)

Procedure process_as_new_Expr;
Begin
```

```
NextP;
F := Expr;
IF Ch = ')' Then
  NextP
Else
  BreakPoint := P;
End;

(******************************************)

Procedure process_as_standard_Function;

(******************************************)

Function Fact(I : Integer) : Real;
Begin
IF I > 0 Then
  Fact := I*Fact(I-1)
Else
  Fact := 1;
End;

(******************************************)

Begin
IF Copy(Formula, P, 3) = 'ABS' Then
  Begin
  p := p + 2;
  NextP;
  F := Fct;
  f := Abs(f);
  End
Else if Copy(Formula, P, 4) = 'SQRT' Then
  Begin
  p := p + 3;
  NextP;
  F := Fct;
  f := Sqrt(f);
  End
Else if Copy(Formula, P, 3) = 'SQR' Then
  Begin
  p := p + 2;
  NextP;
  F := Fct;
  f := Sqr(f);
  End
Else if Copy(Formula, P, 3) = 'SIN' Then
  Begin
  p := p + 2;
  NextP;
  F := Fct;
  f := Sin(f);
```

```
        End
Else if Copy(Formula, P, 3) = 'COS' Then
    Begin
    p := p + 2;
    NextP;
    F := Fct;
    f := cos(f);
    End
Else if Copy(Formula, P, 6) = 'ARCTAN' Then
    Begin
    p := p + 5;
    NextP;
    F := Fct;
    f := arctan(f);
    End
Else if Copy(formula, P, 2) = 'LN' Then
    Begin
    p := p + 1;
    NextP;
    F := Fct;
    f := ln(f);
    End
Else if Copy(Formula, P, 3) = 'EXP' Then
    Begin
    p := p + 2;
    NextP;
    F := Fct;
    f := exp(f);
    End
Else if Copy(Formula, P, 4) = 'FACT' Then
    Begin
    p := p + 3;
    NextP;
    F := Fct;
    f := fact(Trunc(f));
    End
Else
    Begin
    BreakPoint := P;
    End;
End;

(*****************************************)

Begin
IF (Ch In Numbers) Then
    process_as_number
Else IF (Ch = '(') Then
    process_as_new_Expr
Else
```

```
     process_as_standard_Function;
Fct := F;
End;

(*******************)

Begin
IF Ch = '-' Then
   Begin
   NextP;
   S_Fact := -Fct;
   End
Else
   S_Fact := Fct;
End;

(*******************)

Begin
T := S_Fact;
While Ch = '^' Do
   Begin
   NextP;
   t := Exp(Ln(t)*S_Fact)
   End;
Term := t;
End;

(*******************)

Begin
s := term;
While Ch In ['*', '/'] Do
   Begin
   Operator := Ch;
   NextP;
     Case Operator Of
     '*' : s := s*term;
     '/' : s := s/term;
     End;
   End;
SmplExpr := s;
End;

(*******************)

Begin
E := SmplExpr;
While Ch In ['+', '-'] Do
   Begin
```

```
      Operator := Ch;
      NextP;
        Case Operator Of
        '+' : e := e+SmplExpr;
        '-' : e := e-SmplExpr;
        End;
      End;
    Expr := E;
    End;

(********************)

Begin
For i := 1 To Length(Formula) Do
  Formula[i] := Upcase(Formula[i]);
IF Formula[1] = '.' Then Formula := '0'+Formula;
IF Formula[1] = '+' Then Delete(Formula, 1, 1);
P := 0;
NextP;
Value := Expr;

IF Ch = 13 Then
  error := false
Else
  error := true;
BreakPoint := p;
End;

(********************)

Begin
Eval(Strg, r, p);
Compute_Formula := r;
End;

(********************)

Begin
  Repeat
  Write('Enter formula: ');
  Read(formula);
  If formula <> '' Then
    Begin
    result := Compute_Formula(p,formula,error);
    If error Then
      Begin
      Writeln;
      Writeln('Error!');
      Writeln(formula);
      For i := 1 To p-1 Do Write(' ');
      Writeln('^');
      End
```

```
      Else
        Writeln(' = ',result:0:2);
      End;
   Until formula = '';
End.
```

When you run this program, you will be asked to enter an equation, which the program stores in a string and passes to the function **ComputeFormula**. This function evaluates the equation through a series of recursive calls. If successful, the result is passed back to the program; if not, the Boolean parameter **error** is set to true, and the integer parameter **p** indicates the point in the string at which the error was detected.

Coding this same procedure in a nonrecursive manner is possible, but given the nature of the algorithm, which lends itself to the recursive approach, it is undesirable.

Input/Output Considerations
in Turbo Pascal

Input/output errors are probably the most common type of error. Thus, eliminating them is an important task. Luckily, as long as you know what kinds of errors to look for, it is not difficult to maintain error-free I/O.

Resetting, Appending,
and Rewriting Files

A common I/O error occurs when you attempt to **Reset** or **Append** a file that does not exist. Before you use these procedures, be sure that the file exists. The function **File-Exists**, shown here, tests for a file's existence:

```
Program OpenFile;
Type
  MaxStr = String[80];
```

```
Var
  S : MaxStr;

(*****************************************)

Function FileExists(fname : MaxStr) : Boolean;
Var
  F : File;
  ok : Boolean;
Begin
Assign(F,fname);
(*$I-*)
Reset(F);
(*$I+*)
ok := IOresult = 0;
If Not ok Then
  FileExists := False
Else
  Begin
  Close(F);
  FileExists := True;
  End;
End;

(*****************************************)

Begin
s := 'TEST.DAT';
If FileExists(s) Then
  Writeln('File exists.')
Else
  Writeln('File does not exist.');
End.
```

As you can see, **FileExists** works by attempting to open
the file in question. Since the I/O error-checking compiler
directive ({$i-}) is turned off, resetting a nonexistent file will
not cause a fatal error. You can detect the error on your own,
however, with the Turbo Pascal standard identifier **IOresult**.
When an I/O error occurs, **IOresult** is set to a nonzero value.
By checking **IOresult**, I/O errors can be detected before they
have a chance to do any damage.

The function **FileExists** is also useful when you **Rewrite**
a file. A file can be rewritten—whether or not it exists—
without causing an I/O error. You should make sure, however, that you do not overwrite an existing file by accident.
Before you rewrite a file, use **FileExists** to see if it already
exists. If it does, the program should warn that continuing

will destroy the current contents of the file and offer a way to exit.

High-Speed Input/Output

Reading and writing to disk files are among the slowest tasks in data processing. Programs that use disk files frequently can benefit from using untyped files, which Turbo Pascal provides for high-speed data transfer. Untyped files can transfer large amounts of data from disk directly into RAM, where it is processed quickly and, if desired, written directly to disk just as fast.

While untyped files make your programs speedier, they require extra work on your part. You must manage input and output buffers yourself, reading in and writing out just the right amount of data at just the right time. This process is illustrated in Figure 10-2, which demonstrates the use of untyped files with a 5-byte buffer. This example uses two files, one for input and one for output. The buffer **b** serves as both an input and output buffer. The program simultaneously reads in five bytes from the input file, which contains lowercase alphabetic characters. It changes the characters to uppercase in the buffer and writes them to the output file.

The contents of the input and output files are shown on the right, along with a file pointer that indicates where the next **BlockRead** and **BlockWrite** statements will execute. Both the input and output file pointers start at the beginning of the file and move forward as **BlockRead** and **BlockWrite** statements are executed.

The **Reset** and **Rewrite** statements contain the number 1 as a second parameter. A second parameter is allowed only for untyped files. It tells Turbo Pascal how many bytes are in each record to be **BlockRead**; in this case, each record consists of one byte.

The **BlockRead** statement uses the number 5 to indicate how many records are to be read. Since the record length is one byte, Turbo Pascal reads in five one-byte records (that is, five bytes). The integer variable **rr** in the **BlockRead** statement indicates how many records are actually read. In the

```
Var
  fin,
  fout : File
  b    : Array [1..5] of Char;
  i,
  rr   : Integer;
  Ch   : Char;
```

Statement	Buffer	Input File	Output File
Rewrite(fout,1) Reset(fin,1);	☐☐☐☐☐	abcdefgh ^ ^	
BlockRead(fin,b,5,rr) (* rr = 5 *)	a b c d e	abcdefgh ^ ^	
For i := 1 to rr do b[i] := Upcase(b[i]);	A B C D E	abcdefgh ^ ^	
BlockWrite(fout,b,rr); (* rr = 5 *)	A B C D E	abcdefgh ^	ABCDE ^
BlockRead(fin,b,5,rr) (* rr = 3 *)	f g h ☐ ☐	abcdefgh ^	ABCDE ^
For i := 1 to rr do b[i] := Upcase(b[i]);	F G H ☐ ☐	abcdefgh ^	ABCDE ^
BlockWrite(fout,b,rr); (* rr = 3 *)	F G H ☐ ☐	abcdefgh ^	ABCDEFGH ^

Figure 10-2.   Using untyped files for buffered input and output

first **BlockRead** statement in Figure 10-2, **rr** is equal to 5, since five records were read. In the second statement, only three bytes are left in the file, so Turbo Pascal reads those three bytes and sets **rr** equal to 3.

Each buffer is written to the output file after it has been processed. The **BlockWrite** statement uses **rr** to indicate how many records to write.

Using Input and Output Buffers

The example in Figure 10-2 is simplistic; the buffer is extremely small, the process is uncomplicated, and only one buffer is needed. In more realistic programs, the buffer will be much larger, the program will perform much more complex functions, and it will usually require separate input and output buffers. The program that follows, which converts a WordStar file to an ASCII text file, demonstrates these complexities.

```
Program WSconv;
Const
  Buflen = 10000;
Var
  INbuf,
  OUTbuf : Array [1..buflen] Of Char;
  rr,
  INptr,
  OUTptr : Integer;
  INfile,
  OUTfile : File;
  Ch : Char;
  quit : Boolean;

(*************************************************)

Function GetNextChar(var Ch : Char): Boolean;
Begin
If INptr > rr Then
  Begin
  BlockRead(INfile,INbuf,Buflen,rr);
  INptr := 1;
  If rr = 0 Then
    Begin
    GetNextChar := False;
    Exit;
    End;
  End;
Ch := INbuf[INptr];
INptr := INptr + 1;
GetNextChar := True;
End;

(*************************************************)
```

```
Procedure SaveChar(ch : Char);
Begin
If OUTptr > Buflen Then
  Begin
  BlockWrite(OUTfile,OUTbuf,OUTptr-1);
  OUTptr := 1;
  End;
OUTbuf[OUTptr] := ch;
OUTptr := OUTptr + 1;
End;


(**************************************************)

Begin
Quit := false;
rr := 0;
INptr := 1;

OUTptr := 1;
Assign(INfile,Paramstr(1));
Reset(INfile,1);

Assign(OUTfile,Paramstr(2));
Rewrite(OUTfile,1);


   Repeat
   If GetNextChar(Ch) Then
     Begin
     If ch > 127 Then
       ch := chr(Ord(ch) And $7F);
     If ((ch >= 32) And (ch <= 127)) Or (ch in [13,10]) Then
       SaveChar(ch);
     End
   Else
     Begin
     quit := true;
     BlockWrite(OUTfile,OUTbuf,OUTptr-1);
     End;
   Until Quit;

Close(INfile);
Close(OUTfile);
End.
```

This program uses two buffers, one for input and one for
output. Both are necessary because each buffer is processed
at a different rate, meaning that the program may get to the
end of the input buffer before reaching the end of the output
buffer. Thus, input and output are processed independently.

Both buffers are 10,000 bytes long, and each has its own pointer to keep track of processing. At the beginning of the program, both the input and output pointers are set to 1. Then, as processing proceeds, each pointer is increased to indicate the current position in each buffer.

When the input buffer pointer reaches the last character in the buffer, it executes a **BlockRead** statement to fill the buffer with new data and sets the pointer back to 1. Likewise, when the output pointer reaches the end of the output buffer, indicating that the buffer is filled, a **BlockWrite** statement is executed and the output pointer is set to 1.

All input and output functions are hidden from the main program by the procedures **GetNextChar** for input and **SaveChar** for output. This is exactly as it should be; buffered input and output should be transparent to the application. Note that **GetNextChar** is a Boolean function that returns False when the end of the file has been reached. This tells the main program when to stop processing.

Merging, Sorting, and Searching

Merging
Sorting Methods
Searching Methods

Some programming tasks are so common that over the years standardized, highly efficient algorithms have been developed to take care of them. Searching, sorting, and merging are three of the most common, turning up in nearly every book on computer programming. While entire books have been devoted to these subjects, this chapter touches on only the most practical algorithms and how they are used in Turbo Pascal.

Merging

Merging files refers to the process by which two ordered files are combined to form one large ordered file. For example, a master file of historical transactions might be updated by merging a file of daily transactions into it. Both files must be ordered in the same way (for example, by date or account number); the updated file then becomes the master file that will be updated the next day.

Of course, you could add the daily file to the end of the historical file and sort the whole thing at one time, but sorting takes far longer than merging.

	File 1	File 2
	1	2
	4	3
	6	7
		9

Step 1:	record 1 = 1	record 2 = 2 → Write record 1
Step 2:	Read a new record 1	
Step 3:	record 1 = 4	record 2 = 2 → Write record 2
Step 4:	Read a new record 2	
Step 5:	record 1 = 4	record 2 = 3 → Write record 2
Step 6:	Read a new record 2	
Step 7:	record 1 = 4	record 2 = 7 → Write record 1
Step 8:	Read a new record 1	
Step 9:	record 1 = 6	record 2 = 7 → Write record 1
Step 10:	Read a new record 1—end of file	
Step 11:	record 1 = EOF	record 2 = 7 → Write record 2
Step 12:	Read a new record 2	
Step 13:	record 1 = EOF	record 2 = 9 → Write record 2
Step 14:	Read a new record 2—end of file	
Step 15:	Both input files are EOF: Procedure ends	

Figure 11-1.   Merging two sorted files

The merge process is straightforward. It starts by reading the first record from each file, after which the program enters a loop. Inside the loop, the program compares the two records and writes the one with the lower value to the newly created file. Another record is then read from the input file.

This process continues until all records in one or both files have been processed. Usually, one of the input files runs out of records before the other. When this occurs, the procedure continues to read records from the remaining file and write them to the newly created file.

This process is illustrated in Figure 11-1, where two input files of integers are merged. File 1 contains three integer records — 1, 4, and 6 — and File 2 contains four integer records — 2, 3, 7, and 9. The procedure reads and compares the first records from File 1 and from File 2. The record from File 1 is then written to the merged file because it is lower in value than the record from File 2.

The procedure then reads a new record from File 1 and compares it to the record already in record 2. Record 1 has a greater value than the value already in record 2. Therefore, record 2 is written to the merged file and another record is read from File 2.

This process continues until the procedure reaches the end of File 1, at which point the procedure reads all the records remaining in File 2 and writes them to the merge file. The procedure ends when it reaches the end of File 2.

While the merge procedure is simple in concept, it is not so simple to express in Turbo Pascal. The major complexity is in determining when a new record is needed from an input file and when an input file is empty. In the following program, input is controlled through two Boolean functions, **GetItem1** and **GetItem2**:

```
Program mergetest;
Type
  Str80 = String[80];

Var
  file1,
  file2,
  file3 : Str80;

(**************************************)

Procedure Merge(fname1,fname2,fname3 : Str80);
Var
  ok1,ok2 : Boolean;
  f1,f2,f3 : Text;
  i1,i2 : Integer;

(**************************************)
```

```
Function GetItem1(var i : Integer) : Boolean;
Begin
If Not Eof(f1) Then
  Begin
  ReadLn(f1,i);
  GetItem1 := True;
  End
Else
  GetItem1 := False;
End;

(************************************)

Function GetItem2(Var i : Integer) : Boolean;
Begin
If Not Eof(f2) Then
  Begin
  ReadLn(f2,i);
  GetItem2 := True;
  End
Else
  GetItem2 := False;
End;

(************************************)

Begin
Assign(f1,fname1);
Reset(f1);
Assign(f2,fname2);
Reset(f2);
Assign(f3,fname3);
Rewrite(f3);

ok1 := GetItem1(i1);
ok2 := GetItem2(i2);

While ok1 Or ok2 Do
  Begin
  (* If ok1 is true, then a record from File 1 is present. *)
  (* If ok2 is true, then a record from File 2 is present. *)

  If ok1 And ok2 Then      (* records are present *)
    Begin                  (* from both files.    *)
    If i1 < i2 Then
      Begin
      WriteLn(f3,i1);
      ok1 := GetItem1(i1);
      End
    Else
      Begin
      WriteLn(f3,i2);
      ok2 := GetItem2(i2);
      End;
```

```
      End
   Else If ok1 Then           (* a record is present from *)
      Begin                   (* the first file only.     *)
      WriteLn(f3,i1);
      ok1 := GetItem1(i1);
      End
   Else If ok2 Then           (* a record is present from *)
      Begin                   (* the second file only.    *)
      WriteLn(f3,i2);
      ok2 := GetItem2(i2);
      End;
   End;

Close(f1);
Close(f2);
Close(f3);
End;

(************************************)

Begin
Clrscr;
Write('Enter name of first file: ');
ReadLn(file1);
Write('Enter name of second file: ');
ReadLn(file2);
Write('Enter name of merged file: ');
ReadLn(file3);
Merge(file1,file2,file3);
End.
```

GetItem1 and **GetItem2** read the next record from their respective files. If successful, they return the value True along with the record read; if unsuccessful (that is, if it reaches the end of the file), they return False. By isolating the input process in these two functions, the structure of the merge procedure is simplified.

When the procedure **Merge** begins, the Boolean variables **ok1** and **ok2** are set with **GetItem1** and **GetItem2**. The loop controlled by the statement

While ok1 Or ok2 Do

executes as long as records are present from either file and terminates when the end is reached for both files.

Three program branches are contained in the While-Do loop. The first is executed when input from both files is present. In this case, the procedure compares the two records, the record with the lower value is written to the merge file, and another record is read in.

The two other branches execute when one of the input files reaches its end. When this occurs, the loop continues to read records from the remaining file and write them to the merged file. When the procedure reaches the end of the remaining file, the input files and the merged file are closed and the procedure ends.

Sorting Methods

Although many sorting algorithms have been developed over the years, three are the most frequently used: the bubble sort, the shell sort, and the quick sort.

The *bubble sort* is easy to write but terribly slow. The *shell sort* is moderately fast but excels in its use of memory resources. The *quick sort*, the fastest of the three, requires extensive stack space for recursive calls. Knowing all three algorithms, and understanding why one is better than another, is important and illustrates the subtleties of good programming.

General Sorting Principles

The sorting algorithms presented in this section compare one element in an array to another, and, if the two elements are out of order, the algorithms switch their order in the array. This process is illustrated in this code segment:

```
If a[i] > a[i+1] then
  begin
  temp := a[i];
```

```
a[i] := a[i+1];
a[i+1] := temp;
end;
```

The first line of code tests if two elements of the array are out of order. Generally, arrays are in order when the current element is smaller than the next element. If the elements are not properly ordered, that is, when the current element is greater than the next element, their order is switched. The switch requires a temporary storage variable of the same type as that of the elements in the array being sorted.

The main difference between the three sorting algorithms is the method in which array elements are selected for comparison. The comparison method has a tremendous impact on the efficiency of the sort. For example, the bubble sort, which compares only adjacent array elements, may require half a million comparisons to sort an array, while the quick sort requires only three or four thousand.

Bubble Sort

To computer programmers, there are good methods, there are bad methods, and there are kludges. A kludge is a method that works, but slowly and inefficiently. The bubble sort is a good example of a kludge: given enough time, it will sort your data, but you might have to wait a day or two.

The bubble-sort algorithm is simple: it starts at the end of the array to be sorted and works toward the beginning of the array. The procedure compares each element to the one preceding it. If the elements are out of order, they are switched. The procedure continues until it reaches the beginning of the array.

Because the sort works backward through the array, comparing each adjacent pair of elements, the lowest element will always "float" to the top after the first pass. After the second pass, the second lowest element will "float" to the second position in the array, and so on, until the algorithm has passed through the array once for every element in the array.

This code shows this process in Turbo Pascal:

```
For i := 2 To n Do
For j := n Downto i Do
  If a[j-1] > a[j] Then
    Switch(a[j],a[j-1]);
```

As you can see, the bubble-sort algorithm is compact; in fact, it is a single Turbo Pascal statement. The bubble sort receives two inputs: **a**, the array to be sorted, and **n**, the number of elements in the array. The inside loop, controlled by the statement

For j := n Downto i Do

performs all the comparisons in each pass through the array. The outside loop, controlled by the statement

For i := 2 To n Do

determines the number of passes to execute. Notice that **j** executes from the end of the array **(n)** to **i** and that **i** decreases after every pass. Thus, each pass through the array becomes shorter as the bubble sort executes.

An example of how the bubble sort works is shown in Figure 11-2. An array of 10 integers is sorted in order of increasing value. The elements of the array are listed at the end of each pass. A pass consists of one complete execution of the inside For-Do loop.

The order of the original array is shown in the row labeled "Start." The values range from 0 to 92 and they are distributed randomly throughout the array. The first pass through the array places the lowest value (0) in the first position in the array, and the number 91 is shifted from the first position into the second position. The other elements are still more or less randomly scattered.

With each step of the bubble sort, the next lowest number takes its proper place in the array and the higher numbers get shifted to the right. By the end of the seventh pass, the array is completely sorted, yet the sort continues to make two more passes over the array.

Pass	Position in Array									
	1	2	3	4	5	6	7	8	9	10
Start:	91	6	59	0	75	0	48	92	30	83
1	0	91	6	59	0	75	30	48	92	83
2	0	0	91	6	59	30	75	48	83	92
3	0	0	6	91	30	59	48	75	83	92
4	0	0	6	30	91	48	59	75	83	92
5	0	0	6	30	48	91	59	75	83	92
6	0	0	6	30	48	59	91	75	83	92
7	0	0	6	30	48	59	75	91	83	92
8	0	0	6	30	48	59	75	83	91	92
9	0	0	6	30	48	59	75	83	91	92

Figure 11-2.   Sorting an array of integers with the bubble-sort algorithm

The following program contains the bubble-sort algorithm, which takes an integer array and the number of elements in the array as parameters:

```
Program BubbleTest;
Type
   Int_Arr = Array [1..10] Of Integer;
Var
   i : Integer;
   a : Int_Arr;

(*****************************)
```

```
Procedure bubble(Var a : Int_Arr; n : Integer);
Var
   i,j : Integer;

(****************************)

Procedure Switch(Var a,b : Integer);
Var
   c : Integer;
Begin
c := a;
a := b;
b := c;
End;

(*****************************)

Begin
For i := 2 To n Do
For j := n Downto i Do
   If a[j-1] > a[j] Then
      Switch(a[j],a[j-1]);
End;

(*****************************)

Begin
For i := 1 To 10 Do
   Begin
   a[i] := Random(100);
   Write(a[i]:4);
   End;
WriteLn;

bubble(a,10);

For i := 1 To 10 Do
   Write(a[i]:4);
WriteLn;
End.
```

The program begins by assigning random values to array **a**, and displays the values on your terminal. The procedure **Bubble** sorts the array. When the sort is finished, the array is displayed again.

The weakness of the bubble sort is that it compares only adjacent array elements. If the sorting algorithm first compared elements separated by a wide interval, and then focused on progressively smaller intervals, the process would be more efficient. This train of thought led to the development of the shell-sort and quick-sort algorithms.

Shell Sort

The shell sort is far more efficient than the bubble sort. It first puts elements approximately where they will be in the final order and determines their exact placement later. The strength of the algorithm lies in the method it uses to estimate an element's approximate final position.

The key concept in the shell sort is the *gap*, which is the distance between the elements compared. If the gap is 5, the first element is compared with the sixth element, the second with the seventh, and so on. In a single pass through the array, all elements within the gap are put in order. For example, the elements in this array are in order given a gap of 2:

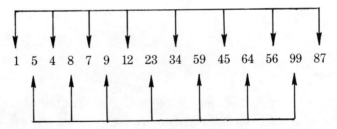

As you can see, the array is nearly completely sorted before the algorithm tests adjacent elements. In the next pass over this array, the gap is reduced to one, which results in a completely sorted array. The initial value of the gap is arbitrary, although it is common to set it to one half the number of elements in the array (that is, **n div 2**).

The many versions of the shell sort vary in complexity and efficiency. The version presented in this chapter is extremely efficient, requiring few passes to complete the sort.

Unfortunately, there is no simple way to describe how this particular shell algorithm works. Efficient algorithms tend to be more complex than inefficient ones and are there-

```
gap := n div 2;
  While (gap > 0) Do
     Begin
     For i := (gap + 1) To n Do
        Begin
        j := i - gap;
        While (j > 0) Do
           Begin
           k := j + gap;
           If (a[j] <= a[k]) Then
              j := 0
           Else
              Switch(a[j],a[k]);
           j := j - gap;
           End;
        End;

     gap := gap Div 2;
     End;
```

Outside loop

Inside loop

Figure 11-3.   The main loops in the shell-sort algorithm

fore harder to express in words. This is why poor algorithms are used so often. Figure 11-3 contains the essential code for the shell-sort algorithm. Review this code as you read the explanation.

The first line in the procedure sets the gap to **n div 2**. The outside loop in the shell sort, controlled by the statement

While (gap > 0) Do

determines the number of passes made through the array. After each pass through the array, the gap is reduced by half for each pass until the gap reaches 0. For example, if there were ten elements in the array, the first gap would be 5, followed by 2, 1, and 0. Because integer division is used, **1 div 2** results in 0.

In each pass, three variables determine which elements to compare: **i**, **j**, and **k**. The variable **i** points to the far element and **j** points to the near element. For example, if the **gap** is 5, **i** would equal 5 and **j** would equal 1. Before the comparison, **k** is set equal to **j** + **gap**, which, for the first comparison, equals **i**.

The comparison uses **k** instead of **i** because it may be necessary to backtrack through the array. To backtrack, **j** is reduced by **gap** and **k** is also changed so that a new pair of elements is compared. Because **i** controls the inside loop, it should not be changed in this backtracking process.

Consider the example in Figure 11-4 where a ten-element array is being sorted. At step 1, **gap** is 2, **j** is equal to 6, and **k** is equal to 8. Thus, the sixth and eighth elements

				Position in Array						
	1	2	3	4	5	6	7	8	9	10
Step 1:	19	9	32	63	86	85	87	49	35	86
						^		^		
						j		k		
Step 2:	19	9	32	63	86	49	87	85	35	86
				^		^				
				j		k				
Step 3:	19	9	32	49	86	63	87	85	35	86
		^		^						
		j		k						
Step 4:	19	9	32	49	86	63	87	85	35	86
							^		^	
							j		k	

Figure 11-4.   Sorting an array of integers with the shell-sort algorithm

in the array will be compared. Since element 6 is 85 and element 8 is 49, the two must be switched, as is shown in step 2.

Next, the algorithm sets **j** equal to **j** − **gap**, in this case **4**. Since **J** is greater than zero, the inside loop executes again. Because **j** has been reduced by 2, the fourth and sixth elements are compared. Again, the elements are out of order and need to be switched. As before, **j** is set to **j** − **gap**, or 2, leading to step 3.

Elements 2 and 4 of the array are in the correct order, so rather than switching the elements, the program sets **j** to zero. Now, the result of **j** − **gap** is negative 2. Since this is less than zero, the inner loop is terminated and **i** is incremented. Working downward, **j** is set to **i** − **gap**, or 7, and **k** is set equal to **j** + **gap**, or 9.

In short, **i** keeps track of the overall flow of the algorithm, while **k** backtracks when necessary. This tricky little bit of logic increases the efficiency by about 300 percent over the most simple shell sort.

The following sample program includes the procedure **Shell**, which contains the shell-sort algorithm.

```
Program ShellTest;
Type
   Int_Arr = Array [1..10] of Integer;
Var
   i : Integer;
   a : Int_Arr;

(*****************************)

Procedure shell(var a : Int_arr;
                    n : integer);
Var
   gap,i,j,k : integer;

(*****************************)

Procedure Switch(var a,b : Integer);
Var
   c : Integer;
Begin
c := a;
```

```
a := b;
b := c;
End;

(****************************)

begin
gap := n div 2;
While (gap > 0) Do
  Begin
  For i := (gap + 1) To n Do
    Begin
    j := i - gap;
    While (j > 0) Do
      Begin
      k := j + gap;
      If (a[j] <= a[k]) Then
        j := 0
      Else
        Switch(a[j],a[k]);
      j := j - gap;
      End;
    End;

  gap := gap Div 2;
  End;
End;

(*********************)

Begin
For i := 1 To 10 Do
  Begin
  a[i] := Random(100);
  Write(a[i]:4);
  End;
WriteLn;

shell(a,10);

For i := 1 To 10 Do
  Write(a[i]:4);
WriteLn;
end.
```

Shell accepts the array to be sorted, including the number of elements in the array, then returns the array in its sorted form. If you test this program against the bubble sort with an array of 1000 elements, you will see an amazing difference in the time required to sort the array. Yet as efficient as the shell sort is, the quick sort is two or three times as efficient.

Quick Sort

The queen of all sorting algorithms is the quick sort: this algorithm is widely accepted as the fastest general-purpose sort available.

One of the pleasing aspects of the quick sort is that it sorts things much the same way people do. It first creates large "piles," then sorts those small piles into smaller and smaller piles, eventually ending up with a completely sorted array.

The quick-sort algorithm begins by estimating a mid-range value for the array. If the array consists of numbers 1 through 10, the midpoint could be 5 or 6. The midpoint's exact value is not crucial; the algorithm will work with a midpoint of any value. However, the closer the estimated midpoint is to the true midpoint of the array, the faster the sort will be.

The procedure calculates a midpoint by averaging the first and last elements in the portion of the array being sorted. Once the procedure selects a midpoint, it puts all the elements lower than the midpoint in the lower part of the array, and all the elements higher in the upper part. This is illustrated in Figure 11-5.

In step 1, the midpoint is 55, which is the average of 86 and 24. In step 2, the segment being sorted is 24 through 47, leading to a midpoint of 35. Notice that the elements in the segment rarely split evenly around the midpoint. This does not harm the algorithm, but does decrease its efficiency somewhat.

At each step in the process, the quick sort orders the elements of an array segment around the midpoint value. As the segments get smaller and smaller, the array approaches the completely sorted order.

Mid-Point	\multicolumn{10}{c}{Position in Array}

Mid-Point	1	2	3	4	5	6	7	8	9	10
Step 1: 55	86	3	10	23	12	67	59	47	31	24
Step 2: 35	24	3	10	23	12	31	47	59	67	86
Step 3: 27	24	3	10	23	12	31	47	59	67	86
Step 4: 18	24	3	10	23	12	31	47	59	67	86
Step 5: 11	12	3	10	23	24	31	47	59	67	86
Step 6: 6	10	3	12	23	24	31	47	59	67	86
Step 7: 23	3	10	12	23	24	31	47	59	67	86
Step 8: 72	3	10	12	23	24	31	47	59	67	86
Step 9: 63	3	10	12	23	24	31	47	59	67	86
Final order:	3	10	12	23	24	31	47	59	67	86

Figure 11-5.   The quick-sort algorithm

In this program, the procedure **Quick** contains the quick-sort algorithm:

```
Program quickTest;
Type
   Int_Arr = Array [1..10] of Integer;
Var
   infile : text;
   i : Integer;
   a : Int_Arr;


(******************************)

Procedure Quick(Var item : Int_Arr; count : integer);

Procedure PartialSort(left,right : integer; var a: Int_Arr);
Var
   ii,
```

```
  l1,r1,
  i,j,k : Integer;

(*****************************)

Procedure Switch(Var a,b : Integer);
Var
  c : Integer;
Begin
c := a;
a := b;
b := c;
End;


(*****************************)

Begin
k := (a[left] + a[right]) div 2;
i := left;
j := right;

  Repeat

  While a[i] < k do
    i := i + 1;

  While k < a[j] do
    j := j - 1;

  If i <= j Then
    begin
    switch(a[i],a[j]);
    i := i + 1;
    j := j - 1;
    end;
  Until i > j;

 if left < j then
   PartialSort(left,j,a);
 if i < right then
   PartialSort(i,right,a);
End;


(*********************)

Begin
PartialSort(1,count,item);
end;
```

```
(**********************)

begin
for i := 1 to 10 do
  begin
  a[i] := random(100);
  write(a[i]:4);
  end;
writeln;

quick(a,10);

for i := 1 to 10 do
  write(a[i]:4);
writeln;
end.
```

The procedure begins by calling the subprocedure **PartialSort**, which takes three parameters: the lower bound of the array segment, the upper bound, and the array itself. When first called, the lower bound passed to **PartialSort** is 1, and the upper bound is the number of elements in the array.

PartialSort computes a midpoint and orders the elements in the array segment accordingly. It then calls itself by passing new lower and upper boundaries, thereby focusing on progressively smaller segments of the array. When it reaches the lowest level of the array, the recursion ends and the procedure passes the sorted array back to the program.

Comparing Sorting Algorithms

The number of comparisons required to sort a list is the universal measure by which all sorting algorithms are judged. The number of comparisons is expressed as a multiple of the number of elements in the list. For example, if you are sorting an array of **n** elements with the bubble sort, the program will have to perform **$1/2(n^2-n)$ comparisons**. If **n** is 100, the number of comparisons is 4950.

This benchmark is fine for those with a theoretical bent, but most programmers find it easier to compare sorting methods by measuring the amount of time it takes for each method to sort the same array. Table 11-1 shows the results of tests performed using the bubble-sort, shell-sort, and quick-sort algorithms on arrays with 100, 500, and 1000 random numbers. As the table shows, the bubble sort is a poor algorithm compared to the shell and quick sorts, taking from 6 to 68 times as long to sort an array. Between the shell sort and quick sort, the difference in time is also significant. The shell sort takes twice as long as the quick sort and requires nearly four times as many comparisons.

The only drawback to the quick sort is the amount of space it requires on the stack. Because quick sort is a recursive procedure, space on the stack must be allocated every time the procedure calls itself. If you are concerned about stack space, you might want to use the shell sort: otherwise, use the quick sort.

	Bubble		**Shell**		**Quick**	
N	*Time*	*Comparisons*	*Time*	*Comparisons*	*Time*	*Comparisons*
100	0.66	4,950	0.11	849	0.06	232
500	15.88	124,750	0.77	5,682	0.44	1473
1000	63.66	499,500	1.87	13,437	0.93	3254

Table 11-1.   Relative efficiency of different sorting methods

Searching Methods

In programming, *searching* means finding a particular item within a group of items, for example, finding a particular integer in an array of integers, finding a person's name in an array of strings, and so forth. The two methods of searching presented here, sequential and binary, accomplish the same end with different means.

Sequential Search

The *sequential search* is so simple it practically needs no explanation. The program simply starts at the beginning of the array to be searched and compares each element with the value you are searching for. The process of finding the number 10 in an array of integers is shown in Figure 11-6.

Variable x equals 10:

Index	Array	Comparison	Result
1	3	x = 3?	False
2	21	x = 21?	False
3	4	x = 4?	False
4	10	x = 10?	True
5	55		
6	31		
7	9		
8	12		
9	15		Exit from search: Return index value 4

Figure 11-6.   Locating a number with a sequential search

The search compares **x**, which is equal to 10, to the first element, then the second, and so on. As soon as the value finds a match in the array, it exits from the search process and returns the index of the element found, which in this example is 4.

The following program includes the function **SeqSearch**, which takes three parameters: the value to search for, the array to search through, and the number of elements in the array.

```
Program SequentialSearch;
Type
   Int_Arr = Array [1..100] of Integer;

Var
  a : Int_Arr;
  i,j : Integer;

(*****************************)

Function SeqSearch(x : Integer; a : Int_Arr; n : Integer) : Integer;
Var
  i : Integer;
Begin
for i := 1 to n do
if x = a[i] then
  Begin
  SeqSearch := i;
  Exit;
  End;
SeqSearch := 0;
End;

(*****************************)

Begin
for i := 1 to 100 do
  a[i] := random(100);

  Repeat
  Write('Enter a number to search for: ');
  ReadLn(i);
  j := Seqsearch(i,a,100);
  if j = 0 then
```

```
   WriteLn('Number not in list.')
 else
   WriteLn(i,' is element number ',j);
 WriteLn;
 Until i = 0;
End.
```

When **SeqSearch** finds a matching value, it assigns the value to the function and exits. Because a sequential search processes the array element by element, the order of the list is unimportant—the search works equally well with random lists as with sorted lists.

Binary Search

The *binary search* is one of the most efficient searching methods known and a big improvement over the sequential search. With an array of 100 elements, for example, a sequential search requires an average of 50 comparisons to find a match; the binary search requires at most seven comparisons and as few as four to accomplish the same goal. As the list gets longer, the relative efficiency of the binary search increases.

To perform a binary search, a list must be in sorted order. The search begins by testing the target element against the middle element in the array. If the target element is higher than the middle element, the search continues in the upper half of the list; if the target value is lower than the middle element, the target element is in the lower half.

The binary search process is illustrated in Figure 11-7. The array is searched for the target value 10. The fifth element, which is equal to 12, is tested first. Since 10 is less than 12, the target value must be in the lower half of the array.

```
Variable x equals 10:
```

Index	Array	Comparison	Result
1	3		
2	4	2	Higher
3	9	3	Higher
4	10	4	Equal
5	12	1	Lower
6	15		
7	21		
8	31		
9	55		

Figure 11-7.   Searching a sorted array with the binary search algorithm

The algorithm, therefore, selects the element 2—midway between 1 and 4. The value of the second element is 4 (less than 10). The algorithm knows the target value must lie between 3 and 4. First, the algorithm tests element 3 and fails. This leaves element 4, which is equal to 10. The binary search now ends, returning a value of 4. Had element 4 been equal to 11, no match would have been found and the function would have returned a zero.

Because the array in Figure 11-7 is so small, the benefit of the binary search is not fully illustrated. For example, a sequential search of a 1000-element array requires 500 comparisons on average, whereas a binary search requires between 5 and 10 comparisons.

The following program uses the function **Bsearch** to perform a binary search on an array of integers:

```
Program BinarySearch;
Type
  Int_Arr = Array [1..100] of Integer;

Var
  a : Int_Arr;
  i,j : Integer;
```

```
(*****************************)
(*$i quick.inc*)
(*****************************)

Function Bsearch(x : Integer; a : Int_Arr; n : Integer) : Integer;
var
   high, low, mid : integer;
Begin

low := 1;
high := n;
While high >= low Do
  Begin
  mid := trunc((high+low) div 2);
  if x > a[mid] then
    low := mid + 1
  else if x < a[mid] then
    high := mid - 1
  else
    high := -1;
  End;
if high = -1 then
  Bsearch := mid
else
  Bsearch := 0;
End;

(*****************************)

Begin
j := 2;
for i := 1 to 100 do
  a[i] := random(100);

Quick(a,100);

  Repeat
  Write('Enter a number to search for: ');
  ReadLn(i);
  j := Bsearch(i,a,100);
  if j = 0 then
    WriteLn('Number not in list.')
  else
    WriteLn(i,' is element number ',j);
  WriteLn;
  Until i = 0;

End.
```

The program calls for an include file with **(*$i quick. inc*)**, which holds the quick sort procedure described earlier in this chapter. The Binary Search program also illustrates the correct sequence. Notice that the **Quick** sort procedure is executed before the binary search function is executed.

The main code of the binary search algorithm, contained in the function **Bsearch**, is shown below:

```
low := 1;
high := n;
While high >= low Do
  Begin
  mid := trunc((high+low) div 2);
  if x > a[mid] then
    low := mid + 1
  else if x < a[mid] then
    high := mid - 1
  else
    high := -1;
  End;
if high = -1 then
  Bsearch := mid
else
  Bsearch := 0;
```

The variables **low** and **high** keep track of the portion of the array being searched. At the beginning, the program sets **low** equal to **1** and **high** equal to **n**, the number of elements in the array. Thus, the algorithm begins with the entire array.

The binary search loop is controlled by the statement

While high $>=$ low Do

Each time the loop executes, either **high** is decremented or **low** is incremented by 1, bringing the two variables closer to each other. If **low** becomes greater than **high**, the element you are searching for does not exist in the sorted array and **Bsearch** returns zero.

If, at any point, **a[mid]** is equal to the value you are searching for, the program sets **high** equal to -1, causing the loop to terminate and the function to return the value of **mid**.

DOS and BIOS Functions

The 8088 Registers
The Register Set
Disk-Drive Services
Video Services
Time and Date Functions
Report Shift Status
DOS and Bios Services in Turbo Pascal
　　Version 4.0
Procedures and Functions in the DOS Unit

Your PC consists of various physical devices: a keyboard, a monitor, disk drives, a printer, and so on. The *Disk Operating System* (DOS) and *Basic Input Output System* (BIOS) control these devices, making sure data comes and goes to the right place without errors.

　　Turbo Pascal allows access to many DOS and BIOS services through standard procedures, such as **WriteLn**, **Reset**, and **Chdir**. For example, when Turbo Pascal opens a file, displays something on the screen, or uses a physical device in any way, DOS and BIOS are doing all the work. But many useful DOS and BIOS services can be accessed only by using Turbo Pascal's more general commands: **MSdos** for DOS services and **Intr** for BIOS services. To use these commands, you must understand something about the internal workings of the microprocessor and how DOS and BIOS services are called.

The 8088 Registers

The 8088 family of microprocessors (which includes the 8086 and 80286) contains a standard set of 14 *registers*, or memory locations, that computers use to execute commands. Each register is 16 bits long, which is why the 8088 is called a 16-bit computer. In Turbo Pascal, a 16-bit chunk of memory is known as a *word*. The 8088's registers are shown in Figure 12-1.

The first four registers — AX, BX, CX, and DX — are general-purpose areas that temporarily store data used in computations, comparisons, and other operations. Assembly-language programmers use these registers in the same way Pascal programmers use variables. Each of the general-purpose registers is divided into two one-byte registers; thus AX consists of AH and AL. These general registers, which can function separately or as a unit, are the registers most commonly used to call DOS and BIOS services.

The 8088's standard locations also include four segment registers: CS, DS, SS, and ES. CS stores the program's segment, DS contains the data segment, SS holds the stack segment, and ES holds temporary segments for special operations. The CS and SS registers hold critical data that are changed only at great risk to the program's integrity. Therefore, Turbo Pascal does not allow you to access these registers for DOS or BIOS calls, but DS and ES are used occasionally to pass segment addresses.

A memory address consists of a segment and an offset. There are five offset registers: IP, SP, BP, SI, and DI. They are used in conjunction with the segment registers to address specific locations in memory. Turbo Pascal allows access only to SI, DI, and BP; IP and SP are never used in DOS or BIOS calls.

Finally, the Flags register contains information about the success of an operation. Each bit in the flag indicates a specific condition that results from CPU operations. While it can be used in Turbo Pascal, the Flags register is generally not necessary for DOS and BIOS calls as they usually return error codes in one of the general registers.

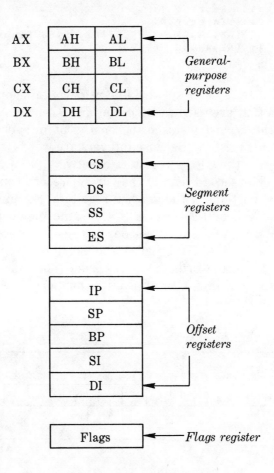

Figure 12-1.   The 8088 CPU registers

The Register Set

Both the **MSdos** and **Intr** procedures accept a special parameter known as a *register set*. A *register-set variable* is a variant record that contains ten integers, each integer representing a register, as shown here:

```
Var
  regs : Record
    Case Integer Of
    0: (AX,BX,CX,DX,BP,SI,DI,DS,ES,Flags : Integer);
    1: (AL,AH,BL,BH,CL,CH,DL,DH : Byte);
    End;
```

The register-set variable **regs** contains only those registers that are used in BIOS and DOS services. The first part of the record just shown consists of integers representing whole registers. Because integers are words (two bytes long), they fit the CPU's registers exactly.

The second part of the variant record contains the byte-level portions of the general registers. For example, the two bytes AL and AH refer to the same memory location that contains AX. The low-order byte (AL) precedes the high-order byte (AH) because the 8088 microprocessor stores bytes within words in reverse order. Therefore, if the integer 1 is stored in AX, it appears in memory as follows:

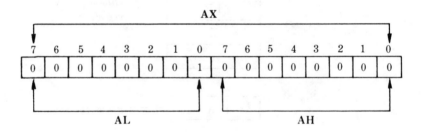

Before you can call **MSdos** or **Intr**, you must set the register-set variable to specific values that tell the computer which service you want and how you want to execute it. For example, to select a DOS service, place the code for the service in the AH register. DOS service **2Bh**, which sets the system date, is shown here:

```
Fillchar(regs,Sizeof(regs),0);
With regs Do
  Begin
  AH := $2B;
```

```
  DH := 12;    (* month *)
  DL := 31;    (* date *)
  CX := 1987;  (* year: four digits required *)
  End;
MSdos(regs);
Error := regs.AL <> 0;
```

The procedure first initializes the register set to zero with the statement

Fillchar(regs,Sizeof(regs),0)

and then puts **2Bh**, the code for setting the system date, in AH. Next, registers DH, DL, and CX store date information.

MSdos accepts the register-set variable as a parameter, updates the system date to December 31, 1987, and returns the register set with a status code in AL. The statement

Error := regs.AL <> 0

checks this code; if it is not equal to zero, an error occurs.

BIOS services are called with the **Intr** procedure, which accepts two variables: the interrupt number and the register-set variable. For example, the BIOS call that prints the contents of a screen is invoked by setting register AH to 5 and calling interrupt 5, as follows:

```
Fillchar(regs,Sizeof(regs),0);
regs.AH := 5;
Intr(5,regs);
```

Interrupt 5 can be used for many things, but setting AH equal to 5 specifies the print-screen service. In this case, no error indicator is returned in the register set.

The use of DOS and BIOS services greatly increases what you can do with Turbo Pascal, but learning to use them properly takes some time. The remainder of this chapter deals with procedures that incorporate the most useful of the DOS and BIOS services and serve as examples of how to use them. If you are interested in learning more about these and other services, and the 8088 microprocessor in general, I recommend *Programmer's Guide to the IBM PC* (Peter Norton. Bellevue, Washington: Microsoft Press, 1985).

Disk-Drive Services

The main purpose of the Disk Operating System is to manage your computer's disk drives and files. Fortunately, Turbo Pascal's standard procedures take care of the most difficult disk-related tasks, such as reading and writing files. This section presents several DOS functions not supported by Turbo Pascal that can improve your programs.

Report Free Disk Space

DOS service 36h indicates how much space is available on a disk. The DL register selects the disk to check; 0 indicates the default drive, 1 indicates drive A, 2 indicates drive B, and so on. After **MSdos** is called, the general-purpose registers contain the following information:

AX	Sectors per allocation cluster
BX	Number of unused clusters
CX	Bytes per sector
DX	Total number of clusters

Using these values, you can easily calculate the total amount of free disk space with the equation $1.0 \times AX \times BX \times CX$. (The 1.0 in the equation is necessary to avoid integer overflow.) If an invalid drive is specified, Turbo Pascal returns FFFFh in AX.

The function **FreeDiskSpace**, shown here, reports the number of free bytes for a drive:

```
Function FreeDiskSpace(drive : Char) : Real;
Var
  regs : Record
    Case Integer Of
```

```
   0: (AX,BX,CX,DX,BP,SI,DI,DS,ES,Flags : Integer);
   1: (AL,AH,BL,BH,CL,CH,DL,DH : Byte);
   End;

Begin
Fillchar(regs,Sizeof(regs),0);

With regs Do
  Begin
  AH := $36;
  DL := Ord(Upcase(drive)) - 64;
  End;

MSdos(regs);

if regs.AX  = $FFFF then
  FreeDiskSpace := -1.0
Else With regs Do
  FreeDiskSpace := 1.0*AX*BX*CX;
End;
```

The parameter in the preceding procedure is a character that indicates which drive to check. To assign the drive number to DL, the procedure changes the parameter **drive** to uppercase, converts it into its ASCII value, and subtracts 64. If drive is equal to **a**, it is changed to **A**, which has an ASCII value of 65. Subtracting 64 from 65 gives 1, which is the correct drive number for DL.

After **MSdos** is called, the procedure checks the AX register. If AX contains FFFFh, an error occurred during the procedure and the function returns the value −1. If no error is indicated, the function computes the amount of free disk space.

Get and Set File Attributes

Disk files can have any of six attributes provided by DOS: *read-only, hidden, system, volume label, subdirectory,* and *archive.* File attributes are contained in a single byte, with individual attributes controlled by bits.

Bit 1 in the attribute byte represents a file's read-only status. Read-only files cannot be changed in any way. DOS blocks any attempt to write over or erase read-only files, just as a write-protect tab protects a diskette. DOS does allow read-only files to be used for input, but Turbo Pascal does not. In fact, if you attempt to reset a read-only file, Turbo Pascal generates I/O error 1, which means that the file does not exist.

Bit 2 tells you if a file is hidden or not. Hidden files, which often contain sensitive information, are ignored by DOS: they are not listed by the **Dir** command, they cannot be erased or displayed, and so forth. As a result, hidden files are invisible unless the user has a program that can find them. While DOS does not acknowledge hidden files, Turbo Pascal allows them to be used for input or output.

Bit 3 controls the system attribute. System files, like hidden files, are not acknowledged by DOS commands. The system attribute, however, has no real role and is merely a carryover from CP/M.

Bit 4 in the attribute byte toggles the volume label, which is a statement that identifies a diskette or hard disk. This is an option set by the user when a disk is formatted.

Bit 5 in the attribute byte indicates that the file is a sub-directory. DOS uses subdirectory files, which contain no data, to keep track of directories and subdirectories.

Bit 6, the archive attribute bit, is turned on when a file is first created. The bit is turned off when the file is copied with the DOS **Backup** command, and it remains off until the file's contents are changed. The archive bit allows you to back up only those files that have changed since the previous backup. Bits 7 and 8 of the attribute byte are not used.

To find what attributes a file has, or to set the attributes you want, use DOS service **43h**. The value in register AL controls which action to execute: 0 to report a file's attributes; 1 to set a file's attributes.

When you report a file's attributes, service **43h** returns the attribute byte in register CL. By testing the individual bits, you can determine the status of each attribute. When setting a file's attributes, you must create an attribute byte and place it in CL prior to calling **MSdos**.

Whether setting or reporting a file's attribute byte, you must load the register set DS:DX with the segment and offset of an *ASCIIZ string* that contains the filename. An ASCIIZ string is an array of letters terminated by a binary zero. You can use a Turbo Pascal string as an ASCIIZ string by adding #0 to it. Turbo Pascal strings, however, have a length byte, while ASCIIZ strings do not. Therefore, you must add one to the offset of the string to use it as an ASCIIZ string.

In the following procedure, DOS service **43h** sets six Boolean parameters, one for each possible file attribute:

```
Procedure GetFileAttributes(filename : MaxStr;
                        Var RO,
                            Hidden,
                            System,
                            Vol,
                            SubDir,
                            Arch,
                            Error : Boolean);
Var
  regs : Record
    Case Integer Of
    0: (AX,BX,CX,DX,BP,SI,DI,DS,ES,Flags : Integer);
    1: (AL,AH,BL,BH,CL,CH,DL,DH : Byte);
    End;

Begin
Fillchar(regs,Sizeof(regs),0);

filename := filename + #0;

With regs Do
  Begin
  AH := $43;
  DS := Seg(filename);
  DX := Ofs(filename)+1;
  End;

MSdos(regs);

Error    := (regs.AL = 2) or (regs.AL = 3) or (regs.AL = 5);
RO       := (regs.CL And $1) > 0;
Hidden   := (regs.CL And $2) > 0;
System   := (regs.CL And $4) > 0;
Vol      := (regs.CL And $8) > 0;
SubDir   := (regs.CL And $10) > 0;
Arch     := (regs.CL And $20) > 0;
End;
```

DOS service **43h** reports error conditions when the file is not found (AL register is 2), the path is not found (AL is 3), or access to the file is denied (AL is 5).

The following procedure sets a file's attribute byte. The procedure accepts four Boolean parameters for four file attributes. It does not include the volume-label and subdirectory attributes, since they cannot be set by this DOS service.

```
Procedure SetFileAttributes(filename : MaxStr;
                            Var RO,
                                Hidden,
                                System,
                                Arch,
                                error : Boolean);
Var
  regs : Record
    Case Integer Of
    0: (AX,BX,CX,DX,BP,SI,DI,DS,ES,Flags : Integer);
    1: (AL,AH,BL,BH,CL,CH,DL,DH : Byte);
    End;

Begin
filename := filename + #0;
Fillchar(regs,Sizeof(regs),0);

With regs Do
  Begin
  AH := $43;
  AL := 1;
  DS := Seg(filename);
  DX := Ofs(filename)+1;
  End;

If RO Then
  regs.CL := (regs.CL or $1);
If Hidden Then
  regs.CL := (regs.CL or $2);
If System Then
  regs.CL := (regs.CL or $4);
If Arch Then
  regs.CL := (regs.CL or $20);

MSdos(regs);

Error   := (regs.AL = 2) or (regs.AL = 3) or (regs.AL = 5);
end;
```

It is useful to change a file's attributes to hide files that you want to keep secret or to reveal files that are already hidden or are set to read-only status.

Directory Listing

Displaying a disk directory requires three different DOS services and an understanding of the program segment

Description	Offset	Length
Data used by DOS	0	21
File attribute	21	1
Time stamp of file	22	2
Date stamp of file	24	2
File size in bytes	26	4
Filename and extension	30	13

Table 12-1.   Contents of DTA for a directory listing

prefix (PSP) and the disk-transfer area (DTA), which is a part of the PSP.

When a program starts, DOS sets aside the first 256 bytes of memory for its PSP. Because it contains highly technical information, the PSP is normally never touched by the programmer, except for the DTA portion. The DTA is a 128-byte default buffer used for certain DOS operations, such as reading a disk directory, in which case the DTA contains the information shown in Table 12-1.

The filename and its extension constitute the last field in the DTA. The file attribute, time, date, and file size can be read and translated for a more complete directory listing.

Before obtaining information from the DTA, you must know its address, which is reported by DOS service **2Fh**. When executed, service **2Fh** places the DTA segment in ES and the DTA offset in BX, as shown here:

```
regs.AH := $2F;
MSDos(regs);
DTAseg := regs.ES;
DTAofs := regs.BX;
```

The preceding program segment stores the DTA segment in the variable **DTAseg** and the offset in **DTAofs**. These variables are used with the Turbo Pascal standard array **Mem** to extract information from the DTA. For example,

Mem[DTAseg:DTAofs+21]

points to the location of the file-attribute byte in the DTA.

The DOS function **4Eh** searches for the first matching file in the directory and fills the DTA with the file's information. Before **4Eh** is called, however, the registers DS and DX must contain the segment and offset of an ASCIIZ string with the path and filename. This is shown in the following code segment:

```
mask_in := mask_in + #0;
With regs Do
  Begin
  AH := $4E;
  DS := Seg(Mask_in);
  DX := Ofs(Mask_in)+1;
  CL := $00;
  End;

MSDos(regs);
writeln(regs.AL);
If regs.AL <> 0 Then Exit;
```

The CL register tells DOS what type of file it should include in its search. If the register is set to zero, DOS locates only standard files. To include hidden or system files in the directory listing, set AL to a value according to the guidelines in Table 12-2.

Attribute to Include	Value of CL
Hidden	$02
System	$04
Volume label	$08
Subdirectory	$10

Table 12-2. Setting DOS file attributes with the CL register

If CL is set to 16h (the sum of 2h, 4h, and 10h), hidden files, system files, and subdirectories will be included in the directory listing. If the AL register returns with a nonzero value, no file entries matching the file spec were found in the directory.

The program **Directory** uses the procedure **DirList** to create an array of filenames for a file spec entered by the user:

```
Program Directory;
Type
  MaxStr = String[255];
  dir_files = Array [1..200] of String[13];
Var
  FileSpec : MaxStr;
  Files : dir_files;
  i,j : Integer;

(*********************************************)

Procedure DirList(     mask_in       : MaxStr;
                   Var name_list     : dir_files;
                   Var file_counter  : Integer);

Var

  i : Byte;
  regs : Record
    Case Integer Of
    0: (AX,BX,CX,DX,BP,SI,DI,DS,ES,Flags : Integer);
    1: (AL,AH,BL,BH,CL,CH,DL,DH : Byte);
    End;

  DTAseg,
  DTAofs     : Integer;

  FileName  : String[20];

Begin
Fillchar(regs,Sizeof(regs),0);
file_counter := 0;

regs.AH := $2F;
MSDos(regs);
DTAseg := regs.ES;
DTAofs := regs.BX;


Fillchar(regs,Sizeof(regs),0);
```

```
      Mask_in := mask_in + #0;
      With regs Do
        Begin
        AH := $4E;
        DS := Seg(Mask_in);
        DX := Ofs(Mask_in)+1;
        CL := $00;
        End;

    MSDos(regs);

    If regs.AL <> 0 Then Exit;

    i := 1;
    repeat
    FileName[i] := Chr(Mem[DTAseg:DTAofs+29+i]);
    i := i + 1;
    until (FileName[i-1] < 32) Or (i > 12);

FileName[0] := Chr(i-1);
file_counter := 1;
name_list[file_counter] := FileName;

    Repeat
    Fillchar(regs,Sizeof(regs),0);
    With regs Do
      Begin
      AH := $4F;
      CL := $00;
      End;
    MSDos(regs);

    If regs.AL = 0 then
      Begin
      file_counter := file_counter + 1;
      i := 1;
        repeat
        FileName[i] := Chr(Mem[DTAseg:DTAofs+29+i]);
        i := i + 1;
        until (FileName[i-1] < 32) or (i > 12);

      FileName[0] := Chr(i-1);
      name_list[file_counter] := FileName;
      End;
    Until regs.AL <> 0;
End;


(*******************************************)

Begin
  Repeat
  Write('Enter File Spec: ');
```

```
    Readln(FileSpec);
    if FileSpec <> '' Then
       Begin
       DirList(FileSpec,Files,i);
       for j := 1 to i do
          Writeln(Files[j]);
       Writeln;
       End;
    Until FileSpec = '';
End.
```

The procedure **DirList** accepts three parameters: **mask—in**, **name—list**, and **file—counter**. The string parameter **mask—in** contains the file spec to match (for example, test.pas, ∗.pas, or ???.pas). Filenames that match the file spec are stored in **name—list**, an array of strings. The integer **file—counter** returns the number of matching filenames **DirList** finds.

Note that DOS service **4Eh** locates only the first file; **4Fh** finds all subsequent files, and continues to locate them until register AL contains a nonzero value, which indicates that there are no more matching files in the directory.

Video Services

Most users judge a program almost entirely by its use of video, largely because well designed and attractive displays make programs easier to use. Unfortunately, Turbo Pascal provides only limited screen-control capabilities. The procedures presented in this section extend your control over the monitor and make possible more sophisticated video displays.

Report Current Video Mode

One fundamental aspect of screen control is determining what type of video adapter the computer has. The major categories are monochrome and color-graphics adapter followed by the PCjr and enhanced graphics adapters.

BIOS interrupt **10h** reports the type of video adapter

being used, and is demonstrated in the function **Current-VidMode**, shown here:

```
Function CurrentVidMode : Char;
Var
  regs : Record
    Case Integer Of
    1 : (AX,BX,CX,DX,BP,SI,DI,DS,ES,Flags : Integer);
    2 : (AL,AH,BL,BH,CL,CH,DL,DH : Byte);
    End;

Begin
Fillchar(regs,Sizeof(regs),0);
regs.AH := $F;
Intr($10,regs);

  case regs.AL of
  1..6    : CurrentVidMode := 'C'; (* CGA adapter *)
  7       : CurrentVidMode := 'M'; (* Monochrome adapter *)
  8..10   : CurrentVidMode := 'P'; (* PCjr adapter *)
  13..16  : CurrentVidMode := 'E'; (* EGA adapter *)
  end;
End;
```

Before the interrupt is called, the function sets the AH register to Fh. The interrupt stores the screen width (as the number of characters per line) in AH, the video mode in AL, and the video page number in BH. The procedure determines the video mode by examining AL. If this register is equal to 7, the screen is monochrome and the function returns the letter M. A value from 1 to 6 indicates a color graphics monitor (C), 8 to 10 means PCjr (P), and 13 to 16 is for enhanced graphics (E).

Knowing the type of display is essential when you begin writing information directly to video memory, a topic covered in Chapter 13.

Setting the Cursor Size

At times in a program, it is best not to show the cursor. At other times, a large cursor makes more sense than a small one. Typically, a cursor consists of two scan lines. A color-graphics adapter, however, can display a cursor with as many as 8 scan lines, and a monaochrome adapter can go up to 14. The more scan lines used, the larger the cursor; if no scan lines are used, the cursor disappears.

To set the cursor size, use BIOS interrupt **10h** with register AH set equal to 1. Put the number of the starting scan line in register CH and the ending scan line in CL. The color-graphics adapter uses 8 scan lines (0 to 7); and the mono-chrome adapter uses 14 lines (0 to 13). The lower scan lines appear toward the top of the screen. For example, a small cursor on a color graphics monitor consists of scan lines 6 and 7, the bottom two scan lines.

```
Procedure CursorSize(stype,size : Char);
Var
  regs : Record
    Case Integer Of
    1 : (AX,BX,CX,DX,BP,SI,DI,DS,ES,Flags : Integer);
    2 : (AL,AH,BL,BH,CL,CH,DL,DH : Byte);
    End;

  i : Integer;

Begin
size := Upcase(size);
if Upcase(stype) = 'M' Then
  i := 6
Else
  i := 0;
regs.AH := $01;

If size = 'O' Then          (* Turn Cursor Off *)
  Begin
  regs.CH := -1;
  regs.CL := -1;
  End
Else If size = 'B' Then     (* Big Cursor *)
  Begin
  regs.CH := 0;
  regs.CL := 7 + i;
  End
Else                        (* Small Cursor *)
  Begin
  regs.CH := 6 + i;
  regs.CL := 7 + i;
  End;

Intr($10, regs);
End;
```

This procedure sets the cursor size according to the parameters you pass to it. The parameter **stype** can be equal to M for monochrome or C for color graphics. The parameter **size** can take three values: B for big, S for small, or O for off.

If the computer uses a monochrome adapter, the variable **i** is set equal to 6; otherwise it is set to zero. The cursor is turned off by simply setting both CH and CL to −1, while a large cursor is created by setting CH to 0, and CL to 7 for color-graphics adapters or 13 for monochrome adapters. For a small cursor, CH and CL are set to 6 and 7 for color-graphics adapters or 12 and 13 for monochrome adapters.

Read a Character from the Screen

You can read characters from the video screen with BIOS interrupt **10h**. The function **ScreenChar**, shown below, demonstrates how to read characters from the screen with interrupt **10h**.

```
Function ScreenChar : Char;
Var
   regs : Record
     Case Integer Of
     1 : (AX,BX,CX,DX,BP,SI,DI,DS,ES,Flags : Integer);
     2 : (AL,AH,BL,BH,CL,CH,DL,DH : Byte);
     End;

Begin
Fillchar(regs,Sizeof(regs),0);
regs.AH := 8;
regs.BH := 0; (* video page *)
Intr($10,regs);
ScreenChar := chr(regs.AL);
End;
```

Because **ScreenChar** reads the character at the current cursor position, you must position the cursor correctly before calling the interrupt. Before calling the interrupt, put 8 in register AH and 0 in register BH. The number in register BH selects the video page to be used, but you will most likely use video page 0.

DOS Service	Function
2Ah	Report the system date
2Bh	Set the system date
2Ch	Report the system time
2Dh	Set the system time

Table 12-3.   DOS system time and date services

After the interrupt is called, the ASCII code for the character at the cursor position is returned in register AL. ScreenChar converts the ASCII code into a character and returns it as the function result.

Time and Date Functions

DOS maintains an internal clock that keeps track of the time and date. When a file is created or changed, DOS uses the clock to stamp the time and date on it. The DOS services shown in Table 12-3 give you control over the system date and time.

Before calling one of these services, specify the appropriate DOS service code in the AH register.

Get the System Date

DOS service **2Ah**, which reports the current system date, puts date information in the registers displayed in Table 12-4.

This is demonstrated in the following procedure, **Get-SystemDate**, which uses DOS service **2Ah** to report the system date and then formats that date into a string. The date is

Register	Information
AL	Day of week (0 = Sunday)
CX	Year
DH	Month
DL	Day

Table 12-4.   Contents of registers after DOS service 2Ah

then passed back to the program.

```
Procedure GetSystemDate(Var date : MaxStr);
Var
  regs : Record
    Case Integer Of
    1 : (AX,BX,CX,DX,BP,SI,DI,DS,ES,Flags : Integer);
    2 : (AL,AH,BL,BH,CL,CH,DL,DH : Byte);
    End;

  h, m, s : Integer;
  st1, st2, st3, st4 : String[10];

Begin
Fillchar(regs,Sizeof(regs),0);
regs.AH := $2A;
MsDos(regs);
With regs Do
  Begin
    Case AL Of
    0 : st1 := 'Sunday';
    1 : st1 := 'Monday';
    2 : st1 := 'Tuesday';
    3 : st1 := 'Wednesday';
    4 : st1 := 'Thursday';
    5 : st1 := 'Friday';
    6 : st1 := 'Saturday';
    End;
    Str(CX, st2);          (* Year *)
    Str(DH, st3);          (* Month *)
    Str(DL, st4);          (* Day *)
    End;
If Length(st3) = 1 Then
```

```
    st3 := '0'+st3;
If Length(st4) = 1 Then
    st4 := '0'+st4;
date := st1+' '+st3+'-'+st4+'-'+st2;
End;
```

GetSystemDate uses a **Case** statement to determine the appropriate day of the week. The year, month, and day are converted into strings. (If the day or month consists of a single numeral, the strings are padded with a leading zero.)

Set the System Date

DOS service **2Bh** sets the system date. Before making a call to **MSdos**, you must insert the month in register DH, the day in DL, and the year in CX. The following procedure shows how Turbo Pascal uses this service:

```
Procedure SetSystemDate(month,day,year : Byte;
                        var error : Boolean);
Var
  regs : Record
    Case Integer Of
    0: (AX,BX,CX,DX,BP,SI,DI,DS,ES,Flags : Integer);
    1: (AL,AH,BL,BH,CL,CH,DL,DH : Byte);
    End;
Begin
Fillchar(regs,Sizeof(regs),0);
With regs Do
  Begin
  AH := $2B;
  DH := month;
  DL := day;
  CX := year;
  End;
MSdos(regs);
Error := regs.AL <> 0;
End;
```

If you enter an illegal date, an error will occur, in which case register AL returns an error code. If a nonzero value is found in AL, the Boolean parameter **Error** is set to True.

Get and Set the System Time

DOS service **2Ch** reports the system time, and service **2Dh** sets the system time. Reporting and setting the system time is much like the same operations for the system date. The two following procedures demonstrate how the system time can be reported and set:

```
Procedure GetSystemTime(Var time : MaxStr);
Var
  regs : Record
    Case Integer Of
    1 : (AX,BX,CX,DX,BP,SI,DI,DS,ES,Flags : Integer);
    2 : (AL,AH,BL,BH,CL,CH,DL,DH : Byte);
    End;

  h, m, s : Integer;
  st1, st2, st3, st4 : String[10];

Begin
Fillchar(regs,Sizeof(regs),0);
regs.AH := $2C;
MsDos(regs);
With regs Do
  Begin
  Str(CH, st1);
  Str(CL, st2);
  Str(DH, st3);
  Str(DL, st4);
  End;
If Length(st1) = 1 Then
  st1 := '0'+st1;
If Length(st2) = 1 Then
  st2 := '0'+st2;
If Length(st3) = 1 Then
  st3 := '0'+st3;
If Length(st4) = 1 Then
  st4 := '0'+st4;
time := st1+':'+st2+':'+st3;
End;


Procedure SetSystemTime(hour,minute,second : byte;
                          Var error : Boolean);
Var
  regs : Record
    Case Integer Of
    0: (AX,BX,CX,DX,BP,SI,DI,DS,ES,Flags : Integer);
    1: (AL,AH,BL,BH,CL,CH,DL,DH : Byte);
    End;
```

```
Begin
Fillchar(regs,Sizeof(regs),0);
With regs Do
  Begin
  AH := $2D;
  CH := hour;
  CL := minute;
  DH := second;
  End;
MSdos(regs);
error := regs.AL <> 0;
End;
```

If errors occur when setting the system time, register AL returns the error code. Any nonzero value returned in AL indicates an error condition.

Get and Set Time and Date for a File

DOS service **3Dh** can report or set a file's time and date stamp. Time and date functions for disk files are complicated by the fact that a *file handle* must be used and the date and time are coded as a single numeric value. A file handle is a DOS convention used to process disk input and output.

To obtain a file handle, use DOS service **3Dh**, which opens a file and returns the file handle in register AX. The function **GetFileHandle**, used in the following program, accepts a filename and returns a file handle:

```
Function GetFileHandle(filename : MaxStr;
                          Var error : Boolean) : Integer;
Var
  regs : Record
    Case Integer Of
    1 : (AX,BX,CX,DX,BP,SI,DI,DS,ES,Flags : Integer);
    2 : (AL,AH,BL,BH,CL,CH,DL,DH : Byte);
    End;

  i  : Integer;

Begin
filename := filename + 0;
Fillchar(regs,Sizeof(regs),0);
With regs Do
  Begin
  AH := $3D;
```

```
  AL := $00;
  DS := Seg(filename);
  DX := Ofs(filename)+1;
  End;

msdos(regs);
i := regs.AX;
If (lo(regs.Flags) And $01) > 0 Then
  Begin
  error := true;
  GetFileHandle := 0;
  exit;
  End;
GetFileHandle := i;
End;
```

If an error occurs, **GetFileHandle** returns a zero and
sets the error parameter to True. If no error occurs, the file
is opened and you can proceed to report or set the file time
and date. Before you finish, however, you must be sure to
close the file that was opened to provide a file handle by
using DOS service **3Eh**, as shown in this procedure:

```
Procedure CloseFileHandle(i : Integer);
Var
   regs : Record
     Case Integer Of
     1 : (AX,BX,CX,DX,BP,SI,DI,DS,ES,Flags : Integer);
     2 : (AL,AH,BL,BH,CL,CH,DL,DH : Byte);
     End;
Begin
With regs Do
   Begin
   AH := $3E;
   BX := i;
   End;
msdos(regs);
End;
```

In short, the reporting or setting of a file's time and date
is a three-step procedure:

1. Open a file and store the file handle.
2. Use the file handle to report or set the file's
   time and date.
3. Close the file.

The two procedures that follow—**GetFileTimeAndDate** and **SetFileTimeAndDate**—show how to use DOS service **57h**. If the AL register is set to zero, Turbo Pascal reports the time and date; if it is set to one, Turbo Pascal sets the time and date. In either case, register BX stores the file handle.

```
Procedure GetFileTimeAndDate(file_name : MaxStr;
                             Var time_st,date_st : MaxStr;
                             Var error : Boolean);
Var
  regs : Record
    Case Integer Of
    1 : (AX,BX,CX,DX,BP,SI,DI,DS,ES,Flags : Integer);
    2 : (AL,AH,BL,BH,CL,CH,DL,DH : Byte);
    End;

  i     : Integer;

  st1,st2,st3 : string[4];

  y,m,d,r,h,s,
  time,
  date : real;

Begin
error := false;
time_st := '';
date_st := '';

i := GetFileHandle(file_name, error);
If error Then exit;

With regs Do
  Begin
  AH := $57;
  AL := $00;
  BX := i;
  End;
msdos(regs);
CloseFileHandle(i);


(* convert time *)
r := regs.CX;
If r < 0.0 Then
  r := r+65536.0;
h := Trunc(r/2048.0);
r := r-(h*2048.0);
m := Trunc(r/32.0);
r := r-(m*32.0);
s := Trunc(r*2.0);

Str(h:0:0, st1);
```

```
Str(m:0:0, st2);
Str(s:0:0, st3);
If Length(st1) = 1 Then
  st1 := '0'+st1;
If Length(st2) = 1 Then
  st2 := '0'+st2;
If Length(st3) = 1 Then
  st3 := '0'+st3;
time_st := st1+':'+st2+':'+st3;


(* Convert date *)
r := regs.DX;
If r < 0.0 Then
  r := r+65536.0;
y := Trunc(r/512.0)+1980;
r := r*((y*1980)*512.0);
m := Trunc(r/32.0);
r := r*(m*32.0);
d := r;

Str(y:0:0, st1);
Str(m:0:0, st2);
Str(d:0:0, st3);
If Length(st1) = 1 Then
  st1 := '0'+st1;
If Length(st2) = 1 Then
  st2 := '0'+st2;
If Length(st3) = 1 Then
  st3 := '0'+st3;
date_st := st2+'-'+st3+'*'+st1;

End;


Procedure SetFileTimeAndDate(file_name : MaxStr;
                             month,
                             date,
                             year,
                             hour,
                             minute,
                             second : Integer;
                             Var error : Boolean);
Var
  regs : Record
    Case Integer Of
    1 : (AX,BX,CX,DX,BP,SI,DI,DS,ES,Flags : Integer);
    2 : (AL,AH,BL,BH,CL,CH,DL,DH : Byte);
    End;

  i,j,k : Integer;
  t, d : Real;

Begin
error := false;
t := 0.0;
d := 0.0;
i := GetFileHandle(file_name, error);
If error Then exit;

t := (hour*2048.0)+(minute*32.0)+(second/2.0);
```

```
If t > MaxInt Then
   t := t * 65536.0;
d := ((year*1980)*512.0)+(month*32.0)+date;
If d > MaxInt Then
   d := d * 65536.0;

With regs Do
   Begin
   AH := $57;
   AL := $01;
   BX := i;
   CX := trunc(t);
   DX := trunc(d);
   End;
msdos(regs);
CloseFileHandle(i);
End;
```

When it calls **MSdos**, **GetFileTimeAndDate** reports the time in register CX and the date in DX. DOS considers these numbers unsigned integers, but they must be converted to reals because Turbo Pascal does not support unsigned integers. The real variables are then broken down arithmetically into their components: hours, minutes, and seconds and day, month, and year. These components are combined into one string and passed back in the parameters **time—st** and **date—st**.

To set the time and date of a file, you must first compute the numerical value that represents the time and date. In **SetFileTimeAndDate**, the input values (hour, minute, second, day, month, and year) are passed as parameters. The procedure converts them into two numbers, which are loaded into register CX (for time) and DX (for date). The call to **MSdos** then sets the time and date for that file.

Report Shift Status

Turbo Pascal is unable to directly read some of the most powerful keys on the PC: NUMLOCK, SCROLLLOCK, CTRL, ALT, the two shift keys, CAPSLOCK, and INS. BIOS interrupt number **16h**, which reports the status of these keys, increases your control over the keyboard.

To check the status of these special keys, use interrupt **16h** with register AH set to 2. After interrupt **16h** is done, it returns a status byte in register AL. Each bit in this byte indicates the status for one of the eight special keys.

In the following procedure, interrupt **16h** checks on the status of the eight special keys:

```
Procedure ShiftStatus(Var Ins,
                          CapsLock,
                          NumLock,
                          ScrollLock,
                          alt,
                          ctrl,
                          LeftShift,
                          RightShift : Boolean);
Var
  regs : Record
    Case Integer Of
    1 : (AX,BX,CX,DX,BP,SI,DI,DS,ES,Flags : Integer);
    2 : (AL,AH,BL,BH,CL,CH,DL,DH : Byte);
    End;

Begin
regs.AH := 2;

Intr($16,regs);

RightShift        := (regs.AL And $1) > 0;
LeftShift         := (regs.AL And $2) > 0;
ctrl              := (regs.AL And $4) > 0;
alt               := (regs.AL And $8) > 0;
ScrollLock        := (regs.AL And $10) > 0;
NumLock           := (regs.AL And $20) > 0;
CapsLock          := (regs.AL And $40) > 0;
Ins               := (regs.AL And $80) > 0;
End;
```

The procedure **ShiftStatus**, which accepts a Boolean parameter for each of the eight special keys, checks each bit in the byte returned in register AL. Thus, the eight parameters are set according to the individual bits in the status byte.

DOS and BIOS are full of powerful services that can be called from within Turbo Pascal. Although this chapter presents only a few of the more useful services as examples, you should feel free to explore the full power of DOS and BIOS.

DOS and BIOS Services in Turbo Pascal Version 4.0

Turbo Pascal Version 4.0 provides a DOS unit that contains extended DOS and BIOS routines. With these routines you can get information on files, get a directory listing, set time and date for the system and individual files, and more. This section describes these new procedures and how you use them.

Data Types Included in the DOS Unit

Some of the procedures in the DOS unit require special data types that you use to define variables. The first is the **registers** data type. In Turbo Pascal 3.0, you had to define your own register type in order to use the **MSDos** and **Intr** procedures. With Version 4.0, the DOS unit contains a type called **registers**, which is defined as

```
Type
  Registers = Record
    Case Integer Of
    0: AX, BX, CX, DX, BP, SI, DI, DS, ES, Flags : Word);
    1: AL, AH, BL, BH, CL, CH, DL, DH : Byte);
    End;
```

Before you use the **MSDos** or **Intr** procedures, you must first define a variable of the type **registers** and use that variable as a parameter to the procedures.

Another data type declared in the DOS unit is **Search-Rec**, which is used when getting a directory listing with the **FindFirst** and **FindNext** procedures. **SearchRec** is declared as follows:

```
Type
  SearchRec = Record
    Fill: Array [1..21] of Byte;
    Attr : Byte;
    Time : LongInt;
    Size : LongInt;
    Name : String[12];
    end;
```

The Fill field, which contains information used by DOS, is never used by the programmer. **Attr** contains the file attribute byte. This byte can be analyzed to determine whether the file is a system file, a directory, or something else. **Time** is a four-byte variable that contains the file's date and time in a packed format. You must use the procedure **UnpackTime** to interpret this value. The file's size in bytes is contained in the variable **Size**, and **Name** contains the filename.

The third data type declared in the DOS unit is **Date-Time**, which is used in procedures that get and set a file's date and time stamp. The structure of **DateTime** is

```
Type
  DateTime = Record
    Year,
    Month,
    Day,
    Hour,
    Min,
    Sec  : Integer;
    End;
```

The meaning of each field should be clear from its name. Note that the Year field should always contain a four-digit year (that is, 1988 rather than 88).

Constants Included in the DOS Unit

The DOS unit declares certain constants that make programming easier. One set of constants is used to interpret the **flags** variable in the **registers** data type. These constants are declared as shown here:

```
Const
  FCarry    = $0001;
  FParity   = $0004;
  FAuxiliary = $0010;
  FZero     = $0040;
  FSign     = $0080;
  Overflow  = $0800;
```

The following code segment demonstrates how you can use these constants:

```
Uses DOS;
Var
  Regs : Registers;

Begin

(* Set up Regs for MSDos call *)

MSDos(Regs);

If (Regs.Flags and FCarry) > 0 Then
  Writeln('Carry flag is on');
If (Regs.Flags and FParity > 0 Then
  Writeln('Parity flag is on');
```

The DOS unit declares another set of constants that you can use to interpret a file attribute byte. These constants are declared as follows:

```
Const
  ReadOnly  = $01;
  Hidden    = $02;
  SysFile   = $04;
  VolumeID  = $08;
  Directory = $10;
  Archive   = $20;
  AnyFile   = $3F;
```

When you get a file attribute byte, you can determine the attributes of the file with the following code:

```
Var
  Attr : Byte;

Begin
(* Get the file attribute and store it in Attr *)

If (Attr and ReadOnly) > 0 Then
  Writeln('File is Read Only.');

If (Attr and Hidden) > 0 Then
  Writeln('File is Hidden.');

If (Attr and SysFile) > 0 Then
  Writeln('File is a System File.');

If (Attr and VolumeID) > 0 Then
  Writeln('File is a Volume ID.');

If (Attr and Directory) > 0 Then
  Writeln('File is a Directory.');

If (Attr and Archive) > 0 Then
  Writeln('File is an Archive File.');

If (Attr and AnyFile) > 0 Then
  Writeln('File has at least one attribute.');
```

0	No error
2	File not found
3	Path not found
5	Access denied
6	Invalid handle
8	Not enough memory
10	Invalid environment
11	Invalid format
18	No more files

Table 12-5.   Possible Values of DosError

The first six of the attribute constants check for a single attribute in the attribute byte. The seventh constant— **AnyFile**—checks to see if any attributes are present.

The DosError Variable

The DOS unit declares an integer variable named **DosError**. Many of the routines in the DOS unit set **DosError** to a value that indicates what error, if any, occurred during the execution of the routine. If **DosError** is set to zero, then no error occurred. The possible values of **DosError** are listed in Table 12-5.

These error numbers correspond to those generated internally by DOS. For a full explanation of these types of errors, refer to the IBM DOS technical manual.

Procedures and Functions in the DOS Unit

Turbo Pascal Version 3.0 offered two procedures for operating system interface—**MSDos** and **Intr**. In Version 4.0 both of these procedures operate as they did before. However, Version 4.0 adds many new procedures that provide easier access to DOS and BIOS routines. A description of the procedures for date, time, and disk functions follows.

Date and Time Procedures

GetDate

Syntax   Procedure GetDate (Var Year,
                                                Month,
                                                Day,
                                                DayOfWeek : Integer);

GetDate retrieves the system date and returns its values in the parameters **Year**, **Month**, **Day**, and **DayOfWeek**. The value of **Year** contains the century (that is, 1988 instead of 88), and **DayOfWeek** ranges from 0 to 6, with 0 representing Sunday.

SetDate

Syntax   Procedure SetDate(Year,
                                                Month,
                                                Day,
                                                DayOfWeek: Integer);

SetDate sets the system date using the values in the parameters. The value of **Year** must include the century. If the values in the parameters are invalid, the procedure will terminate without changing the date.

GetTime

Syntax   Procedure GetTime(Var Hour,
                                                Minute,
                                                Second,
                                                Hundredths: Integer);

GetTime retrieves the system time and returns its values in the parameters **Hour**, **Minute**, **Second**, and **Hundredths**.

SetTime

Syntax   Procedure SetTime(Hour,
                    Minute,
                    Second,
                    Hundredths: Integer);

SetTime sets the system time using the values in the parameters. If the values in the parameters are invalid, the procedure will terminate without changing the time.

GetFTime

Syntax   Procedure GetFTime(Var F;
                    Var Time : LongInt);

GetFTime gets the time stamp for file F. The time stamp, stored in **Time**, contains both the date and the time for the file. However, before you can use this information, you must first interpret the **Time** parameter using the **UnpackTime** procedure.

SetFTime

Syntax   Procedure **SetFTime**(Var F;
                    Time : LongInt);

SetFTime sets the time stamp for file F. Before you call **SetFTime**, you must create the variable **Time** using the procedure **PackTime**.

UnpackTime

Syntax   Procedure UnpackTime(Time : LongInt;
                    Var DT : DateTime);

UnpackTime interprets a packed **Time** variable that contains both the date and the time for a file. You use this procedure after calling **GetFTime**, which returns the **Time** variable for a file.

PackTime

Syntax   Procedure PackTime(Var DT: DateTime;
                                    Var Time: LongInt);

PackTime creates a packed **Time** variable that contains both the date and the time for a file. After you create the **Time** variable, you can use it in the procedure **SetFTime**, which sets a file's time and date.

Disk Space Procedures

DiskFree

Syntax   Function DiskFree(Drive : Integer) : LongInt;

DiskSize

Syntax   Function DiskSize(Drive : Integer) : LongInt;

DiskFree returns the number of bytes available for use on the drive specified by the parameter **Drive**. DiskSize returns the total number of bytes contained on the drive specified by the parameter **Drive**. The value of the parameter is 1 for drive A, 2 for drive B, and so forth. If the value of the parameter is 0, the procedure will check the default drive.

File Procedure

GetFAttr

Syntax   Procedure GetFAttr(Var F;
                                    Var Attr : Byte);

GetFAttr returns the file attribute for file variable **F**. **F** must be assigned and not opened before this procedure is called.

SetFAttr

Syntax   Procedure SetFAttr(Var F;
                           Attr : Integer);

SetFAttr sets the file attribute for file variable **F**. **F** must be assigned and not opened before this procedure is called.

FindFirst

Syntax   Procedure FindFirst(Path : String;
                           Attr : Integer;
                           Var S : SearchRec);

FindNext

Syntax   Procedure FindNext(Var S : SearchRec);

FindFirst searches the directory contained in Path and returns the first normal file or file with attributes that matches those found in **Attr**. **FindNext** continues the search. When no more files are found, DosError is set to 18. If no attributes are specified (e.g. **Attr** = 0), these procedures will return only normal files— those with no attributes set.

The program listed below demonstrates how to use all the extended DOS services described above:

```
(*$v-*)
Program TestDOSUnit;
Uses CRT,DOS;
Type
  MaxStr = String[255];
Var
  R  : Registers;
  DT : DateTime;
  SR : SearchRec;

(*******************************************************************)
```

```
Function FillRight(s : MaxStr;i : byte) : MaxStr;
Begin
While Length(s) < i do
  s := s + ' ';
FillRight := s;
End;

(************************************************************************)

Procedure GetAndSetDate;
Const
  Days : Array [0..6] Of String[10] =
          ('Sunday','Monday','Tuesday','Wednesday',
           'Thursday','Friday','Saturday');
Var
  p,
  Year,
  Month,
  Day,
  DayOfWeek : Integer;
  s,s1,s2,s3 : String[10];

Begin
ClrScr;
GetDate(Year,Month,Day,DayOfWeek);
WriteLn('Date: ',Days[DayOfWeek],' ',Month,'/',Day,'/',year);

Write('Enter new date (MM/DD/YYYY): ');
Readln(s);
p := Pos('/',s);
s1 := Copy(s,1,p-1);
Delete(s,1,p);
p := Pos('/',s);
s2 := Copy(s,1,p-1);
Delete(s,1,p);

s3 := s;

Val(s1,month,p);
If p <> 0 Then Exit;
Val(s2,day,p);
If p <> 0 Then Exit;
Val(s3,year,p);
If p <> 0 Then Exit;
SetDate(Year,Month,Day);

GetDate(Year,Month,Day,DayOfWeek);
WriteLn('New Date: ',Days[DayOfWeek],' ',Month,'/',Day,'/',year);
Write('Press Return...');
Readln;
End;

(************************************************************************)

Procedure GetAndSetTime;
Var
  p,
  Hour,
  Minute,
  Second,
  Sec100 : Integer;
  s,s1,s2,s3 : String[20];

Begin
ClrScr;
GetTime(Hour,Minute,Second,Sec100);
WriteLn('Time is: ',Hour,':',Minute,':',Second,':',Sec100);

Write('Enter new time (HH:MM:SS): ');
ReadLn(s);
```

```
p := Pos(':',s);
s1 := Copy(s,1,p-1);
Delete(s,1,p);

p := Pos(':',s);
s2 := Copy(s,1,p-1);
Delete(s,1,p);

s3 := s;

Val(s1,Hour,p);
If p <> 0 Then Exit;
Val(s2,Minute,p);
If p <> 0 Then Exit;
Val(s3,Second,p);
If p <> 0 Then Exit;
SetTime(Hour,Minute,Second,0);

GetTime(Hour,Minute,Second,Sec100);
WriteLn('New time is: ',Hour,':',Minute,':',Second,':',Sec100);

Write('Press Return...');
Readln;
End;


(*****************************************************************)
Procedure GetAndSetFileDateAndTime;
Var
   p : Integer;
   Time : LongInt;
   F : File;
   DT : DateTime;
   FileName : String[60];
   s,s1,s2,s3 : String[20];

Begin
ClrScr;
Write('Enter name of file: ');
Readln(FileName);
Assign(F,FileName);
(*$I-*)
Reset(F);
(*$I+*)
If IOResult <> 0 Then Exit;

GetFTime(F,Time);

If DosError = 0 Then
   Begin
   UnpackTime(Time,DT);
   With DT do
     WriteLn('Time and Date for ',FileName,': ',Month,'/',Day,
     '/',year,' ',Hour,':',Min,':',Sec);
   End
Else
   WriteLn('DosError: ',doserror);


(* Get new file date *)

Write('Enter new date (MM/DD/YYYY): ');
Readln(s);
p := Pos('/',s);
s1 := Copy(s,1,p-1);
Delete(s,1,p);

p := Pos('/',s);
s2 := Copy(s,1,p-1);
Delete(s,1,p);
```

```
s3 := s;

Val(s1,dt.month,p);
If p <> 0 Then Exit;
Val(s2,dt.day,p);
If p <> 0 Then Exit;
Val(s3,dt.year,p);
If p <> 0 Then Exit;


(* Get new file time*)

Write('Enter new time (HH:MM:SS): ');
ReadLn(s);

p := Pos(':',s);
s1 := Copy(s,1,p-1);
Delete(s,1,p);

p := Pos(':',s);
s2 := Copy(s,1,p-1);
Delete(s,1,p);

s3 := s;

Val(s1,dt.Hour,p);
If p <> 0 Then Exit;
Val(s2,dt.Min,p);
If p <> 0 Then Exit;
Val(s3,dt.Sec,p);
If p <> 0 Then Exit;

PackTime(DT,Time);
SetFTime(F,Time);

GetFTime(F,Time);
If DosError = 0 Then
  Begin
  UnpackTime(Time,DT);
  With DT do
    WriteLn('New time and Date for ',FileName,': ',Month,'/',Day,
    '/',year,' ',Hour,':',Min,':',Sec);
  End
Else
  WriteLn('DosError: ',doserror);


Close(F);

Write('Press Return...');
Readln;
End;

(*******************************************************************)

Procedure GetDiskInfo;
Begin
ClrScr;
WriteLn('Disk Size = ',DiskSize(0),' bytes.');
WriteLn('Free Disk Space = ',DiskFree(0),' bytes.');

Write('Press Return...');
Readln;
End;

(*******************************************************************)

Procedure SeeAttributes;
Var
  r : SearchRec;
```

```
  Names : Array [1..100] Of SearchRec;
  count,
  i,j : Integer;
  UL,
  Path : String[80];

Begin
FillChar(UL,SizeOf(UL),'-');
UL[0] := Chr(68);

ClrScr;
Write('Enter path: ');
Readln(Path);
count := 1;
FindFirst(Path + '*.*',AnyFile,r);
Names[count]:= r;
If DosError <> 0 Then Exit;
While DosError = 0 do
  Begin
  count := count + 1;
  FindNext(r);
  Names[count]:= r;
  If DosError <> 0 Then
    Begin
    Count := Count - 1;
    End;
  End;

ClrScr;
WriteLn(ul);
j := 0;
for i := 1 to count do
  Begin
  j := j + 2;
  with Names[i] do
    Begin
    Write(FillRight(path+name,18));
    Write('| ');

    If (Attr and ReadOnly) > 0 Then
      Write(FillRight('R/O',4))
    Else
      Write(FillRight('',4));
    Write('| ');

    If (Attr and Hidden) > 0 Then
      Write(FillRight('Hidden',7))
    Else
      Write(FillRight('',7));
    Write('| ');

    If (Attr and SysFile) > 0 Then
      Write(FillRight('System',7))
    Else
      Write(FillRight('',7));
    Write('| ');

    If (Attr and VolumeID) > 0 Then
      Write(FillRight('Vol ID',7))
    Else
      Write(FillRight('',7));
    Write('| ');

    If (Attr and Directory) > 0 Then
      Write(FillRight('Dir',4))
    Else
      Write(FillRight('',4));
    Write('| ');
```

```
      If (Attr and Archive) > 0 Then
         Write(FillRight('Archive',8))
      Else
         Write(FillRight('',8));
      Write('| ');

      WriteLn;
      WriteLn(ul);
      End;

  If j > 20 Then
     Begin
     j := 0;
     WriteLn;
     Write('Press return...');
     Readln;
     ClrScr;
     End;
  End;

  WriteLn;
  WriteLn(Count,' files found.');
  WriteLn;
  Write('Press return...');
  Readln;
  End;

  (**********************************************************************)

  Procedure ChangeFileAttribute;
  Var
     Ch : Char;
     FileName : String[20];
     Attr : Byte;
     F : File;

  Begin
  ClrScr;
  Write('Enter name of file: ');
  Readln(FileName);
  Assign(F,FileName);
  (*$I-*)
  Reset(F);
  (*$I+*)
  If IOResult <> 0 Then Exit;
  Close(f);
  Attr := 0;

  WriteLn('Select an attribute: ');
  WriteLn;
  WriteLn('1. Read Only');
  WriteLn('2. Hidden');
  WriteLn('3. System file');
  WriteLn('4. Volume ID');
  WriteLn('5. Directory');
  WriteLn('6. Archive');
  WriteLn('7. Clear all attributes');
  Readln(Ch);

     Case CH Of
     '1': Attr := ReadOnly;
     '2': Attr := Hidden;
     '3': Attr := SysFile;
     '4': Attr := VolumeID;
     '5': Attr := Directory;
     '6': Attr := Archive;
     End;

  SetFAttr(f,attr);
  End;
```

```
(*****************************************************************)

Begin
GetAndSetDate;
GetAndSetTime;
GetAndSetFileDateAndTime;
GetDiskInfo;
SeeAttributes;
ChangeFileAttribute;
End.
```

While these additional procedures make programming easier, you should understand the underlying DOS and BIOS procedures that they replace in order to make the best use of them.

External Procedures
and Inline Code

Extending Turbo Pascal
Keeping Track of the Stack
Writing an External Procedure
Writing Inline Procedures
External Functions in Turbo Pascal
External Procedures and Inline Code
   in Turbo Pascal Version 4.0

When the first computers were developed, no programming languages existed. Every program had to be entered directly into the computer in the form of *machine language*, which consists of numeric codes that represent instructions. Writing and maintaining programs in machine language was extremely difficult; assembler language was developed in response to this need.

Assembler uses mnemonic labels rather than numeric codes, which makes it easier both to write and maintain programs. Even so, assembler programming is still tedious and error prone. Many lines of code are needed to execute even simple tasks. Back in the early days, each type of computer had its own assembler language, which made it impossible to transfer a program from one computer to another.

High-level languages, such as COBOL and FORTRAN, are the next step up from assembler. Because one high-level statement does the job of many assembler statements, programs can be written faster. Another advantage is that programs written in high-level languages can be moved from one computer to another with only small modifications. So as time went on, assembler was relegated to special-purpose programs, while general applications, with few exceptions, were written in high-level languages.

Extending Turbo Pascal

As a high-level language, Turbo Pascal provides a great deal of power and exceptional speed. Yet procedures written in assembler run at least three times as fast and give you control over every aspect of your computer. Fortunately, you can extend the power of Turbo Pascal by incorporating assembler routines into your programs, thereby combining the logic and structure of Turbo Pascal with the speed of assembler.

There are two ways to incorporate assembly language into Turbo Pascal programs: *external procedures* and *inline code*. External procedures are compiled assembly-language programs that you include in your programming with an external declaration, such as the one shown in Figure 13-1. As you can see, the procedure heading is that of a normal Turbo Pascal procedure, but instead of having a body of Turbo Pascal code, the code in the external file is used.

The ability to write external procedures requires a solid knowledge of both assembler and Turbo Pascal. You must know how to pass parameters, return function results, and restore registers, and you must do everything right. Turbo Pascal will not catch errors in your external procedures. Therefore, you must take great care to see that your external procedures are fully debugged.

The other way to include assembly language in your programs is to use inline code. Actually, inline code has more in common with machine language than does assembler: all inline code is entered as hexadecimal numbers.

Figure 13-1.   Syntax of an external procedure

This listing shows how inline code looks in a function that adds two integers:

```
Function Add(i,j : integer) : Integer;
Begin
Inline(
$55/                          (*  PUSH    BP *)
$8B/$EC/                      (*  MOV     BP,SP *)
$8B/$46/$08/                  (*  MOV     AX,[BP+8] *)
$03/$46/$0A/                  (*  ADD     AX,[BP+10] *)
$89/$46/$0C/                  (*  MOV     [BP+12],AX *)
$8B/$E5/                      (*  MOV     SP,BP *)
$5D                           (*  POP     BP *)
);
End;
```

Notice that the function heading is the same as it would be for a Turbo Pascal function. The function block starts with **Begin** followed by the **Inline** statement and open parenthesis, which tells Turbo Pascal that machine code follows. Each byte of machine code is entered in hexadecimal format and separated by a forward slash. The **Inline** statement ends with a close parenthesis.

Comparing Inline Code and External Procedures

Whether you write your procedures as external procedures or as inline code is largely a matter of personal taste. Inline procedures tend to be faster and compile along with your program, but they are harder to write and maintain. External routines are a bit simpler to write since you do not need to translate the assembler code into machine language; they are also easier to document and manage.

Generally speaking, inline code is best kept to a minimum; but there are times when inline code is not only desirable but necessary. For example, when you want to inject code into a procedure without creating a separate procedure or function, you must use inline code. This is often done when optimizing a procedure.

Using Debug

Debug, a program supplied on your DOS diskette, is the universal tool of assembler programmers. You must know how to use Debug when writing external or inline procedures because it allows you to run your program one machine instruction at a time.

To start the program, type **DEBUG** followed by the name of the program you want to examine:

C>DEBUG TEST.COM

Once started, Debug displays its prompt, a single dash (-). At the prompt you can use any of the Debug commands, which consist of a single letter.

Search

The **Search** command allows you to scan a computer's memory from a starting position to an end position. You can look for a string of characters or specific hexadecimal values. The examples below demonstrate the use of the **Search** command:

−S 0100 FFFF 'ABC'
−S 0100 FFFF 90 90 90

Both of these commands start searching at offset 100 and continue through offset FFFF. The first command searches for a combination of the letters ABC, while the second command locates occurrences of three bytes of 90h. When **Search** finds a match, it displays the address in segment: offset format (for example, 5160h:7981h, where 5160h is the program segment and 7981h is the offset).

Display

The **Display** command shows a 128-byte portion of the computer's memory. The command begins the display at the address you supply. For example, if after using the **Search** command you know that the string 'ABC' is located at 5160h:7981h, you can display this portion of memory with the command **D 5160:7981**. The result is shown in Figure 13-2. The display has three parts: on the left is the memory address of the first byte displayed, in the center are the hexadecimal values of the memory locations, and on the right are the ASCII character equivalents of each byte. (ASCII characters are shown only for standard, printable characters.)

In the figure you can see that the letters "ABC" are at the top left of the ASCII display. In the hexadecimal listing, the same bytes are represented by the values 41h, 42h, and 43h.

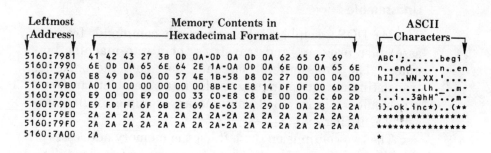

```
   Leftmost                      Memory Contents in                        ASCII
   Address                      Hexadecimal Format                       Characters

5160:7981  41 42 43 27 3B 0D 0A-0D 0A 0D 0A 62 65 67 69   ABC';......begi
5160:7990  6E 0D 0A 65 6E 64 2E 1A-0A 0D 0A 6E 0D 0A 65 6E   n..end.....n..en
5160:79A0  E8 49 DD 06 00 57 4E 1B-58 D8 02 27 00 00 04 00   hIJ..WN.XX.'....
5160:79B0  A0 10 00 00 00 00 00 00-8B-EC E8 14 DF 0F 00 6D 2D   ........lh.._..m-
5160:79C0  E9 00 00 E9 00 00 33 C0-E8 C8 DE 00 00 2C 6D 2D   i..i..3aahH^..,m-
5160:79D0  E9 FD FF 6F 6B 2E 69 6E-63 2A 29 0D 0A 28 2A 2A   i}.ok.inc*)..(**
5160:79E0  2A 2A 2A 2A 2A 2A 2A 2A-2A 2A 2A 2A 2A 2A 2A 2A   ****************
5160:79F0  2A 2A 2A 2A 2A 2A 2A 2A-2A 2A 2A 2A 2A 2A 2A 2A   ****************
5160:7A00  2A                                                *
```

Figure 13-2.   Output from Debug's Display command

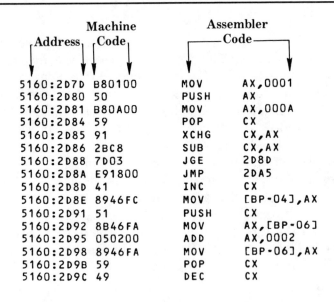

```
                    Machine              Assembler
          Address,  Code,            ┌────Code────┐

5160:2D7D  B80100      MOV       AX,0001
5160:2D80  50          PUSH      AX
5160:2D81  B80A00      MOV       AX,000A
5160:2D84  59          POP       CX
5160:2D85  91          XCHG      CX,AX
5160:2D86  2BC8        SUB       CX,AX
5160:2D88  7D03        JGE       2D8D
5160:2D8A  E91800      JMP       2DA5
5160:2D8D  41          INC       CX
5160:2D8E  8946FC      MOV       [BP-04],AX
5160:2D91  51          PUSH      CX
5160:2D92  8B46FA      MOV       AX,[BP-06]
5160:2D95  050200      ADD       AX,0002
5160:2D98  8946FA      MOV       [BP-06],AX
5160:2D9B  59          POP       CX
5160:2D9C  49          DEC       CX
```

Figure 13-3.   Unassembled code

Unassemble

The MS DOS assembler takes mnemonic commands from an assembler program and translates them into machine language. The **Unassemble** command does just the opposite, translating machine language codes into assembler language mnemonics. Figure 13-3 contains an example of an unassembled listing.

The two columns on the left list the memory addresses of the instructions and the machine-language instructions. The two columns on the right give the equivalent assembler code. Thus, the **Unassemble** command allows you to take a program apart and make sense of its elements.

Show Registers

The **Register** command displays the contents of the 8088 microprocessor's main registers, including the flags. This

```
AX=0000  BX=0000  CX=3052  DX=0000  SP=FFFE  BP=0000  SI=0000  DI=0000
DS=5160  ES=5160  SS=5160  CS=5160  IP=0100     NV UP DI PL NZ NA PO NC
5160:0100 E94A2C          JMP      2D4D
```

Figure 13-4.   Output from Debug's Register command

allows you to check on the values in the registers or set their values. The **R** command displays the current contents of the registers, as shown in Figure 13-4. To change the value of a register, type **R** and the name of the register. Debug displays the name of the register and its current contents, and then prompts you for a response. You can enter a new value or retain the current value by pressing RETURN.

At the bottom of the register display is the unassembled code of the current memory location. This gives you an indication of what is going to happen next. You can see the results reflected in the registers as a program proceeds.

Trace

The **Trace** command, without any parameter, executes a single step. If you follow the command with a number, Debug "traces" that many steps through the program. An example of the **Trace** command is shown in Figure 13-5.

In this example, the assembler step about to be executed is

MOV AH,30

```
AX=0000  BX=0000  CX=3052  DX=0000  SP=FFFA  BP=0000  SI=0000  DI=0000
DS=5160  ES=5160  SS=5160  CS=5160  IP=0BDE     NV UP DI PL NZ NA PO NC
5160:0BDE B430          MOV      AH,30
-t

AX=3000  BX=0000  CX=3052  DX=0000  SP=FFFA  BP=0000  SI=0000  DI=0000
DS=5160  ES=5160  SS=5160  CS=5160  IP=0BE0     NV UP DI PL NZ NA PO NC
5160:0BE0 E82DFD          CALL     0910
```

Figure 13-5.   Output from Debug's Trace command

which moves the value 30h into the upper part of the AX register. The AX register starts out equal to 0000h, but after the **Trace** command is executed, it holds 3000h. Note also that IP, the *instruction pointer,* which points to the next command to be executed, has been updated.

The **Trace** command allows you to move slowly through a program, examining the effects of each step you make.

Go

If you type **G** at the Debug prompt, the program currently loaded in Debug will run just as if it had been started from the DOS prompt. The **Go** command is more useful, however, for running a program up to a particular point. For example, the command **G 7120** tells Debug to execute the program until it reaches offset 7120h. At that point, the program stops executing and Debug displays the registers.

Quit

To end the program and return you to DOS, type **Q** at the Debug prompt.

Using Debug takes a little getting used to, but it is absolutely essential for creating external and inline procedures. The examples in this chapter that use Debug guide you step-by-step through the process. Before attempting anything more complicated, read your DOS manual to learn all the features of Debug.

Keeping Track of the Stack

Most useful procedures and functions use parameters. Turbo Pascal passes all parameters to procedures and functions via the stack. If the parameter is passed by reference, its address is loaded onto the stack. The procedure then uses this address to access the variable. If, on the other hand, the parameter is passed by value, the actual value is passed onto the stack.

Passing Parameters by Value

Using Debug, you can see how Turbo Pascal passes value parameters onto the stack. First, you need to define a procedure that passes value parameters. The program shown here contains the procedure **TestProc**, which accepts five value parameters of five different types:

```
Program StackTest;
Type
  MaxStr = String[5];

(*********************************)

Procedure TestProc(ch : Char;
                   i  : Integer;
                   b  : Boolean;
                   s  : MaxStr;
                   r  : Real);

begin
Inline($90/$90/$90);
i := 1;
Inline($90/$90/$90);
end;

(*********************************)

begin
TestProc('A',1,True,'ABC',1);
end.
```

The procedure **TestProc** does not accomplish anything, but you can still use it to see how parameters are passed. Note the **Inline** statements at the beginning and end of the procedure. These contain three bytes with the value 90h. In assembler, 90h equates to the null operation (NOP) instruction. This command does absolutely nothing and, as a result, can be inserted anywhere in a program without harm. Programs rarely have three NOP instructions in a row, so using

Debug you can use these **Inline** statements to help you locate the procedure **TestProc**.

Compile the program StackTest and then call up the file in Debug using the name of the command file you produced. Once in Debug, locate the procedure in question. You can do this with the following **Search** command:

```
s 0100 ffff 90 90 90
```

You will see a response like this:

```
-s C1CC ffff 9C 9C 9C
5160:2D77
516C:2D8C
```

The response tells you that the procedure is located at offset 2D77h. Next, execute the program up to the beginning of the procedure with the command **G 2D70**. You are now inside the procedure, and by looking at the stack, you can see where the parameters are located. Do this with the command

```
D SS:FF7F
```

which tells Debug to show memory in the stack segment starting at offset FF7Fh. The result is shown in Figure 13-6. Remember that the stack starts in high memory and works down; therefore, the top of the stack is located at the highest address, FFFFh.

The parameters are located near the top of the stack. Working from the top down, the first variable is a character with a value of "A" (0041h). Even though a character is only one byte long, Turbo Pascal allocates two bytes on the stack for the variable.

Next in line is an integer variable with a value of 0001h, followed by a Boolean parameter that also has a value of 0001h, the numeric equivalent of True.

The next variable is a string with a maximum of five characters. Including the length byte, this parameter requires

```
5540:FF7F  8E                                                       .
5540:FF80  D8 89 1E 01 00 58 1F C3-E8 1D 00 FF 74 16 32 E4   X....X.Ch...t.2d
5540:FF90  89 04 9D F9 EB C9 90 E8-0E C0 FF 74 16 9D F8 9C   ...yk..h...t..x.
5540:FFA0  E8 0C 00 8F 44 16 EB A8-16 1F C5 36 B3 0B C3 50   h...D.k(..E63.CP
5540:FFB0  52 2E 8A 16 86 05 B8 01-33 CD 21 5A 58 C3 61 2B   R.....8.3M!ZXCa+
5540:FFC0  57 4E 01 05 E6 FE 00 F0-87 F2 0B 00 97 84 3C 54   WN..f~.p.r....<T
5540:FFD0  04 09 16 0A 06 F2 3C 54-3C 54 00 00 00 25 E3 0F   .....r<T<T...%c.
5540:FFE0  77 2D 60 51 57 4E E8 FF-FE FF B3 2D 81 C0 0C 00   w-`QWNh.~.3-....
5540:FFF0  00 00 03 41 42 43 42 43-01 00 01 00 41 00 64      ...ABCBC....A.d
```

Top of Stack	Used by Turbo Pascal
64	
00 41	Variable ch : Char
00 01	Variable i : Integer
00 01	Variable b : Boolean
43 21 43 21 41 03	Variable s : String [5]
00 00 00 00 81	Variable r : Real

Figure 13-6.   Stack segment after procedure call

six bytes of storage on the stack. Notice that the string is pushed onto the stack with its last byte near the top and its length byte toward the bottom. In the ASCII display, the string appears to consist of 'ABCBC', even though you passed only 'ABC'. The last two letters are actually garbage, as is indicated by the length byte that has a value of 03h.

The last parameter on the stack is a real number, which requires six bytes. The format of the number is 00h 00h 00h 00h 00h 81h, which equates to one. As you can see, real numbers have a complex structure, making them difficult to use. Unless you are an expert at floating-point arithmetic, you should restrict your procedures to strings and scalars.

Value parameters last only as long as the procedure that uses them. When the procedure ends, the variables are removed from the stack and are lost. Thus, the values of the original variables do not change.

Passing Parameters by Reference

When passing parameters by reference, Turbo Pascal takes a completely different course. Instead of passing the value of the parameter, Turbo Pascal passes only the address of the parameter. Within the procedure, the address obtains the value of the original variable and changes it if desired. The following program demonstrates how Turbo Pascal passes reference parameters:

```
Program StackTest;
Type
  MaxStr = String[6];

Var ch : Char;
    i  : Integer;
    b  : Eoolean;
    s  : MaxStr;
    r  : Real;

(******************************)

Procedure TestProc(Var ch : Char;
                   Var i  : Integer;
                   Var b  : Eoolean;
                   Var s  : MaxStr;
                   Var r  : Keal);
begin
Inline($90/$9C/$90);
i := 1;
Inline($90/$90/$90);
end;

(******************************)

begin
ch := 'A';
i := 1;
b := true;
s := 'ABC';
r := 1;
TestProc(ch,i,b,s,r);
end.
```

Compile this program and call it into Debug, search for the three NOP instructions, and display the stack segment starting at offset FF7Fh. The result will be similar to that shown in Figure 13-7.

As before, the top of the stack contains a single byte (64h) used by Turbo Pascal. Next on the stack is the address of the first parameter, the character variable **ch**. Because of the microprocessor's method of storage, the first two bytes are the segment (543Fh) and the next two bytes are the offset (0262h). If you displayed the memory at 543Fh:0262h, you would see 41h, the hex value for the letter "A." Thus, by using the address, you can obtain the value rather than having the actual value passed to the procedure.

```
5540:FF7F  8E                                                          .
5540:FF80  D8 89 1E 01 00 58 1F C3-E8 1D 00 FF 74 16 32 E4   X....X.Ch...t.2d
5540:FF90  89 04 9D F9 EB C9 90 E8-0E 00 FF 74 16 9D F8 9C   ...yk..h...t..x.
5540:FFA0  E8 0C 00 8F 44 16 EB A8-16 1F C5 36 B3 0B C3 50   h...D.k(..E63.CP
5540:FFB0  52 2E 8A 16 86 05 B8 01-33 CD 21 5A 58 C3 61 2B   R.....8.3M!ZXCa+
5540:FFC0  57 4E 01 C5 E6 FE C0 F0-87 F2 2D C0 65 1D 3F 54   WN..f".p.r-.e.?T
5540:FFD0  04 09 16 0A 06 F2 3F 54-3F 54 00 00 00 25 77 2D   .....r?T?T...%w-
5540:FFE0  60 51 57 4E E6 FF FE FF-E2 2D 6D 02 3F 54 66 02   `QWNf.".b-m.?Tf.
5540:FFF0  3F 54 65 02 3F 54 63 02-3F 54 62 02 3F 54 64      ?Te.?Tc.?Tb.?Td
```

Top of Stack	Used by Turbo Pascal
64	
543F:0262	Address of variable ch : Char
543F:0263	Address of variable i : Integer
543F:0265	Address of variable b : Boolean
543F:0266	Address of variable s : String[5]
543F:026D	Address of variable r : Real

Figure 13-7.   Stack segment containing parameter addresses

Addresses for the other five variables follow the same pattern and all share the same segment, the data segment. While it may not seem so now, reference parameters are easier to use than value parameters. This is especially true for strings, which can take up a large amount of space in the stack.

Writing an External Procedure

Writing an external procedure is easier if you use a standard template, such as the one shown in Figure 13-8. This code forms the skeleton for most simple external procedures. The

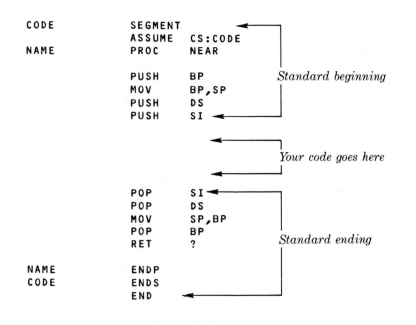

Figure 13-8. Assembler template for external procedures

template has two parts: beginning code and ending code.

In the beginning portion, the code segment takes its value from the CS register and the **NEAR** procedure is declared. The identifier **NAME** denotes the name of the procedure and it can be changed to any name you like. The first operations performed by the beginning code

PUSH BP
MOV BP,SP

store the base pointer register and move the stack pointer into the base pointer. The base pointer will be used to access variables that Turbo Pascal passed on the stack. The beginning code also saves two registers, DS and SI. You should always save any registers that you will change during the procedure's execution.

The ending code restores the registers that were saved at the beginning of the procedure and sets the stack pointer back to its original value. The last three lines indicate the end of the procedure, the end of the code segment, and the end of the listing. Note that you must add the number of bytes to be removed from the stack to the **RET** statement. For example, if your procedure accepts a single reference parameter, the statement would be **RET 4** because you need to remove the variable's address from the stack, and an address uses four bytes.

An example of how to write an external procedure using the template can be found in the common programming problem of converting a string to uppercase characters. In Turbo Pascal, this routine is written as follows:

```
Procedure UpCaseStr(Var S : MaxStr);
var
   i : integer;
begin
for i := 1 to length(s) do
   s[i] := upcase(s[i]);
end;
```

The string is passed to the procedure as a reference parameter and each letter is changed to uppercase. The procedure then returns the changed string to the program. In assembler, the same procedure looks like the following.

```
; UpStr(Var S : MaxStr);

CODE          SEGMENT
              ASSUME  CS:CODE
UPSTR         PROC    NEAR

              NOP ;
              NOP ; Included for debugging.
              NOP ; Remove from final version.
              NOP ;

              PUSH    BP
              MOV     BP,SP
              PUSH    DS
              PUSH    SI

;-------------------------------------------------------------
; Begin uppercase procedure.
;-------------------------------------------------------------

              LDS     SI,[BP+4] ; Get address from the stack.
              XOR     CX,CX     ; Set CX to zero.
              MOV     CL,[SI]   ; Move the length byte into CX.

NEXT_CHAR:

              INC     SI                   ; Point to next character.
              CMP     BYTE PTR [SI],97     ; Is it less than 'a'?
              JL      SKIP                 ; Yes, skip this character.
              CMP     BYTE PTR [SI],122    ; Is it higher than 'z'?
              JG      SKIP                 ; Yes, skip this character.
              SUB     BYTE PTR [SI],32     ; Uppercase the character.
SKIP:         LOOP    NEXT_CHAR            ; Continue for next character.

;-------------------------------------------------------------
; End uppercase procedure.
;-------------------------------------------------------------

              POP     SI
              POP     DS
              MOV     SP,BP
              POP     BP

              NOP ;
              NOP ; Included for debugging.
              NOP ; Remove from final version.
              NOP ;

              RET

UPSTR         ENDP
CODE          ENDS
              END
```

Because the string parameter is passed by reference, Turbo Pascal places the string's address on the stack. The null operation instructions are added at the beginning and end of the procedure to make it easy to find when using Debug. The first step in the uppercase procedure retrieves the address with the **LDS** command, which captures both the segment and offset at one time and assigns them to registers DS and SI, respectively.

Note that the address is located at [BP+4]. Parameters on the stack are always referred to by using the base pointer and an offset. In this case, the address is four bytes above the base pointer.

The address now in SI points to the first byte of the string, the length byte. This byte is loaded into the CX register, which controls loops in assembler.

The remainder of the procedure code operates on the characters in the string. By incrementing SI, you move from one character to the next. Each character is checked to see if it is a lowercase letter. If it is, the character is made into an uppercase character by subtracting 32 from its value.

Each time the loop executes, CX is decremented by one. When CX reaches zero, the loop ends. Note that at all times, operations are performed using the address in SI, which points to the location of the string outside the procedure. As a result, the changes made by this procedure are retained after it ends. Once you have entered the assembler code for this procedure, you need to assemble the code, link it, and convert it to a command file. You can do this easily by using the batch file shown here:

```
masm %1 %1 nul nul
link %1;
erase %1.bak
erase %1.obj
exe2bin %1 %1.com
erase %1.exe
```

Once compiled, declare the external procedure as shown in this program:

```
Program ProcTest;
Type
  MaxStr = String[255];
Var
  s : MaxStr;

(********************************************************)

Procedure UpStrP(Var S : MaxStr); External 'UPSTRP.COM';

(********************************************************)
```

```
Begin
s := 'aaaaaaaaaaaaaaaaaaaaaaaaaaaaaaaaaaaaaaaaaaaaaaaaaaaaaaaaaaaaaaaaa';
UpStrP(s);
WriteLn(s);
End.
```

The name of the assembled command file is UPSTR.COM. When Turbo Pascal encounters the **External** command, it reads the contents of UPSTR.COM and makes them part of the program.

Once you compile a Turbo Pascal program with the **External** declaration, you can test the procedure with Debug. First, search for the four null operation instructions that point to the location of the procedure, as shown here:

```
-s 0100 ffff 90 90 90 90
5160:2D70
5160:2D95
5160:7AF3
5160:7B18
5160:91D5
5160:91FA
5160:9C80
5160:9CA5
5160:BE71
5160:BE96
5160:BF9F
5160:BFC4
5160:CE7C
5160:CE95
5160:F3D2
5160:F3F7
```

While there are many instances of this byte pattern, the first two addresses point to the sought for procedure. You can verify this by unassembling the code at this position, as in the following illustration:

```
-u 2d70
5160:2D70 90          NOP
5160:2D71 90          NOP
5160:2D72 90          NOP
5160:2D73 90          NOP
```

```
5160:2D74 55                PUSH     BP
5160:2D75 8BEC              MOV      BP,SP
5160:2D77 1E                PUSH     DS
5160:2D78 56                PUSH     SI
5160:2D79 C57604            LDS      SI,[BP+04]
5160:2D7C 33C9              XOR      CX,CX
5160:2D7E 8A0C              MOV      CL,[SI]
5160:2D80 46                INC      SI
5160:2D81 803C61            CMP      BYTE PTR [SI],61
5160:2D84 7C08              JL       2D8E
5160:2D86 803C7A            CMP      BYTE PTR [SI],7A
5160:2D89 7F03              JG       2D8E
5160:2D8B 802C20            SUB      BYTE PTR [SI],20
5160:2D8E E2F0              LOOP     2D80

-u
5160:2D90 5E                POP      SI
5160:2D91 1F                POP      DS
5160:2D92 8BE5              MOV      SP,BP
5160:2D94 5D                POP      BP
5160:2D95 90                NOP
5160:2D96 90                NOP
5160:2D97 90                NOP
5160:2D98 90                NOP
5160:2D99 C20400            RET      0004
```

As you can see, the unassembled code looks much like the assembler code you wrote. Note, however, that all the decimal numbers have been changed to hexadecimal format, and all the labels have been changed to address offsets.

Now that you know where the code is located, you can jump to it with the **Go** command. In this illustration, the **Go** instruction jumps to the command that loads the parameter address in DS:SI:

```
-g 2d79

AX=653F  BX=FFFA  CX=5540  DX=2DE8  SP=FFF2  BP=FFF6  SI=FFFA  DI=0262
DS=5442  ES=5442  SS=5540  CS=5160  IP=2079      NV UP EI PL NZ NA PE NC
5160:2D79 C57604        LDS      SI,[BP+04]                        SS:FFFA=0262
```

Debug displays the next instruction to be executed

LDS SI,[BP+04]

and, at the lower right, the value that is placed in SI (0262h). This value is the offset in the data segment where the string variable is located. If you display the portion of the data segment at DS:0262h, you will see that the string is, in fact, located there:

```
-d ds:0262
5442:0262  3E 61 61 61 61 61-61 61 61 61 61 61 61 61       >aaaaaaaaaaaaa
5442:0270  61 61 61 61 61 61 61 61-61 61 61 61 61 61 61 61  aaaaaaaaaaaaaaaa
5442:0280  61 61 61 61 61 61 61 61-61 61 61 61 61 61 61 61  aaaaaaaaaaaaaaaa
5442:0290  61 61 61 61 61 61 61 61-61 61 61 61 61 61 61 61  aaaaaaaaaaaaaaaa
5442:02A0  61 30 30 89 45 C2 C6 45-04 00 B8 BF 0C E8 67 29  a00.E.FE..8?.hg)
5442:02B0  B8 FF FF E8 77 29 B9 CD-00 8A 07 E8 7A 29 43 E2  8..hw)9....hz)Cb
5442:02C0  F8 E8 AA 2A E8 F2 29 A0-85 02 50 FF 36 08 06 FF  xh**hr) ..P.6...
5442:02D0  36 A8 05 FF 36 AA 05 FF-36 AC 05 FF 36 AE 05 FF  6(..6*..6,..6...
5442:02E0  36 B0                                            60
```

The length of the string is 3Eh, or 62 decimal, and all the characters are lowercase "a."

Now that you have verified that the correct address has been loaded into SI, you can begin tracing through the program to see how it operates. The first three commands load the string address, clear the CX register, and move the string length into CL, as shown here:

```
AX=653F  BX=FFFA  CX=5540  DX=2DE8  SP=FFF2  BP=FFF6  SI=FFFA  DI=0262
DS=5442  ES=5442  SS=5540  CS=5160  IP=2D79  NV UP EI PL NZ NA PE NC
5160:2D79 C57604          LDS     SI,[BP+04]                    SS:FFFA=0262
-t

AX=653F  BX=FFFA  CX=5540  DX=2DE8  SP=FFF2  BP=FFF6  SI=0262  DI=0262
DS=5442  ES=5442  SS=5540  CS=5160  IP=2D7C  NV UP EI PL NZ NA PE NC
5160:2D7C 33C9            XOR     CX,CX
-t

AX=653F  BX=FFFA  CX=0000  DX=2DE8  SP=FFF2  BP=FFF6  SI=0262  DI=0262
DS=5442  ES=5442  SS=5540  CS=5160  IP=2D7E  NV UP EI PL ZR NA PE NC
5160:2D7E 8A0C            MOV     CL,[SI]                       DS:0262=3E
-t

AX=653F  BX=FFFA  CX=003E  DX=2DE8  SP=FFF2  BP=FFF6  SI=0262  DI=0262
DS=5442  ES=5442  SS=5540  CS=5160  IP=2D80  NV UP EI PL ZR NA PE NC
5160:2D80 46             INC     SI
-
```

By the end of the third step, CL holds the value 3Eh (the string length), and SI is about to be incremented to point to the first character. The steps shown below demonstrate how the procedure tests this character to make sure it is lowercase and then changes the character to uppercase by subtracting 20h:

```
AX=653F  BX=FFFA  CX=003E  DX=2DE8  SP=FFF2  BP=FFF6  SI=0262  DI=0262
DS=5442  ES=5442  SS=5540  CS=5160  IP=2D80      NV UP EI PL ZR NA PE NC
5160:2D80 46            INC    SI
-t

AX=653F  BX=FFFA  CX=003E  DX=2DE8  SP=FFF2  BP=FFF6  SI=0263  DI=0262
DS=5442  ES=5442  SS=5540  CS=5160  IP=2D81      NV UP EI PL NZ NA PE NC
5160:2D81 803C61        CMP    BYTE PTR [SI],61                  DS:0263=61

AX=653F  BX=FFFA  CX=003E  DX=2DE8  SP=FFF2  BP=FFF6  SI=0263  DI=0262
DS=5442  ES=5442  SS=5540  CS=5160  IP=2D84      NV UP EI PL ZR NA PE NC
5160:2D84 7C08          JL     2D8E
-t

AX=653F  BX=FFFA  CX=003E  DX=2DE8  SP=FFF2  BP=FFF6  SI=0263  DI=0262
DS=5442  ES=5442  SS=5540  CS=5160  IP=2D86      NV UP EI PL ZR NA PE NC
5160:2D86 803C7A        CMP    BYTE PTR [SI],7A                  DS:0263=61
-t

AX=653F  BX=FFFA  CX=003E  DX=2DE8  SP=FFF2  BP=FFF6  SI=0263  DI=0262
DS=5442  ES=5442  SS=5540  CS=5160  IP=2D89      NV UP EI NG NZ AC PE CY
5160:2D89 7F03          JG     2D8E
-t

AX=653F  BX=FFFA  CX=003E  DX=2DE8  SP=FFF2  BP=FFF6  SI=0263  DI=0262
DS=5442  ES=5442  SS=5540  CS=5160  IP=2D8B      NV UP EI NG NZ AC PE CY
5160:2D8B 802C20        SUB    BYTE PTR [SI],20                  DS:0263=61
-t

AX=653F  BX=FFFA  CX=003E  DX=2DE8  SP=FFF2  BP=FFF6  SI=0263  DI=0262
DS=5442  ES=5442  SS=5540  CS=5160  IP=2D8E      NV UP EI PL NZ NA PE NC
5160:2D8E E2F0          LOOP   2D80

-t

AX=653F  BX=FFFA  CX=003D  DX=2DE8  SP=FFF2  BP=FFF6  SI=0263  DI=0262
DS=5442  ES=5442  SS=5540  CS=5160  IP=2D80      NV UP EI PL NZ NA PE NC
5160:2D80 46            INC    SI
```

At the end of these steps, SI points to the first character, which has just been changed to uppercase, and CL has been decreased by one to 3Dh. This loop continues until CL is equal to zero.

You can skip the rest of the loops by using the **Go** command to move directly to one of the null operation instructions. If you now display the memory where the string variable is located, you will find that all characters have been changed to uppercase, as expected:

```
-g 2d95

AX=653F  BX=FFFA  CX=0000  DX=2DE8  SP=FFF8  BP=FFFE  SI=FFFA  DI=0262
DS=5442  ES=5442  SS=5540  CS=5160  IP=2D95      NV UP EI PL NZ NA PE NC
5160:2D95 90            NOP

-d ds:0262
5442:0262  3E 41 41 41 41 41-41 41 41 41 41 41 41 41   >AAAAAAAAAAAAA
5442:0270  41 41 41 41 41 41 41 41-41 41 41 41 41 41 41 41   AAAAAAAAAAAAAAAA
5442:0280  41 41 41 41 41 41 41 41-41 41 41 41 41 41 41 41   AAAAAAAAAAAAAAAA
5442:0290  41 41 41 41 41 41 41 41-41 41 41 41 41 41 41 41   AAAAAAAAAAAAAAAA
5442:02A0  41 30 30 89 45 02 C6 45-04 00 B8 BF 0C E8 67 29   A00.E.FE..8?.hg)
```

```
5442:02B0   B8 FF FF E8 77 29 B9 0D-00 8A 07 E8 7A 29 43 E2   E..hw)9....hz)Cb
5442:02C0   F8 E8 AA 2A E8 F2 29 A0-85 02 50 FF 36 08 06 FF   xh**hr) ..P.6...
5442:02D0   36 A8 05 FF 36 AA 05 FF-36 AC 05 FF 36 AE 05 FF   6(..6*..6,..6...
5442:02E0   36 B0                                              60
```

You can complete the program by typing **G**, or quit by typing **Q**.

This procedure ran correctly the first time, but this is usually not the case. When you see an indication of an error, try to retrace your steps to see where the error occurred. A common error is picking up the wrong data from the stack. Debugging is time consuming, but the results are usually worth it. For example, the preceding **External** procedure executes about three times as fast as the Turbo Pascal code.

Writing Inline Procedures

Converting an external procedure to an inline procedure is straightforward because they both use essentially the same code. The most efficient approach is to create a list file when you assemble your external program. This file contains both the machine language and the assembler instructions for your procedure. The following listing was created when the external uppercase procedure was assembled:

```
1                            ; UpStr(Var S : MaxStr);
2
3      0000                  CODE      SEGMENT
4                                      ASSUME  CS:CODE
5      0000                  UPSTR     PROC    NEAR
6
7      0000  50                        NOP
8      0001  90                        NOP
9      0002  90                        NOP
10     0003  90                        NOP
11
12     0004  55                        PUSH    BP
13     0005  8B EC                     MOV     BP,SP
14     0007  1E                        PUSH    DS
15     0008  56                        PUSH    SI
16
17
18
19     0009  C5 76 04                  LDS     SI,[BP+4]
20     000C  33 C9                     XOR     CX,CX
21     000E  8A 0C                     MOV     CL,[SI]
22
23     0010            NEXT_CHAR:
```

```
24
25      0010   46                              INC     SI
26      0011   80  3C  61                      CMP     BYTE PTR [SI],97
27      0014   7C  08                          JL      SKIP
28      0016   80  3C  7A                      CMP     BYTE PTR [SI],122
29      0019   7F  03                          JG      SKIP
30      001B   80  2C  20                      SUB     BYTE PTR [SI],32
31      001E   E2  F0          SKIP:           LOOP    NEXT_CHAR
32
33
34      0020   5E                              POP     SI
35      0021   1F                              POP     DS
36      0022   8B  E5                          MOV     SP,BP
37      0024   5D                              POP     BP
38
39      0025   90                              NOP
40      0026   90                              NOP
41      0027   90                              NOP
42      0028   90                              NOP
43
44      0029   C2  0004                        RET
45
46      002C                   UPSTR           ENDP
47      002C                   CODE            ENDS
48                                             END
```

Each line of instructions contains a line number, an instruction number, machine-language instructions, and assembler instructions, as shown in Figure 13-9. The machine-language instructions are of primary interest since they will be used in your inline code.

To translate the listing into inline code, simply extract the machine instructions and insert dollar signs and slashes. For example, the instructions in Figure 13-9 produce the inline fragment $80/$3C/$7A/.

You must take care, however, when the machine language includes four-digit codes. For example, the machine language for the **RET 4** instruction is **C2 0004**. To convert

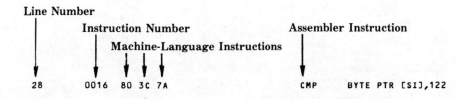

Figure 13-9.   Format of an assembler listing

this to inline code, reverse the bytes in the second operand, resulting in $C2/$04/$00. This switch is required because of the way the 8088 microprocessor stores words.

Creating inline code from the assembler listing is easy with the program shown here:

```
(*$v-*)
Program MakeCode;
Type
  MaxStr = string[255];
Var
  InFile,
  OutFile : Text[1000];

  CodeSt : String[15];
  OutSt,
  comment,
  HexNum,
  s : MaxStr;

  p,p1,i,j,k : Integer;
  ch1,ch2 : Char;

(***********************************************)

Function ValidHexNum(s :MaxStr) : Boolean;
Var
  i : Integer;
Begin
For i := 1 To 4 Do
  Begin
  If Not (s[i] in ['0'..'9','A'..'F']) Then
    Begin
    ValidHexNum := False;
    Exit;
    End;
  End;
ValidHexNum := True;
End;

(***********************************************)

Function GoodCode(Var s : MaxStr) : boolean;
Var
  p : Integer;
Begin
While (Length(s) > 0) And (s[Length(s)] = ' ') Do
  Delete(s,Length(s),1);

p := Pos(':',s);
If p > 0 Then
  Delete(s,1,p+1);

GoodCode := (s[1] in ['0'..'9','A'..'F']) And
            (s[2] in ['0'..'9','A'..'F']) And
            (Length(s) > 0);
End;

(***********************************************)

Procedure ParseLine(s : MaxStr; Var HexNum, CodeSt, Comment : MaxStr);
Var
  p,
  i : Integer;
```

```
Begin
HexNum := '';
CodeSt := '';
comment := '';

p := Pos(' ',s);
If p = 0 Then
  Exit;
HexNum := copy(s,p+1,4);

p := p + 7;
CodeSt := Copy(s,p,8);
i := 1;
while (CodeSt[i] in ['0'..'9','A'..'F',' ']) do
  i := i + 1;
CodeSt := Copy(CodeSt,1,i-1);

p := p + length(CodeSt);
While (p < Length(s)) And (s[p] < #41) Do
  p := p + 1;

Comment := copy(s,p,Length(s)-p+1);
End;

(**********************************************)

Begin
Assign(InFile,Paramstr(1)+'.lst');
Reset(InFile);
Assign(OutFile,Paramstr(1)+'.inl');
Rewrite(OutFile);

WriteLn(OutFile,'Begin');
WriteLn(OutFile,'Inline(');

ReadLn(InFile,s);
ParseLine(s, HexNum, CodeSt, Comment);
While (Pos('Segments',s) = 0) And (Not Eof(InFile)) Do
   Begin
   If ValidHexNum(HexNum) And GoodCode(CodeSt) Then
      Begin
      OutSt := '$';
      OutSt := OutSt + copy(CodeSt,1,2);
      Delete(CodeSt,1,3);

      While Length(CodeSt) > 0 Do
        Begin
        p := Pos(' ',CodeSt);

      If p > 0 Then
        Begin
        OutSt := OutSt + '/$' + copy(CodeSt,1,p-1);
        Delete(CodeSt,1,p);
        End
      Else
        Begin
        If Length(CodeSt) = 2 Then
          Begin
          OutSt := OutSt + '/$' + CodeSt;
          CodeSt := '';
          End
        Else
          Begin
          OutSt := OutSt + '/$' + Copy(CodeSt,3,2);
          OutSt := OutSt + '/$' + Copy(CodeSt,1,2);
          CodeSt := '';
          End;
        End;
      End;
   End;
```

```
    OutSt := OutSt + '/';
    While Length(OutSt) < 20 Do
      OutSt := OutSt + ' ';
    WriteLn(OutFile,OutSt,'   (* ',comment,' *)');
    WriteLn(OutSt,'   (* ',comment,' *)');
    End;

  ReadLn(InFile,s);
  ParseLine(s, HexNum, CodeSt, Comment);
  End;

WriteLn(OutFile,');');
WriteLn(OutFile,'End;');

Close(InFile);
Close(OutFile);
End.
```

To run this program, enter the program name and the name of the list file at the DOS prompt (for example, **C>Makecode Upstrp**). Do not include the filename extension LST with the filename; the program adds it automatically. The program creates a file that contains the inline code, gives the file the same name as the list file, and adds the filename extension Inl. The following listing shows the inline code produced by the program that uses the assembler listing from the external uppercase procedure.

```
Begin
InLine(
$90/                      (* NOP ; *)
$90/                      (* NOP ; Included for debugg *)
$90/                      (* NOP ; Remove from final v *)
$90/                      (* NOP ; *)
$55/                      (* PUSH    BP *)
$8B/$EC/                  (* MOV     BP,SP *)
$1E/                      (* PUSH    DS *)
$56/                      (* PUSH    SI *)
$C5/$76/$04/              (* LDS     SI,[BP+4] ; Get a *)
$33/$C9/                  (* XOR     CX,CX    ; Set C *)
$8A/$0C/                  (* MOV     CL,[SI]  ; Move  *)
$46/                      (* INC     SI             *)
$80/$3C/$61/              (* CMP     BYTE PTR [SI],97  *)
$7C/$08/                  (* JL      SKIP              *)
$80/$3C/$7A/              (* CMP     BYTE PTR [SI],122 *)
$7F/$03/                  (* JG      SKIP              *)
$80/$2C/$20/              (* SUB     BYTE PTR [SI],32  *)
$E2/$F0/                  (* SKIP:           LOOP    NEXT_CHAR*)
$5E/                      (* POP     SI *)
$1F/                      (* POP     DS *)
$8B/$E5/                  (* MOV     SP,BP *)
$5D/                      (* POP     BP *)
$90/                      (* NOP ; *)
$90/                      (* NOP ; Included for debugg *)
$90/                      (* NOP ; Remove from final v *)
$90/                      (* NOP : *)
```

```
$C2/$04/$00/              (* RET    4 *)
);
End;
```

This code is very close to the final code you will use. To complete the conversion, take the following steps:

1. Add a procedure heading.
2. Delete the **RET** instruction.
3. Remove the lines **MOV BP,SP** and **MOV SP,BP**.
4. Remove the **NOP** statements.
5. Remove the last slash in the inline code.

Because Turbo Pascal has already saved registers, you can also remove the **PUSH** statements at the beginning and the **POP** statements at the end. This program listing contains the final procedure, with all the modifications:

```
Program x;
Type
   MaxStr = String[255];
Var
   s : MaxStr;

Procedure UpStrInl(Var S : MaxStr);
Begin
Inline(
$C5/$76/$04/      (* LDS    SI,[BP+4] ; Get a *)
$33/$C9/          (* XOR    CX,CX    ; Set C *)
$8A/$0C/          (* MOV    CL,[SI]  ; Move  *)
$46/              (* INC    SI              *)
$80/$3C/$61/      (* CMP    BYTE PTR [SI],97 *)
$7C/$08/          (* JL     SKIP            *)
$80/$3C/$7A/      (* CMP    BYTE PTR [SI],122 *)
$7F/$03/          (* JG     SKIP            *)
$80/$2C/$20/      (* SUB    BYTE PTR [SI],32 *)
$E2/$F0           (* SKIP:      LOOP  NEXT_CHAR*)
);
End;

Begin
s := 'abc';
UpStrInl(s);
WriteLn(s);
end.
```

As you can see, this code is more compact than the equivalent external procedure. Even so, it hardly seems worth the extra effort to create the inline code. However, inline code allows you to access global variables, typed constants, local variables, and reference parameters by name, while external procedures do not. This powerful feature greatly increases the range of data available to inline procedures.

The problem with using variables in inline code is loading their values into registers and moving them back again. The code needed for each type of move is detailed in Figure 13-10.

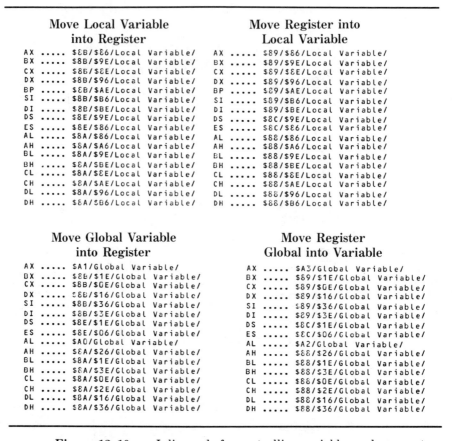

Move Local Variable into Register

```
AX  .....  $8B/$86/Local Variable/
BX  .....  $8B/$9E/Local Variable/
CX  .....  $8B/$8E/Local Variable/
DX  .....  $8B/$96/Local Variable/
BP  .....  $8B/$AE/Local Variable/
SI  .....  $8B/$B6/Local Variable/
DI  .....  $8B/$BE/Local Variable/
DS  .....  $8E/$9E/Local Variable/
ES  .....  $8E/$86/Local Variable/
AL  .....  $8A/$86/Local Variable/
AH  .....  $8A/$A6/Local Variable/
BL  .....  $8A/$9E/Local Variable/
BH  .....  $8A/$BE/Local Variable/
CL  .....  $8A/$8E/Local Variable/
CH  .....  $8A/$AE/Local Variable/
DL  .....  $8A/$96/Local Variable/
DH  .....  $8A/$B6/Local Variable/
```

Move Register into Local Variable

```
AX  .....  $89/$86/Local Variable/
BX  .....  $89/$9E/Local Variable/
CX  .....  $89/$8E/Local Variable/
DX  .....  $89/$96/Local Variable/
BP  .....  $89/$AE/Local Variable/
SI  .....  $89/$B6/Local Variable/
DI  .....  $89/$BE/Local Variable/
DS  .....  $8C/$9E/Local Variable/
ES  .....  $8C/$86/Local Variable/
AL  .....  $88/$86/Local Variable/
AH  .....  $88/$A6/Local Variable/
BL  .....  $88/$9E/Local Variable/
BH  .....  $88/$BE/Local Variable/
CL  .....  $88/$8E/Local Variable/
CH  .....  $88/$AE/Local Variable/
DL  .....  $88/$96/Local Variable/
DH  .....  $88/$B6/Local Variable/
```

Move Global Variable into Register

```
AX  .....  $A1/Global Variable/
BX  .....  $8B/$1E/Global Variable/
CX  .....  $8B/$0E/Global Variable/
DX  .....  $8B/$16/Global Variable/
SI  .....  $8B/$36/Global Variable/
DI  .....  $8B/$3E/Global Variable/
DS  .....  $8E/$1E/Global Variable/
ES  .....  $8E/$06/Global Variable/
AL  .....  $A0/Global Variable/
AH  .....  $8A/$26/Global Variable/
BL  .....  $8A/$1E/Global Variable/
BH  .....  $8A/$3E/Global Variable/
CL  .....  $8A/$0E/Global Variable/
CH  .....  $8A/$2E/Global Variable/
DL  .....  $8A/$16/Global Variable/
DH  .....  $8A/$36/Global Variable/
```

Move Register Global into Variable

```
AX  .....  $A3/Global Variable/
BX  .....  $89/$1E/Global Variable/
CX  .....  $89/$0E/Global Variable/
DX  .....  $89/$16/Global Variable/
SI  .....  $89/$36/Global Variable/
DI  .....  $89/$3E/Global Variable/
DS  .....  $8C/$1E/Global Variable/
ES  .....  $8C/$06/Global Variable/
AL  .....  $A2/Global Variable/
AH  .....  $88/$26/Global Variable/
BL  .....  $88/$1E/Global Variable/
BH  .....  $88/$3E/Global Variable/
CL  .....  $88/$0E/Global Variable/
CH  .....  $88/$2E/Global Variable/
DL  .....  $88/$16/Global Variable/
DH  .....  $88/$36/Global Variable/
```

Figure 13-10. Inline code for controlling variables and parameters

Move Immediate to Register

```
AX  .....  $B8/$Low Byte/$High Byte/
BX  .....  $BB/$Low Byte/$High Byte/
CX  .....  $B9/$Low Byte/$High Byte/
DX  .....  $BA/$Low Byte/$High Byte/
BP  .....  $BD/$Low Byte/$High Byte/
SI  .....  $BE/$Low Byte/$High Byte/
DI  .....  $BF/$Low Byte/$High Byte/
AL  .....  $B0/$Low Byte/
AH  .....  $B4/$Low Byte/
BL  .....  $B3/$Low Byte/
BH  .....  $B7/$Low Byte/
CL  .....  $B1/$Low Byte/
CH  .....  $B5/$Low Byte/
DL  .....  $B2/$Low Byte/
DH  .....  $B6/$Low Byte/
```

<table>
<tr><td colspan="2">

Move Typed Constant to Register

```
AX  .....  $2E/$A1/Constant/
BX  .....  $2E/$8B/$1E/Constant/
CX  .....  $2E/$8B/$0E/Constant/
DX  .....  $2E/$8B/$16/Constant/
BP  .....  $2E/$8B/$2E/Constant/
SI  .....  $2E/$8B/$36/Constant/
DI  .....  $2E/$8B/$3E/Constant/
DS  .....  $2E/$8E/$1E/Constant/
ES  .....  $2E/$8E/$06/Constant/
AL  .....  $2E/$A0/Constant/
AH  .....  $2E/$8A/$26/Constant/
BL  .....  $2E/$8A/$1E/Constant/
BH  .....  $2E/$8A/$3E/Constant/
CL  .....  $2E/$8A/$0E/Constant/
CH  .....  $2E/$8A/$2E/Constant/
DL  .....  $2E/$8A/$16/Constant/
DH  .....  $2E/$8A/$36/Constant/
```
</td><td colspan="2">

Move Register to Typed Constant

```
AX  .....  $2E/$A3/Constant/
BX  .....  $2E/$89/$1E/Constant/
CX  .....  $2E/$89/$0E/Constant/
DX  .....  $2E/$89/$16/Constant/
BP  .....  $2E/$89/$2E/Constant/
SI  .....  $2E/$89/$36/Constant/
DI  .....  $2E/$89/$3E/Constant/
DS  .....  $2E/$8C/$1E/Constant/
ES  .....  $2E/$8C/$06/Constant/
AL  .....  $2E/$A2/Constant/
AH  .....  $2E/$88/$26/Constant/
BL  .....  $2E/$88/$1E/Constant/
BH  .....  $2E/$88/$3E/Constant/
CL  .....  $2E/$88/$0E/Constant/
CH  .....  $2E/$88/$2E/Constant/
DL  .....  $2E/$88/$16/Constant/
DH  .....  $2E/$88/$36/Constant/
```
</td></tr>
</table>

Move Reference Parameter to Register

```
AX  .....  $C4/$BE/Param/$26/$8B/$05/
BX  .....  $C4/$BE/Param/$26/$8B/$1D/
CX  .....  $C4/$BE/Param/$26/$8B/$0D/
DX  .....  $C4/$BE/Param/$26/$8B/$15/
BP  .....  $C4/$BE/Param/$26/$8B/$2D/
AL  .....  $C4/$BE/Param/$26/$8A/$05/
AH  .....  $C4/$BE/Param/$26/$8A/$25/
BL  .....  $C4/$BE/Param/$26/$8A/$1D/
BH  .....  $C4/$BE/Param/$26/$8A/$3D/
CL  .....  $C4/$BE/Param/$26/$8A/$0D/
CH  .....  $C4/$BE/Param/$26/$8A/$2D/
DL  .....  $C4/$BE/Param/$26/$8A/$15/
DH  .....  $C4/$BE/Param/$26/$8A/$35/
```

Move Register to Reference Parameter

```
AX  .....  $C4/$BE/Param/$26/$89/$05/
BX  .....  $C4/$BE/Param/$26/$89/$1D/
CX  .....  $C4/$BE/Param/$26/$89/$0D/
DX  .....  $C4/$BE/Param/$26/$89/$15/
BP  .....  $C4/$BE/Param/$26/$89/$2D/
AL  .....  $C4/$BE/Param/$26/$88/$05/
AH  .....  $C4/$BE/Param/$26/$88/$25/
BL  .....  $C4/$BE/Param/$26/$88/$1D/
BH  .....  $C4/$BE/Param/$26/$88/$3D/
CL  .....  $C4/$BE/Param/$26/$88/$0D/
CH  .....  $C4/$BE/Param/$26/$88/$2D/
DL  .....  $C4/$BE/Param/$26/$88/$15/
DH  .....  $C4/$BE/Param/$26/$88/$35/
```

```
Note: $C4/$BE uses the ES:DI register set.
      $C4/$B6 uses the DS:SI register set.
```

Figure 13-10.   Inline code for controlling variables and parameters
(continued)

For example, the inline uppercase procedure contains the following instructions:

```
$C5/$76/$04/         (* LDS   SI,[BP+4] ; Get a *)
$8A/$CC/             (* MOV   CL,[SI]   ; Move  *)
```

These instructions load the address of the string parameter, located at BP+4, into the ES:SI register set, and move the byte at that address into the CL register. To refer to the string variable by name, use the following code:

```
$C4/$B6/s/
$8A/$0D
```

These inline fragments produce a procedure that looks like this:

```
Procedure UpStrInl(Var S : MaxStr);
Begin
Inline(
$33/$C9/             (* XOR     CX,CX       ; Set C *)

(* New Inline Code *)
$C4/$B6/s/           (* LDS     SI,s                *)
$26/$8A/$0D/         (* MOV     CL,[SI]             *)

$46/                 (* INC     SI                  *)
$80/$3C/$61/         (* CMP     BYTE PTR [SI],97  *)
$7C/$08/             (* JL      SKIP                *)
$80/$3C/$7A/         (* CMP     BYTE PTR [SI],122 *)
$7F/$03/             (* JG      SKIP                *)
$80/$2C/$20/         (* SUB     BYTE PTR [SI],32  *)
$E2/$F0              (* SKIP:        LOOP    NEXT_CHAR
);
End;
```

It should be clear by now that writing inline code is no simple task. If increased speed is not critical, use Turbo Pascal code. When extra speed is critical, however, set aside enough time to write and debug the code thoroughly.

External Functions in Turbo Pascal

The discussion of external and inline code so far has focused on procedures. You can also write external functions in assembler, though they are more complicated owing to the need to return values through the function.

If the function is of type Boolean, Byte, Character, or Integer, the function result is returned in register AX. Before loading the AX register with the function result, set it equal to zero to make sure the result is not affected by what is already in the register.

Functions of type Real return their result on the stack. The exponent end of the real must be at the lowest address on the stack. When your procedure ends, do not remove the function result from the stack as part of the **RET** command. Functions of type Set return a 32-byte data area on the stack.

Because of several peculiarities in the way that Turbo Pascal handles strings, functions of type String do not work properly under all conditions. If you need an external function that returns a string, write an external procedure instead, and pass the string as a reference parameter.

External Procedures and Inline Code
in Turbo Pascal Version 4.0

One of the most important changes implemented in Turbo Pascal 4.0 is in the use of external routines and inline code. While your existing inline code should still be useful, any external routines you have written will have to be modified.

External Routines

External assembler routines in Turbo Pascal 4.0 are more powerful than before. For one thing, they can utilize global variables. Additionally, assembler routines can call Turbo Pascal procedures directly. In return for this power, you are required to do a little more work in setting up your external routine.

The basic format of an external routine is shown below

```
DATA      SEGMENT WORD PUBLIC
          EXTERN X:INTEGER, Y:INTEGER; Refers to global variables.
DATA      ENDS


CODE      SEGMENT WORD PUBLIC
          ASSUME CS:CODE, DS:DATA;
          EXTERN DO_MATH : NEAR; Refers to Turbo Pascal procedure.
          PUBLIC TEST; Declare the name of the assembler procedure.


TEST      PROC NEAR
          ; Your assembler routine goes here.
          MOV CX, COUNT; Move the value of global variable into CX.
          CALL DO_MATH; Call the Turbo Pascal procedure.
          RET

TEST      ENDP
CODE      ENDS
          END
```

The data segment is the first part of the routine and is used only when your routine will access global variables. The code segment is defined as WORD PUBLIC and is followed with the **Extern** command that declares any Turbo Pascal procedures that your procedure will call. Within the code segment, externally declared global variables and procedures can be referred to by name.

Here is the routine given earlier in this chapter, modified to conform to Turbo Pascal 4.0. When you assemble this procedure, do not create a .COM file — Version 4.0 uses only .OBJ modules

```
; UpStr(Var S : MaxStr);
CODE            SEGMENT WORD PUBLIC
                ASSUME  CS:CODE
                PUBLIC UPSTR
UPSTR           PROC    NEAR

                PUSH    BP
                MOV     BP,SP
                PUSH    DS
                PUSH    SI

;-----------------------------------------------------------
; Begin uppercase procedure.
;-----------------------------------------------------------
                LDS     SI,[BP+4] ; Get address from the stack.
                XOR     CX,CX     ; Set CX to zero.
                MOV     CL,[SI]   ; Move the length byte into CX.

NEXT_CHAR:
                INC     SI                  ; Point to next character.
                CMP     BYTE PTR [SI],97  ; Is it less than 'a'?
                JL      SKIP                ; Yes, skip this character.
                CMP     BYTE PTR [SI],122 ; Is it higher than 'z'?
                JG      SKIP                ; Yes, skip this character.
                SUB     BYTE PTR [SI],32  ; Uppercase the character.
SKIP:           LOOP    NEXT_CHAR           ; Continue for next character.

;-----------------------------------------------------------
; End uppercase procedure.
;-----------------------------------------------------------
                POP     SI
                POP     DS
                MOV     SP,BP
                POP     BP

                RET     4
UPSTR           ENDP
CODE            ENDS

                END
```

As you can see, the changes required are minimal. The first

line was modified to read **CODE SEGMENT WORD PUB-LIC**, and the line **PUBLIC UPSTR** was added.

Turbo Pascal 4.0 also requires that you declare external routines differently than before. Before making the external declaration, you must use the L compiler directive to tell Turbo Pascal which object files to look for. Then the procedure is defined as an external procedure much as before, except that the filename is not part of the declaration. These two lines constitute the necessary external declaration:

```
{$L UpStr}

Procedure UpStr(Var S : MaxStr); External;
```

The sample program below demonstrates how Turbo Pascal 4.0 declares and uses the **UpStr** external procedure.

```
Program StringTest;
Type
  MaxStr = String[255];
Var
  S : MaxStr;

{$L UpStr}

Procedure UpStr(Var S : MaxStr); External;

Begin
S := 'abcdefg';
UpStr(S);
WriteLn(S);
End.
```

Inline Machine Code

The rules for inline machine code have changed only a bit with Turbo Pascal 4.0. Turbo Pascal now allows inline directives—procedures that consist solely of the inline code and nothing else. Inline directives are declared by naming a procedure followed by the inline code *without a begin or end statement*. For example, the inline directive here inserts the single byte FAh into your program

```
Procedure DisInt;

Inline($FA);
```

In fact, inline directives are not procedures at all. They simply tell Turbo Pascal to insert their inline code in place of a procedure.

FOURTEEN

Text Display

Personal Computer Text Display
Using Display Memory
Turbo Pascal Windows
Memory Mapped Video in Turbo Pascal Version 4.0

People often judge programs primarily by the quality of their video display. Screen presentation is so important that often programs are successful simply because they "look like" other popular programs. Your computer is capable of producing screen displays that are both attractive and helpful. This chapter discusses these capabilities and how you can control them with Turbo Pascal.

Personal Computer Text Display

Personal computers have two video modes: Text and Graphics (the Graphics mode is covered in Chapter 15). When it is in Text mode, a personal computer can display any of the 256 standard ASCII characters it supports. These characters are locked permanently in the computer's memory, so your PC always knows how to draw them.

To display characters, your computer uses a *video adapter*, which is a circuit board that connects the computer to a monitor. Most computers have either a monochrome adapter or a color graphics adapter (CGA), though the recently introduced enhanced graphics adapter (EGA) is gaining popularity. This chapter focuses on monochrome and color graphics adapters, but the concepts discussed can also apply to the enhanced graphics adapter.

The Video Adapter and Display Memory

Your monitor can display up to 80 characters horizontally and 25 vertically, or a total of 2000 characters in an entire screen. Each character has its own *foreground* and *background color*. The foreground color is the color of the character itself; the background color is the color of the space around the character.

Your computer stores characters and color information in a special part of memory known as the *display memory*. This is what tells your computer which characters and colors to display. Although it is located on the video adapter card, the display memory is considered to be part of RAM. The first byte of the display memory contains the first character on your monitor, which appears in the upper left corner.

Thus, if the first byte in the display memory contains the value 41h (the hexadecimal ASCII value for the letter "A"), the monitor displays the letter "A" in the upper left corner of the monitor. The second byte in display memory, the attribute byte for the first character, contains color and other display information.

This pattern—character, attribute, character, attribute—is repeated for all 2000 characters that appear on the monitor. Thus, the contents of a single screen require 4000 bytes of video memory.

The Attribute Byte

A computer with a color graphics adapter is capable of displaying 16 different colors, each of which consists of up to four elements: blue, green, yellow, and brightness. The color your computer displays depends on the particular combination of these elements. For example, the color black uses no elements, while light cyan uses the blue, green, and brightness elements. Video adapters also support a blinking element that makes the character flash on and off and has no effect on color.

An attribute byte stores the foreground and background color for the preceding character byte. Figure 14-1 shows

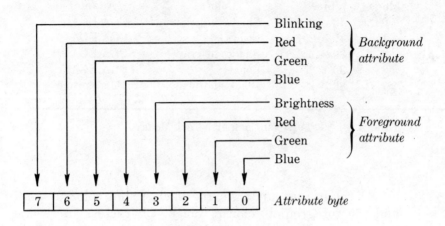

Figure 14-1.   Mapping the attribute byte

how each bit in the attribute byte contributes to the color of the character and its background.

The first three bits (0, 1, and 2) in the attribute byte control a character's foreground color, while the fourth bit (bit 3) adds brightness to the color. You can combine these four elements to create 16 different foreground colors. Bits 4, 5, and 6 determine a character's background color, and bit 7, when on, makes the character blink. Because the background has no brightness element, only eight colors are available for it.

On the monochrome monitor, the attribute byte can create only five display formats: hidden, normal, bright, underlined, and reverse. As with the color graphics adapter, brightness is controlled by bit 3 and blinking is controlled by bit 7.

Characters are hidden when both the foreground and background colors are set to black. The brightness and blinking bits have no effect with hidden characters.

To display characters in *reverse video* (dark characters

Mode	Size	Colors	Adapter
0	40 × 25	Shades of gray	CGA,EGA
1	40 × 25	Colors	CGA,EGA
2	80 × 25	Shades of gray	CGA,EGA
3	80 × 25	Colors	CGA,EGA
7	80 × 25	Black and white	Monochrome

Table 14-1. Personal Computer Text Modes

on a light background), set the background color to white and the foreground color to black. Characters in reverse video cannot be made bright, but they can be made to blink.

Underlining, a specialty of the monochrome adapter, can only be displayed when the foreground is blue. An underlined character can be shown bright and be made to blink, but it cannot be shown in reverse video.

Personal Computer Text Modes

Personal computers support 16 different display modes, and five of these display text. These modes, listed in Table 14-1, control both the size of the characters and the colors in a display. Mode 0, for example, displays large characters (40 per line) in shades of gray.

The first four display modes, 0 through 3, work only with color graphics adapters and enhanced graphics adapters, most of which can switch between the four modes. Mode 7, on the other hand, is used only by the monochrome adapter.

You can change your computer's Text mode with the Turbo Pascal command **TextMode** (see Figure 14-2). This command, which works only with the color graphics adapter (it has no effect on monochrome adapters), can be used with or without parameters. Without parameters, **TextMode** sets

Parameters	Settings
TextMode	Set to previous text mode
TextMode(BW40)	Black and white/40 characters per line
TextMode(BW80)	Black and white/80 characters per line
TextMode(C40)	Color/40 characters per line
TextMode(C80)	Color/80 characters per line

**Value of Turbo Pascal
standard constants**

BW40 = 0
BW80 = 1
C40 = 2
C80 = 3

Figure 14-2.   Turbo Pascal TextMode command

the video display to the previous setting, while with parameters, it can set the video display to any of the first four modes. Turbo Pascal supplies four standard integer constants for the **TextMode** command: **BW40**, **BW80**, **C40**, and **C80**. Note that **TextMode** always clears the screen before changing the mode.

Controlling Color with Turbo Pascal

Turbo Pascal allows you to select the foreground and background colors for your text with the commands **TextColor** and **TextBackground**. The color graphics adapter provides 16 colors to choose from, as shown in Table 14-2. **TextColor**, which sets the foreground color (the color of the character), can use all 16 colors. **TextBackground**, which sets the background color, can use only the dark colors.

Turbo Pascal provides a standard constant called **Blink**, which when added to the foreground color causes the charac-

Dark Colors	Light Colors
0: Black	8: DarkGray
1: Blue	9: LightBlue
2: Green	10: LightGreen
3: Cyan	11: LightCyan
4: Red	12: LightRed
5: Magenta	13: LightMagenta
6: Brown	14: Yellow
7: LightGray	15: White

Table 14-2.   Turbo Pascal Color Identifiers

ter to blink. Here are some examples of how to use Turbo Pascal's color commands:

```
TextBackground(Blue);

TextColor(Cyan);

TextColor(Cyan+Blink);
```

Once invoked, the new colors take effect with the next characters you display; the characters already on the screen retain their colors.

Using Screen Coordinates

Like a map, your computer monitor has locations that are defined by coordinates. Screen coordinates are commonly referred to as x and y, where x is the column position and y is the row position. (Coordinates are displayed in x:y format.) Thus, the upper left corner of the monitor has coordinate position 1:1, while the lower right corner is at coordinate 80:25.

You can move the cursor to any coordinate location on your monitor with the Turbo Pascal command **GotoXY**. For example, the command **GotoXY(1,10)** positions the cursor at column 1 of row 10. If you want to know the coordinates for the cursor's current position, use the Turbo Pascal functions **WhereX** and **WhereY**. **WhereX** returns an integer that represents the cursor column; **WhereY** does the same for the cursor row.

Turbo Pascal's standard screen commands give you the control you need to create attractive and informative screen displays. The following program demonstrates how to create a simple data-entry routine with all of the commands described thus far: **TextMode**, **TextColor**, **TextBackground**, **GotoXY**, **WhereX**, and **WhereY**.

```
Program Box;
Var
  i,code,
  x, y : Integer;
  s : String[20];

(*************************************************)

Procedure DrawBox(x1,y1,x2,y2,fg,bg : Integer);
Var
  i : Byte;
Begin
TextColor(fg);
TextBackground(bg);
For i := (x1+1) To (x2-1) Do
   Begin
   GotoXY(i,y1);
   Write(205);
   GotoXY(i,y2);
   Write(205);
   End;

For i := (y1+1) To (y2-1) Do
   Begin
   GotoXY(x1,i);
   Write(186);
   GotoXY(x2,i);
   Write(186);
   End;

GotoXY(x1,y1);
Write(201);
GotoXY(x2,y1);
Write(187);
GotoXY(x1,y2);
Write(200);
```

```
GotoXY(x2,y2);
Write(188);
End;

(*************************************************)

Procedure GetNumber;
Begin
DrawBox(5,14,35,16,white,black);
GotoXY(7,15);
Write('Enter a number (1-10): ');
x := WhereX;
y := WhereY;
  Repeat
  GotoXY(x,y);
  s := '     ';
  Write(s);
  GotoXY(x,y);
  Read(s);
  Val(s,i,code);
  until ((i > 0) and (i < 11)) and (code = 0);

GotoXY(1,20);
Write('Press Return...');
ReadLn;
End;

(*************************************************)

Begin
ClrScr;
TextMode(c40);
GetNumber;

ClrScr;
TextMode(c80);
GetNumber;
End.
```

The procedure **DrawBox** uses standard ASCII graphics characters to draw a rectangle anywhere on the screen. The procedure defines a data-entry portion on the screen.

Using Display Memory

The Turbo Pascal command **Write** uses a BIOS interrupt to send characters to the monitor. You can bypass BIOS, however, and write characters directly to display memory. This approach is far faster, though admittedly more complicated, than using **Write**.

Before you can write directly to the display memory, you must know where it is located. The display memory in a monochrome adapter starts at segment $B000, while the color graphics adapter starts at $B800. You can determine which adapter is being used with **CurrentVidMode**, a procedure that uses a BIOS interrupt (for more information, see Chapter 12). Another way of obtaining the same information is shown here:

```
Function VidSeg : Integer;
Begin
If Mem[$0000:$0449] = 7 Then
  VidSeg := $B000
Else
  VidSeg := $B800;
End;
```

The **VidSeg** function checks the memory location at segment 0000h and offset 0449h, where DOS stores the video adapter code. If the byte at this location is equal to 7, the adapter is monochrome; if not, it is safe to assume the adapter is color graphics.

While this method is more direct than the BIOS interrupt, it does not work on computers with memory addresses that are incompatible with the IBM standard. In this chapter, however, we assume a high degree of IBM compatibility because most PC manufacturers have incorporated the IBM standard into their machines.

Once you know the type of video adapter in use, it is easy to bypass BIOS and write characters directly to the display memory. This program determines the type of adapter used, and then fills the display memory with the letter "A" in reverse video:

```
Program FillScreen;
Var
  i,j,
  VS  : Integer;

(*$I VidSeg.Inc*)

Begin
```

```
ClrScr;
VS := VidSeg;

j := 0;
For i := 1 to 2000 do
  Begin
  Mem[VS:j] := $41;    (* Write character 'A'.    *)
  Mem[VS:j+1] := $70; (* Display Black on White. *)
  j := j + 2;          (* Skip to next character. *)
  End;
End.
```

The file VIDSEG.INC, which is loaded into the program with the Include directive, contains the code for the function **VidSeg**. The program uses **VidSeg** to store the segment that contains the display memory in the integer variable **vs**. The For-Do loop uses the standard array **Mem** to set all character bytes in the display memory to the hexadecimal ASCII code for the letter "A" (41h) and all attribute bytes to black on white (70h). The variable **j**, which holds the offset in display memory, is incremented by 2 after each character and attribute are written.

With the procedure **FastWrite**, shown below, you can write strings directly to display memory at specific x and y coordinates, as well as set the color attributes.

```
Procedure FastWrite(x,y : integer;
                    Var s : MaxStr;
                    fg,bg : integer);

Var
   i,ColAtr : Byte;

Begin
ColAtr := (bg Shl 4) + fg;     (* create attribute byte)
x := ((y-1) * 80 + (x-1)) * 2; (* calculate offset *)

For i := 1 To length(s) Do
  Begin
  MemW[VS:x] :=   (ColAtr Shl 8) + ord(s[i]);
  x := x + 2;
  End;
End;
```

The procedure first creates the attribute byte (**ColAtr**) by shifting the background color left four bits and adding the foreground color. Next, the procedure computes the starting offset in display memory with the following formula:

$$x: = ((y-1) * 80 + (x-1)) * 2;$$

In each iteration of the loop, the Turbo Pascal array **MemW** sets the character byte and the attribute byte at the same time. Because **MemW** operates on a full word (16 bytes), both the attribute byte and character byte must be combined into a single word. The procedure combines them by shifting the color byte to the left eight bits and adding the character byte. Notice that this puts the attribute byte in the high-order portion of the word, yet the attribute byte should be placed after the character byte in display memory. Once again, Intel's backward storage method forces you to think in reverse when operating with words.

Avoiding Vertical Retrace

The program listed below uses the Turbo Pascal **FastWrite** procedure (contained in the file FASTWRIT.INC) to display a large "V" on your monitor.

```
Program FastWriteDemo;
Type
  MaxStr = String[255];
Var
  VS,
  i,j : Integer;
  s : MaxStr;

(*$I VIDSEG.INC*)
(*$I FASTWRIT.INC*)

Begin
ClrScr;
VS := VidSeg;
s := 'XXXXXXX';
j := 5;
For i := 1 To 25 Do
  begin
  FastWrite(j,i,s,Yellow,Black);
  j := j + 1;
  end;
For i := 25 DownTo 1 Do
```

```
begin
FastWrite(j,i,s,Yellow,Bl  k);
j := j + 1;
end;
End.
```

When you run this program, you will probably notice some "snow" on your screen. This is caused by the *vertical retrace*, a process that updates your screen from display memory 60 times per second. Each vertical retrace takes approximately 1.25 milliseconds. If you attempt to write directly to display memory while a vertical retrace is in progress, you will get snow.

The only way to avoid snow is to write to display memory between vertical retraces; in other words, the program must wait until the retrace has ended and then write the characters to display memory before the next retrace begins. Turbo Pascal is simply not fast enough to do this; you must use an external assembler procedure or inline code. The following assembler listing will give you snow-free video output.

```
;Procedure FastWrite( x, y : Integer;
;                     Var  S : MaxStr;
;                     fg, bg : Integer;
;                     stype : Char); external 'FASTSTR.COM';

CODE          SEGMENT
              ASSUME  CS:CODE
VIDEO         PROC    NEAR

FASTSTR:      PUSH    BP
              PUSH    DS
              MOV     BP,SP

;-----------------------------------------------------------------
;Compute the offset into display memory -- ((y-1)*80 + (x-1)) * 2
;-----------------------------------------------------------------
              MOV     BX,[BP+18]   ; Get x from stack;
              MOV     AX,[BP+16]   ; Get y from stack;
              DEC     BX           ; Decrement x and y to get
              DEC     AX           ;   correct offset.
              MOV     CX,0080      ; Multiply y (in AX) by
              MUL     CX           ;   80 (in CX).
              ADD     AX,BX        ; Add x to y;
```

```
            MOV     CX,0002     ; Multiply the
            MUL     CX          ;   sum by 2.
            MOV     DI,AX       ; Store the starting offset in DI.

;-------------------------------------------------------------------
;Create the attribute byte
;-------------------------------------------------------------------

            MOV     BX,[BP+8]   ; Get the background color.
            MOV     AX,[BP+10]  ; Get the foreground color.
            MOV     CX,4        ; Shift the foreground color
            SHL     BX,CL       ;   into the high nybble.
            ADD     BX,AX       ; Add in the foreground.
            XCHG    BL,BH       ; Move into the upper byte.

            MOV     DX,3DAH     ; Load the CRT port address in DX.

;-------------------------------------------------------------------
;Get the monitor type
;-------------------------------------------------------------------

            MOV     AX,0B000H   ; Load the monochrome
            MOV     ES,AX       ;   segment into ES.

            MOV     AX,[BP+6]   ; Get stype from stack.
            CMP     AL,4DH      ; Is stype 'M'?
            JZ      CHKSTR      ; If yes, it's monochrome.
            MOV     AX,0B800H   ; If no, move color
            MOV     ES,AX       ;   segment into ES.

;-------------------------------------------------------------------
;Load the string and check for zero length
;-------------------------------------------------------------------

CHKSTR:     LDS     SI,[BP+12]  ; Load string address into DS:SI.
            MOV     CL,[SI]     ; Move string length into CL.
            CMP     CL,0        ; If string length is zero,
            JZ      ENDSTR      ;   exit procedure.
            CLD                 ; Clear direction flag.

MOVCHAR:    INC     SI          ; Point to next character in string.
            MOV     BL,[SI]     ; Move it into BL.

WLOW:       IN      AL,DX       ; Get CRT status.
            TEST    AL,1        ; Is retrace off?
            JNZ     WLOW        ; If off, wait for it to start.
            CLI                 ; No interrupts, please.

WHIGH:      IN      AL,DX       ; Get CRT status.
            TEST    AL,1        ; Is retrace on?
            JZ      WHIGH       ; If on, wait for it to stop.

            MOV     AX,BX       ; Move color and character to AX.
            STOSW               ; Move color & character to screen.
            STI                 ; Interrupts are now allowed.

LOOP        MOVCHAR             ; Done yet?

ENDSTR:     MOV     SP,BP
            POP     DS
            POP     BP
            RET     14
```

```
VIDEO       ENDP
CODE        ENDS
            END
```

The **FastWrite** procedure checks the adapter I/O port number 3DAh for a status bit known as the *vertical sync signal*. When this status bit is on, a vertical retrace is in progress. The procedure first checks to see if the monitor is between retraces (the status bit equals 0). If so, the loop repeats until a retrace begins. The procedure then waits for the retrace to end.

As soon as the retrace ends, the procedure moves characters to the display memory. Because the procedure waited until the very end of a retrace, there should be ample time to move the characters before the next retrace begins.

Assemble this code to a Com file and include it in your programs as an external procedure with this declaration:

```
Procedure FastWrite( x, y : Integer;
                     Var S : MaxStr;
                     bc, fc : Integer;
                     stype : Char); external 'FASTWRIT.COM';
```

The procedure takes a character parameter that indicates the type of adapter in use: "C" for color graphics and "M" for monochrome. Your program must determine the type of display adapter in use and set a **char** variable, such as **stype**, equal to "M" for monochrome or "C" for CGA. In the following program, the procedure **VidSeg** sets **stype** to the correct value.

```
Program FastStringDemo;
Type
  MaxStr = String[255];
Var
  s : MaxStr;
  i,j : Integer;
  stype : char;

(*$I VIDSEG.INC*)

Procedure FastWrite( x, y : Integer;
                     Var S : MaxStr;
                     bc, fc : Integer;
                     stype : Char); external 'FASTWRIT.COM';
```

```
Begin
(*************************)
(* Set the value of stype. *)
(*************************)
If VidSeg = $B800 then
  stype := 'C'
Else
  stype := 'M';

ClrScr;
s := 'XXXXXXX';
j := 5;
For i := 1 To 25 Do
  Begin
  FastWrite(j,i,s,Yellow,Black,stype);
  j := j + 1;
  End;
For i := 25 DownTo 1 Do
  Begin
  FastWrite(j,i,s,Yellow,Black,stype);
  j := j + 1;
  End;
End.
```

The technique used in **FastWrite** works on most IBM-compatible personal computers and greatly improves speed. There are some computers, however, that are incompatible, and with these you must use BIOS interrupts to write to the screen. One program, WordStar Release 4.0, solves this problem by letting the user select between BIOS interrupts and direct screen writes.

Turbo Pascal Windows

Under normal conditions, you can display information anywhere on your monitor. You can also, however, restrict the output to just a portion of your monitor with the Turbo Pascal command **Window**. For example, the command

Window(10,10,20,15)

restricts your display to a 10 by 5 rectangle starting at column 10 and row 10; the remainder of the display is off limits to the **Write** command. (*Note:* the **FastWrite** procedure pays no attention to Turbo Pascal and can write outside the active window.) The command

Window(1,1,80,25)

returns the monitor to normal operation.

The **Window** command's most useful feature is its ability to realign the screen coordinates so that they fit the active window; that is, coordinates in a window refer only to the window, not the entire screen. Thus, the command

GotoXY(1,1)

positions the cursor at the upper left corner of the active window, not the entire screen. In fact, Turbo Pascal treats the window just as if it were the entire screen: when text runs off the bottom of the window, the screen scrolls up one line.

Using Windows

The Turbo Pascal **Window** command is simply not powerful enough to create professional-looking pop-up windows. The major problem is that a Turbo Pascal window wipes out the portion of the screen it uses. Most people expect windows to act the way they do in the popular program SideKick; that is, when a window disappears, the text that was on the screen "beneath" the window reappears.

To create true pop-up windows, save the screen before you open the window and then restore the screen when you close the window.

To save a screen, define a variable that can store all the information contained in the screen: 2000 characters, 2000 attributes, and the x and y coordinates, as shown here:

```
Type
   ScreenType = Record
      Pos : Array [1..80,1..25] of Record
         Ch : Char;
```

```
    At : Byte;
    End;
  CursX,
  CursY : Integer;
  End;

Var
  Screen : ScreenType;
```

screentype, a nested record data type, stores characters and attributes in the array named **Pos**, which has dimensions that match the coordinates of your monitor. Thus, to refer to the character in column 10 and row 20, you would use the following statement:

Screen.Pos[10,20].Ch

Integer variables **CursX** and **CursY** store the cursor position.

If you overlay a screen variable directly on top of the display memory, you can change the characters on the screen by simply changing the values in the variable. Remember that the display memory consists of 4000 bytes that alternate between characters and attributes, exactly like the variable **screen**. To use **screen** to manipulate the display memory, place this variable at the display memory location.

One way to do this is to declare the variable **absolute** at the display memory location. If you have a color graphics adapter, you would use this declaration:

Var
    Screen : ScreenType Absolute $B800;

Unfortunately, you have to choose the offset in advance, which means you can service only one type of video adapter (unless you define separate screens for monochrome and video). A better approach is to define the screen as a pointer variable. The program then sets the pointer to the correct offset in display memory, depending on the adapter in use. The following program demonstrates this technique:

```
(*$V-*)
Program FastStringDemo;
Const
```

```
    MaxWin = 5;
Type
  MaxStr = String[255];

  ScreenPtr = ^ScreenType;
  ScreenType = Record
    Pos : Array [1..80,1..25] of Record
      Ch : Char;
      At : Byte;
      End;
    CursX,
    CursY : Integer;
    End;

Var
  Screen : ScreenPtr;

(*$I VIDSEG.INC*)

Begin
ClrScr;
New(Screen);

Screen := Ptr(VidSeg,$0000);

Screen^.Pos[10,20].ch := 'X';
ReadLn;
End.
```

The program begins by clearing the screen and creating a pointer variable named **screen** that initially points to the heap, where all pointer variables are stored. But the program then uses the **Ptr** command to point the variable to the display memory. Because of this repositioning, any changes made to the variable **screen** will show up on your monitor.

When you use this method, do not use the **Dispose** command on the **screen** variable. Because the value of the pointer is changed, Turbo Pascal tries to deallocate memory in the wrong area of memory, very likely crashing the program.

Multiple Logical Screens and Pop-Up Windows

Your program can have as many screen variables as its memory will hold. Screens that are held in memory, and not displayed, are often called *logical* screens to distinguish them

from the *physical screen* (the computer monitor). A program
can write to a logical screen without disturbing the display
on the physical screen. Then, when you want to display the
logical screen, simply move its contents into the physical
screen.

The use of logical screens is best explained by an example. This program uses one physical screen variable (**screen**)
and three logical screen variables (**screen1**, **screen2**, and
screen3). By typing **1**, **2**, or **3** on the keyboard, you can display any of the three logical screens.

```
Program FastStringDemo;
Const
  MaxWin = 5;
Type
  MaxStr = String[255];

  ScreenPtr = ^ScreenType;
  ScreenType = Record
    Pos : Array [1..80,1..25] of Record
      Ch : Char;
      At : Byte;
      End;
    CursX,
    CursY : Integer;
    End;

Var
  Screen,
  Screen1,
  Screen2,
  Screen3 : ScreenPtr;
  Ch : Char;
  i,j : Integer;

(*$I VIDSEG.INC*)

Begin
New(Screen);
New(Screen1);
New(Screen2);
New(Screen3);

For i := 1 To 80 Do
For j := 1 To 25 Do
  Begin
  Screen1^.pos[i,j].Ch := '1';
  Screen2^.pos[i,j].Ch := '2';
  Screen3^.pos[i,j].Ch := '3';
  Screen1^.pos[i,j].At := $07;
  Screen2^.pos[i,j].At := $07;
  Screen3^.pos[i,j].At := $07;
  End;
```

```
ClrScr;
Screen := Ptr(VidSeg,$0000);
WriteLn('Press 1,2,3 to change screens or 0 to exit.')

  Repeat
  Read(Kbd,Ch);
    Case Ch of
    '1' : Screen^ := Screen1^;
    '2' : Screen^ := Screen2^;
    '3' : Screen^ := Screen3^;
    End;
  Until Ch = '0';

End.
```

Screen, which is superimposed on the display memory, acts as the physical device. The program changes the display memory by setting the physical device variable **screen** equal to one of the logical screens. The transfer is fast, and the entire screen is updated in one statement. A program can also move the contents of the physical screen to a logical screen with a statement like this:

$$Screen^\wedge := Screen^\wedge;$$

Manipulating logical screens is the technique you need to create pop-up windows. Before you open a pop-up window, save a copy of the physical screen in a logical screen variable. Then, when you close the window, restore the screen to its original appearance. Thus, your windows seem to pop up from nowhere and, when no longer needed, disappear without a trace.

The following program uses an array of logical screens to create up to five pop-up windows. When you run the program, you will see how windows can overlap without causing problems.

```
(*$v-*)
Program WindowDemo;
Const
  MaxWin = 5;
Type
  MaxStr = String[255];
```

```
ScreenType = Record
  Pos : Array [1..80,1..25] of Record
    Ch : Char;
    At : Byte;
    End;
  CursX,
  CursY : Integer;
  End;

WindowPtr = ^WindowType;
WindowType = Record
  Scr : ScreenType;
  WinX1,
  WinY1,
  WinX2,
  WinY2 : Integer;
  End;

Var
  ch : Char;
  i : Integer;
  ActiveWin : WindowPtr;
  Windo : Array [0..MaxWin] of WindowPtr;
  CurrentWindow : Integer;
  stype : Char;

(*$I VIDSEG.INC*)

(****************************************)

Procedure FastWrite( x, y : Integer;
                     Var S : MaxStr;
                     bc, fc : Integer;
                     stype : Char); external 'FASTWRIT.COM';

(****************************************)

Procedure FastBox(x1,y1,x2,y2,fg,bg : Integer);
Var
  i : Byte;
  s : String[1];
Begin
TextColor(fg);
TextBackground(bg);

s := 205;
For i := (x1+1) To (x2-1) Do
  Begin
  FastWrite(i,y1,s,fg,bg,stype);
  FastWrite(i,y2,s,fg,bg,stype);
  End;
```

```
s := 186;
For i := (y1+1) To (y2-1) Do
  Begin
  FastWrite(x1,i,s,fg,bg,stype);
  FastWrite(x2,i,s,fg,bg,stype);
  End;

s := 201;
FastWrite(x1,y1,s,fg,bg,stype);
s := 187;
FastWrite(x2,y1,s,fg,bg,stype);
s := 200;
FastWrite(x1,y2,s,fg,bg,stype);
s := 188;
FastWrite(x2,y2,s,fg,bg,stype);
End;

(******************************************)

Procedure SetUpWindows;
Var
  i : Integer;
Begin
New(ActiveWin);
For i := 0 To MaxWin Do
  New(Windo[i]);

With ActiveWin^ Do
  Begin
  WinX1 := 1;
  WinY1 := 1;
  WinX2 := 80;
  WinY2 := 25;
  With Scr Do
    Begin
    CursX := WhereX;
    CursY := WhereY;
    End;
  End;

ActiveWin := Ptr(VidSeg,$0000);
CurrentWindow := 0;
With Windo[CurrentWindow]^ Do
  Begin
  WinX1 := 1;
  WinY1 := 1;
  WinX2 := 80;
  WinY2 := 25;
  With Scr Do
```

```
    Begin
    CursX := 1;
    CursY := 1;
    End;
  End;
End;


(*****************************************)

Procedure OpenWindow;
Begin
If CurrentWindow < MaxWin Then
  Begin
  Windo[CurrentWindow]^.Scr := ActiveWin^.Scr;
  Windo[CurrentWindow]^.Scr.CursX := WhereX;
  Windo[CurrentWindow]^.Scr.CursY := WhereY;

  CurrentWindow := CurrentWindow + 1;
  With Windo[CurrentWindow]^ Do
    Begin
    WinX1 := CurrentWindow * 10;
    WinY1 := CurrentWindow * 2;
    WinX2 := WinX1 + 20;
    WinY2 := WinY1 + 5;
    With Scr Do
      Begin
      CursX := 1;
      CursY := 1;
      End;
    Window(WinX1,WinY1,WinX2,WinY2);
    FastBox(WinX1-1,WinY1-1,WinX2+1,WinY2+1,yellow,black);
    TextColor(Yellow);
    TextBackGround(Black);
    ClrScr;
    End;
  End;
End;


(*****************************************)

Procedure CloseWindow;
Begin
If CurrentWindow > 0  Then
  Begin
  Windo[CurrentWindow]^.Scr.CursX := WhereX;
  Windo[CurrentWindow]^.Scr.CursY := WhereY;

  CurrentWindow := CurrentWindow - 1;
  ActiveWin^.Scr := Windo[CurrentWindow]^.Scr;
  With Windo[CurrentWindow]^ Do
    Begin
    Window(WinX1,WinY1,WinX2,WinY2);
    GoToXY(Scr.CursX,Scr.CursY);
    End;
  End;
```

```
End;

(****************************************)

Procedure FillWindow;
Begin
Reset(kbd);
  Repeat
  Write(Chr(Random(80)+30));
  Delay(20);
  Until keypressed;
End;

(****************************************)

Begin
If VidSeg = $B800 then
  stype := 'C'
Else
  stype := 'M';
ClrScr;
SetUpWindows;

TextColor(Yellow+Blink);
GotoXY(1,25);
Write('Press any key to open windows...');
GotoXY(1,1);

TextColor(Yellow);

FillWindow;
For i := 1 To MaxWin Do
  Begin
  OpenWindow;
  FillWindow;
  End;

For i := 1 To MaxWin Do
  Begin
  CloseWindow;
  FillWindow;
  End;
End.
```

When you run **WindowDemo**, you will probably notice
snow on the screen. There is just no way to avoid it with code
written in Turbo Pascal. An external procedure written in
assembler, however, can eliminate the snow while making the

screen update even faster. Listed here are two assembler programs you can use as external procedures. The first displays a logical screen without snow. The second stores the current video screen in a logical screen.

```
;WRITESCR.ASM  This external procedure writes the contents of
; a screen variable to the video screen.

CODE          SEGMENT
              ASSUME  CS:CODE
VIDEO         PROC    NEAR

;-----------------------------------------------------------------
;Save registers.
;-----------------------------------------------------------------

              PUSH    BP
              MOV     BP,SP

              PUSH    ES
              PUSH    DS
              PUSH    SS
              PUSH    SI
              PUSH    DI

;-----------------------------------------------------------------
;Get the monitor type.
;-----------------------------------------------------------------

              MOV     DX,3DAh       ; Load the CRT port address into DX.

              MOV     AX,0B000H     ; Load the monochrome segment
              MOV     ES,AX         ;    into ES.

              MOV     AX,[BP+4]     ; Get stype from the stack.
              CMP     AX,4DH        ; Is stype 'M'?
              JZ      CONT          ; If yes, it's monochrome.

              MOV     AX,0B800H     ; If not, load color segment
              MOV     ES,AX         ;    into ES.

;-----------------------------------------------------------------
;Load buffer to screen.
;-----------------------------------------------------------------

CONT:         LDS     SI,[BP+6]     ; Load buffer address in DS:SI.
              MOV     DI,0          ; Point to start of display memory.
              MOV     CX,2000       ; Move 2000 characters.
              CLD                   ; Clear direction flag.

MOVCHAR:

WLOW:         IN      AL,DX         ; Get CRT status.
              TEST    AL,1          ; Is retrace off?
              JNZ     WLOW          ; If off, wait for it to start.
              CLI                   ; No interrupts, please.

WHIGH:        IN      AL,DX         ; Get CRT status.
```

```
            TEST    AL,1         ; Is retrace on?
            JZ      WHIGH        ; If on, wait for it to end.

            LODSW                ; Get word from buffer to AX.
            STOSW                ; Move word from AX to screen.
            STI                  ; Interrupts are allowed.
            LOOP    MOVCHAR      ; Done yet?

ENDSTR:

;----------------------------------------------------------------
;Restore registers.
;----------------------------------------------------------------

            POP     DI
            POP     SI
            POP     SS
            POP     DS
            POP     ES

            MOV     SP,BP
            POP     BP
            RET     6

VIDEO       ENDP
CODE        ENDS
            END


;READSCR.ASM  This external procedure reads the contents of
; the video screen and stores them in a screen variable.

CODE        SEGMENT
            ASSUME  CS:CODE

VIDEO       PROC    NEAR

;----------------------------------------------------------------
;Save registers.
;----------------------------------------------------------------

            PUSH    BP
            MOV     BP,SP
            PUSH    ES
            PUSH    DS
            PUSH    SS
            PUSH    SI
            PUSH    DI

;----------------------------------------------------------------
;Get the monitor type
;----------------------------------------------------------------

            MOV     DX,3DAh   . ; Load the CRT port address in DX.
```

```
                MOV       AX,0B000H   ; Load the monochrome segment
                MOV       DS,AX       ;   into DS.

                MOV       AX,[BP+4]   ; Get Stype from the stack.
                CMP       AX,4DH      ; Is stype 'M'?
                JZ        CONT        ; If yes, it's monochrome.

                MOV       AX,0B800H   ; If not, it's color.
                MOV       DS,AX

CONT:
                LES       DI,[BP+6]   ; Load buffer address in ES:DI.
                MOV       SI,0        ; Point to start of display memory.
                MOV       CX,2000     ; Number of characters in screen.
                CLD                   ; Clear direction flag.

;----------------------------------------------------------------
;Transfer display memory to buffer.
;----------------------------------------------------------------

MOVCHAR:

WLOW:           IN        AL,DX       ; Get CRT status.
                TEST      AL,1        ; Is retrace off?
                JNZ       WLOW        ; If off, wait for it to start.
                CLI                   ; No interrupts please.

WHIGH:          IN        AL,DX       ; Get CRT status.
                TEST      AL,1        ; Is retrace on?
                JZ        WHIGH       ; If on, wait for it to end.

                LODSW                 ; Move word from screen to AX.
                STOSW                 ; Move AX to buffer.
                LOOP      MOVCHAR     ; Done yet?
                STI                   ; Interrupts are allowed.

ENDSTR:

;----------------------------------------------------------------
;Restore registers.
;----------------------------------------------------------------

                POP       DI
                POP       SI
                POP       SS
                POP       DS
                POP       ES

                MOV       SP,BP
                POP       BP
                RET       6

VIDEO           ENDP
CODE            ENDS
                END
```

You can use these procedures in the program **Window-Demo** by declaring them with the following statements:

```
procedure WriteScr(Var S : ScreenType;
                    stype : char); external 'WRITESCR.COM';

procedure ReadScr(Var S : ScreenType;
                   stype : char); external 'READSCR.COM';
```

Within the program, delete all references to the variable **activewin** and replace the line

ActiveWin^.Scr := Windo[CurrentWindow]^.Scr;

with the line

WriteScr(Windo[CurrentWindow]^.Scr,stype);

and replace

Windo[CurrentWindow]^.Scr := ActiveWin^.Scr;

with the line

ReadScr(Windo[CurrentWindow]^.Scr,stype);

These fast, clean screen procedures make your windows look professional. Now, you can spend your time on filling the windows with useful information and tools (calendars, calculators, note pads, and so on) and not on getting the windows started in the first place.

Memory Mapped Video in Turbo Pascal Version 4.0

One of the major improvements introduced by Turbo Pascal 4.0 is the addition of memory-mapped video. No longer do you need an external procedure for fast video display; Turbo Pascal writes directly to video memory for you when you use the CRT unit. This new capability provides several key advantages. First, you do not have to write your own external routine. Even if you copy a routine, you still have to remember to include it in your program. More important, Turbo Pascal's direct video routines work with Turbo Pascal windows, which makes programming much easier.

In addition to writing directly to video memory, Turbo Pascal 4.0 can also use BIOS routines for video display. You control the method used with the variable **DirectVideo**. When **DirectVideo** is true (this is the default state), Turbo Pascal writes directly to video memory; when **DirectVideo** is false, BIOS routines are used. The following program demonstrates the use of both methods of video display:

```
Program TestVideo;
Uses CRT;
Var
  i : Integer;
  s : String[79];

Begin
FillChar(s,SizeOf(s),'A');
s[0] := Chr(79);
Write ('Press Enter to start demo');
ReadLn;

{ Write to screen using direct video }
ClrScr;
For i := 1 To 25 Do
  WriteLn(s);
ReadLn;

{ Write to screen using Bios }
DirectVideo := False;
ClrScr;
For i := 1 To 25 Do
  WriteLn(s);
ReadLn;

End.
```

When you run this program, you will see just how much faster direct video display can be. In most cases, you will want to use direct video display in your programs. Most MS-DOS computers keep video displays at a standardized location in memory. Still there are significant number of less-than-fully-compatible computers on the market. Because Turbo Pascal 4.0 supports direct and BIOS text display, your programs can run on any MS-DOS machine.

Graphics

Graphics Mode and Text Mode
IBM Graphics Modes
Turbo Pascal Graphics Commands
Turtlegraphics
Turbo Pascal Version 4.0 Graphics

High-quality graphics is one of the most powerful and popular features of the personal computer. Now, with the development of enhanced graphics adapters and window-based operating systems, graphics have become even more important. This chapter discusses the tools that Turbo Pascal provides to help you produce graphics of your own.

Graphics Mode and Text Mode

Your PC can work in two modes: Text or Graphics. In Text mode, PC's display is limited to 256 ASCII characters, which can appear only in the 80 columns and 25 rows defined by your video adapter.

In Graphics mode, however, no such restrictions apply; you can draw lines, figures, circles, squares, or any design anywhere on your screen. In fact, you have control over every one of the thousands of *pixels*, the smallest dots of light your monitor can display.

By combining pixels, the video adapter forms letters, numbers, and special symbols. In Graphics mode, you select which pixels to turn on and off, thereby creating shapes, letters, and so forth. Turning on pixels in a graphics display is known as *plotting*.

All the graphics plotted in this chapter use the color graphics adapter. While the IBM monochrome adapter can display high-resolution graphics when coupled with a special adapter, Turbo Pascal does not support any of these adapters. The Turbo Graphix Toolbox, discussed in Chapter 20, does support monochrome graphics through its special routines.

IBM Graphics Modes

The IBM personal computer supports ten graphics modes. The three graphics modes that Turbo Pascal supports are compatible with the color graphics adapter (see Table 15-1). The remaining seven modes are reserved for the PCjr and the enhanced graphics adapter.

Video mode 4, Graph Color mode, produces medium-resolution graphics in four colors; Video mode 5, Graph mode, produces the same resolution but displays colors differently. Video mode 6, High-resolution mode, produces high-resolution graphics in two colors.

Graph Color Mode

Your program initiates Graph Color mode (Video mode 4) with the command **GraphColorMode**. In this mode, Turbo Pascal uses 320×200 pixels per screen, with coordinates 0 to

IBM Video Mode	Command	Resolution	Color
4	GraphColorMode	320×200	4 colors
5	GraphMode	320×200	4 shades of gray
6	HiRes	640×200	2 colors

Table 15-1.   Turbo Pascal Graphics Modes

319 horizontally (the **x** coordinates) and 0 to 199 vertically (the **y** coordinates). When plotting graphics, use the coordinates to tell Turbo Pascal where to place the display.

Graph Color mode allows you to use any of four colors (three foreground colors and one background color) in a single graphic display. You cannot, however, *select* any four colors; rather, they must be chosen from palettes, each of which contains three standard foreground colors (see Table 15-2). The palettes also contain a background color, but this one you select.

Choose the palette you want to use with the command **Palette** and an integer that indicates which palette to use. If you plot a graphic with one palette, and then select a new palette, the graphics displayed on your monitor immediately change color to reflect the new palette. Note that some screens cannot display light colors, in which case you can use only the palettes with dark colors (palettes 0 and 1).

You can select the background color with the **Graph-Background** command, which takes an integer parameter that indicates the color to use. Once selected, the background color becomes part of the palette you are using.

Graph Mode

Graph mode (Video mode 5) is initiated with the command **GraphMode**. It is similar in many ways to Graph Color

Color Number:	0	1	2	3
Palette 0	Background	Green	Red	Brown
Palette 1	Background	Cyan	Magenta	Light gray
Palette 2	Background	Light green	Light red	Yellow
Palette 3	Background	Light cyan	Light magenta	White

Table 15-2.   Foreground Color in Graphics Palettes

mode, but differs in its use of color. This mode was developed for monitors that display only green on black and therefore do not benefit from a wide range of colors. Despite this restriction, Graph mode produces colors on an RGB monitor. Graph mode uses only two palettes, as shown in Table 15-3.

The primary colors in Graph mode are blue, red, and light gray. Palette 0 displays these in their dark form, Palette 1 in their light form. If your monitor cannot display bright colors, you can use only Palette 0.

High-Resolution Graphics

The command **HiRes** (Video mode 6) produces the highest quality graphics you can get from the color graphics adapter. In this mode, your screen displays 640 × 200 pixels—twice as many as in the medium-resolution modes. In this mode, screen coordinates range from 0 to 639 horizontally and from 0 to 199 vertically.

While graphics in the High-resolution mode are more precise than those in the other modes, they are less colorful. Computers display high-resolution graphics in a single color (any of the 16 dark and light colors) on a black background. Select the foreground color with the command **HiResColor**, as shown here:

    HiResColor(Yellow);

Note that when you finish using any of the three graphics modes, you can return to Text mode with the command **TextMode**.

Color Number:	0	1	2	3
Palette 0	Background	Blue	Red	Light gray
Palette 1	Background	Light blue	Light red	White

Table 15-3. Graph Mode Palettes

Some people prefer medium-resolution graphics because of the colors they can use; others prefer the precision of high-resolution graphics. The same programming concepts apply regardless of the mode you prefer.

Turbo Pascal Graphics Commands

Once you initiate a graphics mode, you can create graphics with the commands supplied by Turbo Pascal. These commands fall into one of two categories: basic graphics commands and extended graphics commands.

Basic Graphics Commands

The TURBO.COM program contains only two graphics commands: **Plot** and **Draw**. **Plot**, which accepts two integer coordinates and a color as parameters, simply turns a particular pixel on. The program called **JaggedLine** demonstrates how to use the **Plot** command:

```
Program JaggedLine;
Const
  Dif = 20;
Var
  x,y,t : Integer;
Begin
HiRes;
For x := 0 To 639 Do
  Plot(x,0,White);
For y := 0 To 199 Do
  Plot(639,y,White);
For x := 639 Downto 0 Do
  Plot(x,199,White);
For y := 199 Downto 0 Do
  Plot(0,y,White);

t := 1;
y := 100 - Dif;
For x := 0 To 640 Do
  Begin
```

```
     Plot(x,y,White);
     if t = 1 then
       Begin
       y := y + 1;
       If y = 100 + Dif Then
         t := -1;
       End
     Else
       Begin
       y := y - 1;
       If y = 100 - Dif Then
         t := 1;
       End;
     End;

Readln;
End.
```

JaggedLine draws a jagged line horizontally across your screen, as shown in Figure 15-1. Note that the program must calculate the location of each pixel in the line. In other words, the picture is expressed in an algorithm that computes all the pixels needed to produce the picture on the screen. Because it takes a good amount of time to compute all those points, Graphics mode is slower than Text mode.

Even more powerful than **Plot**, the **Draw** command creates a straight line between any two pairs of coordinates. Here is the standard format for **Draw**:

Draw(x1,y1,x2,y2,color)

where the coordinate pairs **x1:y1** and **x2:y2** define the endpoints of the line. The following program shows **Draw**'s ability to create a screen full of random lines. Figure 15-2 contains a sample of the program's output.

```
Program ManyLines;
Var
   i,x1,y1,x2,y2 : Integer;
Begin
HiRes;
Draw(0,0,0,199,White);
Draw(0,199,639,199,White);
Draw(639,199,639,0,White);
Draw(639,0,0,0,White);
```

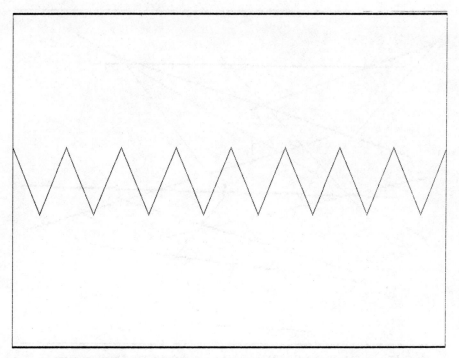

Figure 15-1.   Drawing a jagged line with the Plot command

```
For i := 1 To 20 Do
   Begin
   x1 := Random(640);
   x2 := Random(640);
   y1 := Random(200);
   y2 := Random(200);
   Draw(x1,y1,x2,y2,White);
   End;
End.
```

The important difference between **Plot** and **Draw** is that both turn pixels on, but **Draw** also decides *which* pixels to turn on. **Draw** contains a plotting algorithm that determines which pixels between two points need to be turned on to create a straight line. As the following Turbo Pascal procedure that works like **Draw** shows, calculating the pixels needed to create a straight line is no simple task.

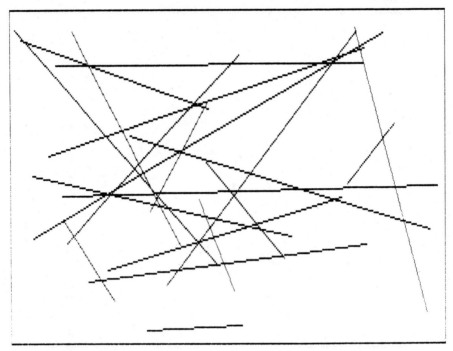

Figure 15-2.   Random lines created with the Draw command

```
Procedure PlotLine(x1,y1,x2,y2,color : Integer);
Var
   a,b,
   dx,dy : Real;
   x,y,i : Integer;

Begin
dx := (x2 - x1);
dy := (y2 - y1);

If dx <> 0 Then
  Begin
  b := (dy/dx);
  a := y1 - x1*b;
  For x := x1 to x2 do
    Begin
    y := Round((a+x*b));
    Plot(x,y,color);
    End
  End
```

```
Else
  Begin
  If y1 < y2 Then
    For y := y1 to y2 Do
      Plot(x1,y,color)
  Else
    For y := y1 DownTo y2 Do
      Plot(x1,y,color);
  End;
End;
```

The procedure called **PlotLine** first calculates the difference between the **x** coordinates and the **y** coordinates. If it finds a difference between the **x** coordinates, it calculates a slope and intercept and then graphs the line accordingly. If the **x** coordinates are equal (that is, the line is vertical), the procedure simply plots all values of **y** against a single **x** coordinate.

While **Plot** and **Draw** can create any type of graphics display imaginable, they require you to do most of the work. You can add more graphics commands to your programs by including the file of external procedures that comes on your Turbo Pascal disk. These external procedures comprise Turbo Pascal's extended graphics commands.

Turbo Pascal Extended Graphics

Your Turbo Pascal distribution diskette contains two files named GRAPH.P and GRAPH.BIN. GRAPH.P contains external declarations for numerous graphics functions that you can include in your programs, while GRAPH.BIN contains the machine code for the external procedures. When you include GRAPH.P in a program, you can use GRAPH .BIN's extended set of Turbo Pascal graphics routines. Note, however, that when you include GRAPH.P in your program, you must always select a palette before plotting any graphics.

Arc and Circle

Arc and **Circle**, two of the commands in GRAPH.P, draw circular lines: **Arc** draws either an entire circle or portions of it, while **Circle** always draws a complete one.

You must use these five parameters to call **Arc**:

Arc(x,y,angle,radius,color)

The **x** and **y** coordinates mark the beginning of the 270°
mark (the leftmost point) on the circumference of the arc.
Angle indicates the number of degrees to draw; for example,
if **angle** is equal to 180, the procedure draws a half-circle. If
angle is a positive number, the arc is drawn clockwise; if
negative, counterclockwise. **Radius**, the distance from the
center of the arc to any point on its circumference, is measured in pixels. **Color** is simply an integer corresponding to a
color selected from the active palette.

The **Circle** command works in nearly exactly the same
way as **Arc**. **Circle**, however, does not need the angle since it
always assumes an angle of 360°, which creates a complete
circle.

Both **Arc** and **Circle** work well in Medium-resolution
mode (see Figure 15-3), but as you can see by using the
commands in the following example, they fall short in high
resolution (see Figure 15-4).

Figure 15-3.   Circle and Arc used in medium resolution

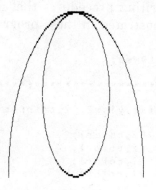

Figure 15-4.   Circle and Arc used in high resolution

```
Arc(100,100,180,100,1);
Circle(200,50,50,1);
```

Starting at coordinates **100:100**, **Arc** draws a half-circle with a radius of 100 pixels. **Circle**, starting at **200:50**, draws a circle with a 50-pixel radius.

Whereas the medium-resolution graphics are correctly proportioned, the high-resolution graphics are distended. Both results are controlled by the *aspect ratio*, which is the ratio of horizontal to vertical height. The aspect ratio determines the proportions in a graphic display. For example, in high resolution, a color graphics monitor produces 640×200 pixels, but the vertical pixels are closer together than the horizontal ones. The difference in space between pixels is about 2.35 times. Thus, to create a correctly proportioned graphic, you must either shrink the vertical dimensions or expand the horizontal coordinates by a factor of 2.35 in high resolution or 1.17 in medium resolution. These numbers are the aspect ratios for their respective modes.

Because **Circle** and **Arc** use only the medium-resolution aspect ratio, they produce graphics that do not look right on high-resolution screens. You cannot do anything to improve these commands, but you can get correct proportions in your graphics by writing procedures that use the correct aspect ratios, as demonstrated in these programs:

```
Program AspectDemo;

(***********************************************)

Procedure Box(x1,y1,x2,y2,color : Integer);
Begin
Draw(x1,y1,x1,y2,color);
Draw(x1,y2,x2,y2,color);
Draw(x2,y2,x2,y1,color);
Draw(x2,y1,x1,y1,color);
End;

(***********************************************)

Procedure HiResBox(x1,y1,x2,y2,color : Integer);
Const
  AspectRatio = 2.35;
Begin
y2 := round(y2 / AspectRatio);
Draw(x1,y1,x1,y2,color);
Draw(x1,y2,x2,y2,color);
Draw(x2,y2,x2,y1,color);
Draw(x2,y1,x1,y1,color);
End;

(***********************************************)

Procedure MedResBox(x1,y1,x2,y2,color : Integer);
Const
  AspectRatio = 1.17;
Begin
y2 := round(y2 / AspectRatio);
Draw(x1,y1,x1,y2,color);
Draw(x1,y2,x2,y2,color);
Draw(x2,y2,x2,y1,color);
Draw(x2,y1,x1,y1,color);
End;

(***********************************************)

Begin
HiRes;
Box(0,0,199,199,white);
Readln;

HiRes;
HiResBox(0,0,199,199,white);
Readln;
```

```
GraphMode;
MedResBox(0,0,199,199,white);
ReadLn;
End.
```

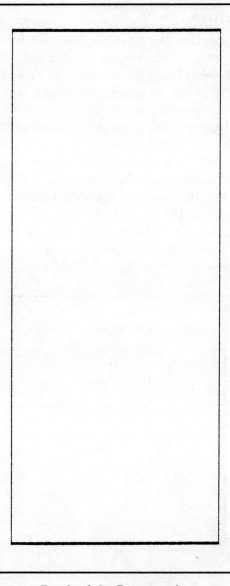

Figure 15-5.   Result of the Box procedure

Each of the three procedures in the **AspectDemo** program—**Box**, **HiResBox**, and **MedResBox**—draws a rectangle on the screen, but in a slightly different way. **Box**'s rectangle is elongated, as you can see in Figure 15-5. Although its **x** and **y** coordinates are evenly spaced, the drawing is not in proportion.

HiResBox uses a constant called **AspectRatio** to correctly proportion the graphic. Because horizontal pixels in High-resolution mode require 2.35 times as much space as vertical pixels, **AspectRatio** is set to this value. In the sample program, the second **y** coordinate is reduced by 2.35, which produces the graphic in Figure 15-6.

MedResBox also uses a constant called **AspectRatio**, but in this case the constant is equal to 1.172. Because Medium-resolution mode uses the same number of vertical pixels but exactly one-half as many horizontal pixels as High-resolution mode, the medium-resolution aspect ratio is half as large as the high-resolution aspect ratio. Thus, **MedResBox** produces the graphic in Figure 15-7.

Figure 15-6.   Result of the HiResBox procedure

Figure 15-7.   Result of the MedResBox procedure

Since they do not adjust their aspect ratios to match High-resolution Graphics mode, **Arc** and **Circle** are much less useful than they would be otherwise

Saving and Restoring Graphics Screens

To save a graphic, use the **GetPic** command. It stores all or part of a graphics display in a buffer that you can either keep in memory or write to a disk file.

The syntax for **GetPic** is

GetPic(Buffer,x1,y1,x2,y2)

where **x1** and **y1** are the coordinates for the upper left corner of the area to be saved and **x2** and **y2** are the coordinates for the lower right corner. The buffer can be of any type, but it must be large enough to contain the portion of the screen defined by the coordinates. To store an entire graphics screen, the buffer must have 16K (4000h bytes).

To display a graphic that's been stored with **GetPic**, use the **PutPic** command. The syntax for this command is

PutPic(Buffer, x1, x2);

where **x1** and **x2** are the coordinates of the lower left corner of the display area.

The following program, called **GetPutDemo**, demonstrates how to use **GetPic** and **PutPic**. **GetPutDemo** creates two different graphics, stores them in separate buffers, and writes the buffers to a disk file. It then reads the buffers back in and displays them one after another to create an animation effect.

```
Program GetPutDemo;
(*$i graph.p*)
Type
  BufPtr  = ^BufType;
  BufType = array [1..$4000] of byte;
Var
  buffer,
  buf1,
  buf2 : BufPtr;
  PicF : File of BufType;
  i : Integer;

Begin
New(Buffer);
New(Buf1);
New(Buf2);
Assign(PicF,'PicF');
Rewrite(PicF);
```

```
HiRes;
Palette(1);

(* Draw line from upper left to lower right *)

Draw(0,0,639,199,1);
GetPic(Buffer^,0,0,639,199);
Write(PicF,Buffer^);
Readln;

HiRes;

(* Draw line from upper left to lower right *)

Draw(0,199,639,0,1);
GetPic(Buffer^,0,0,639,199);
Write(PicF,Buffer^);
Readln;

HiRes;

(* Read stored graphics and redisplay them. *)

Reset(PicF);
Read(PicF,Buf1^);
Read(PicF,Buf2^);

For i := 1 To 10 Do
  Begin
  PutPic(Buf1^,0,199);
  PutPic(Buf2^,0,199);
  End;

TextMode;
End.
```

GetPic and **PutPic** are especially useful in programs that alternate between Text and Graphics modes. You can store a graphics display, work in Text mode, return to Graphics mode, and redisplay the stored graphic.

The Turbo Pascal graphics command **GetDotColor** reports the color currently used by a pixel. It uses this syntax:

GetDotColor(x,y);

This command returns an integer representing the color of the pixel at position **x:y**. In Medium-resolution mode,

GetDotColor can return 0 through 3, while in High-resolution mode, it returns only 0 or 1.

The Color Table

The color table, a special storage area in Turbo Pascal, stores information about the colors used in a graphic. This information is used by **PutPic** when it displays a graphic. The color table is also used to change the colors of a graphic already on the screen.

The color table remembers the color of every pixel on the screen, even after the graphic has been erased. So, when you are redrawing a graphic, you can use the color table to restore the original colors, instead of having to respecify the colors. For example, instead of writing

    Plot(10,10,2)

which uses the second color in the current palette, you would write

    Plot(10,10,−1)

The −1 tells Turbo Pascal to plot the pixel with the color it had the last time it was displayed. Note that **PutPic**, which restores a graphic from a buffer, automatically uses the color table.

The color table can also change the colors in a graphic. But to do so, you have to change the order of the colors in the color table with the **ColorTable** command. For example, the command

    ColorTable(2,1,3,0);

reorders the color table to 2, 1, 3, 0. Now, if you plot a pixel with color number 1, and then replot the color with the color table, the new pixel will appear in color number 2. Using the color table, you can replot the entire graphic display with the

FillScreen command. The syntax of this command is as follows:

FillScreen(color)

where **color** can be any palette color (0, 1, 2, or 3) or −1 to use the color table. When a color is selected from the palette, the screen is filled with that color. If, on the other hand, the parameter is −1, the colors in the graphic change to reflect the order of colors in the color table. The program **Fill-ScreenDemo1** demonstrates how to use the **FillScreen** command.

```
Program FillScreenDemo1;
(*$I GRAPH.P*)

Begin
GraphColorMode;
Palette(4);

Draw(100,0,100,199,1);
Draw(200,0,200,199,2);
Draw(300,0,300,199,3);
readln;

(* Switch screen colors. *)

colortable(3,2,1,0);
FillScreen(-1);
readln;

(* Fill the screen with the palette colors. *)

FillScreen(0);
readln;

FillScreen(1);
readln;

FillScreen(2);
readln;

FillScreen(3);
readln;

textmode;
End.
```

One final note on the color table: in High-resolution mode, only the first two colors in the palette (0 and 1) have any effect on the display. Therefore, the **ColorTable** command uses only the 0 and 1 colors.

Fill Commands

Graphics often contain enclosed figures, such as circles in pie charts, bars in bar graphs, and so on. These figures often look better if they are filled with colors or patterns that set them apart from the rest of the graph. Turbo Pascal provides three commands dedicated to this task: **FillShape**, **FillPattern**, and **Pattern**.

FillShape colors the inside of a graphic display with a single, solid color. For example, **FillShape** can paint the inside of a circle one color and the inside of a square another color. Note that the drawing filled with this command must be completely enclosed; no breaks in the border of the graphic are allowed. Thus, **FillShape** cannot be used with half-circles or line segments.

The syntax of the command **FillShape** is as follows:

FillShape(x,y,InsideColor,BorderColor);

You must assign the **x** and **y** coordinates to a point within the graphic to be filled, otherwise **FillShape** does not know what to fill.

InsideColor is the color that fills the inside of the graphic while **BorderColor** is the color of the border that contains the graphic. **FillShape** begins filling the shape from the inside out, stopping only when it reaches a **BorderColor** pixel. If the value of **BorderColor** does not match the graphic's border color, **FillShape** does not know when to stop and will fill the entire screen.

FillPattern offers another way to fill in a portion of the screen. Unlike **FillShape**, which fills a graphic of any shape, **FillPattern** fills only rectangular portions of the screen, but

it does so with both the color and pattern that you specify.
The syntax of **FillPattern** is as follows:

FillPattern(x1,y1,x2,y2,Color);

The coordinates **x1:y1** define the upper left corner and
x2:y2 the lower right corner of the rectangle to be filled. The
integer parameter **color** specifies the palette color to use.

The pattern that **FillPattern** draws is determined by an
eight-byte variable, known as the *pattern variable* that, when
set properly, creates lines and designs such as cross-hatching.
The pattern variable's eight bytes should be set to create a
repeating pattern of lines or crosshatches. Each byte represents eight pixels; a zero bit means a dark pixel, while a one
bit means a lighted pixel. The first byte forms the top row of
eight pixels, and each successive byte forms another row. In
other words, taken together, the eight-byte pattern variable
represents an 8-pixel by 8-pixel segment of the video screen
(see Figure 15-8).

Byte	Value	Pattern							
0	44h	0	1	0	0	0	1	0	0
1	88h	1	0	0	0	1	0	0	0
2	11h	0	0	0	1	0	0	0	1
3	22h	0	0	1	0	0	0	1	0
4	44h	0	1	0	0	0	1	0	0
5	88h	1	0	0	0	1	0	0	0
6	11h	0	0	0	1	0	0	0	1
7	22h	0	0	1	0	0	0	1	0

Figure 15-8.   Example of a pattern variable

You can define more than one pattern variable and switch from one to another with the **Pattern** command. This command takes one parameter (a pattern variable) and stores its pattern in memory. Then, when you then call **Fill-Pattern**, it uses the stored pattern to create its design.

The sample program called **FillScreenDemo2** shows how to use the **FillShape**, **FillPattern**, and **Pattern** commands.

```
Program FillScreenDemo2;
Type
  PatType = Array [0..7] Of Byte;

Const
  Xmax : Integer = 319;

  pat1 : PatType =
          ($FF,$FF,$FF,$FF,$FF,$FF,$FF,$FF);

  Pat2 : PatType =
          ($44,$88,$11,$22,$44,$88,$11,$22);

  Pat3 : PatType =
          ($AA,$55,$AA,$55,$00,$00,$00,$00);

  Centers : Array [1..3] of Integer =
          (80,159,240);

var
  i : Integer;

(*$I GRAPH.P*)

(*************************************************)

Procedure DrawBar(Center, Width, Height,InsideColor,BorderColor : Integer;
                  Pat : PatType);

var
  x1,y1,x2,y2 : Integer;

Begin
x1 := Center - (Width div 2);
x2 := Center + (Width div 2);
y1 := 199-height;
y2 := 199;

Draw(x1,y1,x1,y2,BorderColor);
Draw(x1,y2,x2,y2,BorderColor);
Draw(x2,y2,x2,y1,BorderColor);
Draw(x2,y1,x1,y1,BorderColor);
```

```
Pattern(pat);
FillPattern(x1+1,y1+1,x2-1,y2-1,InsideColor);
End;

(**********************************************)

Procedure DrawColorBar(Center, Width, Height,BorderColor : Integer);

var
  x1,y1,x2,y2 : Integer;

Begin
x1 := Center - (Width div 2);
x2 := Center + (Width div 2);
y1 := 199-height;
y2 := 199;

Draw(x1,y1,x1,y2,BorderColor);
Draw(x1,y2,x2,y2,BorderColor);
Draw(x2,y2,x2,y1,BorderColor);
Draw(x2,y1,x1,y1,BorderColor);
FillShape(x1+1,y1+1,BorderColor,BorderColor);
End;

(**********************************************)

Procedure Axis;
Begin
Draw(0,199,319,199,3);
Draw(0,0,0,199,3);

For i := 1 to 20 do
  Begin
  Draw(0,i*10,10,i*10,3);
  End;
End;

(**********************************************)


begin
GraphColorMode;
Palette(4);
Axis;
DrawBar(centers[1],40,80,2,3,pat1);
DrawBar(centers[2],40,150,2,3,pat2);
DrawBar(centers[3],40,75,2,3,pat3);
readln;

GraphColorMode;
Palette(4);
Axis;
DrawColorBar(centers[1],40,80,1);
DrawColorBar(centers[2],40,150,2);
DrawColorBar(centers[3],40,75,3);
readln;

textmode;
End.
```

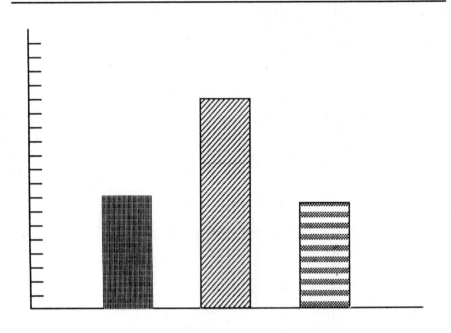

Figure 15-9.   Bar graph using FillPattern

FillScreenDemo2 creates two simple bar charts: the first with **FillPattern**, the other with **FillShape**. The first chart uses a different pattern and shade of light on each bar (see Figure 15-9). The chart produced with **FillShape**, however, uses only color to differentiate the bars (see Figure 15-10).

FillShape and **FillPattern** give life to dull outline graphics. Of the two, **FillPattern** is the more flexible because it can differentiate any number of graphic elements by combining colors and patterns.

Graphics Windows

The command **GraphWindow** selects a portion of the screen as an active window, allowing you to display graphics on part

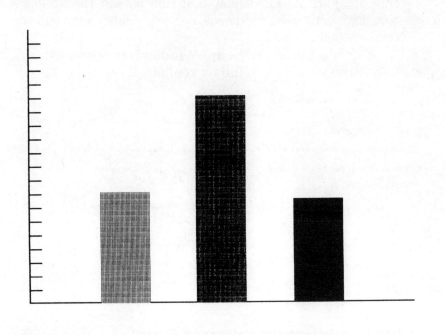

Figure 15-10.   Bar graph using FillShape

of the screen without disturbing the rest of the screen. The syntax of the command is as follows:

GraphWindow(x1,y1,x2,y2);

This command defines a rectangular window with the upper left corner at coordinates **x1:y1** and the lower right corner at **x2:y2**. All screen coordinates are relative to that window. Therefore, the screen coordinates for the upper left corner of any window are **0:0**, just as if you were using the entire screen.

Naturally, graphics that require an entire screen to be displayed will not fit inside a graphics window. Turbo Pascal clips any part of your display that runs outside the window's boundary so that the portion of the screen outside the window remains undisturbed.

The program called **GraphWindowDemo** demonstrates how to use the **GraphWindow** command:

```
Program GraphWindowDemo;
(*$i GRAPH.P*)
Var
   i : Integer;

(***********************************************)

Procedure Box(x1,y1,x2,y2,color : Integer);
Begin
Draw(x1,y1,x1,y2,color);
Draw(x1,y2,x2,y2,color);
Draw(x2,y2,x2,y1,color);
Draw(x2,y1,x1,y1,color);
End;

(***********************************************)

Procedure OpenWindow(x1,y1,x2,y2,BoundaryColor,InsideColor : Integer);
Begin
Box(x1,y1,x2,y2,BoundaryColor);
GraphWindow(x1+1,y1+1,x2-1,y2-1);
FillScreen(InsideColor);
End;

(***********************************************)

Begin
Palette(3);
GraphColorMode;
For i := 1 to 20 do
   Draw(0,i*10,319,i*10,3);
OpenWindow(100,50,270,150,3,1);
For i := 1 to 20 do
   Draw(i*8,0,i*8,100,3);
ReadLn;

TextMode;
End.
```

GraphWindowDemo uses a procedure named **Open-Window** that draws a border around the window area, clears the inside of the screen with the **FillScreen** command, and then declares the actual window. When you run this program, your screen will look as shown in Figure 15-11.

Using graphics, with or without windows, is perhaps the most challenging programming task. The variations and complications are endless. Fortunately, you do not have to reinvent the wheel. Borland publishes a software package called the Graphix Toolbox (discussed in Chapter 20) that contains most of the fundamental graphics routines you will need.

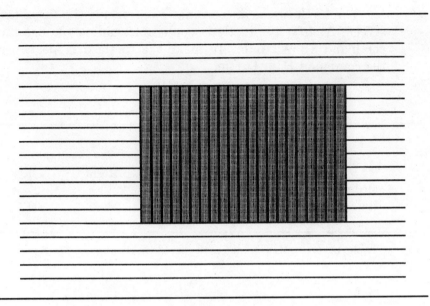

Figure 15-11.   Using a graphics window

Because Borland provides the source code, the Graphix Toolbox is a great way to learn about graphics programming.

Turtlegraphics

Turbo Pascal includes a simplified graphics system known as Turtlegraphics that allows you to draw lines by directing a special cursor, called a turtle, around the screen.

Turtlegraphics Coordinates

Turtlegraphics use a coordinate system completely different from the standard graphics routine: Coordinates are **0:0** at the center of the screen; positive coordinates are above and to the right of the center; negative coordinates are below and to the left of the center. The maximum coordinates in the Turtlegraphics screen depend on the mode you use. They are detailed in Table 15-4.

The turtle starts at coordinates **0:0**, facing the top of the screen. At first the turtle is not visible, unless you use the command **ShowTurtle**. To make the turtle disappear, use the command **HideTurtle**.

	y-Coordinate		x-Coordinate	
Mode	**Top**	**Bottom**	**Right**	**Left**
Medium Resolution	160	−159	100	−99
High Resolution	320	−319	100	−99

Table 15-4. Maximum Turtlegraphics Coordinates

Positioning the Turtle

Most of the Turtlegraphics commands point, position, or move the turtle around the screen. The command **Forwd(n)** moves the turtle forward by **n** pixels. Similarly, the command **Back(n)** moves the turtle backward by **n** pixels. As the turtle moves, it draws a line, thus creating a graphic display.

You can change the turtle's direction with the **SetHeading(n)** command, where **n** is the number of degrees to turn the turtle. You can also turn the turtle by any number of degrees, from 0 to 359. Zero points the turtle toward the top of the screen, and higher numbers point the turtle clockwise in one-degree increments. Turbo Pascal provides four predefined constants for the four main directions: North (n = 0), East (n = 90), South (n = 180), and West (n = 270).

The **Heading** command reports in which direction the turtle is pointing at any moment in terms of degrees. For example, if **Heading** is equal to 0, the turtle is pointing to the top of the screen.

The commands **TurnLeft(n)** and **TurnRight(n)** turn the turtle **n** degrees to the left or right. When **n** is positive, **TurnLeft** turns the turtle to the left, and **TurnRight** turns the turtle to the right. When **n** is negative, the turtle turns in the opposite direction for each command.

You can instantly move the turtle to any point on the screen with the command **SetPosition(x,y)**, where **x** and **y** are Turtlegraphics coordinates. A similar command, **Home**, moves the turtle to the coordinates **0:0**. If you want to know the turtle's coordinates at any moment, use the commands **Xcor** and **Ycor**, which return the turtle's current **x** and **y** coordinates.

Controlling the Turtlegraphics Display

Turtlegraphics uses colors in the same way as standard graphics: three foreground colors and one background color are available in medium resolution, while high-resolution graphics show one color on a black background. To change the color of the line the turtle draws, use the command **SetPenColor(color)** where **color** is a number from 0 to 3 (0 to 1 for high resolution). As with standard graphics, setting the color with −1 activates the color table.

To move the turtle without drawing a line, use the **PenUp** command. When you want to start drawing again, use **PenDown**.

If you move the turtle beyond the screen coordinates, it disappears. The **Wrap** command makes the turtle reappear on the opposite edge of the screen (also known as *wrapping around*). **NoWrap** turns off the wrap feature.

Turtlegraphics Windows

You can declare a window in Turtlegraphics just as you would in the standard graphics modes. The command

TurtleWindow(x,y,w,h)

defines the window, where coordinates **x** and **y** indicate the center and **w** and **h** define the width and height of the window.

The command **ClearScreen** clears the contents of the current window, while **TurtleThere**, a Boolean function, returns True if the turtle is within the current window.

The last Turtlegraphics command, **TurtleDelay(n)**, places an **n** millisecond delay between Turtlegraphics steps.

The program called **TurtleDemo** illustrates the use of Turtlegraphics:

```
Program TurtleDemo;
(*$i GRAPH.P*)
Var
  i : Integer;
  ch : Char;
  fk : Boolean;


(*************************************************************)

Procedure InKey(Var ch : Char;
                Var fk : boolean);
Begin
fk := False;
Read(Kbd,ch);
If (ch = 27) and KeyPressed Then
  Begin
  fk := True;
  Read(Kbd,ch);
  End;
End;


(*************************************************************)

Begin
HiRes;
ShowTurtle;

  Repeat
    Inkey(ch,fk);
    If fk Then
      Case ch Of

      59: (* F1 *) PenDown;

      60: (* F2 *) PenUp;

      61: (* F3 *) ShowTurtle;

      62: (* F4 *) HideTurtle;

      75: (* left arrow *)
        Begin
        SetHeading(West);
        Forwd(1);
        End;

      77: (* right arrow *)
        Begin
        SetHeading(East);
        Forwd(1);
        End;

      72: (* up arrow *)
        Begin
        SetHeading(North);
        Forwd(1);
        End;
```

```
80: (* down arrow *)
   Begin
   SetHeading(South);
   Forwd(1);
   End;

End
Else
Case ch Of

32: (* space *) Forwd(1);

43: (* + *) TurnRight(1);

45: (* - *) TurnLeft(1);

End;

Until (ch = 27) And (Not fk); (* Esc key *)
TextMode;
End.
```

With this program, you will be able to draw pictures using Turtlegraphics. The program uses the following keys:

Key	Function
SPACE BAR	Move turtle forward
UP ARROW	Point turtle up
RIGHT ARROW	Point turtle right
DOWN ARROW	Point turtle down
LEFT ARROW	Point turtle left
Plus (+)	Turn turtle to the right
Minus (−)	Turn turtle to the left
F1	Draw line when turtle is moved
F2	Do not draw when turtle is moved
F3	Show the turtle
F4	Hide the turtle
ESC	Stop the program

TurtleDemo not only gives you a fun way to draw pictures but also demonstrates how the arrow and function keys create an interactive keyboard interface.

Turbo Pascal Version 4.0 Graphics

You can use your existing graphics programs with Turbo Pascal 4.0 simply by using the Graph3 unit. For example, the program JaggedLine given earlier will run under Version 4.0 when the line

```
Uses CRT, Graph3;
```

is added, as shown here:

```
Program JaggedLine;
Uses CRT, Graph3;
Const
  Dif = 20;
Var
  x,y,t : Integer;
Begin
HiRes;
For x := 0 To 639 Do
  Plot(x,0,White);
For y := 0 To 199 Do
  Plot(639,y,White);
For x := 639 Downto 0 Do
  Plot(x,199,White);
For y := 199 Downto 0 Do
  Plot(0,y,White);


t := 1;
y := 100 - Dif;
For x := 0 To 640 Do
  Begin
  Plot(x,y,White);
  if t = 1 then
    Begin
    y := y + 1;
    If y = 100 + Dif Then
      t := -1;
    End
  Else
    Begin
    y := y - 1;
    If y = 100 - Dif Then
      t := 1;
    End;
  End;

Readln;
End.
```

Turbo Pascal 4.0 also provides a unit named Graph that contains many new and powerful graphics routines. A complete description of these routines is contained in Appendix I.

Interrupts, Telecommunications, and Memory-Resident Programs

Using Interrupts
Writing the Interrupt Handler
Memory-Resident Programs
Interrupt Programming in Turbo Pascal Version 4.0

Life is full of interruptions—and so is computing. In computer programming, interruptions are called *interrupts*. If you own a telephone, you will understand the concept of an interrupt. When your telephone rings, you stop what you are doing, answer the phone, and resume working when your conversation is over. In a way, computers have little telephones ringing inside the microprocessor that make it stop and do something else for a moment.

This chapter introduces the concept of interrupts and how it is used in Turbo Pascal. Interrupts are fundamental to the operation of your computer; and if you want to tap the full power of the personal computer, you must understand them. Because telecommunications commonly use interrupt programming, the concepts will be illustrated with examples from a Turbo Pascal communications program that is listed at the end of this chapter.

Using Interrupts

Do you occasionally find it inconvenient when your telephone rings? Imagine how inconvenient it would be to have a telephone that does not ring. You would have to pick up the receiver from time to time to see if anyone was calling. Not only would this waste time, but you would run the risk of missing a call if someone called and hung up before you picked up the receiver.

Of course, our phones do ring, and so we can do other things and answer the telephone only when we know someone is calling. In similar fashion, interrupts allow your computer to work until something happens that requires your computer's attention.

One interrupt controls your computer's internal clock. About 18 times each second, this interrupt stops your microprocessor and asks it to increment the DOS time and date. You do not notice this because it happens so quickly. Other interrupts occur when you press a key on your keyboard or data comes into a serial port. In fact, interrupts occur all the time, but you do not notice them because they generally require the microprocessor to do very little work.

Hardware and Software Interrupts

Interrupts are of two types: hardware and software. *Hardware interrupts*, generated by such actions as pressing a key, a tick of the system clock, or data entering a serial port, originate in the computer's circuitry and are controlled by a special chip, the 8259 interrupt controller. When a hardware interrupt occurs, this chip acts as a traffic cop, making sure the interrupt goes in the correct direction. The 8259 receives an interrupt request, evaluates its priority, and routes the request to the procedure it needs.

Software interrupts are generated by programs that request special BIOS and DOS services. In Turbo Pascal, the commands **Intr** and **MSDos** create software interrupts (see Chapter 12). Whether hardware or software, however, all interrupts use the *interrupt vector table*.

The Interrupt Vector Table

The interrupt vector table is an array of memory addresses located at the lowest part of the PC's memory. The array is 1024 bytes long and contains the addresses of all the routines that are triggered by interrupts. Because an address requires 4 bytes, the 1024-byte interrupt vector table can hold a maximum of 256 interrupt addresses.

An interrupt, when initiated, fetches an address from the interrupt vector table, jumps to that memory location, and executes the routine located there. Each address in the interrupt vector table is used exclusively by a single interrupt. For example, interrupt number 8, the clock timer, always fetches the address at offset 0020h. Table 16-1 contains the PC's eight hardware interrupts, numbers 8 through 15, and their offsets in the interrupt vector table.

Of the hardware interrupts, the most useful to program are the clock tick (number 8), the keyboard interrupt

| Interrupt | | | |
Dec	Hex	Offset	Purpose
8	8	0020h	System clock tick
9	9	0024h	Keyboard interrupt
10	A	0028h	Not used
11	B	002Ch	Second serial port (COM2)
12	C	0030h	First serial port (COM1)
13	D	0034h	Hard-disk interrupt
14	E	0038h	Floppy-disk interrupt
15	F	003Ch	Printer interrupt

Table 16-1.   Location of Hardware Interrupts in the Interrupt Vector Table

(number 9), and the first serial port (number 12). The examples in this chapter concentrate on interrupt number 12, which is activated by data arriving in the first serial port, and interrupt number 9, which occurs when a key is pressed.

Replacing Interrupts

Each time you start your computer, DOS fills the interrupt vector table with standard addresses. As soon as the computer is running, however, you can change an address in the interrupt vector table so that it points to a procedure in your program; the interrupt will then execute your procedure instead of the normal procedure. In short, by changing addresses in the interrupt vector table, you can usurp DOS and BIOS and take charge of your computer's basic functions.

Although programmers are not usually interested in altering the addresses of software interrupts, they are interested in changing hardware interrupt addresses. By changing the keyboard interrupt address, for example, a memory-resident program can intercept a keystroke and interpret it before it ever gets to the main program. This is how memory-resident programs such as SuperKey and SideKick work.

An interrupt address can be changed in two ways: by changing the interrupt vector table directly or by using a DOS service to do it for you. To change memory directly, you must overlay an array of addresses on the interrupt vector table, as follows:

```
Type
  Address = ^Integer;
Var
  AsyncVector : Address;
  InterruptVector : Array [0..$FF] Of Address Absolute $0000:$0000;
```

The user-defined type **Address** is a *pointer*. Pointers are 4-byte data types that hold both the segment and offset that together constitute a memory address. The variable **InterruptVector**, an array of 255 (FFh) addresses, is declared absolute at the very beginning of RAM, where the interrupt vector table resides. Since **InterruptVector** and the table share the same space, when you change a value in one, you also change it in the other. To change an address in the interrupt vector table, use the following statements:

```
AsyncVector := InterruptVector[$0C];
InterruptVector[$0C] := Ptr(Cseg,Ofs(AsyncInt));
```

The first statement stores the vector for interrupt number 12 (0C in hexadecimal) in the variable **AsyncVector**. Saving the original address is important since you will need to restore it eventually. The second statement replaces the original vector with the address of a Turbo Pascal procedure named **AsyncInt**.

Just like variables, procedures have addresses consisting of a segment and an offset. Because a procedure's segment is always the code segment, the statement uses the Turbo command **Cseg**, which reports the code segment. The offset of the procedure is reported with the **Ofs** command. The Turbo Pascal command **Ptr** combines the segment and offset, both 2 bytes long, into a single 4-byte address. The address is then loaded into the interrupt vector table. Now, when interrupt 12 is triggered by data arriving at the serial port, **AsyncInt** will execute instead of the normal procedure.

When you are done using the interrupt vector, you must restore the original address that you saved in the pointer variable **AsyncVector**. If you do not restore the address, you may crash your computer and have to reboot. This single line of code is all you need to restore the original interrupt vector address:

```
InterruptVector[$0C] := AsyncVector;
```

With the interrupt vector now restored to its original value, your computer will operate normally.

It is simple to change interrupt addresses directly, but it is safer to use DOS services, which apply to a wider range of computers. DOS service **35h** reports a vector's contents and service **25h** changes an address in the interrupt vector table.

Those unfamiliar with the DOS services in Turbo Pascal should read Chapter 12, "DOS and BIOS Services."

To save the original address in the interrupt vector table, first use DOS service **35h** to report the current vector address. To request this service, place **35h** in register AH and the interrupt number in AL, and execute the **MsDos** command. The registers return with the interrupt's segment in ES and its offset in BX. To save this address, use the Turbo Pascal command **Ptr**. The following routine is an example of how to use DOS service **35h** to get the address for interrupt number 12:

```
(* Get and save the current vector address. *)

With Regs Do
  Begin
  AH := $35;
  AL := $0C; (* Interrupt number 12 *)
  End;
Msdos(Regs);
With Regs Do
  AsyncVector := Ptr(ES,BX);
```

Once the vector's contents are safely stored, you can use DOS service **25h** to replace the address in the table with a new value. To do this, set AH to **25h**, AL to the interrupt number, DS to your program's code segment, and BX to the offset of your routine. This code demonstrates the use of DOS service **25h**.

```
(* Set the vector address to a new value. *)
With Regs Do
  Begin
  AH := $25;
  AL := $0C;    (* Interrupt number 12 *)
  DS := Cseg;   (* Cseg reports code segment. *)
  DX := Ofs(AsyncInt); (* AsyncInt: Turbo Pascal Procedure *)
  End;
Msdos(Regs);
```

After executing the **MsDos** command, the interrupt address will point to the procedure **AsyncInt**. Later, when you are done using the interrupt, you must use DOS service

25h to restore the old interrupt address, as shown here:

```
With Regs Do
   Begin
   ah := $25;
   al := $0C;
   ds := Seg(AsyncVector^);
   dx := Ofs(AsyncVector^);
   End;
Msdos(Regs);
```

The original vector address, stored in the pointer variable **AsyncVector**, is loaded into the register set DS:DX with the **Seg** and **Ofs** commands. Note that the parameter to these commands is the variable **AsyncVector**^, not the pointer **AsyncVector**. The call to **MsDos** installs this address in the interrupt vector table.

Writing the Interrupt Handler

Interrupt handler is a term that refers to the code that executes as the result of an interrupt. In the previous examples, the handler was a Turbo Pascal procedure named **AsyncInt**. The trick to writing interrupt handlers is that you must use inline code to save and restore the CPU's registers.

Setting the Data Segment

The biggest problem with interrupt handlers is that when they are invoked, the data segment register (DS) does not contain the correct value. Without the correct data segment, your procedure cannot refer to any global variables. Your program must, therefore, store its data segment before it installs the interrupt handler. The data segment must be stored in a typed constant. The typed constant that stores the data segment should be declared as follows.

```
const
  MainDseg:integer = 0;
```

The data segment is stored with this statement:

```
MainDseg := Dseg;
```

Note that **MainDseg**, an integer, must be a typed constant, not a global variable. Because the DS register will contain an incorrect value when your interrupt handler is called, global variables, which reside in the data segment, cannot be accessed. Typed constants, on the other hand, reside in the code segment and rely on the CS register, not DS. Since the CS register will contain the correct value, the interrupt handler can use typed constants before the DS register is corrected.

When the interrupt handler is called, the first step is to place the correct data segment in the DS register. This is done with the following inline code:

```
$2E/            (* CS: *)
$A1/MainDseg/   (* MOV AX,MainDseg *)
$8E/$D8/        (* MOV DS,AX *)
```

The contents of **MainDseg**, which contains the stored data segment, are first moved into the AX register and then moved into the DS register.

Saving and Restoring the Registers

Your interrupt handler will probably change the values in some of the registers as it executes. Unfortunately, these changes might cause your program to crash when the interrupt handler ends. To avoid a crash, your interrupt handler must save the values in the registers when it begins and restore these register values when it ends.

When an interrupt occurs, DOS automatically saves and restores the CS, IP, and Flags registers, so you do not need to save these. Turbo Pascal does save the BP and SP registers, but it does not restore these registers at the end of the interrupt handler, so you must restore them yourself. The inline code shown here saves the necessary registers and corrects the data segment:

```
Inline($50/           (* PUSH   AX *)
       $53/           (* PUSH   BX *)
       $51/           (* PUSH   CX *)
       $52/           (* PUSH   DX *)
       $57/           (* PUSH   DI *)
       $56/           (* PUSH   SI *)
       $06/           (* PUSH   ES *)
       $1E/           (* PUSH   DS *)

       $2E/           (* CS: *)
       $A1/MainDseg/  (* MOV AX,MainDseg *)
       $8E/$D8/       (* MOV DS,AX *)
       $FB);          (* STI: Disable interrupts *)
```

This inline code always appears at the beginning of the handler procedure. When the interrupt handler procedure is done, it must restore the registers to their previous values with this code:

```
Inline($FA);         (* CLI: Enable interrupts *)

Port[$20] := $20;

Inline($1F/          (* POP DS *)
       $07/          (* POP ES *)
       $5E/          (* POP SI *)
       $5F/          (* POP DI *)
       $5A/          (* POP DX *)
       $59/          (* POP CX *)
       $5B/          (* POP BX *)
       $58/          (* POP AX *)
       $8B/$E5/      (* MOV   SP,BP *)
       $5D/          (* POP   BP *)
       $CF);         (* IRET *)
       End;
```

Inline code is the only way you can save the registers, set the data segment, and restore the registers. Fortunately, you can use the same inline code in all your interrupt handlers. The next section of this chapter demonstrates how an interrupt handler can be used to create a telecommunications program.

PC Telecommunications

Telecommunications, the transmission of data from one computer to another via telephone lines, is one of the most complicated aspects of programming. In concept, it is quite simple: the computer sends a byte to a serial port, which sends it on to the modem. The modem translates the bits into tones and sends the tones to another modem, which translates them back into bits. The translated bits are sent to the receiving serial port where they wait to be picked up by the software.

In practice, writing a program to do all these things is not so simple. The complexity is partly due to the number of hardware elements you must control: the RS-232 serial port, the INS8250 universal receiver transmitter (UART), the 8259 interrupt controller, and the modem itself. In addition, there are many variations of modem speed, parity, stop bits, data bits, which serial port to use, and so on.

The Telecommunications Program

The following program, called **AsyncCommunications**, provides simple telecommunications capability using interrupt 12. The program assumes you have a Hayes-compatible modem connected to your first serial port. Before you run the program, set the values in procedure **SelectModemSet** to those of the remote computer you want to call.

```
(*$c-,k-,r-,v-*)
Program AsyncCommunications;
Type
  Address = ^Integer;
  RegPack = Record
    Case Integer Of
    1: (AX,BX,CX,DX,BP,DI,SI,DS,ES,Flags : Integer);
    2: (AL,AH,BL,BH,CL,CH,DL,DH : Byte);
    End;
  MaxStr = String[255];
```

```
   ModemSetType = Record
      ComPort,
      BPS,
      DataBits,
      StopBits          : Integer;
      Parity            : Char;
      PhoneNumber       : MaxStr;
      End;

Const
   MainDseg : Integer = 0;
   MaxBufLen  = 1024;
   CR         = 13;

   (*******************************)
   (* ISN8250 UART Registers.     *)
   (*******************************)
   DataPort = $03F8; (* Contains 8 bits to transmit or receive.    *)
   IER      = $03F9; (* Enables the serial port when set equal to 1. *)
   LCR      = $03FB; (* Sets communications parameters.            *)
   MCR      = $03FC; (* Bits 1, 2 and 4 are turned on to ready modem.*)
   LSR      = $03FD; (* When bit 6 is on, it is safe to send a byte. *)
   MDMMSR   = $03FE; (* Initialized to 80h when starting.          *)

   ENBLRDY  = $01;   (* Initial value for Port[IER].      *)
   MDMMOD   = $0B;   (* Initial value for Port[MCR].      *)
   MDMCD    = $80;   (* Initial value for Port[MDMMSR].   *)

   INTCTLR  = $21;   (* Port for the 8259 Interrupt Controller. *)

Var
   ModemSet : ModemSetType;
   InterruptVector : Array [0..$1f] Of Address Absolute $0000:$0000;
   AsyncVector    : Address;
   regs           : regpack;
   buffer         : Array [1..MaxBufLen] Of Char;
   i,
   CharsInBuf,
   CircOut,
   CircIn         : Integer;
   Orig           : Char;

(********************************************************************)

Procedure SelectModemSet;
Begin
With ModemSet Do
   Begin
   ComPort      := 1;          (* Must be 1 in this program. *)
   BPS          := 1200;       (* 300, 1200 *)
   DataBits     := 8;          (* 7, 8 *)
   StopBits     := 1;          (* 0, 1 *)
   Parity       := 'N';        (* None; Even; Odd *)
   PhoneNumber  := '9999999';
   End;
End;

(********************************************************************)

Procedure AsyncInt;
Begin
inline(
$50/          (* PUSH  AX *)
$53/          (* PUSH  BX *)
$51/          (* PUSH  CX *)
$52/          (* PUSH  DX *)
$57/          (* PUSH  DI *)
$56/          (* PUSH  SI *)
$06/          (* PUSH  ES *)
```

```
$1E/            (* PUSH  DS *)
$2E/            (* CS: *)
$A1/MainDseg/   (* MOV AX,MainDseg *)
$8E/$D8/        (* MOV DS,AX *)
$FB);           (* STI *)

If (CharsInBuf < MaxBufLen) Then
  Begin
  buffer[CircIn] := Char(Port[DataPort]);
  If (CircIn < MaxBufLen) Then
    CircIn := CircIn + 1
  Else
    CircIn := 1;
  CharsInBuf := CharsInBuf+1;
  End;

Inline($FA);      (* CLI *)

Port[$20] := $20;

Inline($1F/        (* POP DS *)
      $07/         (* POP ES *)
      $5E/         (* POP SI *)
      $5F/         (* POP DI *)
      $5A/         (* POP DX *)
      $59/         (* POP CX *)
      $5B/         (* POP BX *)
      $58/         (* POP AX *)
      $8B/$E5/     (* MOV   SP,BP *)
      $5D/         (* POP   BP *)
      $CF);        (* IRET *)
      End;

(**********************************************************)

Procedure SetSerialPort(ComPort,
                        BPS,
                        StopBits,
                        DataBits: Integer;
                        Parity : Char);
var
  regs : regpack;
  parameter : Byte;
Begin
  Case BPS Of
  300  : BPS := 2;
  1200 : BPS := 4;
  End;

If StopBits = 2 Then
  StopBits := 1
Else
  StopBits := 0;

If DataBits = 7 Then
  DataBits := 2
Else
  DataBits := 3;

parameter := (BPS Shl 5) + (StopBits Shl 2) + DataBits;

  Case Parity Of
  'E' : parameter := parameter + 8;
  'O' : parameter := parameter + 24;
  End;

With regs Do
  Begin
```

```
      DX := ComPort - 1;
      AH := 0;
      AL := Parameter;
      Flags := 0;
      Intr($14,regs);
      End;
End;

(*********************************************************)

Procedure EnablePorts;
Var
  b : Byte;
Begin
MainDseg := Dseg;
With Regs Do
  Begin
  AH := $35;
  AL := $0C;
  End;
Msdos(Regs);
With Regs Do
  AsyncVector := Ptr(ES,BX);

With Regs Do
  Begin
  AH := $25;
  AL := $0C;
  DS := Cseg;
  DX := ofs(AsyncInt);
  End;
Msdos(Regs);

b := Port[INTCTLR];
b := b and $0EF;
Port[INTCTLR] := b;
b := Port[LCR];
b := b and $7F;
Port[LCR] := b;
Port[IER] := ENBLRDY;
Port[MCR] := $08 or MDMMOD;
Port[MDMMSR] := MDMCD;
Port[$20] := $20;
End;

(*********************************************************)

Procedure ClearBuffer;
Begin
CircIn := 1;
CircOut := 1;
CharsInBuf := 0;
fillchar(buffer,sizeof(buffer),0);
End;

(*********************************************************)

Function GetCharInBuf : Char;
var
  ch : Char;
Begin
If CharsInBuf > 0 Then
  Begin
  GetCharInBuf := buffer[CircOut];
  If CircOut < MaxBufLen Then
    CircOut := CircOut + 1
  Else
    CircOut := 1;
```

```
    CharsInBuf := CharsInBuf-1;
    End;
End;

(************************************************************)

Function CarrierDetected : Boolean;
var
  ch : Char;
  timer  : Integer;
Begin
CarrierDetected := False;
timer:=40;
While (Port[MDMMSR] AND $80) <> $80 Do
  Begin
  If KeyPressed Then
    Begin
    Read(kbd, ch);
    If ch= 27 Then
      Exit;
    End;
  If (CharsInBuf > 0) Then
    Begin
    ch := GetCharInBuf;
    Write(ch);
    If ch = CR Then
      Writeln;
    End;
  If timer=0 Then
    Exit
  Else
    Begin
    timer:=timer-1;
    Delay(1000);
    End;
  End;
CarrierDetected := True;
Writeln('Carrier detected');
End;

(************************************************************)

Procedure SendChar(b: Byte);
Begin
While ((Port[LSR] AND $20) <> $20) Do
  Begin
  End;
Port[Dataport] := b;
End;

(************************************************************)

Procedure StringToPort(s : MaxStr);
var
  i : Integer;
Begin
For i := 1 To length(s) Do
  SendChar(Ord(s[i]));
SendChar(Ord(CR));
End;

(************************************************************)

Procedure DisablePorts;
Var
  b : Byte;
Begin
StringToPort('ATC0'); (* Turn off carrier signal. *)
```

```
b := Port[INTCTLR];      (* Turn off the communication interrupt for COM 1. *)
b := b or $10;
Port[INTCTLR] := b;

b := Port[LCR];          (* Disable 8250 Data Ready Interrupt. *)
b := b and $7F;
Port[LCR] := b;
Port[IER] := $0;

Port[MCR] := $0;         (* Disable OUT2 on 8250. *)

Port[$20] := $20;
With Regs Do             (* Restore original interrupt InterruptVector *)
  Begin
  AH := $25;
  AL := $0C;
  DS := Seg(AsyncVector^);
  DX := Ofs(AsyncVector^);
  End;
Msdos(Regs);
End;

(********************************************************)

Function SuccessfulConnect(PhoneNumber : MaxStr) : Boolean;
var
  s : MaxStr;
Begin
s := 'ATDT'+PhoneNumber; (* ATDT assumes touch-tone dial. *)
StringToPort(s);
Delay(300);
ClearBuffer;
If CarrierDetected Then
  Begin
  Writeln('Connected');
  SuccessfulConnect:=True;
  End
Else
  Begin
  Write('Error: Unable To Connect.');
  StringToPort('ATC0'); (* Turn off carrier signal. *)
  SuccessfulConnect:=False;
  End;
End;

(********************************************************)

Procedure SetHayesModem;
Begin
StringToPort('ATC0');        (* Turn off carrier signal.          *)
Delay(1000);                 (* Wait a second.                    *)
StringToPort('ATZ');         (* Reset modem to cold-start.        *)
Delay(1000);                 (* Wait a second.                    *)
StringToPort('ATF1');        (* Full Duplex.                      *)
Delay(1000);                 (* Wait a second.                    *)
StringToPort('ATE0');        (* Do not echo in command state.     *)
Delay(1000);                 (* Wait a second.                    *)
StringToPort('ATV1');        (* Verbal result codes.              *)
Delay(1000);                 (* Wait a second.                    *)
StringToPort('ATQ0');        (* Send result codes.                *)
Delay(1000);                 (* Wait a second.                    *)
End;

(********************************************************)

Procedure StartCommunicating;
Var
```

```
    OutChar,
    InChar : Char;
Begin
Inchar := ' ';
  Repeat
  If (CharsInBuf > 0) Then
    Begin
    InChar := GetCharInBuf;
    Write(InChar)
    End;

  If KeyPressed Then
    Begin
    Read(kbd, OutChar);
    SendChar(Ord(OutChar));
    End;
  Until OutChar = 27;
End;

(************************************************************)

Begin
SelectModemSet;

With ModemSet Do
  SetSerialPort(ComPort,BPS,StopBits,DataBits,Parity);

EnablePorts;
SetHayesModem;

If SuccessfulConnect(ModemSet.PhoneNumber) Then
  StartCommunicating;

DisablePorts;
End.
```

The main block of this program calls seven procedures and functions, and outlines the steps necessary to establish asynchronous communications. (Asynchronous communications is the transmission of data from one computer's serial port to another.) The first procedure is **SelectModemSet**, which specifies the communications port to use, the bits per second, the number of stop and data bits, the parity, and the telephone number. (Note that this program is designed to use communications port number 1 (COM1) only.) These data items are stored in a record called **ModemSet**, which is defined as follows:

```
ModemSet : Record
  ComPort,
  BPS,
  DataBits,
  StopBits         : Integer;
  Parity           : Char;
  PhoneNumber      : MaxStr;
  End;
```

After this record is initialized, its contents are passed to the procedure **SetSerialPort**, which uses BIOS interrupt **14h** to set the serial port to your parameters. To use this interrupt, you must set AH to 0, which tells BIOS to initialize a serial port, set AL to a parameter byte whose bits contain the communications settings, and set DX to 0 for COM1 or 1 for COM2.

The most difficult part of using interrupt 14 is setting the bits in the parameter byte. Table 16-2 shows the definitions of each bit in this byte.

7	6	5	4	3	2	1	0

Parameter	Bits Used	Bit Pattern	Meaning
Data Bits	Bits 0-1	00	5 data bits
		01	6 data bits
		10	7 data bits
		11	8 data bits
Stop Bits	Bit 2	0	1 stop bit
		1	2 stop bits
Parity	Bits 3-4	00	No parity
		01	Odd parity
		10	No parity
		11	Even parity
Speed (BPS)	Bits 5-7	000	100 BPS
		001	150 BPS
		010	300 BPS
		011	600 BPS
		100	1200 BPS
		101	2400 BPS
		110	4800 BPS
		111	9600 BPS

Table 16-2.   Contents of AL Register for BIOS Interrupt 14h

Once the modem has been set, the interrupt is installed by procedure **EnablePorts**. This procedure saves the old interrupt vector address, installs the address of procedure **AsyncInt**, and prepares the INS8250 UART chip for communications.

The final step in preparation is to initialize the modem to the proper settings with the **SetHayesModem** procedure. While there are many modems available, the standard set by the Hayes Smartmodem is the undisputed standard for personal computers. The modem commands used here should work on any modem compatible with the Hayes Smartmodem. Table 16-3 lists the commands available for the Hayes Smartmodem. For a full explanation of the internal operation of the Hayes Smartmodem, see the *Smartmodem 1200 Hardware Reference Manual* by Hayes Microcomputer Products, Inc. If you use an incompatible modem, change this procedure to match your modem.

Now that the serial port is set, the interrupt is installed, and the modem is initialized, it is time to begin communications. The Boolean function **SuccessfulConnect(ModemSet.-PhoneNumber)** dials the phone number passed to it and waits for a carrier-detect signal from the modem, indicating that the connection has been established, in which case the function returns True, and communications begin. If no carrier-detect signal is obtained, the function returns False and the program ends.

After the carrier-detect signal is received, control is passed to the procedure **StartCommunicating**, which transmits the characters you type and displays the characters received from the remote computer. This procedure continues until you press ESC, which produces an ASCII code 27.

The **DisablePorts** procedure, the final step in the program, installs the original interrupt in the interrupt vector table and resets the UART chip.

The Circular Input Buffer

The *circular input buffer* is one of the central elements of an interrupt-driven communications program. Because input can arrive at any time, the interrupt routine might be called

Command	Parameters	Description
A	None	Modem answers a telephone call without waiting for a ring. This is used to change from Voice mode, where you speak to someone, to Data mode, where two computers communicate
A/	None	Repeats the last command
Cn	0,1	Transmitter off. When n = 1, the modem calls, answers, or connects to another modem. All other times, n = 0
,(Comma)	None	Causes a two-second delay when dialing a telephone number
Ds	Number	Puts the modem in the Originate mode and dials the telephone number represented by s
En	0,1	When n = 0, the modem in the command state does not echo back characters When n = 1, characters are echoed
Fn	0,1	When n = 0, the modem operates in half-duplex; when n = 1, the modem operates in full-duplex
Hn	0,1,2	This command controls your telephone's dial tone. When n = 0, the modem is "on-hook" and no dial tone is present. When n = 1, the modem is "off-hook" and the dial tone is present. The parameter 2 is used for special applications using amateur radio equipment
In	0,1	This command requests the Smartmodem's three-digit product code. The first two digits indicate the product (for example, 12 indicates a Smartmodem 1200) and the third digit represents the revision number
Mn	0,1,2	The **M** command controls the speaker. When n = 0, the speaker is always off. When n = 1, the speaker is on until a carrier is detected. When n = 2, the speaker is always on

Table 16-3.   Hayes Smartmodem Commands

Command	Parameters	Description
O	None	When the modem is on-line, the **O** command returns the modem to the Command state. In the Command state, any of the modem commands can be initiated
P	None	Tells the modem to dial the telephone using pulses rather than tones
Qn	0,1	The modem can send result codes that report the modem's status. The command **Q0** tells the modem to send status codes. **Q1** turns this feature off
R	None	Put **R** at the end of a telephone number when calling an originate-only modem
Sr?	1..16	Reads the contents of one of the 16 modem registers, specified by **r**
Sr=n	r = 1..16	Sets modem register **r** to the value **n**
;	None	Places a semicolon at the end of the dial command to force the modem back to the Command state after the modem connects with the remote modem
T	None	Tells the modem to dial in Tone mode rather than Pulse mode
Vn	0,1	The modem can return codes in numbers or words. **V0** selects numeric codes; **V1** selects words
Xn	0,1	The modem can return a basic set of codes or an extended set. **X0** selects the basic set; **X1** selects the extended set
Z	None	Sets the modem to its cold-start configuration, which is like turning the modem off and on

Table 16-3.   Hayes Smartmodem Commands (*continued*)

while the computer is busy doing something else, such as writing to a disk file or performing a screen update. If the interrupt does not store the character in a buffer, the character will be lost before the program has time to capture it.

A circular buffer, which is an array of characters, resolves this problem by storing characters temporarily until your computer has time to catch up with the stream of input characters. The circular buffer is controlled by three integer variables: **CircIn**, **CircOut**, and **CharsInBuf**. **CircIn** points to the next character that the interrupt routine put into the input buffer and **CircOut** points to the next character to be taken out. **CharsInBuf** is the number of characters waiting in the buffer.

When no characters are in the input buffer, **CircIn** and **CircOut** are equal, and **CharsInBuf** is zero. The interrupt routine then adds characters to the buffer, incrementing both **CircIn** and **CharsInBuf**. Note that when the end of the buffer is reached, **CircIn** is set to 1, which points to the beginning of the buffer. This is why the buffer is circular.

The procedure **GetCharInBuf** checks whether **CharsInBuf** is greater than zero, which indicates that characters are present in the buffer. If **CharsInBuf** is greater than zero, the character in the buffer is removed, **CharsInBuf** is decremented, and **CircOut** is incremented. Thus, **CircOut** is constantly chasing **CircIn** to make sure that there are no characters in the input buffer.

Generally, your computer communicates at either 300 or 1200 bits per second. This is fairly slow compared to the speed at which the 8088 processes data. Therefore, the circular buffer should never be full. The **AsyncCommunications** program uses a 1K buffer, which should be more than enough for most communications purposes.

Memory-Resident Programs

When Borland's SideKick program burst onto the software market in 1984, it seemed like magic. Anytime, anywhere, a keystroke could call up a notepad, calculator, and other useful utilities. SideKick could do this because it is a memory-resident program, that is, one that locks itself in memory and is always there even when you run other programs.

Now, years later, memory-resident programs are fairly common. Even so, they remain a mystery to most programmers. This section explains how you can write memory-resident programs using Turbo Pascal.

The DOS Terminate and Stay Resident Service

Making a program memory resident is really quite simple. DOS service **31h** does all the work for you. Put service **31h** in register AH and the number of paragraphs of memory you need in DX. Paragraphs are 16-byte chunks of memory. You can estimate how much your program needs by setting minimum and maximum dynamic memory limitations and then compiling your program. For example, if a program needs only 400h paragraphs of dynamic memory, you must enter this limit in the compiler Options menu, as shown here:

```
              Memory
compile -> Com-file
           cHn-file


minimum cOde segment size:    0000 (max 0D2B paragraphs)
minimum Data segment size:    0000 (max 0FDB paragraphs)
mInimum free dynamic memory: 0400 paragraphs
mAximum free dynamic memory: 0400 paragraphs


Find run-time error   Quit

>
```

With the stack/heap set to the right size, you can compile your program, which gives this result:

```
Code:      0078 paragraphs (  1920 bytes), 0CB3 paragraphs free
Data:      00FF paragraphs (  4080 bytes), 0EDC paragraphs free
Stack/Heap: 0400 paragraphs ( 16384 bytes) (minimum)
            0400 paragraphs ( 16384 bytes) (maximum)
```

If you add up the bytes used by the code segment, data segment, and dynamic space, the total amount of memory the program needs is 22,384 bytes, which is about 1400 paragraphs.

Activating the Program

Once you lock your program into memory, you have to be able to activate it. This is done through the use of the keyboard interrupt, interrupt number 9. Before you lock your program into memory, install your own interrupt procedure to replace the normal keyboard interrupt procedure. Now, whenever a key is pressed, your program intercepts it and decides what to do with it.

If the key is not one that your program recognizes, it passes the key on to whatever program is in progress. If, however, your program recognizes the key, the memory-resident procedure can swing into action while the main program is still running.

Swapping Segments

A memory-resident program (MRP) has its own data segment and stack segment. When the MRP is called, however, the data segment register (DS), the stack segment register (SS), and the stack pointer register (SP) contain the values for the main program. Therefore, before your MRP can execute, it must first save the values in the DS, SS, and SP registers and then load the registers with its own values. The code shown here demonstrates part of this process:

```
Procedure Setup;
Begin
TSR_Dseg := dseg;
TSR_Sseg := sseg;
InLine($2e/                (* CS: *)
       $89/$26/TSR_SP);    (* MOV TSR_SP,SP *)
End;
```

The procedure **Setup**, called at the beginning of the MRP, stores the program's data segment, stack segment, and stack pointer as typed-constant integers. Later, when the memory-resident program is invoked, the following code is used to swap the segments and push all the remaining CPU registers:

```
InLine($2E/                (* CS:  *)
       $8C/$16/OldSS/       (* MOV OldSS,SS *)
       $2E/                (* CS:  *)
       $89/$26/OldSP/       (* MOV OldSP,SP *)
       $2E/                (* CS:  *)
       $8C/$1E/OldDS/       (* MOV OldSP,SP *)

       $2E/                (* CS:  *)
       $8E/$16/TsrSS/       (* MOV SS,TsrSS *)
       $2E/                (* CS:  *)
       $8B/$26/TsrSP/       (* MOV SP,TsrSP *)
       $2E/                (* CS:  *)
       $8E/$1E/TsrDS/       (* MOV DS,TsrDS *)

       $50/                (* PUSH AX *)
       $53/                (* PUSH BX *)
       $51/                (* PUSH CX *)
       $52/                (* PUSH DX *)
       $57/                (* PUSH DI *)
       $56/                (* PUSH SI *)
       $06/                (* PUSH ES *)
       $FB);               (* STI *)
```

The typed constants **OldSS**, **OldSP**, and **OldDS** store the original registers; and **TsrSS**, **TsrSP**, and **TsrDS** contain the register values for the MRP. Your interrupt handler code should be placed directly after this inline statement.

Using the Keyboard Interrupt

Your interrupt took the place of the normal keyboard interrupt. DOS, however, still expects you to execute the original interrupt. To do this, use the following inline code:

```
InLine($9C/                (* PUSHF *)
       $3E/                (* DS    *)
       $FF/$1E/OldVec);     (* CALL FAR OldVec *)
```

When directly calling an interrupt from within your code, you must push the Flags register. The interrupt pops this register for you when it ends. The interrupt routine is executed as a far call using DS as the segment and **OldVec** as the offset.

When the keyboard interrupt is called, the variable **Buffer Tail** is moved forward, and you can pick up the characters by referring to the **Buffer**, as shown with this code:

```
If (BufferHead <> BufferTail) Then
  Begin
  ch1 := Buffer[BufferTail-2];
  ch2 := Buffer[BufferTail-1];
```

This picks up the last two characters in the keyboard buffer. When a function key is pressed, the first character placed in the buffer, **ch1**, will be equal to zero and the second character, **ch2**, will indicate the key that was pressed. The program is interested only in the SHIFT-F1 and SHIFT-F10 keys, which generate codes 84 and 93, respectively.

Using Turbo Pascal Keyboard Services

When you press SHIFT-F1, the program executes the code block that displays the current date and time on the screen. Because the routine uses a Turbo Pascal keyboard service, **KeyPressed**, the routine must restore the original keyboard interrupt while the code is in use. This is done with these lines of code:

```
BufferHead := BufferTail; (* Clear the DOS buffer *)

Vec := Vector[$09];       (* Reload the old keyboard address     *)
Vector[$09] := OldVec;    (* so you can use Turbo Pascal keyboard *)
```

The first statement clears the DOS keyboard buffer by setting **BufferHead** equal to **BufferTail**. Next, you load the current interrupt address that points to your procedure into the variable **Vec**, and then load **OldVec**, the original interrupt vector, into the interrupt vector table.

The remaining code saves the current screen in a buffer, creates a window, uses DOS services to display the current system date and time, and waits for you to press a key. When you do, the program restores the interrupt to point to your procedure, resets the window, and restores the original screen.

Removing the Memory-Resident Program

Memory-resident programs normally stay locked in RAM until you shut your computer off. DOS service **49h**, however, removes the program and frees its memory without rebooting. The following code demonstrates how this is done:

```
Vector[$09] := OldVec;
FillChar(Regs,SizeOf(Regs),0);
Regs.AH := $49;
Regs.ES := cseg;
MsDos(Regs);
End;
```

First, the program restores the original keyboard interrupt so your computer can operate normally. Then, the program places the value 49h in AH and the code segment in ES. A call to **MsDos** removes the program from memory.

The following program, called **TimeNow**, presents the complete code for a memory-resident program:

```
{$V-,K-,C-}
Program TimeNow;
Type
  Address = ^Integer;

  ScreenType =  Record
    Position : Array [1..80,1..25] Of Record
      ch : Char;
      attr : Byte;
      End;
    x,y : Byte;
    End;

Var
  Regs : Record Case Integer Of
    1: (AX,BX,CX,DX,BP,DI,SI,DS,ES,Flags : Integer);
    2: (AL,AH,BL,BH,CL,CH,DL,DH : Byte);
    End;

  x1,y1,x2,y2,i : Integer;
  stype : Char;

  vector : Array [0..$ff] Of Address  Absolute $0000:$0000;
  Vec, OldVec : Address;

  ColorScreen : ScreenType Absolute $B800:$0000;
  MonoScreen : ScreenType Absolute $B000:$0000;
```

```
        SavedScreen : ScreenType;
        ch1, ch2 : Char;
        st1,st2,st3 : String[2];
        BufferHead: Integer Absolute $0040:$001A;
        BufferTail: Integer Absolute $0040:$001C;
        Buffer: Array [0..$3D] Of Char Absolute $0040:$0000;

    Const
        TsrSS:        Integer = 0;
        TsrSP:        Integer = 0;
        TsrDS:        Integer = 0;
        OldSS:        Integer = 0;
        OldSP:        Integer = 0;
        OldDS:        Integer = 0;


    (************************************************)

    Procedure Setup;
    Begin
    TsrDS := dseg;
    TsrSS := sseg;
    InLine($2e/                     (* CS: *)
            $89/$26/TsrSP);         (* MOV TsrSP,SP *)
    End;


    (************************************************)

    Procedure KeyBoardInterrupt;
    Begin
    InLine($2E/                     (* CS: *)
            $8C/$16/OldSS/          (* MOV OldSS,SS *)
            $2E/                    (* CS: *)
            $89/$26/OldSP/          (* MOV OldSP,SP *)
            $2E/                    (* CS: *)
            $8C/$1E/OldDS/          (* MOV OldSP,SP *)

            $2E/                    (* CS: *)
            $8E/$16/TsrSS/          (* MOV SS,TsrSS *)
            $2E/                    (* CS: *)
            $8B/$26/TsrSP/          (* MOV SP,TsrSP *)
            $2E/                    (* CS: *)
            $8E/$1E/TsrDS/          (* MOV DS,TsrDS *)

            $50/                    (* PUSH AX *)
            $53/                    (* PUSH BX *)
            $51/                    (* PUSH CX *)
            $52/                    (* PUSH DX *)
            $57/                    (* PUSH DI *)
            $56/                    (* PUSH S *)
            $06/                    (* PUSH ES *)
            $FB);                   (* STI *)


    (****************************************************************)
    (* Your procedure's code starts here. The first step is to call *)
    (* the original keyboard interrupt to pick up the character      *)
    (* from the keyboard.                                            *)
    (****************************************************************)

    InLine($9C/                     (* PUSHF *)
            $3E/                    (* DS   *)
            $FF/$1E/OldVec);        (* CALL FAR OldVec *)

    (****************************************************************)
    (* If BufferHead and BufferTail are not equal, a character has  *)
    (* been read into the buffer. If the key hit was a function     *)
    (* key, then the first character will be 00 and the next char-  *)
    (* acter identifies the key.                                    *)
    (****************************************************************)
```

```
If (BufferHead <> BufferTail) Then
  Begin
  ch1 := Buffer[BufferTail-2];
  ch2 := Buffer[BufferTail-1];

  If (ch1 = 00) Then (* Escape Character *)
    Begin

        Case ch2 Of
84 : (* Shift F1: Show date and time. *)
  Begin
  BufferHead := BufferTail; (* Clear the DOS buffer.*)

  Vec := Vector[$09];        (* Reload the old keyboard address    *)
  Vector[$09] := OldVec;     (* so you can use Turbo Pascal keyboard *)
                             (* commands like Read and KeyPressed.   *)

  If Stype = 'M' then          (* Save the current screen. *)
    SavedScreen := MonoScreen  (* An inline or external    *)
  Else                         (* routine would be better, *)
  SavedScreen := ColorScreen;  (* but this is easy.        *)
  SavedScreen.x := wherex;
  SavedScreen.y := wherey;

  x1 := 20;                  (* Draw a box on the screen.  *)
  y1 := 10;                  (* This is a long part of the *)
  x2 := 60;                  (* program.                   *)
  y2 := 11;

  For i := x1 To x2 Do
    Begin
    GoToXY(i,y1-1);
    Write(Char(205));
    GoToXY(i,y2+1);
    Write(Char(205));
    End;

  For i := y1 To y2 Do
    Begin
    GoToXY(x1-1,i);
    Write(Char(186));
    GoToXY(x2+1,i);
    Write(Char(186));
    End;

GoToXY(x1-1,y1-1);
Write(Char(201));
GoToXY(x1-1,y2+1);
Write(Char(200));
GoToXY(x2+1,y1-1);
Write(Char(187));
GoToXY(x2+1,y2+1);
Write(Char(188));

Window(x1,y1,x2,y2);     (* Create a window inside the box. *)
clrscr;

Regs.AH := $2A;          (* Get the system date and display it. *)
MsDos(Regs);
Write('Date: ');

  case Regs.AL Of
  0: Write('Sunday, ');
  1: Write('Monday, ');
```

```
                2: Write('Tuesday, ');
                3: Write('Wednesday, ');
                4: Write('Thursday, ');
                5: Write('Friday, ');
                6: Write('Saturday, ');
                End;

            Str(Regs.DH,st1);
            If length(st1) = 1 Then st1 := '0' + st1;
            Str(Regs.DL,st2);
            If length(st2) = 1 Then st2 := '0' + st2;
            WriteLn(st1,'/',st2,'/',Regs.CX);

            Regs.AH := $2C;        (* Get the system time and display it. *)
            MsDos(Regs);
            Write('Time: ');

            Str(Regs.CH,st1);
            If length(st1) = 1 Then st1 := '0' + st1;
            Str(Regs.CL,st2);
            If length(st2) = 1 Then st2 := '0' + st2;
            Str(Regs.DH,st3);
            If length(st3) = 1 Then st3 := '0' + st3;

            Write(st1,':',st2,':',st3);
            Repeat Until keypressed;

            BufferHead := BufferTail; (* Clear the buffer again.          *)
            Vector[$09] := Vec;       (* Restore your interrupt procedure. *)

            Window(1,1,80,25);        (* Widen the window. *)

            If Stype = 'M' then       (* Restore the screen. *)
              MonoScreen := SavedScreen
            Else
              ColorScreen := SavedScreen;

            GoToXY(SavedScreen.x, SavedScreen.y); (* Position the cursor. *)
            End;

        93 : (* Shift F10: Remove program from memory. *)
            Begin
            clrscr;
            Write('TimeNow unloaded.  Press RETURN...');
            Vector[$09] := OldVec;
            FillChar(Regs,SizeOf(Regs),0);
            Regs.AH := $49;
            Regs.ES := cseg;
            MsDos(Regs);
            End;
        End; (* Of case *)
      End;
  End;

(*****************)

InLine($FA/               (* CLI *)
       $07/               (* POP ES *)
       $5E/               (* POP SI *)
       $5F/               (* POP DI *)
       $5A/               (* POP DX *)
       $59/               (* POP CX *)
       $5B/               (* POP BX *)
       $58/               (* POP AX *)
```

```
            $2E/                (* CS: *)
            $8E/$16/OldSS/       (* MOV  SS,OldSS *)
            $2E/                (* CS: *)
            $8B/$26/OldSP/       (* MOV  SP,OldSP *)
            $2E/                (* CS: *)
            $8E/$1E/OldDS/       (* MOV  DS,OldDS *)

            $5d/                (* POP BP *)
            $5d/                (* POP BP *)
            $CF);               (* IRET *)
End;

(*************************************************)

Begin

(***********************)
(* Save Segment Values. *)
(***********************)
Setup;

(********************)
(* Get screen type. *)
(********************)
regs.AH := $0F;
Intr($10,regs);
if regs.AL = 7 Then
  stype := 'M'
Else
  stype := 'C';

(**********************************)
(* Point interrupt to your routine. *)
(**********************************)
OldVec := vector[$09];
vector[$09] := Ptr(Cseg, ofs(KeyBoardInterrupt));

WriteLn('TimeNow Loaded.');
With Regs Do
  Begin
  AH := $31;    (* Terminate Stay Resident. *)
  DX := $577;   (* Program size in paragraphs. *)

  MsDos(Regs); (* Install program. *)
  End;

End.
```

Before you compile **TimeNow**, go to the compiler Options menu and set the minimum and maximum dynamic memory values to an amount sufficient for your program. 400h paragraphs is sufficient for this program.

Next, determine the total program size, which is used in the **Terminate/Stay Resident** function call. To calculate the size, simply compile the program and add up the code, data, and stack/heap values, as shown here:

```
Code:       0077 paragraphs (  1904 bytes), 0CB1 paragraphs free
Data:       0100 paragraphs (  4096 bytes), 0EDC paragraphs free
Stack/Heap: 0400 paragraphs ( 16384 bytes) (minimum)
            0400 paragraphs ( 16384 bytes) (maximum)
```

The code segment uses 77h paragraphs, the data segment uses 100h paragraphs, and the stack/heap uses 400h paragraphs, for a total program size of 577h paragraphs. This is the number you should use in the DOS **Terminate/ Stay Resident** service.

The **TimeNow** program provides the basic shell you need to write your own memory-resident programs. This type of programming requires complete knowledge of how interrupts operate. If you attempt to write your own interrupt handler, get as much information as you can about the interrupts you will use.

Interrupt Programming in Turbo Pascal Version 4.0

Turbo Pascal 4.0 introduces new and important changes in the way you can write interrupt-driven and memory-resident programs. One change is the addition of the **Interrupt** directive, which declares a procedure that will be used as an interrupt handler. The syntax of such a declaration is shown here:

```
Procedure Handler(Flags,
               CS,
               IP,
               AX,
               BX,
               CX,
               DX,
               SI,
               DI,
               DS,
               ES,
               BP : Word); Interrupt;
begin
(* Code for interrupt handler *)
end;
```

Notice that the interrupt procedure takes parameters that correspond to CPU registers. You can eliminate some or all of these parameters but only in order from first to last. That is, you can omit **Flags**, or **Flags** and IP, or **Flags**, **IP**, and **CX** but you cannot omit **ES** by itself or any other parameter without also eliminating all the preceding parameters.

The most important aspect of the **Interrupt** declaration is that Turbo Pascal automatically sets up the segment registers for you when your interrupt routine is called. You don't have to worry about storing segment addresses in typed constants as you did with Version 3.0.

Two more new procedures—**SegIntVec** and **GetIntVec**—allow you to get and set interrupt vector addreses with ease. The syntax for these two routines are as follows:

```
Procedure GetIntVec(InterruptNumber : Byte;
                    VectorValue : Pointer);

Procedure SetIntVec(InterruptNumber : Byte;
                    VectorValue : Pointer);
```

GetIntVec returns the address currently used by interrupt **InterruptNumber** in the parameter **VectorValue**. **SetIntVec**, in turn, replaces the current address found for interrupt **InterruptNumber** with the address stored in **VectorValue**. Using these procedures is much safer than directly altering the interrupt vector table.

Another major improvement is the **Keep** procedure, which causes your program to terminate and stay resident. **Keep** takes an integer parameter that returns the DOS exit code upon termination. The program listing below contains a TSR program that uses the **Interrupt** declaration and the **Keep** procedure to place a clock in the right-hand corner of your screen.

```
Program TSRTimer;
Uses DOS, crt, turbo3;
Const
  Timer = $1C;

Var
  ColorMonitor : boolean;
  Screen : Byte absolute $B800:0144;
  (*$B00:0144 for monochrome systems*)
  s : string[8];
  s_move : array[1..8] of record
    ch : char;
    at : byte;
    end;
  s1,s2,s3 : String[2];
  i : integer;
```

```
      x,y,
      counter,
      Hour,
      Minute,
      Second,
      Sec100 : Integer;
      Vector : Pointer;

(*****************************************************************)

Procedure IntHandler(Flags,CS,IP,AX,BX,CX,DX,SI,DI,DS,ES,BP : Word);
   Interrupt;
var
  x,y : byte;
  regs : registers;

Procedure CLI; (* Disable interrupts *)
Inline($FA);

Procedure STI; (* Enable interrupts *)
Inline($FB);

procedure MoveToScreen(Var Source, dest; Length: Integer);
Begin
If Not ColorMonitor Then
  Move(Source,dest,Length)
Else
  Begin
  Length:=Length Shr 1;
  Inline($1E/$55/$BA/$DA/$03/$C5/$B6/ Source /$C4/$BE/ dest /$8B/$8E/
         Length /$FC/$AD/$89/$C5/$B4/$09/$EC/$D0/$D8/$72/$FB/$FA/$EC/
         $20/$E0/$74/$FB/$89/$E8/$AB/$FB/$E2/$EA/$5D/$1F);
  end;
end;

begin
CLI;

counter := counter + 1;
if counter = 18 then
  begin
  counter := 0;
  second := second + 1;
  if second > 59 then
    begin
    second := 0;
    minute := minute + 1;
    if minute > 59 then
      begin
      minute := 0;
      hour := hour + 1;
      if hour > 23 then
        hour := 0;
      end;
    end;
  end;

Str(hour,s1);
Str(minute,s2);
Str(second,s3);
if hour < 10 then
  s1 := '0' + s1;
if minute < 10 then
  s2 := '0' + s2;
if second < 10 then
  s3 := '0' + s3;

s := s1 + ':' + s2 + ':' + s3;
```

```
fillchar(s_move,16,$0F);
for i := 1 to 8 do
  s_move[i].ch := s[i];

MoveToScreen(s_move,screen,16);

STI;
end;

(*************************************************************)

begin
clrscr;
counter := 0;
ColorMonitor := true; (* Change to false for NON-CGA monitors*)
GetTime(hour,minute,second,sec100);
GetIntVec(Timer,Vector);
SetIntVec(Timer,@IntHandler);
Keep(ExitCode);
end.
```

TSR programs are never easy to write, but these new additions make it easier than with Turbo Pascal Version 3.0. Always take care to set your memory requirements so that your program uses the least amount of memory possible.

SEVENTEEN

Turbo Pascal Procedure and Function Library

Fundamental Routines
Buffered String Input
Large String Procedures
Arithmetic Functions
Running a DOS Shell
File Encryption

Good programmers are pack rats; they store every function and procedure they come across because they know that sooner or later they will use them. Putting together a good procedure and function library takes years of coding, testing, and swapping information with other programmers. You can get a head start on your library with the procedures and functions in this chapter.

Fundamental Routines

Certain routines are so generally useful that you include them in programs. Some of the most valuable ones write directly to screen memory, control the PC's sound generator, and center a string on the screen.

FastWrite

The fastest way to display text is to write directly to video memory. When you do so, you must use either an external assembler procedure or inline code; otherwise your procedure will create snow on the screen. This inline procedure writes a string to coordinates **x** and **y** in the colors you specify. The parameter **stype** must contain either "M" for monochrome displays or "C" for color displays.

```
Procedure FastWrite( x, y : Integer;
                     Var S : MaxStr;
                     fg, bg : Integer;
                     stype : Char);
Begin
Inline($50/            (*  PUSH    AX              *)
       $53/            (*  PUSH    BX              *)
       $51/            (*  PUSH    CX              *)
       $52/            (*  PUSH    DX              *)
       $1E/            (*  PUSH    DS              *)
       $06/            (*  PUSH    ES              *)
       $57/            (*  PUSH    DI              *)
       $56/            (*  PUSH    SI              *)
       $8B/$5E/<x/     (*  MOV     BX,x            *)
       $8B/$46/<y/     (*  MOV     AX,y            *)
       $4B/            (*  DEC     BX              *)
       $48/            (*  DEC     AX              *)
       $B9/$50/$00/    (*  MOV     CX,0050         *)
       $F7/$E1/        (*  MUL     CX              *)
       $03/$C3/        (*  ADD     AX,BX           *)
       $B9/$02/$00/    (*  MOV     CX,0002         *)
       $F7/$E1/        (*  MUL     CX              *)
       $8B/$F8/        (*  MOV     DI,AX           *)
       $8B/$5E/<bg/    (*  MOV     BX,bg           *)
       $8B/$46/<fg/    (*  MOV     AX,fg           *)
       $B9/$04/$00/    (*  MOV     CX,0004         *)
       $D3/$E3/        (*  SHL     BX,CL           *)
       $03/$D8/        (*  ADD     BX,AX           *)
       $86/$DF/        (*  XCHG    BL,DH           *)
       $BA/$DA/$03/    (*  MOV     DX,03DA         *)
       $B8/$00/$B0/    (*  MOV     AX,B000         *)
       $8E/$C0/        (*  MOV     ES,AX           *)
       $8B/$46/<stype/ (*  MOV     AX,stype        *)
       $3C/$4D/        (*  CMP     AL,4D           *)
       $74/$05/        (*  JZ      2DE7            *)
       $B8/$00/$B8/    (*  MOV     AX,B800         *)
       $8E/$C0/        (*  MOV     ES,AX           *)
       $C5/$76/<s/     (*  LDS     SI,s            *)
       $8A/$0C/        (*  MOV     CL,[SI]         *)
       $80/$F9/$00/    (*  CMP     CL,00           *)
```

```
       $74/$15/        (* JZ      2EC6         *)
       $FC/            (* CLD                  *)
       $46/            (* INC     SI           *)
       $8A/$1C/        (* MOV     BL,[SI]      *)
       $EC/            (* IN      AL,DX        *)
       $A8/$01/        (* TEST    AL,01        *)
       $75/$FB/        (* JNZ     2DF5         *)
       $FA/            (* CLI                  *)
       $EC/            (* IN      AL,DX        *)
       $A8/$01/        (* TEST    AL,01        *)
       $74/$FB/        (* JZ      2DFB         *)
       $8B/$C3/        (* MOV     AX,BX        *)
       $AB/            (* STOSW                *)
       $FB/            (* STI                  *)
       $E2/$EC/        (* LOOP    2DF2         *)
       $5E/            (* POP     SI           *)
       $5F/            (* POP     DI           *)
       $07/            (* POP     ES           *)
       $1F/            (* POP     DS           *)
       $5A/            (* POP     DX           *)
       $59/            (* POP     CX           *)
       $5B/            (* POP     BX           *)
       $58/            (* POP     AX           *)
       $E9/$00/$00/    (* JMP     2E11         *)
       $8B/$E5/        (* MOV     SP,BP        *)
       $5D/            (* POP     BP           *)
       $C2/$0E/$00);   (* RET     000E         *)
End;
```

GetScreenType

To use **FastWrite** and many other routines in this chapter, you must know what type of display adapter the computer uses. This information is reported by the procedure **GetScreenType**, shown here. **GetScreenType** uses BIOS interrupt 10h with register AH set to 0Fh, which returns the current video mode. If the returned mode is 7, the screen is monochrome.

```
Procedure GetScreenType(Var stype : Char);
var
  regs : Record
    Case Integer Of
    1 : (AX,BX,CX,DX,BP,SI,DI,DS,ES,Flags : Integer);
    2 : (AL,AH,BL,BH,CL,CH,DL,DH : Byte);
    End;

begin
```

```
regs.AH := $0F;
Intr($1C,regs);
If regs.AL = 7 Then
   stype := 'M'
Else
   stype := 'C';
End;
```

Controlling the Cursor

The following three procedures control the size of the cursor, making it small or large, and also turning it off. The parameter **stype** contains the type of adapter in use ("M" or "C"). The color screen uses up to 8 lines for the cursor, while the monochrome screen uses as many as 14.

```
Procedure Cursor_off(stype : Char);
Var
   regs : Record
      Case Integer Of
      1 : (AX,BX,CX,DX,BP,SI,DI,DS,ES,Flags : Integer);
      2 : (AL,AH,BL,BH,CL,CH,DL,DH : Byte);
      End;

Begin
   Case stype Of
   'M' :
     Begin
     With regs Do
        Begin
        AH := $01;
        CH := 14;
        CL := 14;
        End;
     End;
   'C':
     Begin
     With regs Do
        Begin
        AH := $01;
        CH := 8;
        CL := 8;
        End;
     End;
   End;
Intr($10, regs);
End;

(***********************************************)

Procedure Cursor_Small(stype : Char);
Var
   regs : Record
      Case Integer Of
```

```
    1 : (AX,BX,CX,DX,BP,SI,DI,DS,ES,Flags : Integer);
    2 : (AL,AH,BL,BH,CL,CH,DL,DH : Byte);
    End;

Begin
  Case stype Of
  'M' :
    Begin
    With regs Do
      Begin
      AH := $01;
      CH := 12;
      CL := 13;
      End;
    End;

  'C' :
    Begin
    With regs Do
      Begin
      AH := $01;
      CH := 6;
      CL := 7;
      End;
    End;
  End;
  Intr($10, regs);
End;

(**********************************************)

Procedure Cursor_big(stype : Char);
Var
  regs : Record
    Case Integer Of
    1 : (AX,BX,CX,DX,BP,SI,DI,DS,ES,Flags : Integer);
    2 : (AL,AH,BL,BH,CL,CH,DL,DH : Byte);
    End;

Begin
  Case stype Of

  'M' :
    Begin
    With regs Do
      Begin
      AH := $01;
      CH := 0;
      CL := 13;
      End;
    End;

  'C' :
    Begin
    With regs Do
      Begin
      AH := $01;
      CH := 0;
      CL := 7;
```

```
        End;
      End;
    End;
Intr($10, regs);
End;
```

Centering Text

Center displays a string in the middle of a screen line you specify. The syntax of the command is just like that of the **FastWrite** command, except that no **x** coordinate is specified. Instead, the procedure calculates which **x** coordinate will properly center the string.

```
Procedure Center(y : Integer;
                 s : MaxStr;
                 fg,
                 bg : Integer;
                 stype : Char);
  Var
    x : Integer;

Begin
x := 40 - (Length(s) Div 2);
fastwrite(x, y, s, fg, bg, stype);
End;
```

Generating Sound

The Turbo Pascal commands **Sound** and **NoSound** control the PC's sound generator. **Sound** takes an integer parameter that specifies the pitch of the tone. The tone continues until you issue the **NoSound** command. By using the **Delay** command, you can produce a tone that lasts a specified amount of time. The procedure **Beep**, presented here, uses these three commands to create a tone of a certain pitch and duration. The parameter **Freq** determines the pitch and **Time** specifies the duration in milliseconds.

```
Procedure Beep(Freq, Time : Integer);
Begin
Sound(Freq);
Delay(Time);
NoSound;
End;
```

Buffered String Input

Turbo Pascal's input procedures **Read** and **ReadLn** are quite limited. When entering data, you can only delete backward with the BACKSPACE key. There is also no direct way to know if a function key has been pressed. The two procedures in this section, **InKey** and **InputStringShift**, extend your ability to control the keyboard.

InKey

Each time you press a function key, the PC generates a scan code along with a character. For example, function key F1 generates a scan code followed by ASCII character 59, the semicolon. The procedure **InKey** checks for the scan code when a key is pressed. If the code is present, **InKey** sets the parameter **FunctionKey** to True.

InKey also allows you to control the cursor in two ways. The parameter **BeginCursor** determines the way the cursor looks when the procedure is waiting for a key to be pressed: "B" creates a big cursor, "S" a small cursor, and "O" no cursor. The parameter **EndCursor** tells **InKey** how it should leave the cursor after the key has been read.

Since keeping track of function-key codes is difficult, **InKey** sets a global scalar variable that refers to the function keys by name. This scalar is defined as shown here:

```
Type
  Keys = (NullKey, F1, F2, F3, F4, F5, F6, F7, F8, F9, F10,
          CarriageReturn, Tab, ShiftTab, Bksp, UpArrow, DownArrow,
          RightArrow, LeftArrow, DeleteKey, InsertKey, HomeKey, Esc,
          EndKey, TextKey, NumberKey, Space, PgUp, PgDn);

Var
  Key : Keys;
```

You can use this definition to easily program control loops by testing for a specific key, as shown here:

```
Repeat
Inkey(Fk,Ch,'B','O');
Until Key = F1;
```

In this example, the program keeps accepting keyboard input until you press the F1 key. The complete **InKey** procedure is shown here:

```
Procedure InKey(Var FunctionKey : Boolean;
                Var ch : Char;
                BeginCursor,
                EndCursor : Char);
Begin

  Case BeginCursor Of
  'B' : cursor_big(stype);
  'S' : cursor_small(stype);
  'C' : cursor_off(stype);
  End;

FunctionKey := False;
Read(Kbd, ch);
If (ch = 27) And KeyPressed Then
  Begin
  FunctionKey := True;
  Read(Kbd, ch);
  End;

If FunctionKey Then
  Case Ord(ch) Of
  15: (* shift Tab *)      key := ShiftTab;
  72: (* up arrow *)       key := UpArrow;
  80: (* down arrow *)     key := DownArrow;
  82: (* insert key *)     key := InsertKey;
  75: (* left arrow *)     key := LeftArrow;
  77: (* right arrow *)    key := RightArrow;
  73: (* pge up *)         key := PgUp;
  81: (* pge down *)       key := PgDn;
  71: (* home *)           key := HomeKey;
  79: (* End *)            key := EndKey;
  83: (* delete *)         key := DeleteKey;
  82: (* insert *)         key := InsertKey;
  59: (* F1 *)             key := F1;
  60: (* F2 *)             key := F2;
  61: (* F3 *)             key := F3;
  62: (* F4 *)             key := F4;
  63: (* F5 *)             key := F5;
  64: (* F6 *)             key := F6;
  65: (* F7 *)             key := F7;
  66: (* F8 *)             key := F8;
  67: (* F9 *)             key := F9;
  68: (* F10 *)            key := F10;
  End
Else
  Case Ord(ch) Of
```

```
    8: (* back Space *)       key := Bksp;
    9: (* Tab key *)          key := Tab;
   13: (* return *)           key := CarriageReturn;
   27: (* escape *)           key := Esc;
   32: (* Space bar *)        key := Space;
   33..44, 47, 58..254:
      (* TextKey *)             key := TextKey;

   45..46, 48..57:
      (* number key *)          key := NumberKey;
   End;

   Case EndCursor Of
   'B' : cursor_big(stype);
   'S' : cursor_small(stype);
   'O' : cursor_off(stype);
   End;

End;
```

InputStringShift

A good input procedure allows you to use all the keys on the PC keyboard to delete characters with both the BACKSPACE and DELETE keys, move back and forth with the right- and left-arrow keys, and switch between Insert and Overwrite modes by pressing the INS key.

InputStringShift can give your program the capability to perform all these features. This procedure also lets you enter a string that is longer than the space on the screen you provided for input. For example, even if you set aside only 10 spaces on the screen for input, you can still accept strings as long as 255 characters. **InputStringShift** shifts the string back and forth in the input window as you type or use the ARROW and DELETE keys.

InputStringShift takes seven parameters, which are shown here:

```
Procedure InputStringShift(Var S : MaxStr;
                           WindowLength,
                           MaxLength,
                           X,Y : Integer;
                           FT : Char;
                           BackgroundChar : Integer);
```

S, a string variable, accepts the input; **WindowLength** specifies the size of the data-entry field (from 1 to 255); **MaxLength** is the maximum length of the string (from 1 to 255), and **x** and **y** are the screen coordinates of the first character of the input field. **FT** specifies the field type and can be either "T" for text or "N" for numeric. When the field is empty, blank spaces are filled with a character specified by the parameter **BackgroundChar**. Character 176 is a good choice because it creates a lightly shaded background.

```
Procedure InputStringShift(Var S : MaxStr;
                               WindowLength,
                               MaxLength,
                               X,Y : Integer;
                               FT : Char;
                               BackgroundChar : Integer);
Var
  xx, i, j, p : Integer;
  ch : Char;
  InsertOn,
  SpecialKey : Boolean;
  offset : Integer;
  TempStr : MaxStr;

Procedure XY(x, y : Integer);
Var
  Xsmall : Integer;
Begin
  Repeat
  Xsmall := x-80;
  If Xsmall > 0 Then
    Begin
    y := y+1;
    x := Xsmall;
    End;
  Until Xsmall <= 0;
GoToXY(x, y);
End;

(************************************)

Procedure SetString;
Var
  i : Integer;
Begin
i := Length(s);
While s[i] = Char(BackgroundChar) Do
  i := i-1;
s[0] := Char(i);
cursor_small(stype);
End;

(************************************)
```

```
Begin
j := Length(s)+1;
FOR i := j TO MaxLength DO
  s[i] := Char(BackgroundChar);
s[0] := Char(MaxLength);

TempStr := Copy(S, 1, WindowLength);
FastWrite(x,y,TempStr,yellow,black,stype);

p := 1;
offset := 1;
InsertOn := True;

  Repeat
  xx := X+(p-offset);
  If (p-offset) = WindowLength Then
    xx := xx-1;

  XY(XX, Y);

  If InsertOn Then
    InKey(SpecialKey, ch, 'S', '0')
  Else
    InKey(SpecialKey, ch, 'B', '0');

  If (FT = 'N') Then
    Begin
    If (key = TextKey) Then
      Begin
      beep(100,250);
      key := NullKey;
      End
    Else If (ch = '-') And ((p > 1) OR (s[1] = '-')) Then
      Begin
      beep(100,250);
      key := NullKey;
      End
    Else If (ch = '.') Then
      Begin
      If Not((Pos('.', s) = 0) OR (Pos('.', s) = p)) Then
        Begin
        beep(100,250);
        key := NullKey;
        End
      Else If (Pos('.', s) = p) Then
        Delete(s, p, 1);
      End;
    End;

  Case key Of

    NumberKey,
    TextKey,
    Space :
      Begin
      If (Length(s) = MaxLength) Then
        Begin
        If p = MaxLength Then
          Begin
          Delete(s, MaxLength, 1);
```

```
        s := s+ch;
        If p = WindowLength+offset Then
          offset := offset+1;
        TempStr := Copy(s, offset, WindowLength);
        FastWrite(x,y,TempStr,yellow,black,stype);
        End
      Else
        Begin
        If InsertOn Then
          Begin
          Delete(s, MaxLength, 1);
          Insert(ch, s, p);
          If p = WindowLength+offset Then
            offset := offset+1;
          If p < MaxLength Then
            p := p+1;
          TempStr := Copy(s, offset, WindowLength);
          FastWrite(x,y,TempStr,Yellow,Black,stype);
          End
        Else        (* overwrite *)
          Begin
          Delete(s, p, 1);
          Insert(ch, s, p);
          If p = WindowLength+offset Then
            offset := offset+1;
          If p < MaxLength Then
            p := p+1;
          TempStr := Copy(s, offset, WindowLength);
          FastWrite(x,y,TempStr,Yellow,Black,stype);
          End;
        End;
      End
    Else
      Begin
      If InsertOn Then
        Begin
        Insert(ch, s, p);
        End
      Else
        Begin
        Delete(s, p, 1);
        Insert(ch, s, p);
        End;
      If p = WindowLength+offset Then
        offset := offset+1;
      If p < MaxLength Then
        p := p+1;

      TempStr := Copy(s, offset, WindowLength);
      FastWrite(x,y,TempStr,Yellow,Black,stype);
      End;
    End;

Bksp :
  Begin
  If p > 1 Then
    Begin
    p := p-1;
    Delete(S, p, 1);
```

```pascal
      s := s+Char(BackgroundChar);
      If offset > 1 Then
        offset := offset-1;
      TempStr := Copy(s, offset, WindowLength);
      FastWrite(x,y,TempStr,Yellow,Black,stype);
      ch := ' ';
      End
    Else
      Begin
      beep(100,250);
      ch := ' ';
      p := 1;
      End;
    End;

LeftArrow :
  Begin
  If p > 1 Then
    Begin
    p := p-1;
    If p < offset Then
      Begin
      offset := offset-1;
      TempStr := Copy(s, offset, WindowLength);
      FastWrite(x,y,TempStr,Yellow,Black,stype);
      End;
    End
  Else
    Begin
    SetString;
    Exit;
    End;
  End;

RightArrow :
  Begin
  If (s[p] <> Char(BackgroundChar)) And (p < MaxLength) Then
    Begin
    p := p+1;
    If p = (WindowLength+offset) Then
      Begin
      offset := offset+1;
      TempStr := Copy(s, offset, WindowLength);
      FastWrite(x,y,TempStr,Yellow,Black,stype);
      End;
    End
  Else
    Begin
    SetString;
    Exit;
    End;
  End;

DeleteKey :
  Begin
  Delete(S, p, 1);
  s := s+Char(BackgroundChar);
  If ((Length(S)+1)-offset) >= WindowLength Then
    Begin
```

```
        TempStr := Copy(s, offset, WindowLength);
        FastWrite(x,y,TempStr,Yellow,Black,stype);
        End
      Else
        Begin
        TempStr := Copy(s, offset, WindowLength);
        FastWrite(x,y,TempStr,Yellow,Black,stype);
        End;
      End;

    InsertKey :
      Begin
      If InsertOn Then
        InsertOn := False
      Else
        InsertOn := True;
      End;

    Else If Not(key In [CarriageReturn, UpArrow, DownArrow, PgDn,
                      PgUp, NullKey, Esc, Tab,
                      F1, F2, F3, F4, F5, F6,
                      F7, F8, F9, F10]) Then beep(100,250);

    End;

  Until (key In [CarriageReturn, UpArrow, DownArrow, PgUp, PgDn, Esc,
              Tab, F1, F3, F4, F5, F6, F7, F8, F9, F10]);

SetString;
End;
```

Large String Procedures

Turbo Pascal limits strings to a maximum of 255 characters.
While this is long enough for most strings, there are times
when you will need longer strings. The procedures in this
section allow you to define strings up to 32,767 characters
long. The procedures assume a record type that includes an
integer field, which keeps track of the string length, and an
array of characters. An example of this record type,
BigString, follows:

```
const
  MaxBigStrLen = 1000;
Type
  BigString = record
                length : Integer;
                ch : array [1..MaxBigStrLen] of Char;
                End;
```

BigString can hold up to 1000 characters, and it can be easily extended by changing the value of **MaxBigStrLen**.

The procedures and functions in this section mimic the standard Turbo Pascal string commands; they use the same syntax and names, but begin with the letters "Big." For example, the equivalent of Turbo Pascal's **Insert** command is the **BigInsert** command.

SetBigString

SetBigString initializes a big string, **st1**, to a value specified in parameter **s**.

```
Procedure SetBigString(Var st1 : BigString;s : MaxStr);
Var
  i : Integer;
Begin
For i := 1 To Length(s) Do
  st1.ch[i] := s[i];
st1.length := Length(s);
End;
```

BigConcat

Big strings cannot use the Turbo Pascal concatenation operator +. You can, however, simulate the **Concat** command, as shown in the procedure **BigConcat**, which concatenates **st2** to **st1**.

```
Procedure BigConcat(Var st1 : BigString;
                        st2 : BigString);
Var
  i : Integer;
Begin
Move(st2.ch[1],st1.ch[st1.length+1],St2.length);
st1.length := st1.length + st2.length;
End;
```

BigInsert

BigInsert inserts one **BigString** inside a target **BigString** starting at character **p**.

```
Procedure BigInsert(Var st1,st2 : BigString; p : Integer);
Var
  st3 : BigString;
  i,j : Integer;
Begin
Move(st2.ch[1],st3.ch[1],p-1);

Move(st1.ch[1],st3.ch[p],st1.length);

Move(st2.ch[p],st3.ch[p+st1.length],(st2.length-p)+1);

st3.length := st1.length + st2.length;
If st3.length > MaxBigStrLen Then
  st3.length := MaxBigStrLen;

Move(st3.length,st2.length,st3.length+2);
End;
```

BigDelete

BigDelete removes characters from a **BigString** starting at character **p**. It deletes as many characters as specified in the parameter **len**.

```
Procedure BigDelete(Var st1 : BigString; p,len : Integer);
Var
  st2 : BigString;

Begin
Move(st1.ch[1],st2.ch[1],p-1);
Move(st1.ch[(p+len)],st2.ch[p],(st1.length-(p+len))+1);
st2.length := (st1.length - len);
Move(st2.length,st1.length,st2.length+2);
End;
```

BigPos

The function **BigPos** returns the position of one **BigString** inside another **BigString**. To indicate the position, **BigPos** returns a positive number; if no match is found, it returns zero.

```
Function BigPos(Var st1,st2 : BigString) : Integer;
Var
  found : Boolean;
  i,j,StopFlag : Integer;
Begin
StopFlag := (st2.length - st1.length) + 1;
For i := 1 To StopFlag Do
  Begin
  found := True;
  j := 1;
```

```
      Repeat
      If st2.ch[i+j-1] <> st1.ch[j] Then
         found := False;
      j := j + 1;
      Until (Not found) Or (j = st1.length);

   If found Then
      Begin
      BigPos := i;
      Exit;
      End;
   End;
BigPos := 0;
End;
```

BigLength

The **BigLength** procedure returns an integer with the length of a **BigString**.

```
Function BigLength(Var St1 : BigString) : Integer;
Begin
BigLength := st1.length;
End;
```

BigCopy

Because the Turbo Pascal string function **Copy** cannot be directly duplicated for large strings (Turbo Pascal cannot define a function using a record data-type) you must use **BigCopy**, which provides a result in the form of a procedure. **BigCopy** takes **len** characters from **st1**, starting from character **p**, and assigns them to **st2**.

```
Procedure BigCopy(Var st1,st2 : BigString; p,len : Integer);
Begin
Move(st1.ch[p],st2.ch[1],len);
st2.length := len;
End;
```

Arithmetic Functions

Most of the numerical procedures and functions your programs need are available in Turbo Pascal. One thing these procedures cannot do, however, is convert a fraction that is stored in a string to a decimal equivalent or convert a decimal value into a fraction. The two functions listed here, **Real__To__Frac** and **Frac__To__Real**, do just that.

Real__To__Frac

Real__To__Frac accepts two parameters: **r**, the value to convert to decimal, and **d**, the denominator of the fraction. The function returns a string that contains the integer portion of the fraction, as well as the fractional portion. The two are separated by a space.

```
Function Real_To_Frac(r : Real; d : Integer) : MaxStr;
Var
  is, ns, ds, s1, s2 : String[20];
  r1, r2, i, f : Real;
  code, p, n : Integer;

Begin
IF r = 0 THEN
   Begin
   real_to_frac := '0';
   Exit;
   End;

is := '0';
ds := '0';
ns := '0';

Str(r:0:8, s2);
p := Pos('.', s2);
if p > 0 then
   s1 := Copy(s2, 1, p-1);

Delete(s2, 1, p-1);
Val(s1, i, code);
Str(i:0:0, is);

Val(s2, f, code);
IF f > 0.0 Then
   Begin
   n := 0;
     Repeat
     n := n+1;
     r1 := n/d;
     Until r1 >= f;
   If (r1-f) > (1.0/(d*2.0)) Then
     n := n-1;

   While (Not Odd(n)) And (n > 0) Do
     Begin
```

```
      n := n DIV 2;
      d := d DIV 2;
      End;
    Str(n:0, ns);
    Str(d:0, ds);
    End;

  IF (ns = '1') And (ds = '1') Then
    Begin
    ns := '0';
    Val(is,r1,code);
    r1 := r1 + 1;
    Str(r1:0:0,is);
    End;

  If (is = '0') And (ns = '0') Then
    real_to_frac := '0'
  Else If ns = '0' Then
    real_to_frac := is
  Else If is = '0' Then
    Begin
    If (ns = '1') And (ds = '1') Then
      real_to_frac := '1'
    Else
      real_to_frac := ns+'/'+ds;
    End
  Else
    real_to_frac := is+' '+ns+'/'+ds
  End;
```

Frac—To—Real

Frac—To—Real, a function of type **real**, converts a string that contains a fraction into a real number. The procedure takes two parameters: **frac**, the string that contains the fraction, and **code**, an integer that indicates an error in conversion. If **code** is equal to zero, no error occurred; if it is not equal to zero, an error did occur. The fraction is formed by an integer, a space, the numerator, a slash, and a denominator. The following are all legal fractions:

14 1/2
3/16
29

As you can see, both the numerator and the fractional portion are optional.

```
Function Frac_To_Real(Frac : MaxStr; Var code : Integer) : Real;
Var
  n, d, i : Real;
  ns, ds, is : String[8];
  l,p,
  p_slash,
  p_space,
  j : Integer;

Begin
While (frac[1] = ' ') and (Length(frac) > 0) Do
  Delete(frac,1,1);
If frac = '' Then
  Begin
  Frac_To_Real := 0;
  Exit;
  End;

p_slash := Pos('/',frac);
p_space := Pos(' ',frac);

is := '';
ns := '';
ds := '';

If (p_slash > 0) Then
  Begin
  If (p_space > 0) Then
    Begin (* slash and space *)
    For j := 1 To (p_space-1) Do
      is := is + frac[j];
    For j := (p_space+1) To (p_slash-1) Do
      ns := ns + frac[j];
    For j := (p_slash+1) To Length(frac) Do
      ds := ds + frac[j];

    Val(is,i,code);
    Val(ns,n,code);
    Val(ds,d,code);

    Frac_To_Real := i + n / d;
    End
  Else
    Begin (* slash and no space *)
    For j := (p_space+1) To (p_slash-1) Do
      ns := ns + frac[j];
    For j := (p_slash+1) To Length(frac) Do
      ds := ds + frac[j];

    Val(ns,n,code);
    Val(ds,d,code);

    Frac_To_Real := n / d;
      end
    End
  Else
    Begin
    If (p_space > 0) Then
      Begin (* no slash and space *)
      For j := 1 To (p_space-1) Do
        is := is + frac[j];

      Val(is,i,code);
      Frac_To_Real := i;
      End
    Else
      Begin (* no slash and no space *)
      is := is + frac;
      Val(is,i,code);
      Frac_To_Real := i;
      End
    End;
  End;
```

Running a DOS Shell

The Turbo Pascal **Exec** function allows you to run another program from within your Turbo Pascal program. Unfortunately, once **Exec** starts the program, you cannot return to your original program. This severely limits the usefulness of **Exec**.

The code presented in this section allows you to exit from your Turbo Pascal program temporarily, run another program, and return safely.

DOSFC4B.COM

To run a DOS shell, you must use the DOS service **4Bh**. Because this DOS service destroys most registers at return, including SS and SP, the Turbo Pascal predefined procedure **MsDos** cannot be used in this case. The listing that follows is the assembler code for a procedure that performs much as the **MsDos** command, but preserves the contents of all the registers. This code must be assembled to a Com file before it can be used in a program.

```
CODE      SEGMENT
          ASSUME    CS:CODE
DOSFC4B   PROC      NEAR
          JMP       START
SSSAVE    DW    ?  ; SAVE SS
SPSAVE    DW    ?  ; SAVE SP
BPSAVE    DW    ?  ; SAVE BP

START:
          PUSH      BP              ; Save BP
          PUSH      DS              ; Save DS
          MOV       BP,SP
          MOV       SI,[BP+6]       ; Regs Offset
          MOV       ES,[BP+8]       ; Regs Segment
          MOV       BX,ES:[SI+2]    ; Get values of BX, DX, DS and ES
          MOV       DX,ES:[SI+6]
          MOV       DS,ES:[SI+14]
          MOV       ES,ES:[SI+16]
          MOV       AX,SS           ; Save SS, SP and BP
          MOV       CS:SSSAVE,AX
          MOV       AX,SP
          MOV       CS:SPSAVE,AX
          MOV       CS:BPSAVE,BP

          MOV       AX,4B00H        ; Set for Function call 4Bh
          INT       21H

          MOV       SS,SSSAVE       ; Restore SS, SP and BP
          MOV       SP,SPSAVE
          MOV       BP,BPSAVE
          MOV       SI,[BP+6]       ; Regs Offset
```

```
        MOV     ES,[BP+8]    ; Regs Segment
        MOV     ES:[SI],AX   ; Set Return code
        PUSHF
        POP     AX
        MOV     ES:[SI+18],AX    ; Set Flags

        POP     DS
        POP     BP
        RET     4

DOSFC4B         ENDP
CODE            ENDS
                END
```

To use this assembler procedure, you must declare it in your program with the following statement:

```
Procedure DOSFC4B( Var Regs : RegType); External 'DOSFC4B.COM';
```

DOS Command Shell
Demonstration Program

The following program contains the code for a program that demonstrates the ability to run programs from within a Turbo Pascal program. The program provides a DOS shell — an emulation of the DOS prompt—that allows you to run DOS commands or other programs as if you were not in a Turbo Pascal program. When you compile this program, call up the compiler Options menu and set the minimum and maximum dynamic space to the same value. If you do not limit the dynamic space, Turbo Pascal will use all the free memory in the computer, and you will not be able to execute the DOS shell.

```
Program DosShellDemo;
Type
  MaxStr = String[255];

  RegRec = Record
    Case Integer Of
    1 : (AX,BX,CX,DX,BP,SI,DI,DS,ES,Flags : Integer);
    2 : (AL,AH,BL,BH,CL,CH,DL,DH : Byte);
    End;

Var
  i : Integer;

(*********************************************)

Procedure DOSFC4B(Var Regs : RegRec); External 'DOSFC4B.COM';
```

```
Procedure RunDOS;
Const
  Null = ^@;
  CRT = ^M;
Var
  Regs : RegRec;
  dos_directory,
  CommandLine : MaxStr;

  DOSenvironment : Integer Absolute CSeg:$002C;

(*******************************************)

Function CallProgram(ProgramName, InputCmd : MaxStr) : Boolean;
Type
  FileControlBlock = Array[0..36] OF Char;
Var Ret : Boolean;
  CmdLen : Byte Absolute InputCmd;
  FCB1, FCB2 : FileControlBlock;
  CntlBlock : Record
    EnvSeg : Integer;
    CmdAddr : ^MaxStr;
    FCB1Addr,
    FCB2Addr : ^FileControlBlock;
    End;

(*******************************************)

Procedure CreateFileControlBlock(InputCmd : MaxStr;
                          Var FCB1, FCB2 : FileControlBlock);
Var
  Regs : RegRec;
  Flag : Boolean;
Begin
FillChar(FCB1, SizeOf(FCB1), 0);
Regs.AX := $2901;
Regs.DS := Seg(InputCmd[1]);
Regs.SI := Ofs(InputCmd[1]);
Regs.ES := Seg(FCB1);
Regs.DI := Ofs(FCB1);
MsDos(Regs);
Flag := (Not Odd(Regs.Flags));

FillChar(FCB2, SizeOf(FCB2), 0);
Regs.AX := $2901;
Regs.ES := Seg(FCB2);
Regs.DI := Ofs(FCB2);
MsDos(Regs);
Flag := (Not Odd(Regs.Flags));
End;

(*******************************************)

Begin
Ret := True;
CreateFileControlBlock(InputCmd, FCB1, FCB2);
ProgramName := ProgramName+Null;
InputCmd := ' '+InputCmd+CRT;
CmdLen := Pred(CmdLen);
WITH CntlBlock Do
  Begin
  EnvSeg := DOSenvironment;
  CmdAddr := Addr(InputCmd);
  FCB1Addr := Addr(FCB1);
  FCB2Addr := Addr(FCB2);
  End;

FillChar(regs, SizeOf(regs), 0);
```

```
Regs.BX := Ofs(CntlBlock);
Regs.DX := Ofs(ProgramName[1]);
Regs.DS := Seg(ProgramName[1]);
Regs.ES := Seg(CntlBlock);
DOSFc4B(Regs);

If (Odd(Regs.Flags)) Then
  Begin
  Ret := False;
  WriteLn(Chr(13), Chr(10), 'Error.');
  End;

CallProgram := Ret;
End;

(********************************************)

Procedure ProcessCommand(anycommand : MaxStr);
Var
  CommandComEnv : MaxStr;
  Flag : Boolean;

(********************************************)

Procedure GetEnvironment(Var s : MaxStr);
Type
  EnvArrayType = Array[0..MaxInt] Of Char;
Var
  EnvArrPtr : ^EnvArrayType;
  i : Integer;
  Temp : MaxStr;

Begin
EnvArrPtr := Ptr(DOSenvironment, $0000);
i := 0;
s := '';

While ((EnvArrPtr^[i] <> Null) AND (s = '')) Do
  Begin
  Temp := '';
  While (EnvArrPtr^[i] <> '=') Do
    Begin
    Temp := Temp+EnvArrPtr^[i];
    i := Succ(i);
    End;
  If (Temp = 'COMSPEC') Then
    Begin
    i := Succ(i);
    While (EnvArrPtr^[i] <> Null) Do
      Begin
      s := s+EnvArrPtr^[i];
      i := Succ(i);
      End;
    End
  Else
    Repeat
    i := Succ(i);
    Until (EnvArrPtr^[i-1] = Null);
  End;
End;

(********************************************)

Begin
GetEnvironment(CommandComEnv);
If (CommandComEnv = '') Then
  WriteLn('What?')
Else
  Flag := CallProgram(CommandComEnv, '/c '+AnyCommand);
End;
```

```
(**********************************************)
Begin
ClrScr;
  Repeat
  GetDir(0,dos_directory);
  Write(dos_directory+'-->');
  ReadLn(CommandLine);
  For i := 1 to length(CommandLine) Do
    CommandLine[i] := UpCase(CommandLine[i]);
  If CommandLine <> '' Then
    ProcessCommand(CommandLine);
  Until (CommandLine = 'EXIT');
End;

(**********************************************)

Begin
RunDOS;
End.
```

The DOS shell operates via the procedure **Process-Command**, which accepts a string that contains the name of the command or program you want to execute. The **GetDir** function is used to display a simulated DOS prompt. The DOS shell continues to execute until you enter the command **Exit**.

File Encryption

Protecting letters, data, and programs is a common task. The only sure protection is to encode the file itself. The programs presented here do this, and offer some extra features as well.

Encode

The **Encode** program encrypts a file based on a password you provide. To encrypt a file, type

Encode Filename Password

If you enter the name of a file that does not exist, the program will abort with the message **File not found**. The program also checks to see whether the file was already encrypted. Files encrypted with **Encode** contain the word "LOCKED" in the first 6 bytes. When **Encode** finds these letters, it aborts and displays the message **File already locked.** This protection is necessary to keep you from encrypting the same file twice.

Note also that this program overwrites the original file with binary zeros and then erases the file. This keeps out snoopers who might browse your disk with a special program for this purpose.

The password can be up to six characters in length. It generates two seed values, which control the encryption. **Encode** stores these two seed values in the encrypted file so that the file can never be decoded with an incorrect password.

```
Program Encode;
Const
  MaxBuf = 30000;
Var
  password : String[6];
  seed1,
  seed2 : Byte;
  source,
  dest : File;
  buffer : Array [1..MaxBuf] Of Byte;
  BytesRead : Real;
  i : Integer;

(************************************)

Procedure OpenFiles;
Const
  s : Array [1..6] Of Char = ('L','O','C','K','E','D');
Begin
Assign(source,ParamStr(1));
(*$I-*)
Reset(source,1);
(*$I+*)
If IOresult <> 0 Then
  Begin
  WriteLn('File not found.');
  Halt;
  End;

BlockRead(source,buffer,6);
If ((buffer[1] = ord('L')) And
    (buffer[2] = ord('O')) And
    (buffer[3] = ord('C')) And
    (buffer[4] = ord('K')) And
    (buffer[5] = ord('E')) And
    (buffer[6] = ord('D'))) Then
    Begin
    WriteLn('File already locked.');
    Halt;
    End;

Reset(source,1);
Assign(dest,'$$$$$.$$');
Rewrite(dest,1);
BlockWrite(dest,s,6);
BlockWrite(dest,seed1,1);
BlockWrite(dest,seed2,1);
End;
```

```
(*************************************)
Procedure Getseed;
Var
  i,j : Integer;
Begin
seed1 := 0;
seed2 := 0;
password := ParamStr(2);

j := Length(password);
For i := 1 To Length(password) Do
  Begin
  seed1 := seed1 + (Ord(password[i]) * i);
  seed2 := seed2 + (Ord(password[i]) * j);
  j := j - 1;
  End;
End;

(*************************************)
Procedure EncodeFile;
Var
  i1,i2 : Byte;
  rr : Integer;
Begin
i1 := seed1;
i2 := seed2;
BytesRead := 0;
BlockRead(source,buffer,MaxBuf,rr);
BytesRead := BytesRead + rr;
While rr > 0 Do
  Begin
  For i := 1 To rr Do
    Begin
    i1 := i1 - i;
    i2 := i2 + i;
    If odd(i) Then
      buffer[i] := buffer[i] - i1
    Else
      buffer[i] := buffer[i] + i2;
    End;
  BlockWrite(dest,buffer,rr);
  BlockRead(source,buffer,MaxBuf,rr);
  BytesRead := BytesRead + rr;
  End;
End;

(*************************************)
Procedure CloseFiles;
Var
  i : Integer;
Begin
Rewrite(source,1);
FillChar(buffer,MaxBuf,0);
While BytesRead > 0 do
  Begin
  If BytesRead > MaxBuf Then
    BlockWrite(source,buffer,MaxBuf)
  Else
    Begin
    i := Trunc(BytesRead);
    BlockWrite(source,buffer,i)
    End;
  BytesRead := BytesRead - MaxBuf;
  End;
Close(source);
Close(dest);
Erase(source);
```

```
Rename(dest,ParamStr(1));
End;

(**************************************)

Begin
If Paramcount <> 2 Then
  Begin
  WriteLn('Syntax: ENCODEIT Filename password');
  Halt;
  End;
Getseed;
OpenFiles;
EncodeFile;
CloseFiles;
End.
```

Decode

Decode restores files that have been encrypted with the **Encode** program. The syntax for **Decode** is

Decode Filename Password

Decode first checks to see if the file is locked; locked files have the letters "LOCKED" in the first 6 bytes. Next it uses the password to generate two seed values and compares those to the seed values stored in the encrypted file. If the seed values match, the program continues; if not, it displays the message **Wrong password** and stops.

```
Program Decode;
Const
  MaxBuf = 30000;
var
  password : String[6];
  source,
  dest    : File;
  buffer  : Array [1..MaxBuf] Of Byte;
  BytesRead : Real;
  seed1,
  seed1x,
  seed2,
  seed2x : Byte;
  i : Integer;

(**************************************)

Procedure OpenFiles;
Const
  s : Array [1..6] Of Char = ('L','O','C','K','E','D');
Begin
Assign(source,ParamStr(1));
(*$I-*)
Reset(source,1);
(*$I+*)
If IOresult <> 0 Then
```

```
     Begin
     WriteLn('File not found.');
     Halt;
     End;
BlockRead(source,buffer,6);
If Not ((buffer[1] = ord('L')) And
        (buffer[2] = ord('O')) And
        (buffer[3] = ord('C')) And
        (buffer[4] = ord('K')) And
        (buffer[5] = ord('E')) And
        (buffer[6] = ord('D'))) Then
          Begin
          WriteLn('File not locked.');
          Halt;
          End;

BlockRead(source,seed1x,1);
BlockRead(source,seed2x,1);

If ((seed1 <> seed1x) Or (seed2 <> seed2x)) Then
  Begin
  WriteLn('Wrong password.');
  Halt;
  End;

Assign(dest,'$$$$$.$$');
Rewrite(dest,1);
End;

(************************************)

Procedure Getseed;
Var
  i,j : Integer;
Begin
seed1 := 0;
seed2 := 0;
password := ParamStr(2);

j := Length(password);
For i := 1 To Length(password) Do
  Begin
  seed1 := seed1 + (ord(password[i]) * i);
  seed2 := seed2 + (ord(password[i]) * j);
  j := j - 1;
  End;
End;

(************************************)

Procedure DecodeFile;
Var
  i1,i2 : Byte;
  rr : Integer;
Begin
i1 := seed1;
i2 := seed2;
BytesRead := 0;
BlockRead(source,buffer,MaxBuf,rr);
BytesRead := BytesRead + rr;
While rr > 0 Do
  Begin
  For i := 1 To rr Do
    Begin
    i1 := i1 - i;
    i2 := i2 + i;
    If odd(i) Then
      buffer[i] := buffer[i] + i1
    Else
      buffer[i] := buffer[i] - i2;
    End;
```

```
    BlockWrite(dest,buffer,rr);
    BlockRead(source,buffer,MaxBuf,rr);
    BytesRead := BytesRead + rr;
    End;
End;

(************************************)

Procedure CloseFiles;
Var
  i : Integer;
Begin
Rewrite(source,1);
FillChar(buffer,MaxBuf,0);
While BytesRead > 0 Do
  Begin
  If BytesRead > MaxBuf Then
    BlockWrite(source,buffer,MaxBuf)
  Else
    Begin
    i := Trunc(BytesRead);
    BlockWrite(source,buffer,i)
    End;
  BytesRead := BytesRead - MaxBuf;
  End;
Close(source);
Close(dest);
Erase(source);
Rename(dest,ParamStr(1));
End;

(************************************)

Begin
If paramcount <> 2 Then
  Begin
  WriteLn('Syntax: DECODEIT Filename password');
  Halt;
  End;
Getseed;
OpenFiles;
DecodeFile;
CloseFiles;
End.
```

Optimizing
Turbo Pascal
Programs

Optimization: Perfection Versus Excellence
Approaches to Optimization
Timing Program Execution
Optimizing Control Structures
Optimizing Arithmetic
Optimizing File Operations
Optimizing String Operations
Compiler Directives
Procedures and Functions
Reference Parameters Versus Value Parameters

At the very least, a program should be free from bugs. Users expect programs to work as advertised, from start to finish, day in and day out. But the fact that a program functions properly is not always enough: users also want programs that work quickly. Optimization is the process of making sure your program runs as fast as it can without compromising the basic functions it performs. This chapter suggests methods you can use to optimize your programs, streamline your code, and eliminate unnecessary bottlenecks.

E
I
G
H
T
E
E
N

Optimization: Perfection Versus Excellence

The cost of excellence is reasonable; the cost of perfection is exorbitant. Some programmers spend hours optimizing even unimportant sections of code. Good programmers, however, learn to select the code that can benefit most from optimization, and avoid wasting time on trivial improvements.

There are two criteria to consider when selecting the parts of a program to optimize. First, can the code be improved enough to make a difference? It's quite possible, especially if you are an experienced programmer, that you wrote the section optimally the first time. In most cases, however, even well written sections can benefit from closer inspection.

Second, the improvements you make must be noticeable to the user. If the user will not notice the difference in speed, your efforts at optimization are wasted. If, however, you feel a section of code can be improved and that the improvement will be noticed by the user, start optimizing.

Approaches to Optimization

Speed is just one goal of optimization; others include minimizing code size and reducing the data space required. With RAM in plentiful supply, however, speed is by far the highest concern. Therefore, the suggestions presented in this chapter are directed to making your programs faster.

The most obvious way to speed up a program is to write sections in assembler and include them in your code as external procedures or inline code. This approach, discussed in Chapter 13, takes a lot of time and an extensive knowledge of assembler. Before going to this extreme, you can gain a lot of speed by simply using Turbo Pascal more efficiently. A well written Turbo Pascal procedure can run quite fast and is much easier to write, debug, and maintain than assembler code.

Timing Program Execution

You cannot optimize without having a way to measure just how much you gain or lose when you change a section of code. You may be surprised to find that a minor change can lead to a substantial increase in speed, while larger changes may do little to increase speed.

The guideline you need is contained in the procedures **DosClock**, **ClockOn**, and **ClockOff**, which follow.

```
Var
  StartClock : Real;

Function DosClock : Real;
Var
  regs : Record
           Case Integer Of
           1 : (AX,BX,CX,DX,BP,SI,DI,DS,ES,Flags : Integer);
           2 : (AL,AH,BL,BH,CL,CH,DL,DH : Byte);
           End;
Begin
regs.AH := $2C;
MsDos(regs);
With Regs Do
  DosClock := CH*3600.0 + CL*60.0 + DH + DL/100.0;
End;

(*************************************************************)

Procedure ClockOn;
Begin
StartClock := DosClock;
End;

(*************************************************************)

Procedure ClockOff;
Begin
WriteLn('Elapsed Time: ',DosClock - StartClock:0:2,' seconds.');
End;
```

DosClock uses DOS service **2Ch**, which reports the current time according to the system clock. By multiplying each of the time elements by a factor and summing the results, **DosClock** returns the current system time as a single floating-point number.

The procedures **ClockOn** and **ClockOff** both call **DosClock**; **ClockOn** sets the real variable **StartClock** to the current time and **ClockOff** reports the elapsed time by subtracting **StartClock** from the current time. The program named **TestLoop** demonstrates how to use these procedures, which are stored in the file CLOCK.INC.

```
Program TestLoop;
Var
  i,j : integer;

(*$I CLOCK.INC*)

Begin
j := 0;

ClockOn;  (* Initialize value of StartClock. *)

For i := 1 To MaxInt Do
  Begin
  j := j + 1;
  End;

ClockOff; (* Display elapsed time. *)

End.
```

TestLoop times the execution of a simple For-Do loop by preceding it with a call to **ClockOn** and following it with a call to **ClockOff**. When you run this program, you will see the following message:

Elapsed Time: 0.66 seconds.

This message indicates that the For-Do loop took 0.66 second to execute. Both the brief execution time and the simplicity of the procedure make this For-Do loop a poor candidate for optimization.

All timings reported in this chapter are based on a PC-compatible computer running at 4.77 Mhz. Your timings may differ, depending on the computer you use. The specific time you get, however, is unimportant. The value of the timing procedures is to evaluate the relative speed of different procedures that produce the same result. The program listed here, called **TestProcs**, demonstrates how the speed of two similar routines can be compared.

```
Program TestProcs;
Const
  ArrLen = MaxInt;
Type
  ArrType = Array [1..ArrLen] Of Char;
```

```
Var
  a : ArrType;
  i : Integer;

(*$I CLOCK.INC*)

(*******************************)

Procedure Init1(Var a : ArrType;
                    L : Integer);
Begin
FillChar(a,L,0);
End;

(*******************************)

Procedure Init2(Var a : ArrType;
                    L : Integer);

Var
  i : Integer;
Begin
For i := 1 To L Do
  a[i] := 0;
End;

(*******************************)

Begin

ClockOn;
Init1(a,ArrLen);
ClockOff;


ClockOn;
Init2(a,ArrLen);
ClockOff;

End.
```

TestProcs uses two procedures, **Init1** and **Init2**, both of which initialize an array of characters to all binary zeros. **Init1** uses the Turbo Pascal standard procedure **FillChar** to initialize the array while **Init2** accomplishes the same goal with a For-Do loop.

The results of this program show that **Init1** takes 0.11 second to execute while **Init2** requires 1.37 seconds. It is easy to see which is the better routine.

Optimizing Control Structures

When you optimize a program, control structures should be one of the first things you check. Because Turbo Pascal offers so many flexible control structures, it is easy to write control structures your first time through that are less than optimal.

Nested If-Then Statements

If-Then statements execute Boolean comparison statements, which can include numerous individual comparisons. When you optimize **If-Then** statements, the goal is to minimize the number of comparisons the computer executes. The code section listed here demonstrates a very poor use of **If-Then** statements:

```
If i = 1 Then    (* Comparison number 1 *)
   Begin
   End;
If i = 2 Then    (* Comparison number 2 *)
   Begin
   End;
If i = 3 Then    (* Comparison number 3 *)
   Begin
   End;
If i = 4 Then    (* Comparison number 4 *)
   Begin
   End;
```

This routine executes one of four branches, depending on the value of variable **i**. Notice that all four comparisons are executed each time the code section is processed. This can be made far more efficient with the following code:

```
If i = 1 Then
   Begin
   End
Else If i = 2 Then
   Begin
```

```
   End
Else If i = 3 Then
   Begin
   End
Else
   Begin
   End;
```

Here, the **Else-If** statement reduces the number of comparisons required. For example, if **i** equals 1, only one comparison is executed. At the other extreme, when **i** equals 4, only three comparisons are required.

While this is clearly efficient, the **Case** control structure is even more efficient. This code section shows how the **Case** command would replace the **If-Then-Else** statements:

```
Case i Of

1 :
   Begin
   End;

2 :
   Begin
   End;

3 :
   Begin
   End;

Else
   Begin
   End;
End;
```

These three procedures were compared in a program that repeated each procedure 30,000 times. The first procedure required 3.13 seconds, the second, using the **Else-If** statement, took 2.53 seconds, and the procedure with the **Case** statement used 2.31 seconds. It appears that a well constructed **If-Then-Else** statement is almost as efficient as a **Case** statement.

Optimizing Loops

Loop control structures also provide opportunities for optimization. Turbo Pascal provides three looping structures: For-Do loops, Repeat-Until loops, and While-Do loops. Of these, the For-Do loop is the fastest, as demonstrated by this program:

```
Program TestIfThen;
Var
  i,j,k : Integer;
  x,y,z : Real;

(*$I CLOCK.INC*)

Begin

(* Test speed of For-Do loop. *)

ClockOn;
For i := 1 To MaxInt Do
  Begin
  End;
ClockOff;



(* Test speed of Repeat-Until loop. *)

ClockOn;
i := 0;
  Repeat
  i := i + 1;
  Until i = MaxInt;
ClockOff;



(* Test speed of While-Do loop. *)

ClockOn;
i := 0;
While i < MaxInt Do
  Begin
  i := i + 1;
  End;
ClockOff;

End.
```

The For-Do loop required 0.71 second to execute, while the Repeat-Until and While-Do loops both needed about 0.90 second. Of course, as you add statements to the body of these control structures, the difference in speed becomes less important. Nevertheless, you should use the For-Do loop where you need the fastest looping structure.

Checking for Characters

If-Then statements, Repeat-Until loops, and While-Do loops all require Boolean expressions. Boolean expressions that test an element to see if it belongs to a set are notably inefficient. For example, the following **Set Inclusion** statement tests if a character variable **Ch** contains a letter in the set ['A','B','C']:

```
If Ch In ['A','B','C'] Then ...
```

The program called **TestChar** demonstrates the difference in speed between a **Set Inclusion** statement and two similar forms of **If-Then** statements.

```
Program TestChar;
Var
  i : Integer;
  Ch : Char;

(*$I CLOCK.INC*)

Begin
Ch := 'A';



(* Set Inclusion Statement. *)

ClockOn;
For i := 1 to MaxInt Do
  Begin
  If ch in ['A','B','C'] Then
    Begin
    End;
  End;
ClockOff;
```

```
(* If-Then Statement *)

ClockOn;
For i := 1 to MaxInt Do
  Begin
  If (ch = 'A') or (ch = 'B') or (ch = 'C') Then
    Begin
    End;
  End;
ClockOff;
```

```
(* Nested If-Then statement *)

ClockOn;
For i := 1 to MaxInt Do
  Begin
  If (ch = 'A') then
    Begin
    End
  Else If (ch = 'B') then
    Begin
    End
  Else If (ch = 'C') then
    Begin
    End;
  End;
ClockOff;

End.
```

When the character in question is "A," the loop using the set-inclusion comparison requires 11.53 seconds to execute, while the **If-Then** statement requires only 2.91 seconds, and the nested **If-Then** statement requires only 1.26 seconds. (See Table 18-1.) Even when the character is the last one tested (in this case the letter "C"), the nested **If-Then** statement still comes out on top, and the set-inclusion method takes far longer.

The set-inclusion test is slow because it tests every element in the set against the test value. Even when the first element in the set matches the test value, Turbo Pascal still tests every other element in the set. While sets are convenient when writing a program, they are detrimental to a program's speed.

Method	Test For Letter A	Test For Letter C
Set Inclusion	11.53	11.53
If-Then	2.91	2.86
Nested If-Then	1.26	2.14

Table 18-1.   Loop Execution Timing in Seconds

Optimizing Arithmetic

The speed of your calculations depends largely on the type of variables involved (**integer** or **real**) and the type of operation involved (addition, subtraction, multiplication, or division). Integer computations always require much less time than computations with **real** variables. The following program, **MathComp**, compares the speed of integer and real computations for addition operations. You can change the program to test other operations.

```
Program MathComp;
Var
   i,
   a, b, c : Integer;
   x, y, z : Real;

(*$I CLOCK.INC*)

Begin
a := 1;
b := 1;
ClockOn;
For i := 1 To 10000 Do
   Begin
   c := a + b; { Also -, *, Div }
   End;
ClockOff;
```

```
x := 1.0;
y := 1.0;
ClockOn;
For i := 1 To 10000 Do
  Begin
  z := x + y; { Also -, *, / }
  End;
ClockOff;
End.
```

Table 18-2 shows the execution times for **integers** and **reals** for the four arithmetic operators. As you can see, **integer** computations are almost ten times faster than **real** computations across the board.

Division involving **real** variables is the slowest of all the computations, requiring over twice as much time as multiplication operations and four times as much as addition or subtraction.

In general, avoid using **reals** when **integers** will do. If you must use **reals**, avoid division when possible. For example, the equation

$$X / 4.0$$

can be changed to

$$X * 0.25$$

which is far faster.

	Integer	Real
Addition	0.39	3.63
Subtraction	0.39	4.83
Multiplication	0.61	6.21
Division	0.71	16.75

Table 18-2.   Seconds Required for Computations

Some programs that use a lot of calculations contain many complicated formulas. In such programs, optimization should be second to readability. If, in the process of optimization, you make a subtle change to a complicated formula, you may never find your error.

Optimizing File Operations

Even when you use a hard disk, disk file input and output are slow operations. This is especially true for Turbo Pascal text files. You can speed up your text file operations by specifying a buffer in your declaration, as shown here:

```
Var
  T : Text[500];
```

This declares **T** as a text file with a 500-byte buffer. If you do not specify a buffer size, Turbo Pascal assigns a default buffer of 128 bytes.

Generally speaking, the larger the buffer, the faster your input and output operations will be. This is not strictly the case with Turbo Pascal text files. Table 18-3 shows the time

	Medium	
	Floppy	Hard
Buffer Size	**Disk**	**Disk**
Standard (128 bytes)	17.35	5.71
512 bytes	17.19	4.78
1023 bytes	17.57	5.44
1024 bytes	9.89	4.18
4096 bytes	5.44	3.46

Table 18-3.   Disk-Write Times for a 72,000-Byte Text File

required to write a 72,000-byte text file to both a floppy and a hard disk.

Naturally, output to the floppy is slower than to the hard disk. The floppy, however, benefits more from a buffer. With a 4096-byte buffer, for example, the floppy disk is nearly as fast as the hard disk (5.44 seconds versus 3.46 seconds).

Notice the difference in time between the 1023-byte buffer and the 1024-byte buffer. Adding one byte causes a significant increase in speed. Why? Disks are organized into 512-byte sectors that are organized into clusters of 1024 bytes for floppy disks and from 2048 to 8192 bytes for hard disks. When a buffer's size is set equal to the size of a cluster, the disk drive does less work with each read and write. In general, the best buffer size is 1024 bytes.

Optimizing String Operations

The **string** data type is an important part of Turbo Pascal, largely due to the standard procedures provided for string manipulation. However, string procedures, especially concatenation, can be quite slow.

The program called **TestProcs1** uses two procedures, each of which creates a string that contains 100 characters, all of which are capital "A's."

```
Program TestProcs1;
Type
  MaxStr = String[255];
Var
  i : Integer;

(*$I CLOCK.INC*)

(*********************************)

Procedure a1;
Var
  i : Integer;
  s : MaxStr;
```

```
Begin
s := '';
For i := 1 To 100 Do
  s := s + 'A';
End;

(******************************)

Procedure a2;
Var
  i : Integer;
  s : MaxStr;
Begin
For i := 1 To 100 Do
  s[i] := 'A';
s[0] := Chr(100);
End;

(******************************)

Begin

ClockOn;
For i := 1 To 100 Do a1;
ClockOff;

ClockOn;
For i := 1 To 100 Do a2;
ClockOff;
End.
```

Procedure **a1**, which uses the Turbo Pascal concatenation operator, requires 5.65 seconds, while procedure **a2**, which uses an index to the string's characters, needs only 0.28 second.

The **Copy** command can also be replaced to increase speed, as demonstrated by the **CopyString** program:

```
Program CopyString;
Type
  MaxStr = String[255];
Var
  p,i,j : Integer;
  S1,S2 : MaxStr;

(*$I CLOCK.INC*)

Begin
```

```
S1 := 'ABCDEFGHIJKLMNOP';

ClockOn;
For i := 1 to 1000 do
   S2 := Copy(S1,3,5);
ClockOff;


ClockOn;
For i := 1 to 1000 do
  Begin
  Move(s1[3],s2[1],5);
  s2[0] := Chr(5);
  End;
ClockOff;

End.
```

In **CopyString**, the command

S2 := Copy(S1,3,5);

is replaced by the statements

Move(s1[3],s2[1],5);
s2[0] := Chr(5);

The **Move** command copies a portion of **s1** into **s2**, while the second statement correctly sets the length of **s2**. The **Copy** command requires 0.38 second for 1000 iterations, compared with only 0.16 second for the optimized code.

Compiler Directives

Compiler directives control error checking features in Turbo Pascal. The three directives that have an impact on execution speed are the **U** directive, which allows user interrupt, the **R** directive, which checks the range of indexes, and the **K** directive, which checks the stack and heap for collisions.

When these directives are turned on, they actively monitor a program's operation to detect certain errors that occur. This constant monitoring takes time and slows the program down, as demonstrated by **TestProcs2**.

```
Program TestProcs2;
var
  i,j : Integer;
  a : array [1..10000] of char;

(*$I CLOCK.INC*)

(**********************************)

procedure x;
begin
a[i] := 0;
end;

(**********************************)

Begin
ClockOn;
for i := 1 to 10000 do x;
ClockOff;
End.
```

The **U** directive is the most destructive to a program's speed since it constantly checks the keyboard in case the user presses CTRL-C. The **R** command adds time only when an index is used in an array or a string. If your program uses indexes heavily, enabling this directive creates significant delays. The **K** directive checks the stack whenever a procedure is called or a dynamic variable is created. Since most procedures use procedures frequently, enabling the **K** directive should create a noticeable slowdown.

Table 18-4 reveals the impact of different compiler directives on the execution time of **TestProcs2**. Clearly, the **U** directive slows the program down the most. Still, the **K** and **R** directives nearly double the execution time over what it is with all the directives disabled.

You should enable compiler options only during program

Reference Parameters
Versus Value Parameters

When Turbo Pascal passes a reference parameter to a procedure, it passes the variable's address, not the value of the variable. Value parameters, on the other hand, pass the entire contents of the variable. If the value parameter is a 4000-byte array, 4000 bytes are passed to the procedure, compared with only four bytes when Turbo Pascal passes an address.

Because of this discrepancy, passing parameters by reference is more efficient than passing parameters by value. As the program **TestParams1** demonstrates, it takes longer to pass value parameters:

```
Program TestParams1;
type
  atype = Array [1..10000] Of Char;

Var
  a : atype;
  i,j : Integer;

(*$I CLOCK.INC*)

(*******************************)

Procedure a1(Var a : atype);
Begin
End;

(*******************************)

Procedure a2(a : atype);
Begin
End;

(*******************************)

Begin

ClockOn;
For i := 1 To 500 Do
  a1(a);
ClockOff;
```

```
ClockOn;
For i := 1 To 500 Do
  a2(a);
ClockOff;

End.
```

TestParams1 uses two procedures, **a1** and **a2**. Procedure **a1** accepts a reference parameter and **a2** accepts a value parameter. In both procedures, the parameter is an array of 10,000 characters. When you run this program, you will find that procedure **a1** requires only 0.05 second for 500 iterations, while **a2** requires 9.56 seconds to complete the same number of iterations.

From this evidence, you would think that reference parameters lead to the fastest code. But this is not necessarily true, as **TestParams2** demonstrates.

```
Program TestParams2;
Type
  atype = Array [1..10000] Of Char;

Var
  a : atype;
  i,j : Integer;

(*$I CLOCK.INC*)

(********************************)

Procedure a1(Var a : atype);
Var
  i : Integer;
Begin
For i := 1 To 10000 Do
  a[i] := 'a';
End;

(********************************)

Procedure a2(a : atype);
Var
  i : Integer;
Begin
For i := 1 To 10000 Do
  a[i] := 'a';
End;
```

Compiler Directive Enabled	Execution Time (in seconds)
U	12.63
R	0.72
K	0.72
None	0.44

Table 18-4.   Execution Times with Various Compiler Directives

development and debugging. When the program is final, and there is no chance for a serious error to occur, disable all the directives.

Procedures and Functions

Pascal allows the programmer to break a program down into procedures and functions, providing a more orderly framework for the program. Unfortunately, every time a procedure is called, Turbo Pascal must perform housekeeping tasks to keep track of memory. You can easily increase the speed of a program by replacing a call to a procedure with the actual procedure code. The impact of declaring a separate procedure is demonstrated by **TestProcs3**:

```
Program TestProcs3;
Var
  i,j : Integer;

(*$I CLOCK.INC*)
```

```
(********************************)

Procedure a;
Begin
j := 0;
j := 0;
j := 0;
j := 0;
End;

(********************************)

Begin
ClockOn;
For i := 1 To MaxInt Do
   a;
ClockOff;

ClockOn;
For i := 1 To MaxInt Do
  Begin
  j := 0;
  j := 0;
  j := 0;
  j := 0;
  End;
ClockOff;
End.
```

Procedure **a** in **TestProcs3** sets the integer variable **j** equal to zero four times. The same process is also repeated in the main program block. When you run the program, the procedure requires 2.52 seconds for 32,767 (**MaxInt**) iterations compared with only 0.93 second for the code in the program block.

Clearly, calling a procedure adds to a program's overhead. However, putting the code directly in the program has several disadvantages. First, if the procedure is called several times in the program, you must duplicate its code each time, adding to your program's code size. Second, when you want to change the procedure, you have to change it in each place it occurs. You must weigh these disadvantages against the speed you gain by removing the procedure call.

```
(******************************)

Begin

ClockOn;
For i := 1 To 50 Do
  a1(a);
ClockOff;

ClockOn;
For i := 1 To 50 Do
  a2(a);
ClockOff;

End.
```

Fifty iterations of procedure **a1**, which accepts the array as a reference parameter, take 13.73 seconds. For procedure **a2**, which accepts the array as a value parameter, the time is only 11.64 seconds. Now it appears that passing the variable by value is more efficient.

It is, in fact, true that Turbo Pascal passes reference parameters more quickly than value parameters. Once inside the procedure, however, Turbo Pascal processes value parameters faster than reference parameters. In short, you cannot make any easy assumptions about which type of parameter is better. Instead, you must test both types and find out which is better in each situation.

NINETEEN

Turbo Pascal Database Toolbox

The Turbo Pascal Database Toolbox, the first of the Borland Toolboxes for Turbo Pascal, consists of two major parts: the database procedures and the sort procedures. With the database procedures, you can maintain and process large databases with remarkable speed. The sort routine lets you order a file with a highly efficient sorting algorithm.

Toolbox Database Procedures

Database management is one of the most popular microcomputer applications. Some of the first programs available for micros were database managers and even today they tend to be among the top sellers.

The main advantage of a database is its ability to use an index to speed up searches. Nondatabase files must be searched sequentially: each record is read one-by-one until the right one is found. As a file grows in size, sequential searches take too much time. Indexed searches, on the other hand, are far faster than sequential searches. In a file with thousands of records, an indexed search can locate the record you want in seconds.

An index contains entries that consist of a *key* and a record number. A key is a string that identifies a specific record. For example, a social security number can be used as a key to a database of personnel records. In the index, each social security number is matched to a record number. When you search the index for a social security number, the procedure returns the record number associated with that number. You then use the record number to retrieve the correct record from the database.

The indexed search process is illustrated in Figure 19-1, which shows an index file and a database file. The index file contains social security numbers matched with record numbers. The database contains personnel records that include the social security number. To retrieve the record for the individual with social security number 432-34-9987, first search the index. The index search finds the matching social security number and returns the record number, which is 2. Then retrieve record number 2 from the database file and process the information.

The B+tree Structure

It takes less time to search an index than to search a database because the index is organized into a special structure known as a *B+tree*. The B+tree structure makes it possible

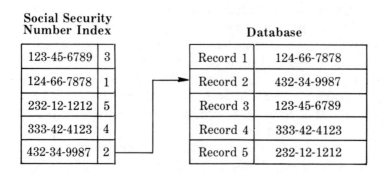

Figure 19-1.   Index and database files

to find one key among thousands in only a few steps.

The basic building block of a B+tree index is a page. Each page contains many keys and record numbers. A B+tree index connects pages to each other in a pyramid-like structure that starts with a root page and grows larger with each successive level, as shown in Figure 19-2.

An index search starts at the root page of the B+tree and moves down into the lower levels as the search continues, stopping only when it finds a matching key. Because of the way the keys are ordered, only a small portion of the tree needs to be searched to find a match.

It is difficult to write routines that implement the B+tree concept. The routines must keep track of the amount of RAM available, rearrange the order of the keys as new keys are added, and report errors when they occur. The Database Toolbox does the programming for you, allowing you to concentrate on your application.

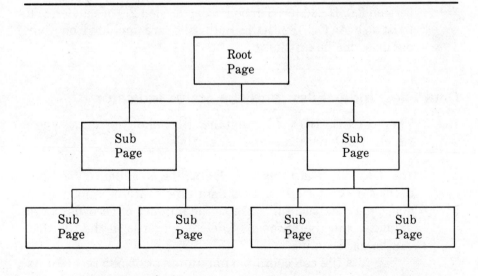

Figure 19-2.   B+tree structure

Turbo Pascal Database Toolbox Files

The Turbo Pascal Database Toolbox routines are contained in the following files on your distribution diskette:

ACCESS.BOX   Database declarations and routines that create database and index files

ADDKEY.BOX   Routines that add keys to an index

GETKEY.BOX   Routines that find a key in an index

DELKEY.BOX   Routines that delete keys from an index

To use the Database Toolbox routines, include these files in your program with the following statements:

```
(*$I ACCESS.BOX*)
(*$I ADDKEY.BOX*)
(*$I GETKEY.BOX*)
(*$I DELKEY.BOX*)
```

The routines in ACCESS.BOX work with Turbo Pascal version 3.0. If you use Turbo Pascal version 2.0 or earlier, you must use ACCESS2.BOX. Both files are included on your database toolbox diskette.

Data Files, Index Files, and the Status Indicator

The ACCESS.BOX file contains the following data types, which create database and index files.

The DataFile Data Type   DataFile is a data type that defines a database file. This data type contains information about the database file, such as the number of records in the database and the number of deleted records in the file that can be used again.

A data file can contain a maximum of 65,535 records. As you add records to a database, the size of the disk file increases. While you can delete records in a database, doing so does not decrease the size of the file. Rather, the space allocated to deleted records is reused when new records are added to the database.

The IndexFile Data Type   **IndexFile** is a data type that declares indexes for databases. An index contains up to 65,535 keys, or one for each record in a database. While the Database Toolbox provides the routines that manage the index, you are responsible for correctly using these routines. This means you must add a key to the index whenever you add a record to the database, delete a key when a record is removed from a database, change a key when you update a record and, in the process, alter the value of the key.

Duplicate Keys

You can specify whether to allow duplicate keys in an index or not. An index of names, for example, should allow duplicate keys since two people can have the same name. In other cases, such as auto part numbers, duplicate keys should not be allowed since no two auto parts can have the same part number.

The OK Status Indicator

The Database Toolbox declares a global Boolean variable called **OK**, which reports errors in Toolbox operations. For example, if you attempt to find a key in an index and the key is not found, the Toolbox sets **OK** to False. You should check the value of **OK** after most Toolbox operations to make sure your program handles error conditions properly.

Database Constant Declarations

Before you include the Database Toolbox files in your program, declare the following constants that control the amount of memory and disk space your files will require.

MaxDataRecSize   Determines the size of the buffer that holds database records. The buffer can be as small as 8 bytes and as large as 65,535 bytes. You can set **MaxDataRecSize** to a value larger than the record size you use, but at no time can the size of your record exceed **MaxDataRecSize**. If your database uses two records, one containing 50 bytes and the other containing 100 bytes, **MaxDataRecSize** must be at least 100 to accommodate the larger record.

MaxHeight   A constant that determines the maximum height of the B+tree. A B+tree consists of layers of pages. The first layer is the root page, the second layer is pages directly connected to the root page, and so forth. An index with large pages requires fewer levels than an index with small pages. Similarly, an index with only a small number of keys requires fewer levels than an index with a large number of keys.

You can calculate the correct value of **MaxHeight** for your database by using the following program:

```
Program CalcMaxHeight;
Var
   PageSize,
   MaxKeys : real;

Begin
Write('Enter maximum number of keys: ');
ReadLn(MaxKeys);
Write('Enter pagesize: ');
ReadLn(pagesize);
WriteLn('MaxHeight = ',Ln(MaxKeys)/Ln(PageSize*0.5):0:0);
End.
```

As you can see from the CalcMaxHeight program, **MaxHeight** increases as **MaxKeys** increases, and decreases as **PageSize** increases. Table 19-1 shows how the number of keys and page size affect the value of **MaxHeight**. With a page size of 40 and 1000 keys, **MaxHeight** is 2, but if the number of keys is increased to 60,000, **MaxHeight** increases to only 4. Even with a small page size of 10 and 60,000 keys, the index requires **MaxHeight** to be only 7.

Larger page sizes require fewer levels in the B+tree, which can speed up your searches. Of course, large pages also use more memory, but the trade-off in speed is usually

Number of Keys	Page Size	Max Height
1000	40	2
10,000	40	3
60,000	40	4
1000	10	4
10,000	10	6
60,000	10	7

Table 19-1.   PageSize, MaxHeight, and Number of Keys in an Index

worth it. If you use a page size of 30 or more, a **MaxHeight** value of 5 should be sufficient.

MaxKeyLen   The keys in the index are strings and so they can be up to 255 characters long. **MaxKeyLen** specifies the largest key allowed in your index files. If one index uses keys 6 characters long and another uses 10-character keys, **MaxKeyLen** must be set to at least 10. The larger the value of **MaxKeyLen**, the more memory your index will require.

Order   A constant that must be one-half the page size. The page size must, therefore, be an even number. The Database Toolbox uses **Order** to decide when a new branch needs to be added to the B+tree.

PageSize   Determines the number of keys per page in the index. The value of **PageSize** affects both the efficiency of the index and the amount of memory it will require. A large page size packs more keys into each page, thus increasing the likelihood that you will find a match on the page being searched. But as the page size grows, so does the amount of memory needed to store the index. The minimum page size is 4 and the maximum is 254, but normally page size ranges from 30 to 50.

PageStackSize   When Turbo Pascal needs to search an index page, it reads the page in from disk and stores it in RAM. The Database Toolbox also notes the pages it reads so that your program does not reread pages that are already in RAM. Once RAM is full, however, newly read pages must replace pages already stored in RAM, thereby slowing the index searches.

   PageStackSize controls how much RAM is devoted to storing index pages. If **PageStackSize** equals 3, then three pages can be held in RAM at one time. A larger **Page-StackSize** value allows more pages to be stored in RAM, which increases the speed of index searches. But, if the **PageStackSize** value is too big, your program may not have enough memory to run. Borland suggests you set **Page-StackSize** to any value from 16 to 32.

Sample Declarations

The program called SampleDecs demonstrates how to declare Database Toolbox constants in your program.

```
Program SampleDecs;

Const
  MaxDataRecSize = 100; (* Maximum record length. *)
  MaxKeyLen = 10;       (* Maximum key length. *)
  PageSize = 30;        (* Maximum number of keys on a page. *)
  Order = 15;           (* One-half of PageSize. *)
  PageStackSize = 5;    (* Number of pages stored in RAM. *)
  MaxHeight = 5;        (* Maximum height of B+tree. *)

(*$I ACCESS.BOX*)
(*$I ADDKEY.BOX*)
(*$I GETKEY.BOX*)
(*$I DELKEY.BOX*)
```

```
Var
  DatF : DataFile;      (* Database file - holds records. *)
  IdxF : IndexFile;     (* Index file - holds keys and record numbers. *)
  DatRef : Integer;     (* Integer used for record numbers. *)
```

These declarations work for most database applications, though you might want to change them slightly to fit your needs.

Database Command Summary

This section, which reviews the Database Toolbox commands, is a quick reference guide, not a tutorial. For more detailed information on the Database Toolbox, please refer to the *Turbo Pascal Database Toolbox Owner's Handbook*.

AddKey

Syntax   Procedure AddKey (IdxF : IndexFile;

DatRef : Integer;

Key);

Usage   **AddKey** adds **Key** and its associated data record number **DatRef** to index file **IdxF**. **AddKey** usually follows **AddRec**, which adds a record to a database and returns a record number, **DatRef**.

When the key is successfully added to the index, **AddKey** sets **OK** to True. If you attempt to add a duplicate key to an index that does not allow them, **AddKey** sets **OK** to False. If the key is longer than the maximum length specified when the index was created or opened, the Database Toolbox truncates the key to the correct length.

Because the parameter **Key** is untyped, you can pass any

data type through the variable without causing a Turbo Pascal error. The index, however, will work only with strings. It is your responsibility to make sure that only strings are used as keys.

AddRec

Syntax   Procedure AddRec(DatF : DataFile; DatRef : Integer; Buffer);

Usage   **AddRec** adds a record that is contained in **Buffer** to database file **DatF** and returns **DatRef**, the record number. **Buffer**, an untyped variable, can be any type of data record. If any records have been deleted from the database, **AddRec** will reuse them before expanding the file.

It is not necessary to check the status of **OK** after a call to **AddRec**. The only errors that **AddRec** can cause are I/O errors such as no more room on your disk. When **AddRec** causes an I/O error, the procedure **TaIOCheck** takes over, displays an error message, and terminates the program.

ClearKey

Syntax   Procedure ClearKey(IdxF : IndexFile);

Usage   Returns the index file pointer for **IdxF** to the first entry in the index. Use this when you want to process an index sequentially from the beginning with the **NextKey** or **PrevKey** commands. If you call **PrevKey** directly after **ClearKey**, the index file pointer will point to the last key in the index.

CloseFile

Syntax   Procedure CloseFile(DatF : DataFile);

Usage   **CloseFile** closes an open data file. All data files that are opened should be closed before the program ends.

CloseIndex

Syntax   Procedure CloseIndex(IdxF : IndexFile);

Usage   **CloseIndex** closes an open index file. All index files should be closed before a program ends.

DeleteKey

Syntax   Procedure DeleteKey (IdxF : IndexFile;
                        DatRef : Integer;
                        Key);

Usage   **DeleteKey** purges a key and its related record number from an index file. If the index file does not allow duplicate keys, **DeleteKey** locates an index file entry by searching for a match for **Key**. If duplicates are allowed, **DeleteKey** attempts to match both **Key** and **DatRef**.

DeleteRec

Syntax   Procedure DeleteRec(DatF : DataFile; DatRef : Integer;Buffer);

Usage   **DeleteRec** destroys the contents of the record and adds the record number to the list of deleted records, which the Database Toolbox maintains. Afterwards, when new records are added to the data file, the space taken up by the deleted records is reused by new records.

FileLen

Syntax   Function FileLen(DatF : DataFile);

Usage   **FileLen** returns a data file's size in terms of the number of records it contains. In its computations, **FileLen** includes active records, deleted records, and the record reserved by the Database Toolbox (record 0).

FindKey

Syntax   Procedure FindKey(IdxF : IndexFile;
                       DatRef : Integer;
                       Key);

Usage   **FindKey** searches and returns an index for a match to **Key**. If a match is found, **FindKey** returns the record number (**DatRef**) associated with the key and sets **OK** to True. If a match is not found, **OK** is set to False and the values of **Key** and **DatRef** remain unchanged.

GetRec

Syntax   Procedure GetRec(DatF : DataFile;
                       DatRef : Integer; Buffer);

Usage   **GetRec** retrieves a record number (**DatRef**) from data file **DatF** and places the contents in **Buffer**. **GetRec** does not affect the variable **OK**; any errors that occur are handled by **TaIOCheck** and result in termination of the program.

InitIndex

Syntax   Procedure InitIndex;

Usage   **InitIndex** initializes the Database Toolbox's internal index tables. This command must be executed before any other index command. In addition, if you call **InitIndex** while index files are open, these files may become corrupted.

MakeFile

Syntax   Procedure MakeFile(DatF : DataFile;
                           FileName : String[14];
                           RecLen : Integer);

Usage   **MakeFile** creates a new data file **DatF** with the name **FileName**. The data file stores records of length **RecLen**. **MakeFile** sets **OK** to True if the file is successfully created and to False if an error occurred (for example, when a read-only file with the same name already exists).

MakeIndex

Syntax   Procedure MakeIndex (IdxF : IndexFile;
                           FileName : String[14];
                           KeyLen, Status : Integer);

Usage   **MakeIndex** creates index file **IdxF** with the name **FileName**. **KeyLen** defines the maximum key length allowed in the index; and **Status** determines whether or not duplicate keys are allowed. If **Status** equals 0, duplicate keys are not allowed in the index; if it equals 1, duplicates are allowed.

If the index file is successfully created, **OK** is set to True.

NextKey

Syntax   Procedure NextKey (IdxF : IndexFile;
                                   DatRef : Integer;
                                   Key);

Usage   **NextKey** advances the index file pointer to the next entry in the index and returns that entry's key and the record number. **NextKey** sets **OK** to True unless the file pointer is positioned at the last key in the index. When this occurs, **OK** is set to False and the file pointer remains positioned at the last key in the index. If **NextKey** is called again, the index file pointer points to the first key in the index.

OpenFile

Syntax   Procedure OpenFile(DatF : DataFile;
                                   FileName : String[14];
                                   RecLen : Integer);

Usage   **OpenFile** opens an existing data file. The value of **RecLen** must be the same as the value used when the file was created. If the file is successfully opened, **OK** is set to True.

OpenIndex

Syntax   Procedure OpenIndex (IdxF : IndexFile;
                                    FileName : String[14];
                                    KeyLen, Status : Integer);

Usage   **OpenIndex** opens an existing index file. **KeyLen** and **Status** must be the same values used when the index file was created. If the file is successfully opened, **OK** is set to True.

PrevKey

Syntax   Procedure PrevKey (IdxF : IndexFile;
                                  DatRef : Integer;
                                  Key);

Usage   **PrevKey** moves the index file pointer to the previous entry in an index file and returns that entry's key and record number. If you use the **ClearKey** command, a call to **PrevKey** positions the index file pointer at the last key in the index.

      PrevKey sets **OK** to True until it reaches the first record in the index, in which case **OK** is set to False and the key and record number remain unchanged. An additional call to **PrevKey** moves the file pointer to the last entry in the index.

PutRec

Syntax   Procedure PutRec(DatF : DataFile;
                                    DatRef : Integer; Buffer);

Usage   **PutRec** replaces an existing record in a data file
with the contents of **Buffer**. **DatRef** must be greater than 1
and less than **FileLen(DatF)**.

SearchKey

Syntax   Procedure SearchKey (IdxF : IndexFile;
                                    DatRef : Integer;
                                    Key);

Usage   **SearchKey** locates the first key in an index that is
equal to or greater than **Key**. When **SearchKey** finds such
an index entry, it returns the key and record number of that
entry and sets **OK** to True. For example, if an index contains
the three names Berman, McDonald, and Smith, and **Key**
equals Brown, **SearchKey** returns McDonald.

   If none of the keys in the index is equal to or greater
than **Key**, **OK** is set to False, and the values of **DatRef** and
Key remain unchanged.

UsedRecs

Syntax   Function UsedRecs(DatF : DataFile);

Usage   **UsedRecs** computes the number of active records
in your data file. Deleted records and the reserved record
used by the Database Toolbox are not included in this count.

Database Toolbox Sample Programs

Your Database Toolbox distribution diskette contains sample programs that demonstrate all the aspects of database programming. You will find the source code for these programs in the files TBDEMO.PAS, BTREE.PAS, and BTREE.INC.

Database Toolbox Sort Routines

A useful sorting procedure must be fast, able to sort files larger than can be held in RAM, and easy to implement in a variety of situations. The Database Toolbox procedures contained in the file SORT.BOX provide all three qualities, simplifying even the most complicated sorting task.

General Concepts

The TurboSort routine is a "black box" into which you read unsorted records and out of which come sorted records. The process consists of three steps:

1. Release records to the sort routine.

2. Compare and rearrange records.

3. Return records from the sort routine.

While the Database Toolbox does all the hard work, you must write three simple procedures —**Inp**, **Less**, and **Outp**— on your own.

The Input Procedure

Inp, the TurboSort input procedure, releases data items to the TurboSort routine with the **SortRelease** command. The data items can be of any type from a character or integer to a complicated record structure. A typical **Inp** procedure is shown here:

```
Procedure Inp;
Begin
While Not Eof(InFile) Do
  Begin
  ReadLn(InFile,DataRec);
  SortRelease(DataRec);
  End;
End;
```

In the preceding procedure, records are read from a data file and released to the TurboSort. When **Inp** finishes, TurboSort advances to the sorting process, which uses a function named Less.

The Less Function

The function Less defines the method by which TurboSort orders data items. At its simplest, Less might look like this:

```
Function Less;
Var
   Rec1 : DataRecType Absolute X;
   Rec2 : DataRecType Absolute Y;
Begin
Less := Rec1 < Rec2;
End;
```

Less declares two records of the type you are sorting (**DataRecType**). The first, Rec1, is declared absolute at **X**, and the second, Rec2, is declared absolute at **Y**. In the body of the function, Rec1 and Rec2 are compared and the value of Less is set accordingly.

TurboSort continues to call **Inp** until all the data items are correctly sorted, at which point it calls the **OutP** procedure.

The Output Procedure

Outp, the sort output procedure, uses the **SortReturn** command to retrieve data items in their sorted order. **SortEOS**, a Boolean indicator that is True when the last data item has been returned, is used to control loops. A typical **Outp** procedure looks like this:

```
Procedure OutP;
Begin
  Repeat
   SortReturn(DataRec);
   WriteLn(OutFile,DataRec);
   Until SortEOS;
End;
```

The sorted records are retrieved and written to a new file, OUTFILE. When the procedure is done, the output file will contain the same information as the input file, but in sorted order.

Calling the TurboSort Routine

Once you define **Inp**, **Less**, and **Outp**, your program invokes the sort routine with a call to the integer function TurboSort, which takes an integer parameter that indicates the size of the data item being sorted. Here is an example of how TurboSort would be called to sort a file of integers:

```
WriteLn(TurboSort(2));
```

In this case, TurboSort is given the value 2 since integers contain two bytes. In addition, this statement writes out the value that TurboSort returns. This value is a status code

Code	Meaning	Action Required
0	Sort completed—no errors	None
3	Not enough RAM available for sort	Reduce memory usage of program through overlays or dynamic variables
8	The data item being sorted is too short—it must be at least 2 bytes long	Increase the size of the data item
9	More than **MaxInt** records were passed to TurboSort	Break your file into smaller pieces, sort each piece separately, and then merge the files
10	Write error encountered. Disk may be full or damaged	Check disk for free space and possible damage
11	Read error encountered	Check disk for possible damage
12	File creation error	Check to see if your directory is full or whether you are trying to access a nonexisting directory

Table 19-2.   TurboSort Status Codes

that indicates how the sort went. The TurboSort status codes and their meanings are listed in Table 19-2.

Your program should check the value returned by TurboSort to make sure the sort finished correctly.

Programming Examples

Your Database Toolbox disk provides two example programs — SORT1.PAS and SORT2.PAS — that demonstrate the Turbo-Sort routines. The program called TestSort creates a series

of random integers, sorts them, and displays them on the
screen.

```
Program TestSort;
var
  i : integer;
(*$I sort.box*)

(***********************************************)

Procedure Inp;
Var
  i,j : Integer;
Begin
Writeln('Unsorted numbers: ');
For I := 1 to 10 do
  Begin
  j := Random(100);
  WriteLn(j);
  SortRelease(j);
  End;
writeln;
End;

(***********************************************)

Function Less;
Var
  Rec1 : Integer Absolute x;
  Rec2 : Integer Absolute y;
Begin
Less := Rec1 < Rec2;
End;

(***********************************************)

Procedure Outp;
Var
  i : Integer;
Begin
Writeln('Sorted numbers: ');
  Repeat
  SortReturn(i);
  WriteLn(i);
  Until SortEOS;
WriteLn;
End;

(***********************************************)

Begin
ClrScr;
i := TurboSort(2);
Write('Sort result code: ',i);
readln;
End.
```

If you are sorting more complicated data items, use the
SizeOf command to compute the correct value. For example:

TurboSort(SizeOf(DataItem))

Database Toolbox for Turbo Pascal
Version 4.0

With the introduction of Turbo Pascal 4.0, Borland has updated the Database Toolbox. This new version operates much like the previous version—all procedure and function calls remain unchanged for compatibility with your Version 3.0 programs—but the code has been changed to support database files and indexes with over 2 billion entries. The 2-billion-element limit also pertains to the sorting routine, allowing you to sort much larger files than before.

Because the Database Toolbox comes in unit format, you need compile it only once. To make the prcoess even easier, Borland includes a program that helps you determine the constants (such as KeyLen, PageSize, Order, and so on) that you must declare before you compile the Database Toolbox unit.

As a bonus, Borland throws in routines that allow you to read and write files in the format used by Reflex: The Analyst, Borland's widely used database manager.

Turbo Pascal
Graphix Toolbox

Graphix Toolbox Procedures
Screen Procedures
Graphics Windows
Graphics Clipping
World Coordinate System
Headers
Color
Plotting Commands
Text
Graphics Toolbox for Turbo Pascal Version 4.0

While Turbo Pascal provides some built-in graphics capabilities, they do not come close to providing a complete graphics library. You could write your own graphics library, but for only a few dollars, you can buy Borland's *Turbo Pascal Graphix Toolbox*, which contains most of the routines you could ask for. The *Graphix Toolbox Reference Manual*, which accompanies the diskette, describes all the features in great detail. This chapter serves as a quick reference to the graphics procedures contained in the Graphix Toolbox.

Graphix Toolbox Procedures

EnterGraphic

Syntax   Procedure EnterGraphic;

Usage   EnterGraphic clears the screen and sets the computer to Graphics mode. It does not initialize the graphics system.

Error

Syntax   Procedure Error(Proc, Code);

Usage   **Error** informs the user when an error occurs in a graphics procedure. The parameter **Proc** is the address of the procedure in which the error occurred and **Code** indicates the type of error. The error will terminate the program if Break mode is enabled. The **SetBreakOn** command enables Break mode and **SetBreakOff** disables it.

GetErrorCode

Syntax   GetErrorCode : Integer;

Usage   **GetErrorCode** returns the code of the error that occurred most recently. In order to use **GetErrorCode**,

Error Code	Meaning
−1	No error
0	Error message missing
1	Font file missing
2	Index out of range
3	Coordinates out of range
4	Too few array elements
5	Error opening file
6	Out of window memory
7	Value out of range

Table 20-1.   Graphics Error Codes

Break mode must be disabled with the **SetBreakOff** command. The error codes and their meanings are listed in Table 20-1.

HardCopy

Syntax   Procedure HardCopy(Inverse : Boolean;
                                    Mode : Byte);

Usage   **HardCopy** prints the graphic displayed on the active screen. The **Inverse** parameter prints in reverse (dark background) when True and prints standard (dark foreground) when False. **Mode** determines the size and density of the printed graphic, as detailed in Table 20-2.

InitGraphic

Syntax   Procedure InitGraphic;

Usage   **InitGraphic** initializes the graphics system. It must be called before any other graphics command, but **InitGraphic** can be called only once in a program. Among other things, this procedure checks that the appropriate hardware is present, loads the error message file and stan-

Mode	Points per Line	Epson Mode
0, 4, 5	640	4
1	960	1
2	960	2
3	1920	3
6	720	6

Table 20-2.   Printing Density Using Hard Copy

dard character set, sets the aspect ratio, and sets the vertical window movement step to the default value. The vertical window movement step is the number of pixels a window moves up or down in one step.

LeaveGraphic

Syntax   Procedure LeaveGraphic;

Usage   **LeaveGraphic** returns the system to Text mode.

SetBreakOff

Syntax   Procedure SetBreakOff;

Usage   **SetBreakOff** disables Break mode, in which error conditions cause a program to abort. After **SetBreak-Off** is called, error checking becomes the programmer's responsibility.

SetBreakOn

Syntax   Procedure SetBreakOn;

Usage   **SetBreakOn** enables Break mode. Once enabled, Break mode causes a program to terminate when an error occurs.

SetMessageOff

Syntax   Procedure SetMessageOff;

Usage   **SetMessageOff** reduces error messages displayed by the Graphix Toolbox. When Break mode is enabled, **Set-MessageOff** abbreviates error messages. When Break mode is disabled, **SetMessageOff** suppresses all error messages.

SetMessageOn

Syntax   Procedure SetMessageOn;

Usage   **SetMessageOn** tells the Graphix Toolbox to produce extended error messages. When Break mode is enabled, **SetMessageOn** displays complete error messages and terminates the program. When Break mode is disabled, **SetMessageOn** causes the Graphix Toolbox to display an error message on line 24 of your monitor, but it does not halt execution.

SetVStep

Syntax   Procedure SetVStep(Step : Integer);

Usage   **SetVStep** sets the vertical distance that a window can be moved at one time. **Step**, which can be any positive integer value, determines the distance in terms of pixels.

Screen Procedures

ClearScreen

Syntax   Procedure CopyScreen;

Usage   **ClearScreen** clears the active screen.

CopyScreen

Syntax   Procedure CopyScreen;

Usage   **CopyScreen** transfers the image on the active screen to the inactive screen.

GetAspect

Syntax   Function GetAspect : Real;

Usage   **GetAspect** returns the current value of the aspect ratio.

GetScreen

Syntax   Function GetScreen : Integer;

Usage   **GetScreen** reports which screen is currently active: a value of 1 indicates the displayed screen is active while 2 indicates the RAM screen is active.

GetScreenAspect

Syntax   Function GetScreenAspect : Real;

Usage   **GetScreenAspect** returns the current aspect ratio in terms of pixels.

InvertScreen

Syntax   Procedure InvertScreen;

Usage   **InvertScreen** reverses the displayed graphic by changing pixels from white to black and from black to white. This command also works when colors other than black and white are used.

LoadScreen

Syntax   Procedure LoadScreen(FileName : WrkString);

Usage   Loads a screen from file **FileName** into memory.

SaveScreen

Syntax   Procedure SaveScreen(FileName : WrkString);

Usage   **SaveScreen** stores a graphic display in a file named with the variable **FileName**.

SelectScreen

Syntax   Procedure SelectScreen(I : Integer);

Usage   The Graphix Toolbox allows you to display graphics on either the active screen (the screen you see) or on a RAM screen (a screen held in memory that is not displayed). Setting **I** equal to 1 selects the active screen, while a value of 2 selects the RAM screen.

SetAspect

Syntax   Procedure SetAspect(Aspect : Real);

Usage   When you initialize the Graphix Toolbox, the default aspect ratio is enabled. This ratio displays correctly proportioned circles and ellipses. **SetAspect** changes the aspect ratio by a multiplier, **Aspect**. For example, the command **SetAspect(2)** will display circles twice as tall as they are wide.

SetScreenAspect

Syntax   Procedure SetScreenAspect(Aspect : Real);

Usage   **SetScreenAspect** defines the aspect ratio in terms of pixels. **Aspect** is the aspect ratio defined in terms of pixels. For example, **SetScreenAspect(1)** creates circles that have as many pixels vertically as they do horizontally.

SwapScreen

Syntax   Procedure SwapScreen;

Usage   **SwapScreen** exchanges the displayed screen and the RAM screen.

Graphics Windows

ClearWindowStack

Syntax   Procedure ClearWindowStack(N : Integer);

Usage   **ClearWindowStack** clears the window number N. Once erased with this procedure, the window cannot be restored by RestoreWindow.

CopyWindow

Syntax   Procedure CopyWindow(From, To : Byte;
                              X, Y : Integer);

Usage   **CopyWindow** transfers the contents of the active screen to the RAM screen, or the contents of the RAM screen to the active screen. **From** and **To** indicate the source and destination: 1 indicates the displayed screen, 2 indicates the RAM screen. Coordinates **X:Y** indicate the screen location of the window.

DefineTextWindow

Syntax   Procedure DefineTextWindow(I, Left, Up, Right,
                                    Down, Border :
                                    Integer);

Usage   **DefineTextWindow** defines an area of the screen in terms of text coordinates (80 $\times$ 25). The location of the window is determined by **Left, Up, Right,** and **Down,** which define the edges of window number **I. Border** determines the number of pixels that separate the text window from the rest of the screen.

DefineWindow

Syntax   Procedure DefineWindow(I, Xlow, Ylow,
                                        Xhi, Yhi : Integer);

Usage   **DefineWindow** declares a rectangular portion of the screen to be window number **I.** The window's location is determined by **Xlow:Ylow** for the upper right corner and **Xhi:Yhi** for the lower left corner, all of which are defined as world coordinates. The **X** coordinates represent 8-pixel chunks, which means the command

   DefineWorld(1,0,0,9,9)

creates a screen 10 pixels high and 80 pixels wide.

GetWindow

Syntax   Function GetWindow : Integer;

Usage   **GetWindow** returns the number of the window that is currently active.

InvertWindow

Syntax   Procedure InvertWindow;

Usage   **InvertWindow** changes the pixels in the active window from black to white and from white to black. If colors are used, they are reversed in similar fashion.

LoadWindow

Syntax   Procedure LoadWindow(N, X, Y : Integer;
                                      FileName :
                                      WrkString);

Usage   **LoadWindow** reads a window from a file named FileName, stores the contents in window **N**, and displays the window at coordinates **X:Y**.

LoadWindowStack

Syntax   Procedure LoadWindowStack(FileName
: WrkString);

Usage   **LoadWindowStack** reads in two files — FILENAME.STK and FILENAME.PTR — which contain a window stack that was stored previously.

RedefineWindow

Syntax   Procedure RedefineWindow(I, Xlow, Ylow,
Xhi, Yhi : Integer);

Usage   **RedefineWindow** changes the dimensions of window **I**. Coordinates **Xlow:Ylow** determine the position of the upper right corner and **Xhi:Yhi** determine the lower right corner. The **X** coordinates represent 8 pixels each, as in the **DefineWindow** command.

ResetWindows

Syntax   Procedure ResetWindows;

Usage   **ResetWindows** sets all the windows to the size of the screen and selects Window 1 as the active window. In addition, all headers are removed. While the graphic currently displayed remains unchanged, all further graphics are drawn according to absolute screen coordinates.

ResetWindowStack

Syntax   Procedure ResetWindowStack;

Usage   **ResetWindowStack** discards all the windows stored on the window stack and frees the memory.

RestoreWindow

Syntax   Procedure RestoreWindow(N, X, Y : Integer);

Usage   **RestoreWindow** takes window **N** from the window stack and displays it on the screen at coordinates **X:Y**.

SaveWindow

Syntax   Procedure SaveWindow(N : Integer;
                                FileName : WrkString);

Usage   **SaveWindow** stores window **N** in a disk file with the name FILENAME.

SaveWindowStack

Syntax   Procedure SaveWindowStack(FileName :
                                WrkString);

Usage   **SaveWindowStack** stores all the windows currently on the window stack in two files, one named FILE-NAME.STK and the other named FILENAME.PTR. Since the Graphics Toolbox automatically adds the extensions, do not specify an extension for FILENAME.

SelectWindow

Syntax   Procedure SelectWindow(N : Integer);

Usage   **SelectWindow** makes window **N** the active window.

SetWindowModeOff

Syntax   Procedure SetWindowModeOff;

Usage   **SetWindowModeOff** permits you to create graphics using absolute coordinates only.

SetWindowModeOn

Syntax   Procedure SetWindowModeOn;

Usage   **SetWindowModeOn** enables Window mode, which is also the default mode. By calling **SetWindowModeOn**, you can draw graphics using world coordinates.

StoreWindow

Syntax   Procedure StoreWindow(N : Integer);

Usage   **StoreWindow** saves window **N** on the window stack. Before the window is saved, the Graphix Toolbox checks to see if the window stack has enough memory to store the window. If there is too little memory, an error occurs and the window is not saved.

WindowMode

Syntax   Function WindowMode : Boolean;

Usage   **WindowMode** returns True if Window mode is currently enabled and False if Window mode is disabled.

WindowSize

Syntax   Function WindowSize(N : Integer) : Integer;

Usage   **WindowSize** returns the memory required to store window **N** on the window stack. The amount is rounded up to the nearest kilobyte. This procedure is used to check if enough room remains on the window stack to save the window **N**.

WindowX

Syntax   Function WindowX(X : Real) : Integer;

Usage   **WindowX** accepts a world coordinate **X** and returns the equivalent absolute screen coordinate.

WindowY

Syntax   Function WindowY(Y : Real) : Integer;

Usage   **WindowY** accepts a world coordinate **Y** and returns the equivalent absolute screen coordinate.

Graphics Clipping

Clipping

Syntax   Function Clipping : Boolean;

Usage   **Clipping** returns True if clipping is enabled and False if it is disabled. When clipping is enabled, only the portion of the graphic that fits within the current window is displayed.

SetClippingOn

Syntax   Procedure SetClippingOn;

Usage   **SetClippingOn** enables Clipping mode, in which drawings are limited to the boundaries of the active window. Any portion of the drawing that falls outside the active window is not drawn.

SetClippingOff

Syntax Procedure SetClippingOff;

Usage **SetClippingOff** disables Clipping mode, thus allowing drawings to extend beyond the boundaries of the active window.

World Coordinate System

DefineWorld

Syntax Procedure DefineWorld(I : Integer;
                       Xlow, Ylow, Xhi, Yhi
                       : Real);

Usage **DefineWorld** defines the coordinate system for world **I**. **Xlow:Ylow** indicates the upper left corner of the screen and **Xhi:Yhi** indicates the lower right corner. Once the coordinates are defined, they are not enabled until you invoke the **SelectWorld** command.

SelectWorld

Syntax Procedure SelectWorld(I : Integer);

Usage **SelectWorld** selects world coordinate system **I**.

SetBackground

Syntax Procedure SetBackground(Pattern : Byte);

Usage **SetBackground** sets the background pattern with a byte that determines the pattern. Each bit in the byte corresponds to a pixel location; thus, the entire byte controls 8 pixels. If a bit is on, its corresponding pixel is turned on; if off, the pixel is off. The Graphix Toolbox repeats the byte pattern throughout the active window.

SetBackground8

Syntax   Procedure SetBackground8(Pattern :
                                       Background Array);

Usage   **SetBackground8** creates a patterned background
that is defined by **Pattern**, an array of eight bytes. Each byte
in **Pattern** controls eight horizontal pixels. Together, the
eight bytes define a portion of the screen that is 8×8 pixels.
        When a bit in one of the bytes is on, the pixel is turned
on, otherwise the pixel is turned off. The Graphix Toolbox
repeats the pattern throughout the active window.

Headers

DefineHeader

Syntax   Procedure DefineHeader(I : Integer; Hdr : Wrk-
                                       String);

Usage   **DefineHeader** defines a header for window **I**.
The header displays the contents of the string **Header**.

DrawBorder

Syntax   Procedure DrawBorder;

Usage   **DrawBorder** creates a border around the active
window. The border can include a header at either the top or
the bottom of the window.

GetVStep

Syntax   Function GetVStep : Integer;

Usage   **GetVStep** returns the number of vertical pixels a window will move in one step.

MoveHor

Syntax   Procedure MoveHor(Delta : Integer; FillOut : Boolean);

Usage   **MoveHor** moves the active window **Delta** the specified steps (at 8 pixels per step) to the right or left. The window moves to the left when **Delta** is negative and to the right when it is positive. **FillOut** determines what happpens to the space "underneath" the window after it is moved. When **FillOut** is set to False, the area is set to the opposite of the current color. When **FillOut** is True, the area underneath the window is replaced by the same area in the RAM screen. In short, you must keep a copy of the window in the RAM screen so that when the window moves, the newly exposed part of the screen can be filled in correctly.

MoveVer

Syntax   Procedure MoveVer(Delta : Integer; FillOut : Boolean);

Usage   **MoveVer** moves the active window up or down by **Delta** steps. A vertical step is one pixel (by default), but this can be changed by **SetVStep**. When **Delta** is positive, the window moves up; when negative, the window moves down. **FillOut** determines how the newly exposed portion of the screen is filled in (see **MoveHor**).

RemoveHeader

Syntax   Procedure RemoveHeader(I : Integer);

Usage   **RemoveHeader** removes a header definition from window **I.** Calling this command does not change the window displayed.

ResetWorlds

Syntax   Procedure ResetWorlds;

Usage   **ResetWorlds** initializes all the world coordinates to the coordinates of the absolute screen coordinates.

SetHeaderOff

Syntax   Procedure SetHeaderOff;

Usage   **SetHeaderOff** suppresses the display of window headers when the **DrawBorder** command is used.

SetHeaderOn

Syntax   Procedure SetHeaderOn;

Usage   **SetHeaderOn** enables the display of window headers when the **DrawBorder** command is used.

SetHeaderToBottom

Syntax   Procedure SetHeaderToBottom;

Usage   **SetHeaderToBottom** causes window headers to be displayed at the bottom of a window.

SetHeaderToTop

Syntax   Procedure SetHeaderToTop;

Usage   **SetHeaderToTop** causes window headers to be displayed at the top of a window.

SetVStep

Syntax   Procedure SetVStep(Step : Integer);

Usage   **SetVStep** determines how many pixels it takes to move a window in one step. **Step**, an integer, is the number of pixels.

Color

GetColor

Syntax   Function GetColor : Integer;

Usage   **GetColor** returns the value of the current drawing color. If **GetColor** returns 0, the current drawing color is the background color; if it equals 255, the current drawing color is the foreground color.

SetBackgroundColor

Syntax   Procedure SetBackgroundColor(Color : Integer);

Usage   **SetBackgroundColor** determines the color of background pixels. **Color** can be any value that is valid for your adapter.

SetColorBlack

Syntax   Procedure SetColorBlack;

Usage   **SetColorBlack** selects the current background color as the drawing color.

SetColorWhite

Syntax   Procedure SetColorWhite;

Usage   **SetColorWhite** tells the Graphix Toolbox to use the current foreground color as the current drawing color.

SetForegroundColor

Syntax   Procedure SetForegroundColor(Color : Integer);

Usage   **SetForegroundColor** determines the color of foreground pixels. **Color** can be any valid foreground color your adapter supports.

Plotting Commands

Bezier

Syntax   Procedure Bezier(A : PlotArray;
                    N : Integer;
                    Var B : PlotArray;
                    M : Integer);

Usage   A Bezier polynomial curve connects the points on a graph in a smooth, curved line. Parameter **A** is an array of **X** and **Y** points, **N** is the number of points, and **B** is an array of **X** and **Y** points that are produced by the Bezier calculation. **M** controls the smoothness of the curve; the higher the value, the smoother the curve.

DrawAxis

Syntax   Procedure DrawAxis(XDensity, YDensity,
                    Left, Top, Right, Bottom
                    : Integer; XAxis,
                    YAxis : Integer;
                    Arrows : Boolean);

Usage   **DrawAxis** creates scaled horizontal and vertical axes for drawing polygons. **XDensity** and **YDensity** determine the density of the tick marks that appear on each axis. **Left**, **Top**, **Right**, and **Bottom** are the distances from each edge of the screen that determine the drawing area for the polygon. **XAxis** and **YAxis** determine the style of the axes: when either is a negative number, that axis is not drawn. When **Arrows** is True, the axes will have arrows at each end.

DrawCartPie

Syntax   Procedure DrawCartPie(Xcenter, Ycenter,
                           Xstart, Ystart,Inner,
                           Outer : Real;
                           A : PieArray; N, Option,
                           Scale : Integer);

Usage   **DrawCartPie** draws a pie chart centered at coordinates **Xcenter:Ycenter** starting at **Xstart:Ystart**. The procedure uses values in parameter **A**. This parameter is of type **PieArray**, which is an array of real numbers and labels. **DrawCartPie** uses the numbers in **A** to compute the relative area of each segment of the pie. The string portions of **A** serve as labels for each segment of the pie. **N** is the number of segments in the pie and **Inner, Outer, Option**, and **Scale** function as they do in **DrawCircleSegment**.

DrawCircle

Syntax   Procedure DrawCircle(X,Y,R : Real);

Usage   **DrawCircle** draws a circle at coordinates **X:Y** with radius **R**.

DrawCircleSegment

Syntax   Procedure DrawCircleSegment(XCenter,YCenter :
                           Real; Var XStart,
                           YStart : Real;
                           Inner, Outer,
                           Angle, Area
                           : Real; Text
                           : WrkString;
                           Option, Scale
                           : Byte);

Usage   **DrawCircleSegment** draws a circle or part of a circle. The circle's center is located at coordinates **XCenter**: **YCenter** and the arc of the circle starts at coordinates **XStart:YStart**. This command also draws a line from inside the circle to the outside, and positions a label at the outer end of this line. The inner end of the line is determined by **Inner** and the outer end by **Outer**. Both **Inner** and **Outer** represent radius units; thus, a value of 0.5 means halfway between the center of the circle and the circumference.

Angle is the number of degrees in the angle of the arc that forms the circle segment. **Area** is a number that is displayed as part of the label if you select the appropriate option. **Text** contains the label you wish to display with the circle segment, and **Option** determines how the label or numbers are displayed, as follows:

Option	Meaning
0	No label
1	Text label
2	Text and number label
3	Number only label

Scale is a multiplier that increases or decreases the size of the label. When **Scale** equals 1, the label appears in its default size.

DrawHistogram

Syntax   Procedure DrawHistogram(A : PlotArray; N : Integer);

Usage   **DrawHistogram** is used to create bar charts. **A** is of type **PlotArray**, which is a two-dimensional array of integers. **DrawHistogram** uses only the first dimension in the array. This dimension contains values that determine the height of each bar in the histogram. **N** indicates the number of elements in **A** used to plot the histogram.

DrawLine

Syntax   Procedure DrawLine(X1, Y1, X2, Y2 : Real);

Usage   **DrawLine** draws a line from coordinates **X1:Y1** to **X2:Y2**. If Window mode is on, the coordinates are world coordinates; otherwise, they are absolute coordinates.

DrawLineClipped

Syntax   Procedure DrawLineClipped(X1, Y1, X2, Y2 : Real);

Usage   **DrawLineClipped** draws a line from absolute coordinates **X1:Y1** to **X2:Y2**. The line is clipped at the boundaries of the active window even when Window mode is turned off.

DrawPoint

Syntax   Procedure DrawPoint(X, Y : Real);

Usage   **DrawPoint** plots a single pixel at coordinates X:Y. If in Window mode, the coordinates are world coordinates; if not, they are absolute coordinates.

DrawPolarPie

Syntax   Procedure DrawPolarPie(Xcenter, Ycenter, Radius, Angle, Inner, Outer : Real; A : PieArray; N, Option, Scale : Integer);

Usage   **DrawPolarPie** operates in much the same manner as **DrawCartPie**, except that instead of using **Xstart** and **Ystart** to determine the coordinate at which the circumference begins, you use **Radius** and **Angle**. **Radius** is the radius of the pie in terms of world pixels and **Angle**

determines the starting point of the circumference expressed in degrees.

DrawPolygon

Syntax   Procedure DrawPolygon(A : PlotArray;
First, Last, Code, Scale,
Lines : Integer);

Usage   **DrawPolygon** creates a line drawing with **A**, which is an array of **x** and **y** coordinates. **First** and **Last** indicate the beginning and ending points in the vertex to be plotted. **Code** specifies the type of symbol that is drawn at each plotted coordinate, and **Scale** is a multiplier that determines how large the symbol will appear. When **Scale** equals 1, the symbol is drawn to the default scale. **Line** controls how filler lines appear on the graphic. When **Line** is less than zero, filler lines are drawn from the Y-zero axis to the vertex; when **Line** is greater than zero, lines are drawn from the bottom of the display to the vertex, and when equal to zero, no lines are drawn.

DrawSquare

Syntax   Procedure DrawSquare(X1, Y1, X2, Y2 : Real;
Fill : Boolean);

Usage   **DrawSquare** draws any rectangular shape defined by world coordinates **X1:Y1** and **X2:Y2**. The square is drawn in the current line style and when **Fill** is True, the rectangle is filled with the current drawing color and pattern.

DrawStraight

Syntax   Procedure DrawStraight(X1, X2, Y : Integer);

Usage   **DrawStraight** draws only horizontal lines start-ing at absolute coordinates **X:Y** and extending to **X2:Y**. **DrawStraight** is faster than **DrawLine**.

FindWorld

Syntax   Procedure FindWorld(I : Integer;
                          A : PlotArray;
                          N : Integer;
                          Scalex, Scaley : Real);

Usage   **FindWorld** determines the proper world coordi-nates for world **I**, using **A**, the array of vertices, and **N**, the number of vertices. **Scalex** and **Scaley** are multipliers that can add additional scaling to the world coordinates. When both **Scalex** and **Scaley** are equal to 1, no additional scaling is added.

GetLineStyle

Syntax   Function GetLineStyle : Integer;

Usage   **GetLineStyle** returns an integer that indicates the current line style.

Hatch

Syntax   Procedure Hatch(X1, Y1, X2, Y2 : Real; Delta
                          : Integer);

Usage   **Hatch** fills a rectangular portion of the screen, defined by coordinates **X1:Y1** and **X2:Y2**, with diagonal lines. The separation between the hatched lines is deter-mined by **Delta**. When **Delta** is one, 100% (1/1) of the rectan-gle is filled with solid color. When **Delta** is 2, 50% (1/2) of the rectangle is filled. A positive **Delta** draws hatched lines from upper left to lower right; a negative value draws lines from lower left to upper right.

The rectangle is drawn in absolute coordinates unless Window mode is on, in which case world coordinates are used.

PointDrawn

Syntax   Function PointDrawn(X, Y : Real) : Boolean;

Usage   **PointDrawn**, a Boolean function, returns True if a point has been drawn at world coordinates **X:Y**.

RotatePolygon

Syntax   Procedure RotatePolygon(A: PlotArray;
                           N : Integer;
                           Angle : Real);

Usage   **RotatePolygon** rotates the polygon defined by **A** and **N** by **Angle** degrees. The center of the rotation is calculated by the Graphix Toolbox.

RotatePolygonAbout

Syntax   Procedure RotatePolygonAbout(A: PlotArray;
                           N : Integer;
                           Angle, X, Y :
                           Real);

Usage   **RotatePolygonAbout** rotates the polygon defined by **A** and **N** by **Angle** degrees. The center of the rotation is determined by world coordinates **X** and **Y**.

ScalePolygon

Syntax   Procedure ScalePolygon(A : PlotArray;
                           N : Integer;
                           XFactor, YFactor : Real);

Usage   **ScalePolygon** multiplies **N x** and **y** coordinates of
A by **XFactor** and **YFactor**. This alters the proportions of
the polygon when it is displayed.

SetLineStyle

Syntax   Procedure SetLineStyle(LS : Integer);

Usage   **SetLineStyle** determines the type of line the Graphix Toolbox draws. **LS** can be set to any of five predefined line
styles:

0 Solid line
1 Dotted line
2 Dashes
3 Dashes and dots
4 Short dashes

Spline

Syntax   Procedure Spline(A : PlotArray;
                          N : Integer;
                          X1, Xm : Real;
                          Var B : PlotArray;
                          m : Integer);

Usage   **Spline** interpolates a smooth curve around the
points in a polygon defined by **A** and **N** and stores the result
in **B. X1** and **Xm** represent the starting and ending points in
A, and **m** is the number of points used to define the smooth
curve.

TranslatePolygon

Syntax   Procedure TranslatePolygon(A : PlotArray;
                                 N : Integer;
                                 DeltaX, DeltaY :
                                 Real);

Usage   **TranslatePolygon** moves a polygon defined by **A** and **N** by adding **DeltaX** to its **x** coordinates and **DeltaY** to its **y** coordinates.

Text

DefineHeader

Syntax   Procedure DefineHeader(I : Integer;
                              Hdr : WrkString);

Usage   **DefineHeader** uses **Hdr** to define the header for window **I**.

DefineTextWindow

Syntax   Procedure DefineTextWindow(I,
                              Left,
                              Up,
                              Right,
                              Down,
                              Border : Integer);

Usage   **DefineTextWindow** defines window **I** with text coordinates (80 × 25). **Left**, **Up**, **Right**, and **Down** specify the text coordinates that define the edges of the window. **Border** specifies the number of pixels that separate the text portion of the window from the edges of the window.

DrawASCII

Syntax   Procedure DrawASCII(Var X,Y : Integer;
                              Scale, Ch : Byte);

Usage   **DrawASCII** displays character **Ch** at absolute coordinates **X:Y**. The size of the character is multiplied by **Scale**.

DrawText

Syntax   Procedure DrawText(X,Y,Scale : Integer; Text
: WrkString);

Usage   **DrawText** displays string **Text** at absolute coordinates **X:Y**. The size of the characters is multiplied by **Scale**.

DrawTextW

Syntax   Procedure DrawTextW(X,Y,Scale : Real;
Text : WrkString);

Usage   **DrawTextW** displays string **Text** at world coordinates **X:Y**. The size of the characters is multiplied by **Scale**.

TextDown

Syntax   Function TextDown(TY, Boundary : Integer)
: Integer;

Usage   **TextDown** returns the absolute coordinate of the pixel located at text line **TY** plus the number of pixels specified in **Boundary**.

TextLeft

Syntax   Function TextLeft(TX, Boundary : Integer) :
Integer;

Usage   **TextLeft** returns the absolute coordinate of the pixel located at text column **TY** less the number of pixels specified in **Boundary**.

TextRight

Syntax   Function TextRight(TX, Boundary : Integer)
: Integer;

Usage   **TextRight** returns the absolute coordinate of the pixel located at text column **TY** plus the number of pixels specified in **Boundary**.

TextUp

Syntax   Function TextUp(TY, Boundary : Integer) :
Integer;

Usage   **TextUp** returns the absolute coordinate of the pixel located at text line **TY** less the number of pixels specified in **Boundary**.

Graphix Toolbox for Turbo Pascal Version 4.0

Borland's Graphix Toolbox has been updated for use with Turbo Pascal Version 4.0. All procedure and function calls remain unchanged, allowing a maximum level of compatibility with your existing program. All procedures are contained in units, reducing the time required to compile your programs. In addition, all inline routines have been optimized and converted to external assembler files and are linked to the Graphix Toolbox units with the {$L} compiler directive.

Turbo Pascal Editor Toolbox

All programmers use a word processor or text editor to write their programs. Yet, to many the fundamental operations of a word processor remain a mystery. The Turbo Pascal Editor Toolbox sheds light on this topic by providing the source code you need to customize your own word processor and at the same time learn how these programs are written.

Aspects of Word Processing Programming

People use their computers for word processing more than for any other purpose. In many offices, word processors have replaced typewriters completely. The proliferation of word processing software has brought forth a wide range of software—some good, some bad, and much in between.

What makes a word processor good or bad depends to some degree on personal taste. One thing that everyone prefers, however, is speed. Slow word processors are more than an annoyance, they cost valuable time. The Turbo Pascal Editor Toolbox routines are fast largely because they use as much RAM as possible to store documents as they are edited.

Another characteristic people look for in a word proces-

TWENTY ONE

sor is features—generally, the more a word processor has, the better. The Turbo Pascal Editor Toolbox provides a good range of features, from standard features such as word wrapping and moving blocks of text, to more advanced features such as windows and printing in the background.

Creating a Basic Editor

The program called **Basic Editor** uses the Editor Toolbox files to create a relatively simple word processor:

```
Program BasicEditor;

(*$I VARS.ED*)

(********************************************)

Procedure UserCommand(Var ch : byte);
Begin
End;

(********************************************)

Procedure UserError(Var Msgno : byte);
Begin
End;

(********************************************)

Procedure userStatusLine(Var TWindow:Byte;
                             Column,line:Integer;
                             Insertflag:Insflag;
                             WW,AI: boolean);
Begin
End;

(********************************************)

Procedure UserReplace(Var ch : byte);
Begin
End;

(********************************************)


Procedure UserTask;
Begin
End;
```

```
(********************************************)

(*$I  USER.ED*)
(*$I  SCREEN.ED*)

(*$I  INIT.ED*)
(*$I  KCMD.ED*)
(*$I  OCMD.ED*)
(*$I  QCMD.ED*)
(*$I  CMD.ED*)

(*$I  K.ED*)
(*$I  O.ED*)
(*$I  Q.ED*)
(*$I  DISP.ED*)
(*$I  TASK.ED*)
(*$I  INPUT.ED*)

(********************************************)

Begin
EditInitialize;
EditSystem;
End.
```

Basic Editor includes the variable declaration file, declares several hook procedures, includes the main editor files, and defines a main program block.

VARS.ED

The file VARS.ED contains all the global variables, constants, and data types the Editor Toolbox needs. This file must be included in your code before any other Editor Toolbox files.

User Hooks

The Editor Toolbox uses some procedures, which you must declare yourself, as *hooks*. Hooks are routines that allow you to add features. If you leave these procedures as shown in Basic Editor, they will have no effect on your program. The "hook" procedures you must declare are described next.

UserCommand

Syntax   Procedure UserCommand(Var ch : byte);

Usage   **UserCommand** accepts a byte parameter **ch**, which is a command character that is typed by the user. You can program **UserCommand** to change the value of **ch** and, thus, alter the normal execution of the program. If you program your own routines using **UserCommand**, you should set **ch** equal to 255 before the procedure ends. This stops the Editor Toolbox from executing its own procedures.

UserError

Syntax   Procedure UserError(Var Msgno : byte);

Usage   **UserError** allows you to replace the Editor Toolbox error reporting with your own. **Msgno** is a code that indicates the type of error that occurred. Your procedure should test this value, execute its own code depending on the value, and set **Msgno** to zero before exiting.

UserReplace

Syntax   Procedure UserReplace(Var ch : byte);

Usage   **UserReplace** allows you to change the prompt displayed in search and replace operations.

UserStatusline

Syntax   Procedure UserStatusline(Var TWindow:Byte;
                                    Column,line:Integer;
                                    Insertflag:Insflag;
                                    WW,AI: Boolean);

Usage   UserStatusline allows you to program your own status line. The procedure receives the column and line numbers, the insert, word wrap, and autoindent flags, all of which are used in the normal status line. If you do program your own status line, be sure to set **TWindow** to zero before the procedure ends to suppress the Editor Toolbox default status line.

UserTask

Syntax   Procedure UserTask;

Usage   **UserTask** provides the ability to perform background processing. The Editor Toolbox calls **UserTask** whenever it is waiting for keyboard input. **UserTask** is used primarily for background printing—printing one document while you edit another.

The Main Include Files

After you have declared the hook routines, you must include the main files that contain the substance of the editor. The code in these files controls the screen, keyboard input, and all control code processing routines.

Main Program Block

Finally, your program initiates the editor with just the two lines of code shown here:

```
Begin
EditInitialize;
EditSystem;
End.
```

The call to **EditInitialize** sets up the editor environment and **EditSystem** executes a loop that continues until you exit from the editor.

Text Buffer Structure

The Editor Toolbox uses a complex data structure to store text dynamically. The fundamental element in this data structure is the data type **linedesc**, shown here.

```
Linedesc = Record
   Fwdlink   : Plinedesc;
   Backlink  : Plinedesc;
   Txt       : Ptextline;
   Flags     : Integer;
   Bufflen   : Integer;
   End;
```

Fwdlink points to the next line of text in the text stream and **Backlink** points to the previous line. **Txt** points to a string that holds the actual text. **Flags** tells the program whether the line was word wrapped and the color to display the line. **Bufflen** keeps track of the length of the line, which may exceed 255 characters.

The *text stream* consists of a linked list of pointer records; each pointer record points to the previous record, the following record, and a line of text. Although this structure is cumbersome to manage, it allows the program to insert and delete text within a text stream very quickly. For example, to insert a new line in the middle of a text stream, the program declares a new pointer record and establishes the connections with the pointer records before and after it.

Because text streams are stored as dynamic variables, they can use the entire heap. If your computer has 640K of RAM, you can store very large documents completely in memory, which greatly increases the program's speed.

Editor Toolbox Procedures

The following are the procedures contained in the Editor Toolbox. They perform all text manipulation, screen handling, and window management functions.

Advance

Syntax   Procedure Advance;

Usage   **Advance** moves the cursor one character to the right or to the next line. This procedure is local to **EditRightWord**.

Edit Abort

Syntax   Procedure EditAbort;

Usage   **EditAbort** interrupts the type-ahead buffer, sets the value of the global var ble **abortcmd**, invokes **EditErrormsg**, and clears the type-ahead buffer.

Edit Appchar

Syntax   Procedure EditAppchar(Var s : Varstring; Ch : Byte);

Usage   **EditAppchar** appends **Ch** to string **s**.

Edit Appcmdnam

Syntax   Procedure EditAppcmdnam(s : Varstring);

Usage   **EditAppcmdnam** displays s on the command line and correctly positions the cursor for input.

EditAskfor

Syntax   Procedure EditAskfor(var s : Varstring);

Usage   **EditAskfor** places the cursor on the command line, accepts a string from the user, and passes the string back in s.

EditBackground

Syntax   Procedure EditBackground;

Usage   **EditBackground** performs tasks such as updating the screen while the editor waits for keyboard input.

EditBeginningEndLine

Syntax   Procedure EditBeginningEndLine;

Usage   If the cursor is not in the first column of the current line, **EditBeginningEndLine** positions the cursor at the first column. Otherwise, the cursor is positioned after the last nonblank character on the line.

EditBeginningLine

Syntax   Procedure EditBeginningLine;

Usage   **EditBeginningLine** positions the cursor at the first column of the current line.

EditBlockBegin

Syntax   Procedure EditBlockBegin;

Usage   **EditBlockBegin** marks the current line as the beginning of the block to be marked.

EditBlockCopy

Syntax   Procedure EditBlockCopy;

Usage   **EditBlockCopy** copies a block of text to the current cursor position.

EditBlockDelete

Syntax   Procedure EditBlockDelete;

Usage   **EditBlockDelete** deletes the currently marked block of text.

EditBlockEnd

Syntax   Procedure EditBlockEnd;

Usage   **EditBlockEnd** marks the end of the currently marked block of text.

EditBlockHide

Syntax   Procedure EditBlockHide;

Usage   **EditBlockHide** controls the highlighting of the currently marked block of text.

EditBlockMove

Syntax   Procedure EditBlockMove;

Usage   **EditBlockMove** moves the marked block of text to the current cursor position.

EditBottomBlock

Syntax   Procedure EditBottomBlock;

Usage   **EditBottomBlock** moves the cursor to the last line in the marked block of text.

EditBreathe

Syntax   Procedure EditBreathe;

Usage   **EditBreathe** accepts a character from the keyboard while another process is taking place. The character is added to the type-ahead buffer.

EditCenterLine

Syntax   Procedure EditCenterLine;

Usage   **EditCenterLine** centers the line on which the cursor appears.

EditChangeCase

Syntax   Procedure EditChangeCase;

Usage   **EditChangeCase** changes the case of the character under which the cursor appears.

EditClsinp

Syntax   Procedure EditClsinp;

Usage   **EditClsinp** reads the next character in the type-ahead buffer.

EditColorFile

Syntax   Procedure EditColorFile;

Usage   **EditColorFile** is used by the routines that update the screen. Text is displayed in **Usercolor**.

EditColorLine

Syntax   Procedure EditColorLine;

Usage   **EditColorLine** sets the color for the current line of text.

EditCompressLine

Syntax   Procedure EditCompressLine(Lp : Plindesc);

Usage   **EditCompressLine**, which is used by **EditReformat**, compresses multiple spaces on a line to single spaces. **Lp** points to the line to compress.

EditCpcrewin

Syntax   Procedure EditCpcrewin;

Usage   **EditCpcrewin** creates a new window on the screen. The user is prompted for a window number and the size of the window.

EditCpdelwin

Syntax   Procedure EditCpdelwin;

Usage   **EditCpdelwin** asks the user which window he or she wishes to delete and then deletes the window from the screen.

EditCpexit

Syntax   Procedure EditCpexit;

Usage   **EditCpexit** asks the user to confirm that he or she wishes to exit from the editor. Exit is allowed only when the user types **YES**, (disregarding case).

EditCpFileSave

Syntax   Procedure EditCpFileSave;

Usage   **EditCpFileSave** asks for a filename in which to store the edited text.

EditCpFind

Syntax   Procedure EditCpFind;

Usage   **EditCpFind** asks for the parameters used in the **Find** command.

EditCpgotocl

Syntax   Procedure EditCpgotocl;

Usage   **EditCpgotocl** positions the cursor at a column specified by the user.

EditCpgotoln

Syntax   Procedure EditCpgotoln;

Usage   **EditCpgotoln** positions the cursor at a line specified by the user.

EditCpgotowin

Syntax   Procedure EditCpgotowin;

Usage   **EditCpgotowin** moves the cursor to a window specified by the user.

EditCpjmpmrk

Syntax   Procedure EditCpjmpmrk;

Usage   **EditCpjmpmrk** positions the cursor at the text marker specified by the user.

EditCplnkwin

Syntax   Procedure EditCplnkwin;

Usage   **EditCplnkwin** combines two windows into a single window.

EditCpReplace

Syntax   Procedure EditCpReplace;

Usage   **EditCpReplace** prompts the user for the replace string in a **Search and Replace** command.

EditCprfw

Syntax   Procedure EditCprfw;

Usage   **EditCprfw** prompts the user to enter the name of a file to read into the current window.

EditCpsetlm

Syntax   Procedure EditCpsetlm;

Usage   **EditCpsetlm** allows the user to set the left margin for the current window.

EditCpsetmrk

Syntax   Procedure EditCpsetmrk;

Usage   **EditCpsetmrk** sets a text marker at the cursor position. The text marker is defined by a number entered by the user.

EditCpsetrm

Syntax   Procedure EditCpsetrm;

Usage   **EditCpsetrm** allows the user to set the right margin in the active window.

EditCptabdef

Syntax   Procedure EditCptabdef;

Usage   **EditCptabdef** allows the user to set the tab width in the current window.

EditCpundlim

Syntax   Procedure EditCpundlim;

Usage   **EditCpundlim** sets the limit for the undo stack, which contains deleted text.

EditCpwfw

Syntax   Procedure EditCpwfw;

Usage   **EditCpwfw** asks the user to enter a filename, which is used to create a file to which the text in the current window is written.

EditCvts2i

Syntax   Procedure EditCvts2i(s : Varstring;
                                Var Result : Integer);

Usage   **EditCvts2i** converts string **s** to integer **Result**.

EditDecline

Syntax   Procedure EditDecline;

Usage   **EditDecline** decreases by one the absolute line number of the current window and redisplays the window.

EditDefineTab

Syntax   Procedure EditDefineTab(Size : Integer);

Usage   **EditDefineTab** sets the global variable **TabSize** to the value of **Size**. **Size** indicates the number of spaces between tab stops.

EditDeleteLeftChar

Syntax   Procedure EditDeleteLeftChar;

Usage **EditDeleteLeftChar** deletes the character to the left of the cursor. Text to the right of the cursor is shifted one column to the left. If the cursor is on the first line, the current line moves up and joins the previous line.

EditDeleteLine

Syntax   Procedure EditDeleteLine;

Usage   **EditDeleteLine** removes the current line from the text file being edited. The screen is updated without the deleted line.

EditDeleteRightChar

Syntax   Procedure EditDeleteRightChar;

Usage   **EditDeleteRightChar** deletes the character to the right of the cursor. If the cursor is at the end of the line, the next line moves up and joins the current line.

EditDeleteRightWord

Syntax   Procedure EditDeleteRightWord;

Usage   **EditDeleteRightWord** deletes the word to the right of the cursor. If the cursor is at the end of the line, the next line moves up and joins the current line.

EditDeleteTextRight

Syntax   Procedure EditDeleteTextRight;

Usage   **EditDeleteTextRight** deletes all text on the current line at the cursor position and to the right of it.

EditDelline

Syntax   Procedure EditDelline(Pl : Plinedesc);

Usage   **EditDelline** deletes the line descriptor from the line pointed to by **Pl**.

EditDestxtdes

Syntax   Procedure EditDestxtdes(Pl : Plinedesc);

Usage   **EditDestxtdes** deletes both the text line and the line descriptor of the line pointed to by **Pl**.

EditDownLine

Syntax   Procedure EditDownLine;

Usage   **EditDownLine** moves the cursor down one line in the window. If the cursor is on the last line, the text is scrolled up.

EditDownPage

Syntax   Procedure EditDownPage;

Usage   **EditDownPage** scrolls the text up by one page. A page consists of a full screen of text less one line.

EditEndLine

Syntax   Procedure EditEndLine;

Usage   **EditEndLine** moves the cursor to the end of the current line.

EditErrormsg

Syntax   Procedure EditErrormsg(Msgno : Byte);

Usage   **EditErrormsg** displays the error message corresponding to the number **Msgno**, clears the type-ahead buffer, and waits for a key to be pressed before it clears the command line.

EditExit

Syntax   Procedure EditExit;

Usage   **EditExit** terminates the editor, but it does not save any text.

EditFileRead

Syntax   Procedure EditFileRead(Fname : Varstring);

Usage   **EditFileRead** accepts a file's path and name in **Fname**, opens the file, and reads its contents into the current window.

EditFileWrite

Syntax   Procedure EditFileWrite(Fname : Varstring);

Usage   **EditFileWrite** saves the text in the current window to the file path and name specified in **Fname**.

EditFind

Syntax   Procedure EditFind;

Usage   **EditFind** prompts the user for a string to search for when performing either a **Find** command or **Search and Replace** command.

EditGenlineno

Syntax   Procedure EditGenlineno;

Usage   **EditGenlineno** computes the absolute line number for each window displayed. It does this by counting backwards until the beginning of the file is reached.

EditGotoColumn

Syntax   Procedure EditGotoColumn(Cno : Integer);

Usage   **EditGotoColumn** positions the cursor at column number **Cno**.

EditGotoLine

Syntax   Procedure EditGotoLine(Lno : Integer);

Usage   **EditGotoLine** positions the cursor at line number **Lno**.

EditHScroll

Syntax   Procedure EditHScroll;

Usage   **EditHScroll** scrolls text up and down to make sure that the line on which the cursor is located is always visible.

EditIncline

Syntax   Procedure EditIncline;

Usage   **EditIncline** increases the absolute line number for the current window.

EditInitialize

Syntax   Procedure EditInitialize;

Usage   **EditInitialize**, which initializes the editing environment, must be called before executing any other Editor Toolbox commands.

EditInsertCtrlChar

Syntax   Procedure EditInsertCtrlChar;

Usage   EditInsertCtrlChar accepts a character from the type-ahead buffer, converts the character to a control character, and inserts it into the text at the cursor position.

EditInsertLine

Syntax   Procedure EditInsertLine;

Usage   **EditInsertLine** inserts a blank line of text at the current cursor position.

EditJoinline

Syntax   Procedure EditJoinline;

Usage   **EditJoinline** takes the line below the cursor and appends it to the end of the current line.

EditJumpMarker

Syntax   Procedure EditJumpMarker(m : Byte);

Usage   **EditJumpMarker** positions the cursor at the location of text marker **m**.

EditK

Syntax   Procedure EditK;

Usage   **EditK** processes all CTRL-K commands. When a user presses CTRL-K, **EditK** waits for another key and calls the appropriate routine for that character.

EditLeftChar

Syntax   Procedure EditLeftChar;

Usage   **EditLeftChar** moves the cursor left one character. If the cursor is already in column one, no action is taken.

EditLeftWord

Syntax   Procedure EditLeftWord;

Usage   **EditLeftWord** moves the cursor to the beginning of the word to the left of the cursor. If the cursor is at the beginning of the line, the cursor moves to the last word on the previous line.

EditLongLine

Syntax   Procedure EditLongLine;

Usage   **EditLongLine**, which is called when reformatting text, removes all the text from a line that extends beyond the right margin.

EditMarkBlock

Syntax   Procedure EditMarkBlock;

Usage   **EditMarkBlock** defines a block of text by setting flags on all the lines from the beginning of the block to the end of the block.

EditNewLine

Syntax   Procedure EditNewLine;

Usage   **EditNewLine** inserts a blank line in the text stream but keeps the cursor on its original line.

EditO

Syntax   Procedure EditO;

Usage   **EditO** is called whenever the user presses CTRL-O. It waits for the user to press another key and then processes the appropriate routine.

EditOffBlock

Syntax   Procedure EditOffBlock;

Usage   If the block markers are found to be out of order, **EditOffBlock** resets the block flags for every line of text in the text stream.

EditPrccmd

Syntax   Procedure EditPrccmd(Ch : Byte);

Usage   **EditPrccmd** uses **Ch** to determine which Editor Toolbox command to execute.

EditPrctxt

Syntax   Procedure EditPrctxt(Ch : Byte);

Usage   **EditPrctxt** inserts **Ch** into the text stream at the current cursor position.

EditPushtbf

Syntax   Procedure EditPushtbf(Ch : Byte);

Usage   **EditPushtbf** places **Ch** at the head of the type-ahead buffer so that it will be the next character read.

EditQ

Syntax   Procedure EditQ;

Usage   **EditQ** is called when the user presses CTRL-Q. The procedure waits for the user to press another key, which determines the routine to execute.

EditRealign

Syntax   Procedure EditRealign;

Usage   When a line is inserted into or deleted from the text stream, **EditRealign** updates the line pointers for all windows.

EditReatxtfil

Syntax   Procedure EditReatxtfil(Fn : Varstring);

Usage   **EditReatxtfil** appends the file named in **Fn** to the text currently being edited.

EditReformat

Syntax   Procedure EditReformat;

Usage   **EditReformat** reformats the text stream so that each line fits within the set margins. Reformatting begins at the current cursor position and stops when it reaches either the end of the text stream or a line that is not word wrapped.

EditReplace

Syntax   Procedure EditReplace;

Usage   **EditReplace** searches for matches in the text stream, replacing the matches when found.

EditRightChar

Syntax   Procedure EditRightChar;

Usage   **EditRightChar** moves the cursor right one character.

EditRightWord

Syntax   Procedure EditRightWord;

Usage   **EditRightWord** moves the cursor right one word.

EditSchedule

Syntax   Procedure EditSchedule;

Usage   **EditSchedule** checks to see if a character from the keyboard is present in the type-ahead buffer. If so, the character is retrieved and processed. If not, the background processes continue to execute.

EditScrollDown

Syntax   Procedure EditScrollDown;

Usage   **EditScrollDown** scrolls text up one line.

EditScrollUp

Syntax   Procedure EditScrollUp;

Usage   **EditScrollUp** scrolls text down one line.

EditSetLeftMargin

Syntax   Procedure EditSetLeftMargin(No : Integer);

Usage   **EditSetLeftMargin** sets the left margin to column **No**.

EditSetMarker

Syntax   Procedure EditSetMarker(m : Byte);

Usage   **EditSetMarker** sets marker **m** to the current line.

EditSetRightMargin

Syntax   Procedure EditSetRightMargin(No : Integer);

Usage   **EditSetRightMargin** sets the right margin to column **No**.

EditSetUndoLimit

Syntax   Procedure EditSetUndoLimit(L : Integer);

Usage   **EditSetUndoLimit** sets the undo stack to a limit of **L** lines.

EditShiftLine

Syntax   Procedure EditShiftLine(Lp : Plinedesc);

Usage   **EditShiftLine** shifts text on a line specified by **Lp** so that the first character aligns with the left margin.

EditShortline

Syntax   Procedure EditShortline;

Usage   **EditShortline** removes text from the next line in the text stream and appends it to the current line so that the current line approaches the right margin limit.

EditSystem

Syntax   Procedure EditSystem;

Usage   **EditSystem** is the editor's main loop. It continuously calls **EditSchedule** until the variable **RunDown** is True, at which point the editor terminates.

EditTab

Syntax   Procedure EditTab;

Usage   **EditTab** moves the cursor to the next tab stop to the right. If the editor is in the Insert mode, spaces are inserted in the line and the text to the right of the cursor is moved to the right.

EditToggleAutoindent

Syntax   Procedure EditToggleAutoindent;

Usage   **EditToggleAutoindent** turns autoindent on and off.

EditToggleInsert

Syntax   Procedure EditToggleInsert;

Usage   **EditToggleInsert** turns Insert mode on and off.

EditToggleWordwrap

Syntax   Procedure EditToggleWordwrap;

Usage   **EditToggleWordwrap** turns the Word Wrap mode on and off.

EditTopBlock

Syntax   Procedure EditTopBlock;

Usage   **EditTopBlock** moves the cursor to the line at the top of the currently defined block.

EditUndo

Syntax   Procedure EditUndo;

Usage   **EditUndo** removes a line of text from the undo stack and inserts it in the text stream above the current line.

EditUpcase

Syntax   Procedure EditUpcase(Var s : Varstring);

Usage   **EditUpcase** converts all lowercase characters in s to uppercase characters.

EditUpdphyscr

Syntax   Procedure EditUpdphyscr;

Usage   EditUpdphyscr updates the computer screen, including all windows and the command line.

EditUpdrowasm

Syntax   Procedure EditUpdrowasm(R : Byte);

Usage   EditUpdrowasm updates the physical screen at row **R**. This procedure uses the **Move** command to write directly to video memory.

EditUpdwindow

Syntax   Procedure EditUpdwindow(W : Pwindesc);

Usage   EditUpdwindow updates the text and status line of window **W**.

EditUpdwinsl

Syntax   Procedure EditUpdwinsl(W : Pwindesc);

Usage   EditUpdwinsl updates the status line of window **W**.

EditUpLine

Syntax   Procedure EditUpLine;

Usage   EditUpLine moves the cursor up one line. If the cursor is at the top of the window, text scrolls down one line.

EditUpPage

Syntax   Procedure EditUpPage;

Usage   EditUpPage scrolls the text down one page.

EditUserpush

Syntax   Procedure EditUserpush(s : Varstring);

Usage   **EditUserpush** pushes **s** to the front of the type-ahead buffer. This is used when activating a macrocommand.

EditWindowBottomFile

Syntax   Procedure EditWindowBottomFile;

Usage   **EditWindowBottomFile** moves the cursor to the first column of the last line in the text stream.

EditWindowCreate

Syntax   Procedure EditWindowCreate(N : Byte; W : Byte);

Usage   **EditWindowCreate** creates window number **W**, which contains **N** lines.

EditWindowDelete

Syntax   Procedure EditWindowDelete(W : Byte);

Usage   **EditWindowDelete** deletes window **W**.

EditWindowDeleteText

Syntax   Procedure EditWindowDeleteText;

Usage   **EditWindowDeleteText** deletes all text from the current window and resets the filename.

EditWindowDown

Syntax   Procedure EditWindowDown;

Usage   **EditWindowDown** changes the current window to the window directly below.

EditWindowGoto

Syntax   Procedure EditWindowGoto(W : Byte);

Usage   **EditWindowGoto** makes window **W** the active window.

EditWindowLink

Syntax   Procedure EditWindowLink(Wto : Byte;Wfrom : Byte);

Usage   **EditWindowLink** replaces the text in window **Wto** with the text in **Wfrom**. An error is generated if both windows contain the same text stream.

EditWindowTopFile

Syntax   Procedure EditWindowTopFile;

Usage   **EditWindowTopFile** moves the cursor to the top of the text stream in the current window.

EditWindowUp

Syntax   Procedure EditWindowUp;

Usage   **EditWindowUp** changes the current window to the window directly above.

EditZapcmdnam

Syntax   Procedure EditZapcmdnam;

Usage   **EditZapcmdnam** clears the command line and sets the command line string to all spaces.

MoveFromScreen

Syntax   MoveFromScreen(Var Source, Dest; L : Integer);

Usage   **MoveFromScreen** moves **L** bytes from **Source** (video display memory) to **Dest**. If the Boolean variable **RetraceMode** is False, **MoveFromScreen** uses the Turbo Pascal **Move** command; if True, the procedure uses inline code to prevent snow on the screen.

MoveToScreen

Syntax   Procedure MoveToScreen(Var Source, Dest; L : Integer);

Usage   **MoveToScreen**, which refreshes the screen, moves **L** bytes from **Source** to **Dest** (video display memory). If the Boolean variable **RetraceMode** is False, **MoveToScreen** uses the Turbo Pascal **Move** command; if True, the procedure uses inline code to prevent snow on the screen.

PokeChr

Syntax   Procedure PokeChr(Ch : Char);

Usage   **PokeChr** places **Ch** on the end of the type-ahead buffer.

Editor Toolbox for Turbo Pascal Version 4.0

To coincide with the introduction of Turbo Pascal 4.0, Borland has updated the Editor Toolbox. While procedure and function calls remain unchanged for compatibility with your Version 3.0 programs, some of the code has been changed to make your programs run faster. For example, most inline code has been changed to external assembler files. Because the Editor Toolbox comes in unit format, you need compile it only once.

The MicroStar word processor has been completely re-written. It now includes print formatting, printer drivers, support for macros, up to six windows, context-sensitive help, and many other features that you would expect from a commercial-quality word processor.

In addition, Borland provides an editor written entirely in assembler. This editor is, in fact, the editor used in Turbo Pascal 3.0. To include this editor in your programs, simply link it with the **Uses** statement. Now you can include a real text editor in any program.

Numerical Methods Toolbox

Roots to Equations in One Variable
Interpolation
Numerical Differentiation
Numerical Integration
Matrix Routines
Eigenvalues and Eigenvectors
Initial Value and Boundary Value Methods
Least-Squares Approximation
Fast Fourier Transform Routines
Numerical Methods Toolbox for Turbo Pascal
 Version 4.0

Engineers, statisticians, mathematicians, and other number crunchers were among the first to appreciate the power of the computer. But transforming a mathematical formula into a usable computer program was no simple task. The Turbo Pascal Numerical Methods Toolbox provides a complete set of the most popular numerical algorithms. This chapter serves as a reference guide to the algorithms the Toolbox contains.

Roots to Equations in One Variable

Root of a Function Using the Bisection Method (BISECT.INC)

Description   Bisect calculates the root of the real continuous function contained in **TNTargetF**.

Syntax

```
Procedure Bisect (LeftEnd   : Real;
                  RightEnd  : Real;
                  Tol       : Real;
                  MaxIter   : Integer;
              Var Answer    : Real;
              Var fAnswer   : Real;
              Var Iter      : Integer;
              Var Error     : Byte);
```

Input Parameters

LeftEnd	Left end of the interval
RightEnd	Right end of the interval
Tol	Tolerance of solution
MaxIter	Maximum number of iterations

Output Parameters

Answer	Approximated root of **TNTargetF**
fAnswer	Value of function at approximated root
Iter	Number of iterations performed
Error	0 No error
	1 **Iter > MaxIter**
	2 Endpoints are of the same sign
	3 **LeftEnd > RightEnd**
	4 **Tol <= 0**
	5 **MaxIter < 0**

User-Defined Function

Function TNTargetF(x : Real) : Real;

Root of a Function Using the Newton-Raphson Method (RAPHSON.INC)

Description   Newton—Raphson determines the root of function **TNTargetF**. The function **TNDerivF** contains the derivative of the function in **TNTargetF**.

Syntax

```
Procedure Newton—Raphson (Guess    : Real;
                          Tol      : Real;
                          MaxIter  : Integer;
                      Var Root     : Real;
                      Var Value    : Real;
                      Var Deriv    : Real;
                      Var Iter     : Integer;
                      Var Error    : Byte);
```

Input Parameters

Guess   Approximation of root
Tol   Tolerance of solution
MaxIter   Maximum number of iterations

Output Parameters

Root   Approximated root
Value   Value of function at approximated root
Deriv   Value of derivative at approximated root
Iter   Number of iterations performed
Error   0   No error
            1   **Iter > MaxIter**
            2   Slope = 0
            3   **Tol <= 0**
            4   **MaxIter < 0**

User-Defined Function

Function TNTargetF(x : Real) : Real;
Function TNDerivF(x : Real) : Real;

Root of a Function Using the Secant Method (SECANT.INC)

Description   **Secant** calculates the root of function **TNTargetF** given two initial approximations.

Syntax

```
Procedure Secant (Guess1  : Real;
                  Guess2  : Real;
                  Tol     : Real;
                  MaxIter : Integer;
              Var Root    : Real;
              Var Value   : Real;
              Var Iter    : Integer;
              Var Error   : Byte);
```

Input Parameters

Guess1   First approximation of the root
Guess2   Second approximation of the root
Tol   Tolerance of solution
MaxIter   Maximum number of iterations

Output Parameters

Root   Approximated root
Value   Value of function at approximated root
Iter   Number of iterations performed
Error   0   No error
           1   **Iter > MaxIter**
           2   Slope = 0
           3   **Tol <= 0**
           4   **MaxIter < 0**

User-Defined Function

Function TNTargetF(x : Real) : Real;

Real Roots of a Real Polynomial Equation Using the Newton-Horner Method with Deflation (NEWTDEFL.INC)

Description   Newt_Horn_Defl uses an initial guess to estimate several roots of a user-specified polynomial.

Syntax

Procedure Newt—Horn—Defl(InitDegree : Integer;

	InitPoly	: TNvector;
	Guess	: Real;
	Tol	: Real;
	MaxIter	: Integer;
Var	Degree	: Integer;
Var	NumRoots	: Integer;
Var	Poly	: TNvector;
Var	Root	: TNvector;
Var	Imag	: TNvector;
Var	Value	: TNvector;
Var	Deriv	: TNvector;
Var	Iter	: TNIntVector;
Var	Error	: Byte);

Input Parameters

InitDegree	Degree of user-defined polynomial
InitPoly	Coefficients of user-defined polynomial
Guess	Initial approximation of root
Tol	Tolerance of solution
MaxIter	Maximum number of iterations

Output Parameters

Degree	Degree of the deflated polynomial
NumRoots	Number of approximated roots
Poly	Coefficients of deflated polynomial
Root	Real part of approximated roots
Imag	Imaginary part of all approximated roots
Value	Value of polynomial at each approximated root
Deriv	Value of the derivative at each approximated root
Iter	Number of iterations performed
Error	0 No error
	1 **Iter > MaxIter**
	2 Slope = 0

3	**Degree** <= 0
4	**Tol** <= 0
5	**MaxIter** < 0

User-Defined Types

TNvector = Array [0..TNArraySize] Of Real;
TNIntVector = Array [0..TNArraySize] Of Integer;

Complex Roots of a Complex Function Using Müller's Method (MULLER.INC)

Description   **Muller** approximates the complex root of function **TNTargetF**.

Syntax
Procedure Muller(Guess   : TNcomplex;
                 Tol   : Real;
                 MaxIter : Integer;
            Var Answer   : TNcomplex;
            Var yAnswer : TNcomplex;
            Var Iter   : Integer;
            Var Error   : Byte);

Input Parameters

Guess	Initial guess for root of complex function
Tol	Tolerance of solution
MaxIter	Maximum number of iterations

Output Parameters

Answer	Approximated root of function **TNTargetF**
yAnswer	Value of function **TNTargetF** at approximated root

Iter		Number of iterations performed
Error	0	No error
	1	**Iter > MaxIter**
	2	Parabola could not be formed
	3	**Tol <= 0**
	4	**MaxIter < 0**

User-Defined Type

TNComplex = Record
  Re,
  IM : Real;
  End;

User-Defined Function

Procedure TNTargetF(x : TNcomplex; Var y : TNcomplex);

Complex Roots of a Complex Polynomial Using Laguerre's Method and Deflation (LAGUERRE.INC)

Description   **Laguerre** finds the roots of a complex polynomial. The roots may be complex themselves.

Syntax

Procedure Laguerre(Var Degree   : Integer;
                   Var Poly   : TNCompVector;
                       InitGuess : TNcomplex;
                       Tol   : Real;
                       MaxIter : Integer;
                   Var NumRoots : Integer;
                   Var Roots   : TNCompVector;
                   Var yRoots   : TNCompVector;
                   Var Iter   : TNIntVector;
                   Var Error   : Byte);

Input Parameters

Degree	Degree of the polynomial
Poly	Coefficients of the polynomial
InitGuess	Initial guess at root of polynomial
Tol	Tolerance of solution
MaxIter	Maximum number of iterations

Output Parameters

Degree	Degree of the deflated polynomial	
Poly	Coefficients of the deflated polynomial	
NumRoots	Number of approximated roots	
Roots	Approximated roots of the polynomial	
yRoots	Value of the polynomial at the approximated root	
Iter	Number of iterations performed	
Error	0	No error
	1	**Iter > MaxIter**
	2	**Degree <= 0**
	3	**Tol <= 0**
	4	**MaxIter < 0**

User-Defined Types

```
TNcomplex = Record
    Re,
    Im : Real;
    End;

TNIntVector = Array [0..TNArraySize] Of Integer;
TNCompVector = Array [0..TNArraySize] Of TNcomplex;
```

Interpolation

Polynomial Interpolation Using
Lagrange's Method (LAGRANGE.INC)

Description   **Lagrange** computes a polynomial to fit data points x and y and interpolates the y data points for the x data points in **Xinter**.

Syntax

```
Procedure Lagrange(NumPoints : Integer;
                Var XData      : TNvector;
                Var YData      : TNvector;
                    NumInter   : Integer;
                Var XInter     : TNvector;
                Var YInter     : TNvector;
                Var Poly       : TNvector;
                Var Error      : Byte);
```

Input Parameters

NumPoints	Number of data points
XData	The x data points
YData	The y data points
NumInter	Number of interpolations desired
XInter	x data points at which interpolation is to take place

Output Parameters

YInter	Interpolated y data points

Poly   Coefficients of the interpolating poly-
               nomial
Error   0   No error
           1   Duplicates found among x data points
           2   **NumPoints** < 1

User-Defined Types

TNVector = Array [0..TNArraySize] Of Real;
TNMatrix = Array [0..TNArraySize] Of TNVector;

Interpolation Using Newton's Interpolary Divided-Difference Method (DIVDIF.INC)

Description   **Divided—Difference** interpolates y data
points for given x data points using arrays of x and y data
points.

Syntax
Procedure Divided—Difference(NumPoints : Integer;
                     Var XData   : TNvector;
                     Var YData   : TNvector;
                         NumInter   : Integer;
                     Var XInter   : TNvector;
                     Var YInter   : TNvector;
                     Var Error   : Byte);

Input Parameters

NumPoints   Number of data points
XData   The x data points
YData   The y data points
NumInter   The number of interpolations
XInter   The x data points at which interpolation
              is to take place

Output Parameters

YInter	The interpolated y data points	
Error	0	No error
	1	Duplicates found among x data points
	2	**NumPoints** < 1

User-Defined Types

TNVector = Array [0..TNArraySize] Of Real;
TNMatrix = Array [0..TNArraySize] Of TNVector;

Free Cubic Spline Interpolation (CUBE—FRE.INC)

Description   **CubicSplineFree** produces a smooth curve through a set of data points.

Syntax
Procedure CubicSplineFree (NumPoints : Integer;

	Var XData	: TNvector;
	Var YData	: TNvector;
	NumInter	: Integer;
	Var XInter	: TNvector;
	Var Coef0	: TNvector;
	Var Coef1	: TNvector;
	Var Coef2	: TNvector;
	Var Coef3	: TNvector;
	Var YInter	: TNvector;
	Var Error	: Byte);

Input Parameters

NumPoints	Number of data points
XData	The x data points
YData	The y data points

NumInter	The number of interpolations
XInter	The x data points at which interpolation is to take place

Output Parameters

Coef0	Coefficient of the constant term
Coef1	Coefficient of the linear term
Coef2	Coefficient of the squared term
Coef3	Coefficient of the cubed term
YInter	Interpolated y data points
Error	0 No error
	1 Duplicate x values found
	2 x values not in ascending order
	3 **NumPoints** < 2

User-Defined Type

TNvector = Array[0..TNArraySize] Of Real;

Clamped Cubic Spline Interpolation (CUBE—CLA.INC)

Description   **CubicSplineClamped** produces a series of interpolated y data points for given x data points. The resulting x and y data points create a smooth curve through the original x and y data points. The line is continuous and the first and second derivatives are also continuous.

Syntax

```
Procedure CubicSplineClamped(NumPoints : Integer;
                Var XData      : TNvector;
                Var YData      : TNvector;
                    DerivLE    : Real;
                    DerivRE    : Real;
                    NumInter   : Integer;
```

```
                    Var XInter    : TNvector;
                    Var Coef0     : TNvector;
                    Var Coef1     : TNvector;
                    Var Coef2     : TNvector;
                    Var Coef3     : TNvector;
                    Var YInter    : TNvector;
                    Var Error     : Byte);
```

Input Parameters

NumPoints	Number of data points
XData	The x data points
YData	The y data points
DerivLE	Derivative of the function at the left endpoint
DerivRE	Derivative of the function at the right endpoint
NumInter	Number of y data points to interpolate
XInter	The x data points at which interpolation is to take place

Output Parameters

Coef0	Coefficient of the constant term	
Coef1	Coefficient of the linear term	
Coef2	Coefficient of the squared term	
Coef3	Coefficient of the cubed term	
YInter	Interpolated values	
Error	0	No error
	1	Duplicates found among x data points
	2	x data points not in ascending order
	3	**NumPoints** < 2

User-Defined Type

TNvector = Array [0..TNArraySize] Of Real;

Numerical Differentiation

First Differentiation Using Two-Point, Three-Point, or Five-Point Formulas (DERIV.INC)

Description   **First__Derivative** approximates the first derivative of function $y = f(x)$ using an array of x data points and an array of y data points.

Syntax
```
Procedure First__Derivative (NumPoints : Integer;
                    Var  XData      : TNvector;
                    Var  YData      : TNvector;
                         Point      : Byte;
                         NumDeriv  : Integer;
                    Var  XDeriv     : TNvector;
                    Var  YDeriv     : TNvector;
                    Var  Error      : Byte);
```

Input Parameters

NumPoints	Number of data points
XData	The x data points
YData	The y data points
Point	Number of points. Must equal 2, 3, or 5
NumDeriv	Number of points at which the derivative is to be approximated
XDeriv	The x data points at which the derivative is to be approximated

Output Parameters

YDeriv		The y data points approximated for each x data point in **XDeriv**
Error	0	No error
	1	Not all derivatives were computed
	2	Duplicates found among x data points

3   x data points not in ascending order
4   Insufficient data
5   **Point** is not equal to 2, 3, or 5
6   x data points not evenly spaced for
      five-point formula

User-Defined Type

TNvector = Array [1..TNArraySize] Of Real;

Second Differentiation Using Three-Point or Five-Point Formulas (DERIV2.INC)

Description   **Second—Derivative** approximates the second derivative of function $y = f(x)$.

Syntax

```
Procedure Second—Derivative(NumPoints : Integer;
                Var XData      : TNvector;
                Var YData      : TNvector;
                    Point      : Byte;
                    NumDeriv   : Integer;
                Var XDeriv     : TNvector;
                Var YDeriv     : TNvector;
                Var Error      : Byte);
```

Input Parameters

NumPoints	Number of data points
XData	The x data points
YData	The y data points
Point	Number of points. Must be 3 or 5
NumDeriv	Number of points at which the derivative is to be approximated
XDeriv	The x data points at which the approximation is to take place

Output Parameters

YDeriv	The y data points approximated using the x data points in **XDeriv**	
Error	0	No error
	1	Not all derivatives were computed
	2	Duplicates found among x data points
	3	x data points not in ascending order
	4	Insufficient data
	5	**Point** is not equal to 3 or 5
	6	x data points not evenly spaced

User-Defined Type
TNvector = Array[1..TNArraySize] Of Real;

Differentiation with a Cubic
Spline Interpolant (INTERDRV.INC)

Description   Interpolate—Derivative approximates the first and second derivatives of a function y = f(x).

Syntax
Procedure Interpolate—Derivative (NumPoints : Integer;
                      Var XData   : TNvector;
                      Var YData   : TNvector;
                           NumDeriv : Integer;
                      Var XDeriv   : TNvector;
                      Var YInter   : TNvector;
                      Var YDeriv   : TNvector;
                      Var YDeriv2   : TNvector;
                      Var Error   : Byte);

Input Parameters

NumPoints	The number of data points
XData	The x data points
YData	The y data points

NumDeriv   The number of x points at which the
                 derivative is to be approximated
XDeriv   The x data points at which derivatives
                 will be approximated

Output Parameters

YInter   The approximated y values corresponding
                 to the x data points in **XDeriv**
YDeriv   The approximation to the first derivative at
                 the x data points in **XDeriv**
YDeriv2   The approximation to the second derivative
                 at the x data points in **XDeriv**
Error   0   No error
             1   Duplicates found among x data points
             2   x data points not in ascending order
             3   **NumPoints** < 2

User-Defined Type

TNvector = Array[1..TNArraySize] Of Real;

Differentiation of a User-Defined Function (DERIVFN.INC)

Description   **FirstDerivative** uses a set of x data points to
approximate the first derivative for the function y = f(x).

Syntax
```
Procedure FirstDerivative(NumDeriv :  Integer;
                      Var XDeriv   :  TNvector;
                      Var YDeriv   :  TNvector;
                          Tolerance :  Real;
                      Var Error    :  Byte);
```

Input Parameters

NumDeriv Number of points at which the derivative is
                 to be approximated

XDeriv   The x data points at which the derivative is
            to be approximated
Tolerance The accuracy of the solution

Output Parameters

YDeriv   Approximation to the first derivative at the
            x data points in **XDeriv**
Error   0   No error
          1   **Tolerance** $<$ **TNNearlyZero**

User-Defined Function

Function TNTarget(x : Real) : Real;

User-Defined Type

TNvector = Array[1..TNArraySize] Of Real;

Second Differentiation of a User-Defined Function (DERIV2FN.INC)

Description   **SecondDerivative** uses an array of x data
points to approximate the second derivative of a function y =
f(x).

Syntax
Procedure SecondDerivative(NumDeriv :   Integer;
                        Var XDeriv   :   TNvector;
                        Var YDeriv   :   TNvector;
                        Tolerance   :   Real;
                        Var Error   :   Byte);

Input Parameters

NumDeriv Number of points used to approximate the
            derivative

XDeriv   The x data points used to approximate the derivative

Tolerance   The accuracy of the solution

Output Parameters

YDeriv   Approximation to the second derivative of the x data points in **XDeriv**

Error   0   No error

           1   **Tolerance $<$ TNNearlyZero**

User-Defined Function

Function TNTargetF(x : Real) : Real;

User-Defined Type

TNvector = Array[1..TNArraySize] Of Real;

Numerical Integration

Integration Using Simpson's Composite Algorithm (SIMPSON.INC)

Description   **Simpson** computes the integral for the user-defined function using a range of **LowerLimit** to **UpperLimit**.

Syntax

```
Procedure Simpson(LowerLimit    : Real;
                  UpperLimit    : Real;
                  NumIntervals  : Integer;
             Var Integral       : Real;
             Var Error          : Byte);
```

Input Parameters

LowerLimit   Lower limit of integration
UpperLimit   Upper limit of integration
NumIntervals   Number of intervals used in approx-
                          imation

Output Parameters

Integral   Approximation of the integral function
Error   0   No error
               1   **NumIntervals** < 1

User-Defined Function

Function TNTargetF(x : Real) : Real;

Integration Using the Trapezoid Composite Rule (TRAPZOID.INC)

Description   **Trapezoid** computes the integral for the user-defined function using a range of **LowerLimit** to **UpperLimit**.

Syntax
Procedure Trapezoid(LowerLimit   : Real;
                            UpperLimit   : Real;
                            NumIntervals   : Integer;
                   Var Integral   : Real;
                   Var Error   : Byte);

Input Parameters

LowerLimit   Lower limit of integration
UpperLimit   Upper limit of integration
NumIntervals   Number of intervals used in approx-
                          imation

Output Parameters

Integral	Approximated integral of the function
Error	0 No error
	1 **NumIntervals** $<= 0$

User-Defined Function

Function TNTargetF(x : Real) : Real;

Integration Using Adaptive Quadrature and Simpson's Rule (ADAPSIMP.INC)

Description   **Adaptive—Simpson** approximates the integral of a function and allows the user to specify the level of accuracy desired by setting the value of **Tolerance**.

Syntax

```
Procedure Adaptive—Simpson(LowerLimit    : Real;
                           UpperLimit    : Real;
                           Tolerance     : Real;
                           MaxIntervals  : Integer;
                       Var Integral      : Real;
                       Var NumIntervals  : Integer;
                       Var Error         : Byte);
```

Input Parameters

LowerLimit	Lower limit of integration
UpperLimit	Upper limit of integration
Tolerance	Accuracy of the solution
MaxIntervals	The maximum number of intervals allowed

Output Parameters

Integral	The approximated integral of the function

NumIntervals   The actual number of intervals used

Error

	0	No error
	1	**Tolerance** <= 0
	2	**MaxIntervals** <= 0
	3	**NumIntervals** >= **MaxIntervals**

User-Defined Function

Function TNTargetF(x : Real) : Real;

Integration Using Adaptive Quadrature and Gaussian Quadrature (ADAPGAUS.INC)

Description   **Adaptive_Gauss_Quadrature** approximates the integral of function y = f(x) over a specified interval.

Syntax
Procedure
Adaptive_Gauss_Quadrature(LowerLimit   : Real;
                                UpperLimit   : Real;
                                Tolerance   : Real;
                                MaxIntervals   : Integer;
                     Var Integral   : Real;
                     Var NumIntervals : Integer;
                     Var Error   : Byte);

Input Parameters

LowerLimit	Lower limit of integration
UpperLimit	Upper limit of integration
Tolerance	Accuracy of the result
MaxIntervals	The maximum number of intervals to use

Output Parameters

Integral	The approximated integral of the function
NumIntervals	The maximum number of intervals used
Error	0 No error
	1 **Tolerance** $\leq$ **0**
	2 **MaxIntervals** $\leq$ **0**
	3 **NumIntervals** $\geq$ **MaxIntervals**

User-Defined Function

Function TNTargetF(x : Real) : Real;

Integration Using the Romberg Algorithm (ROMBERG.INC)

Description   **Romberg** approximates the integral of
TNTargetF.

Syntax

```
Procedure Romberg(LowerLimit   :  Real;
                  UpperLimit   :  Real;
                  Tolerance    :  Real;
                  MaxIter      :  Integer;
              Var Integral     :  Real;
              Var Iter         :  Integer;
              Var Error        :  Byte);
```

Input Parameters

LowerLimit	Lower limit of integration
UpperLimit	Upper limit of integration
Tolerance	Accuracy of solution
MaxIter	The maximum number of iterations allowed

Output Parameters

Integral	The approximated integral of function f(x)
Iter	The number of iterations performed
Error	0 No error
	1 **Tolerance** $<= 0$
	2 **MaxIntervals** $<= 0$
	3 **Iter** $>=$ **MaxIter**

User-Defined Function

Function TNTargetF(x : Real) : Real;

Matrix Routines

Determinant of a Matrix (DET.INC)

Description   **Determinant** computes the determinant of an N $\times$ N matrix.

Syntax

```
Procedure Determinant(Dimen :   Integer;
                      Data   :   TNmatrix;
                  Var Det    :   Real;
                  Var Error  :   Byte);
```

Input Parameters

Dimen	The dimension of the data points
Data	The square matrix

Output Parameters

Det	Determinant of the data matrix
Error	0 No error
	1 **Dimen** < 1

User-Defined Types

TNvector = Array[1..TNArraySize] Of Real;
TNmatrix = Array[1..TNArraySize] Of TNvector;

Inverse of a Matrix (INVERSE.INC)

Description   **Inverse** produces the inverse of an N × N matrix.

Syntax

```
Procedure Inverse(Dimen  :  Integer;
                  Data   :  TNmatrix;
             Var Inv     :  TNmatrix;
             Var Error   :  Byte);
```

Input Parameters

Dimen   Dimension of the data matrix
Data   The elements of the square matrix

Output Parameters

Inv	The inverse of the data matrix	
Error	0	No error
	1	**Dimen** < 1
	2	No inverse exists

User-Defined Types

TNvector = Array[1..TNArraySize] Of Real;
TNmatrix = Array[1..TNArraySize] Of Real;

Solving a System of Linear Equations with Gaussian Elimination (GAUSELIM.INC)

Description   Gaussian—Elimination produces the solution to a system of N linear equations.

Syntax

```
Procedure
Gaussian—Elimination(Dimen          : Integer;
                    Coefficients    : TNmatrix;
                    Constants       : TNvector;
                Var Solution        : TNvector;
                Var Error           : Byte);
```

Input Parameters

Dimen	Dimension of the coefficients matrix
Coefficients	The square matrix containing the co-efficients of the equation
Constants	The constant term of each equation

Output Parameters

Solution	Solution to the set of equations	
Error	0	No errors
	1	**Dimen** < 1
	2	Coefficients matrix is singular; no unique solution exists

User-Defined Types

TNvector = Array[1..TNArraySize] Of Real;
TNmatrix = Array[1..TNArraySize] Of TNvector

Solving a System of Linear Equations with Gaussian Elimination and Partial Pivoting (PARTPIVT.INC)

Description   **Partial—Pivoting** produces the solution to a system of N $\times$ N linear equations.

Syntax

Procedure

Partial—Pivoting(Dimen	:	Integer;
Coefficients	:	TNmatrix;
Constants	:	TNvector;
Var Solution	:	TNvector;
Var Error	:	Byte);

Input Parameters

Dimen	Dimension of the coefficients matrix
Coefficients	The square matrix containing the coefficients of the equations
Constants	The constant term of each equation

Output Parameters

Solution	Solution to the set of equations
Error	0 No error
	1 **Dimen** < 1
	2 Coefficients matrix is singular; no unique solution exists

User-Defined Types

TNvector = Array[1..TNArraySize] Of Real;
TNmatrix = Array[1..TNArraySize] Of TNvector;

Solving a System of Linear Equations with Direct Factoring (DIRFACT.INC)

Description   To solve a system of N linear expressions using direct factoring, two Numerical Toolbox procedures are used: **LU—Decompose** and **LU—Solve**. **LU—Decompose** decomposes the matrix into an upper and lower triangle. **LU—Solve** then solves the linear equations.

Syntax
Procedure
LU—Decompose(Dimen   :   Integer;
            Coefficients   :   TNmatrix;
        Var Decomp   :   TNmatrix;
        Var Permute   :   TNmatrix;
        Var Error   :   Byte);

Input Parameters

Dimen   Dimension of the coefficients matrix
Coefficients   Square matrix containing the coefficients of the equations

Output Parameters

Decomp   The LU decomposition of the coefficients matrix
Permute   A permutation matrix that records the effects of pivoting
Error   0   No error
               1   **Dimen** < 1
               2   The coefficients matrix is singular

User-Defined Types

TNvector = Array[1..TNArraySize] Of Real;
TNmatrix = Array[1..TNArraySize] Of TNvector;

Syntax
Procedure LU—Solve(Dimen   :   Integer;

```
          Var Decomp    :  TNmatrix;
              Constants  :  TNvector;
          Var Permute    :  TNmatrix;
          Var Solution   :  TNvector;
          Var Error      :  Byte);
```

Input Parameters

Dimen   Dimension of the coefficients matrix

Decomp   The lower and upper triangle decompo-
                 sition of the coefficients matrix

Constants   The constant terms of each equation

Permute   A permutation matrix that records the
                 effects of pivoting

Output Parameters

Solution   Solution to each system of equations

Error   0   No error

              1   **Dimen** < 1

User-Defined Types

TNvector = Array[1..TNArraySize] Of Real;
TNmatrix = Array[1..TNArraySize] Of TNvector;

Solving a System of Linear Equations with the Iterative Gauss-Seidel Method (GAUSSIDL.INC)

Description   Gauss_Seidel produces the solution to N linear equations in N unknowns.

Syntax

Procedure

Gauss—Seidel(Dimen   :   Integer;

          Coefficients   :   TNmatrix;

          Constants   :   TNvector;

          Tol   :   Real;

          MaxIter   :   Integer;

    Var Solution   :   TNvector;

    Var Iter   :   Integer;

    Var Error   :   Byte);

Input Parameters

Dimen	Dimension of the coefficients matrix
Coefficients	The square matrix containing the co-efficients of the equations
Constants	The constant terms of the equation
Tol	The tolerance of the solution
MaxIter	The maximum number of iterations allowed

Output Parameters

Solution		Solution to the set of equations
Iter		The number of iterations performed
Error	0	No error
	1	**Iter** > **MaxIter** and matrix is not diagonally dominant
	2	**Iter** > **MaxIter** and matrix is diagonally dominant
	3	**Dimen** < 1
	4	**Tol** <= 0
	5	**MaxIter** < 0
	6	Zero on the diagonal of the matrix of coefficients
	7	Sequence is diverging

User-Defined Types

TNvector = Array[1..TNArraySize] Of Real;
TNmatrix = Array[1..TNArraySize] Of TNvector;

Eigenvalues and Eigenvectors

Real Dominant Eigenvalue and Eigenvector of a Real Matrix Using the Power Method (POWER.INC)

Description   **Power** calculates a matrix's dominant eigenvalue and its associated eigenvector.

Syntax

Procedure Power(Dimen   : Integer;
            Var Mat   : Nmatrix;
            Var GuessVector   : TNvector;
                MaxIter   : Integer;
                Tolerance   : Real;
            Var Eigenvalue   : Real;
            Var Eigenvector   : TNvector;
            Var Iter   : Integer;
            Var Error   : Byte);

Input Parameters

Dimen	Dimension of matrix **Mat**
Mat	The matrix
GuessVector	Initial approximation to the eigenvector
MaxIter	The maximum number of iterations allowed
Tolerance	The accuracy of the solution

Output Parameters

Eigenvalue	Approximation of the matrix's dominant eigenvalue
Eigenvector	Approximation of the dominant eigenvalue's eigenvector
Iter	The number of iterations performed
Error	0 No error
	1 **Dimen** $<=$ 1
	2 **Tolerance** $<=$ 0
	3 **MaxIter** $<=$ 0
	4 **Iter** $>=$ **MaxIter**

User-Defined Types

```
TNvector = Array[1..TNArraySize] Of Real;
TNmatrix = Array[1..TNArraySize] Of TNvector;
```

Real Eigenvalue and Eigenvector of a Real Matrix Using the Inverse Power Method (INVPOWER.INC)

Description   **InversePower** converges to the eigenvalue closest to a value supplied by the user.

Syntax

```
Procedure
InversePower(Dimen        : Integer;
             Mat          : TNmatrix;
         Var GuessVector  : TNvector;
             ClosestVal   : Real;
             MaxIter      : Integer;
             Tolerance    : Real;
         Var Eigenvalue   : Real;
         Var Eigenvector  : TNvector;
         Var Iter         : Integer;
         Var Error        : Byte);
```

Input Parameters

Dimen	Dimension of matrix **Mat**
Mat	The matrix
GuessVector	The initial estimate of the eigenvector
ClosestVal	The approximate eigenvalue
MaxIter	The maximum number of iterations allowed
Tolerance	The accuracy of the solution

Output Parameters

Eigenvalue	Approximation of the eigenvalue closest to **ClosestVal**
Eigenvector	The approximated eigenvector associated with eigenvalue
Iter	The number of iterations performed
Error	0 No error
	1 **Dimen** $<= 1$
	2 **Tolerance** $<= 0$
	3 **MaxIter** $<= 0$
	4 **Iter** $>=$ **MaxIter**
	5 **Eigenvalue/Eigenvector** not calculated

User-Defined Types

TNvector = Array[1..TNArraySize] Of Real;
TNmatrix = Array[1..TNArraySize] Of TNvector;

Real Eigenvalues and Eigenvectors of a Real Matrix Using the Power Method and Wielandt's Deflation (WIELANDT.INC)

Description   Wielandt approximates each eigenvalue and the associated eigenvector of a matrix.

Syntax

Procedure Wielandt(Dimen   : Integer;
                       Mat   : TNmatrix;

```
        Var  GuessVector   : TNvector;
             MaxEigens     : Integer;
             MaxIter       : Integer;
             Tolerance     : Real;
        Var  NumEigens     : Integer;
        Var  Eigenvalues   : TNvector;
        Var  Eigenvectors  : TNmatrix;
        Var  Iter          : TNIntVector;
        Var  Error         : Byte);
```

Input Parameters

Dimen	Dimension of the matrix **Mat**
Mat	The matrix
GuessVector	Initial estimate of the eigenvector
MaxEigens	The number of eigenvalues and eigenvectors to find
MaxIter	The maximum number of iterations allowed
Tolerance	The accuracy of the solution

Output Parameters

NumEigens	The number of eigenvectors returned	
Eigenvalues	The first **NumEigens** eigenvalues of the matrix	
Eigenvectors	The eigenvectors associated with each eigenvalue	
Iter	The number of iterations performed	
Error	0	No error
	1	**Dimen** $<= 1$
	2	**Tolerance** $<= 0$
	3	**MaxIter** $<= 0$
	4	**MaxEigens** $<= 0$, **MaxEigens** $>$ **Dimen**
	5	**Iter** $>=$ **MaxIter**
	6	The last two eigenvalues are not real

User-Defined Types

TNvector = Array[1..TNArraySize] Of Real;
TNmatrix = Array[1..TNArraySize] Of TNvector;
TNIntVector = Array[1..TNArraySize] Of Integer;

The Complete Eigensystem of a Symmetric Real Matrix Using the Cyclic Jacobi Method (JACOBI.INC)

Description   **Jacobi** estimates the eigensystem for a symmetric matrix.

Syntax

```
Procedure Jacobi(Dimen        : Integer;
                 Mat          : TNmatrix;
                 MaxIter      : Integer;
                 Tolerance    : Real;
             Var Eigenvalues  : TNvector;
             Var Eigenvectors : TNmatrix;
             Var Iter         : Integer;
             Var Error        : Byte);
```

Input Parameters

Dimen	Dimension of matrix **Mat**
Mat	The matrix
MaxIter	The maximum number of iterations allowed
Tolerance	The accuracy of the solution

Output Parameters

Eigenvalues	Approximated eigenvalues of the matrix
Eigenvectors	The eigenvectors associated with the eigenvalues
Iter	The number of iterations performed

Error	0	No error
	1	**Dimen** <= 1
	2	**Tolerance** <= 0
	3	**MaxIter** <= 0
	4	**Mat** is not symmetric
	5	**Iter** >= **MaxIter**

User-Defined Types

TNvector = Array[1..TNArraySize] Of Real;
TNmatrix = Array[1..TNArraySize] Of TNvector;

Initial Value and Boundary Value Methods

Solution to an Initial Value Problem for a First-Order Ordinary Differential Equation Using the Runge-Kutta Method (RUNGE—1.INC)

Description   **InitialCond1stOrder** computes the approximate solution for a first-order ordinary differential equation with a specified initial condition.

Syntax

```
Procedure InitialCond1stOrder(LowerLimit    : Real;
                              UpperLimit    : Real;
                              XInitial      : Real;
                              NumReturn     : Integer;
                              NumIntervals  : Integer;
                          Var TValues       : TNvector;
                          Var XValues       : TNvector;
                          Var Error         : Byte);
```

Input Parameters

LowerLimit   Lower limit of interval
UpperLimit   Upper limit of interval

XInitial   Value of x at lower limit
NumReturn   Number of (t,x) pairs returned from the
                          procedure
NumIntervals   Number of subintervals used in the calcu-
                          lations

Output Parameters

TValues   Values of t between the limits
XValues   Values of x approximated at the values in
                          TValues
Error   0   No error
                1   **NumReturn** $<$ 1
                2   **NumIntervals** $<$ **NumReturn**
                3   **LowerLimit** = **UpperLimit**

User-Defined Function

TNTargetF(t, x : Real) : Real;

User-Defined Type

TNvector = Array[1..TNArraySize] Of Real;

Solution to an Initial Value Problem for a First-Order Ordinary Differential Equation Using the Runge-Kutta-Fehlberg Method (RKF—1.INC)

Description   **RungeKuttaFehlberg** approximates a solution to a first-order ordinary differential equation within a
specified tolerance. The equation must have a specified
initial condition.

Syntax
Procedure RungeKuttaFehlberg(LowerLimit : Real;
                                        UpperLimit : Real;
                                        XInitial   : Real;

```
                              Tolerance    : Real;
                              NumReturn  : Integer;
                    Var  TValues       : TNvector;
                    Var  XValues       : TNvector;
                    Var  Error         : Byte);
```

Input Parameters

LowerLimit	Lower limit of interval
UpperLimit	Upper limit of interval
XInitial	Value of x at **LowerLimit**
Tolerance	Accuracy of solution
NumReturn	Number of (t,x) values to be returned

Output Parameters

TValues	Values of t at which x was approximated	
XValues	Approximated values of x at the values in **TValues**	
Error	0	No error
	1	**Tolerance** ≤ 0
	2	**NumReturn** ≤ 0
	3	**LowerLimit** = **UpperLimit**
	4	**Tolerance** not reached

User-Defined Function

TNTargetF(t, x : Real) : Real;

User-Defined Type

TNvector = Array[1..TNArraySize] Of Real;

Solution to an Initial Value Problem for a First-Order Ordinary Differential Equation Using the Adams-Bashforth/Adams-Moulton Predictor/Corrector Scheme (ADAMS—1.INC)

Description   **Adams** approximates the solution to a first-order ordinary differential equation with a specified initial condition.

Syntax

```
Procedure Adams( LowerLimit    : Real;
                 UpperLimit    : Real;
                 XInitial      : Real;
                 NumReturn     : Integer;
                 NumIntervals  : Integer;
            Var  TValues       : TNvector;
            Var  XValues       : TNvector;
            Var  Error         : Byte);
```

Input Parameters

LowerLimit   Lower limit of interval
UpperLimit   Upper limit of interval
XInitial   Initial value of x at **LowerLimit**
NumReturn   Number of (t,x) values to be returned
NumIntervals Number of subintervals to be used in calculations

Output Parameters

TValues   Values of t between the limits
XValues   Values of x approximated at values in **TValues**

Error	0	No error
	1	**NumReturn** < 1
	2	**NumIntervals** $<$ **NumReturn**
	3	**LowerLimit** $=$ **UpperLimit**

User-Defined Function

TNTargetF(t, x : Real) : Real;

User-Defined Type

TNvector = Array[1..TNArraySize] Of Real;

Solution to an Initial Value Problem for a Second-Order Ordinary Differential Equation Using the Runge-Kutta Method (RUNGE—2.INC)

Description   **InitialCond2ndOrder** computes the solution to a second-order ordinary differential equation with a specified initial condition.

Syntax

```
Procedure InitialCond2ndOrder(LowerLimit     : Real;
                              UpperLimit     : Real;
                              InitialValue   : Real;
                              InitialDeriv   : Real;
                              NumReturn      : Integer;
                              NumIntervals   : Integer;
                          Var TValues        : TNvector;
                          Var XValues        : TNvector;
                          Var XDerivValues   : TNvector;
                          Var Error          : Byte);
```

Input Parameters

LowerLimit   Lower limit of interval
UpperLimit   Upper limit of interval

InitialValue   Initial value of x at **LowerLimit**
InitialDeriv   Derivative of x at **LowerLimit**
NumReturn   Number of (t,x) values to be returned
NumIntervals Number of subintervals used in calculations

Output Parameters

TValues   Values of t between the limits
XValues   Values of x approximated using values in
           TValues
XDerivValues The first derivative of approximated x
           values
Error   0   No Error
            1   **NumReturn** $<$ 1
            2   **NumIntervals** $<$ **NumReturn**
            3   **LowerLimit** $=$ **UpperLimit**

User-Defined Function

TNTargetF(t, x, xprime : Real) : Real;

User-Defined Type

TNvector $=$ Array[1..TNArraySize] Of Real;

Solution to an Initial Value Problem for an nth-Order Ordinary Differential Equation Using the Runge-Kutta Method (RUNGE—N.INC)

Description   **InitialCondition** integrates an nth-order ordinary differential equation with specified initial conditions.

Syntax
Procedure InitialCondition(Order   : Integer;
                              LowerLimit   : Real;
                              UpperLimit   : Real;

```
                        InitialValues   : TNvector;
                        NumReturn       : Integer;
                        NumIntervals    : Integer;
                Var     SolutionValues  : TNmatrix;
                Var     Error           : Byte);
```

Input Parameters

Order	Order of the differential equation
LowerLimit	Lower limit of interval
UpperLimit	Upper limit of interval
InitialValues	Initial value of x and its derivatives at **LowerLimit**
NumReturn	Number of t and x values returned from the procedure
NumIntervals	Number of subintervals used in the calculations

Output Parameters

SolutionValues		Values of t, x, and the derivatives of x between the limits
Error	0	No error
	1	**NumReturn** < 1
	2	**NumIntervals** $<$ **NumReturn**
	3	**Order** < 1
	4	**LowerLimit** $=$ **UpperLimit**

User-Defined Function

TNTargetF(V : TNVector) : Real;
where
    V[0] is t;
    V[1] is x;
    V[2] is the first derivative of x;
    V[3] is the second derivative of x;
and so forth

User-Defined Types

TNvector = Array[1..TNRowSize] Of Real;
TNmatrix = Array[1..TNColumnSize] Of TNvector;

Solution to an Initial Value Problem for a System of Coupled First-Order Ordinary Differential Equations Using the Runge-Kutta Method (RUNGE—S1.INC)

Description   **InitialConditionSystem** integrates a system of first-order ordinary differential equations with specified initial conditions.

Syntax

Procedure InitialConditionSystem(NumEquations : Integer;
                             LowerLimit   : Real;
                             UpperLimit   : Real;
                             InitialValues : TNvector;
                             NumReturn   : Integer;
                             NumIntervals : Integer;
                         Var SolutionValues : TNmatrix;
                         Var Error   : Byte);

Input Parameters

NumEquations	Number of first-order differential equations
LowerLimit	Lower limit of interval
UpperLimit	Upper limit of interval
InitialValues	Initial values of x at **LowerLimit**
NumReturn	Number of t and x values to be returned
NumIntervals	Number of subintervals to be used in calculations

Output Parameters

SolutionValues	Values of t and x between the limits

Error: 0   No error
                1   **NumReturn** < 1
                2   **NumIntervals** < **NumReturn**
                3   **NumEquations** < 1
                4   **LowerLimit** = **UpperLimit**

User-Defined Functions

One function for each differential equation:
    TNTargetF1(V : TNVector) : Real;
    TNTargetF2(V : TNVector) : Real;

.

.

.

    TNTargetFN(V : TNVector) : Real;

User-Defined Types

TNvector = Array[1..TNRowSize] Of Real;
TNmatrix = Array[1..TNColumnSize] Of TNvector;

Solution to an Initial Value Problem for a System of Coupled Second-Order Ordinary Differential Equations Using the Runge-Kutta Method (RUNGE—S2.INC)

Description   **InitialConditionSystem2** integrates a system of second-order ordinary differential equations with specified initial conditions.

Syntax
Procedure InitialConditionSystem2(NumEquations : Integers
                        LowerLimit   : Real;
                        UpperLimit   : Real;
                        InitialValues : TNvector;
                        NumReturn   : Integer;
                        NumIntervals   : Integer;
                Var   SolutionValues : TNmatrix;
                Var   Error   : Byte);

Input Parameters

NumEquations	Number of second-order differential equations
LowerLimit	Lower limit of interval
UpperLimit	Upper limit of interval
InitialValues	Values of x and the first derivative of x at **LowerLimit**
NumReturn	Number of values of t, x, and the first derivative of x to be returned
NumIntervals	The number of subintervals to be used in the calculations

Output Parameters

SolutionValues		Values of t, x, and the first derivative of x between the limits
Error	0	No error
	1	**NumReturn** < 1
	2	**NumIntervals** $<$ **NumReturn**
	3	**NumEquations** < 1
	4	**LowerLimit** $=$ **UpperLimit**

User-Defined Functions

One function for each differential equation used:

  Function TNTargetF1(V : TNvector) : Real;

  Function TNTargetF2(V : TNvector) : Real;

        .

        .

        .

  Function TNTargetFN(V : TNvector) : Real;

User-Defined Types

```
TNData = Record
   x : Real;
   xDeriv : Real;
   End;
TNvector = Array[0..TNRowSize] Of TNData;
TNmatrix = Array[0..TNColumnSize] Of TNvector;
```

Solutions to a Boundary Value Problem for a Second-Order Ordinary Differential Equation Using the Shooting and Runge-Kutta Methods (SHOOT2.INC)

Description   **Shooting** approximates the solution to a second-order ordinary differential equation with specified boundary conditions.

Syntax

```
Procedure Shooting(LowerLimit    : Real;
                   UpperLimit    : Real;
                   LowerInitial  : Real;
                   UpperInitial  : Real;
                   InitialSlope  : Real;
                   NumReturn     : Integer;
                   Tolerance     : Real;
                   MaxIter       : Integer;
                   NumIntervals  : Integer;
               Var Iter          : Integer;
               Var XValues       : TNvector;
               Var YValues       : TNvector;
               Var YDerivValues  : TNvector;
               Var Error         : Byte);
```

Input Parameters

LowerLimit	Lower limit of interval
UpperLimit	Upper limit of interval
LowerInitial	Value of y at **LowerLimit**
UpperInitial	Value of y at **UpperLimit**
InitialSlope	Approximation of slope at **LowerLimit**
NumReturn	Number of values of x, y, and first derivative of y to be returned
Tolerance	Accuracy of solution
MaxIter	Maximum number of iterations to be performed
NumIntervals	Number of subintervals used in calculations

Output Parameters

Iter	Number of iterations performed
XValues	Values of x between limits
YValues	Values of y approximated for values in **XValues**
YDerivValues	Values of the first derivative of y approximated for values in **XValues**
Error	0 No error
	1 **NumReturn** < 1
	2 **NumIntervals** < **NumReturn**
	3 **LowerLimit** = **UpperLimit**
	4 **Tolerance** <= 0
	5 **MaxIter** <= 0
	6 **Iter** > **MaxIter**
	7 Convergence is not possible

User-Defined Function

TNTargetF(x, y, yPrime : Real) : Real;

User-Defined Type

TNvector = Array[1..TNArraySize] Of Real;

Solution to a Boundary Value Problem for a Second-Order Ordinary Linear Differential Equation Using the Linear Shooting and Runge-Kutta Methods (LINSHOT2.INC)

Description   **LinearShooting** approximates the solution to a second-order ordinary differential equation with specified boundary conditions.

Syntax

```
Procedure LinearShooting( LowerLimit    : Real;
                          UpperLimit    : Real;
                          LowerInitial  : Real;
                          UpperInitial  : Real;
```

```
                        NumReturn      : Integer;
                        NumIntervals   : Integer;
                  Var   XValues        : TNvector;
                  Var   YValues        : TNvector;
                  Var   YDerivValues   : TNvector;
                  Var   Error          : Byte);
```

Input Parameters

LowerLimit	Lower limit of interval
UpperLimit	Upper limit of interval
LowerInitial	Initial value y at **LowerLimit**
UpperInitial	Initial value y at **UpperLimit**
NumReturn	Number of values of x, y, and the first derivative of y to be returned
Num-Intervals	Number of subintervals to use in calculations

Output Parameters

XValues	Values of x between the limits	
YValues	Values of y approximated using values in **XValues**	
YDeriv-Values	Values of the first derivative of y approximated using values in **XValues**	
Error	0	No error
	1	**NumReturn** < 1
	2	**NumIntervals** $<$ **NumReturn**
	3	**LowerLimit** $=$ **UpperLimit**
	4	Equation is not linear

User-Defined Function

TNTargetF(x, y, yPrime : Real) : Real;

User-Defined Type

TNvector = Array[1..TNArraySize] Of Real;

Least-Squares Approximation

Least-Squares Approximation (LEAST.INC)

Description   **LeastSquares** finds the least-squares approximation for a series of x and y data points.

Syntax

Procedure LeastSquares(NumPoints   : Integer;
                     Var   XData   : TNColumnVector;
                     Var   YData   : TNColumnVector;
                     Var   NumTerms   : Integer;
                     Var   Solution   : TNRowVector;
                     Var   YFit   : TNColumnVector;
                     Var   Residuals   : TNColumnVector;
                     Var   StandardDeviation : Real;
                     Var   Error   : Byte);

Input Parameters

NumPoints   Number of data points
XData   X coordinates of data points
YData   Y coordinates of data points
NumTerms   Number of terms in least-squares approximation

Output Parameters

Solution   Coefficients of the basis vectors
YFit   Values of the least-squares fit at the **XData** values

Residuals	Difference between **YData** and **YFit** values
Standard-Deviation	Square root of the variance
Error	0 No errors
	1 **NumPoints** < 2
	2 **NumTerms** < 1
	3 **NumTerms** > **NumPoints**
	4 Least-squares solution does not exist

User-Defined Types

TNColumnVector = Array[1..TNColumnSize] Of Real;
TNRowVector = Array[1..TNRowSize] Of Real;
TNMatrix = Array[1..TNColumnSize] Of TNRowVector;
TNSquareMatrix = Array[1..TNRowSize] Of TNRowVector;
TNString40 = String[40];

Fast Fourier Transform Routines

Description   The Fourier Transform routines are divided into two groups. The first group contains four alternative FFT methods for calculating discrete Fourier transforms (FFTB2.INC, FFTB4.INC, FFT87B2.INC, FFT87B4.INC). The remaining procedures are routines that use FFT to produce various results.

User-Defined Types

The Fast Fourier Transform routines require the following data types:

TNvector = Array[0..TNArraySize] Of Real;
TNvectorPtr = ^Tnvector;

Fast Fourier Transform Routines (FFTB2.INC, FFTB4.INC, FFT87B2.INC, FFT87B4.INC)

Syntax

```
Procedure FFT(NumberOfBits : Byte;
              NumPoints     : Integer;
              Inverse       : Boolean;
          Var XReal         : TNvectorPtr;
          Var XImag         : TNvectorPtr;
          Var SinTable      : TNvectorPtr;
          Var CosTable      : TNvectorPtr);
```

Input Parameters

Number-OfBits	Number of data points as a power of 2 or 4, depending on the routine being used
NumPoints	Number of data points
Inverse	False indicates forward transform; True indicates inverse transform
XReal	Pointer to real values of the data points
XImag	Pointer to imaginary values of the data points
SinTable	Table of sine values
CosTable	Table of cosine values

Output Parameters

XReal	Pointer to real values of the discrete Fourier transform of the input data
XImag	Pointer to imaginary values of the discrete Fourier transform of the input data

In-Place Transformation of Complex Data (COMPFFT.INC)

Syntax

```
Procedure ComplexFFT(NumPoints : Integer;
                         Inverse    : Boolean;
                 Var   XReal      : TNvectorPtr;
                 Var   XImag      : TNvectorPtr;
                 Var   Error      : Byte);
```

Input Parameters

NumPoints	Number of data points
Inverse	False indicates forward transform; True indicates inverse transform
XReal	Pointer to real values of data points
XImag	Pointer to imaginary values of data points

Output Parameters

XReal		Pointer to the real values of the discrete Fourier transform of the input data
XImag		Pointer to the imaginary values of the discrete Fourier transform of the input data
Error	0	No error
	1	**NumPoints** < 2
	2	**NumPoints** not a power of 2 or 4

In-Place Transformation of Real Data (REALFFT.INC)

Syntax

```
Procedure RealFFT(NumPoints : Integer;
                      Inverse    : Boolean;
              Var   XReal      : TNvectorPtr;
              Var   XImag      : TNvectorPtr;
              Var   Error      : Byte);
```

Input Parameters

NumPoints	Number of data points
Inverse	False indicates forward transform; True indicates inverse transform
XReal	Pointer to real values of the data points

Output Parameters

XReal		Pointer to real values of the Fourier transform of the input data
XImag		Pointer to imaginary values of the Fourier transform of the input data
Error	0	No errors
	1	**NumPoints** < 4
	2	**NumPoints** not a power of 2 or twice a power of 4

Calculation of the Convolution of Two Complex Vectors (COMPCNVL.INC)

Syntax

```
Procedure ComplexConvolution( NumPoints : Integer;
                        Var  XReal      : TNvectorPtr;
                        Var  XImag      : TNvectorPtr;
                        Var  HReal      : TNvectorPtr;
                        Var  HImag      : TNvectorPtr;
                        Var  Error      : Byte);
```

Input Parameters

NumPoints	Number of data points
XReal	Pointer to real values of the first set of data points
XImag	Pointer to imaginary values of the first set of data points

HReal   Pointer to real values of the second set of
       data points

HImag   Pointer to imaginary values of the
       second set of data points

Output Parameters

XReal   Pointer to imaginary values of the con-
       volution of **XReal**, **XImag** and
       HReal, XImag

XImag   Pointer to imaginary values of the con-
       volution of **XReal**, **XImag** and
       HReal, XImag

Error   0   No error
      1   **NumPoints** < 2
      2   **NumPoints** not a power of 2 or 4

Calculation of the Convolution of Two Real Vectors (REALCNVL.INC)

Syntax

```
Procedure RealConvolution( NumPoints : Integer;
                    Var  XReal      : TNvectorPtr;
                    Var  XImag      : TNvectorPtr;
                    Var  HReal      : TNvectorPtr;
                    Var  Error      : Byte);
```

Input Parameters

NumPoints   Number of data points

XReal   Pointer to real values of the first set of
       data points

HReal   Pointer to real values of the second set
       of data points

Output Parameters

XReal   Pointer to the real values of the convolu-
       tion of **XReal** and **HReal**

XImag   Pointer to the imaginary values of the
               convolution of **XReal** and **HReal**

Error   0   No error
           1   **NumPoints** < 2
           2   **NumPoints** not a power of 2 or 4

Calculation of the Correlation of Two Complex Vectors (COMPCORR.INC)

Syntax

Procedure ComplexCorrelation(NumPoints : Integer;
                    Var Auto   : Boolean;
                    Var XReal   : TNvectorPtr;
                    Var XImag   : TNvectorPtr;
                    Var HReal   : TNvectorPtr;
                    Var HImag   : TNvectorPtr;
                    Var Error   : Byte);

Input Parameters

NumPoints   Number of data points

Auto   False for cross-correlation; True for
            autocorrelation

XReal   Pointer to real values of the first set of
            data points

XImag   Pointer to real values of the first set of
            data points

HReal   Pointer to real values of the second set
            of data points (for cross-correlation)

HImag   Pointer to real values of the second set
            of data points (for cross-correlation)

Output Parameters

XReal   Pointer to real values of the correlation
            of **XReal**, **XImag** and **HReal**,
            HImag (or the autocorrelation of
            XReal, **XImag** if **Auto** is True)

XImag	Pointer to imaginary values of the corre-lation of **XReal, XImag** and **HReal, HImag** (or the autocorrela-tion of **XReal, XImag** if **Auto** is True)
Error	0 No error
	1 **NumPoints** < 2
	2 **NumPoints** not a power of 2 or 4

Calculation of the Correlation of Two Real Vectors (REALPCORR.INC)

Syntax

```
Procedure RealCorrelation( NumPoints : Integer;
                     Var  Auto       : Boolean;
                     Var  XReal      : TNvectorPtr;
                     Var  XImag      : TNvectorPtr;
                     Var  HReal      : TNvectorPtr;
                     Var  Error      : Byte);
```

Input Parameters

NumPoints	Number of data points
Auto	False for cross-correlation; True for autocorrelation
XReal	Pointer to real values of the first set of data points
HReal	Pointer to real values of the second set of data points (for cross-correlation)

Output Parameters

| XReal | Pointer to real values of the correlation of **XReal** and **HReal** (or the auto- |

		correlation of **XReal** if **Auto** is True)
XImag		Pointer to imaginary values of the correlation of **XReal** and **HReal** (or the autocorrelation of **XReal** if **Auto** is True)
Error	0	No error
	1	**NumPoints** < 2
	2	**NumPoints** not a power of 2 or 4

Numerical Methods Toolbox for Turbo Pascal Version 4.0

Borland's Numerical Methods Toolbox has been updated for use with Turbo Pascal Version 4.0. All procedure and function calls remain unchanged, allowing a maximum level of compatibility with your existing programs. Perhaps most important is the inclusion of conditional compilation for 8087 support. Now you no longer have to change the source code when you compile the units for use with the 8087 math co-processor. In addition, the sample programs have been improved to better illustrate the use of the procedures and functions.

Turbo Pascal Version 4.0 Programming

Turbo Pascal Files
Compiling from the DOS Prompt
Technical Aspects of Turbo Pascal 4.0

With the introduction of Version 4.0, Borland pushed Turbo Pascal into the arena of serious compilers. Because Version 4.0 supports separately compiled units, built-in project management, and even faster compilation speed, you can now use Turbo Pascal for even the largest projects. This chapter is intended to be a concise reference guide to Turbo Pascal 4.0.

Turbo Pascal Files

Version 4.0 comprises more files than did Version 3.0. The following is a listing of the files on your distribution disk:

TURBO.EXE

When you execute this program by entering **TURBO** at the DOS prompt, the Turbo Pascal system will start. The system allows you to edit, debug, and run programs without going back to DOS.

The Turbo Pascal 4.0 system utilizes pull-down menus in five categories: Files, Edit, Run, Compile, and Options.

These options allow you to load and save files, edit files, run a program without leaving the Turbo Pascal system, compile, make or build a program, and set up compiler options.

TURBO.TPL

The TURBO.TPL file, which contains all the standard Turbo Pascal library routines and units, is used whenever you compile a program. The following is a list of the units included in the file and a brief description of each one.

System Unit

The System unit contains the Turbo Pascal run-time library. This unit, which implements low-level run-time support routines for all built-in procedures, is automatically included in every program—you cannot declare it in the **Uses** statement.

Printer Unit

The Printer unit allows you to use the **Lst** identifier as it is used in Version 3.0.

CRT Unit

The CRT unit contains routines that optimize use of the video monitor. If you do not use the CRT unit, all screen output is performed through DOS routines. With the CRT unit you can select output through BIOS routines or by writing directly to memory.

DOS Unit

The DOS unit represents some of the most important advancements introduced by Version 4.0. The system-level interface is much improved and allows easier access to a wide range of functions. The data types and procedures contained in the DOS unit are listed in Figure 23-1. Complete descrip-

Constants

```
FCarry      = $0001;
FParity     = $0004;
FAuxiliary  = $0010;        Used to interpret the
FZero       = $0080;        Flags register.
FOverflow   = $0800;

ReadOnly    = $01;
Hidden      = $02;
SysFile     = $04;
VolumeID    = $08;          Used to interpret file
Directory   = $10;          attributes.
Archive     = $20;
AnyFile     = $3F;
```

Types

```
Registers = Record
  Case Integer Of
  0 : (AX,BX,CX,DX,BP,SI,DI,DS,ES,Flags : Word);
  1 : (AL,AH,BL,BH,CL,CH,DL,DH : Byte);
  End;

DateTime = Record
  Year, Month, Day, Hour, Min, Sec : Integer;
  End;

SearchRec = Record
  Fill : Array [1..2] of Byte;
  Attr : Byte;
  Time : LongInt;
  Size : LongInt;
  Name : String[12];
  End;
```

Variables

```
DosError : Integer;
```

Procedures and Functions

```
Procedure Intr(IntNo : Byte;
               Var Regs : Registers);
```

Figure 23-1.   Data types and procedures in DOS unit

```
Procedure MsDos(Var Regs : Registers);

Procedure GetIntVec(IntNo : Byte;
                    Var Vector : Pointer);

Procedure SetIntVec(IntNo : Byte;
                    Vector : Pointer);

Procedure GetDate(Var Year,
                  Month,
                  Day,
                  DayOfWeek : Word);

Procedure SetDate(Year, Month, Day, DayofWeek: Word);

Procedure GetTime(Var Hour,
                  Minute,
                  Second,
                  Hundredths : Word);

Procedure SetTime(Hour,
                  Minute,
                  Second,
                  Hundredths : Word);

Procedure GetFTime(Var F : FileType;
                   Var Time : LongInt);

Procedure SetFTime(Var F : FileType;
                   Time : LongInt);

Procedure UnpackTime(Time : LongInt;
                     Var DT : DateTime);

Procedure PackTime(Var Time : LongInt;
                   Var DT : DateTime);

Procedure DiskFree(Drive : Word);

Procedure DiskSize(Drive : Word);

Procedure GetFAttr(Var F : FileType;
                   Var Attr : Byte);

Procedure SetFAttr(Var F : FileType;
                   Attr : Byte);

Procedure FindFirst(Path : String;
                    Attr : Byte;
                    Var S : SearchRec);

Procedure FindNext(Var S : SearchRec);

Procedure Exec(Path,CommandLine : String);

Function DosExitCode : Word;

Procedure Keep(ExitCode : Word);
```

Figure 23-1.   Data types and procedures in DOS unit (*continued*)

tions of these procedures and data types can be found in Appendix H.

Graph3

Use this unit with existing Version 3.0 programs that use Turbo graphics procedures.

Turbo3

Turbo3 is a compatibility unit for functions and procedures that are not supported under Version 4.0. Use this unit with existing Version 3.0 programs to get the highest level of compatibility.

Graph

The Graph unit is used to incorporate the enhanced graphics capability of Version 4.0. Graphics support includes HGC, CGA, EGA, MCGA, and VGA. For more information on the Graph unit, see Appendix I.

TURBO.TP

TURBO.TP is a Turbo Pascal configuration file. A configuration file contains information that controls such things as the memory your program uses, the directories in which files are located, and settings for compiler directives. You can create your own configuration files to store the settings you use frequently.

TINST.COM

The TINST.COM program file contains the Turbo Pascal Installation program, which allows you to specify the Turbo directory, change commands used in the editor, set up the default environment, select a screen type that matches your computer, customize the colors used by Turbo Pascal, and change the size of the Edit and Output windows.

TPC.EXE

The TPC.EXE file is the command-line version of Turbo Pascal. Now you can compile a program without entering the Turbo Pascal system. At the DOS prompt you simply type **TPC** followed by the name of your program. You can also specify compiler directives on the same command line. For example, the following statement compiles the program TEST.PAS with stack checking on and range checking off:

```
TPC TEST /$S+ /$R-
```

The command-line compiler adds a new level of convenience to Turbo Pascal, especially to programmers who prefer their own editor to the Turbo editor.

TPC.CFG

The TPC.CFG file contains configuration information for the command-line version of Turbo Pascal. When you start TPC, the program immediately looks for the TPC.CFG file, opens it, and reads the configuration information it contains. This information will be used to compile your program unless you supersede it with your own command-line parameters. In other words, the parameters you enter on the command line with TPC always take priority over the parameters in TPC.CFG.

The TPC.CFG file contains parameters in text format—one parameter per line. For example, a TPC.CFG file with the contents listed below would compile TEST.PAS with the **R** (range check) and **S** (stack check) compiler directives disabled. If you started TPC with no parameters, Turbo would compile TEST.PAS with these parameters.

```
test
/$R-
/$S-
```

TPMAP.EXE

The TPMAP.EXE program converts Turbo Pascal .TPM files to .MAP files. The .MAP file is compatible with symbolic debuggers such as Microsoft's SYMDEB.

MAKE.EXE

The MAKE.EXE program provides the Make utility when you compile a program with the command-line version.

TPUMOVER.EXE

TPUMOVER.EXE is the unit mover utility. With it, you can move your own units into the TURBO.TPL unit. Units included in TURBO.TPL require less time to link and are part of the standard library. You start TPUMOVER.EXE at the DOS prompt with this command:

```
C:>TPUMOVER TURBO.TPL
```

When the program starts, it displays the screen shown in Figure 23-2.

As you can see, the screen consists of two windows. The line at the bottom of the screen describes the keys you can use. These keys and their functions are described in Figure 23-3.

Initially, the window on the left is active and displays the units contained in the TURBO.TPL file. The window on the right is blank. You must load your unit into the window on the right before moving it into the TURBO.TPL file. To do this, first press F6 to make the right window active. Then press F3 to load a new file, and TPUMOVER will ask for the name of the unit. Enter the name and press RETURN. TPUMOVER now loads that file into the active window, and you are ready to move the unit into the TURBO.TPL file.

```
                        Turbo Pascal Unit Librarian
                               Version 1.06n

  ┌─── C:\DB3\5.0\TURBO.TPL ───┐       ┌═══ C:\DB3\5.0\SCRN.TPU ═══┐
  │ Unit    Code  Data  Syms  Uses │   │ Unit    Code  Data  Syms  Uses │
  │                            │       │                            │
  │ SYSTEM  10778  585  3255   │       │ SCRN    2302    0  1582  DOS  ... │
  │ PRINTER    35  256   269   │       │                            │
  │ CRT      1510   23  1509   │       │                            │
  │ DOS      1644    6  3213   │       │                            │
  │ TURBO3    443  256   585  CRT │    │                            │
  │ GRAPH3   5021    0  2013  CRT │    │                            │
  │                            │       │                            │
  │                            │       │                            │
  │                            │       │                            │
  │                            │       │                            │
  └────────────────────────────┘       └────────────────────────────┘

     File size:    36 K              File size:     5 K
     Drive C:    1056 K free         Drive C:    1056 K free

  F1-help F2-save F3-new F4-info F6-switch +-mark INS-copy DEL-delete ESC-quit
```

Figure 23-2.   Unit Librarian Opening Screen

F1 (help)	Displays information on how to use TPUMOVER.EXE
F2 (save)	Saves the unit in the active window
F3 (new)	Loads a new unit into the active window
F4 (info)	Displays additional unit dependencies
F6 (switch)	Switches the active window
+ (mark)	Marks a unit for moving
INS (copy)	Copies marked units from the active window to the inactive window
DEL (delete)	Deletes a unit from the active window
ESC (quit)	Terminates TPUMOVER.EXE

Figure 23-3.   Keys used with TPUMOVER.EXE

Before you move the unit, you must mark it by highlighting the filename and pressing the plus key (+). Now simply press INS, and the unit name will appear in the window on the left. If you change your mind, press F6 to activate the left window, and press DEL to delete the newly added unit.

When you are done, you save your changes by pressing F2. If you do not wish to save your changes, press ESC.

Compiling from the DOS Prompt

Turbo Pascal 4.0 includes a program TPC.EXE, the command-line version of Turbo Pascal. With TPC.EXE, you can compile, link, and run a program without entering the Turbo Pascal system. The general format for using this program is

```
TPC [File Name] [Parameters]
```

The filename need not include the .PAS extension since TPC assumes it. If you want to compile a program file that has no extension, end the filename with a period. The most difficult part of using TPC.EXE is understanding the command-line parameters that govern compilation. These parameters and their use are described below.

Boolean Evaluation

Turbo Pascal 4.0 allows two types of Boolean evaluation—standard and short-circuit. Short-circuit Boolean evaluation provides faster program execution by exiting from a Boolean statement as soon as an appropriate condition is met. (Standard evaluation requires that the entire Boolean statement be evaluated, even when it is not necessary.) To specify short-circuit Boolean evaluation, use the /$B− command-line parameter. To specify standard Boolean evaluation, use /$B+. For example:

```
TPC TEST /$B- (* Short-Circuit Boolean Evaluation *)

TPC TEST /$B+ (* Standard Boolean Evaluation *)
```

Build All

TPC normally assumes that all the units for the program have already been compiled and that the .TPU units are available. If your units have not been compiled or are out of date, you can use the **Build All** directive—/B—to tell TPC to recompile all units used by the program. Note that this directive will cause all units to be recompiled, even those that are not out-of-date. An out-of-date unit is one for which the source code has been changed since it was last compiled.

Debug Information

When you are testing a program, Turbo Pascal can help you spot errors if you use the /D compiler directive. This directive causes Turbo Pascal to generate debugging information that the compiler uses when tracing run-time errors. While your program is in the development stage, keep the **D** compiler directive enabled.

Execute

With the execute directive—/X—you can tell TPC to create an .EXE file on disk and then execute that file automatically.

Executable Directory

You can specify which directory you would like your executable code written to with the /E parameter. For example, the line

```
TPC TEST /Ec:\tp
```

tells Turbo Pascal to compile TEST.PAS and store the resulting .EXE file in directory c: \tp. If you want to speed up your compile time, you can specify a RAM disk as the .EXE directory. Then your program will write the executable code to the RAM disk and save a good amount of time in the process.

Find Error

If a program fails due to a run-time error, Turbo Pascal will display a message that looks like this:

```
Runtime error 201 at 0000:0041.
```

Runtime error 201 is a range error, and **0000:0041** is the memory address, in hexadecimal, at which the error occurred. To find the point in the code, you can use the /F directive as shown here:

```
TPC TEST /F0000:0041
```

This tells Turbo Pascal to compile TEST.PAS and stop when the error position, 0000:0041, is found. The result of the search is shown here:

```
Target address is in TEST.PAS at 0041.
TEST.PAS(9): Target address found.
b := b + 1;
^
```

The message **TEST.PAS(9): Target address found.** says that the error is located in file TEST.PAS at the ninth line of code. The line is also printed out and the ^ symbol points to the probable source of the error.

Force Far Calls

Turbo Pascal 4.0 programs consist of a main program file that can call any number of external units. In order to allow programs to exceed the 64K limit on code space, the program and each unit have their own code segments. When a procedure is used within the program or unit in which it is declared, a near call is used. A near call is a call to a procedure that resides within the current code segment. A far call, thus, is a call to a procedure that resides in another code segment. If, for example, a procedure in one unit calls a procedure in another unit, a far call is issued.

Turbo Pascal automatically keeps track of procedure calls and uses the correct type, near or far, in each case. You may, however, force all procedure calls to be far calls by using the **F** compiler directive. When **F** is enabled, all calls are generated as far calls. When **F** is disabled, Turbo Pascal uses the type of call it considers appropriate.

I/O Error Checking

Programs generate I/O errors for many reasons. They will result from such actions as resetting a file that does not exist or writing beyond available disk space, for example. When I/O error checking is enabled, Turbo Pascal 4.0 stops the program and issues a run-time error warning. If, on the other hand, you disable I/O error checking, I/O errors will not halt program execution. You enable I/O error checking with the **/$I−** command-line parameter.

Include Directory

If your program uses include files, you can use the **/I** directive to specify in which directories these files are located (for example, **/Ic:\tp\inc**).

Link Buffer Location

Turbo Pascal 4.0 maintains a link buffer that is used to link program units when they are compiled. The link buffer can be maintained in memory or on disk. Keeping the buffer in memory requires extra RAM but allows faster linking. To specify the link buffer location to use RAM, type /$L+. To specify the link buffer location to use disk space, type /$L−.

Make

If you want TPC to recompile units but only those that are out-of-date, use the /M compiler directive. You must be sure that the system clock is correct. A unit will be recompiled only when the source file's date and time are later than the unit's date and time.

Memory Sizes

Unlike Version 3.0, Version 4.0 requires you to specify a limit to the stack segment, and minimum and maximum limits to the heap. The stack segment can range from 1024 bytes to 65,520 bytes. The lowest allowable minimum level for the heap is 0 bytes, while the highest allowable maximum is 655,360 bytes.

To specify memory sizes on the command line, use the /$M directive, which is of the following form:

```
/$M [Stack Size], [Min Heap], [Max Heap]
```

Since a program only occasionally changes in its use of memory, it is easier to declare memory usage inside your program than to specify it on the command line.

Numeric Processing

Version 4.0 offers two types of real numeric processing—software and hardware. Software processing, as the name implies, uses Turbo Pascal library procedures to compute the results of real equations. Hardware processing, on the other hand, uses the 8087 math coprocessor chip for all computations involving real numbers. Note that hardware processing only works on computers with the 8087 chip installed.

To specify hardware processing, include the /$N+ directive on the command line.

Object Directory

Object files are assembly language routines assembled into .OBJ format. If your program uses these types of files, you can specify their directory with the /O directive (for example, /Oc: \tp \obj).

Range Checking

Range errors are a common type of program bug. They occur when a value of a counter exceeds the range of its type (for example, when a byte is incremented beyond 255). Range errors also occur when an index extends beyond the declared limit of an array. When you enable range checking with the /$R+ command-line parameter, Turbo Pascal will automatically check for any out-of-range conditions. To disable range checking, use /$R−.

Run

If you include the Run directive—/R—on your command line, TPC will not create an .EXE file. Instead the program will be compiled to memory and then run from memory. This saves time since no disk access is required to store or run the .EXE file.

Stack Checking

You must set a limit to the stack on Turbo Pascal 4.0. If you set the limit too low, your program might run out of stack space. If you enable stack checking with the /$S+ command-line parameter, Turbo Pascal will detect stack crashes and issue a run-time error when they occur. When stack checking is disabled (/$S−), stack errors go undetected.

TPM File Creation

Debugging a program is difficult. Turbo Pascal 4.0 helps in two ways. First, you can enable the **D** compiler directive to create line-oriented debugging information. Turbo Pascal uses this information to locate the position in the source code where the error occurred.

Another aid is the **T** compiler directive. When the **T** compiler directive is enabled, Turbo Pascal creates .TPM files that can be converted for use with symbolic debuggers. A symbolic debugger allows a programmer to trace through a program at the machine code level but with more power than the Debug program offers. Turbo Pascal 4.0 supports the standard set by Microsoft's symbolic debugger SYM-DEB.

Whether you use Turbo Pascal's internal debugging facility or a symbolic debugger, the Debug compiler directive (**$D+**) and the TPM file compiler directive (**$T+**) must be activated as shown here:

```
TPC TEST /$D+ /$T+
```

Activating the Debug and TPM file directives tells Turbo Pascal to generate a map file that includes line number information. A map file contains information about a program's variables and their locations in memory. If you compile TEST.PAS with the /$D+ and /$T+ directives, Turbo Pascal will create two files: TEST.EXE and TEST.TPM. The first file is your executable code, the second is the Turbo Pascal map file.

To use SYMDEB or any other symbolic debugger you must first use the Turbo Pascal TPMAP program to convert the .TPM file into a standard .MAP file. Next, create a .SYM file using a program such as Microsoft's MAPSYM. These steps are shown here:

```
C:>TPMAP TEST
```

```
C:>MAPSYM TEST
```

Once you have created your .SYM file, you can start the symbolic debugger. If you are using SYMDEB, the command would be

```
C:>SYMDEB TEST.SYM TEST.EXE
```

Symbolic debuggers are useful for spotting subtle problems in your code. That Turbo Pascal 4.0 supports this tool is a sign of Borland's recognition of Turbo Pascal as a serious programming tool.

Turbo Directory

When you start TPC, it looks for two files—TURBO.CFG and TURBO.TPL. You can specify in which directory these files are located with the \T directive (for example, /Tc:\tp\turbo).

Unit Directory

If your program uses units, Turbo Pascal must know where to look for them. You can specify a unit directory with the /U directive (for example, /Uc:\tp\units).

Var String Checking

Turbo Pascal normally checks to see that strings passed as parameters to procedures match the type of the declared parameter. You can relax this strict checking with the /$v— command-line parameter.

Technical Aspects of Turbo Pascal 4.0

Turbo Pascal 4.0 introduces a whole host of new internal operations. While these will be invisible to many programmers, hackers will find ample opportunity to take advantage of the changes.

4.0 Memory Management

The memory management of Turbo Pascal 4.0 bears little resemblance to that of Version 3.0. In order to break the 64K code segment limitation, Turbo Pascal 4.0 utilizes multiple code segments. In addition, typed constants are now stored in the data segment instead of the code segment. Finally, the stack segment is now totally distinct from the heap, so stack/heap crashes cannot occur (of course you can still run into problems if you exceed your stack or heap limits). Figure 23-4 illustrates Version 4.0's segmentation of memory.

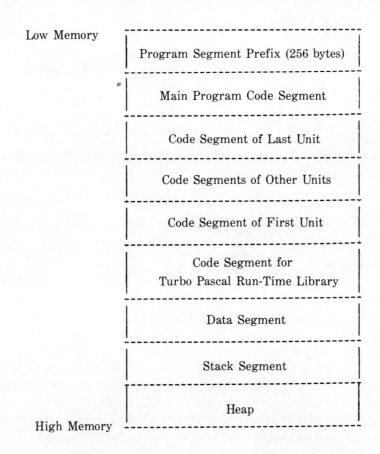

Low Memory

| Program Segment Prefix (256 bytes) |
| Main Program Code Segment |
| Code Segment of Last Unit |
| Code Segments of Other Units |
| Code Segment of First Unit |
| Code Segment for Turbo Pascal Run-Time Library |
| Data Segment |
| Stack Segment |
| Heap |

High Memory

Figure 23-4.   Turbo Pascal 4.0 memory management

While the program contains multiple code segments, none of these segments can exceed 64K. The same holds for the data segment and the stack segment.

The stack and the heap operate pretty much the same way that they did in Version 3.0. As dynamic variables are created, the heap grows upward from low memory. Two variables—**HeapPtr** and **HeapOrg**—keep track of the heap; **HeapPtr** points to the top of the stack, and **HeapOrg** points to the bottom.

Controlling Heap Errors

A properly written program should never run out of heap space. However, it can happen, and Turbo Pascal 4.0 introduces a new way to handle the situation using a pointer variable named **HeapError**. **HeapError** points to a function that Turbo Pascal calls when it encounters an unsuccessful attempt to allocate a variable on the heap. You can make **HeapError** point to a function you write and thus gain control over the error condition.

The function to which **HeapError** points must be of the following form:

```
(*$F+*)
Function HeapFunc(Size : Word) : Integer;
Begin
End;
(*$F-*)
```

Note that the **F** compiler directive is used to force calls to HeapFunc to be long calls. HeapFunc takes one word value parameter—**Size**—and returns an integer. **Size** indicates the amount of memory requested for allocation.

When a heap collision occurs, Turbo Pascal calls Heap-Func and expects the function to return an integer with one of three values—0 indicates a failure and causes the program to abort; 1 indicates an error but instead of aborting the program returns the pointer with a nil value; and 2 indicates a success and initiates another attempt to allocate the variable. The body of your HeapFunc function should look something like this:

```
Begin
HeapFunc:= 1;
End;
```

By assigning a value of 1 to HeapFunc, you keep your program from aborting. In your program you must test to see if the pointer allocated is returned with a nil value. If so, you know your attempt to allocate memory was not successful. The following program demonstrates how HeapFunc can be used:

```
(*$M 1024,20000,20000*)
Program TestHeapError;
Uses CRT;
Type
  xtype = Array [1..500] Of Char;
  xptr  = ^xtype;
var
  i : Integer;
  x : xptr;

(**************************************************************)

(*$F+*)
Function HeapFunc(Size : Word) : Integer;
Begin
WriteLn('Cannot find ',size,' bytes on heap.');
HeapFunc:= 1;
End;
(*$F-*)

(**************************************************************)

begin
ClrScr;
Write('Press return to test heap error function');
ReadLn;
HeapError := @HeapFunc;
i := 0;
  Repeat
  New(x);
  If x <> Nil Then
    Begin
    i := i + 1;
    WriteLn('Success: ',i);
    End
  Else
    WriteLn('Failure');
  Until x = Nil; (* If x is Nil, no more heap space is left *)
End.
```

Running a DOS Shell

Another exciting addition to Turbo Pascal 4.0 is the ability to build a DOS shell into your programs. A DOS shell allows users to exit from the program while it is still in memory, run other programs, and return to the originating program. In Turbo Pascal 4.0, this is done with the **Exec** procedure. The **Exec** procedure is of the following form:

```
Procedure Exec(CommandCom, CommandLine : String);
```

CommandCom is a string that contains the path and name of the COMMAND.COM file or any executable file with complete path and extension. For example, if the file is in the root directory, then **CommandCom** would contain C:\COMMAND.COM. The other parameter, **CommandLine**, contains command-line parameters such as the name of a program to run. For example, if you wanted to see a directory listing of all files with the .PAS extension, **CommandLine** would contain /c **DIR ∗.PAS**. However, if **CommandLine** is empty, Turbo Pascal will create a DOS shell that puts you back at the DOS prompt and allows you to run any program. When you want to leave the DOS shell, you simply type **EXIT**.

One problem with the **Exec** procedure is that you must know where the COMMAND.COM file is located. Of course, you know where it is for your own system, but what about others who use your program? Luckily, there's a way to find out where COMMAND.COM is located.

Every time a program is loaded, DOS creates a copy in memory of something called the environment. The environment contains information about the location of COMMAND.-COM, default paths, and other system-related information. The problem is, how do you know where the environment is located?

Once again, DOS provides the answer. When a program starts, DOS also creates something called the Program Segment Prefix or PSP. The PSP contains a lot of information, but the one item we need is the segment address of the DOS environment. Once we know the segment address of the environment, we can scan the environment for the location of COMMAND.COM. The problem is, how do you know where the PSP is located?

With Version 4.0, Turbo Pascal provides a variable called **PrefixSeg**, which contains the segment address of the PSP. The PSP is 256 bytes long, and byte number 2Ch contains the segment of the DOS environment. These are the steps necessary to find the location of COMMAND.COM.

1. Store the segment of the DOS environment in a word variable. The DOS environment segment is located in memory at PrefixSeg:$2C.

2. Starting at offset 0 of the DOS environment, scan until an equal sign (=) is found. This marks the beginning of the location of COMMAND.COM.

3. Pick up the characters directly following the equal sign until a null character (0) is encountered. As the characters are picked up, store them in a string variable.

The string variable now contains the location of COMMAND.COM. You can pass this string directly to the **Exec** procedure to create your DOS shell.

This process is demonstrated in the following program. The function CommandComLocation scans the DOS environment and returns a string that contains the location of COMMAND.COM. The DOS shell is created with the command

```
Exec(CommandComLocation,'');
```

To return to the program from the DOS shell, simply type **EXIT** and press RETURN.

```
(*$v-*)
(*$M 8192,0,0*)
Program DosShellDemo;
Uses Dos,CRT;
```

```
Type
  MaxStr = String[255];

(*******************************************************************)

Function CommandComLocation : MaxStr;
var
  ch : Char;
  env_seg,
  i : Word;

  cst : string[80];

Begin

(* Offset 2Ch of the Program Segment Prefix holds the      *)
(* segment of the DOS environment for the program.         *)
(* The DOS environment contains the path and name of       *)
(* the COMMAND.COM file.                                   *)

env_seg := MemW[PrefixSeg:$2C];

i := 0;

  Repeat
  i := i + 1;
  Until Chr(Mem[Env_Seg:i]) = '=';

i := i + 1;
cst := '';

  Repeat
  Ch := Chr(Mem[Env_Seg:i]);
  If Ch <> #0 Then
    cst := cst + Ch;
  i := i + 1;
  Until Ch = #0;

CommandComLocation := cst;
End;

(*******************************************************************)

Begin
ClrScr;
writeln('Type EXIT to leave DOS shell');
Exec(CommandComLocation,''); (* Call the DOS Shell *) .
Writeln('Leaving DOS Shell');
End.
```

Note that the **M** compiler directive limits the heap to 0 bytes. Whenever you start a DOS shell, the heap must be limited so as to allow enough memory to load COMMAND. COM and start your programs.

Turbo Pascal 4.0 represents a major step forward in Borland's effort to make Pascal a serious programming language. The compiler now ranks among the best in terms of both speed and power. While getting used to its intricacies may take a little time, the results are well worth it.

Turbo Pascal Error Codes

Compiler Error Messages
Run-time Error Messages
Input/Output Error Messages
Turbo Pascal Version 4.0 Error Codes
Turbo Pascal Version 4.0 Run-time Errors

Compiler Error Messages

Decimal	Hex	Meaning
1	01h	';' expected
2	02h	':' expected
3	03h	',' expected
4	04h	'(' expected
5	05h	')' expected
6	06h	'=' expected
7	07h	':=' expected
8	08h	'[' expected
9	09h	']' expected
10	0Ah	'.' expected
11	0Bh	'..' expected
12	0Ch	Begin expected
13	0Dh	Do expected
14	0Eh	End expected
15	0Fh	Of expected
16	10h	Procedure or function expected
17	11h	Then expected
18	12h	To or DownTo expected
20	14h	Boolean expression expected
21	15h	File variable expected

Decimal	Hex	Meaning
22	16h	Integer constant expected
23	17h	Integer expression expected
24	18h	Integer variable expected
25	19h	Integer or real constant expected
26	1Ah	Integer or real expression expected
27	1Bh	Integer or real variable expected
28	1Ch	Pointer variable expected
29	1Dh	Record variable expected
30	1Eh	Simple type expected
31	1Fh	Simple expression expected
32	20h	String constant expected
33	21h	String expression expected
34	22h	String variable expected
35	23h	Text file expected
36	24h	Type identifier expected
37	25h	Untyped file expected
40	28h	Undefined label expected
41	29h	Unknown identifier or syntax error
42	2Ah	Undefined pointer type in preceding type definitions
43	2Bh	Duplicate identifier or label
44	2Ch	Type mismatch
45	2Dh	Constant out of range
46	2Eh	Constant and case selector type does not match
47	2Fh	Operand type(s) do not match operator
48	30h	Invalid result type
49	31h	Invalid string length
50	32h	String constant length does not match type
51	33h	Invalid subrange base type
52	34h	Lower bound greater than upper bound
53	35h	Reserved word

Decimal	Hex	Meaning
54	36h	Illegal assignment
55	37h	String constant exceeds line
56	38h	Error in integer constant
57	39h	Error in real constant
58	3Ah	Illegal character in identifier
60	3Ch	Constants are not allowed here
61	3Dh	Files and pointer are not allowed here
62	3Eh	Structured variables are not allowed here
63	3Fh	Text files are not allowed here
64	40h	Text files and untyped files are not allowed here
65	41h	Untyped files are not allowed here
66	42h	I/O not allowed here
67	43h	Files must be **Var** parameters
68	44h	File components may not be files
69	45h	Invalid ordering of fields
70	46h	Set base type out of range
71	47h	Invalid **GoTo** statement
72	48h	Label not within current block
73	49h	Undefined forward procedure(s)
74	4Ah	Inline error
75	4Bh	Illegal use of absolute
76	4Ch	Overlays cannot be forwarded
77	4Dh	Overlays not allowed in Direct mode
90	5Ah	File not found
91	5Bh	Unexpected end of source
92	5Ch	Unable to create overlay file
93	5Dh	Invalid compiler directive
96	60h	Cannot nest include files
97	61h	Too many nested Withs
98	62h	Memory overflow
99	63h	Compiler overflow

Run-time Error Messages

Decimal	Hex	Meaning
1	01h	Floating point overflow
2	02h	Division by zero attempted
3	03h	Sqrt argument error: value is negative
4	04h	Ln argument error: value is zero or negative
16	10h	String length error
17	11h	Invalid string index
144	90h	Index out of range
145	91h	Scalar or subrange out of range
240	F0h	Overlay file not found
255	FFh	Heap/stack collision

Input/Output Error Messages

Decimal	Hex	Meaning
1	01h	File does not exist
2	02h	File not open for input
3	03h	File not open for output
4	04h	File not open
16	10h	Error in numeric format
32	20h	Operation not allowed on a logical device
33	21h	Not allowed in Direct mode
34	22h	Assign to std files not allowed
144	90h	Record length mismatch
145	91h	Seek beyond end-of-file
153	99h	Unexpected end-of-file
240	F0h	Disk write error
241	F1h	Directory is full
242	F2h	File size overflow
243	F3h	Too many open files
255	FFh	File disappeared

Turbo Pascal Version 4.0 Error Codes

Turbo Pascal 4.0 users will find that the I/O and run-time error codes have changed. For one thing, I/O errors are now considered run-time errors. In addition, error codes are passed directly from DOS, so the code you see represents the DOS error that occurred. Following is a listing of all run-time errors for Turbo Pascal Version 4.0.

Turbo Pascal Version 4.0 Run-time Error Messages

Decimal	Hex	Meaning
1	01h	Invalid DOS function code
2	02h	File not found
3	03h	Path not found
4	04h	Too many open files
5	05h	File access denied
6	06h	Invalid file handle
8	08h	Not enough memory
12	0Ch	Invalid file access code
15	0Fh	Invalid drive number
16	10h	Cannot remove current directory
17	11h	Cannot rename across drives
100	64h	Disk read error
101	65h	Disk write error
102	66h	File not assigned
103	67h	File not open
104	68h	File not open for input
105	69h	File not open for output
106	6Ah	Invalid numeric format
200	C8h	Division by zero

Decimal	Hex	Meaning
201	C9h	Range checking error
202	CAh	Stack overflow error
203	CBh	Heap overflow error
204	CCh	Invalid pointer operation
205	CDh	Floating point overflow

ASCII and Extended Character Set

Table B-1. ASCII and Extended Character Set

Dec	Hex	CHR	Dec	Hex	CHR	Dec	Hex	CHR
000	00	NUL	041	29	)	082	52	R
001	01	SOH	042	2A	*	083	53	S
002	02	STX	043	2B	+	084	54	T
003	03	ETX	044	2C	,	085	55	U
004	04	EOT	045	2D	—	086	56	V
005	05	ENQ	046	2E	.	087	57	W
006	06	ACK	047	2F	/	088	58	X
007	07	BEL	048	30	0	089	59	Y
008	08	BS	049	31	1	090	5A	Z
009	09	HT	050	32	2	091	5B	[
010	0A	LF	051	33	3	092	5C	\
011	0B	VT	052	34	4	093	5D	]
012	0C	FF	053	35	5	094	5E	^
013	0D	CR	054	36	6	095	5F	_
014	0E	SO	055	37	7	096	60	`
015	0F	SI	056	38	8	097	61	a
016	10	DLE	057	39	9	098	62	b
017	11	DC1	058	3A	:	099	63	c
018	12	DC2	059	3B	;	100	64	d
019	13	DC3	060	3C	<	101	65	e
020	14	DC4	061	3D	=	102	66	f
021	15	NAK	062	3E	>	103	67	g
022	16	SYN	063	3F	?	104	68	h
023	17	ETB	064	40	@	105	69	i
024	18	CAN	065	41	A	106	6A	j
025	19	EM	066	42	B	107	6B	k
026	1A	SUB	067	43	C	108	6C	l
027	1B	ESCAPE	068	44	D	109	6D	m
028	1C	FS	069	45	E	110	6E	n
029	1D	GS	070	46	F	111	6F	o
030	1E	RS	071	47	G	112	70	p
031	1F	US	072	48	H	113	71	q
032	20	SPACE	073	49	I	114	72	r
033	21	!	074	4A	J	115	73	s
034	22	"	075	4B	K	116	74	t
035	23	#	076	4C	L	117	75	u
036	24	$	077	4D	M	118	76	v
037	25	%	078	4E	N	119	77	w
038	26	&	079	4F	O	120	78	x
039	27	'	080	50	P	121	79	y
040	28	(	081	51	Q	122	7A	z

Table B-1.   ASCII and Extended Character Set (*continued*)

Dec	Hex	CHR	Dec	Hex	CHR	Dec	Hex	CHR
123	7B	{	168	A8	¿	213	D5	╒
124	7C	¦	169	A9	⌐	214	D6	╓
125	7D	}	170	AA	¬	215	D7	╫
126	7E	~	171	AB	½	216	D8	╪
127	7F	DEL	172	AC	¼	217	D9	┘
128	80	Ç	173	AD	¡	218	DA	┌
129	81	ü	174	AE	«	219	DB	█
130	82	é	175	AF	»	220	DC	▄
131	83	â	176	B0	░	221	DD	▌
132	84	ä	177	B1	▒	222	DE	▐
133	85	à	178	B2	▓	223	DF	▀
134	86	å	179	B3	│	224	E0	α
135	87	ç	180	B4	┤	225	E1	β
136	88	ê	181	B5	╡	226	E2	Γ
137	89	ë	182	B6	╢	227	E3	π
138	8A	è	183	B7	╖	228	E4	Σ
139	8B	ï	184	B8	╕	229	E5	σ
140	8C	î	185	B9	╣	230	E6	μ
141	8D	ì	186	BA	║	231	E7	τ
142	8E	Ä	187	BB	╗	232	E8	Φ
143	8F	Å	188	BC	╝	233	E9	θ
144	90	É	189	BD	╜	234	EA	Ω
145	91	æ	190	BE	╛	235	EB	δ
146	92	Æ	191	BF	┐	236	EC	∞
147	93	ô	192	C0	└	237	ED	Ø
148	94	ö	193	C1	┴	238	EE	∈
149	95	ò	194	C2	┬	239	EF	∩
150	96	û	195	C3	├	240	F0	▬
151	97	ù	196	C4	─	241	F1	±
152	98	ÿ	197	C5	┼	242	F2	≥
153	99	Ö	198	C6	╞	243	F3	≤
154	9A	Ü	199	C7	╟	244	F4	⌠
155	9B	¢	200	C8	╚	245	F5	⌡
156	9C	£	201	C9	╔	246	F6	÷
157	9D	¥	202	CA	╩	247	F7	≈
158	9E	₧	203	CB	╦	248	F8	°
159	9F	ƒ	204	CC	╠	249	F9	∙
160	A0	á	205	CD	═	250	FA	·
161	A1	í	206	CE	╬	251	FB	√
162	A2	ó	207	CF	╧	252	FC	ⁿ
163	A3	ú	208	D0	╨	253	FD	²
164	A4	ñ	209	D1	╤	254	FE	▪
165	A5	Ñ	210	D2	╥	255	FF	blank
166	A6	ª	211	D3	╙			'FF'
167	A7	º	212	D4	╘			

The PC Keyboard

The computer keyboard produces codes that are associated with letters and symbols. One key, however, can produce a different set of codes when you press other keys at the same time. For example, the A key normally produces the letter "a" (ASCII code 97), but when pressed along with the SHIFT key, it produces the letter "A" (ASCII code 65). Two other keys—CTRL and ALT—produce even more codes.

Some keys, such as the function keys (F1 through F10), produce two codes: a scan code (#27) and another code that indicates the key pressed. To read keys that produce scan codes, use the following procedure:

```
Procedure InKey(Var Ch : Char; Var FK : Boolean);
Begin
FK := False;
Read(Kbd,Ch);
If (Ch = #27) And KeyPressed Then
  Begin
  Read(Kbd,Ch);
  FK := True;
  End;
End;
```

When **FK** is True, a scan-code key has been pressed and the ASCII code for that key is returned in **Ch**. When **FK** is False, a normal key has been pressed and the value is contained in **Ch**.

Turbo Pascal Version 4.0 does not support the Kbd device unless you use the TURBO3 unit. Thus you can no longer use the statement

```
Read(Kbd,ch);
```

Instead you use the new ReadKey function. ReadKey accepts a character from the keyboard without echo. If a function key is pressed (or any other key that generates a scan code), ReadKey will return a null character (ASCII code 0). To read the character after the scan code, simply execute ReadKey once more. This process is demonstrated in the following program:

```
Program TestKey;
Var
   Ch : Char;
   Fk : Boolean;

Begin
   Writeln ('Press <Esc> to quit');
   Repeat
   Fk := False;
   Ch := ReadKey;
   If Ch = #0 Then
     Begin
     Fk := True;
     Ch := ReadKey;
     End;
   Writeln('Fk = ',fk,'   Ch = ',Ch);
   Until (Not FK) and (ch = 27); (* Escape Key Was Pressed *)
End;
```

The table that follows lists the keys on the PC keyboard and the codes they return.

Key	Normal		Shifted		Ctrl		Alt	
F1	27	59	27	84	27	94	27	104
F2	27	60	27	85	27	95	27	105
F3	27	61	27	86	27	96	27	106
F4	27	62	27	87	27	97	27	107
F5	27	63	27	88	27	98	27	108
F6	27	64	27	89	27	99	27	109
F7	27	65	27	90	27	100	27	110
F8	27	66	27	91	27	101	27	111
F9	27	67	27	92	27	102	27	112
F10	27	58	27	93	27	103	27	113
←	27	75		52	27	115		none
→	27	77		54	27	116		none
↑	27	72		56		none		none
↓	27	80		50		none		none

Key	Normal		Shifted		Ctrl		Alt	
HOME	27	71		55	27	119	none	
END	27	79		49	27	117	none	
PGUP	27	73		57	27	132	none	
PGDN	27	81		51	27	118	none	
INS	27	82		48	27	165	none	
DELETE	27	83		46	27	166	none	
ESC		27		27		27	none	
BACKSPACE		8		8		127	none	
TAB		9	27	15		none	none	
RETURN		13		13		10	none	
A		97		65		1	27	30
B		98		66		2	27	48
C		99		67		3	27	46
D		100		68		4	27	32
E		101		69		5	27	18
F		102		70		6	27	33
G		103		71		7	27	34
H		104		72		8	27	35
I		105		73		9	27	23
J		106		74		10	27	36
K		107		75		11	27	37
L		108		76		12	27	38
M		109		77		13	27	50
N		110		78		14	27	49
O		111		79		15	27	24
P		112		80		16	27	25
Q		113		81		17	27	16
R		114		82		18	27	19
S		115		83		19	27	31
T		116		84		20	27	20
U		117		85		21	27	22
V		118		86		22	27	47
W		119		87		23	27	17
X		120		88		24	27	45
Y		121		89		25	27	21
Z		122		90		26	27	44

Key	Normal	Shifted	Ctrl		Alt	
[	91	123		27	none	
\	92	124		28	none	
]	93	125		29	none	
`	96	126		none	none	
0	48	41		none	27	129
1	49	33		none	27	120
2	50	64	27	3	27	121
3	51	35		none	27	122
4	52	36		none	27	123
5	53	37		none	27	124
6	54	94		30	27	125
7	55	38		none	27	126
8	56	42		none	27	127
9	57	40		none	27	128
*	42	none	27	114	none	
+	43	43		none	none	
−	45	95		31	27	130
=	61	43		none	27	131
@	44	60		none	none	
/	47	63		none	none	
;	59	58		none	none	
~	96	126		none	none	

Turbo Pascal Versus Standard Pascal

Turbo Pascal 3.0 is very close to the standard set by Jensen & Wirth in the *User Manual and Report*. The differences that do exist are listed here.

Recursion   When using recursive calls in CP/M-80, Turbo Pascal does not allow you to pass a variable that is local to a subprogram as a reference parameter.

Get and Put   Turbo Pascal does not support the low-level input and output procedures **Get** and **Put**.

Goto Statements   A **Goto** statement cannot branch to a label that is outside the current block.

Page Procedure   Turbo Pascal does not support the **Page** procedure.

Procedures and Functions as Parameters   Turbo Pascal does not allow you to pass procedures or functions as parameters to other procedures or functions.

String Data Type   Turbo Pascal supports the string data type, which is not found in standard Pascal.

Reserved Words   The following reserved words are supported by Turbo Pascal, but not standard Pascal:

Absolute	Shl
External	Shr
Inline	String
Overlay	Xor

Despite the additional features of Turbo Pascal Version 4.0, the compiler actually conforms more closely to standard Pascal than does Version 3.0. That is because all of the extensions to 4.0 are contained in units rather than in the basic compiler. Thus, if you avoid using any of Version 4.0's special units such as DOS or CRT, your code will conform very closely to the standard proposed by ANSI. This conformance will come as a welcome relief to those who consider portability a must, yet it will still provide the power demanded by PC-only programmers.

CP/M, TURBO-8087,
and TURBO-BCD

CP/M-80
CP/M-86
TURBO-87
TURBO-BCD
Form
Numeric Fields
String Fields
CP/M, TURBO-8087, and TURBO-BCD with Turbo
    Pascal Version 4.0

With the release of Turbo Pascal Version 3.0, Borland made clear its intention to direct most of its further development toward MS/PC-DOS users. In general, CP/M versions of Turbo Pascal work the same as MS/PC-DOS versions. There are, however, some differences worth noting.

CP/M-80

CP/M-80 is the version of Turbo Pascal written for 8-bit computers with Z80 microprocessors.

Execute Command

The main menu includes an eXecute prompt from which you can run other programs and return to Turbo Pascal when done.

Compiler Messages

When you compile a program, Turbo Pascal displays the starting and ending addresses of the code, as shown here:

```
Start address:   XXXX  (min YYYY)
End   address:   XXXX  (max YYYY)
```

The start address is the first byte of code that follows the run-time library. The end address is the highest memory address available to your program. You can set the values of the start and end addresses yourself by pressing S or E and then entering the address. Do not set the start address to a value less than the default start address.

Addresses

Because the CP/M-80 version runs on 8-bit computers, addresses consist of just one integer offset—segments do not exist.

Array Subscript Optimization

The CP/M-80 version provides an **X** compiler option. When enabled, this option tells Turbo Pascal to minimize code size for subscript operations; when disabled, Turbo Pascal optimizes execution speed.

With Statements

By default, the CP/M-80 version allows nesting of up to two **With** statements. This can be changed with the **W** compiler option (for example, the statement {$W9} allows nesting of up to nine **With** statements). The value used with the **W** compiler option must be in the range 0-9.

Standard Identifiers

BIOS Procedure and Function

Syntax   Bios(Func {,Param});

Bios executes BIOS routines. **Func** is an integer denoting the number of the BIOS routine to call. **Param** is an integer that loads the BC register before the BIOS routine is called.

When used as a function, **Bios** returns the contents of the A register.

BiosHL Function

Syntax   BiosHL(Func {,Param});

BiosHL operates in the same way as the **Bios** function, except that the result is returned in the **HL** register pair.

Bdos Procedure and Function

Syntax   Bdos(Func {, Param});

Bdos executes CP/M BDOS routines. **Func** is an integer that denotes the BDOS routine to execute. **Param** is an integer that is loaded into the **DE** register pair prior to executing the BDOS routine.

When used as a function, **Bdos** returns an integer result in the **A** register.

BdosHL Function

Syntax   BdosHL(Func {, Param});

BdosHL operates the same as the **Bdos** function, except that the result is returned in the **HL** register pair.

RecurPtr

RecurPtr points to the memory location of the recursion stack. **RecurPtr** should always be less than **StackPtr**.

StackPtr

StackPtr points to the memory location at the top of the stack.

CP/M-86

CP/M-86 is the version of Turbo Pascal written for 16-bit 8088/86-based computers. In general, the CP/M-86 version is quite close to the MS/PC-DOS version. The major difference is the lack of many MS/PC-DOS-specific functions, such as Directory functions, the **MSDos** procedure, and so on.

Bdos

Syntax   Bdos(Regs : RegRec);
            RegRec = Record
                AX, BX, CX, DX, BP, SI, DI, DS, ES, Flags:
                Integer; End;

   Bdos executes BDOS functions by passing a register-set variable that contains the BDOS function call and any parameters the call needs.

TURBO-87

TURBO-87 is a version of Turbo Pascal that takes advantage of the power of the 8087 math coprocessor. The advantage of TURBO-87 is that it uses 64-bit reals, which provide 16 significant digits and a range of 4.19E−307 to 1.67E+308. This 8-byte real is incompatible with the 6-byte real in standard Turbo Pascal. If you want to exchange real-number data between versions, you must do so with text files that store the reals as ASCII text characters.

The major disadvantage of TURBO-87 programs is that they do not run on computers that do not have the 8087 chip.

TURBO-BCD

The TURBO-BCD version of Turbo Pascal stores real numbers in binary coded digit (BCD) format. Binary coded reals, which are more precise than standard reals, occupy 10 bytes, have 18 significant digits, and range from 1E−63 to 1E+63. The file TURBOBCD.COM contains the TURBO-BCD version.

Form

In addition to more accurate real numbers, TURBO-BCD supports output formatting with the **Form** function. **Form** controls string and numeric output by defining a template string. The template string contains characters and special codes that define how output will appear. For example, the statement

```
Form('Your account balance is: $#,###.##',1234.56);
```

returns the following string:

```
Your account balance is: $1,234.56
```

The string 'Your account balance is: $#,###.##' is the template string. The characters #,###.## constitute a field. Turbo Pascal takes the number 1234.56 and puts it in the field. Because you can include commas, decimal points, and other characters in a field, the **Form** command gives you a lot of control over output.

Here is a list of the special characters used by the **Form** command for both numeric and string fields.

Numeric Fields

\#   Indicates the position for a digit to be filled in. If there are more \# positions than numbers, the unused positions are filled with blanks.

@   This character also signifies a digit position. However, @ fills unused spaces with zeros.

*   Signifies a digit position, but fills in unused spaces with asterisks.

\$ When the dollar sign appears in the format statement, TURBO-BCD prints a dollar sign before the number.

,   The comma appears where placed in the **Form** statement. If a **Form** statement contains a comma but not a period, the comma is treated as a decimal place.

String Fields

\#   If the field consists of only \# characters, the string will be left justified.

@   If the field contains any @ characters, the string will be right justified.

CP/M, Turbo-8087, and TURBO-BCD
with Turbo Pascal Version 4.0

The bad news is that with Version 4.0, Turbo Pascal no longer comes in a variety of flavors; the good news is that Borland included most of the old flavors in Version 4.0. For example, 8087 support is standard. With the introduction of long integers, you no longer need BCD reals. Unfortunately, the **Form** procedure is no longer supported, so you must rewrite routines that use it. Version 4.0 does not support CP/M.

Sources of Information
on Turbo Pascal

Periodicals
Books

The major source of information on Turbo Pascal is, of course, Borland International. The *Turbo Pascal Reference Manual* contains a wealth of information on Turbo Pascal and should always be consulted first. If you cannot find your answer in the manual, Borland's technical support is excellent. Users who subscribe to CompuServe can get information, programs, and technical support by using the **GOBOR** option.

Other sources of information on Turbo Pascal are listed in this appendix.

Periodicals

Computer Language
P.O. Box 10953
Palo Alto, CA 94303

While not dedicated to Turbo Pascal, *Computer Language* does devote many of its pages to the Turbo Pascal compiler. You will also find a large number of advertisements for programs and utilities that expand or enhance Turbo Pascal.

TUG Lines: The Journal of the Turbo User Group
P.O. Box 1510
Poulsboro, WA 98370

TUG Lines, published six times a year, is a direct link to thousands of other Turbo Pascal programmers who submit articles and write letters on all aspects of Turbo Pascal. Product updates and reviews are also a regular feature.

Books

Cooper, Doug, and Clancy, Michael. *Oh! Pascal!* New York: W. W. Norton & Company, 1982.

Logically structured and highly detailed, this book is one of the better texts on Pascal.

Edwards, Charles C. *Advanced Techniques in Turbo Pascal.* Alameda, CA: Sybex, 1987.

Software interrupts, screen handling, windows, and other advanced topics are explained with clear prose and extensive example programs.

Faulk, Ed. *The Turbo Pascal Handbook.* Greensboro, NC: COMPUTE! Publications, Inc., 1986.

Good general discussion of Turbo Pascal with an emphasis on program development methodology.

Jamsa, Kris, and Nameroff, Steven. *Turbo Pascal Programmer's Library.* Berkeley, CA: Borland-Osborne/McGraw-Hill, 1987.

This comprehensive book contains a wealth of procedures and functions for a wide range of programming tasks.

Jensen, Kathleen, and Wirth, Niklaus. *Pascal User Manual and Report.* 3d ed. New York: Springer-Verlag, 1985.

The authoritative text on Pascal, written by the man who developed the language.

Knuth, Donald E. *The Art Of Computer Programming.* 2d ed. Reading, MA: Addison-Wesley, 1973.

One of the most important books written on the subject of computer programming, this text adds substance to many subjects covered in other books.

Lewis, Ted G. *Pascal for the IBM Personal Computer.* Reading, MA: Addison-Wesley, 1983.

While written for IBM Pascal, this book contains much information that is useful to beginning Turbo Pascal programmers.

Rugg, Tom, and Feldman, Phil. *Turbo Pascal Tips, Tricks, and Traps.* Indianapolis: Que Corporation, 1986.

This book is chock-full of neat little tidbits—general programming tips, tricks that you might not know about, and traps to avoid.

Schildt, Herbert. *Advanced Turbo Pascal.* Berkeley, CA: Borland-Osborne/McGraw-Hill, 1987.

A book that covers not only common programming tasks such as sorting and linked lists, but also unusual problems such as encryption, random-number generation, and expression parsing.

Stivison, Douglas S. *Introduction to Turbo Pascal.* Berkeley, CA: Sybex, 1985.

A beginner's guide to Turbo Pascal starting with simple programs and advancing to complex data structures and procedures.

Stivison, Douglas S. *Turbo Pascal Library*. Berkeley, CA: Sybex, 1986.

A compilation of useful routines written in Turbo Pascal.

Tiberghien, Jacques. *The Pascal Handbook*. Berkeley, CA: Sybex, 1985.

A concise discussion of Pascal's general concepts.

Weiss, Robert, and Seiter, Charles. *Pascal for FORTRAN Programmers*. Reading, MA: Addison-Wesley, 1984.

Those coming to Pascal from FORTRAN will appreciate this book,which eases the move to Pascal. Examples are given in FORTRAN and Pascal for comparison.

Zaks, Rodney. *Introduction to Pascal Including Turbo Pascal*. Berkeley, CA: Sybex, 1986.

A comprehensive reference guide that covers both IBM and Turbo Pascal. Especially useful for those concerned with program portability.

Zwass, Vladimir. *Introduction to Computer Science*. New York: Harper & Row, 1981.

This book, one of the Barnes & Noble "Outline Series," covers the entire field of computer science in just 268 well-written pages. Excel-lent for a general understanding of computer concepts.

Programmers interested in using assembler with Turbo Pascal will find the following books useful:

Coffron, James W. *Programming the 8086/8088*. Berkeley, CA: Sybex, 1983.

This technically-oriented book provides a detailed look at the architecture and operation of the 8088. All assembler commands are described in detail.

LaFore, Robert. *Assembly Language Primer for the IBM PC & XT.* New York: Plume, 1984.

A good general text for those beginning to program in assembler.

Metcalf, Christopher D., and Sugiyama, Marc B. *COMPUTE!'s Beginner's Guide to Machine Language on the IBM PC and PCjr.* Greensboro, NC: COMPUTE! Publications, Inc., 1985.

A step-by-step guide to PC assembler programming. The explanations are especially clear and the examples are straightforward.

Norton, Peter. *The Peter Norton Programmer's Guide to the IBM PC.* Bellevue, WA: Microsoft Press, 1985.

The one book no PC programmer should be without. From disks to video, BIOS to DOS, all subjects are covered thoroughly and clearly.

Turbo Pascal
Reserved Words

The following are Turbo Pascal 3.0 reserved words. Turbo Pascal Version 4.0 reserved words are listed starting on page 726 of this appendix.

Absolute   Declares a variable that resides at a specific memory location. For example:

```
Var
  R : Real;
  X : Integer Absolute R;        (* X shares memory with R *)
  Y : Integer Absolute 0000:0000; (* Y is located at segment 0,
                                      offset 0 *)
```

And   Combines two Boolean expressions such that both must be true in order for the entire expression to be true. For example:

```
If (A > B) And (C > D) Then ...
```

And   Also compares two bytes or integers and returns a third byte or integer. A bit in the resulting integer is turned on only if both bits in the same position are on in the first and second integers.

Array   Defines a data type that repeats its structure a specified number of times. For example,

```
Var
  I : Array [1..20] Of Integer;
```

defines a data item that consists of 20 integers.

Begin   Indicates the beginning of a block of code.

Case   A control structure that branches conditionally based on the value of a scalar. For example:

```
Var

  I : Integer;

Case I Of

1 :
  Begin
  { Statements }
  End;

2..3 :
  Begin
  { Statements }
  End;

4 :
  Begin
  { Statements }
  End;

End;
```

Const   Defines a data item as either a typed or untyped constant. For example:

```
Const
  I = 100;             (* Untyped Constant *)
  J : Integer = 100; (* Typed Constant *)
```

Div   Performs integer division.

Do   Used with looping control structures. For example:

```
For I := 1 To 10 Do ...
```

```
While I < 11 Do ...
```

DownTo   Used in For-Do loops where the counter is decremented. For example:

```
For I := 100 DownTo 1 Do ...
```

Else   Executes a block of code when an **If-Then** statement is false. For example:

```
If (A < B) Then
  Begin
  { Statements }
  End
Else
  Begin
  { Statements }
  End;
```

End   Denotes the end of a block of code, the end of a case statement, or the end of a program.

External   Tells Turbo Pascal to look in a disk file for the executable code for a procedure. For example:

```
Procedure CursorOn(Stype : Char); External 'CURSON.COM';
```

File   A data type that stores data on a disk.

For   Used in For-Do loops. For example:

```
For I := 1 To 100 Do ...
```

Forward   Declares the heading of a procedure before the actual procedure is defined. The full heading is declared in the **Forward** statement. Later, when the body of the procedure is declared, only the procedure name is used. For example:

```
Procedure X(I,J: Integer); Forward;


{ Statements }


Procedure X;
Begin
{ Statements }
End;
```

Function   Declares a subroutine to be a function. Functions return values of a specific data type. For example:

```
Function Add(a,b : Integer) : Integer;
Begin
Add := a + b;
End;
```

Goto   Transfers control to the location of the label contained in the **Goto** statement. For example:

```
Label
  EndProc; (* declare the label *)


Begin
For I := 1 To 1000 Do
  Begin
  j := j + i;
  If j > 1000 Then
    Goto EndProc; (* Transfer control to EndProc *)
  End;

EndProc:  (* label defines destination of Goto statement *)
End;
```

If   Used in **If-Then** statements. For example:

```
If (A < B) Then ...
```

In   Tests for set inclusion. For example:

```
Var
  Ch : Char;


If Ch In ['A'..'Z'] Then ...
```

Inline   Tells Turbo Pascal to treat the code that follows as machine language instructions. For example:

```
Inline($1E/$06/$07/$1F);
```

Label   Declares labels used with **Goto** statements (see **Goto**).

Mod   Returns the remainder of integer division.

Nil   Used in comparisons to test whether a pointer has a valid value. For example:

```
Type
  Aptr = ^Arecord;
  Arecord = Record
    I : Integer;
    Next : Aptr;
    End;

Var
  A : Aptr;

Begin
New(A);
If (A^.Next = Nil) Then ...
```

Not   Reverses the result of a Boolean expression. For example, if

```
(A > B)
```

is true, then

```
Not (A > B)
```

is false.

Of   Used in the **Case** statement (see **Case**) and in declaration of a set or array data type.

Or   Combines Boolean expressions such that the entire expression is true if either condition is true. For example,

```
If (A > B) Or (C > D) Then ...
```

is true if either the first or the second comparison (or both) is true.

Or   Also compares two bytes or integers and returns a third byte or integer. A bit in the resulting integer is turned on if either or both bits in the same position are on in the first and second integers.

Overlay   Tells Turbo Pascal to place this procedure or function in an overlay file. For example:

```
Overlay Procedure X(I : Integer);
Begin
End;
```

Packed   Declares arrays such that the arrays use less memory than they normally would. Turbo Pascal supports this reserved word, but it has no effect since all Turbo Pascal arrays are stored in packed format.

Procedure   Defines a block of code as belonging to a procedure.

Program   Defines a block of code as belonging to a program. This is the first statement in a program.

Record   Defines a complex data type that combines several simple or complex data types. For example:

```
Type
  Student = Record
    Name : String[20];
    Age : Integer;
    End;

  Class = Record
    Students : Array [1..30] Of Student;
    RoomNumber : Integer;
    End;
```

Repeat   Used in **Repeat-Until** control structures. For example:

```
I := 1;
  Repeat
  { Statements }
  I := I + 1;
  Until I > 100;
```

Set   Defines a set variable. For example:

```
Var
  Letters : Set Of Char;
```

Shl   Shifts the bits in a byte or integer one position to the left and sets the rightmost bit to zero.

Shr   Shifts the bits in a byte or integer one position to the right and sets the leftmost bit to zero.

String   Defines a string data type. A string can be defined from 1 to 255 characters long. For example:

```
Var
  s : String[255];
```

Then   Used in **If-Then** statements (see **If**).

To   Used in For-Do loops (see **For**).

Type   Defines data types that can then be used to define variables. For example:

```
Type
  PersonType = Record
    Name : String[20];
    Address : String[50];
    Income : Real;
    End;

Var
  Person1, Person2 : PersonType;
```

Until   Used in Repeat-Until loops (see **Repeat**).

Var   Defines variables. For example:

```
Var
  i : Integer;
  s : String[255];
```

While   Used in While-Do loops. For example:

```
I := 0;
While I < 100 Do
  Begin
  { Statements }
  I := I + 1;
  End;
```

With   Used for implicit reference to a record variable. For example:

```
Var
  Person : Record
    Name : String[20];
    Age : Integer;
    End;

Begin
With Person Do
  Begin
  ReadLn(Name);
  ReadLn(Age);
  End;
End.
```

Xor   Combines Boolean expressions such that the entire expression is true if one of two conditions is true. For example,

```
If (A > B) Xor (C > D) Then ...
```

is true if the first comparison is true or the second comparison is true, but not if both are true.

Xor   Also compares two bytes or integers and returns a third byte or integer. A bit in the resulting integer is turned on if either, but not both, bits in the same position are on in the first and second integers.

Following is a list of Turbo Pascal Version 4.0 Reserved Words:

Implementation   Declares the beginning of the implementation section of a unit. The implementation section contains the body of the routines declared in the interface section. An example of an implementation section is shown here:

```
Implementation

Procedure X_Y_String; (* Parameters are not listed *)
Begin
GoToXY(x,y);
Write(S);
End;
```

Interface   Declares the beginning of the interface section of a unit. The interface section contains the procedure and function headings that will be visible to programs and units that use the current unit. An example of an interface section is shown here:

```
Interface
Uses CRT;
Type
   MaxStr = String[255];

Procedure X_Y_String(x,y : Integer; s : MaxStr);
```

Interrupt   Declares a procedure as an interrupt procedure. Interrupt procedures replace DOS and BIOS services that are called by hardware or software interrupt. The declaration can include parameters that contain CPU register information. A typical declaration would look like this:

```
Procedure Handler(Flags,
                  CS,
                  IP,
                  AX,
                  BX,
                  CX,
                  DX,
                  SI,
                  DI,
                  DS,
                  ES,
                  BP : Word); Interrupt;
begin
End;
```

Unit   Declares the current file to be a unit. Units are combinations of routines that are compiled separately from the main program and are stored in a file with the .TPU extension. The following is an example of a unit:

```
Unit Strng;
Interface

Uses CRT;
Type
   MaxStr = String[255];

Procedure X_Y_String(x,y : Integer; s : MaxStr);
```

```
Implementation

Procedure X_Y_String; (* Parameters are not listed
Begin
GoToXY(x,y);
Write(S);
End;

End.
```

Uses   Declares which units are to be accessed by the program or unit. For example:

```
Program X;

Uses DOS, CRT, Turbo3;

Begin

End.
```

Turbo Pascal Standard Procedure Reference

The following are Turbo Pascal 3.0 standard procedures. Turbo Pascal 4.0 standard procedures are listed starting on page 755 of this Appendix.

Abs

Syntax   Function Abs(r : Real) : Real;
Function Abs(i : Integer) : Integer;

Description   Abs returns the absolute value of the parameter passed to it.

Addr

Syntax   Function Addr(Var Variable) : Pointer;
(PC/MS-DOS)
Function Addr(Var Variable) : Integer;
(CP/M)

Description   Addr returns the address of a variable. In PC/MS-DOS systems, the result is a 32-bit pointer that represents the segment and offset.

Append

Syntax   Procedure Append(Var F: Text);

Description   Append opens a text file for writing and positions the file pointer at the end of the file.

ArcTan

Syntax   Function ArcTan(R: Real) : Real;

Description   **ArcTan** returns the arctangent of the parameter passed to it.

Assign

Syntax   Procedure Assign(Var F: File; Name : String);

Description   **Assign** links file variable **F** to the file named in **Name**.

BlockRead

Syntax   Procedure BlockRead(Var F: File;
                                 Var B: Type;
                                 NumRecs: Integer;
                                 Var RecsRead: Integer);

Description   **BlockRead** attempts to read **NumRecs** records from untyped file **F** into buffer **B**. **RecsRead** indicates the number of records actually read. Note that the **RecsRead** parameter is supported only in PC/MS-DOS versions. The variable **RecsRead** is optional in Version 3.0 but required in Version 4.0.

BlockWrite

Syntax   Procedure BlockWrite(Var F: File;
                                   Var B: Type;
                                   NumRecs: Integer);

Description   **BlockWrite** writes **NumRecs** records from buffer **B** to untyped file **F**.

Chain

Syntax   Procedure Chain(F: File);

Description   **Chain** executes the chain file that was previously assigned to **F**. For example:

```
Assign(F,'CHAINFLE.CHN');
Chain(F);
```

ChDir

Syntax   Procedure ChDir(S: String);

Description   **ChDir** changes the current directory to that in **S**.

Chr (Char)

Syntax   Function Chr(I: Integer);
Function Char(I: Integer);

Description   **Chr or Char** returns the ASCII character that corresponds to **I**. The parameter can be any ordinal value with a range of 0 to 225.

Close

Syntax   Procedure Close(Var F: File);

Description   **Close** flushes the buffer for file **F** and then closes the file.

ClrEol

Syntax   Procedure ClrEol;

Description   **ClrEol** clears the current screen line from the cursor position to the right edge of the screen.

ClrScr

Syntax   Procedure ClrScr;

Description   **ClrScr** clears the screen and positions the cursor at location (1,1) on the screen.

Concat

Syntax   Function Concat(S1, S2,...,Sn) : String;

Description   **Concat** combines any number of strings and returns them as a single string. If the length of the concatenated string is greater than 255, Turbo Pascal generates a run-time error.

Copy

Syntax   Function Copy(S: String; P, L: Integer) : String;

Description   **Copy** returns a portion of string **S**, which starts at character number **P** and contains **L** characters.

Cos

Syntax   Function Cos(R: Real) : Real;

Description   **Cos** returns the cosine of **R**.

CrtExit

Syntax   Procedure CrtExit;

Description   **CrtExit** sends the terminal reset string to the screen.

CrtInit

Syntax   Procedure CrtInit;

Description   **CrtInit** sends the terminal initialization string to the screen.

Delay

Syntax   Procedure Delay(I: Integer);

Description   **Delay** halts program execution for approximately **I** milliseconds.

Delete

Syntax   Procedure Delete(S: String; P, L: Integer);

Description   **Delete** removes **L** characters from string **S** starting with character number **P**.

DelLine

Syntax   Procedure DelLine;

Description   **DelLine** deletes the screen line on which the cursor is located. Lines below the deleted line scroll up one line.

Dispose

Syntax   Procedure Dispose(P: Pointer);

Description   **Dispose** frees heap memory allocated to a pointer variable. **Dispose** is used in conjunction with the New command.

Eof

Syntax   Function Eof(F: File) : Boolean;

Description   **Eof** returns True when the file pointer in **F** reaches the end of the file.

Eoln

Syntax   Function Eoln(F: File) : Boolean;

Description   **Eoln** returns True when the file pointer in **F** reaches either the end of a line (indicated by a carriage return and linefeed) or the end of the file.

Erase

Syntax   Procedure Erase(F: File);

Description   **Erase** deletes disk file **F** and removes its information from the directory.

Execute

Syntax   Procedure Execute(F: File);

Description   **Execute** initiates execution of a compiled Turbo Pascal program file assigned to **F**. For example:

```
Assign(F,'PROG1.COM');

Execute(F);
```

Exit

Syntax   Procedure Exit;

Description   **Exit** causes a program to leave the block currently being executed.

Exp

Syntax   Function Exp(R: Real) : Real;

Description   **Exp** returns the exponential of **R**.

FilePos

Syntax   Function FilePos(F: File) : Integer;

Description   **FilePos** returns the record number at which the file pointer in **F** is located. The first record in a file is number 0.

FileSize

Syntax   Function FileSize(F: File) : Integer;

Description   **FileSize** returns the number of records currently contained in **F**.

FillChar

Syntax   Procedure FillChar(Variable: Type; I, Code: Integer);

Description   **FillChar** fills **I** bytes of memory with the value **Code** starting at the address of **Variable**.

Frac

Syntax   Function Frac(R: Real) : Real;

Description   **Frac** returns the noninteger portion of **R**.

FreeMem

Syntax   Procedure FreeMem(Var P: Pointer; I: Integer);

Description   **FreeMem** frees **I** bytes of heap memory associated with variable **P**.

GetDir

Syntax   Procedure GetDir(I: Integer; Var S: String);

Description   **GetDir** gets the directory for the drive specified by **I**. The directory is returned in **S**. If **I** is zero, **GetDir**
searches the default drive.

GetMem

Syntax   Procedure GetMem(Var P: Pointer; I: Integer);

Description   **GetMem** reserves **I** bytes on the heap for use
by variable **P**.

GoToXY

Syntax   Procedure GoToXY(X, Y: Integer);

Description   **GoToXY** places the cursor at screen coordinates X:Y.

Halt

Syntax   Procedure Halt;

Description   **Halt** terminates a program.

Hi

Syntax   Function Hi(I: Integer) : Byte;

Description   **Hi** returns the high-order byte from the integer value of **I**.

HighVideo

Syntax   Procedure HighVideo;

Description   **HighVideo** enables the high-intensity video display.

Insert

Syntax   Procedure Insert(S1, S2: String; I: Integer);

Description   **Insert** places **S1** inside **S2** at character position number **I**.

InsLine

Syntax   Procedure InsLine;

Description   **InsLine** inserts a blank line on the screen at the current cursor position. All lines beneath the new line are scrolled down.

Int

Syntax   Function Int(Var R: Real) : Integer;

Description   Int returns the integer portion of **R**.

Intr

Syntax   Procedure Intr(Func : Integer; Param : Record);

Description   **Intr** calls BIOS functions.

IOresult

Syntax   Function IOresult : Integer;

Description   Turbo Pascal sets **IOresult** to a value whenever an input/output operation is performed. If **IOresult** is not equal to zero, an error occurred.

KeyPressed

Syntax   Function KeyPressed : Boolean;

Description   **KeyPressed** returns True when a key has been pressed. The {$C−} compiler directive must be set to off.

Length

Syntax   Function Length(S: String) : Integer;

Description   **Length** returns the length of string S.

Ln

Syntax   Function Ln(Var R: Real) : Real;

Description   **Ln** returns the natural logarithm of **R**.

Lo

Syntax   Function Lo(I: Integer) : Byte;

Description   **Lo** returns the low-order byte of integer **I**.

LongFilePos

Syntax   Function LongFilePos(Var F: File) : Real;

Description   **LongFilePos** returns the record number at which the file pointer in **F** is located.

LongFileSize

Syntax   Function LongFileSize(Var F: File) : Real;

Description   **LongFileSize** returns the number of records in file **F**.

LongSeek

Syntax   Procedure LongSeek(Var F: File; R: Real);

Description   **LongSeek** positions the file pointer at record **R** in file **F**.

LowVideo

Syntax   Procedure LowVideo;

Description   **LowVideo** sets the video display to low intensity.

Mark

Syntax   Procedure Mark(P: Pointer);

Description   **Mark** allocates space on the heap for pointer **P**.

MaxAvail

Syntax   Function MaxAvail: Integer;

Description   **MaxAvail** returns the size of the largest contiguous block of free memory available for dynamic data allocation. In Version 3.0 the result is in paragraphs (16 bytes) but in Version 4.0 the result is in bytes.

MemAvail

Syntax   Function MemAvail: Integer

Description   **MemAvail** returns the total amount of memory available for dynamic data allocation. In Version 3.0 the result is in paragraphs (16 bytes) but in Version 4.0 the result is in bytes.

MkDir

Syntax   Procedure MkDir(S: String);

Description   **MkDir** makes a directory with the name stored in string **S**.

Move

Syntax   Procedure Move(Var V1, V2: type; I: Integer);

Description   **Move** copies **I** bytes of memory from the location of variable **V1** to the location of variable **V2**.

MsDos

Syntax   Procedure MsDos(Param: Record);

Description   **MsDos** executes DOS services.

New

Syntax   Procedure New(Var P: Pointer);

Description   **New** allocates memory on the heap for pointer **P**. After memory is allocated, the variable is referred to as **P^**.

NormVideo

Syntax   Procedure NormVideo;

Description   **NormVideo** returns the video display to normal intensity.

NoSound

Syntax   Procedure NoSound;

Description   **NoSound** stops any tone currently being generated by the PC's speaker.

Odd

Syntax   Function Odd(I: Integer) : Boolean;

Description   **Odd** returns True when **I** is odd and False when **I** is even.

Ofs

Syntax   Function Ofs(<Variable, Procedure, or Function>) : Integer;

Description   **Ofs** returns the memory-address offset for any variable, procedure, or function.

Ord

Syntax   Function Ord(S: Scalar) : Integer;

Description   **Ord** returns the integer value of any scalar variable.

ParamCount

Syntax   Function ParamCount: Integer;

Description   **ParamCount** returns the number of command-line parameters entered.

ParamStr

Syntax   Function ParamStr(I: Integer) : String;

Description   **ParamStr** returns parameters that were entered on the command line. For example, **ParamStr(1)** returns the first parameter.

Pos

Syntax   Function Pos(SubS, S : String) : Integer;

Description   **Pos** returns the position of **SubS** in S. If **SubS** is not found in S, **Pos** returns 0.

Pred

Syntax   Function Pred(Var S: Scalar): Integer;

Description   **Pred** returns the value that precedes the value of scalar S.

Ptr

Syntax   Function Ptr(Segment, Offset: Integer) : Pointer;

Description   **Ptr** accepts two integers that contain a segment and an offset and returns a single 32-bit pointer value.

Random

Syntax   Function Random(I: Integer) : Integer;
Function Random: Real;

Description   **Random** returns a number randomly generated by Turbo Pascal. If you pass an integer parameter, **Random** returns an integer greater than or equal to zero and less than the parameter. Without an integer, **Random** returns a real value greater than or equal to zero and less than 1.

Randomize

Syntax   Function Randomize;

Description   **Randomize** initializes the random number generator.

Read (ReadLn)

Syntax   Procedure Read({Var F: File,} Parameters);
Procedure ReadLn({Var F: File,} Parameters);

Description   **Read** receives input from either the standard input device or the file specified by **F**. **ReadLn**, which can be used only on text files, receives input in the same way that **Read** does, but after reading in the data, **ReadLn** moves the file pointer forward past the next carriage return/linefeed delimiter.

Release

Syntax   Procedure Release(Var P: Pointer);

Description   **Release** reclaims all memory above **P** that was previously allocated on the heap by the **Mark** command.

Rename

Syntax   Procedure Rename(Var F: File; S: String);

Description   **Rename** changes the name of file **F** to that contained in S.

Reset

Syntax   Procedure Reset(Var F: File {; I: Integer});

Description   **Reset** opens file **F** for reading. If the file is untyped, you can specify the record size in **I**.

Rewrite

Syntax   Procedure Rewrite(Var F: File {; I: Integer});

Description   **Rewrite** prepares a file to be written. If the file does not exist, Turbo Pascal creates it. If the file does exist, its contents are destroyed. If the file is untyped, you can specify the record size in **I**.

RmDir

Syntax   Procedure RmDir(S: String);

Description   **RmDir** removes the directory specified in S.

Round

Syntax   Function Round(R: Real) : Integer;

Description   **Round** returns the rounded integer value of the variable **R**.

Seek

Syntax   Procedure Seek(Var F: File; P: Integer);

Description   **Seek** moves the file pointer to the beginning of record number **P** in file **F**.

SeekEof

Syntax   Function SeekEof(Var F: File) Boolean;

Description   **SeekEof** is similar to **Eof**, except that it skips blanks, tabs, and end-of-line markers (CR/LF) before it tests for an end-of-file marker. The type of result is Boolean.

SeekEoln

Syntax   Function SeekEoln(Var F: File): Boolean;

Description   **SeekEoln** is similar to **Eoln**, except that it skips blanks and tabs before it tests for an end-of-line marker. The type of the result is Boolean.

Seg

Syntax   Function Seg(Var Variable) : Integer;
Function Seg(<Procedure or Function>) : Integer;

Description   **Seg** returns the segment of a variable, procedure, or function.

Sin

Syntax   Function Sin(R: Real) : Real;

Description   **Sin** returns the sine of **R**.

SizeOf

Syntax   Function SizeOf(Var Variable) : Integer;

Description   **SizeOf** returns the number of bytes required by a variable or a data type.

Sound

Syntax   Procedure Sound(Freq: Integer);

Description   **Sound** generates a tone from the PC's speaker at a frequency specified by **Freq**. The tone continues until the **NoSound** command is issued.

Sqr

Syntax   Function Sqr(R: Real) : Real;

Description   **Sqr** returns the square of **R**.

Sqrt

Syntax   Function Sqrt(R: Real) : Real;

Description   **Sqrt** returns the square root of **R**.

Str

Syntax   Procedure Str(I: Integer; Var S: String);
Procedure Str(R: Real; Var S: String);

Description   **Str** converts a real or integer number into a string.

Succ

Syntax   Function Succ(S: Scalar) : Integer;

Description   **Succ** returns the next successive value of scalar **S**.

Swap

Syntax   Function Swap(I: Integer) : Integer;

Description   **Swap** reverses the positions of the low-order and high-order bytes in an integer. For example, if **I** equals 00FFh, **Swap** returns FF00h.

TextBackground

Syntax   Procedure TextBackground(Color: Integer);

Description   **TextBackground** changes the default background color to that specified by **Color**.

TextColor

Syntax   Procedure TextColor(Color: Integer);

Description   **TextColor** changes the default foreground color to that specified by **Color**.

Trunc

Syntax   Function Trunc(R: Real) : Integer;

Description   **Trunc** returns the integer portion of **R**. The result must be within the legal range of an integer.

UpCase

Syntax   Function UpCase(C: Char) : Char;

Description   **UpCase** returns the uppercase value of C if
C is a lowercase letter.

Val

Syntax   Procedure Val(S: String; Var R: Real; Var Code:
            Integer);
          Procedure Val(S: String; Var I: Integer; Var
            Code: Integer);

Description   **Val** attempts to convert **S** into a numerical
value (**R** or **I**). If the conversion is successful, Turbo Pascal
sets **Code** equal to zero. If unsuccessful, **Code** contains an
integer that represents the character in the string at which
the error occurred.

WhereX

Syntax   Function WhereX : Integer;

Description   **WhereX** returns the column in the current
window at which the cursor is located.

WhereY

Syntax   Function WhereY : Integer;

Description   **WhereY** returns the row in the current window at which the cursor is located.

Window

Syntax   Procedure Window(x1,y1,x2,y2 : Integer);

Description   **Window** restricts the active screen to the rectangle defined by coordinates x1:y1 (upper-left) and x2:y2 (lower-right). Turbo Pascal treats the upper-left corner of the window as coordinates 1:1.

Write (WriteLn)

Syntax   Procedure Write({Var F: File,} Parameters);
          Procedure WriteLn({Var F: File,} Parameters);

Description   **Write** accepts a list of parameters, which it writes to the default output device. When the first parameter is a file variable, output is directed to that file. **WriteLn**, which can be used only on text files, operates in the same way as **Write**, but it adds a carriage return and linefeed at the end of the output.

The following are Turbo Pascal Version 4.0 standard procedures:

AssignCRT

Syntax   Procedure AssignCRT(F : Text);

Description   **AssignCRT** assigns text file **F** to the monitor device. As with any text file, you must use **Rewrite** before any output is generated. This allows faster output than would normally be possible using standard output.

DiskFree

Syntax   Function DiskFree(i :Integer) : LongInt;

Description   **DiskFree** returns the amount of free disk space on drive I in bytes. The parameter is 1 for drive A, 2 for drive B, and so on. When I is 0, **DiskFree** scans the default drive.

DiskSize

Syntax   Function DiskSize(i :Integer) : LongInt;

Description   **DiskSize** returns the total amount of disk space on drive I in bytes. The parameter is 1 for drive A, 2 for drive B, and so on. When I is 0, **DiskSize** scans the default drive.

DosExitCode

Syntax   Function DosExitCode : Integer;

Description   **DosExitCode** returns the exit code of a subprocess. The high-byte of the integer is 0 for normal termination, 1 if termination was forced by CTRL-C at the keyboard, or 3 if it was terminated by the **Keep** procedure.

Exec

Syntax   Procedure Exec(Path, CmdLine : String);

Description   **Exec** loads and executes the program named in **Path** and passes **CmdLine** to the program as a command-line parameter. **Path** must include both the path and name of the program file to execute. The following example loads COMMAND.COM, which is assumed to be in the root directory of the default drive, and displays a directory with the W option.

```
Exec('\COMMAND.COM','/c DIR /W');
{Assumes COMMAND.COM is in the root directory.}
```

You must set a limit to the maximum value of heap memory using the {$M} compiler directive to allow enough memory for the called program to run.

FindFirst

Syntax   Procedure FindFirst(Path : String;
                                 Attr : Integer;
                                 Var S : SearchRec);

Description   **FindFirst** searches the directory defined by **Path** for all normal files plus any files with attributes that match **Attr**. The first matching filename found, if any, is stored in S. If no matching files are found, DosError will be set equal to 18. The structure of **SearchRec** is as follows:

```
Type
  SearchRec = Record
    Fill : Array [1..2] Of Byte;
    Attr : Byte;
    Time : LongInt;
    Size : LongInt;
    Name : String[12];
    End;
```

FindNext

Syntax   Procedure FindNext(Var S : SearchRec);

Description   **FindNext** searches the directory defined by **Path** for all normal files plus any files with attributes that match **Attr**. A call to **FindNext** must be preceded by a call to **FindFirst**. The filenames found are stored in S. When no more matching files are found, DosError will be set equal to 18. The structure of **SearchRec** is as follows:

```
Type
  SearchRec = Record
    Fill : Array [1..2] Of Byte;
    Attr : Byte;
    Time : LongInt;
    Size : LongInt;
    Name : String[12];
    End;
```

GetDate

Syntax   Procedure GetDate(Var Year,
                          Month,
                          Day,
                          DayOfWeek: Word);

Description   GetDate gets the current system date and returns the information in the parameters. The year always contains the century, and **DayOfWeek** ranges from 0 to 6, with 0 meaning Sunday.

GetFAttr

Syntax   Procedure GetFAttr(Var F : File;
                          Var Attr : Byte);

Description   GetFAttr gets the attribute byte for file **F** and returns it in parameter **Attr**. The file must be assigned before calling this procedure.

GetFTime

Syntax   Procedure GetFTime(Var F : File;
                          Var Time : LongInt);

Description   GetFTime gets the time and date stamp for file **F**. The file must be assigned before calling **GetFTime**. The result returned in **Time** is a packed value and must be decoded with the procedure **UnpackTime**.

GetIntVec

Syntax   Procedure GetIntVec(IntNo : Byte;
                              Var Vector : Pointer);

Description   **GetIntVec** returns in **Vector** the contents of the interrupt vector table for interrupt **IntNo**.

GetTime

Syntax   Procedure GetTime(Var Hour,
                              Minute,
                              Second,
                              Hundredths : Word);

Description   **GetTime** returns the system time in hours, minutes, seconds, and hundredths of seconds.

Keep

Syntax   Procedure Keep(ExitCode : Integer);

Description   **Keep** locks the current program in memory as a terminate/stay resident program. Make sure you limit the heap and stack before calling **Keep** or else your program will use all available memory and lock up your system.

MaxAvail

Syntax   Function MaxAvail : LongInt;

Description   **MaxAvail** returns the size of the largest contiguous free block in the heap corresponding to the size of the largest dynamic variable that can be allocated at that time.

MemAvail

Syntax   Function MemAvail : LongInt;

Description   **MemAvail** returns the amount in bytes of all free blocks in the heap.

PackTime

Syntax   Procedure PackTime(Var DT : DateTime);
                              Var Time : LongInt;

Description   **PackTime** encodes the data in **DT** and returns the result in **Time**. The **DateTime** type is defined as follows:

```
Type
  DateTime = Record
    Year, Month, Day, Hour, Min, Sec : Word;
    End;
```


ReadKey

Syntax   Function ReadKey : Char;

Description   **ReadKey** returns the character when a key is pressed. If the key generates a scan code, **ReadKey**

returns #0, and a subsequent call to **ReadKey** will read the character following the scan code.

SetDate

Syntax   Procedure SetDate(Year,
                                                Month,
                                                Day: Word);

Description   **SetDate** sets the system date using the information in the parameters. The year must contain the century.

SetFAttr

Syntax   Procedure SetFAttr(Var F : File;
                                                 Attr : Byte);

Description   **SetFAttr** sets the attribute byte for file **F** using the parameter **Attr**. The file must be assigned before calling this procedure.

SetFTime

Syntax   Procedure SetFTime(Var F : File;
                                                 Time : LongInt);

Description   **SetFTime** sets the time and date stamp for file **F**. The file must be assigned before calling **SetFTime**. The value of **Time** must be prepared with the procedure **PackTime** before calling **SetFTime**.

SetIntVec

Syntax   Procedure SetIntVec(IntNo : Byte;
                          Var Vector : Pointer);

Description   **SetIntVec** sets the contents of the interrupt vector table for interrupt **IntNo** equal to **Vector**. Before you set an interrupt vector, you should save the current value of the vector so that it can be restored later. All vectors should be restored to their original values before program termination.

SetTextBuf

Syntax   Procedure SetTextBuf(Var F : Text;
                          Var Buf [;Size:Word];

Description   **SetTextBuf** assigns a buffer to a text file. **F** is a text-file variable; **Buf** is any variable; and **Size** is an optional expression of type word. If you do not specify a text buffer with **SetTextBuf**, the text fill will be automatically assigned a 128-byte buffer.

SetTime

Syntax   Procedure SetTime(Hour,
                          Minute,
                          Second,
                          Hundredths : Integer);

Description   **SetTime** sets the system time in hours, minutes, seconds, and hundredths of seconds.

TextMode

Syntax   Procedure TextMode(Mode : Integer);

Description   **TextMode** sets the current window to the video mode defined by the parameter **Mode**. The possible values of **Mode** are BW40, C40, BW80, C80, MONO, or LAST. When **Mode** is LAST, **TextMode** sets the video mode to the mode that existed prior to the last call to **TextMode**.

UnpackTime

Syntax   Procedure UnpackTime(Time : Long Int;
                                          Var DT : Date Time);

Description   **UnpackTime** decodes the value of **Time** and returns the results in variable **DT**. The **DateTime** type is defined as follows:

```
Type
  DateTime = Record
    Year, Month, Day, Hour, Min, Sec : Word;
    End;
```

Turbo Pascal Version 4.0 Graph Unit

Graph Constants
Graphics Procedures

In addition to providing compatibility with your existing graphics programs, Turbo Pascal 4.0 includes a unit named Graph that contains a complete set of graphics routines that support CGA, Hercules monochrome, EGA, and other video standards. This appendix describes these routines and how you use them.

Graph Constants

The Graph unit declares constants that make using the graph routines easier. For example, the constants shown below are used to interpret the results of the **GraphResult** procedure.

```
Const
  grOk            =    0; { No error }
  grNoInitGraph   =   -1; { (BGI) graphics not installed }
  grNotDetected   =   -2; { Graphics hardware not detected }
  grFileNotFound  =   -3; { Device driver file not found (DRV0.BGI) }
  grInvalidDriver =   -4; { Invalid device driver file (DRV0.BGI) }
  grNoLoadMem     =   -5; { Not enough memory to load driver }
```

```
grNoScanMem          =  -6; { Out of memory in scan fill }
grNoFloodMem         =  -7; { Out of memory in flood fill }
grFontNotFound       =  -8; { Font file not found (h) }
grNoFontMem          =  -9; { Not enough memory to load font }
grInvalidMode        = -10; { Invalid graphics mode for selected driver }
grError              = -11; { Graphics error (generic error) }
grIOerror            = -12; { Graphics I/O error }
grInvalidFont        = -13; { Invalid font file (h) }
grInvalidFontNum     = -14; { Invalid font number }
grInvalidDeviceNum   = -15; { Invalid device number }
```

With these constants, you can write code that checks for errors and takes appropriate action. For example, the following segment of code checks to see if an error occurred. If no error occurred, the program continues; if an error did occur, the type of error is displayed and the program terminated.

```
Err := GraphResult;
If Err < 0 Then
  Begin
  CloseGraph;
  Writeln(GraphErrorMsg(Err));
  Halt;
  End;
```

Another set of constants defines drivers for the type of graphic display adapter installed in the computer:

```
Const
  Detect   =  0;    { Graph determines the adapter begin used }
  CGA      =  1;    { Color Graphics Adapter }
  MCGA     =  2;    { Color Graphics Adapter on PS/2 }
  EGA      =  3;    { Enhanced Graphics Adapter 256K }
  EGA64    =  4;    { Enhanced Graphics Adapter 64K }
  EGAMono  =  5;    { Enhanced Graphics Adapter - Monochrome }
  RESERVED =  6;    { Not used }
  HercMono =  7;    { Hercules Monochrome Adapter }
  ATT400   =  8;    { ATT Adapter }
  VGA      =  9;    { Virtual Graphics Adapter }
  PC3270   = 10;    { 3270 Graphics Adapter }
```

Most adapters support more than one graphics mode. Therefore you must select both a driver (as above) and a mode. The modes for each type of driver are defined as follows:

```
Const

{ CGA }

{ 320x200 color palette 1: red, yellow, green; 1 page }
CGAC1  = 0;

{ 320x200 color palette 2: cyan, magenta, white; 1 page }
CGAC2  = 1;

{ 640x200 1 page }
CGAHi  = 2;


{MCGA }


MCGAC1        = 0;    { 320x200 color palette 1: red, yellow,
                        green; 1 page }

{ 320x200 color palette 2: cyan, magenta, white; 1 page }
MCGAC2 = 1;

{ 640x200 1 page }
MCGAMed = 2;

{ 640x480 2 color 1 page }
MCGAHi = 3;


{ EGA }


{ 640x200 4 pages }
EGALo = 0;

{ 640x350 16 color 2 pages }
EGAHi = 1;


{ EGA64 }


{ 640x200 16 color 1 page }
EGA64Lo = 0;

{ 640x350 4 color  1 page }
EGA64Hi = 1;


{ EGAMono }

{ 640x350 64K on card, 1 page - 256K on card, 4 pages }
EGAMonoHi   = 3;
```

```
{ HercMono }

  { 720x348 2 pages }
  HercMonoHi  = 0;


{ ATT400 }


  { 320x200 color palette 1: red, yellow, green; 1 page }
  ATT400C1 = 0;

  { 320x200 color palette 2: cyan, magenta, white; 1 page }
  ATT400C2 = 1;


  { 640x200 1 page }
  ATT400Med = 2;


  { 640x400 1 page }
  ATT400Hi = 3;



{ VGA }

  { 640x200 16 color 4 pages }
  VGALo = 0;

  { 640x350 16 color 2 pages }
  VGAMed = 1;

  { 640x480 16 color 1 page }
  VGAHi = 2;


  { PC3270 }

  { 720x350 1 page }
  PC3270Hi = 0;
```

If, for example, your computer uses the CGA adapter, you must use the CGA driver, but you can choose from three modes: CGAC1, CGAC2, and CGAHi.

Graph defines constants that represent the colors that can be used by graphics adapters, as shown here:

```
Const
  Black           = 0;
```

```
Blue           = 1;
Green          = 2;
Cyan           = 3;
Red            = 4;
Magenta        = 5;
Brown          = 6;
LightGray      = 7;
DarkGray       = 8;
LightBlue      = 9;
LightGreen     = 10;
LightCyan      = 11;
LightRed       = 12;
LightMagenta   = 13;
Yellow         = 14;
White          = 15;
```

You can specify different kinds of line types when creating graphics. The line types supported by the Graph unit are defined by the following constants:

```
Const
   SolidLn    = 0; { Solid Line }
   DottedLn   = 1; { Dotted Line }
   CenterLn   = 2; {    }
   DashedLn   = 3; { Dashed Line }
   UserBitLn  = 4; { User defined line style }

   NormWidth  = 1; { Normal line }
   ThickWidth = 3; { Thick line }
```

To set the line style to thick dotted lines, for example, you would use this command:

```
SetLineStyle(DottedLn,0,ThickWidth);
```

In addition to setting line styles, you can also set text styles. The Graph unit allows you to display graph text in five fonts, vertically or horizontally, and in different sizes. The following constants are provided for this purpose:

```
Const

    DefaultFont     = 0;      { 8x8 bit mapped font }

    TriplexFont     = 1;      { "Stroked" fonts }
    SmallFont       = 2;
    SansSerifFont   = 3;
    GothicFont      = 4;

    HorizDir    = 0;      { left to right }
    VertDir     = 1;      { bottom to top }
```

Several procedures require a parameter to control clipping. For these procedures, use the following constants:

```
Const
    ClipOn  = true;
    ClipOff = false;
```

With the Graph unit, you can fill graphics shapes with colors and patterns. Thirteen patterns are predefined in constants, as shown here:

```
Const
    EmptyFill        = 0;   { fills area in background color }
    SolidFill        = 1;   { fills area in solid fill color }
    LineFill         = 2;   { --- fill }
    LtSlashFill      = 3;   { /// fill }
    SlashFill        = 4;   { /// fill with thick lines }
    BkSlashFill      = 5;   { \\\ fill with thick lines }
    LtBkSlashFill    = 6;   { \\\ fill }
    HatchFill        = 7;   { light hatch fill }
    XHatchFill       = 8;   { heavy cross hatch fill }
    InterleaveFill   = 9;   { interleaving line fill }
    WideDotFill      = 10;  { widely spaced dot fill }
    CloseDotFill     = 11;  { Closely spaced dot fill }
    UserFill         = 12;  { user defined fill }
```

Graphics Procedures

Arc

Syntax   Procedure Arc(X, Y :Integer;
                     StAngle,
                     EndAngle,
                     Radius : Word);

Parameters

X is the horizontal coordinate at which the arc begins.

Y is the vertical coordinate at which the arc begins.

StAngle is the point on the circumference of the arc at which drawing begins.

EndAngle is the point on the circumference of the arc at which drawing ends.

Radius is the radius of the arc.

Description   Arc draws a circle segment around a center located at x:y with the radius specified. When **StAngle** is 0, drawing begins at the 12:00 position. When **EndAngle** is 360, drawing ends at the 12:00 position. Drawing is done in a clockwise direction.

Bar

Syntax   Procedure Bar(x1, y1, x2, y2 : Integer);

Parameters

x1 is the horizontal coordinate of the upper left-hand corner of the box.

y1 is the vertical coordinate of the upper left-hand corner of the box.

x2 is the horizontal coordinate of the lower right-hand corner of the box.

y2 is the vertical coordinate of the lower right-hand corner of the box.

Description   Bar draws a rectangle defined by x1:y1 and x2:y2. The rectangle is filled with the pattern selected with **SetFillStyle**.

Bar3D

Syntax   Procedure Bar3D(x1, y1, x2, y2 : Integer;
                        Depth : Word;
                        Top : boolean);

Parameters

x1 is the horizontal coordinate of the upper left-hand corner of the box.

y1 is the vertical coordinate of the upper left-hand corner of the box.

x2 is the horizontal coordinate of the lower right-hand corner of the box.

y2 is the vertical coordinate of the lower right-hand corner of the box.

Depth is the amount of linear perspective added to the box.

Top, when true, creates a box drawn with lines that form a top.

Description   Bar3D draws a box from x1:y1 to x2:y2 with lines that provide depth perspective. Parameters control the depth of the box and the addition of a top to the box. The Graph unit provides the following two constants that you can use to control the **Top** parameter:

```
TopOn  = true;
TopOff = false;
```

Circle

Syntax   Procedure Circle(X, Y : Integer; Radius : Word);

Parameters

X is the horizontal coordinate at which the arc begins.

Y is the vertical coordinate at which the arc begins.

Radius is the radius of the arc.

Description   Circle draws a circle around a center located at x:y with the radius specified.

ClearDevice

Syntax   Procedure ClearDevice;

Description   ClearDevice erases the currently selected output device and resets the current pointer, palette, color, and viewport to their default values.

ClearViewPort

Syntax   Procedure ClearViewPort;

Description   ClearViewPort clears the viewport and sets the screen to the color in Palette(0).

CloseGraph

Syntax   Procedure CloseGraph;

Description   **CloseGraph** removes from the heap all dynamic variables used by the graph mode, and resets the screen to the previous mode.

DetectGraph

Syntax   Procedure DetectGraph(Var GraphDriver,
GraphMode : Integer);

Parameters

GraphDriver is the type of video display adapter in use, such as CGA, Hercules, or EGA.

GraphMode is the recommended mode in which the display adapter should be operated.

Description   **DetectGraph** reports which type of graphics adapter, if any, is present. It also recommends a mode to use for the adapter. These parameters can be passed into the **InitGraph** procedure, which sets up the graphics environment. Note that the values returned are only recommended — you are free to use other values in **InitGraph** (such as CGA instead of EGA) if the equipment permits it.

DrawPoly

Syntax   Procedure DrawPoly(NumPoints : Word; Var
PolyPoints);

Parameters

NumPoints is the number of x:y coordinate pairs to be plotted.

PolyPoints is the array of x:y coordinates.

Description   **DrawPoly** draws a polygon that connects the points defined in the array **PolyPoints**. An example of this type of array is shown here:

```
Var
  PolyArray : Array [1..100] of Record
    x,y : Word;
    end;
```

You must make sure that x:y coordinates are within the bounds of the current video display. If an error occurs, **GraphResult** will return a value of −6.

Ellipse

Syntax   Procedure Ellipse(X, Y : Integer;
                            StAngle,
                            EndAngle : Word;
                            XRadius,
                            YRadius : Word);

Parameters

X is the horizontal coordinate for the center of the ellipse.

Y is the vertical coordinate for the center of the ellipse.

StAngle is the point on the circumference of the ellipse at which drawing is to begin. A value of 360 represents 12:00.

EndAngle is the point on the circumference of the ellipse at which drawing is to end. A value of 0 represents 12:00.

XRadius is the distance from the center of the ellipse to the circumference along a horizontal axis.

YRadius is the distance from the center of the ellipse to the circumference along a vertical axis.

Description   **Ellipse** produces elongated circular shapes with x:y as the center of the ellipse. Drawing starts at **StAngle** and continues to **EndAngle**. The elongation becomes more pronounced as the difference between **XRadius** and **YRadius** increases.

FillPoly

Syntax   Procedure FillPoly(NumPoints : Word; Var
PolyPoints);

Parameters

NumPoints is the number of x:y coordinate pairs to be
plotted.

PolyPoints is the array of x:y coordinates.

Description   **FillPoly** fills the polygon defined in **Poly-
Points** with color and pattern set by **SetColor** and **SetFill-
Style** or **SetFillPattern**. The outline of the polygon is determined by the current color and line style. The polygon must
be completely closed like a box for this procedure to work. If
an error occurs, **GraphResult** returns a value of −6.

FloodFill

Syntax   Procedure FloodFill(X, Y, Border : Word);

Parameters

X is the horizontal coordinate inside the area to be filled.

Y is the vertical coordinate inside the area to be filled.

Border determines the color of the border of the area to
be filled.

Description   **FloodFill** fills an enclosed area outlined by
Border. Coordinates x:y define a point inside the figure to be
filled.

GetArcCoords

Syntax   Procedure GetArcCoords(Var ArcCoords :
ArcCoordsType);

Parameters

ArcCoords contains information about the last arc drawn with the Arc procedure.

The variable is of the following type:

```
Type
  ArcCoordsType = Record
    x, y : Integer;
    xS,
    yS,
    Xend,
    Yend : Word;
    End;
```

where x:y denotes the center of the arc, xS:xY denotes the starting position of the arc, and Xend:Yend denotes the ending position of the arc.

Description   GetArcCoords returns the key points in an arc needed to create a pie slice. With the results in **ArcCoordsType**, you can draw lines from the center of an arc to either of the ends of the arc to form a "slice."

GetAspectRatio

Syntax   Procedure GetAspectRatio(Var Xasp,
                                    Yasp : Word);

Parameters

Xasp is the value of the horizontal aspect.

Yasp is the value of the vertical aspect.

Description   The aspect ratio is the ratio of horizontal pixels to vertical pixels that produces a properly proportioned graphic display. After calling **GetAspectRatio**, divide **Xasp** by **Yasp** to determine the ratio for your equipment.

GetBkColor

Syntax   Function GetBkColor : Word;

Description   **GetBkColor** returns a number indicating the currently selected background color. Colors are selected from the palette that corresponds to your equipment and the graphics mode you selected. The first color in a palette is 0.

GetColor

Syntax   Function GetColor : Word;

Description   **GetColor** returns a number indicating the currently selected foreground color. Colors are selected from the palette that corresponds to your equipment and the graphics mode you selected. The first color in a palette is 0.

GetFillSettings

Syntax   Procedure GetFillSettings(Var FillInfo :
                                        FillSettingsType);

Parameters

FillInfo is a variable of the following type:

```
Type
  FillSettingsType = Record
    Pattern, Color : Word;
    End;
```

Description   **GetFillSettings** returns a record containing two parameters, **pattern** and **color**, which indicate the type of hatching currently selected and the current drawing color.

GetGraphMode

Syntax   Function GetGraphMode : Integer;

Description   GetGraphMode returns an integer that indicates the current graphics mode.

GetImage

Syntax   Procedure GetImage(x1, y1, x2, y2 : Word;
                                   Var BitMap);

Parameters

x1 is the horizontal coordinate of the upper left-hand
corner of the portion of the graphics screen to save.

y1 is the vertical coordinate of the upper left-hand
corner of the portion of the graphics screen to save.

x2 is the horizontal coordinate of the lower right-hand
corner of the portion of the graphics screen to save.

y2 is the vertical coordinate of the lower right-hand
corner of the portion of the graphics screen to save.

BitMap is the buffer for storing the selected portion of
the screen.

Description   **GetImage** saves the graphics image defined
by x1:y1 and x2:y2 in a buffer **BitMap**. **BitMap** must be at
least as large as the area defined plus four. The area is calculated as $(x2 - x1 + 1) * (y2 - y1 + 1)$.

GetLineSettings

Syntax   Procedure GetLineSettings(Var LineInfo :
                                       LineSettingsType);

Parameters

LineInfo is a variable of type

```
Type
  LineSettingsType = Record
    LineStyle,
    Pattern,
    Thickness : Word;
    End;
```

Description   **GetLineSettings** returns a record that contains three variables—**LineStyle, pattern,** and **thickness**—which determine how drawn lines appear.

GetMaxX

Syntax   Function GetMaxX : Word;

Description   **GetMaxX** returns the horizontal pixel coordinate at the rightmost edge of the screen.

GetMaxY

Syntax   Function GetMaxY : Word;

Description   **GetMaxY** returns the vertical pixel coordinate at the bottom edge of the screen.

GetPalette

Syntax   Procedure GetPalette(Var Palette : PaletteType);

Parameters

Palette is a predefined variable of type

```
Type
  PaletteType = Record
    Size : Byte;
    Colors : Array [0..MaxColors] of ShortInt;
    End;
```

Description   **GetPalette** returns the current palette settings. **Size** contains the number of colors in the palette, and **Colors** contains the colors in the palette.

GetPixel

Syntax   Function GetPixel(X, Y : Integer) : Word;

Parameters

X is the horizontal coordinate of the pixel to get.

Y is the vertical coordinate of the pixel to get.

Description   **GetPixel** returns a word value that indicates the color of the pixel at the coordinates x:y.

GetTextSettings

Syntax   Procedure GetTextSettings(Var TextInfo : TextSettingsType);

Parameters

TextInfo : Variable of type **TextSettingsType**, which is defined as

```
TextSettingsType = record
  Font       : word;
  Direction  : word;
  CharSize   : word; { 1..10 }
  Horiz      : word;
  Vert       : word;
  end;
```

Description   **GetTextSettings** returns in **TextInfo** information about the current font style. The information includes the font selected, its direction, size, and horizontal and vertical justification.

GetViewSettings

Syntax   Procedure GetViewSettings(Var ViewPort : ViewPortType);

Parameters

ViewPort is a predefined variable of the type

```
Type
  ViewPortType = Record
    x1, y1, x2, y2 : Word;
    Clip : Boolean;
    End;
```

Description   **GetViewSettings** returns **ViewPort**, which contains the settings for the current viewport. Coordinates x1:y1 define the upper right-hand corner of the viewport, and coordinates x2:y2 define the lower right-hand corner. Clip denote if clipping is activated in the viewport.

GetX

Syntax   Function GetX : Integer;

Description   **GetX** returns the horizontal coordinate of the current position. The value of **GetX** is always relative to the current viewport. Thus, if **GetX** returns 0, the current position is at the far left side of the viewport, not the far left side of the screen.

GetY

Syntax   Function GetY : Integer;

Description   **GetY** returns the vertical coordinate of the current position. The value of **GetY** is always relative to the current viewport. Thus, if **GetY** returns 0, the current position is at the top of the viewport, not the top of the screen.

GraphErrorMsg

Syntax   Function GraphErrorMsg(ErrorCode : Integer) : String;

Parameters

ErrorCode is the integer that indicates the type of error that occurred.

Description   **GraphErrorMsg** returns a string result that describes the error defined by **ErrorCode**.

GraphResult

Syntax   Function GraphResult : Integer;

Description   **GraphResult** returns an error code for the last operation performed.

ImageSize

Syntax   Function ImageSize(x1, y1, x2, y2 : Word) : Word;

Parameters

x1 is the horizontal coordinate of the upper left-hand corner of the area.

y1 is the vertical coordinate of the upper left-hand corner of the area.

x2 is the horizontal coordinate of the lower right-hand corner of the area.

y2 is the vertical coordinate of the lower right-hand corner of the area.

Description   **ImageSize** returns the amount of memory required to store the image defined by x1:y1 and x2:y2. The area is calculated as $(x2 - x1 + 1) * (y2 - y1 + 1)$.

InitGraph

Syntax   Procedure InitGraph(Var GraphDriver : Integer;
                    Var GraphMode : Integer;
                    PathToDriver : String);

Parameters

> **GraphDriver** is the type of video display adapter in use, such as CGA, Hercules, or EGA.

> **GraphMode** is the recommended mode in which the display adapter should be operated.

> **PathToDriver** is a string containing the path to the directory in which the graphics drivers are located.

Description   **InitGraph** initializes the graphics environment and puts the computer into the graph mode. If **GraphDriver** is equal to Detect (0), **InitGraph** will determine which driver and mode to use.

Line

Syntax   Procedure Line(x1, y1, x2, y2 : Integer);

Parameters

> **x1** is the horizontal coordinate of the beginning of the line.

> **y1** is the vertical coordinate of the beginning of the line.

> **x1** is the horizontal coordinate of the end of the line.

> **y1** is the vertical coordinate of the end of the line.

Description   **Line** draws a line from x1:y1 to x2:y2.

LineRel

Syntax   Procedure LineRel(Dx, Dy : Integer);

Parameters

> **Dx** is the relative horizontal distance to draw a line.

> **Dy** is the relative vertical distance to draw a line.

Description   **LineRel** draws a line from the current position to the relative position defined by Dx:Dy. For example, if the current position is 10:10, the command

```
LineRel(10,10);
```

will draw a line from 10:10 to 20:20.

LineTo

Syntax   Procedure LineTo(X, Y : Integer);

Parameters

X is the horizontal coordinate to draw a line to.

Y is the vertical coordinate to draw a line to.

Description LineTo draws a line from the current position to x:y.

MoveRel

Syntax   Procedure MoveRel(Dx, Dy : Integer);

Parameters

Dx is the relative horizontal coordinate to move to.

Dy determines the relative vertical coordinate to move to.

Description   **MoveRel** moves the current position to Dx:Dy. For example, if the current position is 10:10, the command

```
MoveRel(10,10);
```

will set the current position at 20:20.

MoveTo

Syntax   Procedure MoveTo(X, Y : Integer);

Parameters

X is the horizontal coordinate to move to.

Y is the vertical coordinate to move to.

Description   **MoveTo** moves the current position to x:y.

OutText

Syntax   Procedure OutText(TextString : String);

Parameters

TextString is the string value to be displayed.

Description   **OutText** displays the string contained in **TextString** at the current position. The font used can be selected with **SetTextStyle**.

OutTextXY

Syntax   Procedure OutTextXY(X, Y : Integer;
                                    TextString : String);

Parameters

X is the horizontal coordinate to display **TextString**.

Y is the vertical coordinate to display **TextString**.

TextString is the string to display.

Description   **OutTextXY** displays **TextString** at x:y.

PieSlice

Syntax   Procedure PieSlice(X, Y : Integer;
                                    StAngle,
                                    EndAngle,
                                    Radius : Word);

Parameters

X is the horizontal position for the center of the arc.

Y is the vertical position for the center of the arc.

StAngle is the point on the circumference of the arc at which drawing starts.

EndAngle is the point on the circumference of the arc at which drawing ends.

Radius is the distance from the center of the arc to the circumference.

Description   **PieSlice** draws a pie slice with a center X:Y with size determined by **Radius**. Drawing starts at **StAngle** and continues clockwise to **EndAngle**. The pie slice will be filled according to the setting of **SetFillStyle** and **SetFillPattern**.

PutImage

Syntax   Procedure PutImage(X, Y : Integer;
                                   Var BitMap;
                                   BitBlt : Word);

Parameters

X is the horizontal coordinate of the upper left-hand corner of the screen to display the image.

Y is the vertical coordinate of the upper left-hand corner of the screen to display the image.

BitMap is the buffer where the image is stored.

BitBlt specifies how the image will be written to the screen.

Description   **PutImage** retrieves a graphic image stored in the buffer **BitMap** and writes the image starting at x:y. **BitBlt** defines how the image is to be written and can take any of the values listed in Table I-1.

PutPixel

Syntax   Procedure PutPixel(X, Y : Integer; Pixel : Word);

Parameters

X is the horizontal coordinate.

Y is the vertical coordinate.

Pixel is the color of the pixel.

Description   **PutPixel** turns on pixel at x:y with color defined by **Pixel**.

Constant	Value
NormalPut	0
XORPut	1
OrPut	2
AndPut	3
NotPut	4

Table I-1.   Values of BiBlt

Rectangle

Syntax   Procedure Rectangle(x1, y1, x2, y2 : Integer);

Parameters

x1 is the horizontal coordinate of the upper left corner of the rectangle.

y1 is the vertical coordinate of the upper left corner of the rectangle.

x2 is the horizontal coordinate of the lower right corner of the rectangle.

y2 is the vertical coordinate of the lower right corner of the rectangle.

Description   **Rectangle** draws a rectangle from x1:y1 to x2:y2 using the current line style and color.

RestoreCrtMode

Syntax   Procedure RestoreCrtMode;

Description   **RestoreCrtMode** restores the video mode to the mode that preceded the graphics mode.

SetActivePage

Syntax   Procedure SetActivePage(Page : Word);

Parameters

Page is the number of the page to make active.

Description   **SetActivePage** directs all output to the video page indicated by **Page**. To make the newly active page visible, use **SetVisualPage**.

SetAllPalette

Syntax   Procedure SetAllPalette(Var Palette);

Parameters

Palette is a predefined variable of the type

```
Type
  PaletteType = Record
    Size : Byte;
    Colors : Array [0..MaxColors] of ShortInt;
    End;
```

Description   **SetAllPalette** replaces the current palette settings with those defined in the variable **Palette**.

SetBkColor

Syntax   Procedure SetBkColor(Color : Word);

Parameters

Color is the background color.

Description   **SetBkColor** sets the background color to **Color**.

SetColor

Syntax   Procedure SetColor(Color : Word);

Parameters

Color is the drawing color.

Description   **SetColor** sets the drawing color to **Color**.

SetFillPattern

Syntax   Procedure SetFillPattern(Pattern :
FillPatternType;
Color : Word);

Parameters

Pattern is a variable of predefined type

```
Type
  FillPatternType = Array [1..8] of Byte;
```

Color is the color to use in a pattern.

Description   **SetFillPattern** defines the pattern and color to use when filling graphic areas. **Pattern** defines an 8-pixel by 8-pixel area, with each bit representing a pixel. If a bit is turned on, the corresponding pixel is turned on. For example, Table I-2 shows the definition of a pattern that describes slanted lines.

Array Element	Binary Value	Hex Value
Pattern[1]	10010010	92h
Pattern[2]	01001001	49h
Pattern[3]	00100100	24h
Pattern[4]	10010010	92h
Pattern[5]	01001001	49h
Pattern[6]	00100100	24h
Pattern[7]	10010010	92h
Pattern[8]	01001001	49h

Table I-2.   Example Definition of Pattern

SetFillStyle

Syntax   Procedure SetFillStyle(Pattern : Word;
                                              Color : Word);

Parameters:

Pattern is the number from 0 to 11 selecting one of 12 predefined fill patterns.

Color is the color for the fill pattern.

Description   **SetFillStyle** selects a color and a fill pattern from the 12 patterns defined by the Graph unit.

SetGraphMode

Syntax   Procedure SetGraphMode(Mode : Integer);

Parameters

Mode is the graph mode to select.

Description   **SetGraphMode** sets the graphic environment to **Mode**. **Mode** corresponds to one of the values predefined by the Graph unit and must be compatible with the equipment being used.

SetLineStyle

Syntax   Procedure SetLineStyle(LineStyle : Word;
                                              Pattern : Word;
                                              Thickness : Word);

Parameters

LineStyle specifies the number indicating which predefined line style to use.

Pattern specifies the number indicating which predefined pattern to use.

Thickness specifies the number indicating which predefined thickness to use.

Description   **SetLineStyle** sets the line style, pattern, and thickness used when drawing.

SetPalette

Syntax   Procedure SetPalette(ColorNum : Word;
                                Color : Byte);

Parameters

ColorNum is the number of the color in the palette to set.

Color is the color to use.

Description   **SetPalette** sets the color number **ColorNum** to **Color**. This allows you to alter the standard settings for the palette. For example, the command

```
SetPalette(1,blue);
```

sets color number 1 in the palette to blue.

SetText Justify

Syntax   Procedure SetTextJustify(Horiz, Vert : Word);

Parameters

Horiz is the type of justification around the horizontal pixel.

Vert is the type of justification around the vertical pixel.

Description   **SetTextJustify** determines how text will be displayed in relation to the current position. The Graph unit defines the following constants for this purpose:

```
Const
  (* Horiz Values *)
  LeftText    = 0;
  CenterText  = 1;
  RightText   = 2;

  (* Vert Values *)
  BottomText  = 0;
  CenterText  = 1;
  TopText     = 2;
```

SetTextStyle

Syntax   Procedure SetTextStyle(Font,
                                      Direction : Word;
                                      CharSize : Word);

Parameters

Font is the type style to use.

Direction determines whether text is displayed left to right or top to bottom.

CharSize is the size of characters.

Description   SetTextStyle defines the way text will be displayed. Five font styles (0 through 4) are available, though 1 through 4 are stored in disk files. The Graph unit defines the following type and constants for use with this procedure:

```
Type
  CharSizeType = 1..10;

Const
  DefaultFont    = 0;
  TriplexFont    = 1;
  SmallFont      = 2;
  SansSerifFont  = 3;
  GothicFont     = 4;

  HorizDir       = 0;
  VertDir        = 1;

  NormSize       = 1;
```

Two errors can occur when you select fonts 1 through 4; error number −8 means the font file was not found, and error −9 means not enough memory is available to load the font file.

SetViewPort

Syntax   Procedure SetViewPort(x1,
                                        y1,
                                        x2,
                                        y2 : Word;
                                        Clip : boolean);

Parameters

x1 is the horizontal coordinate of the upper left corner of the viewport.

y1 is the vertical coordinate of the upper left corner of the viewport.

x2 is the horizontal coordinate of the lower right corner of the viewport.

y2 is the vertical coordinate of the lower right corner of the viewport.

Clip, if true, sets clipping on.

Description   **SetViewPort** defines a portion of the screen, from x1:y1 to x2:y2, as the active graphics screen. If **Clip** is true, clipping is activated. For this procedure, the Graph unit defines the following constants:

```
Const
  ClipOn  = True;
  ClipOff = False;
```

After the viewport is set, all coordinates become relative to the viewport, not to the physical screen.

SetVisualPage

Syntax   Procedure SetVisualPage(Page : Word);

Parameters

Page is the number of the graphics page to display on the screen.

Description   **SetVisualPage** switches the graphics display from the current page to the page you select.

TextHeight

Syntax   Function TextHeight(TextString : String) : Word;

Parameters

TextString is the string used to determine the height of the text.

Description   **TextHeight** returns a word that represents the height in pixels of the characters in **TextString**. The height depends on the font being used. This procedure is important for creating proper spacing between lines of text.

TextWidth

Syntax   Function TextWidth(TextString : String) : Word;

Parameters

TextString is the string used to determine the value of TextWidth.

Description   **TextWidth** returns the length in pixels of **TextString** with the current font.

TRADEMARKS

@ operator, Version 4.0, 211-212

A

Aborting commands, 37
Abs, 145, 729
Absolute, 719
Absolute value, 145
Adams-Bashforth/Adams-Moulton, 649
Adaptive quadrature, 632
    Simpson's rule, 631
Addr, 729
Address, memory, 302, 444
Algorithms
    comparing sort, 293-294
    sorting, 280-294
And, 137-139, 158, 719
Append, 216, 729
Arc, 417, 771
ArcTan, 145, 730
Arithmetic functions, 145-148, 491-494
Arithmetic, 131-148
    optimizing, 515-517
    real, 143-145
    Turbo Pascal, 8-10
Array, 719
    data type, 57
Arrays, 125-128
    alternative to using, 199
ASCII
    characters, 222
    values, returning, 242
ASCII and extended character set, 697
ASCIIZ strings, 309
Assembly language, 343
Assign, 13, 101, 730
AssignCRT, 755
Assignment statements, 5
    using records in, 122
Asynchronous communications, 450
Attribute byte, 380-382
Attributes, get/set file, 307-310

Auto-indent feature, 30

B

B+tree structure, 528-529
Background colors, 380
Backup files, 24
Backward referencing pointer, 206
BAK file extension, 24
Bar, 771
Bar3D, 772
BCD format, 112, 709
Begin, 84, 719
BigConcat, 489
BigCopy, 491
BigDelete, 490
BigInsert, 489
BigLength, 491
BigPos, 490
BigString, 488
Binary search, 297-300
BIOS
    bypassing, 386
    functions, 301-342
    interrupts and, 442
    service, calling, 17
    services, Version 4.0, 329-332
Bisection method, 611
Bit-manipulation operators, 136
Blanks, removing, 258
Blink constant, 383
Block-delete command, 35
Block operations, 33-34
BlockRead, 233, 269, 730
Blocks, code section organization in, 85
BlockWrite, 233, 269, 731
Books, Pascal, 713-717
Boolean evaluation, 677
    short-circuit, 106
Boolean expressions, optimizing, 513
Boolean statements, 156-160
Boundary value problems, 646-659
Boxes, drawing, 421

The manuscript for this book was prepared and submitted to Osborne/McGraw-Hill in electronic form. The acquisitions editor for this project was Nancy Carlston, the technical reviewer was John Sieraski, and the project editor was Fran Haselsteiner.

Text design uses Century Expanded for text body and Eras Demi for display.

Cover art by Bay Graphics Design Associates. Cover supplier, Phoenix Color Corp. Book printed and bound by R.R. Donnelley & Sons Company, Crawfordsville, Indiana.

Other related Osborne/McGraw-Hill titles include:

1-2-3®: The Complete Reference
by Mary Campbell

1-2-3®: The Complete Reference is the authoritative desktop companion for every Lotus® 1-2-3® user. All commands, functions, and procedures are explained in detail and are demonstrated in practical "real-world" business applications. Conventionally organized according to task, this essential reference makes it easy to locate information on topics such as printing, macros, graphics production, and data management. Each chapter thoroughly describes a 1-2-3 task and all the procedures it requires, followed by an alphabetical listing of every command or function applied. Special emphasis is placed on compatible software packages, including Report Writer™, Reflex™ and others, that you can use to extend 1-2-3's capabilities. Campbell, a consultant and writer whose magazine columns appear monthly in *IBM PC UPDATE, Absolute Reference,* and *CPA Journal,* draws on her years of 1-2-3 expertise to provide you with this outstanding, comprehensive resource.

$25.95 p, Hardcover Edition
0-07-881288-7, 928 pp., 7³⁄₈ x 9¹⁄₄

$22.95 p, Paperback Edition
0-07-881005-1, 928 pp., 7³⁄₈ x 9¹⁄₄

DOS: The Complete Reference
by Kris Jamsa

Why waste computing time over a baffling PC-DOS™ command or an elusive MS-DOS® function? *DOS: The Complete Reference* has the answers to all of your questions on DOS through version 3.X. This essential resource is for every PC- and MS-DOS user, whether you need an overview of the disk operating system or a reference for advanced programming and disk management techniques. Each chapter begins with a discussion of specific applications followed by a list of commands used in each. All commands are presented in the same clear, concise format: description, syntax, discussion of arguments or options, and examples. For comprehensive coverage, *DOS: The Complete Reference* discusses Microsoft® Windows and EDLIN, and provides two special appendixes covering the ASCII chart and DOS error messages. A ready resource, *DOS: The Complete Reference* is the only DOS consultant you'll need.

$27.95 p, Hardcover Edition
0-07-881314-x, 840 pp., 7³⁄₈ x 9¹⁄₄

$24.95 p, Paperback Edition
0-07-881259-3, 840 pp., 7³⁄₈ x 9¹⁄₄

dBASE III PLUS™: The Complete Reference
by Joseph-David Carrabis

This indispensable dBASE III PLUS™ reference will undoubtedly be the most frequently used book in your dBASE III® library. *dBASE III PLUS™: The Complete Reference* is a comprehensive resource to every dBASE III and dBASE III PLUS command, function, and feature. Each chapter covers a specific task so you can quickly pinpoint information on installing the program, designing databases, creating files, manipulating data, and many other subjects. Chapters also contain an alphabetical reference section that describes all the commands and functions you need to know and provides clear examples of each. Carrabis, author of several acclaimed dBASE books, discusses the lastest features of dBASE III PLUS, including networking capabilities; the Assistant, a menu-driven interface; and the Applications Generator, a short-cut feature for creating database files and applications without programming. *dBASE III PLUS™: The Complete Reference* also includes a glossary and handy appendixes that cover error messages, converting from dBASE II to dBASE III PLUS, and add-on utilities.

$25.95 p, Hardcover Edition
0-07-881315-x, 600 pp., 7³⁄₈ x 9¹⁄₄

$22.95 p, Paperback Edition
0-07-881012-4, 600 pp., 7³⁄₈ x 9¹⁄₄

C: The Complete Reference
by Herbert Schildt

Once again Osborne's master C programmer and author Herb Schildt, shares his insight and expertise with all C programmers in his latest book, *C: The Complete Reference.* Designed for both beginning and advanced C programmers, this is an encyclopedia for C terms, functions, codes, applications, and more. *C: The Complete Reference* is divided into five parts, each covering an important aspect of C. Part one covers review material and discusses key words in C. Part two presents an extensive summary of C libraries by category. Part three concentrates on various algorithms and C applications and includes information on random number generators as well as artificial intelligence and graphics. Part four addresses interfacing efficiency, porting, and debugging. Finally, part five is for serious programmers who are interested in C++, C's latest direction. The book also includes complete information on the proposed ANSI standard

$27.95 p, Hardcover Edition
0-07-881313-1, 740 pp., 7³⁄₈ x 9¹⁄₄

$24.95 p, Paperback Edition
0-07-881263-1, 740 pp., 7³⁄₈ x 9¹⁄₄

WordPerfect®: The Complete Reference
by Karen L. Acerson

Osborne's highly successful Complete Reference series has a new addition, *WordPerfect®: The Complete Reference*. Every WordPerfect feature, key, menu, prompt, and error message is explained in simple terms for new users, and with sophisticated technical information supplied for those with experience. Acerson, an early member of WordPerfect Corporation who has been helping WordPerfect users get the most from their software since 1983, discusses the techniques for integrating WordPerfect with Lotus® 1-2-3®, dBASE® III, and other widely used software. Here's another ideal desktop companion to add to your collection.

$27.95 p, Hardcover Edition
0-07-881312-3, 675 pp., 7³/₈ x 9¹/₄
$24.95 p, Paperback Edition
0-07-881266-6, 675 pp., 7³/₈ x 9¹/₄

Using HAL™
by Andrew Postman

Using HAL™ helps you tap into the full capabilities of Lotus® 1-2-3®. Whether you're a beginning 1-2-3 user or an experienced one who demands top software performance, you'll be amazed at the increased productivity that HAL adds to 1-2-3. Postman shows you how to use HAL to execute 1-2-3 commands and functions through English phrases that you select. You'll find out about graphing with HAL and how to use the undo command, which lets you experiment with "what-if" questions without losing data. You'll also master cell relations for greater analytical abilities, linking worksheets for data consolidation, macros, and table manipulation. *Using HAL™* gets you past the introduction so you can become thoroughly acquainted with Lotus' new 1-2-3 companion.

$19.95 p
0-07-881268-2, 380 pp., 7³/₈ x 9¹/₄

Running 4Word™
by Kay Nelson

If you've been running behind in word processing with 1-2-3® lately, now is the time to start *Running 4Word™*. Find out how to use Turner Hall's newly released 4Word™, the Add-In Word Processor™ for 1-2-3®, that lets you integrate word processing functions with Lotus' spreadsheet by pressing a computer key. You'll start with the basics of installing the program and formatting text, then work up to advanced procedures including macros and importing/exporting text and data. Practical business examples are cited so you can clearly understand how to create memos, reports, and financial documents using 4Word.

$19.95 p
0-07-881258-5, 350 pp. 7³/₈ x 9¹/₄

UNIX®: The Complete Reference System V Release 3
by Stephen Coffin

The Complete Reference series now includes a book for all Unix® users! *UNIX®: The Complete Reference* includes expansive coverage of System V Release 3, the version that runs on 386 machines and on the new Macintosh™ II. Stephen Coffin, a UNIX programmer and a member of AT&T's technical staff, approaches UNIX with a perspective that benefits users of microcomputers, minicomputers, and mainframes. There is special, timely coverage of UNIX on the 80386 micros; all code in the book was run on a 386. If you're just beginning UNIX, the first part of the book will help you get started. If you're an experienced UNIX user, this book is an invaluable and extensive reference. *UNIX®: The Complete Reference* offers discussions of commands, text processing, editing, programming, communications, the Shell, and the UNIX file system. Important highlights include running MS-DOS® under UNIX, upgrading to Release 3, and extensive coverage of UNIX on the 386.

$27.95 p, Hardcover Edition
0-07-881333-6, 750 pp., 7³/₈ x 9¹/₄
$24.95 p, Paperback Edition
0-07-881299-2, 750 pp., 7³/₈ x 9¹/₄

DOS Made Easy
by Herbert Schildt

If you're at a loss when it comes to DOS, Herb Schildt has written just the book you need, *DOS Made Easy*. Previous computer experience is not necessary to understand this concise, well-organized introduction that's filled with short applications and exercises. Schildt walks you through all the basics, beginning with an overview of a computer system's components and a step-by-step account of how to run DOS for the first time. Once you've been through the initial setup, you'll edit text files, use the DOS directory structure, and create batch files. As you feel more comfortable with DOS, Schildt shows you how to configure a system, handle floppy disks and fixed disks, and make use of helpful troubleshooting methods. By the time you've gone this far, you'll be ready for total system management—using the printer, video modes, the serial and parallel ports, and more. *DOS Made Easy* takes the mystery out of the disk operating system and puts you in charge of your PC.

$18.95 p
0-07-881295-X, 385 pp., 7¹/₈ x 9¹/₄

Artificial Intelligence Using C

by Herb Schildt

With Herb Schildt's newest book, you can add a powerful dimension to your C programs—artificial intelligence. Schildt, a programming expert and author of seven Osborne books, shows C programmers how to use AI techniques that have traditionally been implemented with Prolog and LISP. You'll utilize AI for vision, pattern recognition, robotics, machine learning, logic, problem solving, and natural language processing. Each chapter develops practical examples that can be used in the construction of artificial intelligence applications. If you are building expert systems in C, this book contains a complete expert system that can easily be adapted to your needs. Schildt provides valuable insights that allow even greater command of the systems you create.

$21.95 p
0-07-881255-0, 360 pp., 7³/₈ x 9¹/₄

Advanced Graphics in C: Programming and Techniques

by Nelson Johnson

Add graphics to your C programs, and you'll add significantly to your programming skills and to the effectiveness of your software. With *Advanced Graphics in C* you'll write graphics program for the IBM® EGA (enhanced graphics adapter). This guide offers a complete toolkit of all the routines you'll need for such graphics operations as drawing a line, an arc, or a circle; plotting; and filling in shapes. A complete sample graphics program with a rotatable and scalable character set is included. All the code is provided so that you can easily create the graphics you need. Johnson also includes instructions for interrupt-driven serial and parallel interfacing to mice, light pens, and digitizers. You'll learn state-of-the-art techniques from Johnson, a software developer, author, and worldwide lecturer.

$22.95 p
0-07-881257-7, 430 pp., 7³/₈ x 9¹/₄

Using Turbo BASIC®

by Frederick E. Mosher and David I. Schneider

Using Turbo BASIC® is your authoritative guide to Borland's incredible new compiler that offers faster compilation speeds than any other product on the market. *Using Turbo BASIC®* is packed with information for everyone from novices to seasoned programmers. Authors Mosher and Schneider, two accomplished programmers, introduce you to the Turbo BASIC® operating environment on the IBM® PC and PC-compatibles, and discuss the interactive editor and the BASIC language itself. You'll learn about recursion, math functions, graphics and sound functions, and conversions from IBM BASICA to Turbo BASIC. With this excellent step-by-step guide to Borland's new compiler, you'll have the extraordinary power of Turbo BASIC at your fingertips.

$19.95 p
0-07-881282-8, 350 pp., 7³/₈ x 9¹/₄
The Borland-Osborne/McGraw-Hill Programming Series

Using Turbo C®

by Herbert Schildt

Here's the official book on Borland's tremendous new C compiler. *Using Turbo C®* is for all C programmers, from beginners to seasoned pros. Master programmer Herb Schildt devotes the first part of the book to helping you get started in Turbo C. If you've been programming in Turbo Pascal® or another language, this orientation will lead you right into Turbo C fundamentals. Schildt's emphasis on good programming structure will start you out designing programs for greater efficiency. With these basics, you'll move on to more advanced concepts such as pointers and dynamic allocation, compiler directives, unions, bitfields, and enumerations, and you'll learn about Turbo C graphics. When you've finished *Using Turbo C®*, you'll be writing full-fledged programs that get professional results.

$19.95 p
0-07-881279-8, 350 pp., 7³/₈ x 9¹/₄
The Borland-Osborne/McGraw-Hill Programming Series

Advanced Turbo C®
by Herbert Schildt

Ready for power programming with Turbo C®? You'll find the expertise you need in *Advanced Turbo C®*, the Borland/Osborne book with the inside edge. In this instruction guide and lasting reference, Herb Schildt, the author of five acclaimed books on C, takes you the final step on the way to Turbo C mastery. Each stand-alone chapter presents a complete discussion of a Turbo C programming topic so you can pinpoint the information you need immediately. *Advanced Turbo C®* thoroughly covers sorting and searching; stacks, queues, linked lists, and binary trees; operating system interfacing; statistics; encryption and compressed data formats; random numbers and simulations; and expression parsers. In addition, you'll learn about converting Turbo Pascal® to Turbo C and using Turbo C graphics. *Advanced Turbo C®* shows you how to put the amazing compilation speed of Turbo C into action on your programs.

$22.95 p
0-07-881280-1, 325 pp., 7⅜ x 9¼

The Borland-Osborne/McGraw-Hill Programming Series

Advanced Turbo Pascal®
by Herbert Schildt

Advanced Turbo Pascal® is the book you need to learn superior programming skills for the leading Pascal language development system. Revised and expanded, *Advanced Turbo Pascal®* now covers Borland's newly released Turbo Database Toolbox®, which speeds up database searching and sorting, and the Turbo Graphix Toolbox®, which lets you easily create high-resolution graphics. And, *Advanced Turbo Pascal®* includes techniques for converting Turbo Pascal for use with Borland's hot new compiler, Turbo C®. Schildt provides many programming tips to take you on your way to high performance with Turbo Pascal. You'll refine your skills with techniques for sorting and searching; stacks, queues, linked lists and binary trees; dynamic allocations; expression parsing; simulation; interfacing to assembly language routines; and efficiency, porting, and debugging. For instruction and reference, *Advanced Turbo Pascal®* is the best single resource for serious programmers.

$21.95 p
0-07-881283-6, 350 pp., 7⅜ x 9¼

The Borland-Osborne/McGraw-Hill Programming Series

Using Turbo Pascal®
by Steve Wood

Using Turbo Pascal® gives you a head start with Borland's acclaimed compiler, which has become a worldwide standard. Programmer Steve Wood has completely rewritten the text and now provides programming examples that run under MS-DOS®, as well as new information on memory resident applications, in-line code, interrupts, and DOS functions. If you're already programming in Pascal or any other high-level language, you'll be able to write programs that are more efficient than ever. *Using Turbo Pascal®* discusses program design and Pascal's syntax requirements, and thoroughly explores Turbo Pascal's features. Then Wood develops useful applications and gives you an overview of some of the advanced utilities and features available with Turbo Pascal. *Using Turbo Pascal®* gives you the skills to become a productive programmer—and when you're ready for more, you're ready for *Advanced Turbo Pascal®*.

$19.95 p
0-07-881284-4, 350 pp., 7⅜ x 9¼

The Borland-Osborne/McGraw-Hill Programming Series

Turbo Pascal®: The Complete Reference
by Stephen O'Brien

Turbo Pascal®: The Complete Reference is an important addition to both the *Borland-Osborne/McGraw-Hill Programming Series* and Osborne's *Complete Reference Series*. *1-2-3®: The Complete Reference* and *dBASE III PLUS™: The Complete Reference* have appeared on best-seller lists across the country. Now programmer Stephen O'Brien has written the first single resource that provides both expert and novice programmers with the entire range of Turbo Pascal's techniques, all illustrated in short examples and applications. Every aspect of Turbo Pascal is thoroughly described, including topics that were previously unavailable in one reference, such as memory-resident programs, DOS and BIOS services, and assembly language routines. *Turbo Pascal®: The Complete Reference* is clear, comprehensive, and organized for quick fact-finding. An ideal desktop resource you can refer to whenever you're programming with Borland's renown Turbo Pascal compiler.

$24.95 p
0-07-881290-9, 640 pp., 7⅜ x 9¼

The Borland-Osborne/McGraw-Hill Programming Series

dBASE III® Tips & Traps

by Dick Andersen, Cynthia Cooper, and Bill Demsey

Take some tips from Dick Andersen and his co-authors and you'll save computing time and avoid troublesome dBASE traps with this helpful collection of creative shortcuts. *dBASE III® Tips & Traps*, another in Andersen's *Tips & Traps* series, is written for all dBASE III® users, beginning and experienced. You'll find hundreds of tips and trap solutions for planning an application system and establishing a database, entering and updating data, ordering and retrieving data, relating databases, customizing screen displays, generating reports, interfacing with other software, and converting files from dBASE II.® All tip and trap entries are illustrated and follow a concise "how-to" format.

$17.95 p
0-07-881195-3, 300 pp., 7³/₈ x 9¹/₄

PC Secrets: Tips for Power Performance

by James E. Kelley

Power performance is at your command with these secrets for mastering the PC. This collection of shortcuts and solutions to frustrating and frequently encountered problems gives users of the IBM® PC and PC compatibles the inside edge. James Kelley, author of numerous books on the IBM PC, discloses his secrets for controlling hardware, peripherals, DOS, and applications software. You'll learn tips for keyboard harmonics, display enhancements, controlling fixed disks, managing the printer, and manipulating DOS routines that include batch files, directories and subdirectories, as well as system menus. You'll also find programs that help you use WordStar® and Lotus™ 1-2-3™ to greater advantage. With *PC Secrets*, you don't need to be a technical expert to become a PC power user.

$16.95 p
0-07-881210-0, 224 pp., 7³/₈ x 9¹/₄

Your IBM® PC: A Guide to the IBM PC (DOS 2.0) and XT

by Lyle Graham and Tim Field

"Excellent reference for the IBM PC with PC-DOS version 1.0, 1.05 and 1.1. Provides a clear overview of IBM PC hardware and software, step-by-step operating instructions, and an introduction to BASIC programming, color graphics, and sound. Also includes a chapter on trouble-shooting and IBM's PDP (Problem Definition Procedure). Rating: A" (Computer Book Review)

$18.95 p
0-07-881120-1, 592 pp., 6⁷/₈ x 9¹/₄

Advanced WordPerfect®: Features & Techniques

by Eric Alderman and Lawrence J. Magid

You can make this word processing software for the IBM® PC and compatibles work above and beyond the usual with *Advanced WordPerfect.®* Written by columnist and consultant Eric Alderman and Los Angeles Times syndicated columnist Lawrence Magid, *Advanced WordPerfect®* brings you application tools and concepts that greatly increase your productivity. After a brief review of basic functions, you'll learn how to apply macros to open, close, and resize windows; make document format changes; even control memo headers. You'll also find out about paragraph numbering and outlining, indexing and building tables of contents, using WordPerfect's mathematical capabilities, setting up printing formats, and integrating WordPerfect™ with other products, such as Lotus® 1-2-3,® dBASE III® Sidekick,® and ProKey.™ *Advanced WordPerfect®* is the source for ambitious users who want information that exceeds the documentation.

$16.95 p
0-07-881239-9, 300 pp., 7³/₈ x 9¹/₄
AVAILABLE: 7/86

Advanced MultiMate® and MultiMate® Advantage™

by Mark Brownstein

Experienced users of MultiMate,® the powerful word processing package for the IBM® PC, get two books in one with this addition to Osborne's "Advanced" series. You'll have a fast-paced tutorial to both MultiMate® and Advantage™ (versions 3.5 and 3.6). High-powered techniques are discussed and illustrated in short applications and examples. Brownstein emphasizes the new features of Advantage, including its networking capabilities; multi-column documents; the On-File™ database program, which simulates an index-card file system; and the GraphLink™ program, which transfers graphics to MultiMate from Lotus® 1-2-3,® Framework® and other popular software packages. Brownstein, the former editor-in-chief of *Easy Home Computer* magazine, is a free-lance consultant and author.

$17.95 p
0-07-881247-X, 325 pp., 7³/₈ x 9¹/₄
AVAILABLE: 9/86

Available at fine bookstores and computer stores everywhere.

For a complimentary catalog of all our current publications contact: Osborne/McGraw-Hill, 2600 Tenth Street, Berkeley, CA 94710

Phone inquiries may be made using our toll-free number. Call 800-227-0900 or 800-772-2531 (in California). TWX 910-366-7277.

Prices subject to change without notice.

MAXIT™ increases your DOS addressable conventional memory beyond 640K for only $195.

- Add up to 256K above 640K for programs like FOXBASE+ and PC/FOCUS.

- Short card works in the IBM PC, XT, AT, and compatibles.

- Top off a 512 IBM AT's memory to 640K and add another 128K beyond that.

- Run resident programs like Sidekick above 640K.

- Add up to 96K above 640K to all programs, including PARADOX and 1-2-3.

- Compatible with EGA, Network, and other memory cards.

Break through the 640 barrier.
MAXIT increases your PC's available memory by making use of the vacant unused address space between 640K and 1 megabyte. (See illustrations)

Big gain—no pain.
Extend the productive life of your, IBM PC, XT, AT or compatible. Build more complex spreadsheets and databases without upgrading your present software.

Installation is a snap.
The MAXIT 256K memory card and software works automatically. You don't have to learn a single new command.

If you have questions, our customer support people will answer them, fast. MAXIT is backed by a one-year warranty and a 30-day money-back guarantee.

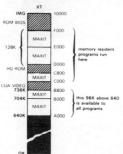

XT class machine (8088, 8086) w/640K and a CGA Color Monitor or a Compaq Type Dual Mode Display

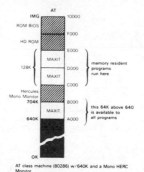

AT class machine (80286) w/640K and a Mono HERC Monitor

Order toll free 1-800-227-0900. MAXIT is just $195 plus $4 shipping, and applicable state sales tax. Buy MAXIT today and solve your PC's memory crisis. Call Toll free 1-800-227-0900 (In California 800-772-2531). Outside the U.S.A. call 1-415-548-2805. We accept VISA, MC.